PRACTICAL ALGORITHMS FOR

3D COMPUTER GRAPHICS

SECOND EDITION

PRACTICAL ALGORITHMS FOR

3D COMPUTER GRAPHICS

SECOND EDITION

R. STUART FERGUSON

THE QUEEN'S UINVERSITY OF BELFAST

UK

CRC Press
Taylor & Francis Group
Boca Raton London New York

CRC Press is an imprint of the
Taylor & Francis Group, an **informa** business
AN A K PETERS BOOK

CRC Press
Taylor & Francis Group
6000 Broken Sound Parkway NW, Suite 300
Boca Raton, FL 33487-2742

First issued in hardback 2017

© 2014 by Taylor & Francis Group, LLC
CRC Press is an imprint of Taylor & Francis Group, an Informa business

No claim to original U.S. Government works

Version Date: 20131112

ISBN-13: 978-1-4665-8252-1 (pbk)
ISBN-13: 978-1-138-42804-1 (hbk)

Visit the Taylor & Francis Web site at
http://www.taylorandfrancis.com

and the CRC Press Web site at
http://www.crcpress.com

Contents

Preface   ix

I   Basic principles   1

1   Introduction   3
   1.1   A note on mathematics for 3D computer graphics   4
   1.2   Getting up to speed and following up   5
   1.3   Assumed knowledge   7
   1.4   Computer graphics and computer games   8
   1.5   The full spectrum   9

2   Basic theory and mathematical results   11
   2.1   Coordinate systems   11
   2.2   Vectors   14
   2.3   Homogeneous coordinates   14
   2.4   The line in vector form   16
   2.5   The plane   17
   2.6   Intersection of a line and a plane   18
   2.7   Closest distance of a point from a line   19
   2.8   Closest distance of approach between two lines   20
   2.9   Reflection in a plane   21
   2.10   Refraction at a plane   22
   2.11   Intersection of a line with primitive shapes   23
   2.12   Transformations   26
   2.13   Parametric curves   41
   2.14   Interpolation   42
   2.15   Bézier curves   46
   2.16   Splines   50
   2.17   Parametric surfaces   56
   2.18   Angular interpolation (quaternions)   58

3   Data structures for 3D graphics   69
    3.1   Integer coordinates   69
    3.2   Vertices and polygons   70
    3.3   Algorithms for editing arrays of structures   76
    3.4   Making an edge list from a list of polygonal faces   79
    3.5   Finding adjacent polygons   81
    3.6   Finding polygons adjacent to edges   84

4   Basic visualization   87
    4.1   The rendering pipeline   88
    4.2   Hidden surface drawing and rasterization   92
    4.3   Anti-aliasing   110
    4.4   Lighting and shading   114
    4.5   Materials and shaders   128
    4.6   Image and texture mapping   134
    4.7   Perlin noise   144
    4.8   Pseudo shadows   149
    4.9   Line drawing   154
    4.10 Tricks and tips   163

5   Realistic visualization   165
    5.1   Radiometric lighting and shading   167
    5.2   Ray tracing   168
    5.3   Ray tracing optimization   171
    5.4   Multi-threading and parallel processing   184

6   Computer animation   187
    6.1   Keyframes (tweening)   187
    6.2   Animating rigid motion   189
    6.3   Character animation   202
    6.4   Inverse kinematics   215
    6.5   Physics   237
    6.6   Animating cloth and hair   246
    6.7   Particle modeling   252

II   Practical 3D graphics   259

7   Real-time 3D: OpenGL   263
    7.1   The basics   266
    7.2   Native programming   273
    7.3   The GL shading language   277
    7.4   The P-buffer and framebuffer objects   290
    7.5   Rendering a particle system using OpenGL   290

7.6   Summing up   292

8   Mobile 3D: OpenGLES   293
    8.1   OpenGLES   294
    8.2   3D on iOS   296
    8.3   3D on Android   304
    8.4   Summing up   313

9   The complete package: OpenFX   319
    9.1   Using OpenFX   321
    9.2   The OpenFX files and folders structure   324
    9.3   Coordinate system and units   327
    9.4   User interface implementation   328
    9.5   The Animation module   331
    9.6   The Designer module   341
    9.7   The Renderer module   350
    9.8   Adding to the software   362
    9.9   Continuing to dissect OpenFX   369

III   Practical algorithms for modeling and procedural textures   371

10 Modeling with polygonal datasets   375
    10.1   Triangulating polygons   376
    10.2   Triangulating polygons with holes   385
    10.3   Subdividing polygonal facets   391
    10.4   Lofting   394
    10.5   Surfaces of revolution   400
    10.6   Beveling   401
    10.7   Orienting surface normals   405
    10.8   Delaunay triangulation   407
    10.9   Boolean modeling   413
    10.10 Metaball modeling and marching cubes   429
    10.11 Texture coordinate generation   442
    10.12 Building polygonal primitives   451

11 Algorithms for procedural textures   453
    11.1   A standard interface   454
    11.2   CPU textures   463
    11.3   GPU textures   492
    11.4   Fur and short hair   497

Bibliography   499

Index   504

Preface

Taken as a whole, the topics covered in this book will enable you to create a complete suite of programs for three-dimensional computer animation, modeling and image synthesis. It is about practical algorithms for each stage in the creative process. The text takes you from the construction of polygonal models of objects (real or imaginary) through rigid body animation into hierarchical character animation and finally down the rendering pipeline for the synthesis of realistic images of the models you build.

The content of the first edition of the book, published in 2001, arose from my experience of working on two comprehensive commercial 3D animation and modeling application programs (*Envisage 3D* and *SoftFX*) for the personal computer in the 1990s. In that time the capabilities of both the hardware and software for creating computer graphics increased almost unimaginably.

Back in 2001 it was hard to envisage how radically the graphics scene would change again as the special purpose graphics processors (GPUs) rolled out, with ever increasing capabilities. Since 2001 we have been finding new and exciting ways to take advantage of the advancements in graphics technology through an open source 3D animation and modeling program called *OpenFX* and in investigating how to enhance the immersive experience with virtual reality [59]. I am sure that the computer games of the future will have to interact with all the human senses and not just our sight. Glimpses of this are here now in the Nintendo Wii and the Microsoft Kinect.

Getting the opportunity to bring this book up to date in a second edition is a marvelous opportunity to include some interesting algorithms that were either still to be found useful or had a very low profile back in 2001. Whilst algorithms and most of the basic principles of computer graphics remain the same, the practicalities have changed unrecognizably in the last twelve years. So the second edition allows us to look at implementations in a new way and part II of the first edition has been completely re-written with three new chapters covering the modern approach to real-time 3D programming and an introduction into 3D graphics for mobile devices.

I've chosen in part II to focus on OpenGL as the preferred API for gaining access to the high-speed hardware, primarily because of its simplicity, long pedigree and platform independence. Many books cover OpenGL in great depth and we have only space in the text to distill and focus on the most important aspects of using the API in practice. But hopefully you will find it useful to see how much can be achieved in a few lines of computer code.

We can also take the opportunity of having the source code of OpenFX available to demonstrate how to deploy our algorithms in practice and get the most out of the programmable graphics hardware through its two rendering engines, one based on the principles we cover in part I and the other on GPU acceleration. One of the new chapters provides a rich set of clues to the design of OpenFX and with the narrative that it provides you should be able to take the OpenFX source code and, for example, write your own radiosity renderer.

As with OpenGL, we do not have space to present long listings in our discussion on OpenFX, so the listings that do appear in the book have been curtailed to focus on the most important members of the key data structures and the entry points and variables used in the functions that constitute in the primary paths of execution in the program.

Like 3D computer graphics, publishing is evolving and so to get the most out of the book please use its website too. Computer codes are more useful in machine readable form, and some topics can benefit from additional briefing papers that we don't have space to include. The example projects associated with part II are only mentioned briefly in the text, but they are accompanied by a comprehensive narrative on the website, including building instructions and platform specifics that really need to be kept up to date on almost a month-by-month basis.

Target readership

I hope that this book will be useful for anyone embarking on a graphics research program, starting work on a new 3D computer game, beginning a career in an industry associated with computer graphics or just wanting a reference to a range of useful graphics algorithms.

I would also hope that the algorithms presented in part III might prove useful for more experienced professional software developers, typically any of you who wish to write *plug-in* modules for any 3D application program or shader code for a games engine commercially available today.

References to websites and other Internet resources

In this edition we are not going to provide references in the form of URLs. We are only providing **one** URL, and that is to the website for the book. On our website you will find a list of the web references we use in the book; by doing this we can continually update the web references and remove or re-vector any links that become outdated, and even add new ones. So, our web address is: http://www.pa3dcg.org/ and for OpenFX: www.openfx.org.

Acknowledgments

In this second edition I would especially like to thank Sarah Chow at Taylor & Francis, not only for offering me the opportunity to update the original book, but also for providing encouragement and very helpful support over the last few months that I have been working on the new book. I'd of course also like to thank Taylor & Francis CRC Press for publishing the work, and its editorial and production team, who have smoothed the production process.

I am very grateful to "JM," who reviewed the manuscript and made, in an amazingly short time, some really valuable observations on how the draft could be improved and reorganized.

I'd also like to reiterate my thanks to those who provided invaluable encouragement to start the project and see it through to first edition: Dan Sprevak, Quamer and Mary Hossain and Ron Praver. And of course, the book would never have seen the light of day without the support of Alice and Klaus Peters at A K Peters.

Finally, I'd of course like to thank my chums at Queen's University, especially the members of the Pensioners' Tea Club, Karen, Merivyn, George and Mr. Moore, who actually are not real pensioners at all, they keep me just on the right side of sanity.

Part I

Basic principles

1

Introduction

Computer graphics embraces a broad spectrum of topics including such things as image processing, photo editing, a myriad of types of computer games and of course special effects for the movies and TV. Even a word processor or presentation package could be said to fall into the category of a graphics program.

Three-dimensional computer graphics (3DCG), the topic covered in this book, began as a separate discipline in the early 1980s where those few fortunate individuals who had access to computing hardware costing tens or hundreds of thousands of dollars began to experiment with the wondrous science of producing, through mathematics alone, pictures that in many cases could not be distinguished from a photograph. The "Voyager" animations of Jim Blinn for NASA were perhaps the first really well publicized use of computer graphics. The title from a television program of the period sums up perfectly the subject of computer graphics: It was *Painting by Numbers*.

We can think of four main applications for 3DCG: computer-aided design, scientific visualization, the ever growing entertainment businesses (cinema and TV animation) and computer games.

There is some overlap between these categories. At the level of the mathematical theory on which graphics algorithms are based they are exactly the same. At the program level however it is usually possible to identify an application as belonging to one of these four categories.

1. In a computer-aided design (CAD) application the most important feature is to be able to use the graphics to present accurate and detailed plans that have the potential to be used for further engineering or architectural work.

2. Scientific visualization is the process of using graphics to illustrate experimental or theoretical data with the aim of bringing into focus trends, anomalies, or special features that might otherwise go unnoticed if they are presented in simple tabular form or by lists of numbers. In this category one might include medical imaging, interpreting physical phenomena and presentations of weather or economic forecasts.

3. Computer animation for the entertainment industry is itself a broad subject where the primary driver is to produce realistic pictures or sequences of

pictures that would be very difficult, impossible or too expensive to obtain by conventional means. The movie, TV and advertising industries have adopted this use of 3D computer animation with great enthusiasm and therefore perhaps it is they who provided the main driving force behind the rapid improvements in realism that can be achieved with 3DCG.

4. In the case of computer game development *fast and furious* is the watchword, with as many twists and turns as can be accomplished in real-time. The quality of images produced from game rendering engines improves at what seems like a constantly accelerating pace and the ingenuity of the game programmers ensures that this is a very active area of computer graphics research and development.

Essentially, this book is targeted at those who work on applications under the broad heading of computer animation, rendering and 3D modeling. If you are interested in scientific visualization the book by Schroeder, Martin and Lorensen [77] is an extensive and valuable resource. Many of their algorithms complement those described here (in chapter 10) and they provide readily adaptable code. In the engineering arena, 3D modeling software is used to design everything from plastic bottles to aircraft. Nowadays the CAD design tools also offer some excellent product visualizations as well as the rigorous technical drawings and plans. With the drawing parts of packages such as Solid Edge [73] achieving maturity the latest developments in these packages has tended to take them into the realm of analysis, for such things as stresses and strains, using mathematical techniques such as finite elements. From the graphics point of view visualizing the results of analysis closes the circle into scientific visualization again. As a result CAD type software lies somewhat outside the scope of this book. Our discussions on the topic will be limited to modeling with primitive planar shapes. The essentials of computer-aided geometric design are well covered in Farin's book [29] and information on solid modeling for CAD/CAM (computer-aided manufacture) can be found in the book by Mortenson [62].

For computer game developers the key element is the ability to render large numbers of polygons in real time. This is probably the most rapidly advancing area of application development and virtually every computer game now relies on the dedicated graphics hardware. A clear distinction is starting to emerge with, on one hand, ever more powerful console systems, whilst on the other hand, 3D games are starting to become popular as cell phone apps. Nearly everything that we discuss in this book has utility on the technical side of the computer games business.

1.1   A note on mathematics for 3D computer graphics

Geometry is the foundation on which computer graphics and specifically 3DCG is built. A familiarity with the basic concepts of geometry and what I can only express as *a "feel" for three dimensions* will make the understanding of existing, and creation of new, 3D algorithms much more straightforward.

In this book only two assumptions are made about the reader's mathematical prowess. First, that you have an appreciation of the Cartesian frame of reference which is used to map three-dimensional space and second, you know the rules for manipulating vectors and matrices. For any reader who wishes to *brush up* on their vector geometry a general introduction is given by Kindle [49].

A recent and excellent compendium of all aspects of the mathematics used in computer graphics is given by Lengyel [54], and the timeless classic *Numerical Recipes* by Press et al. [74] is a hugely valuable resource of source code for algorithms that solve more mathematical problems than we need to think about for computer graphics. And it has excellent accompanying computer codes as well.

1.2 Getting up to speed and following up

This book is not a general introduction to the subject of computer graphics (CG) or even to 3DCG. If you want to acquire background knowledge of hardware, software packages or the current state of what is now a huge industry there are many other excellent sources of information available.

The quantity of reference material that is available and our access to it has changed utterly since the first edition of the book was published. I think it is fair to say that *there is nothing you cannot find out about 3D computer graphics in the semi-infinite universe of the the World Wide Web*. A search engine may be a magnificent and powerful tool, but only if you have a clue about what you are looking for. So there remains a real need for the carefully crafted book, and the classic references have as much value today as they did a decade ago.

Of course, it would be quite ridiculous to dismiss the World Wide Web's semi-infinite library and resources, but its real value comes about because it lets you *get what you need, when you need it*. But we must be selective and have a pointer to follow. This is not as easy as it sound, because pages move, pages get changed, and pages get deleted or become outdated. Our aim is to preserve as much longevity in this book as we can, so all our web references will appear through our online content. There are only two web addresses you need to open the door: the book's website (the address is quoted in the Preface) and that of our open-source 3D application OpenFX (also referenced in the Preface).

As we've just discussed, there will always be a need to refer to some of the classic texts of computer graphics. They not only offer an insight into how the topic evolved but they also provide some of the best explanations for the major breakthroughs in 3D graphics. The following sections cover books that I personally have found very useful in my work.

1.2.1 Classic references

Many of the references cited in the first edition are timeless classics, and although some may be out of print, all can be obtained in a good library or with the click of a mouse from a secondhand bookstore. Some of the most useful ones, then and now are: *Real-Time Rendering* by Akenine-Möller and Haines [1], which describes the most important algorithms in the rendering pipeline and provides links to a wealth of research material. It has proved very popular and several revisions continue to be printed regularly. Watt [89] provides a good introduction to the main concepts of 3D computer graphics, and a comprehensive (but a bit dated) reference on all aspects of CG is that of Foley, Van Dam, Feiner and Hughes [31]. The book by Watt and Watt [87] is useful for filling in specific details on rendering and animation. For the mathematically inclined a rigorous evaluation on a very broad range of CG algorithms can be found in Eberly's book [21].

1.2.2 Specialist references

If you cannot find the algorithm you are looking for in the chapters forming part III then try looking into the five volumes of the Graphics Gems series [6, 34, 41, 50, 66].

The GPU Gems series [30, 64, 71] and the GPU Pro [27] series reinvigorate many of the classic Graphics Gems and packages them for GPU programming. Unfortunately, the GPU Gems series tend to be a bit hard to follow in places and it takes a bit more effort to get good value from the ideas presented there.

As already alluded, computer graphics publications have, in recent years, been carrying titles referring to the programmable graphics hardware (the Graphics Processing Unit, GPU) or to programming for computer games, but unless they are practical works focusing on OpenGL or DirectX programming, they are pretty much presenting the same material as in the classics. However there can be subtle differences of emphasis and terminology and reading the way different authors present the same idea can often lead to a *eureka* moment. *Game Engine Architecture* by Gregory [36] was one of the first books to put the focus on rendering algorithms specifically tailored for computer games programs.

Writing programs for the GPU (called shaders) has virtually become a science in itself and many of the ideas put forward in *Programming Vertex and Pixel Shaders* [28], *Shaders for Game Programmers and Artists* [53], *ShaderX*^{3} [24], *ShaderX*^{4} [25] and *ShaderX*^{5} [26] provide fascinating reading. Some gems of particular use for game developers can be found in Deloura's volume, *Game Programming Gems* [20].

For background and to complement the procedural textures described in chapter 11, the book by Ebert et al. [23] is ideal. It goes on to explore the use of fractals in computer graphics and demonstrates the techniques of volume shading and hypertextures with which realistic images of hair and fur can be created.

1.2.3 Practical references

Probably the best and most practically useful book in relation to geometric modeling algorithms is *O'Rourke's Computational Geometry* [65], which provides a useful alternative view of some of the modeling algorithms that we discuss in chapter 10 and its C code is a masterful implementation of the algorithms.

We already mentioned *The Visualization Toolkit* by Martin and Lorensen [77], an extremely useful library of software and not just a book. And of course the (code with) *Numerical Recipes in C++* [74] is a delight to have on hand when you need code for a mathematical algorithm.

The OpenGL books, the *Red Book* [82] and the *OpenGL SuperBible* [78], form a powerful duo of reference and *how-to* material. There is nothing these books will not show you how to do in real-time 3D graphics with OpenGL.

There are many practically useful references one can call on in the arena of programming the mobile and tablet devices. These specific texts will be identified in chapter 8.

And of course, we could not end this section without mentioning the World Wide Web, but there are just far too many useful references to acknowledge here. And anyway, who wants a 256 character web reference in a book? Consult our website for a collection of our favorite links.

1.3 Assumed knowledge

As stated earlier the assumption is that the reader is familiar with the concepts of the *vector* and has a basic knowledge of *coordinate geometry*. Some experience of using 3D graphics application software would also be an advantage, at least enough to know the significance of the terms *vertex, face/facet, polygon* and *pixel*.

For the programming sections, a knowledge of a **C** like programming language is essential, but since most languages have C (or C++) like syntax some programming experience in any language should let you get to grips with all the practical material. The biggest real challenge in developing computer programs comes in devising algorithms for tasks so that they can be carried out by the rather stupid computer, which after all can only do three things: *move, add, and decide which of two things to do next, depending on what the outcome of the add was*, think about it! [1]

The chapter on graphics programming for mobile devices has to develop its examples using the the C++ like languages of: Objective-C, in the case of Apple's iOS devices, and JAVA for the myriad of Android phones and tablets.

---

[1] And the second biggest challenge is not in coding up the algorithm in C, Java, Fortran, Python, Basic and so on. It is in knowing what Application Programmer Interface (API) function to use to get the computer's operating system or library to give you control of its user interface and peripherals: screen, disk, mouse, keyboard, WiFi and so forth.

To be able to make full use of the *Windows* example programs, it would be a decided advantage if you have used one of the versions of the *Visual Studio* Integrated Development Environment (IDE) and the Windows (Win32) Software Development Kit (SDK). For iOS programming there is little alternative but to develop within the Xcode project environment, and whilst Android applications can be built with commands in a shell or terminal using makefiles, the recommended IDE is one of the versions of Eclipse.

However, when you strip away the details, Visual Studio, Xcode and Eclipse all do basically the same thing and in pretty much the same way, so if you've used one of them, getting started with another is eased considerably. On the down side, mobile device application development is a rapidly evolving scene; not only do system versions change every two or three months but the APIs and even the development environments do too. We are fortunate that, by choosing to focus our mobile programming discussions on the mature OpenGL standard, even if everything else changes, our programs for 3D should not be affected too much.

1.4   Computer graphics and computer games

The theory of computer graphics is now a fairly mature subject, so it is possible to reflect on and examine the mathematics and algorithms safe in the knowledge that they have longevity. The ever increasing computer power and its availability allow the quest for perfection to continue, but the frenetic pace of fundamental research in the 1980s and '90s has relaxed a little. This is not true in the computer games world; the frenzy continues, perhaps with a little more emphasis now on interacting with the non-visual senses, for example as is done in games that make use of the Nintendo Wii-mote, balance board or the Microsoft Kinect.

Despite the interest in new sensors, touch and feel devices and stereoscopy, the games developers are still striving for greater realism in real-time graphics. The current best thinking is that the specialized programmable hardware, the GPU, will continue to improve. GPU manufacturers continue to release ever more powerful processors. One day soon you will be able to ray-trace a million polygons in real-time. Real-time graphics programing forms a significant part of this book.

Programming a GPU poses its own challenges and despite the hardware's standard provision of many of the basic algorithms of 3D graphics, it is essential that you are completely comfortable with the fundamentals in order to squeeze that last few cycles out of the processor; to make your game more realistic and exciting than the next guy's game. Gaming is not just about realistic graphics. The importance of movement and its physical simulation are a vital part of the realism quest. In this book we rank computer animation and realistic physical dynamics as being just as important as realistic rendering. It says a lot, to learn that games developer companies make use of many more artists and actors than they do programmers and software engineers.

1.5 The full spectrum

This book covers the full spectrum of 3D computer graphics. Starting with a blank canvas we must have tools to build numerical descriptions of objects and embed them in a virtual universe, or at least be able to mesh, optimize and decorate the point cloud delivered by a laser scanner. Just having a numerical description of the buildings of a city, the people in it, the mountains of the moon or the flowers in the garden, is like having a computer with no screen, so we must be able to turn the numbers into a beautiful picture. But not even a crystal clear snapshot can do justice to simulating reality. We must also be able to move around, look at things and watch, while the virtual world and its inhabitants go about their lives. Being able to do these things from a basic set of numbers is what this book is about.

The word *practical* in the title highlights the aim of taking the algorithms of computer graphics all the way from their theoretical origins right through into a practical implementation. The book has a companion website where a suite of practical codes and references can be found. And, to really reinforce the focus on practical programs a chapter is devoted to lifting the lid on the OpenFX open source software package to show how it does its modeling, animation, and visualization. After reading chapter 9 you will be able to delve into the OpenFX source code, modify it and use it as a platform for all sorts of interesting projects.

The book is divided into three parts. The first, "basic principles," covers the key concepts of 3D computer graphics. After this brief introduction the focus moves to the fundamental mathematical ideas (chapter 2) that lie at the heart of all the other algorithms discussed in the book. Personally, I find it very satisfying that in just a few pages we can set out *all the maths* you need to produce beautiful photo-realistic pictures.

A computer-generated image of a 3D universe requires that the objects which inhabit it are described using numbers and stored in some form of structured database. Chapter 3 discusses the pros and cons of 3D data organization and describes several algorithms that are useful in manipulating faceted models of the universe's inhabitants.

Chapters 4 and 5 cover the topic of rendering and take a step-by-step approach to the design of algorithms, from the fastest scanline Z buffer procedure to the high-quality ray-traced approach. I have tried to include those little things that generally get overlooked in the grand theoretical texts but are of practical importance, for example, how to optimize your 3D data for ray tracing.

The principles of computer animation discussed in chapter 6 have resonances not just in the business of making animated movies because, when they are used in real-time they underlie some of the vital features of a computer game's engine. Chapter 6 outlines the basic principles of animation techniques and discusses character animation and other motions governed by the laws of physics rather than by having to *move them by hand*. The principles of *inverse kinematics* are introduced and presented in a way specific to computer animation and for use in computer games.

Part II is devoted to the topic of real-time 3D rendering, and dissecting the OpenFX software. In chapter 7 we look at how to use the OpenGL library to take maximum advantage of the computer hardware specifically designed for 3D graphics. With the growth of the use of the *so-called* smart-phone and the fact that these devices include specialist hardware for rendering 3D graphics, it seems very timely to show how easy it is to move a 3D application from the desktop into the pocket. Chapter 8 will show you how to build an environment on the most popular mobile devices for deploying a 3D game or other 3D application. To complete part II, chapter 9 examines the code for OpenFX, which is an open source, fully functional, 3D modeling, animation and visualization application program that puts into practice the algorithms of the book.

Part III is intended for the professional *plug-in* or game engine developer and provides (hopefully) a rich collection of algorithms covering such diverse topics as polygonal modeling procedures (chapter 10) and procedural textures for use with a photo-realistic Z buffer or ray tracing renderer (chapter 11), or in the fragment programs of a GPU.

The chapter on pseudo three-dimensional video transition effects from the first edition has been removed and may now be found in an updated form on the book's website.

The subject of 3D graphics has matured very significantly since the first edition of the book was written back in 2001. Twelve years on, despite the many new algorithms and vast advances in hardware, the core algorithms are just as valid as they were back then, so that's where we will start—read on.

2

Basic theory and mathematical results

This chapter describes the essential mathematical concepts that form the basis for most 3D computer graphics theory. It also establishes the notation and conventions that will be used throughout the book. There are many texts that cover 3D computer graphics in great detail, and if you are unfamiliar with the details considered in this chapter consult other references [2, 15, 89]. For books that cover the mathematical theory in more detail you might consult Foley et al. [31], Rogers and Adams [76] or Mortenson [61].

If you wish you can skip directly to chapter 4 where the main topics of the book begin with details of algorithms for the rendering pipeline. Refer back to the appropriate sections in this chapter when required.

2.1 Coordinate systems

A coordinate system provides a numerical frame of reference for the 3D universe in which we will develop our ideas and algorithms. Two coordinate systems are particularly useful to us, the ubiquitous Cartesian (x, y, z) rectilinear system and the spherical polar (r, θ, ϕ) or (angular) system. Cartesian coordinates are the most commonly used, but angular coordinates are particularly helpful when it comes to directing 3D animations where it is not only important to say where something is located but also in which direction it is looking or moving.

2.1.1 Cartesian

Figure 2.1 illustrates the Cartesian system. Any point P is uniquely specified by a triple of numbers (a, b, c). Mutually perpendicular coordinate axes are conventionally labeled x, y and z. For the point P the numbers a, b and c can be thought of as distances we need to move in order to travel from the origin to the point P. (Move a units along the x axis then b units parallel to the y axis and finally c units parallel to the z axis.)

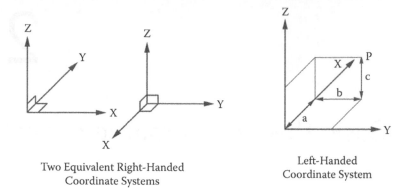

Two Equivalent Right-Handed
Coordinate Systems

Left-Handed
Coordinate System

Figure 2.1: Right- and left-handed coordinate systems with the z axis vertical.

In the Cartesian system the axes can be orientated in either a *left-* or *right-*handed sense. A right-handed convention is consistent with the vector cross product and all algorithms and formulae used in this book assume a right-handed convention.

2.1.2 Spherical polar

Figure 2.2 shows the conventional spherical polar coordinate system in relation to the Cartesian axes. r is a measure of the distance from the origin to a point in space. The angles θ and ϕ are taken relative to the z and x axes respectively. Unlike the Cartesian x, y and z values, which all take the same units, spherical polar coordinates use both distance and angle measures. Importantly, there are some points in space that do not have a unique one-to-one relationship with an (r, θ, ϕ) coordinate value. For example points lying on the positive z axis can have any value of ϕ; $(100, 0, 0)$ and $(100, 0, \pi)$ both represent the same point.

Also, the range of values which (r, θ, ϕ) can take is limited. The radial distance r is such that it is always positive $0 \leq r < \infty$, θ lies in the range $0 \leq \theta \leq \pi$ and ϕ takes values $0 \leq \phi < 2\pi$. There is no unique way to specify a range for ϕ; one could equally well choose $-\pi \leq \phi < \pi$, but to avoid confusion it is best to adhere rigidly to one interval.

It is quite straightforward to change from one coordinate system to the other. When the point P in figure 2.2 is expressed as (r, θ, ϕ) the Cartesian coordinates (x, y, z) are given by the trigonometric expressions:

$$
\begin{aligned}
x &= r \sin \theta \cos \phi \\
y &= r \sin \theta \sin \phi \\
z &= r \cos \theta
\end{aligned}
$$

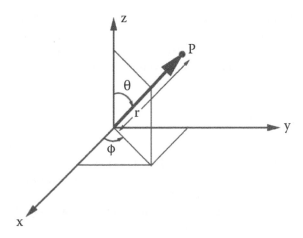

Figure 2.2: The spherical polar coordinate system.

Conversion from Cartesian to spherical coordinates is a little more tricky; it requires an algorithm that tests for the special cases where P lies very close to the z axis. A suitable implementation is presented in listing 2.1.

```
if (x² + y²) < ε {
    r =| z |
    θ = 0
    φ = 0
}
else {
    r = √(x² + y² + z²)
    θ = arcsin(√(x² + y²)/r)
    if (y < 0) {
        φ = 2π − ATAN2(y, x)
    }
    else {
        φ = ATAN2(y, x)
    }
}
```

Listing 2.1: Algorithm for conversion from Cartesian to spherical coordinates.

The parameter ϵ is necessary because no computer can calculate with total accuracy. What value is chosen depends on the relative size of the largest and smallest measurements. For example a 3D animation of atomic and molecular processes would have a very different value of ϵ from one illustrating planetary dynamics.

The function $ATAN2(y, x)$ is provided in the libraries of many computer languages. It returns a value in the range $(-\pi, \pi)$, which is the angle made with the x axis by a line from $(0, 0)$ to (x, y). In the first quadrant this is equivalent to $\arctan(y/x)$, which is of course not defined at $\pi/2$.

2.2   Vectors

The vector, the key to all 3D work, is a triple of real numbers (in most computer languages these are usually called floating point numbers) and is noted in a **bold** typeface, e.g., **P** or **p**. When hand written (and in the figures of this book) vectors are noted with an <u>underscore</u>, e.g., $\underline{P}$.

Care must be taken to differentiate between two ways in which we use vectors in computer graphics: see figure 2.3.

- Position Vector

A position vector runs from the origin of coordinates $(0, 0, 0)$ to a point (x, y, z) and its length gives the distance of the point from the origin. Its components are given by (x, y, z). The essential concept to understand about a position vector is that it is anchored to specific coordinates (points in space). The set of points or *vertices* that are used to describe the *shape* of all models in 3D graphics can be thought of as position vectors.

Thus a point with coordinates (x, y, z) can also be identified as the end point of a position vector **p**. We shall often refer to a point as (x, y, z) or **p**.

- Direction Vector

A direction vector differs from a position vector in that it is **not** anchored to specific coordinates. Frequently direction vectors are used in a form where they have unit length; in this case they are said to be *normalized*. The most common application of a direction vector in 3D computer graphics is to specify the orientation of a surface or ray direction. For this we use a direction vector at right angles (*normal*) and pointing away from the surface. Such *normal* vectors are the key to calculating lighting and surface shading effects.

2.3   Homogeneous coordinates

Section 2.2 focused on two ways of using vectors that are particularly pertinent in 3D computer graphics. However vectors are a much more general mathematical concept, an n-tuple of numbers $(a_1, a_2, .., a_n)$, where $n > 1$ is a vector. A one-dimensional array in a computer program is a vector; a single column matrix $[a_1, a_2, a_3, ...a_n]^T$ is also a vector.

One of the most obvious differences between position and direction vectors is that directions are independent of any translational transformation, whereas the coordinates of a point in 3-space are certainly not independent when the

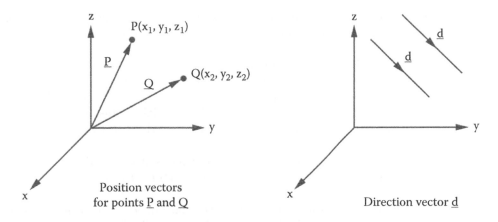

Figure 2.3: Position and direction vectors.

point is moved. In order to be able to treat these vectors consistently we need to introduce the concept of homogeneous coordinates. Since 3D vectors are a logical extension of 2D vectors, and it is easier to understand the concept of homogeneous coordinates in 2D, we will consider these. Hopefully you will be comfortable with the idea of extending them to 3D by adding in a third component, the result of which we present without rigorous proof.

A general two-dimensional line is represented by the well-known equation:

$$ax + by + c = 0 \qquad (2.1)$$

Any point in a plane (x_p, y_p) that lies on the line must satisfy 2.1, that is, $ax_p + by_p + c$ must be identically zero. It is quite legitimate to write 2.1 using matrix notation:

$$[a, b, c][x, y, 1]^T \qquad (2.2)$$

This conveys the same information as 2.1, but it can now be clearly seen that two pairs of *triple numbers* are involved, (a, b, c) and $(x, y, 1)$ Any triple of numbers conforms to the definition of a 3-vector and so the line in 2.1 is fully defined by the vector (a, b, c). The triple $(x, y, 1)$ is also a 3-vector and represents any point that satisfies the equation, i.e., lies on the line in 2.1, for example the point $(x_p, y_p, 1)$.

Equation 2.1 and the line it represents is unchanged if we multiply it by a constant, say w to give:

$$wax + wby + wc = 0 \qquad (2.3)$$

or equivalently:

$$[a, b, c][wx, wy, w]^T \qquad (2.4)$$

From this it is clear that, in this situation, the family of vectors (wx, wy, w) for any w are equivalent. Vectors with this property are called (in the trade) *homogeneous vectors.* Thus, for our specific case where the vector (wx, wy, w) represents the coordinates of a point on a 2D plane it is known as a *homogeneous coordinate.*

In its simplest form we can think of the homogeneous coordinate of the 2D point (x, y) as $(x, y, 1)$. For a point in 3D (x, y, z) we can propose that the equivalent homogeneous coordinate will be (wx, wy, wz, w), or in its simplest form $(x, y, z, 1)$. The last element, the 1, is essential because if it was zero then c in 2.1 would disappear and only lines that pass through the coordinate origin could be specified.

Considering 2D vectors again, we ask, what sort of two-dimensional vector might be represented by the homogeneous vector $(x, y, 0)$ (or more generally $(wx, wy, 0)$)?

We know from basic geometry that the constant c in equation 2.1 defines a whole family of lines with the same gradient (parallel lines) lying in the plane. These lines are not anchored to any point. The representation in equation 2.2 shows us that if the homogeneous vector has a third component of zero, then the c value of the line (a, b, c) is irrelevant in satisfying 2.1. Thus a 2D homogeneous vector $(x, y, 0)$ can be used to define a direction vector that is independent of any origin of coordinates. A 3D direction vector may be similarly described by the homogeneous 4-vector $(x, y, z, 0)$.

After transformations are discussed in section 2.12 it should be evident that 3D direction vectors written in the homogeneous form $(x, y, z, 0)$ are invariant to translational transformations whereas 3D position vectors, written in homogeneous form $(x, y, z, 1)$ and representing points, are not.

There are other subtleties related to 2D and 3D homogeneous coordinates that have a fourth element of zero, but we refer you to books such as those by Zisserman [39] for elaboration.

This way of representing vertex coordinates and surface normal vectors is exactly what we need to handle transformations in 3D graphics.

2.4   The line in vector form

There are two useful ways to express the equation of a line in vector form. For a line passing through a point $\mathbf{P_0}$ and having a direction $\hat{\mathbf{d}}$, then any point $\mathbf{p}$ which lies on the line is given by:

$$\mathbf{p} = \mathbf{P_0} + \mu\hat{\mathbf{d}}$$

$\mathbf{P_0}$ is a position vector and $\hat{\mathbf{d}}$ is a unit length (*normalized*) direction vector.

Alternatively any point $\mathbf{p}$ on a line passing through two points $\mathbf{P_0}$ and $\mathbf{P_1}$ is given by:

$$\mathbf{p} = \mathbf{P_0} + \mu(\mathbf{P_1} - \mathbf{P_0})$$

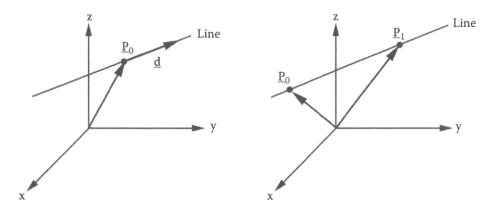

Figure 2.4: Specifying a line.

The parameter μ takes values in the range $-\infty < \mu < \infty$. Note that when $\mu = 0$ then $\mathbf{p} = \mathbf{P_0}$.

On a line passing through two points $\mathbf{p} = \mathbf{P_0}$ when $\mu = 0$ and $\mathbf{p} = \mathbf{P_1}$ when $\mu = 1.0$.

Using two points to express an equation for the line is useful when we need to consider a finite segment of a line. (There are many examples where we need to use segments of lines such as calculating the point of intersection between a line segment and a plane.)

Thus if we need to consider a line segment we can assign $\mathbf{P_0}$ and $\mathbf{P_1}$ to the segment end points with the consequence that any point on the line $\mathbf{p}$ will only be part of the segment if its value for μ in the equation above lies in the interval $[0, 1]$.

2.5   The plane

A plane is completely specified by giving a point on the plane $\mathbf{P_0}$, and the direction $\hat{\mathbf{n}}$ perpendicular to the plane.

To write an equation to represent the plane we can use the fact that the vector $(\mathbf{p} - \mathbf{P_0})$ which lies in the plane must be at right angles to the normal to the plane, thus:

$$(\mathbf{p} - \mathbf{P_0}) \cdot \hat{\mathbf{n}} = \mathbf{0}$$

Alternatively a plane could be specified by taking three points, $\mathbf{P_2}$, $\mathbf{P_1}$ and $\mathbf{P_0}$, lying in the plane. Provided they are not co-linear it is valid to write the equation of the plane as:

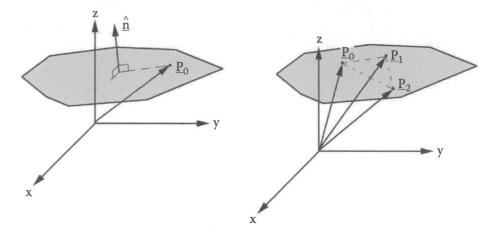

Figure 2.5: Specifying a plane.

$$(\mathbf{p} - \mathbf{P_0}) \cdot \frac{(\mathbf{P_2} - \mathbf{P_0}) \times (\mathbf{P_1} - \mathbf{P_0})}{|\,(\mathbf{P_2} - \mathbf{P_0}) \times (\mathbf{P_1} - \mathbf{P_0})\,|} = 0$$

Figure 2.5 illustrates these two specifications for a plane. It should be noted that these equations apply to planes that extend to infinity in all directions. We shall see later that the intersection of a line with a *bounded* plane plays a very important role in rendering and modeling algorithms.

2.6 Intersection of a line and a plane

The intersection of a line and a plane is a point $\mathbf{p_i}$ that satisfies the equation of the line and the equation of the plane simultaneously. For the line $\mathbf{p} = \mathbf{P_1} + \mu \hat{\mathbf{d}}$ and the plane $(\mathbf{p} - \mathbf{P_p}) \cdot \hat{\mathbf{n}} = 0$ the point of intersection $\mathbf{p}_I$ is given by:

> **if** $(|\hat{\mathbf{d}} \cdot \hat{\mathbf{n}}| < \epsilon)$ there is no intersection
> **else** {
> $\mu = \dfrac{(\mathbf{P_p} - \mathbf{P_1}) \cdot \hat{\mathbf{n}}}{\hat{\mathbf{d}} \cdot \hat{\mathbf{n}}}$
> $\mathbf{p}_I = \mathbf{P_1} + \mu \hat{\mathbf{d}}$
> }

Note that we must first test to see whether the line and plane actually intersect. The parameter ϵ allows for the numerical accuracy of computer calculations and since $\hat{\mathbf{d}}$ and $\hat{\mathbf{n}}$ are of unit length ϵ should be of the order of the machine arithmetic precision.

$$\mathbf{a} = \mathbf{P}_0 - \mathbf{P}_p$$
$$\mathbf{b} = \mathbf{P}_1 - \mathbf{P}_p$$
$$d_a = \mathbf{a} \cdot \mathbf{n}$$
$$d_b = \mathbf{b} \cdot \mathbf{n}$$

```
  if |d_a| ≤ ε_0  and  |d_b| ≤ ε_0  {
     both P_0 and P_1 lie in the plane
  }
  else  {
      d_ab = d_a d_b
       if  d_ab < ε_1  {
          The line crosses the plane
        }
      else  {
         The line does not cross the plane
        }
  }
```

Listing 2.2: Algorithm to determine whether the line joining two points crosses a plane.

2.6.1   Intersection of a line segment with a plane

Given a line segment joining $\mathbf{P}_0$ to $\mathbf{P}_1$ and a plane $(\mathbf{p} - \mathbf{P}_p) \cdot \hat{\mathbf{n}} = \mathbf{0}$ the algorithm of figure 2.2 determines whether the plane and line intersect. Note that this does not actually calculate the point of intersection. It is a good idea to separate the calculation of an intersection point by first testing whether there will be one before going on to determine the point. This is especially useful when we need to consider clipping, see section 4.2.6.

The parameters ϵ_0 and ϵ_1 are again chosen as non-zero values because of the numerical accuracy of floating point calculations.

2.7   Closest distance of a point from a line

Consider the line L passing through the points $\mathbf{P_1}$ and $\mathbf{P_2}$ as shown in figure 2.6. To find the closest distance, l, of the point $\mathbf{p}$ from L we recognize that the projection of the vector $\mathbf{p} - \mathbf{P_1}$ onto $\mathbf{P}_L$ allows us to find the point, $\mathbf{q}$, on L which is closest to $\mathbf{p}$. Thus, the closest distance is given by the steps:

Let $\mathbf{d} = (\mathbf{P_2} - \mathbf{P_1})$
then $\mu = \dfrac{(\mathbf{p} - \mathbf{P_1}) \cdot \mathbf{d}}{\mathbf{d} \cdot \mathbf{d}}$ and $\mathbf{q} = \mathbf{P_1} + \mu \mathbf{d}$
thus $l = |\mathbf{p} - \mathbf{q}|$
When ($\mu < 0$ or $\mu > 1.0$)   {
       $\mathbf{p}$ is closer to the line outside of the segment from $\mathbf{P_1}$ to $\mathbf{P_2}$
   }

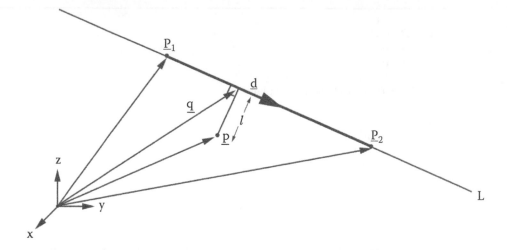

Figure 2.6: Closest distance of a point from a line segment.

As illustrated in figure 2.6 it is only when $0 < \mu < 1$ that the perpendicular from **p** to the line meets the position vector **d**, i.e., between the points $\mathbf{P_1}$, $\mathbf{P_2}$.

This algorithm is useful for a 3D application program where it is necessary to interactively pick a line by touching it, or pointing to it on a display with a user input device such as a mouse.

2.8   Closest distance of approach between two lines

In three-dimensional space two arbitrary lines rarely intersect. However it is useful to be able to find the closest distance of approach between them. In the geometry shown in figure 2.7 the segment AA' (vector **b**) joins the points of closest approach between the lines:

$$\mathbf{p} = \mathbf{P_1} + \lambda\hat{\mathbf{r}}$$
$$\mathbf{p} = \mathbf{P_2} + \mu\hat{\mathbf{d}}$$

At the points of closest approach **b** is perpendicular to both lines and therefore: $\mathbf{b} \cdot \hat{\mathbf{d}} = 0$ and $\mathbf{b} \cdot \hat{\mathbf{r}} = 0$.

To determine the length of **b** consider the alternative ways of specifying the point **x**, i.e., following alternative paths from O to **x**:

$$\mathbf{x} = \mathbf{P_1} + \lambda\hat{\mathbf{r}}$$
$$\mathbf{x} = \mathbf{P_2} + \mu\hat{\mathbf{d}} + \mathbf{b}$$

Thus:

$$\mu\hat{\mathbf{d}} - \mathbf{b} = \lambda\hat{\mathbf{r}} + (\mathbf{P_1} - \mathbf{P_2}) \tag{2.5}$$

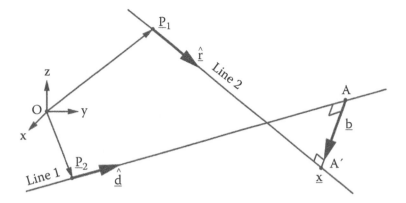

Figure 2.7: Closest distance of approach between two lines.

Once λ and μ are determined the length of $\mathbf{b}$ is readily found:

$$l = \left| \mathbf{P}_1 + \lambda\hat{\mathbf{r}} - (\mathbf{P}_2 + \mu\hat{\mathbf{d}}) \right| \tag{2.6}$$

Taking the dot product of 2.5 with $\hat{\mathbf{r}}$ will eliminate $\mathbf{b}$ and give an expression for λ:

$$\lambda = \mu(\hat{\mathbf{d}} \cdot \hat{\mathbf{r}}) - (\mathbf{P}_1 - \mathbf{P}_2) \cdot \hat{\mathbf{r}} \tag{2.7}$$

The dot product of 2.5 with $\hat{\mathbf{d}}$ eliminates $\mathbf{b}$ and substituting λ using 2.7 gives:

$$\mu = \frac{((\mathbf{P}_1 - \mathbf{P}_2) \cdot \hat{\mathbf{d}}) - ((\mathbf{P}_1 - \mathbf{P}_2) \cdot \hat{\mathbf{r}})(\hat{\mathbf{d}} \cdot \hat{\mathbf{r}})}{1 - (\hat{\mathbf{d}} \cdot \hat{\mathbf{r}})^2} \tag{2.8}$$

With μ known 2.7 gives λ and then the distance of closest approach follows from 2.6.

Note: If the lines are parallel $\left| (\hat{\mathbf{d}} \cdot \hat{\mathbf{r}}) \right| < \epsilon$ (where ϵ is the machine tolerance of zero, approximately 1×10^{-6} for single precision calculations), then the algorithm is terminated before it reaches equation 2.8.

2.9   Reflection in a plane

In many rendering algorithms there is a requirement to calculate a reflected direction given an incident direction and a plane of reflection. The vectors we need to consider in this calculation are of the *direction* type and assumed to be of unit length.

If the incident vector is $\hat{\mathbf{d}}_{in}$, the reflection vector is $\hat{\mathbf{d}}_{out}$ and the surface normal is $\mathbf{n}$, we can calculate the reflected vector by recognizing that because $\hat{\mathbf{d}}_{out}$ and $\hat{\mathbf{d}}_{in}$ are normalized (the argument would work equally well provided

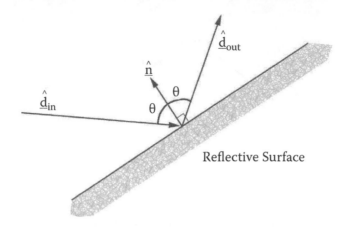

Figure 2.8: Incident and reflection vector.

$\mathbf{d}_{out}$ and $\mathbf{d}_{in}$ are the same length) then vector $(\hat{\mathbf{d}}_{out} - \hat{\mathbf{d}}_{in})$ is co-linear with $\hat{\mathbf{n}}$; figure 2.8 illustrates this, therefore:

$$\hat{\mathbf{d}}_{out} - \hat{\mathbf{d}}_{in} = \alpha\hat{\mathbf{n}} \qquad (2.9)$$

where α is a scalar factor. As the incident and reflected angles are equal

$$\hat{\mathbf{d}}_{out} \cdot \hat{\mathbf{n}} = -\hat{\mathbf{d}}_{in} \cdot \hat{\mathbf{n}} \qquad (2.10)$$

Taking the dot product of both sides of Equation 2.9 with $\mathbf{n}$, substituting in equation 2.10 and using the fact that $\mathbf{n}$ is normalized we obtain for the reflected direction:

$$\hat{\mathbf{d}}_{out} = \hat{\mathbf{d}}_{in} - 2(\hat{\mathbf{d}}_{in} \cdot \hat{\mathbf{n}})\hat{\mathbf{n}}$$

2.10   Refraction at a plane

Photo-realistic renderers require to be able to simulate transparent surfaces where rays of light are refracted as they pass through the boundary between materials of different refractive index. Figure 2.9 shows a refractive surface with an incident vector $\hat{\mathbf{d}}_i$, surface normal $\hat{\mathbf{n}}$ and refracted vector $\hat{\mathbf{d}}_r$. All three vectors are of the direction type.

The physical model of refraction is expressed in Snell's law which states:

$$\frac{n_r}{n_i} = \frac{\sin\theta_i}{\sin\theta_r}$$

where n_i and n_r are transmission constants for the media in which the incident and refracted light rays travel. Snell's law can also be written in vector form:

$$n_i(\hat{\mathbf{d}}_i \times \hat{\mathbf{n}}) = n_r(\hat{\mathbf{d}}_r \times \hat{\mathbf{n}})$$

Since $\hat{\mathbf{d}}_i$, $\hat{\mathbf{d}}_r$ and $\hat{\mathbf{n}}$ all lie in a plane, $\hat{\mathbf{d}}_r$ can be expressed as a linear combination of $\hat{\mathbf{d}}_i$ and $\hat{\mathbf{n}}$:

$$\hat{\mathbf{d}}_r = \alpha\hat{\mathbf{d}}_i + \beta\hat{\mathbf{n}} \tag{2.11}$$

Taking the vector product of both sides of equation 2.11 with $\hat{\mathbf{n}}$ and substituting it for the right-hand side of the vector form of Snell's law gives a value for α which is:

$$\alpha = \frac{n_i}{n_r}$$

The dot product of both sides of equation 2.11 produce a quadratic in β:

$$\hat{\mathbf{d}}_r \cdot \hat{\mathbf{d}}_r = 1 = \alpha^2 + 2\alpha\beta(\hat{\mathbf{n}} \cdot \hat{\mathbf{d}}_i) + \beta^2$$

Only one of the roots of this equation is a physically meaningful solution. The appropriate root is determined by considering an incident ray perpendicular to the surface. Once this is done the meaningful value of β is substituted into 2.11 and rearranged to give a two step calculation for the refracted direction:

$$r = (\hat{\mathbf{n}} \cdot \hat{\mathbf{d}}_i)^2 + \left(\frac{n_r}{n_i}\right)^2 - 1$$

$$\hat{\mathbf{d}}_r = \frac{n_i}{n_r}\left((\sqrt{r} - \hat{\mathbf{n}} \cdot \hat{\mathbf{d}}_i)\hat{\mathbf{n}} + \hat{\mathbf{d}}_i\right)$$

Note that if the term r is negative, reflection (section 2.9) rather than refraction occurs.

2.11   Intersection of a line with primitive shapes

Many 3D algorithms *(rendering and modeling)* require the calculation of the point of intersection between a line and a fundamental shape called a *primitive*. We have already dealt with the calculation of the intersection between a line and a plane. If the plane is bounded we get a primitive shape called a *planar polygon*. Most 3D rendering and modeling application programs use polygons that have either three sides (triangles) or four sides (quadrilaterals). Triangular polygons are by far the most common because it is always possible to reduce an n sided polygon to a set of triangles. Most of the modeling algorithms in this book will refer to triangular polygons. An algorithm to reduce an n sided polygon to a set of triangular polygons is given in chapter 10.

Other important primitive shapes are the planar disc and the volume solids, the sphere and cylinder. There are more complex shapes that can still be termed

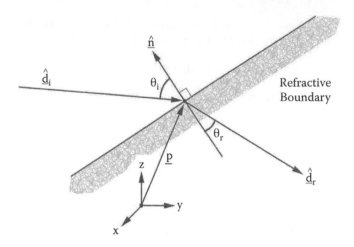

Figure 2.9: Tracing a refracted ray. Note that the incident, refracted and surface normal directions all lie in a plane.

primitive though they are used much less frequently. It is possible to set up analytic expressions for shapes made by lofting a curve along an axis or by sweeping a curve round an axis; see Burger and Gillies [15] for examples. There are a large number of other primitive shapes such as Bézier, spline and NURBS patches and subdivision surfaces to mention a few.

In this section we will examine the most important intersection in the context of software that uses planar polygons as the basic unit for modeling objects.

2.11.1   Intersection of a line with a triangular polygon

This calculation is used time and time again in modeling algorithms (Booleans, capping and normal calculations) and in rendering algorithms (image and texture mapping and in ray tracing). The importance of determining whether an intersection occurs in the interior of the polygon, near one of its vertices, or at one of its edges, or indeed just squeaks by outside, cannot be over emphasized.

This section gives an algorithm that can be used determine whether a line intersects a triangular polygon. It also classifies the point of intersection as being internal, or a point close to one of the vertices or within some small distance from an edge.

The geometry of the problem is shown in figure 2.10. The point $\mathbf{P}_i$ gives the intersection between a line and a plane. The plane is defined by the points $\mathbf{P}_0$, $\mathbf{P}_1$ and $\mathbf{P}_2$, as described in section 2.6. They also identify the vertices of the triangular polygon. Vectors $\mathbf{u}$ and $\mathbf{v}$ are along two of the edges of the triangle under consideration. Provided $\mathbf{u}$ and $\mathbf{v}$ are **not** co-linear the vector $\mathbf{w}$,

$$\mathbf{w} = \mathbf{P}_i - \mathbf{P}_0$$

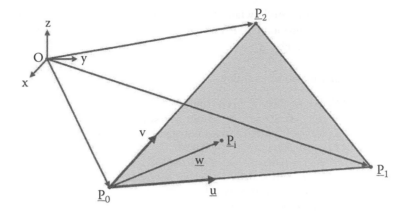

Figure 2.10: Intersection of line and triangular polygon.

lies in the plane and can be expressed as a linear combination of $\mathbf{u}$ and $\mathbf{v}$:

$$\mathbf{w} = \alpha\mathbf{u} + \beta\mathbf{v} \qquad (2.12)$$

Once α and β have been calculated a set of tests will reveal whether $\mathbf{P}_i$ lies inside or outside the triangular polygon with vertices at $\mathbf{P}_0$, $\mathbf{P}_1$ and $\mathbf{P}_2$.

Algorithm overview:

1. To find $\mathbf{P}_i$ we use the method described in section 2.6.

2. To calculate α and β take the dot product of 2.12 with $\mathbf{u}$ and $\mathbf{v}$ respectively. After a little algebra the results can be expressed as:

$$\alpha = \frac{(\mathbf{w} \cdot \mathbf{u})(\mathbf{v} \cdot \mathbf{v}) - (\mathbf{w} \cdot \mathbf{v})(\mathbf{u} \cdot \mathbf{v})}{(\mathbf{u} \cdot \mathbf{u})(\mathbf{v} \cdot \mathbf{v}) - (\mathbf{u} \cdot \mathbf{v})^2}$$

$$\beta = \frac{(\mathbf{w} \cdot \mathbf{v})(\mathbf{u} \cdot \mathbf{u}) - (\mathbf{w} \cdot \mathbf{u})(\mathbf{u} \cdot \mathbf{v})}{(\mathbf{u} \cdot \mathbf{u})(\mathbf{v} \cdot \mathbf{v}) - (\mathbf{u} \cdot \mathbf{v})^2}$$

Since both expressions have the same denominator it need only be calculated once. Products such as $(\mathbf{w} \cdot \mathbf{v})$ occur more than once and therefore assigning these to temporary variables will speed up the calculation. It is very worthwhile optimizing the speed of this calculation because it lies at the core of many *time critical* steps in a rendering algorithm, particularly image and texture mapping functions. **C++** code for this important function is available with the book.

The pre-calculation of $(\mathbf{u} \cdot \mathbf{u})(\mathbf{v} \cdot \mathbf{v}) - (\mathbf{u} \cdot \mathbf{v})^2$ is important, because should it turn out to be too close to zero we cannot obtain values for α or β. This problem occurs when one of the sides of the triangle is of zero length. In practice a triangle where this happens can be ignored because if one of its sides has zero length, it has zero area and will therefore not be visible in a rendered image.

3. Return hit code as follows:

   if $(\alpha < -0.001 \;$ or $\; \alpha > 1.001 \;$ or
       $\beta < -0.001 \;$ or $\; \beta > 1.001)$ miss polygon
   if $((\alpha + \beta) > 1.001)$ miss polygon beyond edge $\mathbf{P}_1 \rightarrow \mathbf{P}_2$
   if $(\alpha \geq 0.0005 \;$ and $\; \alpha \leq 0.9995$
     and $\; \beta \geq 0.0005 \;$ and $\; \beta \leq 0.9995$
     and $\; (\alpha + \beta) \leq 0.9995)$ inside polygon
   else if $(\alpha < 0.0005)$ {
     along edge $\mathbf{P}_0 \rightarrow \mathbf{P}_1$
     if $(\beta < 0.0005)$ at vertex $\mathbf{P}_0$
     else (**if** $\; \beta > 0.9995)$ at vertex $\mathbf{P}_1$
     else On edge $\mathbf{P}_0 \rightarrow \mathbf{P}_1$ not near vertex
   }
   else if $(\beta < 0.0005)$ {
     along edge $\mathbf{P}_0 \rightarrow \mathbf{P}_2$
     if $(\alpha < 0.0005)$ at vertex $\mathbf{P}_0$
     else if $(\alpha > 0.9995)$ at vertex $\mathbf{P}_2$
     else On edge $\mathbf{P}_0 \rightarrow \mathbf{P}_2$ not near vertex
   }
   else if $((\alpha + \beta) > 0.9995)$ on edge $\mathbf{P}_1 \rightarrow \mathbf{P}_2$
   else miss polygon

Note that the parameters -0.001 and so on are not dependent on the absolute size of the triangle because α and β are numbers in the range $[0, 1]$.

Alternative algorithms for ray/triangle intersection are shown in Badouel [34] and Moller [60].

2.12 Transformations

Transformations have two purposes in 3D graphics: *to modify the position vector of a vertex* and *change the orientation of a direction vector*. It is useful to express a transformation in the form of a matrix. In the previous sections we discussed vectors; a vector itself is just a special case of a matrix. If you are unfamiliar with matrices, vectors or linear algebra in general it might be useful to consult other references [7, 17, 57].

The vectors we have used so far apply to the 3D universe and thus have three components (x, y, z). In matrix form they also have three elements and are written in a single column:

$$\begin{bmatrix} x \\ y \\ z \end{bmatrix}$$

This matrix is said to have three rows and one column, a 3×1 matrix. Matrices can have any number of rows and columns; for example a 4×4 matrix might be represented by:

$$\begin{bmatrix} a_{00} & a_{01} & a_{02} & a_{03} \\ a_{10} & a_{11} & a_{12} & a_{13} \\ a_{20} & a_{21} & a_{22} & a_{23} \\ a_{30} & a_{31} & a_{32} & a_{33} \end{bmatrix}$$

It turns out that all the transformations appropriate for computer graphics work, moving, rotating, scaling etc., can be represented by a matrix of size 4×4. Matrices are mathematical objects and have their own algebra just as real numbers do. You can add, multiply and invert a matrix.

Several different notations are used to represent a matrix. Throughout this text we will use the [ ] bracket notation. When we discussed vectors we used a bold type to represent a vector as a single entity. When we want to represent a matrix as an individual entity we will use the notation of a capital letter in square brackets, e.g., $[P]$. Since a 3D vector and a 3×1 matrix represent the same thing we will use the symbols $\mathbf{P}$ and $[P]$ interchangeably.

If a transformation is represented by a matrix $[T]$, a point $\mathbf{p}$ is transformed to a new point $\mathbf{p}'$ by matrix multiplication according to the rule:

$$[p'] = [T][p]$$

The order in which the matrices are multiplied is important; $[T][p]$ is different from $[p][T]$, and indeed one of these may **not** even be defined.

There are two important points which are particularly relevant when using matrix transformations in 3D graphics applications:

1. How to multiply matrices of different sizes.

2. The importance of the order in which matrices are multiplied.

The second point will be dealt with in section 2.12.4. As for the first point, to multiply two matrices the number of columns in the first must equal the number of rows in the second. For example a matrix of size 3×3 and 3×1 may be multiplied giving a matrix of size 3×1. However a 4×4 and a 3×1 matrix cannot be multiplied. This poses a small problem for us because vectors are represented by 3×1 matrices and transformations are represented as 4×4 matrices.

The problem is solved by using homogeneous coordinates in the transformations. We will not make use of all the extra flexibility that working in homogeneous coordinates offers and restrict ourselves to taking advantage of the promotion of a 3D coordinate by adding a fourth component of unity to the vectors that represent positions. Thus the first three elements of a homogeneous coordinate are the familiar (x, y, z) values and the fourth is set to '1' so that now a vector appears as a 4×1 matrix. A transformation applied to a vector in *homogeneous* coordinate form results in another *homogeneous* coordinate vector. For all the work in this book the fourth component of vectors will be set to unity and thus they can be transformed by 4×4 matrices. We will also use transformations that leave the fourth component unchanged. Thus the vector **p** with components (p_0, p_1, p_2) is expressed in homogeneous coordinates as:

$$\mathbf{p} = \begin{bmatrix} p_0 \\ p_1 \\ p_2 \\ 1 \end{bmatrix}$$

Note that many texts use the fourth component for certain transformations and the OpenGL library (used in chapter 7) also offers facilities to use a non-unity value.

The transformation of **p** into **p**′ by the matrix $[T]$ can be written as:

$$\begin{bmatrix} p_0' \\ p_1' \\ p_2' \\ 1 \end{bmatrix} = \begin{bmatrix} t_{00} & t_{01} & t_{02} & t_{03} \\ t_{10} & t_{11} & t_{12} & t_{13} \\ t_{20} & t_{21} & t_{22} & t_{23} \\ t_{30} & t_{31} & t_{32} & t_{33} \end{bmatrix} \begin{bmatrix} p_0 \\ p_1 \\ p_2 \\ 1 \end{bmatrix}$$

2.12.1 Translation

The transformation:

$$[T_t] = \begin{bmatrix} 1 & 0 & 0 & dx \\ 0 & 1 & 0 & dy \\ 0 & 0 & 1 & dz \\ 0 & 0 & 0 & 1 \end{bmatrix}$$

moves the point with coordinates (x, y, z) to the point with coordinates $(x + dx, y + dy, z + dz)$.

The translated point $[p'] = [T_t][p]$ or:

$$\begin{bmatrix} 1 & 0 & 0 & dx \\ 0 & 1 & 0 & dy \\ 0 & 0 & 1 & dz \\ 0 & 0 & 0 & 1 \end{bmatrix} \begin{bmatrix} x \\ y \\ z \\ 1 \end{bmatrix} = \begin{bmatrix} x + dx \\ y + dy \\ z + dz \\ 1 \end{bmatrix}$$

2.12.2   Scaling

The transformation matrix:

$$[T_s] = \begin{bmatrix} s_x & 0 & 0 & 0 \\ 0 & s_y & 0 & 0 \\ 0 & 0 & s_z & 0 \\ 0 & 0 & 0 & 1 \end{bmatrix}$$

scales (expands or contracts) a position vector $\mathbf{p}$ with components (x, y, z) by the factors s_x along the x axis, s_y along the y axis and s_z along the z axis. The scaled vector of $\mathbf{p}'$ is $[p'] = [T_s][p]$.

2.12.3   Rotation

A rotation is specified by an axis of rotation and the angle of the rotation. It is a fairly simple trigonometric calculation to obtain a transformation matrix for a rotation about one of the coordinate axes. When the rotation is to be performed around an arbitrary vector based at a given point, the transformation matrix must be assembled from a combination of rotations about the Cartesian coordinate axes and possibly a translation.

Rotate about the z axis To rotate round the z axis by an angle θ, the transformation matrix is:

$$[T_z(\theta)] = \begin{bmatrix} cos\theta & -sin\theta & 0 & 0 \\ sin\theta & cos\theta & 0 & 0 \\ 0 & 0 & 1 & 0 \\ 0 & 0 & 0 & 1 \end{bmatrix} \tag{2.13}$$

We can see how the rotational transformations are obtained by considering a positive (anti-clockwise) rotation of a point $\mathbf{P}$ by θ round the z axis (which points out of the page). Before rotation $\mathbf{P}$ lies at a distance l from the origin and at an angle ϕ to the x axis, see figure 2.12. The (x, y) coordinate of $\mathbf{P}$ is $(l \cos \phi, l \sin \phi)$. After rotation by θ $\mathbf{P}$ is moved to $\mathbf{P}'$ and its coordinates are $(l \cos(\phi + \theta), l \sin(\phi + \theta))$. Expanding the trigonometric sum gives expressions for the coordinates of $\mathbf{P}'$:

$$\begin{aligned} P_x' &= l \cos \phi \cos \theta - l \sin \phi \sin \theta \\ P_y' &= l \cos \phi \sin \theta + l \sin \phi \cos \theta \end{aligned}$$

Since $l \cos \phi$ is the x coordinate of $\mathbf{P}$ and $l \sin \phi$ is the y coordinate of $\mathbf{P}$ the coordinates of $\mathbf{P}'$ become:

$$\begin{aligned} P_x' &= P_x \cos \theta - P_y \sin \theta \\ P_y' &= P_x \sin \theta + P_y \cos \theta \end{aligned}$$

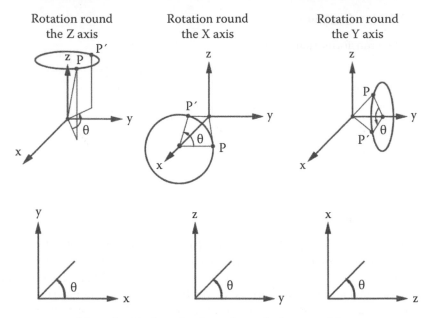

Viewed with the axis of rotation pointing out of the page

Figure 2.11: Rotations, anti-clockwise looking along the axis of rotation, toward the origin.

Writing this in matrix form we have:

$$\begin{bmatrix} P_x{}' \\ P_y{}' \end{bmatrix} = \begin{bmatrix} \cos\theta & -\sin\theta \\ \sin\theta & \cos\theta \end{bmatrix} \begin{bmatrix} P_x \\ P_y \end{bmatrix}$$

There is no change in the z component of **P** and thus this result can be expanded into the familiar 4×4 matrix form by simply inserting the appropriate terms to give:

$$\begin{bmatrix} P_x{}' \\ P_y{}' \\ P_z{}' \\ 1 \end{bmatrix} = \begin{bmatrix} \cos\theta & -\sin\theta & 0 & 0 \\ \sin\theta & \cos\theta & 0 & 0 \\ 0 & 0 & 1 & 0 \\ 0 & 0 & 0 & 1 \end{bmatrix} \begin{bmatrix} P_x \\ P_y \\ P_z \\ 1 \end{bmatrix}$$

Rotation about the y axis To rotate round the y axis by an angle θ, the transformation matrix is:

$$[T_y(\theta)] = \begin{bmatrix} cos\theta & 0 & sin\theta & 0 \\ 0 & 1 & 0 & 0 \\ -sin\theta & 0 & cos\theta & 0 \\ 0 & 0 & 0 & 1 \end{bmatrix}$$

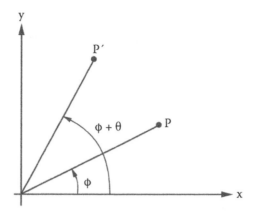

Figure 2.12: Rotation of point **P** by an angle θ round the z axis.

Rotation about the x axis To rotate round the x axis by an angle θ, the transformation matrix is:

$$[T_x(\theta)] = \begin{bmatrix} 1 & 0 & 0 & 0 \\ 0 & cos\theta & -sin\theta & 0 \\ 0 & sin\theta & cos\theta & 0 \\ 0 & 0 & 0 & 1 \end{bmatrix}$$

Note that as illustrated in figure 2.11 θ is positive if the rotation takes place in a clockwise sense when looking from the origin along the axis of rotation. This is consistent with a right-handed coordinate system.

2.12.4 Combining transformations

Section 2.12 introduced the key concept of a transformation applied to a position vector. In many cases we are interested in what happens when several operations are applied in sequence to a model or one of its points (*vertices*). For example: *move the point* **P** *10 units forward, rotate it 20 degrees round the z axis and shift it 15 units along the x axis.* Each transformation is represented by a single 4×4 matrix and the compound transformation is constructed as a sequence of single transformations as follows:

$$\begin{aligned} [p'] &= [T_1][p] \\ [p''] &= [T_2][p'] \\ [p'''] &= [T_3][p''] \end{aligned}$$

where $[p']$ and $[p'']$ are intermediate position vectors and $[p''']$ is the end vector after the application of the three transformations. The above sequence can be combined into:

$$[p'''] = [T_3][T_2][T_1][p]$$

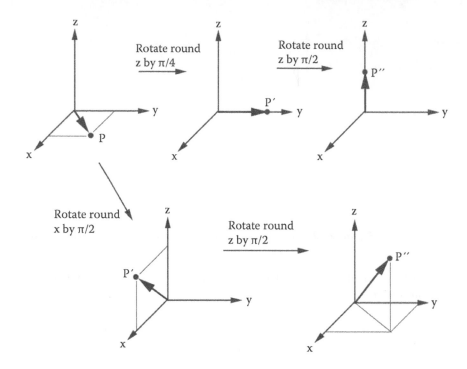

Figure 2.13: Effect of transformations applied in a different order.

The product of the transformations $[T_3][T_2][T_1]$ gives a single matrix $[T]$. Combining transformations in this way has a wonderful efficiency: If a large model has 50,000 vertices and we need to apply 10 transformations, by combining the transformations into a single matrix, 450,000 matrix multiplications can be avoided.

It is important to remember that the result of applying a sequence of transformations depends on the order in which they are applied. $[T_3][T_2][T_1]$ is **not** the same compound transformation as $[T_2][T_3][T_1]$. Figure 2.13 shows the effect of applying the transformations in a different order.

There is one subtle point about transformations that ought to be stressed. The parameters of a transformation (angle of rotation, etc.) are all relative to a **global** frame of reference. It is sometimes useful to think in terms of a local frame of reference that is itself transformed relative to a global frame and this idea will be explored when we discuss key frame and character animation. However it is important to bear in mind that when a final scene is assembled for rendering, all coordinates must be specified in the same frame of reference.

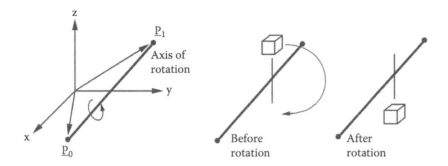

Figure 2.14: Rotation round an arbitrary vector.

2.12.5   Rotation about an arbitrary axis

The transformation corresponding to rotation of an angle α around an arbitrary vector (for example that shown between the two points $\mathbf{P}_0$ and $\mathbf{P}_1$ in figure 2.14) cannot readily be written in a form similar to the rotation matrices about the coordinate axes.

One way to obtain the desired transformation matrix is through the combination of a sequence of basic translation and rotation matrices. (Once a single 4×4 matrix has been obtained representing the composite transformations it can be used in the same way as any other transformation matrix.)

The following outlines an algorithm to construct a transformation matrix to generate a rotation by an angle α around a vector in the direction $\mathbf{P}_1 - \mathbf{P}_0$:

1. Translate $\mathbf{P}_0$ to the origin of coordinates.

2. Align rotation axis $\mathbf{P}_1 - \mathbf{P}_0$ with the x axis.

3. Rotate by angle α round x axis.

4. Make inverse transformation to undo the rotations of step two.

5. Translate origin of coordinates back to $\mathbf{P}_0$ to undo the translation of step one.

The full algorithm is given in listing 2.3. Moller and Haines [1] give a more robust method of rotating around any axis.

It is possible to combine rotational transformations together into a single 3×3 matrix in the case of a rotation by θ around a directional vector $\mathbf{u} = [u_x, u_y, u_z]^T$. In this case any translational element would have to be removed first and then re-applied and θ is anti-clockwise when looking in the direction of $\mathbf{u}$. Thus:

$$[T(\theta)] = [I]cos\theta + \sin\theta[T_c] + (1 - \cos\theta)[T_t] \tag{2.14}$$

Let $\mathbf{d} = \mathbf{P}_1 - \mathbf{P}_0$
$[T_1]$ = a translation by $-\mathbf{P}_0$
$d_{xy} = d_x^2 + d_y^2$
if $d_{xy} < \epsilon$ {
  rotation axis is in the $\mathbf{z}$ *direction*
   if $d_z > 0$ make $[T_2]$ a rotation about z by α
  else $[T_2]$*is* a rotation about z by $-\alpha$
   $[T_3]$*is* a translation by $\mathbf{P}_0$
    return the product $[T_3][T_2][T_1]$
}
$d_{xy} = \sqrt{d_{xy}}$
if $d_x = 0$ and $d_y > 0$ $\phi = \pi/2$
else if $d_x = 0$ and $d_y < 0$ $\phi = -\pi/2$
else $\phi = ATAN2(d_y, d_x)$
$\theta = ATAN2(d_z, d_{xy})$
$[T_2]$*is* a rotation about z by $-\phi$
$[T_3]$*is* a rotation about y by $-\theta$
$[T_4]$*is* a rotation about x by α
$[T_5]$*is* a rotation about y by θ
$[T_6]$*is* a rotation about z by ϕ
$[T_7]$*is* a translation by $\mathbf{P}_0$
Multiply the transformation matrices to give the final result
$[T] = [T_7][T_6][T_5][T_4][T_3][T_2][T_1]$

Listing 2.3: Algorithm for rotation round an arbitrary axis. d_x, d_y and d_z are the components of vector $\mathbf{d}$.

where:

$$[T_c] = \begin{bmatrix} 0 & -u_z & u_y \\ u_z & 0 & -u_x \\ -u_y & u_x & 0 \end{bmatrix}$$

is the cross product matrix and:

$$[T_t] = \begin{bmatrix} u_x^2 & u_x u_y & u_x u_z \\ u_y u_x & u_y^2 & u_y u_z \\ u_z u_x & u_z u_y & u_z^2 \end{bmatrix}$$

is the tensor product. This neat expression is a matrix form of Rodrigues' rotation formulae.

2.12.6 Rotational change of frame of reference

In working with objects that have curved surfaces, or even those with flat surfaces that are not orientated in the direction of one of the axes of the global frame of reference, it is sometimes desirable to define a local frame of reference on every

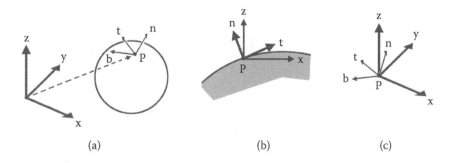

Figure 2.15: Surface local coordinates: (a) A point on an object with position **P** in the global (world) frame of reference has a surface local frame of reference, (b) in a two-dimensional section. (c) The relative orientations of the local and global frames of reference.

point on the surface. For any point on a surface **P** the normal vector **n** is used to define the orientation of the surface and is an important variable in all the lighting models.

The normal is defined through its components (n_x, n_y, n_z) relative to the global frame of reference. However **locally** at the surface, the normal is always vertical. If we can define two other mutually perpendicular vectors at **P** we would have a frame of reference in which the normal was always vertical and any other point or direction could be defined with respect to the local frame of reference. Such a local frame of reference is important when the texturing procedures of image mapping, and especially bump mapping (see section 4.6.2), are considered. Figure 2.15 illustrates the relationship between the local frame of reference and the global frame of reference.

A complete frame of reference requires two additional coordinate vectors. If we stipulate that the frame of reference is orthogonal, then only one additional vector is really needed. It must be perpendicular to **n** and thus it lies in the plane of the surface at **P**. In texture mapping applications, this additional vector is also used to define one of the edges of the map. Even curved surfaces tend to be locally flat when one is close enough to **P**. This additional vector lying in the surface is termed the tangent vector **t**. The third vector is easily obtained by taking the cross product: $\mathbf{b} = \mathbf{n} \times \mathbf{t}$. Each of these local frame vectors are specified by their components in the global frame of reference, thus: (n_x, n_y, n_z), (t_x, t_y, t_z) and (b_x, b_y, b_z).

Given a local frame of reference's basis vectors it is easy to build a rotational transformation that will transform any *direction* vector, defined in the local frame of reference, to its equivalent direction defined in terms of the global frame of reference's basis vector. If the direction **d** is specified relative to the local frame by its components (d_u, d_v, d_w) then in terms of its direction in the global frame of reference it will be given by $\mathbf{d}' = d_u \mathbf{n} + d_v \mathbf{t} + d_w \mathbf{b}$. This linear transformation can be expressed as a 3×3 matrix:

$$
\begin{bmatrix} d_x{}' \\ d_y{}' \\ d_z{}' \end{bmatrix} = \begin{bmatrix} t_x & b_x & n_x \\ t_y & b_y & n_y \\ t_z & b_z & n_z \end{bmatrix} \begin{bmatrix} d_u \\ d_v \\ d_w \end{bmatrix} \tag{2.15}
$$

Equation 2.15 transforms a direction vector specified in the surface local frame of reference to the equivalent in the global frame, that is local to global $[d'] = [T_{lg}][d]$. However in order to determine the direction of a vector, for example the relative location of a light to $\mathbf{P}$, the transformation needed is the one from the global to the local reference frame, that is, $[T_{gl}]$, the inverse of $[T_{lg}]$. It is a well known result that for rotational transformations the inverse of its matrix representation is simply its transpose, that is $[T_{gl}] = [T_{lg}]^{-1} = [T_{lg}]^{T}$.

Thus when the surface normal and surface tangent vectors are known at a point $\mathbf{P}$, any direction vector, specified relative to the global frame of reference, can be transformed into a direction vector relative to the surface local reference frame by multiplying it by the matrix:

$$
\begin{bmatrix} t_x & t_y & t_z \\ b_x & b_y & b_z \\ n_x & n_y & b_z \end{bmatrix} \tag{2.16}
$$

Note: This only applies to direction vectors, so for example if we want to get the relative direction of a light at $\mathbf{L}_p$ to the surface at $\mathbf{P}$ (both specified in a global frame of reference), it is the direction vector $\mathbf{L}_p - \mathbf{P}$ that has to be transformed with the matrix in equation 2.16.

2.12.7   Viewing transformation

Before rendering any view of a 3D scene (see chapter 4) one has to decide from where to view/photograph the scene and in which direction to look (point the camera). This is like setting up a camera to take a picture. Once the camera is set we just click the shutter. The camera projects the image as seen in the viewfinder onto the photographic film and the image is rendered. This is a two stage process: the projection stage will be discussed in section 2.12.8, and now we will consider how to set a viewpoint and direction of view.

In mathematical terms we need to construct a suitable transformation that will allow us to choose a viewpoint (place to set up the camera) and direction of view (direction in which to point the camera). Once we have this *view transformation* it can be combined with any other transformations that need to be applied to the scene or to objects in the scene.

We have already seen how to construct transformation matrices that move or rotate points in a scene. In the same way that basic transformation matrices were combined in section 2.12.5 to create an arbitrary rotation we can build a single matrix, $[T_o]$, that will transform all the points (vertices) in a scene in such

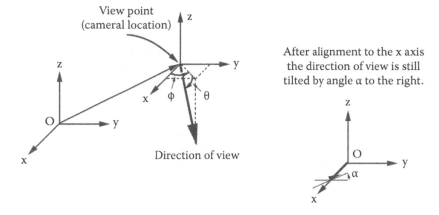

Figure 2.16: Viewpoint and direction of view.

a way that the projection of an image becomes a simple standard process. To do this we arrange that the camera is fixed at the center of the universe, $(0,0,0)$, and locked off to point in the direction $(1,0,0)$ (along the x axis).

There is nothing special about the direction $(1,0,0)$; we could equally well have chosen to fix the camera to look in the direction $(0,1,0)$, the y axis, or even $(0,0,1)$, the z axis. But since we have chosen to let z represent the **up** direction and it is not a good idea to look directly up, $(0,0,1)$ would be a poor choice for viewing. (Note: The OpenGL and Direct3D software libraries for 3D graphics have their z axis parallel to the viewing direction.)

Once $[T_o]$ has been determined it is applied to all objects in the scene. If necessary $[T_o]$ can be combined with other transformation matrices to give a single composite transformation $[T]$.

A viewing transformation depends on:

1. Position of the view point (camera location). (A vector $\mathbf{p}_o$, see figure 2.16.)

2. The direction in which we wish to look: north, south, east or west. This is measured by an angle ϕ which is relative to the **x** axis and lies in the xy plane. ϕ is positive to the right of the **x** axis when looking along **x** from the view point.

3. The amount by which we look up or down. The angle θ measures this relative to the xy plane. It is positive when looking down. Note that when determining a viewing transformation the effect of looking up or down comes into play after the direction of view has been accounted for and therefore it is equivalent to a rotation around the **y** axis.

4. The degree to which our head is tilted to the left or right. This is measured by the angle α. To be consistent with the right-handed frame of reference

and sense of rotation α is positive when the camera tilts to the right as it looks from $\mathbf{p}_o$ along the $\mathbf{x}$ axis.

A viewing transformation appears to operate in reverse to ordinary transformations. For example, if you tilt your head to the left, the world appears to tilt to the right. Note carefully that the angle θ is positive if we are looking down, and negative if we are looking up. If you prefer, you can think of: ϕ as the **heading**, θ as the **pitch** and α as the degree of **banking**. The viewing transformations are also combined in the reverse order to the order in which a transformation is assembled for objects placed in a scene. In that case the rotation around $\mathbf{x}$ is applied first and the translation by $\mathbf{p}_o$ is applied last.

Given the parameters $\mathbf{p}_o$, ϕ, θ and α (illustrated in figure 2.16) the transformation $[T_o]$ is constructed by the following algorithm:

Place observer at $(0,0,0)$ with the transformation:
$[T_1] =$ a translation by $-\mathbf{p}_o$
Rotate the direction of observation into the xz plane with:
$[T_2] =$ a rotation about z by $-\phi$
Align the direction of observation to the $\mathbf{x}$ axis with:
$[T_3] =$ a rotation about y by $-\theta$
Straighten the camera up with transformation:
$[T_4] =$ a rotation about x by $-\alpha$
Multiply the individual transformation matrices to give
one composite matrix representing the viewing transformation:
$[T_0] = [T_4][T_3][T_2][T_1]$

2.12.8 Projection

We saw in section 2.12.7 that after setting up a camera to record an image the view must be projected onto film or electronic sensing device. In the conventional camera this is done with a lens arrangement or simply a *pinhole*. One could also imagine holding a sheet of glass in front of the viewer and then having them trace on it what they see as they look through it. What is drawn on the glass **is** what we would like the computer to produce: a 2D picture of the scene. It's even showing the right way up as in figure 2.17.

It is straightforward to formulate expressions needed to perform this (non-linear) transformation. A little thought must be given to dealing with cases where parts of the scene go behind the viewer or are partly in and partly out of the field of view (this topic is discussed in section 4.2.6). The field of view (illustrated in figure 2.18) governs how much of the scene you see; it can be changed. In photography telephoto and fish-eye lenses have different fields of view. For example the common $50mm$ lens has a field of view of $45.9°$. Because of its shape as a truncated pyramid with a regular base the volume enclosed by the field of view is known as a *frustum*.

One thing we can do with a projective transformation is to adjust the *aspect ratio*. The *aspect ratio* is the ratio of height to width of the rendered image.

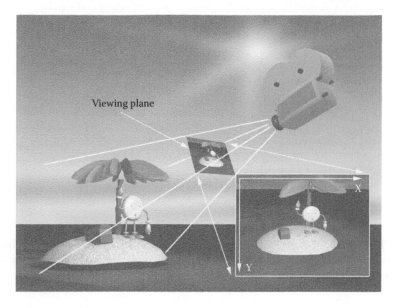

Figure 2.17: Project the scene onto the viewing plane. The resulting two-dimensional image is then recorded or displayed.

For television work it is 4 : 3 and 16 : 9 for basic cine film. The aspect ratio is related to the vertical and horizontal resolution of the recorded image. Get this relationship wrong and your spheres will look egg shaped.

Before formulating expressions to represent the projection we need to define the coordinate system in use for the projection plane. It has become almost universal (however not in the OpenGL library discussed in chapter 7) to represent the computer display as a pair of integers in the range $0 \rightarrow (X_{max} - 1)$ horizontally and $0 \rightarrow (Y_{max} - 1)$ vertically. The coordinate origin $(0,0)$ is in the top left corner, see figure 2.17.

The distance of the projection plane from the viewpoint can be chosen arbitrarily; setting it to one unit simplifies the calculations. Thus if the plane of projection is located at $(1, 0, 0)$ and orientated parallel to the yz plane (i.e., the viewer is looking along the x axis) then the screen coordinates (X_s, Y_s) for the projection of a point (x, y, z) are given by:

$$X_s = \frac{X_{max}}{2} - \frac{y}{x}s_x \qquad (2.17)$$

$$Y_s = \frac{Y_{max}}{2} - \frac{z}{x}s_y \qquad (2.18)$$

The parameters s_x and s_y are scale values to allow for different aspect ratios and fields of view. This effectively lets us change the *zoom* settings for the camera.

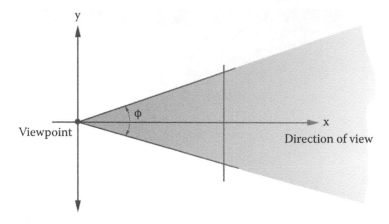

Figure 2.18: The field of view ϕ governs how much of the scene is visible to a camera located at the viewpoint. Narrowing the field of view is equivalent to using a zoom lens.

Obviously, X_s and Y_s must satisfy $0 \leq X_s < X_{max}$ and $0 \leq Y_s < Y_{max}$.

If f_f (measured in mm) is the focal length of the desired camera lens and the aspect ratio is $A_x : A_y$ then:

$$s_x = \frac{X_{max}}{2} \frac{f_f}{21.22} A_x$$

$$s_y = \frac{Y_{max}}{2} \frac{f_f}{21.22} A_y$$

The numerical factor 21.2 is a constant to allow us to specify f_f in standard mm units. For a camera lens of focal length f_f the field of view θ can be expressed as:

$$\theta \simeq 2ATAN2(21.22, f_f)$$

Any point (x, y, z) for which $x < 1$ will not be transformed correctly by equations 2.17 and 2.18 and steps must be made to eliminate them before the projection is applied. This process is called *clipping*. How the clipping is done depends on whether a wireframe or shaded solid is to be rendered and it is discussed in section 4.2.6.

It is possible to express the perspective transformation as a 4×4 matrix. However, when the matrix is applied to a point's homogeneous coordinate in order to find its projected location on the viewing plane, one has to remember to divide the first three components by the fourth before using the 3D coordinate value. Since the projection plane is usually chosen to be perpendicular to one of the coordinate axes, then the value along that axis will become the location of

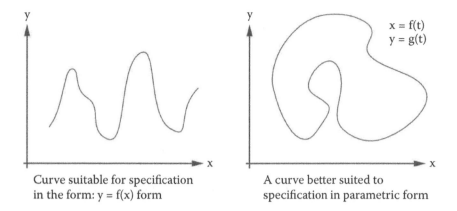

Figure 2.19: Two-dimensional curves.

the clipping plane. For example, the projection matrix for a xz clipping plane located at $y = d$ would be:

$$\begin{bmatrix} 1 & 0 & 0 & 0 \\ 0 & 1 & 0 & 0 \\ 0 & 0 & 1 & 0 \\ 0 & \frac{1}{d} & 0 & 0 \end{bmatrix} \tag{2.19}$$

This transformation sends a homogeneous point $(x, y, z, 1)$ to the homogeneous point $(x, y, z, \frac{y}{d})$, which after projective division becomes $(d\frac{x}{y}, d, d\frac{z}{y}, 1)$, equivalent to the 2D coordinate $(d\frac{x}{y}, d\frac{z}{y})$ on the viewing plane (located at $y = d$).

2.13   Parametric curves

In two dimensions a curve is generally expressed as a function in the form $y = f(x)$. Unfortunately this can be a cumbersome representation to work with. It's fine for curves like the one shown in figure 2.19 (left) but when the curve is closed or loops, like the one in figure 2.19 (right), then a parametric representation is better.

The difficulties of expressing a curve in the form $y = f(x)$ can be illustrated by considering the equation of a circle: $y = \pm\sqrt{x^2 - r^2}$. The problem here is that to draw a curve with a $\pm$ in its equation requires special purpose handling.

A better alternative is to obtain separate functions for x and y in terms of a single parameter θ:

$$x = r\cos\theta \tag{2.20}$$

$$y = r\sin\theta \tag{2.21}$$

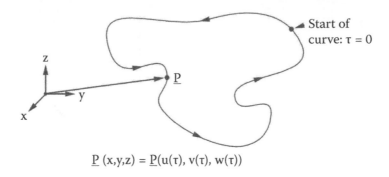

$$\underline{P}\,(x,y,z) = \underline{P}(u(\tau),\,v(\tau),\,w(\tau))$$

Figure 2.20: A three-dimensional parametric curve.

where θ is an angle in the range $[0, 2\pi)$. Equations 2.20 and 2.21 are well behaved: given a θ each returns one value only. This is ideal for plotting because it wouldn't matter if the curve twisted, turned or looped.

Actually, since angles are measured in radians, and radians are a measure of the arc length of a unit circle, θ could also be thought of as a *length along the curve*.

The idea of the parameter having a physical meaning like *length* is a very useful one for curves in both two and three dimensions. We shall use it in section 6.2.2 when studying the animation of objects following paths. An alternative and equally useful parameter is *time*.

Equations 2.20 and 2.21 are specific to a two-dimensional circular curve. For work in three dimensions a set of parametric functions that apply to a general curve can be written in the form:

$$x = u(\tau) \qquad\qquad (2.22)$$
$$y = v(\tau) \qquad\qquad (2.23)$$
$$z = w(\tau) \qquad\qquad (2.24)$$

Here τ is the parameter. Any curve (we shall call it a path) in 3D space, be it a straight line, a Bézier curve, a cubic spline or even a curve constructed from pieces of other curves, can be specified by three functions. Figure 2.20 illustrates a typical three-dimensional parametric curve.

2.14   Interpolation

Suppose we have a set of data containing n $(n > 1)$ pairs of values (x_0, y_0), (x_1, y_1), (x_2, y_2), ... (x_i, y_y), ... (x_{n-1}, y_{n-1}). These can be plotted on a two-dimensional diagram as shown in figure 2.21. Joining the points (x_i, y_i) together

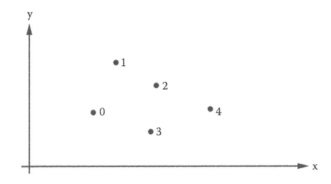

Figure 2.21: Data points for interpolation.

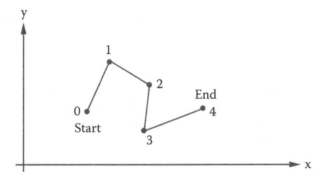

Figure 2.22: Joining up the data points to make a path.

in the order, $0 \to 1 \to 2 \to \ \ldots \ \to i \to \ \ldots \ \to n-1$ will create a path through the points. The path will have a beginning and an end as illustrated in figure 2.22. To draw the path we had to use **interpolation**, that is, *we had to assume what the path looks like as it goes* **through** *the data points.* For the path of figure 2.22, with all its *kinks*, we might be forgiven for thinking that our assumption on how it behaves between the points is a poor one because the path shown in figure 2.23, which also passes through the data points, looks smoother, and for many applications it is therefore a better path.

Since we know nothing more about the path other than the points it passes through, the *which is better* argument is unresolvable. The paths shown in figures 2.22 and 2.23 are only two out of an infinite number of possible paths, all of which pass through the points (x_0, y_0), etc.

The path shown in figure 2.22 was drawn by using the following simple procedure to join up the points:

1. Take the points two at a time and obtain the equation of a straight line

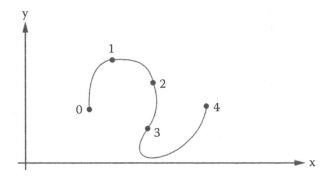

Figure 2.23: Smoothly joining up the data points.

passing through them in parametric form. For example, for points 0 and 1,

$$
\begin{aligned}
x &= x_0 + \mu(x_1 - x_0) \\
y &= y_0 + \mu(y_1 - y_0)
\end{aligned}
$$

2. For each line use its equations to obtain (select values of μs in the range $(0,1)$) x and y values corresponding to points lying on the line. Plot the points on the diagram. When enough of them have been plotted the line will look continuous.

This procedure of finding extra points on the line joining consecutive data points is called *linear* interpolation. To draw a smoother path through the same set of data another type of interpolation is required.

Interpolation procedures that use curves rather than straight lines to plot the path between data points use more than two consecutive points. For example, by taking groups of three points at a time it is possible to specify a quadratic curve for the path between the data points. This is illustrated in figure 2.24 where three quadratic curves make up the path through seven points. Unfortunately there are *kinks* (discontinuous first derivatives) at the points where the curves join. The path looks smooth near point 1 but at point 2 there is a kink. To eliminate the kinks we could consider using four points at a time, but then the kinks would appear at every fourth point. So why not build an $(n-1)$th order curve to go through all the n data points in the path? The reason we cannot consider more than about four or five points as a group is because the calculation becomes *ill-conditioned*. There are ways round the *ill-conditioning* problem but even when that is solved a very *wiggly* path will be produced that looks totally unrealistic. A better approach is to group three or four points together and blend them so that the kinks disappear. For example, a good blend is achieved with the curves making up the path shown in figure 2.25.

The path of figure 2.25 was obtained by *blending* pieces of cubic curves. A cubic curve was constructed to pass through points $0 - 1 - 2 - 3$ but it was only

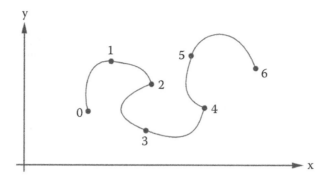

Figure 2.24: Quadratic interpolation using points $(0-1-2)$ and then $(2-3-4)$, etc.

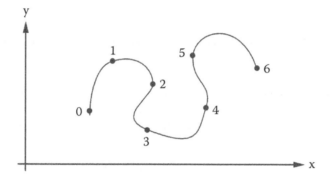

Figure 2.25: Blending cubic curves to make a smooth path.

used to draw that part of the path between points $0-2$. Another cubic was designed to pass through points $1-2-3-4$ but this time it was used to draw (by interpolation from the cubic) the piece of the path between points $2-3$.

There are more elaborate ways to blend curves together and much analysis has been done on the topic. A detailed discussion of such issues can be found in Burger and Gillies [15].

An alternative but effectively similar strategy to that of blending pieces of curves together over a range of points is to insist that at all data points, the slope or gradient of the curve is the same on both sides of the point. This will eliminate *kinks* such as those that are so obvious in figure 2.24.

2.14.1   Linear interpolation

Given two points with position vectors $\mathbf{P_0}$ and $\mathbf{P_1}$ any point lying on a straight line between them satisfies:

$$\mathbf{p} = \mathbf{P_0} + \mu(\mathbf{P_1} - \mathbf{P_0})$$

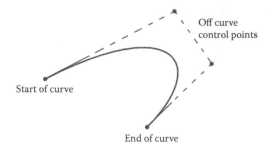

Figure 2.26: Basic Bézier curve with two control points on and two control points off the curve.

Choosing μ such that $0 \leq \mu \leq 1$ returns a linearly interpolated point. When $\mu = \frac{1}{2}$ then $\mathbf{p} = \mathbf{P}_{\frac{1}{2}}$ will lie midway between $\mathbf{P}_0$ and $\mathbf{P}_1$.

In terms of the (x, y, z) coordinates of $\mathbf{p}$ three interpolating equations can be written as

$$
\begin{aligned}
x &= x_0 + \mu(x_1 - x_0) \\
y &= y_0 + \mu(y_1 - y_0) \\
z &= z_0 + \mu(z_1 - z_0)
\end{aligned}
$$

(x_0, y_0, z_0) are the coordinates of $\mathbf{P}_0$ and (x_1, y_1, z_1) is $\mathbf{P}_1$.

2.14.2   Quadratic interpolation

Quadratic interpolation fits a quadratic to three points $\mathbf{P}_0$, $\mathbf{P}_1$ and $\mathbf{P}_2$ to be taken together. The equation

$$
\mathbf{p} = (2(\mathbf{P}_2 - \mathbf{P}_0) - 4(\mathbf{P}_1 - \mathbf{P}_0))\mu^2 - ((\mathbf{P}_2 - \mathbf{P}_0) - 4(\mathbf{P}_1 - \mathbf{P}_0))\mu + \mathbf{P}_0
$$

gives the point $\mathbf{p}$ as μ varies between 0 and 1. When $\mu = \frac{1}{2}$ the point is $\mathbf{p} = \mathbf{P}_1$ and $\mathbf{p} = \mathbf{P}_2$ is reached when $\mu = 1$.

Note that in this case μ is **not** the length of the curve.

2.15   Bézier curves

In the preceding discussion on interpolation it was assumed that to describe a path by a number of component curves they all pass through points from which

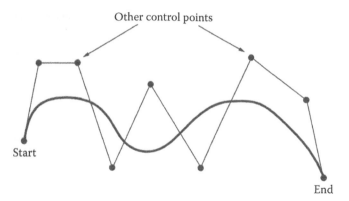

Figure 2.27: Bézier curve with two control points (knots) on and $n-2$ other knots (control points).

their shape was derived. This doesn't have to be the case. It is true however, that for computer graphics work, it is likely that our interest is in paths and curves that *do* pass through all their *control* points. Nevertheless there is one important exception, the Bézier curve.

Curves of this form are named after Pierre Bézier, who worked for the French company Renault and first used them in the design of automobiles. Today perhaps their most common usage is to provide a mathematical descriptions of typefaces and scalable character fonts for the printing industry. The text you are reading was printed by instructing a printer to fill in the outline of each character that has been described by a closed path made up from straight line and Bézier curve segments. PostScript and TrueType fonts that are used by virtually every personal computer to display and print text are specific variants of this method of describing character and other shapes. Figure 2.26 shows a basic Bézier curve constructed from four points. It is readily seen that the curve itself only passes through the first and last point. Bézier curves can have as many *control* points as desired but only the first and last will lie on the curve. For all Bézier curves the direction of the curve as it leaves the first point is toward the second (off curve) point. The direction in which the curve approached the last point is from the penultimate one, see figure 2.29. Many books and journal articles refer to the control points of Bézier and spline curves as *knots*. Figure 2.27 shows a Bézier curve with n knots (control points).

As the number of knots in a Bézier curve increase the properties that make it so useful become diluted, the curve just gets lazy and meanders from start to finish paying little heed to the intervening knots. The most useful Bézier curve turns out to be the simplest 4 knot curve. These 4 knot curves can be readily joined together to make the most complex shapes. Figure 2.28 shows a path with four Bézier segments. Using Bézier segments has the advantage that whilst

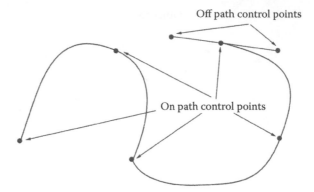

Figure 2.28: Path made from several 4 knot Bézier curves.

it is not too difficult to avoid *kinks* in the path on the occasions when *kinks* are desirable they can be easily incorporated.

The mathematical form of the general Bézier curve of degree n defined by the $n + 1$ control points $\mathbf{P}_0, \mathbf{P}_1, \mathbf{P}_2, \ldots, \mathbf{P}_n$ is given by:

$$\mathbf{B}(u) = \sum_{i=0}^{n} B_{n,i}(u)\mathbf{P}_i \qquad (2.25)$$

where the blending functions $B_{n,i}$ are the *Bernstein polynomials* defined by:

$$B_{n,i}(u) = \frac{n!}{i!(n-i)!}u^i(1-u)^{n-i} \qquad (2.26)$$

In computer graphics the most commonly used Bézier curves are of degree 3. There are several algorithms for drawing Bézier curves: one suitable for any number (n) of knots is the de Casteljau recursive procedure [15]. De Casteljau's algorithm is relatively short but because it is recursive its calculation can be quite slow especially when n is large.

In the case of Adobe's Postscript language [44], font and other curved shapes are described by a set of 4 knot Bézier curves and straight line segments. A 4 knot Bézier curve is specified by a cubic polynomial in parametric form. Figure 2.29 illustrates the effect on the Bézier of moving the knots to different positions. By linking 4 knot Bézier curves together the most complicated calligraphic shapes as illustrated in figure 2.30.

For the four knots (x_0, y_0), (x_1, y_1), (x_2, y_2) and (x_3, y_3), a point (x, y) on the Bézier can be interpolated using:

$$x(t) = a_x t^3 + b_x t^2 + c_x t + x_0 \qquad (2.27)$$
$$y(t) = a_y t^3 + b_y t^2 + c_y t + y_0 \qquad (2.28)$$

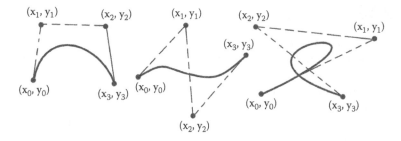

Figure 2.29: Two-dimensional Bézier curves showing the effect of different placement of the *intermediate* points (the knots).

Figure 2.30: Calligraphic shape (the letters CG) made from many 4 knot Bézier curves.

where t is the parameter and

$$x_1 = x_0 + \frac{c_x}{3} \tag{2.29}$$

$$x_2 = x_1 + \frac{c_x + b_x}{3} \tag{2.30}$$

$$x_3 = x_0 + a_x + b_x + c_x \tag{2.31}$$

Usually the (x_0, y_0), (x_1, y_1) etc. are known. a_x, b_x and c_x can be calculated by rearranging equations 2.29, 2.30 and 2.31 to give:

$$
\begin{aligned}
c_x &= 3(x_1 - x_0) \\
b_x &= 3(x_2 - 2x_1 + x_0) \\
a_x &= x_3 + 3(x_1 - x_2) - x_0
\end{aligned}
$$

Similar expression for a_y, b_y etc., can be obtained.

Equations 2.27 and 2.28 are readily extended to give a description of a 4 knot curve in three dimensions. The knots are specified by position vectors and the interpolated points can be obtained by varying the parameter t.

2.16   Splines

Spline is a term that owes it origins to the flexible strip of wood draftsmen used to use to draw curves. Weights would hold the spline in place at the points on the drawing which the curve must pass through. Tracing along the wooden strips produced a smooth and pleasing curve. An examination of the properties of the physical spline suggests a suitable mathematical model for it is a cubic function. A good example of a cubic function is the Hermite curve which is specified in terms of the curve passing through two end points at which two tangent directions are also specified.

The spline that will be examined in this section has the greatest utility in computer graphics because it is constructed so that it passes through all the data points. Since a cubic curve requires four parameters to define it, a spline curve that will fit through more than four data points is usually handled piecewise, where four data points are taken in turn, with the spline function used to determine the course of the curve between the middle two. This form of piecewise spline is ofter referred to as a Catmull-Rom spline.

A cubic spline is written in the form:

$$\mathbf{p}(\tau) = \mathbf{K}_3\tau^3 + \mathbf{K}_2\tau^2 + \mathbf{K}_1\tau + \mathbf{K}_0 \tag{2.32}$$

or equivalently (to speed up its calculation)

$$\mathbf{p}(\tau) = (((\mathbf{K}_3\tau + \mathbf{K}_2)\tau + \mathbf{K}_1)\tau + \mathbf{K}_0)$$

The unknown vector constants $\mathbf{K}_0$, $\mathbf{K}_1$, $\mathbf{K}_2$ and $\mathbf{K}_3$ have to been determined; their components are independent of each other. τ is a parameter having values in the interval $[0, 1]$ such that when $\tau = 0$, $\mathbf{p}(0) = \mathbf{P}_i$, and when $\tau = 1$, $\mathbf{p}(1) = \mathbf{P}_{i+1}$

To determine the unknown vector constants we impose four conditions on 2.32:

1. The spline passes through the point $\mathbf{P}_i$ at the start of the curve.

2. The spline passes through the point $\mathbf{P}_{i+1}$ at the end of the curve.

3. The derivative $\mathbf{P}'_i$ of the spline at $\mathbf{P}_i$ is given.

4. The derivative $\mathbf{P}'_{i+1}$ of the spline at $\mathbf{P}_{i+1}$ is given.

These apply to each of the components of $\mathbf{p}$, i.e., for its x component we need to consider the values: x_i , x_{i+1}, x'_i , x'_{i+1}. Differentiating equation 2.32 w.r.t. τ gives:

$$\mathbf{p}'(\tau) = 3\mathbf{K}_3\tau^2 + 2\mathbf{K}_2\tau + \mathbf{K}_1 \tag{2.33}$$

Substituting for x_i and x_{i+1} in (2.32) with $\tau = 0$ and $\tau = 1$ respectively and then with x'_i and x'_{i+1} in (2.33) while $\tau = 0$ and $\tau = 1$ gives four simultaneous equations for the x component of the $\mathbf{K}$s. Written in matrix form these are:

$$\begin{bmatrix} 0 & 0 & 0 & 1 \\ 1 & 1 & 1 & 1 \\ 0 & 0 & 1 & 0 \\ 3 & 2 & 1 & 0 \end{bmatrix} \begin{bmatrix} K_{3_x} \\ K_{2_x} \\ K_{1_x} \\ K_{0_x} \end{bmatrix} = \begin{bmatrix} x_i \\ x_{i+1} \\ x'_i \\ x'_{i+1} \end{bmatrix}$$

On solution the following expressions are obtained:

$$\begin{aligned} K_{3_x} &= 2x_i - 2x_{i+1} + x'_i + x'_{i+1} \\ K_{2_x} &= -3x_i + 3x_{i+1} - 2x'_i - x'_{i+1} \\ K_{1_x} &= x'_i \\ K_{0_x} &= x_i \end{aligned}$$

If $\mathbf{P}_i$ and $\mathbf{P}_{i+1}$ are part of a set of points making up a path, such as, ... $\mathbf{P}_{i-1}$, $\mathbf{P}_i$, $\mathbf{P}_{i+1}$, $\mathbf{P}_{i+2}$ ..., the $\mathbf{K}$s are obtained using the value of $\mathbf{p}$ at $\mathbf{P}_{i-1}$, $\mathbf{P}_i$, $\mathbf{P}_{i+1}$ and $\mathbf{P}_{i+2}$ as follows:

$$K_{3_x} = -\frac{1}{2}x_{i-1} + \frac{3}{2}x_i - \frac{3}{2}x_{i+1} + \frac{1}{2}x_{i+2} \tag{2.34}$$

$$K_{2_x} = x_{i-1} - \frac{5}{2}x_i + 2x_{i+1} - \frac{1}{2}x_{i+2} \tag{2.35}$$

$$K_{1_x} = -\frac{1}{2}x_{i-1} + \frac{1}{2}x_{i+1} \tag{2.36}$$

$$K_{0_x} = x_i \tag{2.37}$$

Similar expressions may be written for K_{3_y}, K_{3_z}, etc., and thus the constant vectors $\mathbf{K_i}$ become:

$$\mathbf{K_i} = \begin{bmatrix} K_{i_x} \\ K_{i_y} \\ K_{i_z} \end{bmatrix}$$

for $i = 0, 1, 2, 3$.

In summary: The calculations we used to obtain the $\mathbf{K_i}$ vectors are *local*. That is, they only depend on coordinates of the two points between which the cubic is used for interpolation and the two other nearest neighbors. Therefore, when we draw pieces of a path with many points, segments can be drawn independently. There is no need to take a global view of the whole path in order to draw just a little piece of it.

A couple of notes on splines:

- Extending this type of spline for use in three dimensions is relatively easy. A parameter, τ, replaces the variable x and there are two additional polynomials, one in each of the other coordinates.

- Usually τ takes integer values at the control points, i.e. $-1, 0, 1, 2$. In this case there is no relationship between the parameter τ and the distance between the points.

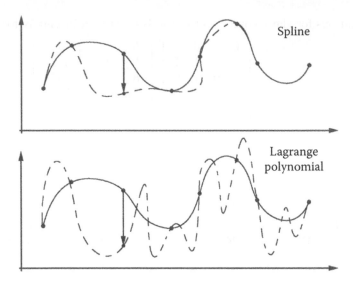

Figure 2.31: Effect of displacing a control point on the shape of spline and Lagrange polynomials.

2.16.1   The natural spline

An alternative view of the calculation of the spline constants arises by considering **all** the fixed points of the spline together in a single step. A set of cubic curves, one for each pair of fixed points, is still obtained but the blending is done implicitly and the overall curve is smooth and well behaved. Well behaved means that if one of the control points is moved the curve will change shape only in its vicinity. Far away, the shape of the curve will not be affected. Contrast this with other interpolation methods, Lagrange polynomial interpolation for example: If a Lagrange polynomial is fitted to the data a change in one control point will show a ripple effect throughout the curve. Some examples of this effect are shown in figure 2.31 where spline and Lagrangian interpolating functions are compared.

To study the idea of a global spline curve we shall examine a two-dimensional set of n points, (x_i, y_i), where the data is ordered so that $x_0 < x_1 < x_2 < \dots < x_{n-2} < x_{n-1}$. Figure 2.32 illustrates the setup.

For the ith interval, between the points (x_i, y_i) and (x_{i+1}, y_{i+1}), the form of the cubic is:

$$y = a_i(x - x_i)^3 + b_i(x - x_i)^2 + c_i(x - x_i) + d_i \qquad (2.38)$$

This curve must be satisfied by both (x_i, y_i) and (x_{i+1}, y_{i+1}). Blending is achieved by assuming that at (x_i, y_i) the slope and curvature are the same as in the previous interval (between points (x_{i-1}, y_{i-1}) and (x_i, y_i)). Slope and curvature are given by first and second derivatives respectively.

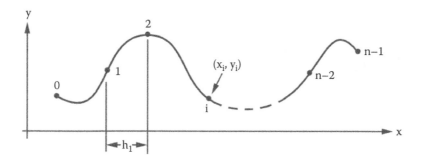

Figure 2.32: A two-dimensional spline curve passing through n data points.

Letting $h_i = (x_{i+1} - x_i)$ and S_i represent the second derivative at the point (x_i, y_i) an equation in which the S_is are unknown may be written for a general point i,

$$h_{i-1}S_{i-1} + 2(h_{i-1} + h_i)S_i + h_iS_{i+1} = 6\left(\frac{y_{i+1} - y_i}{h_i} - \frac{y_i - y_{i-1}}{h_{i-1}}\right) \qquad (2.39)$$

Equation (2.39) is obtained by differentiating (2.38) twice, rearranging and making use of the assumptions about slope and curvature at point i.

Since equation (2.39) applies at the points on the spline (except the first and last) a set of $n - 2$ simultaneous equations may be written for the n values of S_i, that is, an equation for each of the internal points 1, 2, ... $(n - 2)$.

A set of $n - 2$ equations in n unknowns does not have a unique solution and so two additional equations, for S_0 and S_{n-1}, are obtained by specifying some pertinent end conditions. Possible end conditions are:

1. The end cubics approach linearity, $S_0 = S_{n-1} = 0$, the so-called natural boundary conditions.

2. The end cubics approach parabolas, $S_0 = S_1$ and $S_{n-1} = S_{n-2}$.

3. S_0 is a linear extrapolation from S_1 and S_2, and S_{n-1} is a linear extrapolation from S_{n-3} and S_{n-2}.

Using the natural boundary conditions a set of $n - 2$ linear equations in $n - 2$ unknowns (the S_i) are established. In matrix form, these are written as $[H][S] = [Y]$ where:

$[H] =$

$$\begin{bmatrix} 2(h_0 + h_1) & h_1 & 0 & 0 & .. & 0 \\ h_1 & 2(h_1 + h_2) & h_2 & 0 & .. & 0 \\ 0 & h_2 & 2(h_2 + h_3) & h_3 & & \\ .. & .. & .. & .. & .. & .. \\ 0 & .. & 0 & h_{n-4} & 2(h_{n-4} + h_{n-3}) & h_{n-3} \\ 0 & .. & 0 & 0 & h_{n-3} & 2(h_{n-3} + h_{n-2}) \end{bmatrix}$$

$$[S] = \begin{bmatrix} S_1 \\ S_2 \\ S_3 \\ .. \\ .. \\ S_{n-2} \end{bmatrix}$$

$$[Y] = 6 \begin{bmatrix} \left(\dfrac{y_2 - y_1}{h_1} - \dfrac{y_1 - y_0}{h_0} \right) \\ \left(\dfrac{y_3 - y_2}{h_2} - \dfrac{y_2 - y_1}{h_1} \right) \\ \left(\dfrac{y_4 - y_3}{h_3} - \dfrac{y_3 - y_2}{h_2} \right) \\ .. \\ .. \\ \left(\dfrac{y_{n-1} - y_{n-2}}{h_{n-2}} - \dfrac{y_{n-2} - y_{n-3}}{h_{n-3}} \right) \end{bmatrix}$$

The matrix $[H]$ is very sparse (it has many zero elements) and *tridiagonal*. Linear equations with this structure are amenable to very rapid solution by using an algorithm such as the one in McCalla [58].

Once the S_i have been found the constants a_i, b_i, c_i and d_i in equation 2.38 are obtained from:

$$a_i = \frac{S_{i+1} - S_i}{6h_i}$$

$$b_i = \frac{S_i}{2}$$

$$c_i = \frac{y_{i+1} - y_i}{h_i} - \frac{2h_i S_i + h_i S_{i+1}}{6}$$

$$d_i = y_i$$

After that, the cubic polynomial equation (2.38) is used to yield values for y given x in the interval between (x_i, y_i) and (x_{i+1}, y_{i+1}).

2.16.2   Other splines

Splines come in many flavors. The *basis splines*, uniform B-spline, non-uniform
B-splines and recursive B-splines have other mathematical properties that make
them useful in different situations. The common feature among all these splines
is that they are constructed piecewise by blending together a series of functions
$B_i(t)$ within each of the pieces. The $B_i(t)$ are called the basis functions, hence
the B in the name. They are functions of a single parameter t. It is then possible
to determine the location of any point on the curve defined by $n+1$ control points
from:

$$\mathbf{P}(t) = \sum_{i=0}^{n} N_i(t)\mathbf{P}_i \qquad (2.40)$$

where the $\mathbf{P}_i$ are the control points and, in the case of the uniform B-splines:

$$N_i(t) = \begin{cases} B_0(t - t_{i+1}) & \text{if } t \in [t_{i+1}, t_{i+2}) \\ B_1(t - t_i) & \text{if } t \in [t_i, t_{i+1}) \\ B_2(t - t_{i-1}) & \text{if } t \in [t_{i-1}, t_i) \\ B_3(t - t_{i-2}) & \text{if } t \in [t_{i-2}, t_{i-1}) \\ 0 & \text{otherwise} \end{cases} \qquad (2.41)$$

Of course, any single piece in which of $\mathbf{P}(t)$ is to be determined is only affected
by four control points. Thus for segment k

$$\mathbf{P}_k(t) = \sum_{i=0}^{3} N_{i+k-1}(t)\mathbf{P}_{i+k-1} \qquad (2.42)$$

The t_i values in equation 2.41 are called the knot values, since they correspond
to the parameter at each of the curve's knots. The knots are the points on the
curve where it begins and ends as well as those points where the pieces of the
spline join together. Thus a curve with $n+1$ control points will have $n-1$ knots.
The full collection of knot values for a curve is known as the *knot vector*.

   In B-splines the t_i are equally spaced; in the non-uniform B-splines they may
take any value of t, even the same value. The $B_i(t)$ are determined so that the
properties we require for the spline are satisfied. In the case of the non-uniform
and rational B-splines the $N_i(t)$ are determined through a recursive formula that
also depends on the order of the curve, which for cubic splines is 3.

   To plot a B-spline curve specified by $n+1$ control points, incremental values
of the parameter $t \in [0, n-1]$ are substituted into 2.40 and the resulting points
$\mathbf{P}$ joined up. For example, for a curve with 8 control points, the uniform B-spline
knot vector will be $[0, 1, 2, 3, 4, 5]$ and there will be 5 segments.

   We have only touched on the rich mathematics of spline curves in this section.
Bartels et al. [8] present a useful general study of spline theory for both curves
and surfaces. They introduce the highly useful non-uniform rational B-spline
(NURBS) that has proved its utility in CAD applications. Lengyel [54] provides
a detailed derivation of the basis functions for all splines in the family.

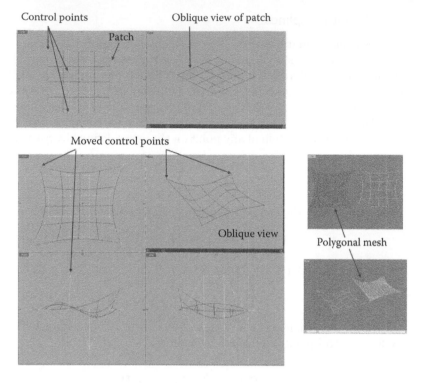

Figure 2.33: A basic NURBS patch is controlled by its network of control points. (Taken from OpenFX.)

2.17   Parametric surfaces

In section 2.16 methods of working with curves in computer graphics were discussed. The Bézier and spline curves introduced there can be extrapolated into a two-dimensional space to facilitate modeling curved surfaces. However, Bézier and simple polynomial based curves cannot model every form of curve, for example a circle cannot be exactly modeled by a Bézier curve. Rational polynomials (one polynomial divided by another) offer the potential to model any shape. Extending rational polynomials into a two variable parameter space offers the potential to represent a surface with any degree of curvature. Making up models from patches described by rational polynomials with the added constraints of position, tangent and curvature continuity offers the potential to model any shapes. Two-dimensional NURBS fulfills all the requirements for patch modeling and have proved popular with CAD designers. Most CAD tools and 3D modeling software offers the facility to use NURBS surfaces, which are straightforward extensions of NURBS curves.

NURBS patches are specified in terms of their control points. Figure 2.33 illustrates a 2D patch with its control points and how it is possible to move the control points interactively to distort the patch into shape to be modeled, whilst the control points of a NURBS patch are the main way in which the patch of a CAD software program is specified by the designer. There are two other attributes that are needed for a full specification of the patch, the *knot* and the *order*. The order of a NURBS patch is the number of control points used in the calculation of the coordinate of any point on the patch. The knots determine how the control points affect the patch. They effectively give weight to how much influence the control points have on determining the coordinate of any point on the surface.

By definition, NURBS patches are 2D surfaces embedded in 3D space, the shape of which is determined by a network of control points $\mathbf{p}_{i,j}(x, y, z)$. The control points are arranged in a 2D grid of surface local coordinates (u, v), where $0 \leq u \leq 1$ and $0 \leq v \leq 1$. The 3D location of any point on the surface $\mathbf{P}$ of a patch is obtained by specifying a value of the patch local coordinate system (u_0, v_0), and use:

$$\mathbf{P}(u, v) = \sum_{i=1}^{k} \sum_{j=1}^{l} R_{i,j}(u, v)\mathbf{p}_{i,j} \tag{2.43}$$

Here, $R(u, v)$ is the rational polynomial that gives a NURBS its properties, l is the number of control points across the surface in the u direction, and l the number in the v direction.

To generate a polygonal mesh for a NURBS patch, a regular array of (u, v) coordinates is passed through equation 2.43 to give an array of 3D coordinates that are connected together in a polygonal mesh, an example of which is depicted in figure 2.34.

The term $R_{i,j}(u, v)$ in equation 2.43 is obtained through a combination of basis functions, $N_{i,n}$, which are polynomials of degree n. The degree of polynomial may be chosen depending on the desired properties, curvature etc., of the surface, and based on this, additional control points are brought into play in calculating $R(u, v)$. Typically $N_{i,n}$ (where i identifies a control point) is obtained in a recursive formulation:

$$N_{i,n} = fN_{i,n-1} + gN_{i+1,n-1}$$

f is a linear function that rises from 0 to 1 and g falls from 1 to 0 over the intervals where N is non-zero. $N_{i,0}$ is a constant function with a value of 1 over the interval between control points $[i, i + 1]$ and 0 elsewhere.

Bringing these terms together allows the expression for $R_{i,j}(u, v)$ to be evaluated:

$$R_{i,j}(u, v) = \frac{N_{i,n}(u)N_{j,m}(v)w_{i,j}}{\sum_{p=1}^{k} \sum_{q=1}^{l} N_{p,n}(u)N_{q,m}(v)w_{p,q}} \tag{2.44}$$

$w_{i,j}$ is the control point's weighting value. For a good practical implementation of the NURBS patch see Peterson's Graphics Gem [41] and further details

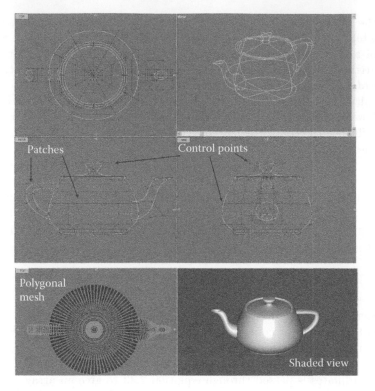

Figure 2.34: NURBS patches can take up any curvature. In this figure, 32 patches are combined to form the model of a highly curved surface. For visualization purposes the patches are converted to a polygonal mesh of the most suitable resolution, which might be viewpoint dependent.

of the basic mathematics of NURBS curves and surfaces may be obtained in Lengyel [54].

2.18   Angular interpolation (quaternions)

Implicit in the previous discussion on interpolation was the use of the Cartesian coordinate system. This is ideal for interpolating position vectors. On the other hand there are many scenarios where it will be required to interpolate direction vectors.

Consider the following:

> *You are standing on the top of a hill with a camera on a motorized tripod looking North. You wish to set the camera so that it pans round to face East taking pictures every 10°.*

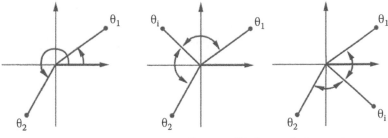

Two possible interpolation angles

Figure 2.35: In this example of angular interpolation there are two possible values for an angle bisecting the angles θ_1 and θ_2.

This is a job for angular interpolation, first direction $0°$, last direction $90°$, and 8 intermediate steps. In this case linear interpolation of the angle is the natural way to obtain the directions to use for the intermediate shots. As we shall see when we consider computer animation a combination of interpolated positions and interpolated angles is a very efficient method of directing the action.

Angles are cyclic of period 2π, therefore the angle α is the same angle as $\alpha + 2\pi$, $\alpha + 4\pi$, ..., $\alpha + 2n\pi$. This makes interpolation a little tricky. As shown in figure 2.35 there are two possible solutions to the problem of finding the angle, θ_i, that lies half way between the two angles θ_1 and θ_2.

This problem of interpolation gets more complex when three dimensions are involved. First, to be able to specify an arbitrary orientation three angles are needed. Section 2.12.7 introduced three measures that describe the orientation of a camera observing a collection of objects. There they were referred to as *heading, pitch* and *roll (bank)*. Three angles specifying an orientation are known as *Euler* angles. However, there are 12 possible conventions for describing Euler angles making their specification rather confusing. We will choose the convention for orientation illustrated in figure 2.36. Thus, in three dimensions, interpolation between two orientations reduces to the problem of obtaining the triple (ϕ, θ, α) given two or more sets of angles $(\phi_0, \theta_0, \alpha_0)$, $(\phi_1, \theta_1, \alpha_1)$, etc.

Unfortunately, orientations specified with Euler angles (ϕ, θ, α) cannot be interpolated in the same way that positions are interpolated because of the periodic way in which angles are defined. This poses something of a problem; however an excellent solution has been waiting in the wings since 1843 when Hamilton [37] developed the mathematics of the quaternion as part of his attempt to find a generalization of the complex number. The significance of the quaternion for computer graphics was first recognized by Shoemake [81].

For the work in this book it is unnecessary to explore the details of the quaternion in depth. We are only interested in using quaternions to help us achieve angular interpolation between given orientations and this simply requires that we

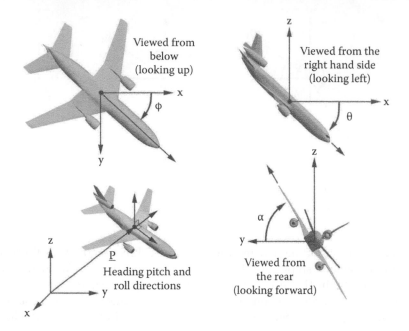

Figure 2.36: One set of Euler angles (ϕ, θ, ϕ) used to specify orientation. In each of the views the third axis is directed into the page. Each angle is specified by a radian measure relative to a base axis and is considered to be positive when the orientation is clockwise if observed from the coordinate origin while looking in the direction of the base axis. For computer animation work it is appropriate to think of an object as having a *rest* orientation, say directed along the **x** axis without any tilt (roll or bank). To pivot the object into some other orientation a series of rotations are applied until it has taken up the orientation specified by the Euler angles (ϕ, θ, α) relative to the reference direction.

can interpolate between quaternions and switch back and forth[1] between equivalent representations of orientation, i.e., Euler angles, quaternions and rotation matrices.

2.18.1   The quaternion

A quaternion q is an ordered pair $(w, \mathbf{v})$ of a scalar and three-dimensional vector $\mathbf{v}$ with components (x, y, z). Like vectors, a *unit length* or normalized quaternion must satisfy:

$$w^2 + x^2 + y^2 + z^2 = 1$$

---

[1]Users of application software generally prefer to specify orientations in terms of Euler angles, pitch, elevation and headings rather than as abstract quaternions.

Quaternions have their own algebra with rules for addition and multiplication. Addition is straightforward: add the scalar components and the vector components. Multiplication is more interesting. Given two quaternions q_1 and q_2 the product is the quaternion:

$$q_1 q_2 = (w, \mathbf{v}) = (w_1 w_2 - \mathbf{v_1} \cdot \mathbf{v_2}, w_1 \mathbf{v_2} + w_2 \mathbf{v_1} + \mathbf{v_1} \times \mathbf{v_2})$$

A conjugate quaternion to q is defined as $\bar{q} = (w, -\mathbf{v})$. Thus, the squared magnitude of q is:

$$q\bar{q} = |q|^2 = w^2 + |\mathbf{v}|^2$$

Note that if q is of unit magnitude its inverse q^{-1} equals its conjugate, $q^{-1} = \bar{q}$ and $q\bar{q} = 1$.

2.18.2   Quaternions and rotations

We have seen in section 2.12.3 that the action of rotating a vector $\mathbf{r}$ from one orientation to another may be expressed in terms of the application of a transformation matrix $[R]$, which when applied to $\mathbf{r}$ to $\mathbf{r'} = [R]\mathbf{r}$ gives it a new orientation. The matrix $[R]$ is independent of $\mathbf{r}$ and will perform the same (**relative**) rotation on any other vector.

One can write $[R]$ in terms of a succession of Euler angle rotations, i.e., as a function $[R(\phi, \theta, \alpha)]$ (the order being vital). However, the same rotation can be achieved by specifying $[R]$ in terms of a unit vector $\hat{\mathbf{n}}$ and a single angle γ. That is, $\mathbf{r}$ is transformed into $\mathbf{r'}$ by rotating it round $\hat{\mathbf{n}}$ through γ.

The angle γ is positive when the rotation takes place in a clockwise direction when viewed along $\hat{\mathbf{n}}$ from its base. The two equivalent rotations may be written as:

$$\begin{aligned} \mathbf{r'} &= [R(\phi, \theta, \alpha)]\mathbf{r} \\ \mathbf{r'} &= [R'(\gamma, \hat{\mathbf{n}})]\mathbf{r} \end{aligned}$$

At first sight it might seem difficult to appreciate that the same transformation can be achieved by specifying a single rotation round one axis as opposed to three rotations round three orthogonal axes; figure 2.37 illustrates this process. There are also a whole range of other subtleties surrounding this issue that are only really resolved through the use of quaternions; Wolf [38] discusses these in depth.

It is also quite difficult to imagine how $(\gamma, \hat{\mathbf{n}})$ might be calculated given the more naturally intuitive and easier to specify Euler angles (ϕ, θ, α). However, there is a need for methods to switch from one representation to another.

In a number of important situations it is necessary to use the $(\gamma, \hat{\mathbf{n}})$ representation. For example the Virtual Reality Modeling Language (VRML) [40] uses the $(\gamma, \hat{\mathbf{n}})$ specification to define the orientation adopted by an object in a virtual world.

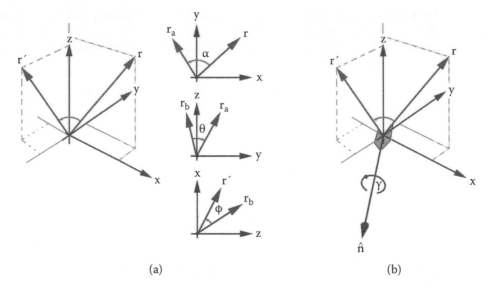

Figure 2.37: Rotation about an arbitrary axis, $\hat{\mathbf{n}}$, chosen to point in a direction that is at right angles to both the initial and final results. (b) will achieve the same result as three consecutive rotations around orthogonal basis vectors (a). Here $\mathbf{r}$ is the initial vector and $\mathbf{r}'$ the result after re-orientation. $\mathbf{r}_a$ and $\mathbf{r}_b$ are intermediate steps.

Watt and Watt [86] derive an expression that gives some insight into the significance of the $(\gamma, \hat{\mathbf{n}})$ specification of a rotational transform by determining $[R]\mathbf{r}$ in terms of $(\gamma, \hat{\mathbf{n}})$:

$$\mathbf{r}' = [R]\mathbf{r} = \cos\gamma\mathbf{r} + (1 - \cos\gamma)(\hat{\mathbf{n}} \cdot \mathbf{r})\hat{\mathbf{n}} + (\sin\gamma)\hat{\mathbf{n}} \times \mathbf{r} \qquad (2.45)$$

This expression is the vital link between rotational transformations and the use of quaternions to represent them. To see this consider two quaternions:

1. $p = (0, \mathbf{r})$, a quaternion formed by setting its scalar part to zero and its vector part to $\mathbf{r}$ (the vector we wish to transform)

2. $q = (w, \mathbf{v})$, an arbitrary quaternion with unit magnitude: $q\bar{q} = qq^{-1} = 1$

The product qpq^{-1} gives the quaternion:

$$qpq^{-1} = (0, ((w^2 - (\mathbf{v} \cdot \mathbf{v}))\mathbf{r} + 2(\mathbf{v} \cdot \mathbf{r})\mathbf{v} + 2w(\mathbf{v} \times \mathbf{r}))) \qquad (2.46)$$

Since q is an arbitrary quaternion of unit magnitude there is no loss of generality by expressing it in the form:

$$q = \left(\cos\left(\frac{\gamma}{2}\right), \sin\left(\frac{\gamma}{2}\right)\hat{\mathbf{n}}\right) \qquad (2.47)$$

Substitute $\cos\left(\dfrac{\gamma}{2}\right)$ for w and $\sin\left(\dfrac{\gamma}{2}\right)\hat{\mathbf{n}}$ for $\mathbf{v}$ in equation 2.46. The vector part of qpq^{-1} is identical, term for term, with the rotation expressed by equation 2.45. Therefore if we express a rotation in the form $[R(\gamma,\hat{\mathbf{n}})]$ its action on a vector $\mathbf{r}$ is equivalent to operating the following four steps:

1. Promote the vector $\mathbf{r}$ to the quaternion $p = (0,\mathbf{r})$.

2. Express $[R(\gamma,\hat{\mathbf{n}})]$ as the quaternion $q = (\cos\dfrac{\gamma}{2}, \sin\dfrac{\gamma}{2}\hat{\mathbf{n}})$.

3. Evaluate the quaternion product $p' = qpq^{-1}$.

4. Extract the transformed vector $\mathbf{r}'$ from the vector component of $p' = (0,\mathbf{r}')$. (Note that the scalar component of operations such as these will always be zero.)

This isn't the end of our story of quaternions because, just as rotational transformations in matrix form may be combined into a single matrix, rotations in quaternion form may be combined into a single quaternion by multiplying their individual quaternion representations together. For example consider rotations $[R_1]$ and $[R_2]$ represented by quaternions q_1 and q_2 respectively. Applying them in turn to $p' = q_1 p q_1^{-1}$ and $p'' = q_2 p' q_2^{-1}$ gives:

$$
\begin{aligned}
p'' &= q_2 p' q_2^{-1} \\
p'' &= q_2(q_1 p q_1^{-1})q_2^{-1} \\
p'' &= (q_2 q_1)p(q_1^{-1}q_2^{-1}) \\
p'' &= q_c p q_c^{-1}
\end{aligned}
$$

Here $q_c = q_2 q_1$ and as quaternions satisfy $(q_2 q_1)^{-1} = q_1^{-1}q_2^{-1}$. We can write $(q_1^{-1}q_2^{-1}) = (q_2 q_1)^{-1}$.

2.18.3 Converting Euler angles to quaternions

From the Euler angles (ϕ,θ,α) shown in figure 2.36 a quaternion that *encapsulates the same information* is constructed by writing quaternions for rotation ϕ about the $\mathbf{z}$, θ about the $\mathbf{y}$ and α about the $\mathbf{x}$ axes:

$$
\begin{aligned}
q_{\mathbf{x}} &= \left[\cos\frac{\alpha}{2}, \sin\frac{\alpha}{2}, 0, 0\right] \\
q_{\mathbf{y}} &= \left[\cos\frac{\theta}{2}, 0, \sin\frac{\theta}{2}, 0\right] \\
q_{\mathbf{z}} &= \left[\cos\frac{\phi}{2}, 0, 0, \sin\frac{\phi}{2}\right]
\end{aligned}
$$

and then multiplying them together as $q = q_z q_y q_x$. The components of q are:

$$
\begin{aligned}
w &= \cos\frac{\alpha}{2}\cos\frac{\theta}{2}\cos\frac{\phi}{2} + \sin\frac{\alpha}{2}\sin\frac{\theta}{2}\sin\frac{\phi}{2} \\
x &= \sin\frac{\alpha}{2}\cos\frac{\theta}{2}\cos\frac{\phi}{2} - \cos\frac{\alpha}{2}\sin\frac{\theta}{2}\sin\frac{\phi}{2} \\
y &= \cos\frac{\alpha}{2}\sin\frac{\theta}{2}\cos\frac{\phi}{2} + \sin\frac{\alpha}{2}\cos\frac{\theta}{2}\sin\frac{\phi}{2} \\
z &= \cos\frac{\alpha}{2}\cos\frac{\theta}{2}\sin\frac{\phi}{2} - \sin\frac{\alpha}{2}\sin\frac{\theta}{2}\cos\frac{\phi}{2}
\end{aligned}
$$

2.18.4   Converting a quaternion to a matrix

In section 2.12.3 it was shown that a rotational transformation in matrix form could be applied to a position vector to pivot it into a new orientation $[p'] = [T_\theta][p]$. A quaternion contains rotational information but it cannot be directly applied to a position vector in the same way that a matrix can. Therefore it is useful to have a method of expressing the rotational information in the quaternion directly as a matrix which, in turn can be used to rotate position vectors.

For a normalized quaternion $[w, x, y, z]$ the corresponding 4×4 matrix is:

$$
\begin{bmatrix}
1 - 2y^2 - 2z^2 & 2xy + 2wz & 2xz - 2wy & 0 \\
2xy - 2wz & 1 - 2x^2 - 2z^2 & 2yz + 2wx & 0 \\
2xz + 2wy & 2yz - 2wx & 1 - 2x^2 - 2y^2 & 0 \\
0 & 0 & 0 & 1
\end{bmatrix}
$$

It is important to note that a 4×4 matrix can encapsulate positional transformations as well as rotational ones. A unit quaternion only describes pure rotations. So, when quaternions are combined the complex rotation they represent is with respect to axes passing through the coordinate origin $(0, 0, 0)$.

2.18.5   Converting a matrix to a quaternion

If the rotational matrix is given by:

$$
[M] = \begin{bmatrix}
a_{00} & a_{01} & a_{02} & 0 \\
a_{10} & a_{11} & a_{12} & 0 \\
a_{20} & a_{21} & a_{22} & 0 \\
0 & 0 & 0 & 1
\end{bmatrix}
$$

and the quaternion q by:

$$
q = [w, x, y, z]
$$

Shoemake's [81] algorithm in listing 2.4 obtains q given $[M]$. The parameter ϵ is the machine precision of zero. A reasonable choice would be 10^{-6} for floating point calculations. Note only elements of $[M]$ that contribute to the rotation are considered in the algorithm.

```
w = ¼(1 + a₀₀ + a₁₁ + a₂₂)
if  w > ε {
    w = √w   w₄ = 1/(4w)
    x = w₄(a₁₂ − a₂₁)   y = w₄(a₂₀ − a₀₂)   z = w₄(a₀₁ − a₁₀)
}
else {
    w = 0
    x = −½(a₁₁ + a₂₂)
    if  x > ε {
        x = √x   x₂ = 1/(2x)   y = x₂a₀₁   z = x₂a₀₂
    }
    else {
        x = 0   y = ½(1 − a₂₂)
        if  y > ε {
            y = √y   z = a₁₂/(2y)
        }
        else {
            y = 0   z = 1
        }
    }
}
```

Listing 2.4: An algorithm for the conversion of rotational transformation matrix M with coefficients $a_{i,j}$ to the quaternion q with coefficients (w, x, y, z).

2.18.6 Converting a quaternion to Euler angles

To convert the quaternion to the equivalent Euler angles, first convert the quaternion to an equivalent matrix, and then use the matrix to Euler angle conversion algorithm. Sadly matrix to Euler angle conversion is unavoidably ill-defined because the calculations involve inverse trigonometric functions. To achieve this conversion use the algorithm shown in listing 2.5 which converts the matrix $[M]$ with elements a_{ij} to Euler angles (ϕ, θ, α).

The angles (ϕ, θ, ϕ) lie in the interval $[-\pi, \pi]$ but they can be biased to $[0, 2\pi]$ or some other suitable range if required.

2.18.7 Interpolating quaternions

One major advantage of using quaternions in 3D computer graphics is that the interpolation between two orientations defined by the Euler angles, say $(\phi_0, \theta_0, \alpha_0)$ and $(\phi_1, \theta_1, \alpha_1)$, is easily done when the orientations are expressed in a quaternion form. It is not possible to interpolate between two orientations when they are specified as a rotation matrices. To illustrate the advantage of quaternions we recall that *linear* interpolation between two position vectors gives a straight

---

$\sin\theta = -a_{02}$

$\cos\theta = \sqrt{1 - \sin^2\theta}$

if $|\cos\theta| < \epsilon$ {

   It is not possible to distinguish heading from pitch and the convention that
   ϕ *is* 0 *is assumed, thus:*

   $\sin\alpha = -a_{21} \quad \cos\alpha = a_{11}$

   $\sin\phi = 0 \quad \cos\phi = 1$

}

else {

   $\sin\alpha = \dfrac{a_{12}}{\cos\theta} \quad \cos\alpha = \dfrac{a_{22}}{\cos\theta}$

   $\sin\phi = \dfrac{a_{01}}{\cos\theta} \quad \cos\phi = \dfrac{a_{00}}{\cos\theta}$

}

$\alpha = ATAN2(\sin\alpha, \cos\alpha)$

$\theta = ATAN2(\sin\theta, \cos\theta)$

$\phi = ATAN2(\sin\phi, \cos\phi)$

Listing 2.5: Conversion from rotational transformation matrix to the equivalent Euler angles of rotation.

line and in Cartesian geometry a straight line is the shortest path between two points. A similarly simple interpolation for quaternions is desirable. Therefore for quaternions the question arises: What is equivalent to a straight line?

A clue to the answer comes from the concept of latitude and longitude. Latitude and longitude are angular directions from the center of the earth to a point on its surface whose position is to be specified. Thus a pair of values *(lat,long)* represent a point on the earth's surface. To go from one place to another by the shortest route one follows a *great circle*, illustrated in figure 2.38. The great circle is the line of intersection between a sphere and a plane that passes through the center of the sphere. Intercontinental flight paths for aircraft follow great circles; for example the flight path between London and Tokyo passes close to the North Pole. We can therefore say that just as the shortest distance between two points in a Cartesian frame of reference is by a straight line, the shortest distance between two *(latitude, longitude)* coordinates is along a *path* following a great circle. The *(latitude, longitude)* coordinates at intermediate points on the *great circle* are determined by interpolation, in this case by *spherical interpolation*.

Quaternions are used for this interpolation. We think of the end points of the path being specified by quaternions, q_0 and q_1. From these a quaternion q_i is interpolated for any point on the great circle joining q_0 to q_1. Conversion of q_i back to *(latitude, longitude)* allows the path to be plotted. In terms of angular interpolation we may think of latitude and longitude as simply two of the Euler angles. When extended to the full set (ϕ, θ, α) a smooth interpolation along the equivalent of a great circle is the result.

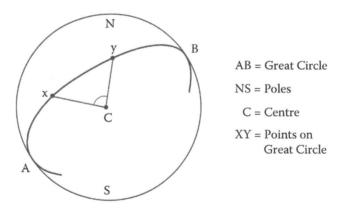

Figure 2.38: A great circle gives a path of shortest distance between two points on the surface of a sphere. The arc between points X and Y is the shortest path.

$\sigma = w_0 w_1 + x_0 x_1 + y_0 y_1 + z_0 z_1$
```
if  σ > 1{
        normalize q0 and q1 by
        dividing the components of q0 and q1 by σ
}
```
$\theta = \cos^{-1}(\sigma)$
```
if  |θ| < ε {
        β0 = 1 - μ  β1 = μ
}
else {
```
$$\beta_0 = \frac{\sin(1-\mu)\theta}{\sin\theta} \quad \beta_1 = \frac{\sin\mu\theta}{\sin\theta}$$
```
}
```
$w_i = \beta_0 w_0 + \beta_1 w_1$
$x_i = \beta_0 z_0 + \beta_1 x_1 \quad y_i = \beta_0 y_0 + \beta_1 y_1 \quad z_i = \beta_0 z_0 + \beta_1 z_1$

Listing 2.6: Implementation of the slerp function.

Using the concept of moving along a great circle as a guide to angular interpolation a *spherical interpolation function, slerp()*, may be derived. The form of this function that works for interpolating between quaternions $q_0 = [w_0, x_0, y_0, z_0]$ and $q_1 = [w_1, x_1, y_1, z_1]$ is given by Shoemake [81] as:

$$slerp(\mu, q_0, q_1) = \frac{\sin(1-\mu)\theta}{\sin\theta} q_0 + \frac{\sin\mu\theta}{\sin\theta} q_1$$

where μ, the interpolation parameter, takes values in the range $[0, 1]$. The angle θ is obtained from: $\cos\theta = q_0 \cdot q_1 = w_0 w_1 + x_0 x_1 + y_0 y_1 + z_0 z_1$. The algorithmic implementation in listing 2.6 of the *slerp()* function for the interpolated quaternion $q_i = [w_i, x_i, y_i, z_i]$ avoids the problem of division by zero when θ is close to zero.

3

Data structures for 3D graphics

The visual appearance of 3D models representing all kinds of objects is dictated by the properties of their surfaces with color being the most important. Often the surface of a model is constructed by building it up from a series of primitive shapes. A polygon with three sides (*a triangle*) is the simplest form of primitive shape. In chapter 2 other simple primitives like the sphere were discussed. Today in computer-aided design (CAD) application programs more complex surface shapes referred to as *patches* have proved popular. These include Bézier and NURBS (non-uniform rational B-spline) patches which have curved edges and continuously varying internal curvature. A model can usually be accurately represented by combining a lot fewer of these more sophisticated surface shapes. Whether using primitive polygons or curved patches to describe a model there are advantages and disadvantages. The simplest polygon is fast to render and easy to manipulate; the more complex patches usually give a better approximation to the original object, especially if it has many curved parts. Occasionally, it is a matter of personal preference which sort of patch to use. For example, a cube is modeled just as effectively with triangular polygons as it is with Bézier patches. Figure 3.1 shows the famous Utah teapot in polygonal and Bézier patch form.

Whatever type of patch is used to describe the surface of a 3D model it must be *located* in space, which means attaching it to three or more *vertices* or points somewhere in 3D space. With appropriate transformations applied to the vertex coordinates a visualization (more commonly called a rendering) can be produced on the computer monitor or other output device.

3.1 Integer coordinates

When the topic of coordinate systems is discussed, Cartesian or possibly polar are the words that come to mind. Very little thought is given to the numbers system used to map out the spaces; it is more or less taken for granted that floating point decimals will be used. In the perfect world of mathematics there is no need to

Figure 3.1: Polygonal and Bézier patch surface representations.

pay the slightest thought to approximation; if two numbers are equal, then they
are equal, and their magnitude is irrelevant. Unfortunately, in the practical and
imperfect world where calculations have to be done by machine, the behavior of
numbers is far from perfect. Only in the case of the integer numbers (lying inside
the range of precision of the computer's word length) can one really say that x
is equal to y when they are being compared in a computer program; otherwise
all one can really say is that if $|x - y| < \epsilon$ we will accept the fact that x and y
are equal.

Being able to say that x equals y is an essential part of most of the algorithms
used in computer graphics: Does this edge hit that polygon, is often a key
question. Three-dimensional computer graphics is founded on 3D geometry,
and 3D geometry is very good at finding those situations where our numerical
mathematics is challenged the most: Does the line hit the polygon on its edge,
or inside, is a *very* hard question to answer. Using one computer that calculates
to an accuracy of ten decimal places may give a different answer to one that
calculates to 20 places of decimals. For this reason we often choose to store the
coordinate data for vertices and other points using integers, and where possible
working with algorithms that manipulate things using only integers, we can then
say with certainty whether x equals y or whether two lines actually are parallel
or not.

A number of the most significant computational geometry algorithms used in
CGI are written to work best with integer coordinates; see O'Rourke [65]. The
OpenFX program (chapter 9) uses integer coordinates to record its 3D data.

3.2   Vertices and polygons

The minimal description of a 3D model requires a list of surface patches and a
list of vertex coordinates. Each entry in the surface patch list must identify the
vertices to which it is connected and have some way of allowing its surface to
take on the appearance of wood, marble, glass or chrome etc. Indeed, one of
the most popular ways to provide a comprehensive set of surface attributes is

for each surface patch to store an index into a table of *materials*. The material provides a color and many other properties. With careful choice of parameter an extremely realistic look to the model can be achieved.

Despite the fact that real-time shading can now be done routinely on basic personal computers it can still be useful to use a wireframe display when designing interactive 3D animations or complex models. Shaded rendering is done in a subsequent step to whatever degree of realism is required, a process that can take minutes or even hours.

A wireframe model is a set of straight lines that join vertices together. The edges of each polygonal surface constitute the members of this set. Sometimes it can be useful to maintain a separate list of edges rather than to have to generate it from the polygons each time a drawing of the wireframe is made. This policy has the advantage of a faster display and since edges are not normally rendered, they can be used to link various parts of a model together for editing purposes.

There are three alternative schemes for storing the geometric description of a model:

1. For the n vertices of each surface polygon store n integers. Each integer identifies an entry in the vertex list. For each entry in the vertex list store the coordinates (x, y, z) of a position vector. Most 3D programs store (x, y, z) as single precision floating point numbers, but a few use integers. If polygon edges are needed then they can be obtained by pairing consecutive vertices.

2. For each surface polygon that is connected to n vertices store n integers. Each integer identifies an entry in the vertex list. For each entry in the vertex list store a position vector giving its (x, y, z) coordinates. If required a separate list for the m edges can be included. It holds two integers for each edge that index entries in the vertex list.

3. For each surface polygon with k edges store k integers identifying the entry in an edge list. An edge list identifies connections between vertices. Normally edges are part of the boundaries of polygons but it is possible to have edges in a model that have no connection with its polygonal surfaces. These will show up in a wireframe drawing of the model but will not be visible in either a hidden line or shaded rendering. For each edge, store two integers to index entries in the vertex list corresponding to the vertices at the end of the edge. For each entry in the vertex list store a position vector giving its (x, y, z) coordinates.

These organizations are summarized in figure 3.2.

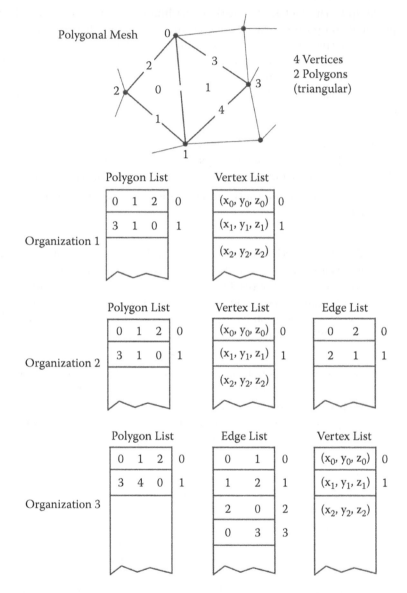

Figure 3.2: Data organization for the description of a 3D piecewise planar model.

To complete the requirements for a useful data structure we add a material index for each polygon and *texture coordinates* to every vertex. *Texture coordinates* allow a two-dimensional frame of reference to cover the surface of a model, rather like the way latitude and longitude are a two-dimensional coordinate system that are used to reference any point on the surface of the earth (a 3D spheroid). Just using a two-dimensional texture coordinate for each vertex has a slight disadvantage because the texturing is only visible in the polygons attached to the vertices; therefore if two adjacent polygons share a common pair of vertices it is not possible to provide a different mapping in the two polygons. Despite the addition of $2n$ numbers per N-gon it is better to record the texture coordinates for all the vertices of a polygon with the polygon.

There is also a good case to be made for including an additional three-dimensional texture coordinate system. It might be local to the whole object mesh, or apply to all surfaces with a specific material, or be defined on a per-vertex, or per-polygon-vertex basis. The reason for this inclusion is that procedural shaders are often three-dimensional; an object might look like it was carved out of marble, granite etc., rather than just look like the material was just painted over its surface.

In addition to this information it is a good idea to add a few temporary variables to the structure for use by modeling and rendering algorithms. For example, some of the algorithms described in chapter 10 require additional members in the data structures for vertices, edges and faces.

3.2.1 Skeletons, bones and materials

Partitioning a polygonal model into sub-units that are linked in a parent–child–grandchild relationship is useful. For example hierarchical linkages are very significant in character animation. An easily implemented and practically useful scheme is one that is analogous to the familiar file-store structure of computer systems, i.e. a root directory with files and subdirectories which themselves contain files and subdirectories and so on to whatever depth you like.

A doubly linked list of *hierarchy* entries is the best way to organize this data. In addition to *previous* and *next* pointers each entry will have a pointer to its *parent*, see figure 3.3. Other data can easily be appended to the structure as necessary. When using the structure for character animation or to reference parts of big model the entries can be given symbolic names, an example of which is shown in figure 3.3.

To complete a hierarchical description every polygon or vertex in the model is identified with one of the hierarchical names. A similar concept is one in which files on a computer disk are identified by the folders in which they are stored.

In a connected network of vertices and facets it is probably more useful to associate vertices, rather than polygons with one of the hierarchical names. To implement this association the vertex data structure shown in figure 3.10 must be extended with the entry h_{id} where, for a vertex h_{id}, identifies which hierarchical name the vertex is associated with. The new structure is shown in figure 3.4. A basic version of a structure that specifies a polygonal surface patch is illustrated in figure 3.5.

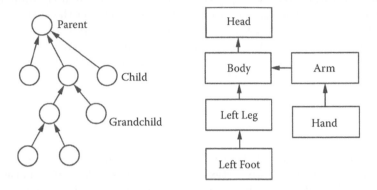

Figure 3.3: A hierarchical data structure for editing and character animation.

$\mathbf{p}$	position vector of vertex
ν, μ	surface texture coordinates
x	temporary integer index
n	number of adjacent vertices
V_{adj}	list of adjacent vertices
h_{id}	pointer to hierarchical element vertex is assigned to

Figure 3.4: Vertex data structure with hierarchical identifier.

V_{id}	list of vertex ids to which polygon is attached
id_{mat}	pointer to a material in materials list
id_{map}	pointer to a texture map in the list of image maps
(ν_i, μ_i)	texture coordinates for each vertex
$\mathbf{n}$	normal to surface plane

Figure 3.5: Typical surface patch data structure.

Notes:

1. The hierarchical names do not record any information about which vertices are assigned to them. Thus if it becomes necessary to modify the vertex lists (by adding or deleting for example) there is no need to update the hierarchy. However, the converse is **not** true. If a name in the hierarchy

is removed then all the vertices must be checked for any reference to the deleted hierarchical name and that reference removed.

2. When used for character animation, assigning each vertex to be attached to only one bone is not always the best strategy. For example, a vertex in the mesh of a forearm of a character that lies close to the elbow should have its position influenced to a certain extent by the bone in the upper arm. There are two ways in which we might try to enhance the model. First, it is easy to arrange that the movement of any of the bones in the skeleton could influence a displacement of a vertex in proportion to their distance from the vertex, with the added possibility of weighting how a particular bone amplifies or attenuates its influence. Or second, a list of bones (instead of just one) can be assigned to influence each vertex and only those in the list used to modify the movement of the vertex, again possibly in proportion to their distance from the vertex.

Both approaches have advantages and it is a good idea to assign extra attributes to each bone's data structure (see figure 3.3), so that additionally: (1) a weight, (2) a range of influence and possibly (3) a rate of influence that declines with distance, may be attributed to each bone. Also, since both two- and four-legged animals can be modeled with at most two bones influencing a third, the inclusion of a second vertex pointer per vertex would allow the influence of sufficient bones to be applied without being polluted by influence from other bones, just because they happen to be close by, but not directly connected.

3.2.2   Material data structures

In section 3.2 it was pointed out that in order to provide details of a surface texture the most efficient way is to maintain a list of materials, any one of which can be applied to the surface. The efficiency of this scheme is easily seen because there will always be a very much larger number of polygons defining an object's shape than there will be materials from which that surface could be built. Another advantage could ensue because separating the material data from the geometric data allows the number of properties that define the material to be increased (or decreased) without the need to modify the geometry describing structures.

The most basic material property that should be included to describe a surface is its color, but there are many other possibilities, e.g., its transparency and reflectivity. These will be discussed later in the book. Painting an image across a surface is perhaps the next most significant technique of giving texture to a surface that would otherwise look very unrealistic if just left a plain color. Painting a picture from an image file is usually referred to as *texture mapping* or *image mapping* and it plays a very important role, because an image map can also be used to simulate reflectivity, surface roughness and transparency. It is probably worth separating the image map from the other material properties by using a separate list. Then one or the other or both can be applied to the same surface.

Often materials, or image maps, or texture maps, or algorithmic textures, are just called *shaders*, but whatever they are called they play an equally important role to the geometry that describes an object's shape.

3.3   Algorithms for editing arrays of structures

When a modeling tool requires making many changes to the contents of its vertex, edge and face data, an organization based on a doubly linked list is very efficient, for example when deleting a vertex from the middle of the list. However, when it is not possible to use a doubly linked list data organization, fast editing functions are needed for things like inserting and or removing items from a basic indexed list.

For 3D data, the order in which polygons and vertices appear in a list is usually unimportant. Therefore, when items are added to a list, they can simply be tagged on to the end. Of course, the memory has to be dynamically extended to accommodate the extra items. To delete items from the list is more complex and if not done efficiently can be unacceptably time consuming. This section presents a very efficient algorithm for the removal of one or more items from anywhere in a list of vertex or polygon data structures.

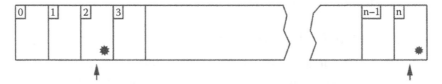

Figure 3.6: Array of *polygon structures* numbered 1 to n.

Figure 3.6 illustrates a representation of the list of polygon structures. Those to be deleted are marked with a *. Each structure will be composed of perhaps 16 to 32 bytes. The last entry n could be removed simply by reallocating the memory space to hold $n - 1$ polygons, but to eliminate polygon 2 the data for polygons 3 to n must be shifted to lower memory before the memory is reallocated. However this shifting operation is very slow and it gets slower if there are other entries to be removed later. Note that the vertex and polygon lists are *dependent*, because each polygon list entry points to an entry in the vertex list; therefore if the vertex list is modified, even if the polygon list is not, the polygon vertex identifiers will need to be updated, a process termed *re-vectoring*.

A very fast scheme can be developed by using the fact that the order of items in the list is unimportant. In this case all that has to be done is to copy the last entry in the list into the place held by the item to be deleted. The list may then be shortened by one entry. If several items are deleted the reduction in the size of the list is done in one step. In the example shown in figure 3.6 copy item $n - 1$ to item 2 (remember item n is also to be deleted).

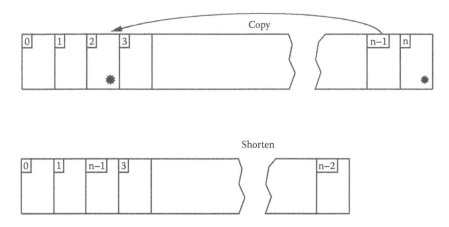

Figure 3.7: Deleting two items from the list of structures.

The whole of the structure can be copied with one call to a fast *memory copy* function (usually available as part of any system API, *Application Programming Interface*). The algorithm works through the list and when it finds an entry to be deleted it copies an entry from the end of the list and shortens the list by one. See the examples illustrated in figures 3.7 and 3.8. When all the entries have been processed one call to the reallocation function tidies up the memory.

The algorithm for removing unwanted entries from a list of *Poly* structures with *Npolys* entries is summarized in listing 3.1.

Note that by not indexing k when the structure is to be deleted we get the chance to immediately delete the one replacing it if it too is flagged for deletion.

This algorithm can be applied to the polygon and vertex lists in exactly the same way. However, as mentioned above, any change to the vertex list will invalidate entries in the polygon and edge lists that point to items in the vertex list. For example, if a polygon is attached to vertices $100, 101, 102$ in the vertex list but vertex 2 is removed from the list then vertices indexed as $100, 102$ or 103 may have moved to a different place in the vertex list. So, if we don't fix up the polygon data a memory violation will probably occur; at the very least the model will be a mess.

The fix is easily done by employing a dummy index variable in the vertex structure. As the algorithm steps through the vertex list copying down from the end to over-write the entries to be erased, it writes into the dummy index of the copied entry *the location where the copy has moved to*. At the end of the pass, but before the vertex list is resized, the polygon list is scanned again so that

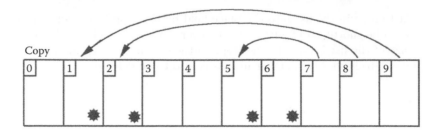

Copy

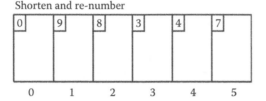

Shorten and re-number

Figure 3.8: Deleting multiple items from the list.

```
i = 0 , k = 0  and  newN = Npolys
repeat  while  i < Npolys {
    if  Poly(k)  flagged for deletion  {
        if  i < Npolys − 1 {
            copy size of Poly structure (bytes)
            from Poly(newN − 1) to Poly(k)
        }
        newN = newN − 1
    }
    else  k = k + 1
    i = i + 1
}
Npolys = newN
```

Listing 3.1: Outline of an algorithm to remove unwanted entries from a list of $Npoly$ $Poly$ structures. The unwanted entries will be *flagged* in some convenient manner.

each reference to an entry in the vertex list is tested. If it points to one of the vertices that has been moved then it is replaced by the new location (stored in the dummy index) that was determined in the first pass. Memory reallocation completes the algorithm. This algorithm is shown in detail in listing 3.2.

Such a scheme is very efficient and uses as few operations as possible when removing items from a 3D data structure which has been stored in a contiguous memory block.

3.4   Making an edge list from a list of polygonal faces

When producing a wireframe drawing of a model or converting between the data formats of alternative 3D CAD and animation packages it is important to be able to build a list of *edges* from a list of *polygons*.

It is straightforward to make a list of edges by creating one edge for each polygon side, but most polygons will share edges. The task of removing multiple entries from the edge list becomes excessively time consuming as the number of polygons increases. In the case of n polygons approximately $3n^2$ tests need to be performed to make sure that the same edge is not recorded more than once in the edge list. When dealing with more than a few hundred polygons it is essential to find a more efficient procedure.

The following gives the outline of an algorithm that deals with the issue more efficiently:

- For each vertex i in the model set up a list to hold the identity of other vertices in the model attached to vertex i by an edge. Initially these lists will be empty.

- Take each polygon in the model in turn and with every edge of the polygon consider the vertices at both ends of the edge.

- Label the vertices j and k. For vertex j look at j's list of adjacent vertices. If it is empty or does not contain vertex k then add k to j's list. For vertex k look at its list of adjacent vertices and if it is empty or does not contain vertex j then add j to k's list.

- When all the polygons have been examined consider each vertex in turn. Call the current one i. For vertex i create an edge between vertex i and all the vertices in i's list of attached vertices. For an example see figure 3.9.

Vertex	Vertex attached to...		Edges
0	0	1,2,3	$0 - 1$
1	1	1,4,6,9	$0 - 2$
2	2	...	$0 - 3$
3	3		$1 - 4$
.	.		$1 - 6$
.	.		$1 - 9$
n	n	7,11,19	

Figure 3.9: Building an edge list from a polygon list.

The advantage of this procedure comes from the fact that the number of comparison tests will be much fewer than would be required by the simplistic approach of checking all polygons against all polygons.

Erase items from the Polygon list but don't
release the recovered memory yet
set $i = 0, k = 0, j = 0$ and $newN = Nverts$
repeat **while** $i < Nverts$ {
    if $Vert(k)$ flagged **for** deletion {
      if $i < Nverts - 1$ {
    copy size of $Vert$ structure (bytes) from $Vert(newN - 1)$ to $Vert(k)$
    $Vert(newN - 1).x = j$ (extra index in $Vert$ structure)
      }
     $newN = newN - 1$
    }
    else   {
     $k = k + 1$
     $j = j + 1$
    }
   $i = i + 1$
 }
$Nvert = newN$

Now process the dependent Poly data structure to fix it up
set $i = 0$
repeat **while** $i < Npolys$ {
  set $j = 0$
  repeat **while** $j < NvertPerPoly$ {
    if $Poly(i).V_{id}(j) \geq Nvert$ {
      $Poly(i).V_{id}(j) = Vert(Poly(i).V_{id}(j)).x$
    }
    $j = j + 1$
  }
  $i = i + 1$
}

To finish: Tidy up the memory allocation for $Poly$ and $Vert$ structures

Listing 3.2: Details of the algorithm to remove unwanted entries from a polygonal database when the database uses a contiguous list rather than a doubly linked list to record the polygons and vertices.

To accommodate the adjacency list it is necessary to augment the vertex data structure with two items, n and V_{adj} as shown in figure 3.10. V_{adj} is a dynamically sized array of vertex identifiers.

Pseudo-code for the above algorithm is given in listings 3.3 and 3.4. Part 1 of the algorithm calls to a subroutine which inserts vertices in the adjacency list and extends it if necessary.

In the subroutine (part 2) the adjacency lists for vertices V_1 and V_2 are checked. If an entry is already present in the list the subroutine returns immediately.

p	position vector of vertex
ν, μ	surface texture coordinates
x	temporary integer index
n	number of adjacent vertices
V_{adj}	list of adjacent vertices

Figure 3.10: Entries in the vertex data structure.

Part 1 Recording
set $i = 0$ and repeat **while** $i < Npolys$ {
    InsertInVertexList $(Poly(i).V_{id}(0), Poly(i).V_{id}(1))$
    InsertInVertexList $(Poly(i).V_{id}(1), Poly(i).V_{id}(2))$
    InsertInVertexList $(Poly(i).V_{id}(2), Poly(i).V_{id}(0))$
    $i = i + 1$
}

Part 2 Building Edges
set $i = 0$ and repeat **while** $i < Nvert$ {
    if $Vert(i).n > 0$ {
        set $j = 0$ and repeat **while** $j < Vert(i).n$ {
        Create edge between vertices i and $Nvert(i).V_{adj}(j)$
      $j = j + 1$
        }
    }
    $i = i + 1$
}

Listing 3.3: Part 1 of the algorithm to make an edge list from a list of connected polygonal facets.

3.5 Finding adjacent polygons

Some of the algorithms to be discussed in later chapters require that every polygon (in a mesh model) knows the identity of its neighboring polygons. A neighboring polygon is one that shares an edge. For the example in figure 3.11 polygons 1 and 2 share an edge as do polygons 2 and 3.

Algorithms that need this information include:

- Delaunay triangulation.

- Subdivision of surfaces.

- Algorithms to make surface normal orientations consistent.

Like the procedure for finding edges given a set of polygons (section 3.4) finding adjacent polygons can be a prohibitively lengthy task if an exhaustive comparison is used.

Subroutine InsertInVertexList(V_1, V_2)
V_1 *and* V_2 *are indexes into the vertex list*

```
if  Vert(V₁).n > 0  {
    set  i = 0  and  repeat  while  i < Vert(V₁).n  {
        if  Vert(V₁).Vadj(i) = V₂  then already present so return
        i = i + 1
    }
}
if  Vert(V₂).n > 0  {
    set  i = 0  and  repeat  while  i < Vert(V₂).n  {
        if  Vert(V₂).Vadj(i) = V₁  then already present so return
        i = i + 1
    }
}
Extend the list  Vert(V₁).Vadj  by 1
Vert(V₁).Vadj(Vert(V₁).n) = V₂
Vert(V₁).n = Vert(V₁).n + 1
```

Listing 3.4: Part 2 of the algorithm to make an edge list from a list of connected polygonal facets. In part 2 the subroutine checks to see if an edge already has an entry in the edge list.

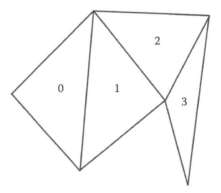

Polygon	Adjacent to		
0	−1	−1	1
1	0	2	−1
2	1	−1	3
3	2	−1	−1

Figure 3.11: Identity of adjacent triangular polygons.

The following algorithm describes a procedure that will be significantly faster than an exhaustive comparison. It is known to work with many thousands of triangular polygons. In principle this procedure is quite similar to the *edge generating* algorithm of section 3.4. However, before it can be used the vertex data structure must be enhanced by adding a counter for the number of adjacent polygons and a list to identify them. Also, the polygon data structure needs a list in which to store the identity of the adjacent facets.

In the case of a triangular polygon the adjacent facet identifier list will be required to hold up to a maximum of three integers. When polygons have one or more edges that are not adjacent to other polygons this can be flagged by storing a −1 as the identity of the neighboring polygon. The augmented data structures are illustrated in figure 3.12.

$\mathbf{p}$	position vector of vertex
ν, μ	surface texture coordinates
x	temporary integer index
n_V	number of adjacent vertices
V_{adj}	list of adjacent vertices
h_{id}	pointer to hierarchical element to assign vertex to
n_F	number of adjacent polygons
F_{adj}	list of adjacent polygons

V_{id}	list of vertex ids to which polygon is attached
id_{mat}	pointer to a material in materials list
id_{map}	pointer to a texture map in the list of image maps
$A_{id}(3)$	list of the ids of polygons with a common side
$\mathbf{n}$	normal to surface plane

Figure 3.12: Vertex and polygon data structures to accommodate calculation and storage of polygon adjacency information.

The detailed pseudo-code implementation of the algorithm is presented in listings 3.5 and 3.6. However, before presenting the algorithm in detail the following gives a simple overview:

1. For each vertex create a list to hold the identity of polygons which are attached to it. Initially all the lists will be empty.

2. Work through all the triangular polygons, j, and consider each of its vertices in turn. For each vertex (call it k) of j add j to k's polygon adjacency list F_{adj}. (For each vertex this builds up a list of which polygon is attached to which vertex.)

3. Again work through all the polygons, call the current one j, and then taking each side in turn, identify the two vertices to which it is attached. Call them i_1 and i_2. For vertices i_1 and i_2, look through each one's list of attached polygons and see if any have an edge between i_1 and i_2 (remembering

to exclude the current polygon j). If they have, then this is the polygon adjacent to polygon j along the side between vertices i_1 and i_2. This can be done by checking all polygons adjacent to i_1 against all polygons adjacent to i_2 and if they have a polygon in common it can only be polygon j or another one with vertices i_1 and i_2 in common, which is the one adjacent to polygon j.

Part 1: Build polygon adjacency list for each vertex
set $i = 0$ and repeat while $i < Npolys$ {
    set $j = 0$ and repeat **while** $j < 3$ {
      $id = Poly(i).V_{id}$
      $n = Vert(id).n_F$
      extend the list $Vert(id).F_{adj}$ to $n + 1$ spaces
      $Vert(id).F_{Adj}(n) = i$
      $Vert(id).n_F = n + 1$
      $j = j + 1$
    }
    $i = i + 1$
}

Listing 3.5: Part 1 of the algorithm to make a list of polygons attached to each vertex from a Facet/Vertex 3D database.

3.6 Finding polygons adjacent to edges

Some of the algorithms to be discussed in later chapters require that every edge knows the identity of its neighboring polygons. For most closed surfaces approximated by a network of polygons an edge will have at most two neighboring polygons.

The algorithm itself is very similar to that for finding polygons adjacent to polygons, described in section 3.5, and example code implementation can be obtained from the website.

Part 2: Build polygon adjacency list for each polygon
i_1 *and* i_2 *are vertex id's for polygon edges*
set $i = 0$ and repeat while $i < Npolys$ {
       set $l = 0$ and repeat while $l < 3$ {
           check all polygons adjacent to i_1 and i_2 to see if any of them
           have an adjacent polygon in common (it must not be of course be i)
           $Poly(i).A_{id}(l) = -1$ /* record -1 if nothing adjacent */
           if $l = 0$ {
             $i_1 = Poly(i).V_{id}(0)$
             $i_2 = Poly(i).V_{id}(1)$
           }
           else if $l = 1$ {
             $i_1 = Poly(i).V_{id}(1)$
             $i_2 = Poly(i).V_{id}(2)$
           }
           else if $l = 2$ {
             $i_1 = Poly(i).V_{id}(2)$
             $i_2 = Poly(i).V_{id}(0)$
           }
           if $Vert(i_1).n_F > 0$ and $Vert(i_2).n_F > 0$ {
             set $j = 0$ and repeat **while** $j < Vert(i_1).n_F$ {
             $t = Vert(i_1).F_{adj}(j)$
               set k=0 and repeat **while** $k < Vert(i_2).n_F$ {
                 $u = Vert(i_2).F_{adj}(k)$
                 u and v are polygons adjacent to i_1 and i_2, if they are the same
                 then the edge between i_1 and i_2 is a boundary of polygons
                 t and u. it is either i or the desired polygon
                 if $u = t$ and $u \neq i$ {
                   $Poly(i).A_{id}(l) = u$
                   jump to   label   /* no need to continue */
                 }
                 $k = k + 1$
               }
             $j = j + 1$
             }
           }
            label:
           $l = l + 1$
       }
     $i = i + 1$
   }

Listing 3.6: Part 2 of the algorithm to make a list of adjacent polygons from a Facet/Vertex 3D database.

4

Basic visualization

In this chapter the mathematical principles of chapter 2 and the structures of chapter 3 come together to produce a collection of algorithms that are used to synthesize images from purely numerical data so that the viewer should instantly be able to exclaim **"That's a ...!"** This synthesis is termed *rendering*, and from the scientific point of view this is a mathematical modeling process of the way light interacts with surfaces, how light travels to the observer's location and how they perceive it.

In the decade or so since publication of the first edition of this book the major mathematical models used in the rendering process have been refined but not radically changed. Most of the physical models and their mathematical implementations were worked out in the 20th century. What has changed and continues to change is the power of the computer used to carry out the calculations. The invention of the specialized graphics processor, the GPU, lies at the heart of these changes and it has enabled visualization models that were previously thought to be impractical to use to become mainstream. Of course, the primary purpose of the GPU is in rendering images in real-time which is principally fueled by the huge market for computer games.

Good as it is, the GPU is still orders of magnitude too slow to calculate in real-time a complete physical model of the light transport process. Even to be able to model some of the most important rendering challenges GPU shaders[1] have to resort to some empirical and heuristic approximations. The GPU hardware's architecture is designed around the *rendering pipeline* concept. A number of the algorithms described in this chapter have their place in the rendering pipeline. Whilst the GPU builds these algorithms in hardware there are always going to be occasions where a software implementation is still essential, especially if you are looking for images with particular qualities. In fact, because the GPU is programmable, a knowledge of the algorithms it uses, how they work and the principles that underlie them is essential if you are going to write programs for the GPU and make the most of its incredible power. The procedural textures (one type of shaders) to be discussed in chapter 11, the OpenGL programs and GPU hardware discussed in chapter 7 and the implementation of an extensible

---

[1]The programs that run in a GPU are called shaders.

software rendering pipeline in chapter 9, can all be *ported* to GPU programs, but only if you have a knowledge of the basics that are covered in this chapter.

In the context of computer graphics, rendering is the process of artificially generating a picture of *something* from a numerical dataset or other form of specification. This usually involves billions of calculations as the picture is synthesized. Continuing advances in computer technology are allowing pictures to be produced more and more rapidly. Some algorithms can deliver an image in only a few milliseconds. However the quest for more and more lifelike pictures requires calculating processes of rapidly increasing complexity. Consequently, no matter how quickly developments in processor technology deliver increased performance, there are always grumblings of discontent among the artists and designers who use computer graphics in their work.

From the point of view of describing algorithms for the rendering task there is a point where a quantum leap in the time it takes to render a picture (an image) occurs. Thus it is useful to classify rendering algorithms in two groups: those that are very fast and those that are not. At one end of the fast rendering spectrum are the *real-time* rendering engines. *Engine* is a term with its origin in the computer games industry where rendering a standard TV or video sized image usually takes a few milliseconds. The real-time engines are relying more and more on the GPU hardware and programmer APIs like OpenGL [82] or DirectX. See for example Sherrod and Jones [79] which is focused on the latest version of DirectX.

It is interesting to note that most of the recent books in the area of real-time graphics tend to place their focus on 3D games programing, which just goes to highlight the dominance of computer games within the 3D graphics scene. A comprehensive introduction to the algorithms for *real-time* rendering may be found in Akenine-Möller and Haines [1], and an excellent and comprehensive source of demonstrator programs exemplifying all aspects of OpenGL is the *OpenGL SuperBible* [78]. We highlight the most salient features of OpenGL in chapter 7 and especially how to use it with the rapidly emerging market of tablet computers and mobile phones in chapter 8.

More realistic rendering (the subject of chapter 5) still requires minutes, or possibly hours, to generate a single picture; however in many cases the result is so good that it is impossible to tell a computer-generated image from a photograph of the real thing.

4.1   The rendering pipeline

The rendering algorithm is termed a pipeline because the steps that are undertaken can be thought of as a progression through a series of actions that are performed in a specific order and with never any need to take a step back, or repeat a step. As the operations of one step are being performed on some of the

Input Model Description

16376 Polygons 10040 Vertices

Polygon List

Polygon	Vertex ID	Material
1	3 1 2	1
2	2 3 4	1
3	...	
	...	
16376	16374 16375 3	10

VertexList

Vertex	Coordinates
1	0.0 5.1 7.1
2	0.0 5.3 7.2
	...
	...
10040	1.8 7.5 6.6

Rendered Output

Figure 4.1: An example of the input to and output from a renderer.

object/scene description data, say at the start of the pipeline, other parts of the data can be undergoing final processing.

4.1.1 The basics of rendering

The basic rendering procedure takes a list of polygons and vertices and produces a picture of the object they represent. The picture (or *image*) is recorded as an array (sometimes referred to as a *raster*) of a large number of little regions of the picture called *pixels* (shortened "picture element"). The raster is organized into rows and each row holds a number of pixels.

Each pixel in the array holds a number to give value to the color or intensity at the equivalent location in the image. Because the number of pixels in a raster is finite (the pixel value represents a small area, not a single point) there will always be some inaccuracy when they are used to display the image they represent. The quality of an image is primarily related to the accuracy with which the pixel color value is recorded and to the number of pixels in the raster. A raster is regarded as a two-dimensional array with a height and a width. For example the high-definition video resolution is of the order of 1920×1080.

All computer monitors use the three primary colors (red, green and blue) model to represent shades of color. At least 7 bits will be required for each primary in order to represent all the $\approx 350,000$ different shades of color that the human eye can distinguish. Since computers like to work in *byte* sized chunks each pixel is most commonly represented by three bytes, one byte each for the red, green and blue primary colors (the so called 24 bit system).

When making movies where the minimum frame rate is at least 30Hz it is essential that some form of digital compression is brought into play to store the image sequences. A lot of work has been done on image and movie compression through standards like the H264 MPEG-4 encoder algorithm. Most animation software can record its output using at least one form of compression codec. Image and movie compression is outside the scope of this book. June's book [47] offers some practical code in this area as a starting point for further experiments. The personal computer is now such a powerful video processor and has such large storage capacity that the ability to record, edit and assemble video in high definition is quite possible on virtually every machine sold. Coupled with the availability of a high-definition camera in every phone, everyone has, more or less, a movie production studio on their lap. Now all they need is a 3D animation program to allow them to make and mix-in special effects to match Hollywood's best efforts.

Even though there are many algorithms that can be classified as rendering procedures they are probably variations on the general theme set out in the following short list of sequential steps (called *the graphics pipeline* [12]):

1. Load the data describing objects in the scene into memory (RAM).

2. Use translation, scaling and rotational transformations to move each object into their appointed position.

3. Apply the viewing transformation. After this step keep a record of the 3D coordinates of each vertex in the scene.

4. Apply the projection transformation to find equivalent coordinates in the viewing plane for all vertices in the scene. Store these 2D projected screen coordinates along with the data recorded in step 3. Store all coordinate data in floating point form.

   Note: *The number of instructions the computer must perform in each of the preceding steps is primarily proportional to the number of vertices in the scene.*

5. For each pixel in the output raster calculate what is visible and record this information.

   The number of instructions the computer must perform in this last step will depend on the rendering algorithm but, more importantly, *it will be proportional to the number of pixels in the raster. However on some hardware the number of times a pixel is overwritten can also make a significant contribution to the execution time.* Therefore, for something even as simple as a cube (8 vertices and 6 polygons) you might still be drawing it into a raster with 500,000 pixels. Any optimization that can be done in this last step will be immensely rewarding.

   It is usual to retain the pixel information in the computer's fast memory until the whole raster has been filled. This block of data is called a **framebuffer**. Once rendering is complete the contents of the framebuffer can be transferred to a mass storage device or copied to the screen. The framebuffer is also an ideal environment in which to carry out additional image processing.

All the renderers we will discuss perform steps 1–4 above and it is only in step 5 that significant differences occur. Procedures for the execution of step 5 form the bulk of the topics to be discussed in this chapter. As we go along we shall see that most of the calculations that a renderer must perform have already been covered in chapter 2.

4.1.2 Hardware rendering and the GPU

There is some flexibility in the order in which some of the rendering algorithm's steps may be be performed. The graphics hardware has tended to set up its pipeline to perform the steps in the specific order: geometry transformation, lighting, rasterization (to map the points, lines, and polygons in the input data onto the pixels in the output image), followed by texture and image mapping, and framebuffer operations (hidden surface removal). In a software renderer it is not necessary to stick to the rigid order that hardware imposes. For example the lighting model could be applied at the stage where the pixel is being shaded (colored, etc.) instead of before rasterization. Indeed, until the programmable GPU became widely available, the hardware based engines did not do a very realistic job of lighting and shading because they only performed a simple Lambertian lighting model at the vertices. Figure 4.2 illustrates the key stages in three variants of the rendering pipeline. Each box is a self contained unit, and in a hardware implementation every stage can be working on different data at the same time. It also shows where programmability is typically added into the pipeline.

By looking at figure 4.2 is should be easy to see why the programmability is primarily separated into the vertex and pixel processors. They are at different parts of the pipeline and are operating on very different entities. It should also be evident that the pixels processing is done further down the pipeline and consequently there is no way that any output from the pixel processing can be fed back to the place where its vertices and the scene geometry are processed. However, the normal direction of information flow does allow for some additional data to be passed from the level of the vertex to the level of the pixel and in this the rasterizer plays an important role. This topic is discussed in section 7.3 where OpenGL GPU programming is discussed.

However the pipeline is envisioned, even if it were to do no texturing and no lighting, just to be able to present the viewer with a drawing in which they can perceive a three-dimensional solid object, it is necessary to avoid drawing those parts of solid objects that aren't visible from the viewpoint. This is the topic of the next important section.

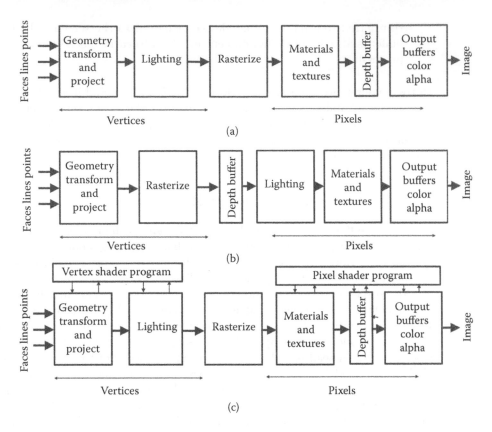

Figure 4.2: The graphics pipeline: (a) This is the basic hardware pipeline in which all the output buffers are located at the end of the pipeline. The lighting model is applied on a per-vertex basis, texturing is done on a per-pixel basis. (b) This variation is used in most software implementations because the lighting is done on a per-pixel basis and the depth (visibility) buffer may be used to eliminate any polygons that are not visible before any lighting or shading calculations are undertaken. (c) A variation on (a) that illustrates stages in the pipeline that are controlled by the GPU programs. However, because of the programmability, the lighting calculations can be postponed until rasterization is performed and the pixels are processed.

4.2   Hidden surface drawing and rasterization

Working with a faceted polygonal specification of an object to be rendered (and after it has been moved into the required position relative to the observer), the first and very simple test for visibility is to remove (*cull*) any polygons that are at the back of the object when viewed from the observer's location. The only requirement to ensure that this test always works is that the object is closed and that there is a consistent labeling of the surface normal vector for each polygon. The usual convention is that the normal **n** points away from the object, from

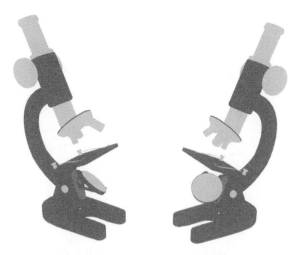

Figure 4.3: A hidden surface drawing.

its surface into the outside. Using this convention, the test for a back-face is simply: if $(\mathbf{n} \cdot \mathbf{v}) < 0)$, then it is a back-face; here $\mathbf{v}$ is the viewing direction vector. Sometimes the surface normal for each face is specified explicitly, but often the direction of $\mathbf{n}$ is implied by the order in which the vertices that surround each face are stored in the object's data structure.

A hidden surface drawing is supposed to shade all the pixels lying inside the polygon after it has been projected onto the viewing plane. However, the only information available about where the projection of a polygon lies in the viewing plane is where its projected vertices lie.

To shade inside the projected polygons it is necessary to devise a procedure that will fill all the pixels that lie within the boundary of the polygon. Filling areas inside a border on a 2D pixel display used to be a very significant task, and is still something that is needed by software like presentation packages that draw bar graphics and pie charts, for example. In the context of 3D surface rendering it is the projections of the polygons onto the viewing plane that need to be filled, a process known as *rasterization*. Some common algorithms used for rasterization are described in section 4.2.5 after the critically important hidden surface procedures are described.

In contrast to a wireframe drawing, in which only the visible edges of the polygons are drawn, the hidden surface procedure attempts to color in the drawing so that the edges separating adjacent polygons of the same shading, and also polygons that are out of sight (hidden by others), are not shown. For example if you look at a solid cube you will be able to see at most 3 of its 6 facets at any one time, or from any one viewpoint. Unlike a wireframe drawing, where a list of edges is sufficient to complete the drawing, a list of polygons must be used to render a hidden surface picture.

Figure 4.4: Examples of non-convex polygons. Any polygon that has a hole in it is always non-convex.

To construct a hidden surface view, each polygon edge is projected onto the viewing plane; then, instead of just drawing the projected edges, pixels lying inside the boundary formed by the projected edges of a polygon are given an appropriate color.

Sadly, if all we did was work through the list of polygons sequentially and fill in appropriate pixels it is certain that the drawing would be a mess. At the very least we would see parts of the model that should have remained hidden. It is the purpose of section 4.2 to describe algorithms that will make sure that those parts of a model which should be obscured from view never get drawn.

Before considering the hidden surface algorithm it is worth pausing to consider the implications of the statement:

Pixels lying inside the boundary formed by the projected edges of a polygon are given an appropriate color.

Finding which pixels lie inside a polygon is itself not always a trivial task especially when the polygon is non-convex. A convex polygon is one in which **any** point in the interior can be joined to **any** vertex on the boundary by a line that does not cross any edge of the polygon. Because there are so many pixels in a raster and in most cases such a high number of polygons are to be filled, any procedure to implement the filling task must be very efficient. We will look at three potential algorithms in section 4.2.5. An even more important task than filling pixels within a specified outline is the calculation of the appropriate color with which to fill those pixels. Determining the color value for any pixel in the output raster is the **most** significant task any rendering algorithm has to perform. It governs the shading, texturing (e.g., wood, marble or decals), and quality of the final image.

Sort the list of polygons so that it is ordered by distance from the viewpoint with the polygon furthest away at the start of the list.

Repeat the following for all polygons in the ordered list   {
    Draw projected polygon into the framebuffer using the procedure
    described in section 4.2.5.
}

Listing 4.1: An outline of the painter's rendering algorithm.

4.2.1   The painter's algorithm

This is the simplest of all the hidden surface rendering techniques. It does not deliver true hidden surface behavior because it cannot resolve polygons which intersect each other or overlap in certain ways. Some shapes that are not amenable to rendering with the painter's algorithm are illustrated in figure 4.5. It does give very good results if there are a large number of similarly sized polygons in a scene because the small inaccuracies are less noticeable.

The painter's procedure relies on the simple observation that if you paint on a surface, you paint *over* anything that had previously been there, hiding it. Therefore if the list of polygons can be arranged so that those polygons nearest the viewer occur at the end of the list you can just paint every polygon into the framebuffer and the nearest ones will overwrite those further away. Once all the polygons have been drawn the result is a hidden surface view. This simple idea can be summarized in the steps given in listing 4.1, which constitutes a possible procedure for step 5 in the basic rendering algorithm of section 4.1.1.

As noted earlier there are occasions where this simple procedure fails. The reason it fails is that in the depth sorting step we have to assume that each polygon is represented by only **one** depth. Polygons however are not just points lying at one value of depth. They cover large portions of the projection plane with different areas on the polygon visible in different pixels. Consequently the depth of the polygon in each of the pixels that it covers will not necessarily be the same. We really need to look at depth on a pixel-by-pixel basis not on a polygon-by-polygon basis. Therefore, if it were possible to depth sort for *every* pixel covered by a polygon we would have a true hidden surface procedure. A method that accomplishes this is discussed in section 4.2.3.

4.2.2   Sorting

The painter's algorithm needs to sort a list of items using a specific criterion (depth from observer). There are many good algorithms that perform the sorting required by the painter's algorithm. One that is in common use is the standard quicksort; another is the basic shell sort.

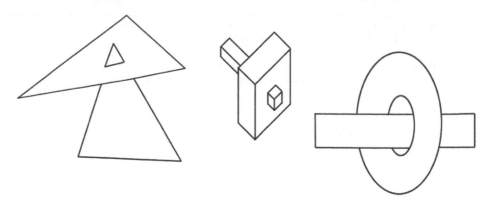

Figure 4.5: Polygon arrangements that confuse the painter's algorithm.

4.2.3   The Z buffer hidden surface algorithm

In the comment at the end of section 4.2.1 the observation was made that the painter's algorithm was inadequate because depth sorting was done on a per polygon basis rather than at every pixel in the raster or framebuffer. Because of the very large number of pixels making up the raster it is quite impractical to carry out a depth sort amongst every polygon for every pixel; *this is one of the drawbacks of a simple ray tracing algorithm.* However an alternative procedure that accomplishes the same task is available, *the Z buffer algorithm.*

Look at figure 4.6; it shows a polygon and its projection onto the viewing plane where an array of pixels is illustrated. Imagine adding a matching array of similar dimension that is capable of recording a real number for each pixel; this is the Z buffer. The main action of the algorithm is to record in the Z buffer at address (i, j) the *distance* from V the viewpoint, to P the point where a line through V and pixel (i, j) intersects polygon k. This action is repeated for all pixels inside the projection of polygon k.

When it comes to drawing another polygon, say l, it too will paint into a set of pixels some of which may overlap those previously filled with data from polygon k. It is now that the Z buffer comes into play. Before information for polygon l is written to the pixel at location (i, j) the Z buffer is checked to see whether polygon l appears to be in front of polygon k. If l is in front of k then the data from l is placed in the framebuffer and the Z buffer depth at location (i, j) is updated to take account of l's depth.

The algorithm is known as the "Z buffer algorithm" because the first programs to use it arranged their frame of reference with the viewpoint at the origin and the direction of view aligned along the z axis. In these programs the distance to any point on the polygon from the viewpoint was simply the point's z coordinate. (OpenGL and Direct3D use this direction for their direction of view.) The Z buffer algorithm is summarized in listing 4.2.

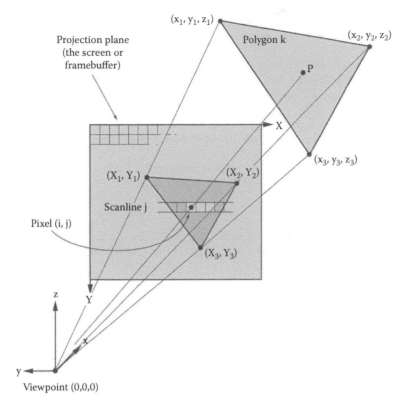

Figure 4.6: Projecting back from the viewpoint through pixel (i, j) leads to a point in the interior of polygon k. (It is also common, in OpenGL for example, for the view vector to be aligned with the z axis.)

There are some important details regarding the Z buffer procedure: Following the convention established in section 2.12.7 the viewpoint V occurs at $(0, 0, 0)$ and the direction of view is along the **x** axis. It is therefore the x component of the point P that is inserted into the Z buffer.

> Note that the x coordinate of P is not quite the same thing as the distance between V and P. However, so long as one is consistent this not important and using the x coordinate requires much less computation than the actual Euclidean distance.

To find P, and hence its x coordinate, we call on the ideas of section 2.6 for the intersection of line and plane. The plane in this case is the polygonal facet k with surface normal **n**. To find a point in the plane we can choose any of the vertices of polygon k, say $\mathbf{P}_0$. It is usual to pre-calculate the normals and record them as part of the data structure associated with every polygon as suggested in chapter 3.

Fill the depth buffer at $Z(i,j)$ with a *'far away'* depth.
i.e. Set $Z(i,j) = \infty$ for all i, j.

```
Repeat for all polygons k {
    For polygon k find pixels (i, j) covered by it. Fill these with the color of
    polygon k. Use the procedure outlined in section 4.2.5.

    With each pixel (i, j) covered by k repeat {
        Calculate the Depth (Δ) of P from V (see figure 4.6)
        If  Δ < Z(i, j) {
            Set pixel (i, j) to color of polygon k
            Update the depth buffer Z(i, j) = Δ
        }
    }
}
```

Listing 4.2: The basic ideas of the Z buffer rendering algorithm.

For the equation of the line we know that it originates at $(0,0,0)$ and that it passes through a pixel in the raster given by equations 2.17 and 2.18 in section 2.12.8. Rearranging these equations and arbitrarily choosing a value of $x = 1$ gives the direction vector $\mathbf{d}$, (with components d_x, d_y, d_z):

$$
\mathbf{d} = \begin{bmatrix} 1 \\ \left(\dfrac{\frac{X_{max}}{2} - X_s}{s_x} \right) \\ \left(\dfrac{\frac{Y_{max}}{2} - Y_s}{s_y} \right) \end{bmatrix}
$$

Following the analysis of section 2.6, the point of intersection is given by $\mathbf{P} = \mu \mathbf{d}$ where:

$$
\mu = \frac{\mathbf{P}_0 \cdot \mathbf{n}}{\mathbf{n} \cdot \mathbf{d}}
$$

Since the x component of $\mathbf{d}$ is unity the x component of $\mathbf{P}$ is μ and in the frame of reference that we are using this is the value that is written into the Z buffer for pixel (i,j).

Using general expressions to determine the Z depth is not an efficient way to do the calculation. It is possible to take advantage of some of the special circumstances under which the depth is determined:

1. The constant $(\mathbf{P}_0 \cdot \mathbf{n})$ is dependent only on the polygon. It could therefore be calculated at the same time as the polygon's normal is determined and stored along with the normal in the data structure allocated to every polygon: say we call it c_k.

2. Filling pixels one scanline after another implies that those parts of the expression for Z which are independent of the horizontal coordinate need only be calculated once per scanline. This will save many arithmetic operations since most pixels on each scanline will need to have a Z depth determined. The z component of $\mathbf{d}$ is constant across the scanline and therefore if we let $d_2 = n_z d_z$, the calculation of Z at pixel (i, j) simplifies to:

$$Z = \frac{c_k}{n_x + n_y d_y + d_2}$$

One division, one multiplication and two additions, quite a significant saving over the direct use of the general expressions.

In practice, graphics hardware often uses *normalized depth* (after perspective division), because this makes it possible to linearly interpolate depth in *screen space* from pixel to pixel within the *viewport*. Screen space and the viewport are discussed more fully in chapter 7 on OpenGL.

Comments:

1. Since the Z buffer works on a per-pixel basis it solves all the problems of the painter's algorithm and (*up to the resolution of a pixel*) it gives a perfect hidden surface visualization.

2. Spending time determining the color to write into framebuffer or display on a monitor only to have it be replaced later when a polygon is found lying closer to the viewpoint is **very** unsatisfactory. It may have taken quite a bit of effort to calculate that color, shading, texturing etc. Here is what might be regarded as an important clue to fast rendering:

   *First calculate what you **can** see, then calculate what you **do** see.*

   Instead of calculating a pixel's color and then storing that in the framebuffer, store the identity of the polygon that can be seen at that pixel. (*Imagine you are standing at the viewpoint and are looking at the scene through a wire grid held at the projection plane. Through each square you will see a polygon in the scene.*) Once the Z buffer algorithm has run its course go through the *identity* buffer, extract the identity of which polygon is visible in the pixel and calculate the appropriate color value, then write that color into the framebuffer. This way the expensive calculations are not wasted and there may be an advantage when one needs to apply anti-aliasing techniques as described in section 4.3. Perhaps a little more memory will be needed but it is certainly worth the expense. When memory resource is scarce the next algorithm is an ideal alternative.

```
repeat for all scanlines, j, in the raster  {
    repeat for all pixels i on scanline, 0 ≤ i < X_max
        Z(i) = ∞  set the scanline Z buffer to a far away depth
        Id(i) = −1   set the polygon ID buffer to indicate no polygon visible
    }
    repeat for all polygons, k, such that 0 ≤ k < Npoly  {
        if   polygon k does not span scanline j {
            skip on to next polygon
        }
    find first, i₁, and last, i₂, pixels covered by polygon k on scanline
    j, use the procedure of section 4.2.5.
    repeat with each i such that i₁ ≤ i ≤ i₂  {
        calculate the depth, Δ, of P (see figure 4.6)
        if  Δ < Z(i)  {
            Id(i) = k   record ID of polygon k for pixel i, j
            Z(i) = Δ   update the depth buffer
        }
    }
    }
    repeat for all i, on scanline j, such that 0 ≤ i < X_max   {
        if  Id(i) ≥ 0   set pixel (i, j) to color of polygon Id(i)
    }
}
```

Listing 4.3: The scanline Z rendering algorithm.

4.2.4   The scanline Z buffer algorithm

This version of the Z buffer algorithm was preferred in practice because it did not need to maintain a full screen Z buffer and so would work in the much smaller memory of an early PC. In most respects it involves the same calculations as the full Z buffer procedure but with a buffer size that is only required to store one row of pixels, called a scanline, at a time. For example, to generate an image at a resolution of 1024×768 requires a full Z and framebuffer of some $786,000$ elements (5.25Mb); using a scanline Z procedure one can get away with a storage requirement for $1,024$ elements or 16kb.

Now of course if the Z buffer is only one row high, it must be applied to each row in the raster (with respect to the example above, 768 times). This means that every polygon has to be checked every time a raster row is processed. In theory this should be much slower than using a full Z buffer but in practice this is not usually the case. To see why just remember that to build up the depth information in the Z buffer each polygon has to be scanline filled over a number of rows anyway. In fact if there is a polygon that nearly fills the whole raster then there is almost exactly the same work to do in both full Z and scanline Z procedures. With a careful organization of the algorithm rendering speed can approach that of the full Z buffer, especially when the *slow* step of *rendering* the pixel (to record *what you do see*) is taken into account.

A typical implementation of the scanline Z algorithm is given in listing 4.3.

The very low memory requirement of the scanline Z buffer algorithm has the added advantage that if you want to simulate transparent or semi-transparent surfaces then two or more scanline buffers can be easily accommodated. Separate scanline buffers are used for the *opaque* and *transparent* surfaces visible in pixel (i,j). A comparison of the *depth* between buffers will tell us whether transparent parts of the surface lie in front of the opaque parts or vice versa. Maintaining two scanline buffers for transparent surfaces allows two overlapping transparent surfaces to be rendered correctly. After about four *transparency* buffers are employed synthetic images of glass objects can look pretty good.

A trick very often used to draw complex shapes (e.g., trees in an architectural flyby) is to paint them on transparent quadrilateral polygons and then render the scene. See section 4.6.1 on transparency mapping.

4.2.5 Rasterization and polygon filling

Three potential algorithms that fill a closed polygonal region specified by a set of coordinates at the vertices of the boundary, $(x_0, y_0) \to (x_1, y_1) \to (x_2, y_2)... \to (x_{n-2}, y_{n-2}) \to (x_{n-1}, y_{n-1}) \to (x_0, y_0)$, are:

1. Recursive Seed Fill

   This is the simplest of all the methods but it is also the slowest. A pixel that lies inside the region to be filled is taken as a *seed*; it is set to record the chosen color. Then the seed's nearest neighbors are found and with each in turn this procedure is executed recursively. The process continues until the boundary is reached.

2. Ordered Seed Fill

   This is a method that many *paint* packages use to color in regions of a drawing. The procedure works by first choosing a seed pixel inside the region to be filled. Each pixel on that row in the raster, to the left and right of the seed, is filled, pixel by pixel, until a boundary is encountered. While scanning that row a series of extra seeds are placed on the rows above and below subject to certain conditions. After all the pixels in the row have been filled any additional seeds placed on other rows are processed in exactly the same manner. This algorithm is also recursive but it has the advantage that the number of recursive calls is dramatically reduced. A full explanation of this and the Recursive Seed Fill can be found in Burger [15].

3. Scanline Fill

   The polygon is filled by stroking across each row in the raster and coloring any pixels on that row if they lie within the polygon, see figure 4.8.

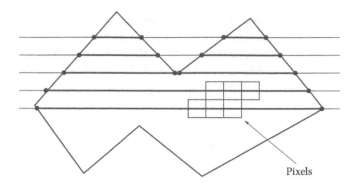

Figure 4.7: Scanline fill by stroking the rows of the output raster.

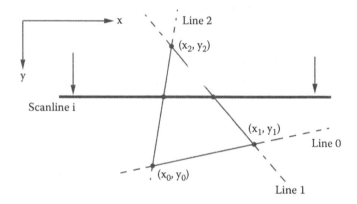

Figure 4.8: Scanline filling a triangular polygon.

This is the most useful filling procedure for a 3D polygon rendering algorithm because it works very efficiently for simple convex shapes. The drawing stage in a large number of rendering algorithms is commonly performed with triangles because a triangle is the simplest polygon and it is also planar. All triangles are convex. Quadrilaterals are easily divided into two triangles and higher order polygons are rare. In any case it is always possible to divide up polygons with more than three sides into two or more triangular facets.

An algorithm to scanline fill a triangular polygon Let the three vertices projected onto the view plane have coordinates $(x_0, y_0), (x_1, y_1)$ and (x_2, y_2), and let c be the color to assign to the pixel. For the geometry illustrated in figure 4.8 the following six step procedure will fill pixels with color c that occur within the triangle $(x_0, y_0) \rightarrow (x_1, y_1) \rightarrow (x_2, y_2)$:

1. Find minimum and maximum y coordinates of the polygon's vertices:

$$y_{min} = \min(y_0, y_1, y_2)$$

and

$$y_{max} = \max(y_0, y_1, y_2)$$

2. Find the largest integer i_0 such that $i_0 \leq y_{min}$ and the smallest integer i_1 such that $i_1 \geq y_{max}$. *Note that this step requires mixing real and integer arithmetic and therefore care must be exercised in coding these statements.* After this step we know that horizontal scanline i, such that $i_0 \leq i \leq i_1$, will cross the polygon somewhere.

3. For all scanlines $i_0 \leq i \leq i_1$ repeat the following steps.

4. Consider each of the lines, $0, 1$ and 2 in figure 4.8 in turn; if a line crosses the scanline between the vertices at either end of the segment find the x coordinate of the intersection with i. If any of the lines are horizontal assume there is no intersection. There will be either two or three such values; three values may occur because one of the vertices of the triangle may lie on scanline i. To obtain the x coordinate of the intersection between scanline i and the side joining (x_1, y_1) to (x_2, y_2), for example, a simplified 2D line intersection calculation is all that is required. The algorithm given in listing 4.4 takes advantage of the fact that the scanline is horizontal and the first thing it does is to check and see if the scanline crosses the triangle at all. (This step will be performed many times, proportional to both the number of polygons and the resolution of the framebuffer so the tests are ordered with the least common one performed first.)

5. Find the minimum and maximum x coordinates, x_{min} and x_{max} of the intersection.

6. Step, j, across the row of pixels from x_{min} to x_{max} setting pixel (j, i) to color c at each step. Use the nearest integer values of x_{min} and x_{max}.

4.2.6 Culling and clipping

For the final two steps (4 and 5) of the basic rendering algorithm to work correctly, it is imperative that the vertices of all facets have an x coordinate $x > 0$ (i.e., in front of the viewpoint) and that the projected coordinates (X, Y) are such that $0 \leq X < X_{max}$ and $0 \leq Y < Y_{max}$. In all the topics we have discussed before, this has been implicitly assumed. However these conditions are not always satisfied in practice. Indeed in some common uses of 3D graphics, e.g., *walk throughs*, these conditions will be met by only a very few of the vertices in the scene.

if $y_1 < i$ and $y_2 < i$ then no intersection
if $y_1 > i$ and $y_2 > i$ then no intersection
$\Delta y = y_2 - y_1$
if $|\Delta y| < \frac{1}{2}$ then line horizontal $\Rightarrow$ no intersection
$\Delta x = x_2 - x_1$
$d = \dfrac{(i - y_1)\Delta x}{\Delta y}$
$x_{int} = x_1 + d$

Listing 4.4: Determining the intersection between raster scanline i and the side joining points (x_1, y_1) to (x_2, y_2).

In order to reduce the number of calculations and remove artifacts that can occur when the conditions given earlier are violated it is necessary to perform culling and clipping. For our work the term culling will apply to the action of discarding **complete** polygons, i.e., those polygons with all their vertices outside the field of view, or in the case of a wireframe drawing, the vertices at both ends of an edge. Clipping will refer to the action of modifying those polygons (or edges) that are partially in and partially out of the field of view. Culling should always be performed first because it is likely to give you the biggest performance gain.

4.2.7 Culling

For 3D graphics there are three important types of cull:

1. Remove polygons behind the viewpoint.

   If the x coordinate of *all* vertices for polygon k are such that $x \leq 1$ then cull polygon k. Note that this is equivalent to removing any polygons that lie behind the projection plane.

2. Remove polygons projected to lie outside the raster.

   If the projected coordinates (X, Y) for **all** the vertices of polygon k are such that $X < 0$ or $X \geq X_{max}$ or $Y < 0$ or $Y \geq Y_{max}$ then cull polygon k.

3. Cull any *back-faces*.

   A *back-face* is any polygon that faces away from the viewpoint. It is called a back-face because if the model were solid then any polygons facing away from the viewer would be obscured from view by polygons closer to the viewer.

   In order to say whether a polygon faces toward or away from an observer a convention must be established. The most appropriate convention to apply is one based on the surface normal vector. Every polygon (which is essentially a bounded plane) has a surface normal vector as defined in

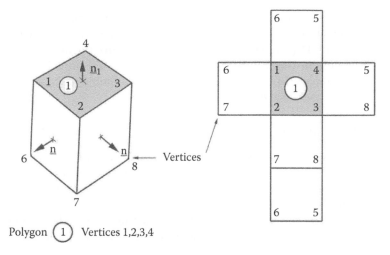

Polygon (1) Vertices 1,2,3,4

Figure 4.9: Surface normal vectors for a cube and a plan of the vertices showing a consistent ordering of the vertices round each polygonal face. For example $\mathbf{n}_1 = (\mathbf{P}_2 - \mathbf{P}_1) \times (\mathbf{P}_3 - \mathbf{P}_1)$.

section 2.5. Since it is possible for a surface normal to point in two opposite directions it is usual to assume that it is directed so that, in a general sense, it points away from the inside of an object. Figure 4.9 shows a cube with the normal vectors illustrated.

If the dot product of the normal vector with a vector from the viewpoint to a point on the polygon is negative the polygon is said to be a *front-face*; if the dot product is positive the polygon is a *back-face*.

Comments:

- There are a number of alternative ways to organize culling. One can use a bounding volume for groups of polygons and organize them in a hierarchical way with one bounding volume, containing multiple bounding volumes containing yet more bounding volumes, etc. Two other culling techniques, view frustum cull and occlusion culling, are proving popular in game engines but their discussion is outside the scope of this chapter. For more information on these culling techniques consult Akenine-Möller and Haines [1].

- Since the normal to a plane can be determined from the position vectors of three points in that plane, a consistent ordering of the vertices around a polygon should be observed whenever possible. Figure 4.9 includes a plan of a cube with vertex orderings consistent with the outward facing normals.

- A cube has a definite inside and outside, it is solid. Some shapes, particularly if in one dimension they are very thin with respect to the other two, might be represented by a single layer of polygons, for example a model of a CD (compact disk) could be made from a *fan* of triangles. A model made in this way has no sense of inside and outside. In such cases it is necessary to think of each polygon as double sided and therefore ignore any back-face culling step altogether.

4.2.8   Clipping

We need to consider clipping in both two and three dimensions. Two-dimensional clipping is important so that memory access violations do not occur in the screen buffer. The algorithm due to Sutherland and Cohen and described by Angel [3] has achieved almost universal usage as the most pertinent procedure for drawing lines in a 2D pixelated raster. The algorithm orders the clipping of lines in a series of tests which eliminate the most common cases first:

1. Both points inside

2. The line does not span the visible area.

The tests are followed by a step to calculate one or two points on the line where it crosses the boundary of the visible area.

In a 3D rendering algorithm, the 2D tests are applied after each polygon has been projected onto the viewing plane. There is no need for intersection calculations since all drawing occurs on one scanline at a time. Thus, the following modifications to the Z buffer algorithm will accomplish 2D clipping:

1. Begin by adding the instructions given in listing 4.5 to the loop that is processing the polygons; a flag is used to indicate whether the polygon should be culled or not.

2. Conclude by inserting the instructions given in listing 4.6 in the procedure to scanline fill the projected polygon.

In a general Z buffer algorithm any 3D clipping should be done before the polygons are projected onto the viewing plane. Clipping is usually done against a set of planes that bound a volume. Polygons (or parts of polygons) that lie inside the volume are retained for rendering. A cubic volume is the simplest to create but since the field of view establishes a pyramidal shaped volume, this is commonly used as the clipping volume. This frustum is arranged so that its sides correspond to the edges of the field of view. The top and bottom of the frustum form the so-called front and back clipping planes. The front clipping plane is used to prevent polygons from extending to the wrong side of the projection plane. The front and back clipping planes are at right angles to the direction of view, see figure 4.10. For the purposes of a Z buffer rendering algorithm, it is essential to use the front clipping plane. A back clipping plane is required

---

While repeating for all polygons k add the following:
```
{
    Set flag
    repeat for all vertices i of polygon k     {
        let (X, Y) be projected coordinates of vertex i
        if  X ≥ 0  and  X < Xmax  {\
          clear the flag and jump to next polygon
        }
        if  Y ≥ 0  and  Y < Ymax  {
          clear the flag and jump to next polygon
        }
    }
    if the flag is set cull the polygon
}
```

Listing 4.5: Amendments to the Z buffer algorithm to cull polygons which lie outside the field of view.

Check scanline, i, to see if it is inside the raster.
if $i < 0$ or $i \geq Y_{max}$ skip to next scanline

On scanline i polygon k spans pixels x_1 to x_2.
Before setting pixel values apply limits to x_1 and x_2.

$$x_1 = \max(0, x_1)$$
$$x_2 = \max(0, x_2)$$
$$x_1 = \min((X_{max} - 1), x_1)$$
$$x_2 = \min((X_{max} - 1), x_2)$$

Listing 4.6: Amendments to the Z buffer algorithm to clip polygons partially lying outside the field of view.

because the Z buffer has finite resolution, an important point if the Z buffer is implemented in hardware using 16 or 24 bits per pixel. Other necessary clipping can be accomplished in the 2D projection plane. For multiple clipping planes it is sufficient to apply them one at a time in succession; for example clip with the back plane, then the front plane, then the side plane, etc. An interesting application of the use of clipping planes is to produce animated cut away views; for example by moving the clipping plane through a model the inside can be revealed gradually.

Clipping a triangular polygon with a clipping plane To see how 3D clipping is achieved we consider the following: Look at figure 4.11. It shows a triangular polygon ABC which is to be clipped at the plane PP' (seen end on). Clipping is accomplished by splitting triangle ABC into two pieces; BDE and $ACED$.

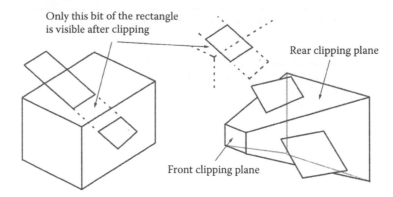

Figure 4.10: Cubic and truncated pyramidal clipping volumes penetrated by a rectangular polygon. Only that portion of the rectangle which lies inside the clipping volume would appear in the rendered image.

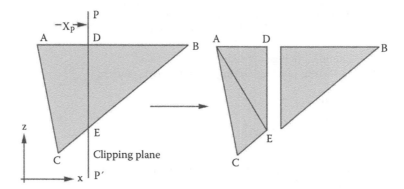

Figure 4.11: Clipping a triangular polygon, ABC, with a yz plane at PP', at $(x_p, 0, 0)$. Clipping divides ABC into two pieces. If the polygons are to remain triangular the piece $ADEC$ must be divided in two.

The pieces are then either removed from, or added to, the polygon database as necessary. For example, when PP' is the back clipping plane triangles ADE and AEC are added to the database, whilst triangle BDC is removed. Points D and E are determined by finding the intersection between the lines joining vertices of the polygon and the clipping plane. The calculation is straightforward (section 2.6 considered a general case) but, since the clipping plane is at right angles to the x axis and because clipping to such a plane is commonly used, it is worth writing expressions specifically for these particular circumstances. Therefore the intersection point, $\mathbf{p}$, between a line joining points $\mathbf{P}_1$ and $\mathbf{P}_2$ and

There are three possible cases to consider as illustrated in figure 4.12.

if edges AB and BC cross PP' {
   calculate point D on edge AB
   calculate point E on edge BC
   Re-label the triangle ABC to have vertices DBE
   Add new triangles ADC and DEC to database
}
else if edges AB and CA cross PP' {
   calculate point D on edge AB
   calculate point E on edge CA
   Re-label the triangle ABC to have vertices ADE
   Add new triangles DBE and BCE to database
}
else if edges BC and CA cross PP' {
   calculate point D on edge CA
   calculate point E on edge BC
   Re-label the triangle ABC to have vertices CDE
   Add new triangles DAE and ABE to database
}

This procedure has ensured that there will be an edge actually in the clipping plane. Polygons will lie on one side or the other. **No** polygons will span the clipping plane. Despite this it is useful to keep a record of all polygons because another clipping plane might be added later. A flag can be used to indicate which triangle lies inside the appropriate clipping volume.

Listing 4.7: Algorithm to clip the triangular polygons ABC with a plane PP' (seen in cross section) as illustrated in figure 4.11.

the yz plane at x_p is given by:

$$
\begin{aligned}
p_x &= x_p \\
p_y &= P_{1y} + \frac{(x_p - P_{1x})}{(P_{2x} - P_{1x})}(P_{2y} - P_{1y}) \\
p_z &= P_{1z} + \frac{(x_p - P_{1x})}{(P_{2x} - P_{1x})}(P_{2z} - P_{1z})
\end{aligned}
$$

Once the coordinates of the points D and E are known the algorithm to clip the triangular polygon ABC is complete and it is given in listing 4.7.

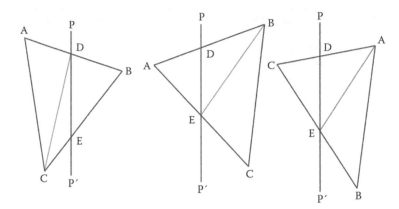

Figure 4.12: Possible configurations for clipping a triangular polygon. Note that in figure 4.7 there is a consistent counterclockwise ordering of the vertices for all the polygons created. This is vital for a consistent sense of inside and outside to be maintained. Although the second and third configurations look the same they are in fact different because the clipping plane crossed edges *AB* and *AC* in the second but edges *BC* and *AC* in the third.

4.3   Anti-aliasing

Aliasing is a term arising from the theory of sampled signals. The manifestation of aliasing depends on how the signal is interpreted, audio, video etc., but in all cases aliasing effects are regarded as undesirable and at least some effort should be devoted to minimizing their interference. Anti-aliasing refers to the steps taken to minimize the deleterious effects of aliasing. For our purposes the only significant problem with aliasing is due to the fact that the output device or framebuffer is of finite resolution. In computer graphics work the artifacts of aliasing are often referred to as the *jaggies* because the finite dimensions of the raster causes a straight line drawn at an angle across it to take on the appearance of a *staircase* rather than a straight line. Aliasing artifacts are also a significant problem in rendering image maps and textures, as discussed in section 4.5.

The obvious way to reduce the aliasing effect is to increase the resolution of the raster or framebuffer. An alternative approach is to use the range of color or brightness provided by the display to smooth out the obvious aliasing artifacts. Figure 4.13 illustrates this alternative technique; on the left it shows a couple of characters from a text font that have been rendered into a pixelated raster. By fading the edges with lighter shades of gray (shown on the right) the curves look smoother and angled straight lines look less jagged. At the bottom of figure 4.13 the effect of the same technique on a straight line is also illustrated. To consider anti-aliasing further it is useful to investigate procedures to anti-alias the drawing of points, lines and pictures.

Figure 4.13: Anti-aliasing by fading the brightness in pixels near the edge of lines and shapes.

4.3.1   Anti-aliasing points

In the context of 3D graphics the most common need to draw points in the framebuffer or on a screen is as the result of a particle model of some sort, for example rain, snow, fireworks etc.

After projection a point **p** will have coordinates (X, Y) which are scaled to lie within the dimensions of the raster, but X and Y will be floating point numbers and to record a color value it is necessary to fill the best guess pixel at some integer coordinate (X_i, Y_j). Unfortunately simply rounding X or Y to the nearest integer will result in aliasing artifacts. The effect will be especially noticeable in a sequence of images where the particles will appear to jitter and move about in fits and starts.

A point can be successfully anti-aliased by spreading out its color value over not only the nearest integer pixel but also into those adjacent to it in the raster. For example, if the projected point is at raster coordinates $(1.3, 3)$ and it has a brightness value of 0.7 (on a $[0, 1]$ scale) pixel the $(1, 3)$ will be assigned a brightness of 0.7 and pixel $(2, 3)$ a brightness of 0.4. This *blending* will give the point the appearance of being located to the left side of pixel $(1, 3)$. Using the notation given in figure 4.14 the instructions in listing 4.8 will draw, with anti-aliasing, a point P with brightness c.

4.3.2   Anti-aliasing lines

To minimize the aliasing effect when drawing lines in a pixelated raster blend the brightness in the pixels of adjacent rows and columns (see figure 4.13). This can be accomplished by modifying the Bresenham line drawing algorithm to that given in listing 4.9.

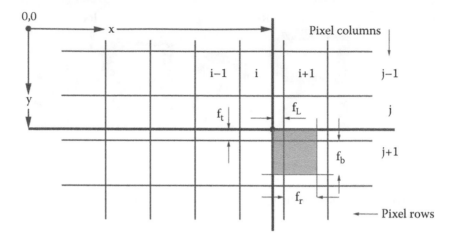

Figure 4.14: When a point, P, is projected to the view plane its coordinates, (X, Y), will not always be dead center in pixel i, j. Blending the brightness of P into adjacent pixels $i, j + 1$, $i + 1, j$ and $i + 1, j + 1$ will help to lessen the effect of the display raster (or framebuffer) being composed of discrete elements.

The projected point is (X, Y) (float data types)
Function $frac(x)$ returns the fractional part of x *
Each pixel is one unit square

$i = X$ //rounded down to integer
$j = Y$
$f_l = 1 - frac(X)$
$f_r = frac(X + 1)$
$f_t = 1 - frac(Y)$
$f_b = frac(Y + 1)$
set pixel (i, j) to value $c \times f_t \times f_l$
set pixel $(i + 1, j)$ to value $c \times f_t \times f_r$
set pixel $(i, j + 1)$ to value $c \times f_b \times f_l$
set pixel $(i + 1, j + 1)$ to value $c \times f_b \times f_r$

Listing 4.8: Using the notation given in figure 4.14 this algorithm will draw, with anti-aliasing, a point P with brightness c.

4.3.3 Anti-aliasing pictures

The simplest way to anti-alias synthesized images is to *supersample*. That is: Divide each pixel into a number of subpixels, render each of them as if they were individual pixels and then average the results. For example divide each pixel into 4 subpixels. An alternative way of doing this is to render into a raster that is twice as wide and twice as high and then average over adjacent groups of 4

```
Δx = x₂ − x₁
Δy = y₂ − y₁
δ = −Δx/2
set x = x₁ and y = y₁
draw pixel at (x, y) with color c
while x < x₂ do {
    δ = δ + Δy
    if δ ≥ 0 {
        y = y + y_inc
        δ = δ − Δx
    }
    x = x + 1
    /* modified section */
    draw pixel at (x, y) with color c(1 − δ/Δx)
    draw pixel at (x, y + 1) with color c·δ/Δx
    /* end modification */
}
```

Listing 4.9: A modified Bresenham's algorithm for rendering anti-aliased lines.

pixels. For example rendering to a raster of 1280×960 and averaging pixels i, j, $i + 1, j$, $i, j + 1$ and $i + 1, j + 1$ will give the same result as rendering to a raster of 640×480 with each pixel divided into 4. This box filtering is quick and easy to apply but in theory the best results are obtained from a $\frac{\sin x}{x}$ filter function.

Because a supersample of n requires $(n - 1)$ additional pixel values to be determined the rendering process slows down as anti-aliasing is applied. For example if it takes one minute to render a frame of TV resolution without anti-aliasing it will take about nine minutes to anti-alias it on a 3×3 supersample. Sadly, for a good enough quality TV sized image it **is** necessary to use at least a 3×3 supersample.

There are a couple of tricks that can be employed to accelerate the anti-aliasing process and both of them rely on the fact that the most noticeable aliasing artifacts occur near edges where color or brightness changes occur.

Techniques to accelerate supersampled anti-aliasing

1. Once the first supersample has been obtained for pixel (i, j) the remaining samples are only rendered if the color differs from that for pixels $(i - 1, j)$ or $(i, j - 1)$ by more than a certain threshold.

2. Use the fact that relatively few calculations are required to determine the identity of the polygon visible in each of the supersamples for pixel (i, j). If the same polygon appears in each supersample then there is no need to perform the more time consuming work of determining a color value for all

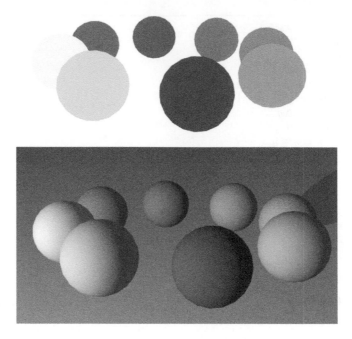

Figure 4.15: (Top) Hidden surface visualization of a group of colored spheres made up from 320 triangular polygons in each sphere, and (bottom) the same view with a simple lighting model.

the supersamples. Simply do it once and record that as the value for pixel (i, j). If different polygons appear in each supersample then we must get color values for those that are different and average the results for pixel (i, j).

Using either of these techniques can lead to significantly reduced rendering times without much loss in picture quality.

4.4 Lighting and shading

Figure 4.15(top) illustrates a simple scene of a colored spheres rendered with a hidden surface algorithm. Only those triangular polygons that should be visible *are* visible but there is definitely still something not very realistic about the image: It certainly doesn't look like a photograph. Figure 4.15 (bottom) shows the same scene after the simplest possible lighting model has been included in the renderer and the level of realism is certainly improved.

It is without doubt the way in which light interacts with surfaces of a 3D model that is the most significant effect that we can simulate to provide visual

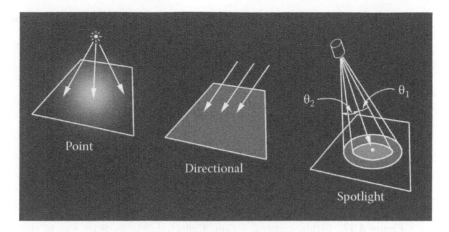

Figure 4.16: Three types of light source.

realism. A hidden surface procedure may determine *what you can see* but it is mainly the interaction with light that determines *what you do see*.

To simulate *lighting* effects it stands to reason that at least the location and color of one or more lights must be known. In addition to this we need to classify the light as being one of the three types illustrated in figure 4.16:

1. A point light source that illuminates in all directions.

2. A directional or parallel light source. In this case the light comes from a specific direction which is the same at all points in the scene. (The illumination from the sun is an example of this type of illumination.)

3. A spotlight illumination is limited to a small region of the scene. The beam of the spotlight is normally assumed to have a graduated edge so that the illumination is a maximum inside a cone of half angle θ_1 and falls to zero intensity inside another cone of half angle θ_2, naturally $\theta_2 > \theta_1$.

For a lot of scenes the type 1 source gives the best approximation to the lighting conditions. In simulated outdoor scenes the sun is so far away that its illumination is simulated as a directional light source with all rays arriving at the scene in a parallel direction.

Before proceeding we should consider the format for recording a value for the surface color and illumination, call it c. In CG programs a model to describe color must be employed. A detailed description of various color models may be found in Watt and Watt [87]. The simplest color model that fulfills all the requirements is one with three components, one for each of the primary colors, red, green and blue, the so-called RGB values. Any color the eye can perceive can be expressed in terms of an RGB triple. Thus c is recorded as c_R, c_G, c_B which are usually stored as unsigned 8 bit integers giving a range for each of 256

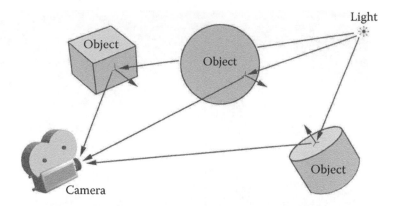

Figure 4.17: Lights, camera, action. Reflected light finds its way to the observer.

discrete values. For preliminary calculation it is more usual to assume that c_R, c_G and c_B are recorded as floating point numbers in the range $[0, 1]$. We will also assume that any light or surface color is also given as an RGB triple in the same range.

There are other models to describe color. HSV (Hue, Saturation Value), and CMYK (Cyan,Magenta,Yellow, blacK) are alternatives that have advantages in certain situations. It is possible to convert back and forward between any of these models if necessary.

To determine the color that is recorded in a pixel the effect of lights need to be combined with the surface properties of the polygon visible in that pixel. The simplest way to do this is to break up the mathematical model for light–surface interaction into a number of terms, each one of which represents a specific physical phenomenon.

In the following expressions s_R, s_G, s_B represent the color of the surface, and l_R, l_G, l_B the color of the light. I_a, I_c, I_d and I_s are the four contributions to the lighting model and we will discuss them shortly. Using this terminology the color c calculated for the pixel in question may be expressed as:

$$c_R = I_a s_R + I_c(I_s + I_d s_R)l_R \qquad (4.1)$$

$$c_G = I_a s_G + I_c(I_s + I_d s_G)l_G \qquad (4.2)$$

$$c_B = I_a s_B + I_c(I_s + I_d s_B)l_B \qquad (4.3)$$

Writing the expressions in this form with s_R and so forth as separate terms facilitates the calculation because the surface color may be determined independently of the remainder of the terms in the lighting model; indeed it might possibly be calculated in a separate module.

To obtain expressions for the four components in our illumination model (I_a, I_c, I_d and I_s) we must consider the spatial relationship between the lights,

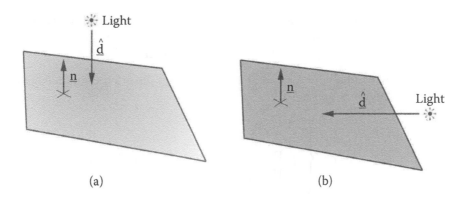

Figure 4.18: Diffuse illumination. (a) The brightest illumination occurs when the incident light direction is at right angles to the surface. (b) The illumination tends to zero as the direction of the incident light becomes parallel to the surface.

the camera and the action; this is illustrated in figure 4.17. In the following expressions we will assume that **p** is the point to be illuminated on the visible polygon which has a surface normal $\hat{\mathbf{n}}$ at **p**. We will now proceed to consider models for the components:

1. *Ambient reflection* (I_a)

   When there are no lights in a scene the picture will be blank. Including a small fraction of the surface color, s_R and so on, helps to simulate the effect of light reflected from the world around the scene. Without it pictures of objects would look like they had been taken in outer space. An image rendered with an ambient light factor of unity is equivalent to a simple hidden surface drawing such as that which produced the *flat* look shown in figure 4.15. The component of a lighting model due to ambient reflection is designated as I_a and it is always constant, i.e., $I_a = k$.

2. *Diffuse reflection* (I_d)

   Diffuse lighting is the most significant component of an illumination model. The term *reflection* is used here because it is light reflected from surfaces which enters the camera. The model we choose to describe in this chapter is a simple Lambertian illumination where a polygon is most brightly illuminated when the incident light strikes the surface at right angles. The illumination falls to zero when the direction of the beam of light is parallel to the surface. This behavior is known as the Lambert cosine law and is illustrated in figure 4.18. The diffuse illumination component I_d for a point light source located at $\mathbf{P}_l$ is thus given by:

$$I_d = \frac{\mathbf{P}_l - \mathbf{p}}{|\mathbf{P}_l - \mathbf{p}|} \cdot \hat{\mathbf{n}}$$

In the case of a directional light source with incident direction $\hat{\mathbf{d}}$ the diffuse component becomes:

$$I_d = -\hat{\mathbf{d}} \cdot \hat{\mathbf{n}}$$

For a spotlight located at $\mathbf{P}_l$, pointing in direction $\hat{\mathbf{d}}$ and having light cone angles θ_1 and θ_2:

$$I_d = \begin{cases} \dfrac{\mathbf{P}_l - \mathbf{p}}{|\mathbf{P}_l - \mathbf{p}|} \cdot \hat{\mathbf{n}} & \text{if } \theta < \theta_1 \\[2ex] \left(\dfrac{\mathbf{P}_l - \mathbf{p}}{|\mathbf{P}_l - \mathbf{p}|} \cdot \hat{\mathbf{n}} \right) \left(1 - \dfrac{(\theta - \theta_1)}{(\theta_2 - \theta_1)} \right) & \text{if } \theta_1 \leq \theta \leq \theta_2 \\[2ex] 0 & \text{if } \theta_2 < \theta \end{cases}$$

where $\cos \theta = \frac{\hat{\mathbf{d}} \cdot (\mathbf{p} - \mathbf{P}_l)}{|(\mathbf{p} - \mathbf{P}_l)|}$.

Section 5.1 in chapter 5 delves a little more deeply into the physics of illumination and offers some pointers to illumination models that are more accurate but at the expense of taking longer (sometimes much longer) to calculate.

3. *Specular reflection (I_s)*

It is the specular component of the light reflected from a surface that makes it look shiny. In practice the effect of specular reflection is to add a *highlight* to parts of a model that have been designated as shiny. The specular highlight takes the color of the light and not that of the surface on which it is visible. To set up a model for specular reflection we need to consider in a little more detail something of its origin.

A perfect mirror reflects all rays of light perfectly and the angle of reflection is equal to the angle of incidence. However shiny surfaces that are not perfect mirrors introduce small random fluctuations in the direction of the reflected rays. These random fluctuations in the direction of the reflected rays of light tend to be small so that they all lie within a cone-shaped volume that has its apex at the point of reflection and its axis lying in the direction that a ray would take if the surface was a perfect mirror (see figure 4.19).

In the lighting model the specular illumination component I_s is normally modeled with the empirical expression suggested by Phong [72]:

$$I_s = \cos^m \phi$$

in which ϕ is the angle between the reflection vector and the vector leading from the viewpoint at $\mathbf{P}_v$ to $\mathbf{p}$ on the surface. To determine ϕ from the known geometry shown in figure 4.19 it is necessary to use a few intermediate steps.

First calculate the vector $\mathbf{b}$ which bisects the vectors between $\mathbf{p}$ and the viewpoint and between $\mathbf{p}$ and $\mathbf{P}_l$. The vector $\mathbf{b}$ takes an angle β between these vectors. From that the angle α is easily determined because $\cos\alpha = \hat{\mathbf{b}} \cdot \hat{\mathbf{n}}$ (the surface normal $\hat{\mathbf{n}}$ is known) while $\mathbf{b}$ is given by:

$$\mathbf{b} = -\frac{\mathbf{p}-\mathbf{P}_l}{|\mathbf{p}-\mathbf{P}_l|} - \frac{\mathbf{p}-\mathbf{P}_v}{|\mathbf{p}-\mathbf{P}_v|}$$

$$\hat{\mathbf{b}} = \frac{\mathbf{b}}{|\mathbf{b}|}$$

In figure 4.19 we note that:

$$\beta = \phi + \theta - \alpha$$

and that:

$$\beta = \theta + \alpha$$

Eliminating β and canceling θ gives:

$$\alpha = \frac{\phi}{2}$$

In terms of the known geometry I_s therefore becomes:

$$\begin{aligned} I_s &= \cos^m\phi \text{ or,} \\ I_s &= (2\cos^2\alpha - 1)^m \text{ or,} \\ I_s &= (2(\hat{\mathbf{b}}\cdot\hat{\mathbf{n}})^2 - 1)^m \end{aligned}$$

The cosine power, m, is the parameter which governs the *shininess* of a surface. Very shiny surfaces have a high m; typical values lie in the range 10 to 99.

If accelerated hardware or fast processors are not available the presence of a power function in the calculation of specular reflection can be quite slow. In this situation it is a good idea to establish a two-dimensional lookup table with a few values of m and the dot product $(\mathbf{b}\cdot\mathbf{n})$. The table can be quite small because the visual appearance of specular highlights does not change too rapidly, perhaps 16 values of m and 1000 values covering the interval $[0,1]$ in which the dot product $\mathbf{b}\cdot\mathbf{n}$ lies. Setting aside a 64k block of memory to store the table will be a very good investment when the time saved in rendering is taken into account. When very fast processors or accelerated hardware is available the memory access time can often exceed the time for a power calculation and in this case it is better to do the calculation.

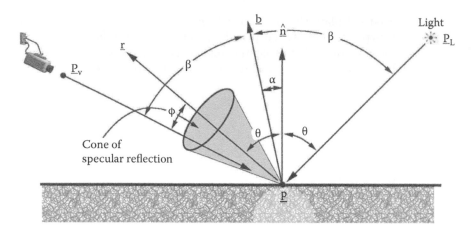

Figure 4.19: Specular reflection.

4. *Depth cueing (I_c)*

   Like any electromagnetic radiation light is attenuated as it travels away
   from its source. The reflected light (mainly diffuse) arriving at the viewpoint has traveled from the light source to the object where it was reflected
   on to the observer. In theory the light intensity should be attenuated with
   distance from its source using an inverse square law but in practice a linear
   fall-off looks much more realistic. Quite often depth cueing can be omitted
   entirely from the model with only mildly noticeable effect. A linear model
   is usually written in the form:

$$I_c = \frac{1}{d_o + d}$$

where d_o is a constant and d is the distance of **p** from the viewpoint.
Assuming that the viewpoint is at $(0, 0, 0)$ and the observer is looking along
the x axis, a good assumption is to let $d = p_x$, the x coordinate of **p**.

If depth cueing is to be used it is also a good idea to perform an *exposure*
test by examining all the polygons and scaling the light intensities so that
the maximum is always unity. If this is not done then it can require quite
a lot of trial and error testing to generate a picture that is neither under-
or overexposed.

Figure 4.20: Shading of two similar polygon models of a sphere. Flat shading on the left and basic Gouraud smooth shading on the right.

Once each component of the illumination model in equation 4.1 is known a general expression for the effect of lighting a surface in the scene at some point $\mathbf{p}$ with n lights becomes:

$$c_R = I_a s_R + I_c \sum_{i=0}^{n-1} (I_s(i) + I_d(i) s_R) l_R(i)$$

$$c_G = I_a s_G + I_c \sum_{i=0}^{n-1} (I_s(i) + I_d(i) s_G) l_G(i)$$

$$c_B = I_a s_B + I_c \sum_{i=0}^{n-1} (I_s(i) + I_d(i) s_B) l_B(i)$$

I_d and I_s depend on the position of light i and on which type of light it is, for example spotlight. If $n > 1$ each term in the lighting model must be limited so that it falls in the range $[0, 1]$, otherwise an overexposed picture will be produced.

Look at figure 4.20. It shows two pictures of the same faceted model of a sphere. The one on the right looks smooth (apart from the silhouetted edges which we will discuss later). It is the way a sphere should look. The one on the left looks like just what it is, a collection of triangular polygons. Although the outline of neither is perfectly circular it is the appearance of the interior that first grabs the attention. This example highlights the main drawback of the representation of an object with a model made up from polygonal facets. To model a sphere so that it looks smooth by increasing the number (or equivalently decreasing the size) of the facets is quite impractical. Tens of thousands of facets would be required just for a simple sphere. However both the spheres shown in figure 4.20 contain the same number of facets and yet one manages to look smooth. How?

The answer is the use of a trick that fools the eye by smoothly varying the shading within the polygonal facets. The point has already been made that if

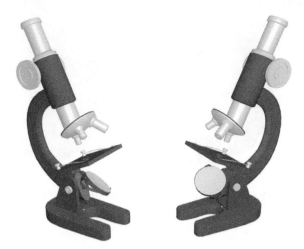

Figure 4.21: After lighting and Phong shading have been added to a hidden surface rendering, the image starts to look much more realistic.

you look at the outlines of both spheres you will see that they are made from straight segments. In the case of the smooth looking sphere it is because the discontinuities in shading between adjacent facets have been eliminated that it looks smooth. To the eye a discontinuity in shading is much more noticeable than a small angular change between two edges.

So how is the smooth shading achieved? There are two useful possibilities: one, the Phong approach, gives a more realistic look than the other, the Gouraud approach. Unfortunately Phong's shading model achieves its realism at the expense of a greater number of calculations, so we will look at them both. Combining shading with lighting makes another major contribution to obtaining a realistic picture of an object from its numerical model as illustrated in figure 4.21, which shows the effect on the test image of adding a shading procedure to the renderer.

4.4.1 Gouraud shading

To simulate smooth shading across a polygon the Gouraud approach is a two step process:

1. Calculate the intensity of the light at each vertex of the model.

2. Use a bi-linear interpolation to obtain the intensity at any point within a polygon from the intensity at the vertices of the polygon.

To calculate the light intensity at vertex i, as shown in Figure 4.22, it is necessary to take account of all the polygons attached to vertex i. Section 4.4 showed how the intensity of the light falling on a point within a polygon can be calculated.

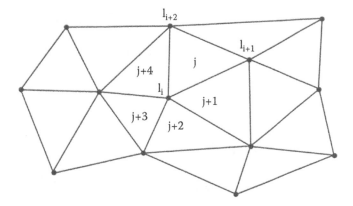

Figure 4.22: Averaging light intensities in polygons j to $j + 4$ adjacent to vertex i will provide an appropriate intensity, I_i, at vertex i. Similarly light intensities I_{i+1} and I_{i+2} are determined from the light falling on polygons adjacent to those vertices.

```
for all vertices i < n   {
    set vertex intensities Iᵢ = 0
}
for all polygons k < m   {
    set running average intensity Iₗ = 0
    for vertices i of polygon k   {
        calculate light intensity at vertex
        l = Poly(k).Vid(i) and update running average intensity Iₗ
        make sure that 0 ≤ Iₗ ≤ 1
    }
}
```

Listing 4.10: The Gouraud shading procedure.

We then average the intensity of the light falling on polygons attached to vertex i. For example: In figure 4.22 polygons j, $j + 1$, $j + 2$, $j + 3$ and $j + 4$ will contribute to the average shading at vertex i. Thus to calculate light intensities at n vertices with m polygons recorded in a list, (say $Poly(k)$, remember polygons store the ID of the vertices that they are attached to, see figure 3.12), use the short algorithm of listing 4.10.

To interpolate the intensity I_p at the point $\mathbf{p}$, as shown in figure 4.23, there are two alternatives:

1. Work directly in three dimensions from the known intensities I_0, I_1, I_2 and the vertices at $\mathbf{P}_0$ and so forth which have coordinates (x_0, y_0, z_0), (x_1, y_1, z_1) and (x_2, y_2, z_2), respectively. Use the procedure described in section 2.11.1 to obtain α and β and then interpolate bilinearly to obtain

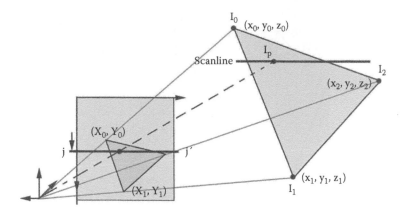

Figure 4.23: To calculate the light intensity at an internal point of a triangular polygon interpolate from the intensity at the polygon's vertices.

I_p:
$$I_p = I_0 + (I_2 - I_0)\alpha + (I_1 - I_0)\beta$$

Finding I_p directly in three dimensions is slow. It would be better if we could do the calculation after the polygon's vertices have been projected onto the viewing plane. We can indeed do this because shading is the last step in the rendering algorithm and all the necessary 3D calculations have already been carried out. This leads to our second alternative.

2. Use the two-dimensional coordinates after projection of the polygon's vertices to the viewing plane, i.e., to points (X_0, Y_0), (X_1, Y_1) and (X_2, Y_2). Further, because the rendering procedure will normally be filling pixels sequentially across a scanline a few additional arithmetic operations can be saved by calculating an increment in intensity I which is added to the value obtained for the previous pixel on the scanline.

For a triangular polygon, k, which spans scanline j (see figure 4.23) starting at pixel i the intensity $I_{i,j}$ can be obtained from the following equations:

$$\Delta = (Y_2 - Y_0)(X_1 - X_0) - (X_2 - X_0)(Y_1 - Y_0)$$
$$\alpha = \frac{(Y_2 - Y_0)(i - X_0) - (X_2 - X_0)(j - Y_0)}{\Delta}$$
$$\beta = \frac{(j - Y_0)(X_1 - X_0) - (i - X_0)(Y_1 - Y_0)}{\Delta}$$
$$I_{i,j} = I_0 + \alpha(I_1 - I_0) + \beta(I_2 - I_0)$$

The intensity in adjacent pixels $I_{i+1,j}$ and so forth is determined by calculating an increment δI from:

$$\delta I = \frac{(Y_1 - Y_2)I_0 + (Y_2 - Y_0)I_1 + (Y_0 - Y_1)I_2}{\Delta}$$

Then for all the remaining pixels on scanline j covered by polygon k the intensity is given by:

$$I_{i+1,j} \;\; = \;\; I_{i,j} + \delta I$$

4.4.2 Phong shading

The Gouraud shading procedure works well for the diffuse reflection component of a lighting model but it does not give a good result when specular reflection is taken into account. Specular highlights occupy quite a small proportion of a visible surface and the direction of the normal at precisely the visible point must be known so that the specular reflection can be determined. Thus Phong's approach was to interpolate the surface normal over a polygon rather than interpolate the light intensity. In the other aspects the procedure is similar to the Gouraud shading algorithm.

Gouraud's algorithm still has its uses because Phong's [72] approach requires much more work. The additional calculations include vector instead of scalar interpolation and a time-consuming square root calculation to normalize the resultant normal before it can be used in the lighting equations. However most of the additional calculation occurs because the diffuse lighting scalar product must be evaluated for every pixel covered by the projection of the polygon and not just its vertices.

Phong shading is done in the following two stages:

1. Calculate a normal vector for each vertex of the model.

2. Use two-dimensional interpolation to determine the normal at any point within a polygon from the normals at the vertices of the polygon.

In stage 1 an analogous procedure to the first step of the Gouraud algorithm is used. In this case however averaging takes place with normal vectors instead of illumination intensities. Figure 4.24 shows a cross section through a coarse (6 sided) approximation of a cylinder. In (a) the facet normals are illustrated, (b) shows the vertex normals obtained by averaging normals from facets connected to a particular vertex and in (c) the effect of interpolation on normal vectors is shown. A smoothly varying surface normal will interact with the incoming light beam to give smoothly varying shading which will also work correctly with the model for specular highlights.

In stage 2 expressions very similar to those that occur in the Gouraud model are derived. For a triangular polygon k that spans scanline j at the leftmost

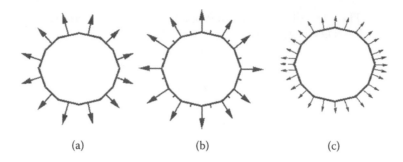

(a)   (b)   (c)

Figure 4.24: In Phong smoothing the surface normals are averaged at the vertices and then the vertex normals are interpolated over the flat facets to give an illusion of a continuously varying curvature.

pixel i the normal vector $\hat{\mathbf{n}}_{i,j}$ is given by:

$$\Delta = (Y_2 - Y_0)(X_1 - X_0) - (X_2 - X_0)(Y_1 - Y_0)$$

$$\alpha = \frac{(Y_2 - Y_0)(i - X_0) - (X_2 - X_0)(j - Y_0)}{\Delta}$$

$$\beta = \frac{(j - Y_0)(X_1 - X_0) - (i - X_0)(Y_1 - Y_0)}{\Delta}$$

$$\begin{bmatrix} n_x \\ n_y \\ n_z \end{bmatrix}_{i,j} = \begin{bmatrix} n_{0x} + \alpha(n_{1x} - n_{0x}) + \beta(n_{2x} - n_{0x}) \\ n_{0y} + \alpha(n_{1y} - n_{0y}) + \beta(n_{2y} - n_{0y}) \\ n_{0z} + \alpha(n_{1z} - n_{0z}) + \beta(n_{2z} - n_{0z}) \end{bmatrix}$$

$$\hat{\mathbf{n}}_{i,j} = \frac{\mathbf{n}_{i,j}}{|\mathbf{n}_{i,j}|}$$

For the remaining pixels on scanline j, i.e., pixels $i+1$, $i+2$ etc., the normals $(\mathbf{n}_{i+1,j}, \mathbf{n}_{i+2,j})$ are determined by calculating an incremental vector $\delta\mathbf{n}$ given by:

$$\begin{bmatrix} \delta n_x \\ \delta n_y \\ \delta n_z \end{bmatrix} = \frac{1}{\Delta} \begin{bmatrix} (Y_1 - Y_2)n_{0x} + (Y_2 - Y_0)n_{1x} + (Y_0 - Y_1)n_{2x} \\ (Y_1 - Y_2)n_{0y} + (Y_2 - Y_0)n_{1y} + (Y_0 - Y_1)n_{2y} \\ (Y_1 - Y_2)n_{0z} + (Y_2 - Y_0)n_{1z} + (Y_0 - Y_1)n_{2z} \end{bmatrix}$$

Normals in the remaining pixels on scanline j covered by polygon k are thus determined sequentially from:

$$\mathbf{n}_{i+1,j} = \mathbf{n}_{i,j} + \delta\mathbf{n}$$

$$\hat{\mathbf{n}}_{i+1,j} = \frac{\mathbf{n}_{i+1,j}}{|\mathbf{n}_{i+1,j}|}$$

Remember: The normal $\hat{\mathbf{n}}_{i,j}$ found by interpolation in the two-dimensional projection plane is still the three-dimensional normal vector at $\mathbf{p}$ on polygon k (which is the point visible in pixel (i, j)).

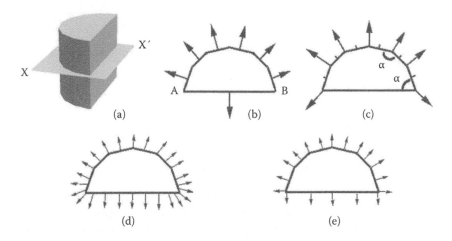

Figure 4.25: A cross section through a cylinder that has been cut in half along its axis.

Before we finish discussing Phong shading there is one very important point that requires a little more thought. Look at figure 4.25: in (a) we see a rendered half cylinder approximated by 6 rectangular facets on the curved side and 1 rectangular facet on the flat (cut) side; in (b) a plan of the section at plane XX' shows the facet normals. Now imagine what happens as stage 1 of Phong's procedure is applied. In (c) the averaged vertex normals are shown and (d) gives the interpolated normals. Even at the points labeled A and B the normal vector varies smoothly including round the sharp corner. This is **not** quite the desired result because the corner will be smoothed out and the distinct edge will just merge into the smooth shading. At points A and B the corners should really be retained. To achieve this make the following modification to the algorithm at stage 1:

- Do not update the running average for the vertex normal unless the angle $\alpha < \dfrac{\pi}{2}$ or the user overrides the decision. (α is illustrated in figure 4.25.)

Figure 4.25(e) shows the effect after this correction is applied. On a practical level to achieve this correction the vertex normals must be stored as part of the polygon data structures (see chapter 3) because a discontinuity between the normals of adjacent polygons cannot be represented if a single vector is stored for each vertex. Thus the data structure associated with each polygon in a model, from figure 3.12, must be updated to that shown in figure 4.26.

V_{id}	list of vertex identifiers to which polygon is attached
$id_{material}$	pointer to material in materials list
$A_{id}(3)$	list of the id's of polygons with a common side
n	normal to surface plane
$\mathbf{e}_{id}$	list of Phong vertex normals

Figure 4.26: Vertex and polygon data structures with vertex normals $\mathbf{e}_{id}$.

4.5   Materials and shaders

Now we consider how the appearance of objects can be enriched without having to go to the computational expense of using a more sophisticated lighting model, or by building a much more highly detailed polygonal model. The basic idea is simple enough. Every surface polygon is assigned a number of attributes, such as color, roughness, shininess, and transparency. It has become common in graphics application software not to record all the surface attributes for every polygonal facet in a model. For one thing, a lot of attributes and an excessive number of polygons will lead to a requirement for excessive storage; however, in practice, the number of different sets of attributes is likely to be quite smaller, an object with 100,000 polygons might only use two colors. Realizing that any face can be assigned a whole range of attributes by building a separate list of *materials* and then assigning a material to a face with a single integer identifier reduces the data storage considerably and significantly increases the flexibility, because, if the list of surface attributes were to change, then it is only necessary to change the format of the few items in the materials list and not the many thousands of polygons.

The idea of a materials list fits very neatly with the hardware rendering engines which do not like to have to change their surface attribute states (color, shininess, smoothing etc.) too often. By sending polygons, grouped together by material, along the rendering pipeline one after another, the number of changes of state is kept to a minimum.

So what does a material contain? Even the best images synthesized from a polygonal model still lack the detail and richness of real surfaces. Imperfections due to wear and tear, regular color variations or natural material properties are very difficult to represent with polygons. Something as simple as text painted onto surfaces or detailed colored patterns would require polygon meshes to have prohibitively large numbers of facets and vertices. Two complimentary techniques, *image mapping* and *procedural texturing*, allow for realistic detail to be added to the images of polygonal or patched models without increasing the number of polygons.

The terms procedural texture and image map nicely discriminate these two approaches, because the procedural (or algorithmic) texture can be thought of as occupying a volume and the image map as being draped over a surface. The procedural texture matches well with the idea of an extended material description, color is a volume filling attribute, and we can think of the object as being carved from a block of material X. Sometimes the 2D image map and the 3D material are recorded in separate lists. The OpenFX software considered in chapter 9 does this. Other terms are often used in computer graphics to refer to a procedural texture or an image map: in OpenGL and DirectX the term *texture map* is used instead of *image map*. In the last few years the term *shader* has become popular to describe programs that run in the GPU, and whilst a GPU shader can do a lot more than deliver a surface material, texture or image map, the term shader is often associated with the algorithms accompanying procedural textures.

Image mapping is probably the first choice of the 3D computer artist or CAD engineer when faced with the need to enhance a plain mesh model; it can make even the simplest model look tremendously lifelike and is the easiest and most adaptable way to add fine detail. The most popular real-time rendering libraries use image mapping extensively (see chapter 7). The theory of image mapping is discussed in section 4.6.

Procedural or algorithmic textures provide some of the most beautiful surfaces seen in computer-generated images. They have the advantage over the image mapping approach that they can be rendered in any resolution and therefore do not exhibit the problems that an image map can suffer from when it is rendered in close up. They do sometimes however show aliasing effects; see Apodaca and Gritz [4].

The aliasing effect from which mapped images suffer is due to the fact that they must be recorded on an array of finite size and thus their pixelated nature becomes all too apparent in close up snapshots. Procedural textures have the additional advantages that they don't require the large amount of memory that may be required to record an image nor is the problem that arises when an essentially flat (two-dimensional) image is mapped on to space filling solids evident. In section 4.4 equations 4.1, 4.2 and 4.3 described how the surface color S, at a point $\mathbf{p}$, is combined with the lighting conditions to produce a color value to represent what is seen at $\mathbf{p}$. The surface color S with its three components s_R, s_G, s_B can encapsulate not just a plain color but perhaps a blend or some other elaborate combination of shades. However, no matter how complex the procedure used to calculate S, the only variables on which it may depend are the position of $\mathbf{p}$, coordinates (x, y, z) or the two-dimensional texture coordinates (X, Y) first introduced in chapter 3; they are also commonly referred to as the u and v coordinates. This can be expressed formally as:

$$S = f(x, y, z, X, Y) \tag{4.4}$$

It is unusual for $f(x, y, z, X, Y)$ to depend on x, y, z at the same time as it depends on X, Y and therefore the term *volume texture* tends to be used for cases where $f()$ is independent of X or Y. Most volume textures tend to be generated from a fixed set of rules, and they are therefore called "procedural textures".

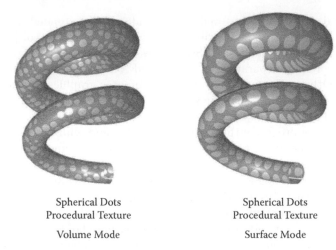

Spherical Dots   Spherical Dots
Procedural Texture   Procedural Texture

Volume Mode   Surface Mode

Figure 4.27: Procedural texture in volume and surface modes. Note the way the dots cling to the surface when texture coordinates are applied to the surface of the shape and how the shape appears to be carved out of a block of *colored spheres* when volume coordinates are used.

When $f()$ is independent of x, y or z the texture is called a surface texture and all image mapping methods fall into this category.

In addition to providing a way to alter the surface color S at $\mathbf{p}$, a texturing procedure might also modulate the direction of the surface normal or modify the transparency of the surface. In fact with a combination of these techniques and some ability to simulate reflections it can become difficult to distinguish a rendered image of the model from a photograph of the real thing.

Procedural textures can be used equally easily with functions of the form $f(x, y, z)$ (volume) or $f(X, Y)$ (surface). Figure 4.27 shows an example of a procedural texture applied to the same object in volume and surface modes. They are excellent for simulating naturally occurring surfaces, wood, marble, granite, clouds, tree bark, veins, etc. The list is almost endless. Chapter 11 details some algorithms to simulate a significant variety of surfaces.

We can establish two general types of procedural texture:

1. Those that use regular geometric patterns.

2. Those that use random patterns.

In many cases an enhanced appearance is achieved by combining the two types. The pattern of irregular paving slabs is one such example. Discolored and weathered bricks is another. Indeed this work has been extended to the concept of volume textures with the possibility of creating realistic clouds, smoke, coral, hair and fur.

The input to the algorithm is a position coordinate (x, y, z), the
mortar % thickness t_m and the colors for brick and mortar.
The output is a color triple s_R, s_G, s_B and a function
$Floor(a)$ is called to return the nearest lower integer to a.
In the C language Floor would be implemented as follows
```
#define  Floor(a)   ((a) < 0.0? ((long)(a)-1L:(long)(a))
```

if integer part of z is divisible by 2   \{
$$x = x + \tfrac{1}{2}$$
$$y = y + \tfrac{1}{2}$$
}
$$x = x - Floor(x)$$
$$y = y - Floor(y)$$
$$z = z - Floor(z)$$

A collection of   **if**'s divide the brick from the mortar
if $z > 1 - t_m$ or $y > 1 - t_m$ or
$\quad (y > \tfrac{1}{2} - t_m$ and $y < \tfrac{1}{2})$ or
$\quad (y < \tfrac{1}{2}$ and $((x > \tfrac{1}{2} - t_m$ and
$\quad x < \tfrac{1}{2})$ or $x > 1 - t_m))$ or
$\quad (y > \tfrac{1}{2}$ and $((x > \tfrac{1}{3} - t_m$ and
$\quad x < \tfrac{1}{3})$ or $(x > \tfrac{7}{10}$ and $x < \tfrac{7}{10} + t_m)))$ {
$\quad$ return the mortar color
}
else {
$\quad$ return the brick color
}

Listing 4.11: An algorithm that creates a brick and mortar procedural texture. For
a given point **p** which has coordinates (x, y, z) it determines whether **p** is inside the
brick or the mortar.

4.5.1 Basic geometric procedural textures

Listing 4.11 presents an algorithm for generating a very simple geometric texture,
i.e., a three-dimensional system of bricks and mortar. Other simple textures that
fall into this category include checks, dots, triangular shapes, stars, hexagonal
patterns and even a digital readout such as might appear on a clock.

The algorithm given in listing 4.11 illustrates a compact interface between
the texturing function and its host renderer. An input of a position, a small set
of parameters and an output of color value are sufficient to control all procedural
functions. In fact we could standardize the parameter list so that the same function can be used by scanline, Z buffer or ray tracing renderers interchangeably.
In fact texturing functions are ideal candidates for implementation as run time
definable libraries, as for example DLLs under the Windows operating system.

4.5.2   Basic random procedural textures

Simply generating random numbers does not lead to the creation of very interesting textures. What is required is a random function which is spatially correlated, that is, the surface attributes at two different locations are similar if the points are close together but if the points are far apart then calculated surface attributes will be quite independent of one another.

A random number generator with just these properties was originally proposed by Perlin [69] in what turned out to be a seminal paper on the topic. Textures based on Perlin's ideas call upon one basic function: the noise generator. Section 4.7 explains in detail the elegance of the noise generator algorithm. Given a position, $\mathbf{p}$, the noise generator returns a scalar value in the range $[0, 1]$; we will write it as: $u = sNoise(\mathbf{p})$. This function has the essential property quoted above and of equal importance for application in rendering: *if called with the same value of* $\mathbf{p}$ *it returns the same noise, therefore although it has random properties they are quite repeatable.*

From $sNoise(\mathbf{p})$ three other useful functions are easily derived:

1. A noise generator that returns a vector given a position, $\mathbf{v} = vNoise(\mathbf{p})$.

2. A function called turbulence, which is similar to the noise function but is smooth in some places while varying rapidly in others, something like the effect achieved when two colors of paint are stirred together. $u = sTurb(\mathbf{p})$ generates a scalar turbulence value.

3. $\mathbf{v} = vTurb(\mathbf{p})$ returns a vector valued turbulence.

These *noise* functions have statistical properties (translational and rotational invariance) that make them particularly useful for 3D graphics work.

The turbulence functions are examples of a *fractal* or $1/f$ noise. They can be easily calculated by adding basic Perlin noises. *The idea is that the noise signal is built up by adding a number of components with the amplitude of each component inversely proportional to its frequency.* Thus low frequency components have large amplitude but the high frequency components have small amplitude.

Comment: The fractal noise function can also be useful for building models of natural shapes, e.g., trees and mountain landscapes.

There are many ways to implement the Perlin noise function. See Ward's gem in Avro [6] for example.

One of the shortest and fastest ways to write a Perlin noise generator is to establish a three-dimensional array of random numbers and then to interpolate linearly from that to obtain a noise value for a specific point $\mathbf{p}$.

Perhaps the most versatile noise texture is that called bozo (see chapter 11 for examples). With appropriate scaling and level setting it can represent many natural phenomena such as clouds and solar corona. An algorithm for the bozo texture is given in listing 4.12. The appearance of the brick and bozo textures are illustrated in figure 4.28.

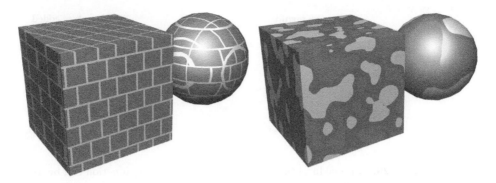

Figure 4.28: The brick and bozo textures generated by the algorithms given in listings 4.11 and 4.12.

The input to the algorithm is a position coordinate (x, y, z), two threshold values t_1 and t_2, three color triples
$c_{1R}, c_{1G}, c_{1B}, c_{1R}, c_{1G}, c_{1B}$ and c_{1R}, c_{1G}, c_{1B}
and a turbulence parameter τ which give the texture its *swirly* look.
The output is a color triple s_R, s_G, s_B The Bozo texture is a threshold of the noise function. At each threshold a color change occurs.

```
if  τ ≠ 0 {
    v = vTurb(p)
    p = p + τv
}
n = sNoise(p)
if  n < t₁ {
    assign color s = c₁ (R,G and B)
}
else if  n < t₂ {
    assign color s = c₂ (R,G and B)
}
else {
    assign color s = c₃ (R,G and B)
}
```

Listing 4.12: An algorithm to create a bozo procedural texture. It calls upon the Perlin noise functions and returns a color setting at a point P with coordinates (x, y, z).

For some practical hints on implementing procedural textures you might consult Worley's book [22].

Procedural textures, especially the noise based ones, give beautiful, richly detailed and realistic looking effects when the vector noise function is used to perturb the direction of the surface normal at P. Doing this has the effect

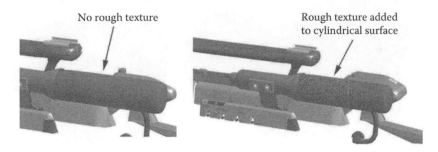

No rough texture

Rough texture added
to cylindrical surface

Figure 4.29: A procedural texture that uses the $vNoise()$ function can be used to *bend* the surface normal.

of giving a rough, bumpy, or pitted appearance to the surface because of the way the Phong lighting model interacts with the surface normal. Figure 4.29 illustrates a procedural texture that modulates the surface normal to give a rough surface. The noise function can also be called upon to alter the transparency or reflectivity of the surface at P. When all of these effects are combined some of the most visually stunning computer-generated images emerge, even from shapes described with only a few hundred polygons.

Before ending this section it is worth pointing out that in step 2 of the rendering algorithm, models are moved or rotated to place them at appropriate positions in the scene. If any surface of that model is covered with a volume texture then the position argument to the noise function should be specified with respect to a frame of reference attached to the model and **not** some global frame. If a global frame of reference for the argument to the noise function were used then an animation of a moving model will give the disturbing appearance that the model is moving through a kind of three-dimensional *sea* of the texture.

4.6 Image and texture mapping

An image map performs a very similar task to that of a two-dimensional procedural texture. It adds detail to surfaces without the need for a very large number of small polygons. In contrast to a procedural texture, image maps provide the model designer much greater control over the appearance of the texture. In essence any image may be used as the source for the image map. (2D drawings or scanned photographs are common sources.) This is particularly useful in product design applications where text, manufacturers' logos or *labels* can be added to a 3D model of the product.

In this section we will consider how two-dimensional pictures are attached to a polygonal 3D model. Figure 4.31 shows a simple rectangular polygon mapped with a small picture applied in several useful ways and we shall consider these later.

The expressions needed to determine the color s at a point, $\mathbf{p}$, within a triangular polygon due to the application of an image map are analogous to those we obtained when considering a procedural texture applied in surface mode. If the vertices of a triangular polygon are $\mathbf{P}_0$, $\mathbf{P}_1$ and $\mathbf{P}_2$, then s, the color to be substituted into the lighting model, is determined by executing the following steps:

1. Use the coordinates of the vertices of the surface polygon relative to $\mathbf{p}$ to determine parameters α and β, where:

$$(\mathbf{p} - \mathbf{P}_0) = \alpha(\mathbf{P}_1 - \mathbf{P}_0) + \beta(\mathbf{P}_2 - \mathbf{P}_0) \tag{4.5}$$

   Section 2.11.1 explains the necessary analysis.

2. Given texture coordinates of (X_0, Y_0), (X_1, Y_1) and (X_2, Y_2) at $\mathbf{P}_0$, $\mathbf{P}_1$ and $\mathbf{P}_2$, respectively, a texture coordinate for the point $\mathbf{p}$, say (X, Y), is determined by:

$$X = X_0 + \alpha(X_1 - X_0) + \beta(X_2 - X_0) \tag{4.6}$$
$$Y = Y_0 + \alpha(Y_1 - Y_0) + \beta(Y_2 - Y_0) \tag{4.7}$$

3. From (X, Y) an index (i, j) into an array of pixels $A_{n,m}$ which record an image of resolution $n \times m$ is determined as follows:

$$i \;=\; \text{nearest integer to } (nX)$$
$$j \;=\; \text{nearest integer to } (mY)$$

4. Copy the pixel color from $A_{i,j}$ to s. How the information in A is stored and addressed is a matter of personal choice as is whether the image is true color (16.7 million colors), hicolor (65536 colors) or paletted (one byte used to address a palette of 256 colors).

Figure 4.30 illustrates the mapping process.

There are two important issues that arise in step 3 above. First to obtain a valid address in A both i and j must satisfy simultaneously $0 \le i < n$ and $0 \le j < m$ or, equivalently, by scaling to a unit square: $0 \le X < 1$ and $0 \le Y < 1$. Thus the question arises as to how to interpret texture coordinates that fall outside the range $[0, 1]$. There are three possibilities all of which prove useful. They are:

1. Do not proceed with the mapping process for any point with texture coordinates that fall outside the range $[0, 1]$; just apply a constant color.

2. Use a modulus function to *tile* the image over the surface so that it is repeated as many times as necessary to cover the whole surface.

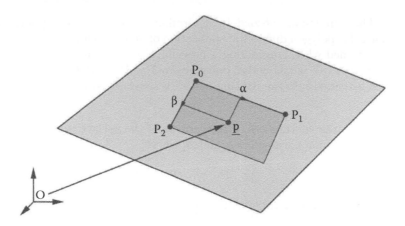

Figure 4.30: Mapping an image into a rectangle with texture coordinates of $(0,0)$ at $\mathbf{P}_0$, $(1,0)$ at $\mathbf{P}_1$ and $(0,1)$ at $\mathbf{P}_2$. At the point $\mathbf{p}$ an appropriate pixel color is determined from the image using the steps given in the text.

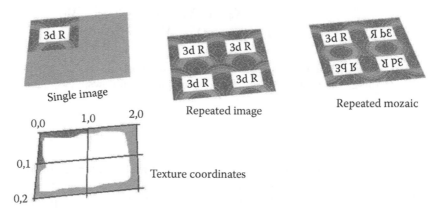

Figure 4.31: Different ways of interpreting mapping coordinates over a flat surface. (a) No mapping outside unit rectangle. (b) Tiling by repeatedly copying the image map. (c) Mosaic tiling. In this case the image map is carefully arranged so that no discontinuous edges are visible when the map is tiled.

3. Tile the image over the surface but choose a group of four copies of the image to generate blocks that themselves repeat without any seams, i.e., a mosaic pattern. To generate a mosaic pattern the α and β values in equation 4.6 and 4.7 are modified to α_m and β_m (a procedure described in the algorithm of listing 4.13).

These three methods of applying an image map to a polygon's surface are illustrated in figure 4.31.

the Floor function is given in figure 4.11

$\alpha_m = (\text{float}) Floor(\alpha)$

$\beta_m = (\text{float}) Floor(\beta)$

$b_x = ((\text{truncate } \alpha_m)(\text{bitwise AND}) \ 1)$

$b_y = ((\text{truncate } \beta_m)(\text{bitwise AND}) \ 1)$

$\alpha_m = \alpha - \alpha_m$

$\beta_m = \beta - \beta_m$

```
if  bx ≠ 0  {
    if  by ≠ 0  {
        αm = 1 − αm
        βm = 1 − βm
    }
    else  {
        αm = 1 − αm
    }
}
else  if  by ≠ 0  {
    βm = 1 − βm
}
```

Listing 4.13: Generating a mosaic repeat pattern for seamless image mapping.

The second issue is the rather discontinuous way of rounding the floating point texture coordinates (X, Y) to the integer address (i, j) ($i = \text{truncate}(x)$ and $j = \text{truncate}(y)$) used to pick the color from the image. A better approach is to use a bilinear (or higher order) interpolation to obtain s which takes into account not only the color in pixel (i, j) but also the color in the pixels adjacent to it. Thus, if the texture coordinates at **p** are (X, Y) we obtain s by using color values from $A_{i-1,j}$, $A_{i+1,j}$, $A_{i,j-1}$ and $A_{i,j+1}$ in addition to the color from $A_{i,j}$. The procedure for this is given in listing 4.14.

Notes:

1. Bilinear interpolation gives good results when the image map is being magnified but not in cases where the image is being reduced in size, as the object being mapped moves away from the camera for example.

2. We have **not** discussed how the vertices are assigned texture coordinates. This topic is covered in chapter 10, section 10.11.

3. The determination of α and β in equation 4.5 is done in three dimensions. Other approaches to texture mapping (as would be done in a hardware rasterizer for example) will implement the interpolation after projection onto the viewing plane. In those circumstances the use of a linear interpolation to obtain the texture look-up coordinates is incorrect and another approach such as perspective-correct barycentric interpolation [54] would need to be used.

$$\delta X = X - \text{float} (i)$$
$$\delta Y = Y - \text{float}(j)$$
if $\delta X > \frac{1}{2}$ {
$\quad \delta X = \delta X - \frac{1}{2}$
$\quad$ **if** $\delta Y > \frac{1}{2}$ {
$\quad\quad \delta Y = \delta Y - \frac{1}{2}$
$\quad\quad s = A_{i,j}(A_{i+i,j} - A_{i,j})\delta X + (A_{i,j-1} - A_{i,j})\delta Y$
$\quad$ }
$\quad$ **else** {
$\quad\quad \delta Y = \frac{1}{2} - \delta Y$
$\quad\quad s = A_{i,j}(A_{i+i,j} - A_{i,j})\delta X + (A_{i,j+1} - A_{i,j})\delta Y$
$\quad$ }
}
else {
$\quad \delta X = \frac{1}{2} - \delta X$
$\quad$ **if** $\delta Y > \frac{1}{2}$ {
$\quad\quad \delta Y = \delta Y - \frac{1}{2}$
$\quad\quad s = A_{i,j}(A_{i-i,j} - A_{i,j})\delta X + (A_{i,j-1} - A_{i,j})\delta Y$
$\quad$ }
$\quad$ **else** {
$\quad\quad \delta Y = \frac{1}{2} - \delta Y$
$\quad\quad s = A_{i,j}(A_{i-i,j} - A_{i,j})\delta X + (A_{i,j+1} - A_{i,j})\delta Y$
$\quad$ }
}

Listing 4.14: Bilinear interpolation to calculate a color value, s, at texture coordinate (X,Y) from an image with color recorded in the pixel array A which has dimension $n \times m$.

4.6.1 Transparency mapping

Transparency mapping follows the same steps as basic image mapping to deliver a color value, s, for use at a point $\mathbf{p}$ on polygon k. However instead of using s directly as a surface color it is used to control a mixture between the color settings for polygon k and a color derived from the next surface recorded in the transparency buffer. (Remember that the Z buffer algorithm can be modified to hold several layers so that if any of them were transparent the underlying surface would show through.) Note that when mixing the proportion of s due to the underlying surface **no** lighting effects are applied. That is, when you look through a window from inside a room it is not the light in the room that governs the brightness of the world outside. Figure 4.32 illustrates the use of a combination of two maps applied to a simple quadrilateral polygon. Incidentally, painting trees on glass is a very useful trick for decorating animated tours of architectural fantasies!

Figure 4.32: An image of a model with just 11 rectangular polygons (some obscured). Ten of them have both a standard image map and a transparency map applied. The polygon representing the ground is made rough by applying a *bumpy* procedural texture.

4.6.2   Bump mapping

Bump mapping, introduced by Blinn [11], uses the color from an image map to modulate the direction of the surface normal vector. Again there is a similarity with those procedural textures that cause the surface normal vectors to tilt away from the direction determined by the Phong shading model. For example this technique can be used to produce the appearance of embossed text. Many animators use a sequence of bump maps to give the illusion of waves on the surface of a lake or the sea although such surfaces are probably more realistically simulated by the *noise* type procedural texture of Perlin [69].

To implement a bump map it is the change in color from one pixel to another which determines the displacement vector that is added to the surface normal of polygon k at point $\mathbf{p}$. Most of the analysis we need in order to calculate the perturbing vector, $\mathbf{\Delta n}$, has been covered already. Bump mapping usually uses the same texture coordinates as are used for basic image mapping. In fact it is essential to do so in cases where an image and bump map are part of the same material; for example a brick surface can look very good with a bump map used to simulate the effect of differential weathering on brick and mortar.

To determine $\boldsymbol{\Delta}\mathbf{n}$ we need to find incremental vectors parallel to two of the sides of polygon k, call them $\boldsymbol{\Delta}\mathbf{n}_1$ and $\boldsymbol{\Delta}\mathbf{n}_2$. Do this by first finding texture coordinates at points close to $\mathbf{p}$ (at $\mathbf{p}$ the texture coordinates are (X, Y) given by equations 4.6 and 4.7). The easiest way to do this is to make small increments, say δ_α and δ_β, in α and β and use equations (4.6) and (4.7) to obtain texture coordinates (X_r, Y_r) and (X_b, Y_b).

Before using the texture coordinates to obtain "bump" values from the map it is necessary to ensure that the distance *in texture space* between (X, Y) and (X_r, Y_r) and between (X, Y) and (X_b, Y_b) is small. To achieve this write:

$$
\begin{aligned}
\Delta_t &= \sqrt{(X_r - X)^2 + (Y_r - Y)^2} \\
X_r &= X + \delta\frac{(X_r - X)}{\Delta_t} \\
Y_r &= Y + \delta\frac{(Y_r - Y)}{\Delta_t}
\end{aligned}
$$

and do the same thing to (X_b, Y_b). These equations include an additional scaling factor δ that will be discussed shortly. The next step is to obtain values from the *bump* image at texture coordinates (X, Y), (X_r, Y_r) and (X_b, Y_b). Using the bilinear interpolation algorithm given in Figure 4.14 three *bump* values s_0, s_1 and s_2, are obtained. It only remains to construct $\boldsymbol{\Delta}\mathbf{n}$ and add it to the normal, $\hat{\mathbf{n}}$, for polygon k. Thus:

$$
\begin{aligned}
\mathbf{d}_1 &= (\mathbf{P}_1 - \mathbf{P}_0) \\
\mathbf{d}_2 &= (\mathbf{P}_2 - \mathbf{P}_0) \\
\boldsymbol{\Delta}\mathbf{n}_1 &= (s_1 - s_0)\left(\frac{\mathbf{d}_1}{|\mathbf{d}_1|}\right) \\
\boldsymbol{\Delta}\mathbf{n}_2 &= (s_2 - s_0)\left(\frac{\mathbf{d}_2}{|\mathbf{d}_2|}\right) \\
\mathbf{n} &= \mathbf{n} + h(\boldsymbol{\Delta}\mathbf{n}_1 + \boldsymbol{\Delta}\mathbf{n}_2) \\
\hat{\mathbf{n}} &= \mathbf{n}/|\mathbf{n}|
\end{aligned}
$$

h is a parameter that facilitates control of the apparent height of the bumps. Its range should be $[0, 1]$.

The choice of δ, δ_α and δ_β will determine how well the algorithm performs. They should be chosen so that they are small relative to the texture coordinate range across the polygon.

4.6.3 Reflection mapping

True reflections can only be simulated with ray tracing or other time-consuming techniques but for quite a lot of uses a *reflection map* can visually satisfy all the requirements. Surfaces made from gold, silver, chrome and even the shiny paint work on a new automobile can all be realistically simulated with a skillfully created reflection map, a technique introduced by Blinn and Newell [10].

An outline of a reflection map algorithm is:

1. With the knowledge that polygon k, at point $\mathbf{p}$, is visible in pixel (i, j) determine the reflection direction $\mathbf{d}$ of a line from the viewpoint to $\mathbf{p}$. (Use the procedure given in section 2.9.)

2. Because step 3 of the basic rendering algorithm transformed the scene so that the observer is based at the origin $(0, 0, 0)$ and is looking in direction $(1, 0, 0)$ the reflected direction $\mathbf{d}$ must be transformed with the inverse of the rotational part of the viewing transformation. The necessary inverse transformation can be calculated at the same time as the viewing transformation.

   Note: The inverse transformation must not include any translational component because $\mathbf{d}$ is a direction vector.

3. Get the Euler angles that define the direction of $\mathbf{d}$. These are the heading ϕ which lies in the range $[-\pi, \pi]$ and pitch θ which lies in the range $[\frac{-\pi}{2}, \frac{\pi}{2}]$. Scale the range of ϕ to cover the width, X_{max}, of the reflection image. Scale the range of θ to cover the height, Y_{max}, of the reflection image.

$$X = \frac{(\pi + \phi)}{2\pi} X_{max}$$
$$Y = \frac{(\frac{\pi}{2} - \theta)}{\pi} Y_{max}$$

4. Use the bilinear interpolation algorithm of figure 4.14 to obtain a color value s from the image in the vicinity of (X, Y).

5. Mix s with the other sources contributing to the color seen at pixel (i, j).

You can think of the reflection mapping process as one where the reflected surface is located at the center of a hollow sphere with the image map painted on its inside. Figure 4.33 illustrates the relationship of object to reflection map. Another reflection mapping procedure that gives good results is the cubic environment due to Greene [35].

When procedural textures, pseudo shadows and reflection maps are added to the Phong shaded rendering of Figure 4.21 a highly realistic looking image (for example, figure 4.34) can be generated without having to pay the very heavy time penalty that ray traced rendering procedures impose.

4.6.4   Mip-mapping

Imagine a tiled floor that extends into the far distance with the textured appearance being the result of applying an image map, something like that shown

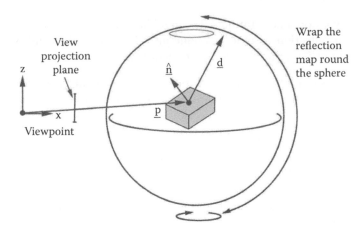

Figure 4.33: A reflection map can be thought of as an image painted on the inside of hollow sphere with the reflective model placed at its center.

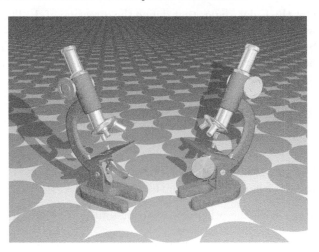

Figure 4.34: Final image of models first shown in figure 4.3 now using a pseudo shadow, procedural texture and reflection map.

in figure 4.35(a). Rendering two adjacent pixels near the bottom of the image where the viewing vector intersects the floor close to the camera will most likely result in a texture look-up that results in the same color value being obtained. Rendering two adjacent pixels near the top of the image where the viewing vector intersects the floor at a great distance from the viewpoint could result in the texture look up returning very different color values. The result of this is that an unpleasant moiré pattern because the image map sampling is subject to aliasing effects and the integrating effect of the imperfect natural vision processes is not present in the basic mathematical imaging model.

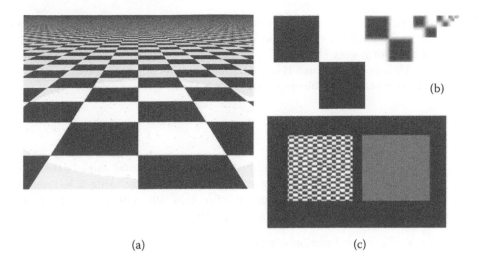

(a)						(c)

Figure 4.35: (a) A checkerboard texture mapped on a plane viewed from an oblique angle. (b) A mip-map that would be suitable to use for the checker texture in (a). (c) Two polygons located at a far distance from the camera, one using the original texture and the other using the mip-map.

However, it is possible to modify the texture look-up process in a way that mitigates seeing the aliasing errors. This process is known as *mip-mapping*. In mip-mapping the original texture map is augmented by making filtered versions of the original image drawn at smaller and smaller resolutions, where each copy has the appearance of being viewed from farther and farther away. Making mip-maps puts control of how a textured surface changes as it moved away from the observer back in the hands of the artist. For example, a black/white checker texture applied to a wall in the far distance will probably just look blandly gray, rather than an unpleasant and high contrast moiré patter.

Which level of the mip-map to use is determined by using the depth z (distance) to the point on the surface that is to be mapped. When a texture map value is needed, the two levels in the mip-map that bracket z, that is $[zm_i, zm_{i+1}]$ are accessed. The color values found in each of the bracketing levels are blended together in the ratio of z to the the interval $[zm_i, zm_{i+1}]$. Figure 4.35(b) shows a mip-map that would be a suitable candidate for a checkerboard texture. It is usual to make the top level image in a mip-map a square with the dimension of 2^n, and each sub-level a dimension of one quarter the size of the level above it. This allows the mip-map to be packed into an image that is only twice the size of the original and allows the lookup software to work with the appropriate levels without too much extra computation. In figure 4.35(c) the effect of using the mip-map is evident. Two polygons (enlarged) are placed far away from the camera and tiled with the image map. On the left the original image is sampled resulting in a high contract pattern with obvious misalignment of the checks. On the right the lowest resolution bitmap, a 1×1 pixel image, is sampled, resulting in a uniform gray shading.

Akenine-Mōller and Haines [1] discuss the mip-map process in detail and consider other possible application algorithms.

4.7   Perlin noise

Most of the rich and beautiful procedural textures and shaders that arise from the theory of fractals [67] are created in practice by using a self similar *noise* generator, often called a Perlin noise function [69], named after its creator. This noise function has the following properties:

- The noise function is **not** totally random (i.e., white noise).

- It must not have frequency components that exceed the sampling frequency.

- It should be reproducible (in the sense of animation.)

- It should be spatially invariant, and periodic (in that it can be used to cover an arbitrary volume of space without exhibiting any edge discontinuities.)

- It should be quick to calculate.

The Perlin noise function (and many other variants) builds on the idea of a space filling integer lattice. When a noise value needs to be calculated at any 3D point (x, y, z) the eight neighboring lattice points are identified as (ix, iy, iz), $(ix + 1, iy, iz)$, $(ix, iy + 1, iz)$ etc. Values of some *quantity* computed at these lattice points are then interpolated throughout the cell to give a noise value at (x, y, z).

The Perlin noise is constructed by generating a smooth function that has the value zero at the integer lattice points and has a given derivative (or gradient) value at the same integer lattice points. This derivative takes the form of a specified 3D gradient vector at each lattice point. The overall function can be called on in computer code simply as:

```
n=(float)Noise(float x, float y, float z);
```

which takes the position (x, y, z) as input arguments and returns a noise value in the range 0 to 1.

4.7.1   The algorithm

It is not possible to store gradients for all possible coordinate points (x, y, z), so one uses a hash function to identify which gradient vector to use at a particular cell corner when calculating the noise value. Thus, a hashed value is

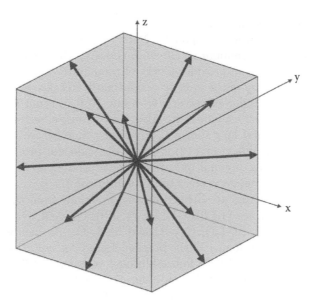

Figure 4.36: The Perlin noise vectors. The 12 vectors are each directed from the center of the cell toward the mid-points of the cubic cell edges.

used to look up gradient vectors from a manageably sized table. The algorithm first calculates the integer coordinates of the base corner of the cell containing (x, y, z), i.e., ix=(**int**)x; iy=(**int**)y; iz=(**int**)z. This cubic cell lies between ix and ix+1, and iy and iy+1, and iz and iz+1. Thus, the coordinate for which the noise value is to be calculated has an offset from the base corner of dx=x−ix; dy=y−iy; dz=z−iz.

Using ix, iy, iz and dx,dy,dz, the eight weight values are computed, one for each corner of the cell. Then trilinear interpolation is used to determine a noise value at (x, y, z). A corner's weight is calculated by randomly selecting a special *gradient* vector and taking its scalar product with the fractional vector, from (dx, dy, dz), to that corner. This may seem a very simple algorithm but its implementation is ingenious and the results of its use speak for themselves.

4.7.2 Defining the gradient vector candidates

Perlin chose 12 possible vectors from which 8 are pseudo-randomly selected, one for each corner of the cell containing (x, y, z). The directions of the candidate vectors are shown in figure 4.36.

To allow for a quick selection, the list of 12 vectors is augmented by duplicating 4 of the vectors, giving a total of 16 candidate gradient vectors. (Doing this will allow us to select a vector by using the low order 4 bits of a random number to identify one of the 16 possibilities.) The key to removing directional bias in the gradients is to skew the set of gradient directions away from the co-ordinate axes and long diagonals. Note: It is not necessary for the direction of the vectors to be random at all, since choosing the 8 corner vectors at random and combining them provides plenty of randomness.

If we allow any of the x, y, or z coordinates to take values of either 0, 1 or -1 we can make 27 different vectors. Of course $(0,0,0)$ is not a well formed direction vector, so we must exclude that. Also, if we choose a vector so that: (1) it avoids the main axis and long diagonal directions, thereby avoiding the possibility of axis-aligned clumping, and (2) it allows the eight dot products to be carried out without requiring any multiplications (thus speeding up the calculations), we are left with 12 candidate vectors from the original 27.

These 12 vectors are defined by the directions from the center of a cube to its edges. They are (1,1,0), (-1,1,0), (1,-1,0), (-1,-1,0), (1,0,1), (-1,0,1), (1,0,-1), (-1,0,-1), (0,1,1), (0,-1,1), (0,1,-1) and (0,-1,-1). As mentioned before, to help increase the performance of the process of *gradient vector selection*, the list of 12 vectors is augmented with four additional vectors: (1,1,0), (-1,1,0), (0,-1,1) and (0,-1,-1). These additional vectors form a regular tetrahedron, so adding them redundantly introduces no visual bias in the texture.

4.7.3   Selecting the gradient vectors

At each cell corner we need to pick randomly one of the gradient vectors (from the list of 16) and form the scalar product of it with the vector from that corner to the point at which we wish to calculate the noise value. For example for corner (ix, iy, iz) the vector product must be formed with (dx, dy, dz). Remember that the randomness must be reproducible, but we can achieve this and make the selection process very fast if we pre-build a table of random associations between the (ix, iy, iz) cell corner positions and gradient vectors. The table will typically have 256 entries. Each entry corresponds to a different combination of the 8 cell corners identifiers. The entry to be selected from the table is chosen by passing the cell corner coordinates (ix, iy, iz) through a hash function (modulo 256.)

4.7.4   Hashing

If the table of pre-computed random numbers contains N (where N is a power of 2) entries, then any ix, iy, and iz values can be mapped into a value between 0 and $N - 1$ by using: ix   mod (N) etc. This is accomplished very rapidly by using the C/C++ & operator, i.e., ix = ix & (N−1). The result is a mapping of any ix into an integer in the range 0 to $N - 1$.

A random selection that still ensures that all cases have a possibility of being selected can be made by: begin with a look-up table populated with the numbers in sequence 0, 1, 2, 3, ..., 254, 255 then shuffle the sequence randomly. The final table might look like this:

```
Ntab[]={95,42,81,  ... 251,255,11 }  ;
```

To choose a random vector for integer coordinate ix we simply look up the table k=Ntab[ix mod (N−1)] and use vector k from the list. (As there are only 16 vectors in the table the actual vector used is k&15.)

To choose one of the vectors based on three lattice corner coordinates, we can still use a single table by repetition of the look-up three times in succession, as in:

$$id = Ntab[Ntab[Ntab[ix] + iy] + iz];$$

This hash function is chosen because it returns results that are more irregular than id=Ntab[ix+iy+iz];, for example.

Note that Ntab has 256 entries whose values lie in the range 0 to 255, so the sum Ntab[ix] + iy could produce a value in the range 0 to 511, which would lie outside the table. However, if the size of the table is doubled, by appending a copy, then the lookup will function perfectly and the result of looking up a value for (ix, iy, iz) will be a random integer in the range 0 to 255.

4.7.5 Calculating the gradient vector and corner weights

The corner weights are obtained for each corner in turn. A cell corner weight is obtained by calculating the dot product of one of the randomly selected gradient vectors with the vector from that corner to (dx, dy, dz). For example at cell corner $(ix + 1, Iy + 1, iz + 1)$ the dot product is formed between the gradient vector and $(dx - 1, dy - 1, dz - 1)$.

The random gradient vector look-up and the scalar product calculation can be done very efficiently in C program code, for example in the function grad (...):

```
(float)grad(int ix, int iy, int iz,
            float dx, float dy, float dz){
  int id;
  float u,v,grad;
  id=Ntab[Ntab[Ntab[ix&(N−1)]+iy&(N 1)]+iz&(N−1)];// Hash
  // Modulo 16 divide by mask off the low order 4 bits.
  id = id & 15;
  if(id < 8 || id == 12 || id == 13)u=dx; else u=dy;
  if(id < 4 || id == 12 || id == 13)v=dy; else v=dz;
  if(id&1)u = −u;
  if(id&2)v = −v;
  grad = u + v;
  return grad;
}
```

Note that we have been very careful to define all our gradient vectors so that they have the property that any two of their elements will have either the value −1, or +1, and that the third element will always have the value 0. With this property the gradient calculation can be done without doing any multiplication.

The function begins by hashing the integer coordinate (ix, iy, iz) and looking up a random vector identifier in the range 0 to 255. It then selects one of the

16 gradient vectors by extracting and using the four low order bits in the vector identifier *id*.

Since the values of dx, dy and dz all lie in the range $[0, 1]$ and the cell size is unity, the output of the grad function could lie in the range $[-2, 2]$. This function is applied at the 8 corners of the cell giving rise to 8 gradient values:

```
g000 = grad(ix  ,iy  ,iz  ,        dx  ,dy  ,dz  );
g100 = grad(ix+1,iy  ,iz  ,        dx−1,dy  ,dz  );
g010 = grad(ix  ,iy+1,iz  ,        dx  ,dy−1,dz  );
g110 = grad(ix+1,iy+1,iz  ,        dx−1,dy−1,dz  );
g001 = grad(ix  ,iy  ,iz+1,        dx  ,dy  ,dz−1);
g101 = grad(ix+1,iy  ,iz+1,        dx−1,dy  ,dz−1);
g011 = grad(ix  ,iy+1,iz+1,        dx  ,dy−1,dz−1);
g111 = grad(ix+1,iy+1,iz+1,        dx−1,dy−1,dz−1);
```

4.7.6 Interpolation

After calculating the gradient values at the cell corners we need to interpolate them in order to get the noise value at (x, y, z) (i.e., the point offset by (dx, dy, dz) from (ix, iy, iz)). However, using linear interpolation among the g000, g100, ... etc. values does not give us a very smooth function, nor does it guarantee that the noise function has continuous first and second derivatives as (x, y, z) moves from one cell into another.

If we pass (dx, dy, dz) through a polynomial function first, we will generate a smooth variation in the noise value and endow it with the properties of continuous first and second derivatives. The polynomial function:

$$f(t) = 6t^5 - 15t^4 + 10t^3$$

(with t in the range $[01]$) satisfies the requirement.

Thus, the interpolation uses the values (wx, wy, wz) at each corner of the cell, where $wx = f(dx)$, $wy = f(dy)$ and $wz = f(dz)$ and each wx, wy, wz lie in the range $[0, 1]$. Consequently, given gradient values g000, g100, etc., we calculate the final value using trilinear interpolation as follows:

```
(float)linInt((float)v, (float)a, (float)b)){
  //perform the linear interpolation:
  return   v*a + (1−v)*b;
}
  ..
x00 = linInt(wx,g000,g100);
x10 = linInt(wx,g010,g110);
x01 = linInt(wx,g001,g101);
x11 = linInt(wx,g011,g111);
y0  = linInt(wy,x00,x10);
y1  =  linInt(wy,x01,x11);
Np  = linInt(wz,y0,y1);
  ..
```

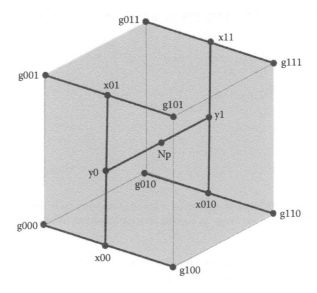

Figure 4.37: The final noise value is obtained by trilinear interpolation between the gradient values obtained at each corner of the cube.

The resulting variable Np is the final value for the Perlin noise at point (x,y,z). Figure 4.37 illustrates the intermediate values in the trilinear interpolation.

This very clever algorithm lies at heart of some of the most beautiful textures and effects that have been seen in CGI images, movies and computer games.

4.8   Pseudo shadows

Shadows are perhaps the most important consequence of lighting that an observer uses when looking at photographs to assess the relative positions of objects. For example, figure 4.38 shows a simple scene with a twisted ribbon that is located somewhere above a flat plane extending to infinity in all directions, *what we might call a ground plane*. If you were asked: How close to the ground is the ribbon? How would you decide from this two-dimensional picture? From the image on the left it's hard to tell, but add the shadow as shown on the right and you can easily tell that the ribbon is located well above the ground. You can also work out the relative position of the light. Unfortunately the calculations that allow perfect shadows to be determined are amongst the most time consuming a renderer can be called upon to execute. Techniques such as "ray tracing" need to be used to determine perfect shadows. This will be considered separately in chapter 5. However, shadows are so important that much faster, but *approximate*, methods have been developed to render shadows. It is these *pseudo* shadow techniques

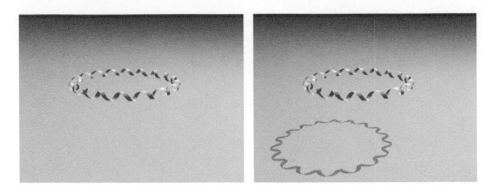

Figure 4.38: Adding shadows to a computer-generated image gives the viewer some very powerful visual clues as to the relative position of objects in a scene.

that will be discussed in this section. The shadow shown in figure 4.38 was generated with just such a technique.

We will consider two approaches to pseudo shadowing which cover most eventualities. They are planar shadows and shadow maps.

4.8.1 Planar shadows

If the surface on which the shadow falls is flat then it is straightforward to find the shadow cast by a polygon. Once found the shadow is projected to the viewing plane where a buffer analogous to the Z buffer is used to hold a *shadow mask*. Because shadows are either on or off, a one byte per pixel mask can accommodate up to 8 different planar shadowed surfaces.

The contents of the shadow mask must be determined in a step that precedes step 5 in the basic rendering algorithms (section 4.1.1). In the final rendering step, as the Z or scanline buffers are being filled at pixel i, j, the following test is added:

> If the point **p** on polygon k is visible in pixel i, j and polygon k is part of one of the planes that has a shadow on it then the shadow buffer at coordinate i, j is checked to see if polygon k is in shadow or not. If it is then the color of pixel i, j is dimmed.

Figure 4.39 illustrates the geometry used to produce a shadow mask for the shadow cast on a plane (normal $\hat{n}$ position $\mathbf{P}_p$) by a triangular polygon (vertices $\mathbf{P}_0$, $\mathbf{P}_1$ and $\mathbf{P}_2$) lit from a point light source at $\mathbf{P}_l$.

In the shadow buffer the shadow cast by a triangular polygon is always triangular too. If we let (X_0, Y_0), (X_1, Y_1) and (X_2, Y_2) be the coordinates in the shadow buffer equivalent to vertices $\mathbf{P}_0$ etc., we can use a scanline filling procedure to set all the appropriate flags in the shadow buffer. To calculate the coordinates (X_0, Y_0) in the shadow buffer equivalent to vertex $\mathbf{P}_0$ in the polygon

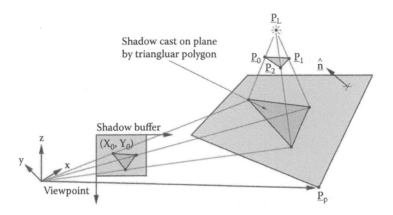

Figure 4.39: Filling the shadow mask with the shadow cast on a flat plane by a triangular polygon.

casting the shadow, first obtain the intersection point of the line passing through $\mathbf{P}_l$ and $\mathbf{P}_0$ and the plane $(\mathbf{p} - \mathbf{P}_p) \cdot \hat{\mathbf{n}} = 0$. Then project that point to (X_0, Y_0) with the same scale factor and aspect ratio used in step 4 of the basic rendering algorithm. Those calculations are detailed in sections 2.6 and 2.12.8.

Planar shadows have sharply defined edges and are essentially perfect, which sometimes is an advantage but at other times may lead to less realistic results. The amount of memory required to hold the shadow buffer is not particularly excessive and depends on the resolution of the output raster. The disadvantage of planar shadows is that they cannot simulate realistic shadows falling on curved or non-planar surfaces. Shadow mapped lights, which we will consider next, do give pretty good looking shadows across any shape of surface.

4.8.2   Shadow maps

Look at figure 4.40. It shows a viewpoint (with associated projection plane) and spotlight directed toward the point $\mathbf{p}$ in the scene. The viewpoint is located at the origin of coordinates and the spotlight is at $\mathbf{P}_L$. Imagine now a viewpoint at the position of the light source $\mathbf{P}_L$ which is looking in the direction of the spotlight, toward the target at $\mathbf{p}$. For a field of view that just encloses the spotlight's cone a projection plane capable of showing everything visible from the light's point of view can be defined. We can use a Z depth buffer associated with this imaginary projection plane to help us render a shadow due to the spotlight. This technique requires us to *pre-render* a view of the scene for each spotlight and fill its *shadow* Z buffer, or what we will call its *shadow map*, as in the standard Z buffer algorithm.

During rendering of the scene when it comes time to determine if a point $\mathbf{p}$ lies in shadow or not, we imagine a line from $\mathbf{p}$ to $\mathbf{P}_L$; it must pass through

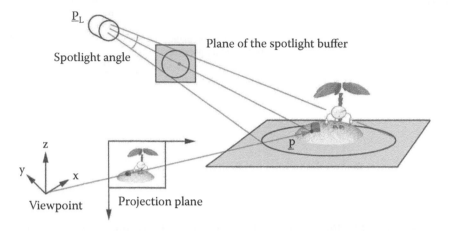

Figure 4.40: A scene with spotlight illumination.

one of the cells in the shadow map associated with the imaginary viewpoint at $\mathbf{P}_L$. That cell records the distance of the nearest point in the scene from the imaginary camera (and spotlight), say d_{min}.

Here then is our test to see if $\mathbf{p}$ lies in shadow: if the distance from $\mathbf{p}$ to $\mathbf{P}_L$ is greater that d_{min} then point $\mathbf{p}$ lies in shadow.

This procedure works because the spotlight shines on a limited area, and so its cone of illumination is bounded and therefore the pseudo camera's field of view can be set to include all parts of the scene illuminated by the spotlight. Because the light's shadow map is of finite resolution the outline of the shadow will be subject to aliasing effects. The more memory allocated to hold the shadow map or the narrower the angle of the spotlight cone the less noticeable the aliasing will be. To reduce the visual impact of the aliasing at the edges of the shadow a degree of blurring can be introduced by averaging shadow values over a number of adjacent cells. This will cause the shadow to have a soft (blurry) edge but that is sometimes more realistic than the harsh crisp shadows produced by the shadow plane approximation.

To implement this technique the instructions in listing 4.15 are inserted in the rendering algorithm after the viewing transformation has been performed. Note that the viewing transformation has been applied to the lights too.

For the scene illustrated in figure 4.40 where the spotlight direction is given by the vector $\mathbf{d} = \mathbf{p} - \mathbf{P}_L$, i.e., a heading of:

$$\phi = ATAN2(d_y, d_x)$$

and pitch:

$$\theta = ATAN2(d_z, \sqrt{d_x^2 + d_y^2})$$

```
Repeat for all spotlights  {
    Build a viewing transformation, [T] for an imaginary camera located at the
    position of the spotlight. Apply [T] to vertices in scene.
    Repeat for all polygons k  {
        Project vertices of polygon k onto the shadow buffer
        plane and fill each entry with the depth to visible surface.
    }
}
```

Listing 4.15: Procedure to fill the shadow map associated with a spotlight.

are used. Transformation $[T]$ is the product $[T] = [T_3][T_2][T_1]$ where

$$[T_1] = \text{a translation by } -\mathbf{P}_L$$

$$[T_2] = \text{a rotation round } z \text{ axis (up) by } -\phi$$

$$[T_3] = \text{a rotation round } y \text{ axis by } -\theta$$

The projection is scaled so that the spotlight's outer cone (half angle θ_2) just fits inside the field of view. Thus, for a shadow buffer resolution of $n \times n$ and vertex coordinates (x', y', z'), after pre-multiplication by $[T]$, the shadow buffer coordinates (X, Y) are obtained from

$$d = \frac{n}{2 \tan \theta_2} \tag{4.8}$$

$$X = \frac{n}{2} - d\frac{y'}{x'} \tag{4.9}$$

$$Y = \frac{n}{2} - d\frac{z'}{x'} \tag{4.10}$$

The shadow map technique is completed by adding the following actions to the final rendering step after the surface color, shading and lighting at $\mathbf{p}$ have been determined; repeat them for all spotlights:

1. Apply transformation $[T]$ to $\mathbf{p}$ to give position (x', y', z'), in the frame of reference where the spotlight is at origin.

2. Apply the projection equations (4.8, 4.9, 4.10) to give (X, Y) and its nearest integer indices (X_i, Y_i).

3. Extract the shadow distance from the shadow map, $d_{min} = Z(X_i, Y_i)$.

4. If $x' > d_{min}$ then $\mathbf{p}$ is in shadow with respect to the spotlight.

Comment:

> While the above procedure works well in most cases it can be subject
> to some unpleasant moiré patterning. This is due to the fact that each
> cell in the shadow map equates to quite a big area in the scene and
> within which there might be a significant depth variation, especially
> when the resolution of the buffer is low. As a result of this when the
> time comes to compare the depth of point **p** with values in the buffer
> then sometimes it will appear to be in and sometimes it will appear
> to be out of shadow. It is very important to set near and far planes
> as close to each other as possible as this gives better precision in the
> shadow map and therefore yields better results.
>
> A simple procedure due to Woo [50] can eliminate the visual distur-
> bance. To apply it, a second (temporary) copy of the light shadow
> map is needed. In this second copy record the depth of the second
> closest polygon from the light and when the full shadow is rendered
> we simply average the depth between the two and use this as the
> shadow depth. In the case when there is only one surface (the sec-
> ond buffer holds infinity) then it cannot cast shadows on anything so
> ignore it. After each spotlight buffer has been checked the memory
> used for the temporary shadow map can be released. One final point:
> The shadow map only needs to be rebuilt in a non-static scene.

4.9   Line drawing

Before the days of the photographic quality printer and the proliferation of the
multi-monitor desktop computer most 3D drawing was presented in line-drawn
form. For 3D diagrams in a book or working drawings, or in an equipment
manual produced by a CAD package, the line-drawn form of a 3D scene or
object still has its uses. Indeed, an outline or (edge and major fold) drawing of
an object is an important component of many automatically generated cartoons.
By superimposing an outline drawing on a scene illuminated with ambient light
only, one has a very passable approximation to the beautiful hand drawn cartoons
generated by the skilled artist. Using a lighting model, like the Gooch shading,
can enhance the cartoon look by producing appropriate specular highlights, and
when combined with a hidden surface line drawing, cartoons can be produced on
an industrial scale without the need for an artist skilled in the art of perspective.
This section will briefly consider the production of line drawn 3D images.

4.9.1   Wireframe

The simplest way to visualize the numerical model for an object is to draw it
in wireframe. A wireframe drawing involves relatively few calculations to render

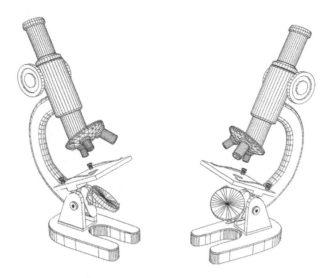

Figure 4.41: A wireframe drawing.

it. The action of step 5 in the rendering algorithm is simply to work through all the polygons that describe the model and taking each side in turn:

1. Check to see if it has been drawn already.

2. If not identify the vertices it is connected to.

3. Retrieve the screen coordinates determined in step 4 of the rendering algorithm.

4. Draw a line connecting these two points in the frame buffer.

If a list of edges in the model is available so much the better since there is no need to check whether or not the edge has been drawn before.

For a wireframe drawing, such as that shown in figure 4.41, to be recorded in the framebuffer or drawn on a raster display, a procedure for rendering lines is required. Both framebuffer and output display are composed of pixels, thus to draw a line from a to b, the pixels through which the line passes must be given an appropriate value to represent the color of the line.

The line drawing procedure should be fast and as simple as possible to implement. Perhaps the most commonly used procedure yet established is due to Bresenham [14] and we will consider this now for the case of a raster equivalent to a two-dimensional array of integer coordinates in the range $(0 \rightarrow X_{max})$ and $(0 \rightarrow Y_{max})$. The algorithm works incrementally from a starting point (x_1, y_1) and the first step is to identify in which one of 8 octants the direction of the end point lies. These octants are identified in figure 4.42. How the algorithm proceeds depends on which octant contains the end point of the line in question.

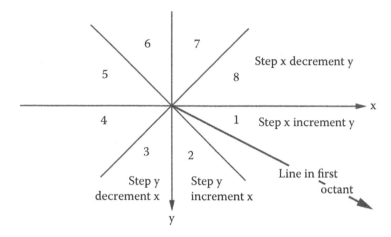

Figure 4.42: The Cartesian octants. Note that the positive y coordinate is downward. When drawing lines the center of the octants is taken to lie at the same place as the first point on the line. The illustrated line lies in the first octant.

A faster procedure reported by Wyvill [34] could be considered, if there are a huge number of lines to be drawn but since most *line* rendering is done by some library API and, for any 3D application the amount of time spent drawing lines is insignificant, Bresenham's procedure is sufficient for most purposes.

In the case of a line lying in the first octant, say between points (x_1, y_1) and (x_2, y_2), it is drawn by stepping one horizontal pixel at a time from x_1 to x_2 and at each step making the decision whether or not to step ± 1 pixel in the y direction. Since the gradient or slope of the line is $\Delta = \dfrac{y_2 - y_1}{x_2 - x_1}$ each horizontal increment will contribute a y displacement of Δ. Of course increments in y must be in integer steps (one pixel at a time) and since $\Delta \ll 1$ is a common occurrence it is usual to accumulate an error term δ that adds small changes at each step, i.e., $\delta = \delta + \Delta$. When $\delta = 1$ the current y coordinate is incremented by 1 while δ is reset to zero. The cycle continues until x_2 is reached.

This basic procedure can be optimized by reformulating the equations so that the calculation is done with integer arithmetic alone and by making comparisons with zero rather than unity. The enhanced procedure goes by the name of *the integer differential line generator* and an algorithm for it is presented in listing 4.16.

For lines in the first octant $y_{inc} = 1$ in the algorithm of figure 4.16. To draw a line in the second octant where $x_{inc} = 1$ the roles of x and y are reversed in figure 4.16, initially $\delta = -\Delta y/2$. The x coordinate is incremented and δ reduced by Δy at each step.

For a general line between any two points the drawing algorithm starts by making appropriate choices for x_{inc} and y_{inc}, if necessary $x_1 \leftrightarrow x_2$ or $y_1 \leftrightarrow y_2$

$\Delta x = x_2 - x_1$
$\Delta y = y_2 - y_1$
$\delta = -\Delta x/2$
set $x = x_1$ and $y = y_1$
draw pixel at (x, y) with color c
while $x < x_2$ **do** {
    $\delta = \delta + \Delta y$
    if $\delta \geq 0$ {
        $y = y + y_{inc}$
        $\delta = \delta - \Delta x$
    }
    $x = x + 1$
    draw pixel at (x, y) with color c
}

Listing 4.16: The basic integer differential line generator algorithm.

$\Delta x = x_2 - x_1$
$\Delta y = y_2 - y_1$
if $|\Delta x| > |\Delta y|$ {
    if $\Delta x < 0$ {
        swap $x_2 \leftrightarrow x_1$
        swap $y_2 \leftrightarrow y_1$
    }
    if $y_2 > y_1$ then $y_{inc} = 1$
    else $y_{inc} = -1$
    Call the first octant algorithm
}
else {
    if $\Delta y < 0$ {
        swap $x_2 \leftrightarrow x_1$
        swap $y_2 \leftrightarrow y_1$
    }
    if $x_2 > x_1$ then $x_{inc} = 1$
    else $x_{inc} = -1$
    Call the second octant algorithm
}

Listing 4.17: Algorithm for the drawing of an arbitrarily directed straight line in a raster display.

are swapped, and in the final step a call is made to first or second octant line drawing procedures. This algorithm is presented in listing 4.17.

As a final thought on wireframe drawing it is worth making the following brief comment: In drawing the wireframe on the projection plane it is assumed that

Figure 4.43: A hidden line drawing from a set of triangular polygons.

straight edges in 3D space project to give straight edges on the 2D projection plane. Fortunately this assumption is true.

4.9.2   Hidden line drawing

A hidden line drawing looks quite similar to a wireframe drawing except that the drawing has a look of some *solidity* about it. We achieve this by not drawing edges which are hidden behind polygons lying closer to the viewpoint. We might call this a kind of *hybrid* hidden line–hidden surface procedure. Hidden line drawings are very useful in CAD applications because it allows engineers to see something of the structure of their design as well as its appearance.

There are two procedures that can be used to generate an accurate hidden line drawing such as that shown in figure 4.43 and of course there are approximate procedures that are fast but can be confused by all but the simplest shapes. Quite a reasonable hidden line drawing of convex shapes can be achieved if a culling process to remove faces that cannot be seen is performed before all the edges of the remaining polygons are drawn as a wireframe. The two procedures we will consider are:

1. As a spin-off from the hidden surface Z buffer procedure.

2. Draw the edges in the scene where they are not obscured by any polygons (the visible edges procedure).

4.9.3   The hidden surface spin-off

This algorithm is summarized in the short algorithm of listing 4.18.

Use either the scanline or full Z buffer procedure to record at each pixel the identity of which polygon is visible.

Work though the raster in the order shown in figure 4.44 and check for a change of recorded value both above and to the left of the current pixel, pixels $i-1, j$ and $i, j-1$

If a difference is detected place a *foreground* color value in the framebuffer otherwise place a background color.

Listing 4.18: Rendering a hidden surface image as a "spin off" from the basic Z buffer procedure.

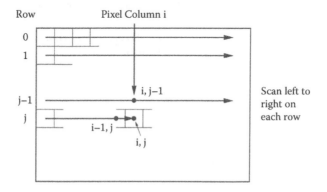

Figure 4.44: Working through a raster to produce a hidden line drawing.

Working from a Z buffer procedure has the big advantage that it accurately represents edges in a hidden line drawing which occur because polygons might intersect. These are edges that can't exist as entries in any polygon and/or edge list describing the scene. For example a drawing of a cylinder poking through a cube (figure 4.45) will have edges that are not part of any polygon in either the cube or the cylinder.

An interesting effect can be achieved with a hidden line drawing based on hidden surface procedures. It arises because adjacent polygonal faces with normal vectors pointing in the same direction are planar and in most situations little benefit is gained by drawing the common edge between adjacent co-planar faces: indeed a picture in which these are omitted can have a much cleaner look. (The drawing in figure 4.43 had a few such edges removed.) However edges between adjacent polygons should not be omitted if the polygons have different colors even if they are co-planar. This idea can be pushed to the limit by relaxing the planarity condition, $\mathbf{n}_1 \cdot \mathbf{n}_2 = 1$, say to: $\mathbf{n}_1 \cdot \mathbf{n}_2 > \theta$ with $\theta \approx \frac{1}{2}$. Doing this will lead to cartoon like drawings like that in figure 4.46 for example.

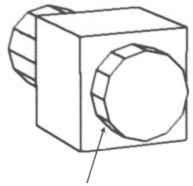

Edges are introduced where cylinder and cube
intersect. They are not in the polygon database

Figure 4.45: A hidden surface drawing showing edges that must be drawn but are not
part of the specification of the models in the drawing.

Figure 4.46: A hidden line drawing with edges drawn only if they are adjacent to the
background, a different model or another polygon such that (1) the color is different
or (2) the angle between them is $> 60°$.

4.9.4   A visible edge hidden line algorithm

Look at figure 4.47 which shows a wireframe drawing of a cube (with the top
removed so that we can see inside it). It has 6 polygons and 12 edges. The edges
labeled $1, 2, 3, 4, 6, 7, 10, 11, 12$ will be fully visible in a hidden line drawing. Edge
9 will be partially visible. To decide whether edge i is visible it has to be tested
against each of the polygons to see whether it lies behind any of them. However
it is not sufficient to treat edge visibility as simply either *visible* or *not visible*

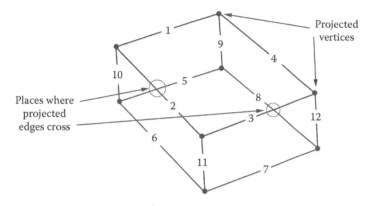

Figure 4.47: Wireframe cube labeling edges and crossovers.

for the whole edge because a case can arise where part of an edge will be visible and part will be obscured. So, before the visibility test can be made the edges must be broken up into appropriate segments.

To see how we can do this look again at figure 4.47, but this time think of it purely as a two-dimensional drawing. Anywhere that the lines cross is a potential site for one of the edges to change from being visible to hidden. These crossing points are the only places where the visibility status of an edge can change. Dividing the lines at these crossing points gives us the segments we need to test for visibility against the polygons in the model. For example, edge 11 will be composed of two segments because it is crossed by edge 5. After the edges have been divided into segments the segments can be tested to see if they are obscured by any polygons. If a segment is not obscured then it is drawn.

Most of the geometric calculations for this algorithm have been covered in chapter 2 and thus only the logical steps in the algorithm are summarized in listing 4.19.

As discussed previously this approach to hidden line drawing does not allow for edges that are introduced by the intersection of polygons. However because the output is a list of line segments the drawing can be made on an output device in any resolution, i.e., it is not subject to the aliasing effect (see section 4.3) that the hidden surface algorithms suffer from. Therefore, it is not necessary to render the picture again in order to work at a higher resolution. This form of output is ideal for recording in the device independent encapsulated postscript format. Another useful alternative procedure for the production of hidden line drawings was developed by Janssen [45].

In the 2D projection plane find the intersections of all projected
edges with all the other projected edges. For each edge make
a list of the segments it is divided into. (Including the coordinates
at the ends of the segments.)

With each line segment make the following tests to see if that segment is
visible, if it is then *draw it*.

Repeat for every projected edge i {
  Repeat for every segment j of edge i {

    Project back from the ends of segment j to the polygon of which
    edge i is a boundary. This gives a *depth* that can be
    associated with the line segment. Call these points $\mathbf{p}_1$
    and $\mathbf{p}_2$ and let their x coordinates be x_1 and
    x_2, which we will use as the depths.

    Repeat tests 1-3 below for every polygon k {
      Test 1:
      In projection: Test if segment j of edge i is inside polygon k.
      If it is not then move on to the next polygon
      Test 2:
      If x_1 and x_2 are both greater than the maximum x coordinate
       of vertices of polygon k then segment i is obscured so jump
      on to next segment.
      Test 3:
      Find the points $\mathbf{q}_1$ and $\mathbf{q}_2$ on polygon k where the
      lines from the viewpoint through $\mathbf{p}_1$ and $\mathbf{p}_2$
      intersect it.
      If the x coordinate of $\mathbf{q}_1 < x_1$ and the x coordinate
      of $\mathbf{q}_2 < x_2$ then segment i is obscured so jump on
      to the next segment.
    }
    If this point is reached then segment j of edge i is not obscured
     so draw it.

  }
}

Listing 4.19: The visual edges algorithm.

4.10 Tricks and tips

The *key* to fast rendering is smart algorithms but efficient programming can also help. Here are a few tricks and tips to speed up the code.

1. Try not to calculate the same things more than once, particularly if it is a time-consuming calculation. After calculation store it in a temporary variable. For example normalizing a vector is slow because it requires a reciprocal square root.

2. When rendering, try to calculate as much as possible on a per-polygon basis before proceeding to the rendering pass. A big scene may have 200,000 polygons and a medium sized anti-aliased image might have the equivalent of 9,000,000 pixels. (This is true for a software renderer; in a hardware pipeline there may be more pixel processors than vertex processors.)

3. When testing several things that will result in a calculation being avoided make the most common test first. See section 4.2.4.

4. Arrange nested loops so that complex calculations are as high in the nest as possible and therefore done as infrequently as possible.

5. Use inline code for short, very often used functions.

6. Sometimes it is more efficient to repeat code than to call a function. For example, in **C** or **C++** programs use macros to add, subtract, copy and take dot and cross products of vectors.

7. Where possible use look up tables. The Perlin noise functions are an excellent case in point. Another candidate is the replacement of the power function in the calculation of specular reflection.

5

Realistic visualization

To improve on the rendering approach described in chapter 4 the first technique that comes to mind is *ray tracing*. There are other techniques for generating high-quality synthetic images but they will not be discussed here. Ray tracing may be slow but it does give superb, almost photographic quality, images and better algorithms are being developed all the time, so that under certain conditions it is even possible to achieve real-time ray tracing. There are many books that describe the theory of ray tracing in detail. One of the most cited books that comprehensively examines the physics of the rendering process is *Physically Based Rendering From Theory to Implementation* [70]. Watt [88] in chapters 7 and 8 covers all the basics of ray tracing and in Glassner [33] the story is continued. Shirley [80] specializes in realistic ray tracing. A full description of a complete package is given by Lindley [56] and there are also quite a few good publicly available freeware and shareware ray tracing programs with code that can be retrieved from many FTP sites and open source repositories.

The idea on which ray tracing is based seems almost too simple to be true but suppose you could:

> *Follow the paths taken by particles of light (photons) on their journey from source, through the scene (as they are scattered back and forth between objects), and on until they are either captured by a camera or eye. Or head off to infinity.*

Then you would be simulating the physical mechanism that enables us to see and take photographs.

In practice this is a hopeless task because of the huge number of photons emitted by a light source and the fact that all but a minute fraction of them will ever be scattered into the camera. Therefore, ray tracing does it in *reverse*. It sends *feelers or rays* from the camera out into the scene. If the feeler rays find anything, they work back toward the sources of illumination and give us a path for the photons to follow from source to photographic plate. To a first approximation the sources of illumination are simply the lights in a scene, but light can be scattered onto a surface from other adjacent surfaces and in the simple ray tracing model these are not accounted for. It is possible to *feel around*, looking for other light emitters, but because the secondary illumination feeler rays cannot look in every possible direction, a finite number are dispatches in pseudo-random directions.

Sometimes all the feeler rays may encounter reflective surfaces and when that happens they have to follow a new path and continue their journey. There are lots of other things that can happen to feeler rays. Sometimes they may divide, with each sub-ray following separate paths. The way in which the ray tracing algorithm handles such situations, and the sophistication of the mathematical models it uses for light/surface interaction, governs the quality of the images produced.

So, we can get away with following a few rays of light, but what about the next question: How few? Our digital camera records its image at a finite number of pixels in a raster and since each pixel holds one value we need send only one feeler ray per pixel—well almost. In section 4.3 we saw that pixelated displays suffer from aliasing. Ray traced images are no exception and thus they require some anti-aliasing. Dispatching more than one ray per pixel and averaging the result is equivalent to the technique of super-sampling. Again here, the additional feeler rays are dispatches in somewhat random directions. The additional of a random element in the ray tracing algorithm sometimes endows it with the moniker *Monte Carlo* ray tracing.

This chapter is primarily concerned with the the ray tracing algorithm because it is very successful, and conceptually it is the simplest realistic visualization procedure. The option to render a scene using ray tracing is offered by most of the mainstream 3D visualization packages, and the code for the OpenFX package which is dissected in chapter 9 exemplifies how it can be done in practice when rendering objects described by a very large number of planar polygons.

Despite the popularity of the ray tracing algorithm some would argue that it does not implement a true model of the illumination process and cannot easily image things like the penumbra of soft shadows, particulate light scattering or the caustics due to light passing through refractive glass. A lot of work has been done on an alternative approach know as radiosity, and this has been used to produce some of the most realistic images ever synthesized. However radiosity is not the perfect solution either. It cannot account for specular reflections for example. Radiosity tends to be explained in abstract mathematical terms in most texts, but a more practically orientated introduction can be found in the book by Ashdown [5]. Although quite old it offers a practical perceptive.

Neither ray tracing nor radiosity are perfect rendering algorithms. Recently it has been suggested by Jensen [46] that both approaches should be augmented by a technique called photon mapping to fill in some of the gaps. It is likely that a hybrid approach will win out. A hybrid rendering engine would include all three ideas, as well as the basic Z-buffer hidden surface approach, so that the advantages of each are used. One thing is certain; whether you go to the computational expense of ray tracing or radiosity it is likely that you will want to use a better illumination model than the simple Lambertian cosine law presented in section 4.4. Before delving in to study ray tracing in detail we will digress a little in the next section to consider the physics of light-material interaction and how more elaborate illumination models may be obtained.

5.1   Radiometric lighting and shading

Light is an electromagnetic (EM) radiation and physicists assign it a wave-particle duality, which means that they can model its behavior using either the behavior of waves or ballistic particles. As observers we mostly perceive light as a reflection from the world around us. This can be the scattered light in a blue sky or the yellow light reflected from a white object lying in the shadow of a yellow object that is in bright sunlight. Accounting for multi-path illumination realistically is one of the major challenges in computer graphics. The light that we perceive has a wavelength lying in that part of the EM spectrum between about 390nm and 700nm, and what we see when a scene is illuminated is the refection due to the way the light interacts with surface materials.

The way light or any other electromagnetic radiation interacts with a surface is usually modeled using the wave approach and is based on the assumption of conservation of energy in which the incident light is either absorbed, transmitted, or reflected. There can also be an emissive component. This model is known as the *radiometric* model as it is valid across the EM spectrum.

A very detailed study of all aspects or the radiometric model of light transport in the context of computer graphics and all other aspects of physical rendering may be found in Pharr and Humphreys [70], which includes a detailed description of a C++ implementation and some beautiful examples of rendered scenes.

In reality, light enters the scene from the light sources. It bounces around the scene, passes through transparent materials or is absorbed, sometimes to be re-emitted. Once an equilibrium has been established, every point on every surface is acting as a small radiator and will be emitting some light, in addition to the active sources (*what we call the lights*). With the exception of the active emitters, most of the emission will be due to reflection. Sampling the light emanating from a point on a surface gives the color that we perceive with our eyes or record in a photograph. Trying to calculate the light emerging from every point on a surface due to the illumination from light emerging from every other point on the surface is the essence of the radiosity algorithm.

This book does not delve into the details of radiosity or the radiometric approach to photo-realistic rendering, however a briefing document on the topic and a closely allied area with high potential, called photon mapping, can be obtained from the website.

5.2   Ray tracing

The standard algorithm for ray tracing follows the first three steps of the basic rendering procedure described in section 4.1.1.

1. Load the data describing objects in the scene to memory.

2. Move each model into its appointed position.

3. Apply the viewing transformation. (Not all ray tracing applications use this step.)

After step 3 instead of projecting the polygons from the scene onto the viewing plane a ray tracer calculates the direction of a feeler ray, $\hat{\mathbf{d}}$, from $(0,0,0)$ so that it passes through the point in the projection plane equivalent to pixel (i,j) of the display raster (which is of size X_{max} by Y_{max}). For a projection plane located at $(1,0,0)$ we can obtain the same field of view for the ray tracer as we get from the Z buffer renderer by using equations 2.17 and 2.18 to calculate $\hat{\mathbf{d}}$ as follows:

$$\begin{bmatrix} d_x \\ d_y \\ d_z \end{bmatrix} = \begin{bmatrix} 1 \\ \left(\dfrac{\frac{X_{max}}{2} - \text{float}(i) + \frac{1}{2}}{s_x} \right) \\ \left(\dfrac{\frac{Y_{max}}{2} - \text{float}(j) + \frac{1}{2}}{s_y} \right) \end{bmatrix}$$

$$\hat{\mathbf{d}} = \mathbf{d}/|\mathbf{d}|$$

The fraction $(\frac{1}{2})$ is included so that the feeler ray passes through the center of the pixel. To jitter the feeler ray for anti-aliasing purposes a different offset in the range $[0,1]$ would be used. The scaling factors s_x and s_y account for field of view and aspect ratio.

When using ray tracing to render a scene it is inappropriate to cull or clip any model or model facet because rays can bounce back and strike models lying behind the camera or out of the field of view.

In the visualization step the *feeler ray* (origin $(0,0,0)$ direction $\hat{\mathbf{d}}$) is followed (traced) out into the scene until it intersects a polygon. Once the point of intersection, $\mathbf{p}$, is located the surface properties can be determined and the pixel set to the appropriate color value, a process that is illustrated in figure 5.1.

If on first hit the ray isn't totally absorbed we can continue to trace its path until it reaches a final destination or is so attenuated that there is nothing to see. It is usual to do this recursively so that the same code is used to trace all rays, not just those originating from the viewpoint. Each time the ray hits a surface a calculation is made of the illumination using the methods described in sections 4.4 and 4.4.2.

While the spotlight shadow effect (described in section 4.8.2) with its soft edges is sometimes used by a ray tracer, the normal procedure to trace shadows

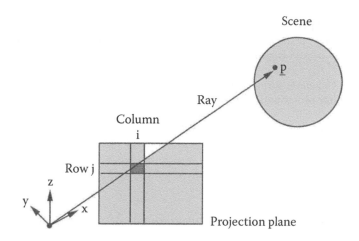

Figure 5.1: Tracing a ray from the viewpoint out through pixel (i, j) until it hits an object in the scene.

Load model descriptions and move them into position.
Apply viewing transformation.
Repeat for all rows, j, in the raster   {
    Repeat for all columns, i, in the raster   {
        Initialize color value, s, (RGB components)
        For pixel (i, j) calculate ray direction $\hat{\mathbf{d}}$
        Set ray origin, $\mathbf{p}$, to $(0, 0, 0)$
        Call recursive function to return s for pixel (i, j)
        DoRay$(\mathbf{p}, \hat{\mathbf{d}}, s)$
        Copy s into the pixel array at address (i, j)
    }
}

Listing 5.1: Ray tracing, part 1: Set up the geometry (view direction, etc.), launch a feeler ray for every pixel and store the color it returns.

is done by checking the path from the visible point $\mathbf{p}$ to each light source. If any facet in a model in the scene intersects this path then $\mathbf{p}$ is deemed to be in shadow.

So the full basic ray tracing algorithm can be summarized in the two parts presented in listings 5.1 and 5.2.

Note the recursive use of the *DoRay()* function in the algorithm of figure 5.2. In the practical implementation of any recursive function care is often taken to ensure that the function doesn't become stuck in an infinite loop. In *DoRay()* this might happen if a ray hits a reflective surface which bounces it to another reflective surface which reflects it back to the first so that it continues to bounce

---

DoRay$(\mathbf{p}, \hat{\mathbf{d}}, s)$ {

Find the identity of the polygon, k, that intersects the ray $\mathbf{p} + \mu\hat{\mathbf{d}}$
at $\mathbf{p}_i$ and is closest to $\mathbf{p}$.

Calculate surface color s_s for polygon k at $\mathbf{p}_i$ $\hat{\mathbf{d}}_t$
use procedural texture or image map if required

If the material properties of k indicate that it is partially
reflective or transparent then cast extra rays.

If reflective get reflective direction $\hat{\mathbf{d}}_r$
DoRay$(\mathbf{p}_i, \hat{\mathbf{d}}_r, s_r)$;

If transparent get transparent direction $\hat{\mathbf{d}}_t$
DoRay$(\mathbf{p}_i, \hat{\mathbf{d}}_t, s_t)$

Get surface normal, $\hat{n}_i$ at $\mathbf{p}_i$, use Phong's interpolation
and any procedural or bump mapping if necessary.

From $\mathbf{p}_i$ send feeler ray to each light source. Test every polygon
 n the model to see if feeler ray intersects
it. If it does then the surface is in shadow..

Combine s_s with s_r and s_t and apply lighting to give
the final s value that is returned.

}

Listing 5.2: Ray tracing, part 2: The key recursive function $DoRay(\mathbf{p}, \hat{\mathbf{d}}, s)$ that does
the key work of a ray tracing algorithm. For a given ray, origin $\mathbf{p}$, direction $\hat{\mathbf{d}}$, determine
the color, s, of the surface seen.

back and forward forever unless the mirrors are less than perfect. In practice the
recursion must be terminated at some preset depth. For most scenes after three
or four reflections the ray can be assumed to have left the scene.

All the calculations and procedures needed for the steps in the basic ray
tracing algorithm have already been studied in chapters 2 and 4. Sophisticated extensions to the basic algorithm tend to be directed at simulating surface
properties, color patterns, transparency lighting and inter-object reflections. By
using more and more rays a better approximation to ambient lighting conditions
and the penumbra of shadows can be included. The red, green and blue primary
color model is only an approximation to the continuous spectrum of illumination
from natural light. Other color models need to be employed in order to develop
more sophisticated physical models of the way light interacts with surfaces. The

dispersion of light through a prism is one example. Recent developments [68] in procedural textures can deliver realistic models of smoke plumes, steam, cloud, hair and fur. However it is the realistic shadows and true reflections that are the **most** significant reasons to call on the use of a ray tracer.

The basic algorithm in figures 5.1 and 5.2 involves an almost impossibly large number of calculations when it is applied to rendering realistic models with more than a few hundred primitive shapes. Note the term *primitive shape*. This could include spheres, torii, swept or lofted analytic curves and even more complex structures built by Boolean operations on basic primitives. Nevertheless your main observation probably was the *hours* it took the computer to trace even an image of moderate resolution. What is worse is that the rendering time increases as the number of models in the scene increases, thus if you need to render a scene with models made up from thousands of polygonal facets, a basic ray tracing renderer is virtually useless.

So the main question is: Why is ray tracing so much slower? The answer lies in the first two lines of the algorithm given in figure 5.2. *For each pixel, test every polygon and find the one closest to the origin of the ray.* This is potentially an enormous number of operations. If the raster is of size $n \times m$ and the scene is described with k polygons, $\approx n \times m \times k \times r$ (r is the average recursion depth) testing and swapping operations must be performed. For example, to synthesize an image of size 640×480 using a 2×2 anti-aliasing supersample with a scene with $20,000$ polygons requires ≈ 24 billion tests. With each test taking many processor cycles you could be waiting a very long time for the image to materialize.

The remainder of this chapter is devoted to techniques that can be used to speed up the ray tracing algorithm. Given favorable circumstances it is possible to produce ray traced images with thousands of polygons in a fraction of the time that it would take using the basic algorithm and perhaps only five or ten times slower than a Z buffer procedure.

5.3 Ray tracing optimization

A huge step in optimizing the ray tracing algorithm would result if we could reduce the number of pixels through which we need to trace rays. So consider this: *In section 5.2 the ray tracing algorithm was designed so that it used the same viewpoint, view direction and field of view as the basic Z buffer renderer.* As a consequence both rendering algorithms will see the same polygons in the same pixels. For the most part the same equations and algorithms are used to determine illumination, Phong shading, procedural texturing and image mapping. Thus we can use a Z buffer algorithm to render the scene and trace additional rays to track reflections, refractions, ambient lighting or for shadow determination.

5.3.1 Hybrid tracing

Just adding a Z buffer to the ray tracing procedure *alone* will result in a huge saving in execution time especially if shadow determination is not required. Without shadows perhaps as few as 1 to 5 % of the image pixels will need to be traced. If shadows are required one of the pseudo techniques described in section 4.8 could still be included as an option in a ray tracing renderer.

Another factor that adds to the advantage of a hybrid algorithm is that the shape of most models is such that often (particularly in animated sequences) there can be a substantial proportion of pixels showing the background color. Making a Z buffer rendering first will identify which pixels are showing background and as a result don't need to be traced at all. Thus, combining Z buffer and ray tracing renderers produces a **hybrid tracer** which performs the steps:

1. Use the Z or scanline buffer to determine the identity of which polygon is visible in each pixel. Store the identity in a list.

2. Jump into the ray tracing procedure using the identity of the polygons from the list as the surface of first hit.

3. Continue with the standard ray tracing procedure from there.

Note:

> For a hybrid tracer it is probably better to use a scanline Z buffer procedure. It saves on memory because the additional buffer which records the identity of the visible polygon has to accommodate only one row of pixels at a time.

Switching to hybrid tracing is particularly useful in saving execution for those scenes with a significant amount of background showing. However if a model should, after projection, cover the whole raster and every visible point on it requires to have its shadow status determined, then other optimization techniques will need to be developed as well.

In essence, what all ray tracing optimization techniques try to do is minimize the number of intersection tests a ray needs to make. This includes secondary rays and shadow feelers. There are two approaches that have received much investigation:

1. Bounding volumes

2. Spatial subdivision

We will look at both of these but in the case where models are constructed from a large number of convex planar polygons. Spatial subdivision will probably be the easiest method to implement, so we will consider that technique in much greater detail. Both optimization methods work by creating some form of hierarchical subdivision prior to tracing any rays. When it comes to following a ray it is hoped that the use of the hierarchical data will obviate the need for a large number of intersection tests.

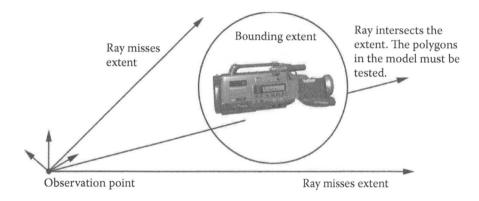

Figure 5.2: A ray need only be tested against surface polygons if it also intersects a bounding extent.

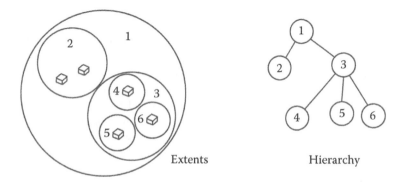

Figure 5.3: Nested bounding volumes and their hierarchical relationship.

5.3.2   Bounding volumes

Bounding volumes, sometimes called extents, are a simple primitive shape, sphere or cube for example, that encloses the whole model. When a ray is traced the first *hit* test is against a very few of these bounding volumes and only when an intersection occurs is it necessary to test the ray against individual surface pieces; figure 5.2 illustrates the idea.

Within a bounding volume it is possible to create nested bounding volumes that gradually break the scene up into smaller and smaller regions with fewer and fewer polygons in each. Figure 5.3 illustrates nested spherical extents and their hierarchical relationship. Should a ray not intersect an extent at one level in the hierarchy then there is no need to test any extent (or polygon bounded by that extent) if it is a descendant of that level.

So the idea of extents is simple in theory but unfortunately it is more difficult to apply it in practice. Look again at the situation in figure 5.2. How would you

Collection of objects

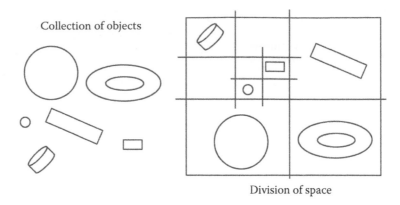

Division of space

Figure 5.4: Subdividing a two-dimensional space into small rectangles so that at most one object is contained in each.

proceed to generate descendant extents for that model after the first and most obvious? It *is* necessary to do so because unless the number of polygon tests can be limited to a few hundred per extent we will still have an interminable wait for the image to develop.

A lot of experiments have been conducted on the use of unusual bounding volumes (see Arvo and Kirk [33], figure 6) but in most cases very good optimization seems only to be obtained when the shape of the models are known and appropriate extents can be designed. For general work a spatial subdivision is probably a better bet.

5.3.3   Spatial subdivision

The idea here is again to break up space into a number of small boxes so that there are as few polygons in each little box as possible. In many ways a very similar idea to that of the bounding extent except that no attempt is made to optimize the *fit* of the extent round the whole or parts of a model. In addition, the regularity of the subdivision means that it is easy to trace rays from one box to another as they pass through the scene.

For explanatory purposes in this section, because it is easier to illustrate the spatial subdivision procedure in two dimensions, most of the diagrams used to illustrate the process are two-dimensional. We should however remember that in reality the process is taking place in three dimensions.

To begin, consider the scene shown in figure 5.4. On the left it illustrates six objects and on the right a spatial subdivision which arranges for each little rectangle to contain at most one object. The subdivision was produced successively with vertical and horizontal cuts so that at any stage rectangles are only divided if they contain more than one object. From figure 5.4 note the following:

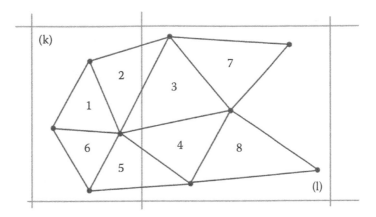

Figure 5.5: Part of a model made from a connected network of polygonal facets.

1. The subdivision is hierarchical. It continues until each rectangle holds only one object or until you reach a maximum user defined depth.

2. The size of the rectangles are not uniform: some are large, some are small. The size is chosen so that the objective, of *"one object in each subdivision"*, is achieved with the fewest number of subdivisions. One way to do this is to recursively choose a dividing line at each step that places half the objects to the right and half to the left of it.

3. The example shows discrete *separated* objects.

All this looks great in theory until we come to consider a model made from a connected network of polygonal facets, then we have a bit of a dilemma! Look at figure 5.5; it shows a small network of connected polygonal facets. No matter how hard we try (how many times we subdivide), there is **no** way that we can separate each polygon so that a rectangle in the subdivision contains only one polygon. The fact that the polygons are connected is responsible for that. The very best we could probably do is associate polygons $1, 2, 3, 4, 5, 6$ with rectangle k and polygons $2, 3, 4, 5, 7, 8$ with rectangle l. We are going to have to accept that in practice a one polygon to one subdivision goal is unattainable. There are two possible solutions: Any polygon that spans a subdivision is split. For example triangle 2 in figure 5.5 could be split into three smaller triangles, one piece will be in rectangle l and two pieces will fall in rectangle k; see figure 5.6. This approach will increase the number of triangles in the model and increase the complexity of the code since image mapping coordinates and so forth will need to be recalculated. An alternative solution is to accept that in some cases the maximum limit of number of polygons per subdivision may be exceeded and design the subdivision algorithm carefully so that it recognizes when further division is pointless.

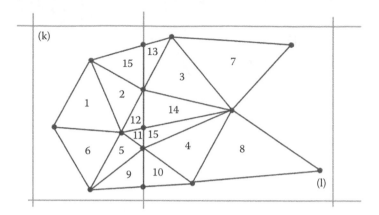

Figure 5.6: Split any polygon that spans a plane of subdivision.

To develop an algorithm for spatial subdivision we begin with the principles illustrated in figure 5.4. Thus the procedure starts with a big region that encloses all polygons: in two dimensions a rectangle, in three dimensions a box. After that, split the region into four (two dimensions) or eight (three dimensions). Continue recursively splitting each subdivision until all of them satisfy the terminating condition.

In 3D this algorithm is called octree decomposition, because it divides a volume into sub-units eight at a time.

5.3.4   Octree decomposition

Before developing the algorithm further let us be clear as to the inputs that are available and what outputs we require.

The inputs are a list of polygons and a list of vertices typically recorded using one of the alternative data structures described in chapter 3. The output we need is a hierarchical representation of the octree decomposition and for each small box, at the ends of the branches of the octree, a list of the polygons which, at least partially, lie inside it. With this information rays can be traced as they travel through the scene moving from one box in the octree to another. Figure 5.7 shows a cubic region of space and how that might be divided up into cubic volumes. That particular subdivision would occur as a result of most of the polygons being located in one corner at the top of the cube.

The algorithm to build an octree will be based on a recursive function that calls itself eight times, once for each branch of the octree. The recursive function will consist of a number of short steps. The data structure that we shall use for each node in the octree is listed in figure 5.8.

The first stage in the octree building algorithm shown in listing 5.3 launches the recursive function. After that recursive subdivision proceeds until the full

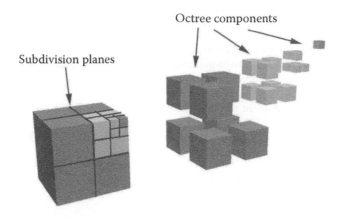

Figure 5.7: The first few subdivisions of a spatial octree decomposition.

x_{min}, x_{max} y_{min}, y_{max} z_{min}, z_{max}	Dimensions of the box associated with octree node k.
n $Poly(i)$	Number of polygons falling inside box for node k. List of identities of the n polygons falling inside the box associated with node k.
$Child(i)$ $Parent$	List of 8 pointers to *child* nodes of node k. Pointer to parent node of node k.

Figure 5.8: Data recorded at each node, k, in the octree.

octree has been established; the steps executed within the recursive function are given in listing 5.4.

Before illustrating the octree decomposition process with an example, a little more detail needs to be given for some of the steps carried out by the recursive function of figure 5.4. Consider the following after looking at figure 5.4:

Step 1 The procedure can be terminated if:

1. The number of polygons attached to node O is less than a preset threshold.

2. The size of the box is smaller than a preset minimum.

3. The octree depth has exceeded a preset limit.

Step 2 There are a number of criteria that could be used. A coordinate average in each of x, y and z at the centroid of the polygons is a logical choice.

Create the first, *root*, node in the octree.

Determine a bounding box that encloses all the polygons in the model.
It might be useful to include a small *guard* region so that nothing
is missed when it comes to tracing rays.

Assign all polygons in the model to the root node's polygon list.

Assign the child and parent pointers to indicate that this node has
no descendants or parent.

Start the recursive procedure by subdividing the *root* node.

Call function   Xtend(Root);

Listing 5.3: The first step in decomposing the octree creates a root node and launches
the recursive subdivision.

Step 3 A fairly quick test is needed here. The centroid of each polygon is a
possible candidate point with which to test for inclusion in one of the subdivided
volumes.

Step 4 This is the most significant step in the algorithm and will require a test
that is capable of determining if any part of a polygon falls within one of the
subdivisions. The test can be performed in a sequence of increasingly complex
checks with the simplest and most clear cut performed first. The following checks
rely on the fact that the box has 12 edges and thus for triangular polygons there
will be an intersection if either: one of the 12 sides of the box intersects the
triangle, or one of the 3 sides of the triangle intersects one of the 6 sides of the
box.

   Thus the checks to apply for polygon k against the volume associated with
node i are:

1. If the maximum x coordinate of every vertex of polygon k is less than the
   minimum x coordinate of the sides of the box for node i then the polygon
   does not overlap the box. The same criteria is applied to the y and z
   coordinates.

2. If the minimum x coordinate of every vertex of polygon k is greater than the
   maximum x coordinate of the sides of the box for node i, then the polygon
   and box **do not** overlap. The same applies to the y and z coordinates.

3. Having performed these simple checks to eliminate candidate overlaps there
   is another quick check that will detect certain overlaps: If any of polygon
   k's vertices lies inside the box for node i, then the box and polygon **do**
   overlap.

Step 1:
 Check the terminating conditions to see if node O should be
 further subdivided or not. If not then exit the function.
Step 2:
 Using the location of all n polygons assigned to node O find
 suitable planes parallel to the x, y, and z axes which
 divide the box associated with node O into 8 smaller boxes.
Step 3:
 Check to see that the division has accomplished something!
 i.e. each subdivided box will contain $< n$ polygons. If not then ext
Step 4:
 Create 8 child nodes for node O and then
 repeat the following for each: $0 \leq i < 8$.   {
   Step 4a:
    Indicate that node i has no descendants, no associated polygons
    and that it is descended from node O.
   Step 4b:
    Assign bounding limits using the planes determined in step 2.
   Step 4c:
    For all the polygons k, assigned to node O check to see
    if they intersect the box associated with child i.
    If there is an intersection then add k to the polygon
    list $Poly(n_c) = k$ and increment n_c, the counter
    for the number of polygons assigned to child i.
 }
Step 5:
 Clear the list of polygons associated with node O. All polygons will
 now have been reassigned to one or more of node O's descendants.
Step 6:
 Extend the octree by calling function $Xtend()$ for
 each of node O's descendants in turn.

Listing 5.4: Function $Xtend(O)$ which uses recursion to subdivide the volume associated with node O.

The following two checks are relatively slow to apply.

4. Each edge of polygon k is tested against each side of the box. This is a two-part check: First determine that the edge crosses the plane containing the side and then check whether the intersection point lies within the bounds of the rectangular side.

 Since the box's sides are conveniently parallel to the reference axes, the general geometry for line–plane intersection described in section 2.6 can be considerably simplified. For example if the side lies in the xy plane at z coordinate z_0, and it is bounded between $[X_{min} - X_{max}]$ and $[Y_{min} - Y_{max}]$, then an edge from $\mathbf{p}_0$ to $\mathbf{p}_1$ may be checked by the following procedure:

if $p_{1z} - p_{0z} < \epsilon$ {
  return *no intersection* line does not cross plane
}
Let $\mu = \dfrac{z_0 - p_{0z}}{p_{1z} - p_{0z}}$
and $\alpha = p_{0x} + \mu(p_{1x} - p_{0x})$
Then **if** $\alpha \leq X_{min}$ or $\alpha \geq X_{max}$ {
  return *no intersection* crosses plane outside box
}
Let $\beta = p_{0y} + \mu(p_{1y} - p_{0y})$
if $\beta \leq Y_{min}$ or $\beta \geq Y_{max}$ {
  return *no intersection* crosses plane outside box
}
return *intersection*

5. The 12 edges are checked against the polygon using the line triangle intersection algorithm described in section 2.11.1.

Even though the above steps have been described for triangular polygons there is no reason why the procedure could not be applied to any convex planar polygon.

5.3.5   A simple octree decomposition example

Let's examine an example of the construction of an octree from the six connected triangular polygons shown in figure 5.9(a). Figures 5.9 and 5.10 illustrate the progressive subdivision and growth of the octree. For ease of illustration the example is restricted to two dimensions.

Figure 5.9(b) shows the box associated with the octree's root node and the identity of the polygons assigned to the root, at this stage all of them. In 5.9(c) the dividing planes at XX' and YY' are shown as added. Using these planes, polygons are assigned to the nodes of the octree as illustrated in figure 5.10(a). Dividing the area for node A into AA, AB, AC and AD as shown in 5.10(b) produces the assignments given in 5.10(c). After this stage we will assume that further subdivision is unnecessary.

One thing to note about the octree spatial subdivision is that sometimes a polygon cannot be uniquely assigned to only one of the subdivided spaces, i.e., to one of the nodes of the octree. There are two ways forward. First, the polygon can simply be assigned to all the octree voxels that it passes through. Of course this will increase the number of polygons that need to be tested as a ray traverses the octree, and it may not be possible to reduce the number of faces in a octree voxel below an acceptable threshold. Second, as an alternative the polygons can be split, i.e., clipped, along the sides of the voxel so that each part (itself a polygon) may be assigned to only one node. Splitting a polygon increases the polygon count and one has to be very careful not to split a polygon when one of its vertices happens to lie in the splitting plane, or if an edge of a polygon lies in

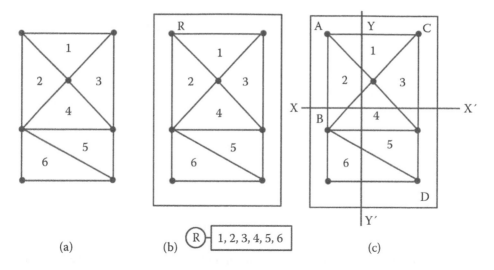

Figure 5.9: Building a very simple octree for 6 connected triangles. (a) The system. (b) The root node, its associated box and octree polygon assignments. (c) Add the dividing lines.

the plane of a split. In these special cases the polygon must be assigned to only one of the adjacent octree voxels. Detecting these special cases are facilitated by using integer coordinates for the vertices and the splitting planes.

Another useful practical trick is to make a copy of the mesh and split the copy leaving the initial mesh intact. The copy that was split is not used for rendering directly. Each split face in the copy keeps a record of the face it was built from in the original mesh. When rays are being traced through the octree, the split copy is used for the ray–polygon intersection tests. When the ray hits a face in the split mesh, the pointer to the face that the split face originated from lets us use the original face to carry out the lighting and shading calculations. By leaving the original mesh intact it is not necessary to fix up vertex normals in the split mesh, or re-interpolate color intensities or texture coordinates at each of the vertices created due to the split, hence the code can be shorter and less prone to errors.

One final comment: *The depth of the octree never need grow too deep. A depth of 20 can accommodate a range of feature sizes as large as from* 1 *to* 10^6.

5.3.6 Tracing rays through an octree

Once a subdivision of space containing the scene is obtained the basic ray tracing algorithm can proceed. However it must be modified so that as a ray is traced through the scene, it moves in increments. Each increment takes the ray from one subdivided volume into the next one along its path, i.e., into one of those

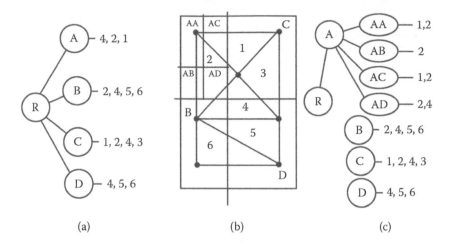

Figure 5.10: Continuing the example from figure 5.9. (a) Octree data after first division. (b) Add the division for node (A). Assume boxes C, D and E have attained their target limit for division so they are not divided again. (c) The octree data and polygon assignments after division of box A.

that are adjacent to the current location of the ray. At each incremental step the following actions are carried out:

1. Identify the octree node i which is the node associated with the volume of space where the ray is currently located.

2. Test the ray for intersection with any polygons in the list held at node i and record the identity id of the polygon which is closest to the origin of the ray. Also note the point of intersection $\mathbf{p}$ between polygon id and the ray.

3. Using polygon id's material and the point $\mathbf{p}$ calculate appropriate surface texture and lighting. If necessary dispatch additional rays to determine reflections, shadows etc.

To determine which node in the octree we should use for i in the above, we have to descend through the tree starting at its root and taking branches according to the rule that $\mathbf{p}$ lies within the box associated with that branch and its node. When we can descend *no* further down the tree: this is node i.

As a simple example consider the case illustrated in figure 5.11 with the equivalent octree given (figure 5.12.) We will assume that the ray originates at $\mathbf{p}$, so the first set of polygons we need to test for intersection are those that intersect the rectangle in which $\mathbf{p}$ lies. To determine this we start at the root R of the octree (figure 5.12), and perform a simple **if–then–else** test to see whether $\mathbf{p}$ lies in the rectangle associated with R; it does. Next, the same test is applied

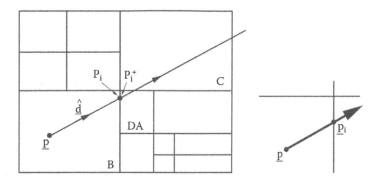

Figure 5.11: Tracing a ray originating at **p** through a subdivided space (a two-dimensional representation of the division).

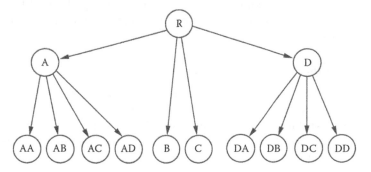

Figure 5.12: The hierarchical octree corresponding to the spatial subdivision shown in figure 5.11. (Again this is a two-dimensional representation of an octree.)

to all immediate descendant nodes, those labeled A, B, C and D. The test shows that **p** does not lie in A but that it does lie in B. Since B has no descendants, we have reached the end of the search and can proceed to test for intersection with any polygon in the list attached to the data structure for octree node B.

If there are no intersections at this stage we need to track the ray into an adjacent box, for this example, the rectangle labeled DA in figure 5.11. This we can do in three steps:

1. Project the ray in direction $\hat{\mathbf{d}}$ to find the spot on the sides of the box associated with node B where the ray leaves box B; call it the point $\mathbf{p}_i$.

2. Project the ray forward by a *small amount* to get another point; call it $\mathbf{p}_i^+$ given by:
$$\mathbf{p}_i^+ = \mathbf{p}_i + \Delta\hat{\mathbf{d}}$$

3. Work down through the octree to find the node whose boundaries are such that $\mathbf{p}_i^+$ lies in its associated box.

Once a new octree node has been identified the process is repeated using $\mathbf{p}_i^+$ as the starting point for the next increment of the ray.

Notes:

1. The small increment Δ used to extend the ray into the next box should be chosen carefully. A magnitude somewhat less than the smallest dimension of the smallest box in the octree will be satisfactory because then there is no chance of $\mathbf{p}_i^+$ falling in a non-neighboring box. In addition Δ must be greater than zero so that even glancing rays get into the neighboring box.

2. The time penalty incurred by tracking rays in this way is not as great as it may seem because finding which branch of the octree holds $\mathbf{p}_i^+$ involves checking relatively few levels of the tree with quite simple comparison tests.

3. The same tracking procedure can be used equally well for rays that originate as a result of a reflection or refraction and for feeler rays checking for shadows.

5.3.7 Following reflected rays

The procedure set out in section 2.9 deals with reflection by generating a secondary ray with its origin at the point where the primary ray intersects the reflective surface. Like all other rays the secondary ray is passed to the basic tracing function $DoRay()$ (figure 5.2). The value $DoRay()$ returns is mixed with lighting and texture values as usual.

5.3.8 Following refracted rays

Using the procedure set out in section 2.10 a secondary ray is generated with its origin at the point where the primary ray intersects the transparent surface. Like all other rays the secondary ray is passed to the basic tracing function $DoRay()$ (figure 5.2). The color value $DoRay()$ returns is mixed with lighting and texture values as usual.

5.3.9 Tracing shadows

A feeler ray from the point $\mathbf{p}$ where the shadow status is to be tested is tracked through the octree subdivision toward each light in the same way as any other ray. If in each subdivision a polygon intersects the ray, then $\mathbf{p}$ is deemed to be in shadow and consequently there is no need to follow the ray any further.

5.4 Multi-threading and parallel processing

Multi-threading can be regarded as the modern term for parallel/concurrent processing. It allows several tasks, even within the same program, to execute at the same time, or appear to execute at the same time. One could perhaps say that the *concept was ahead of its time* and until recently most computer programs were not written as multi-threaded applications. However, *now multi-threading's time has come* because virtually every new computer is designed around a multi-core processor that truly allows a program to do several tasks at the same time.

In theory, ray tracing is an **ideal** application for implementation in a parallel processor because each ray is, to all intents and purposes, independent of all the others. Thus in systems which provide hardware to take advantage of concurrent tasks it makes sense to design a ray tracing algorithm which farms out the tracing of individual rays to different *threads* of execution. However, there is **no** advantage and perhaps even a significant penalty to be incurred if a multi-threaded algorithm is executed by a system with just one processor.

Threaded algorithms must conform to the following standards:

1. Have a separate function which when called carries out all calculations and can be used re-enterently.

2. Variables needed for temporary use within a thread must **not** be placed in memory locations that are available to concurrently executing threads. In practice this means storing all intermediate data on a stack.

3. So-called global variables (accessible to all threads) are usable for *read only* or *write only* access, but not read and write unless some kind of lock is applied when working with these data.

In the case of a ray tracing application program, the geometry of a scene may be recorded in global memory. This description is read and used simultaneously by different threads to trace a ray and calculate a pixel color value which is placed in another globally accessible matrix (the output raster) at an address unique to each thread.

From a practical point of view perhaps the most significant design decision for a multi-processor rendering algorithm is the strategy for dispatching tasks to the host processors. Do we use a separate thread for each pixel, scanline or something else? Since we have already stated that it is very undesirable to create more threads than processors the best idea is to divide the output raster into as many regions as there are processors in the hardware and direct each processor to render all the pixels in its region. This has a *little* drawback because part of the image might need very little processing, say background only, while another might be showing a complex model with multiple reflective surfaces.

A good practical compromise is to use what one might call *interlaced scanlines*. For example in a dual processor environment, processor A renders rows 1, 3, 5, 7 etc., while processor B renders rows 2, 4, 6, 8 etc. The advantages of this approach are first that in any image there will be high correlation between the content of adjacent rows so calculation times will be very similar for all processors. Second, the overheads of spawning threads will not be too great, as might happen if every pixel's calculation dispatched a new thread.

You can observe this strategy in action in the OpenFX application's code that is examined in chapter 9.

6

Computer animation

This chapter starts with an introduction to the most commonly used approach to 3D computer animation, i.e., *keyframe in-betweening (tweening)*. It shows how this is used for the animation of rigid body behavior and illustrates possibilities for the extension of the keyframe approach to cover the more complex topic of character animation. Following the discussion on character animation we will proceed with an explanation of a technique often used for character animation, namely inverse kinematics or IK for short. IK has applications in non-character animation but it is probably its association with articulated models (i.e., characters) that animators would find it most useful. Finally there is a discussion and a few examples of aspects of the simulation of realistic motion that arise from some basic physical laws.

6.1 Keyframes (tweening)

The idea of the keyframe is well known to *paper-and-pencil* animators. It is a "description" of a scene at one instant of time, a key instant. Between key instants it is assumed that nothing "startling" happens. It is the role of the *key* animators to draw the *key* scenes which are used by a team of others to draw a series of scenes filling in the gaps between the keys so that jumps and discontinuities do not appear. This is called *"tweening"* (derived from the rather long and unpronounceable word inbe*tweening*).

To convince an observer that the animation is smooth and flicker free a number of pictures must be flashed quickly before them. Cine film presents 24 pictures per second and television either 25 or 30 per second depending on the system in use. A 30 minute animated feature will require upward of 54,000 images. Each of these pictures, whether for TV or the movies, is known as a frame.

The task of *tweening* is a fairly monotonous repetitive one and thus it is ideally suited to some form of automation with a computer. A half-hour animated movie may only need a couple of thousand keyframes, about 4% of the total length. Some predefined and commonly used actions described by library "scripts" might cut the work of the animators even further. For example engineering designers commonly need to visualize their design rotating in front of the camera; a script or template for rotation about some specified location at a fixed distance from the camera will cut the work of the animator even further.

Thus in computer animation the basic idea is:

> *Set up a description of a scene (place models, lights and cameras in three dimensions) for each keyframe. Then use the computer to calculate descriptions of the scene for each frame in between the keyframes and render appropriate images.*

Most (if not all) computer animation application programs give their users the task of describing the state of the action in keyframes and then they do their best to describe what happens in the snapshots taken during the remaining frames. This is invariably done by interpolating between the description of at least two but possibly three or four keyframes.

Applications programs offer quite a lot of diversity in the power they provide to their users and in how they implement the interpolation but most of them offer the following features:

1. As many models as required can be included in a scene and each can be independently instructed how to behave. A viewpoint emulates the behavior of a camera and can take a specific field of view and other lens properties.

2. Each model is associated with a number of keyframes which specify different features of the actions they might undertake. Probably the most important is to specify where in the scene a model is located. The animator specifies which frame is a keyframe and assigns a location the model is to occupy in the scene corresponding to that frame.

3. The animator is allowed some control of parameters governing the interpolation algorithm used in determining the position of a model at the time of the non-keyframe snapshots.

4. Many other actions of a model in an animation can also be described in terms of a keyframe with parameter values determined by interpolation. To supplement the specification of position, all application programs give the animator the option to specify an orientation (or *attitude*) for the model in a keyframe. Typically, with the three angles, heading, pitch and roll, the angles will be interpolated during the "tween" frames.

5. The option for hierarchical behavior, for example a formation air display, can be animated by describing the motion of the leading aircraft with the others instructed to *follow* it. Hierarchical motion allows quite complex action to be produced with ease. An aerobatic display by a helicopter is

a good example of hierarchical motion. The fuselage follows the display path and the main and tail rotor blades all follow the fuselage whilst at the same time rotating in appropriate planes which themselves tilt as the machine rolls, dives and loops the loop.

In the remaining sections of this chapter we will investigate some details of the theory underlying these features.

6.2   Animating rigid motion

Rigid objects are things like motor vehicles, airplanes, buildings or even people who do not move their arms or legs about. All *fly by* and *walk through* type animations fall into this category. Rigid motion is the simplest type of animation because each model is considered as an immutable entity and the animator only has to specify parameters for its position and orientation.

We saw in section 6.1 that an animation is built up frame by frame with the position and orientation being either specified (because it is a keyframe) or interpolated from at least two keyframes. In three dimensions a point in space is specified by a position vector, $\mathbf{p} = (x, y, z)$. To specify an *orientation* three parameters are required. There are a number of possibilities but the scheme illustrated in figure 2.36 where values of heading, pitch and roll (ϕ, θ, α) are given is a fairly intuitive and easy to work with description of a model's orientation. Once the six numbers $(x, y, z, \phi, \theta, \alpha)$ have been determined for each model a transformation matrix is calculated and inserted into the standard rendering pipeline which then proceeds to paint a picture for that frame. All the other frames are rendered in the same way.

In an animation it is not only the models in view that exhibit action; some of the most important uses for computer graphics arise because the camera (the viewpoint) can move, pivot and tumble. However it doesn't matter whether it is a model built from vertices and polygonal facets, or a light or viewpoint, the behavior of every element associated with a snapshot is uniquely specified by the set of the six numbers $(x, y, z, \phi, \theta, \alpha)$. Chapter 2, section 2.12.7 describes how to calculate terms in the *view* matrix, given an $(x, y, z, \phi, \theta, \alpha)$ for the camera.

Taking all this into account we can write a modified form of the basic rendering algorithm first introduced in section 4.1.1 that serves as quite a comprehensive template for any animation algorithm:

1. Load the description of the action of the animation. The action is described by a list of keyframes for each participating element; an element is either a model, a light or camera. Each keyframe will record the position and orientation of an element for a specific frame. For every model participating in the animation, load its vertex, edge and facet data.

2. Repeat all the remaining steps for every frame i in the animation.

3. Determine the parameters $(x, y, z, \phi, \theta, \alpha)$ for the camera in frame i by interpolation from the record of its keyframes. Build the associated viewing transformation matrix $[T_c]$ by following the steps given in section 2.12.7.

4. Repeat the following for every model k in the animation:

   (a) Determine the parameters $(x, y, z, \phi, \theta, \alpha)$ for model k at frame i by interpolation from the record of these at two or more of the model's keyframes.

   (b) Build a transformation matrix, say $[T_k]$, which will be applied to the vertices of model k so that in effect the vertex coordinates of **all** models participating in the animation will be based on the same *global* frame of reference. $[T_k]$ is obtained by the combination of transformations for orientation and position. The orientation transformation is obtained with sequential rotations about the x, y and z axes by angles α, θ and ϕ, respectively. Moving the model to its position (x, y, z) is given by a translation through $\mathbf{p_o} = [x, y, z]^T$. Thus $[T_k]$ is given by:

   $$\begin{aligned}
   [T_p] &= \text{a translation by } \mathbf{p_o} \\
   [R_x(\alpha)] &= \text{a rotation about } x \text{ by } \alpha \\
   [R_y(\theta)] &= \text{a rotation about } y \text{ by } \theta \\
   [R_z(\phi)] &= \text{a rotation about } z \text{ by } \phi \\
   [T_k] &= [T_p][R_z(\phi)][R_y(\theta)][R_x(\alpha)]
   \end{aligned}$$

   Note that the rotational transformations are applied before the model is moved into position.

   (c) Combine $[T_k]$ with $[T_c]$ to give a single transformation for application to the vertices of model k.

   $$[T_{ck}] = [T_c][T_k]$$

   (d) Apply $[T_{ck}]$ to the vertices of model k. Note that because each frame will probably require a model to alter its location it is essential to hold a copy of the original vertex positions and apply $[T_{ck}]$ to that.

   The final two steps below are taken from the basic rendering algorithm of section 4.1.1.

5. Apply the projection transformation to all vertices.

6. For each pixel in the output raster determine what is visible and record this information.

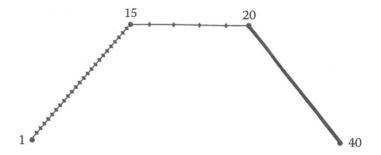

Figure 6.1: Using linear interpolation to plot the movement of an object at, and between, keyframes. The keyframes are plotted with a • and labeled with the frame when they occur.

Note:
In practice animation software will probably not have one long list of vertices and facets. There will be several lists, one for each model in the animation. However, because all vertex coordinates are known relative to the same axes (thanks to the application of the $[T_{ck}]$) no further processing is required.

6.2.1   Position tweening

To find the position of any object (camera, light or model) in an animation during a non-keyframe frame, say i where there are n keyframes such that $0 \leq i < n$, an interpolation of one form or another is performed. The simplest way to do this is by linearly interpolating from the position in two keyframes.

Using the notation of section 2.14.1, let $\mathbf{P}_0$ be the position associated with keyframe l which is chosen so that $l < i$ and there is no other k such that $k < i$ and $k > l$. Then find $\mathbf{P}_1$ which is the position associated with keyframe m chosen so that $m > i$ and there is no other k such that $k > i$ and $k < m$. If we let parameter μ be given by:

$$\mu = \frac{i - l}{m - l}$$

then during frame i the position of the object is given by:

$$\mathbf{p} = \mathbf{P_0} + \mu(\mathbf{P_1} - \mathbf{P_0})$$

For an animation with several keyframes linear interpolation will direct the object to move from the positions plotted at the keyframes as illustrated in figure 6.1.

There are two things to note about the movement shown in the example of figure 6.1:

1. The path taken by the object has abrupt changes of direction at a keyframe. In some situations this might be desirable behavior but for most of the time we would expect a simulation of realistic behavior to make the object follow a smooth curve which passes through the points associated with the keyframes.

2. Unless the ratio of distance between keyframes to time interval between keys is approximately constant in adjacent sections of the path, the object will appear to move erratically and make abrupt changes of speed at keyframes. In the example depicted by figure 6.1 it takes approximately four times as long to cover the distance between keyframes 20 and 40 as it does to cover twice the distance between keyframes 15 and 20.

Avoiding erratic behavior requires some skill on the part of the animator in choosing when to make a keyframe and where the associated position should be. As an alternative it is possible to specify a path which is to be followed during a specific time interval (say between frames f_l and f_m) and instruct the computer to calculate where a model or camera is during the snapshot at frame i.

Higher order interpolation, e.g., with a quadratic polynomial (section 2.14.2) or a cubic spline (section 2.16), will remove the abrupt changes of direction during keyframes. It is important to appreciate that for spline interpolation the movement of any element in an animation must be specified by at least four keyframes. Splines have the big advantage that they will be well behaved; they can have their flexibility adjusted by user-specified parameters so that even for the same control points (at the keyframes) a wide variety of paths are possible. Figure 6.2 illustrates the effect of increasing and decreasing the "tension" in a spline.

To obtain the position $\mathbf{p}$ of camera or model during frame i, using a cubic spline requires the position of four keyframes, $\mathbf{P}_{-1}$ in frame a, $\mathbf{P}_0$ in frame b, $\mathbf{P}_1$ in frame c and $\mathbf{P}_2$ in frame d. These must be chosen so that $a < b < c < d$ and $b < i < c$. This situation is illustrated in figure 6.3.

Equation 2.32 repeated as 6.1 below provides an expression for the determination of any point $\mathbf{p}$ on the spline in terms of parameter τ.

$$\mathbf{p}(\tau) = \mathbf{K}_3\tau^3 + \mathbf{K}_2\tau^2 + \mathbf{K}_1\tau + \mathbf{K}_0 \qquad (6.1)$$

The constants $\mathbf{K}_0$ etc., are determined from $\mathbf{P}_{-1}$, $\mathbf{P}_0$, $\mathbf{P}_1$ and $\mathbf{P}_2$ as given by equations 2.34, 2.35, 2.36 and 2.37.

To make use of the spline it only remains to relate parameter τ to frame i for which $\mathbf{p}$ is required. Before writing an expression let us consider the following:

1. When $\tau = 0$ equation 6.1 gives $\mathbf{p} = \mathbf{P_0}$ and this occurs when $i = b$.

2. If $\tau = 1$ then $\mathbf{p} = \mathbf{P_1}$ and this occurs when $i = c$.

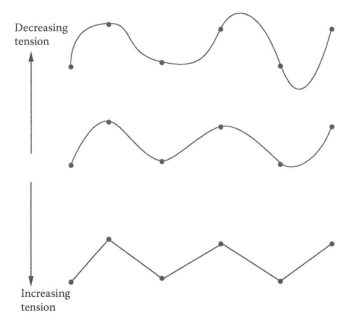

Figure 6.2: Changes in the flexibility (or tension) of a spline allow it to represent many paths through the same control points.

The first relationship between τ and *time* that one might consider is a linear one, effectively parameterizing the spline by time with:

$$\tau = \frac{i - b}{c - b}$$

Although this approach is acceptable it can give rise to a problem when the spline is highly curved. To see this look at figure 6.4; it shows part of a spline curve with four keyframes and three "tween" frames in the interval between the keys.

The curve has a sharp loop between frames 14 and 18. The position of each tween frame is plotted with a cross and corresponds to τ values of 0.25, 0.5 and 0.75. It is evident that the τ values are 0.25 units apart but (*and this is the problem*) in the highly curved segment the distance between the points on the curve corresponding to successive frames is not uniform.

This effect is even more evident on the insert graph of *time vs. distance along curve* which shows significant discontinuities near keyframes 14 and 18. Discontinuities such as these are very noticeable to the observer. An object following this spline will appear to slow down near keyframes and speed up in the middle of segments. Such disturbing behavior may be minimized by reducing the curvature of segments but this requires that the number of keyframes be increased and even then it will not be eliminated.

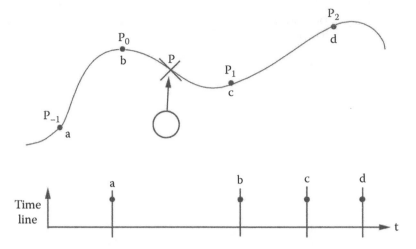

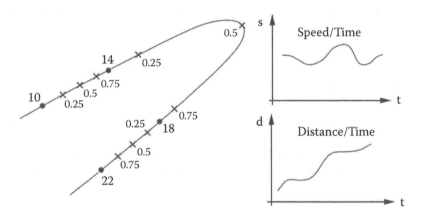

Figure 6.3: Building a spline for interpolation of position in frame i. Below the spline the figure depicts a "timeline" diagram illustrating the time (in frames) of the occurrence of position keyframes. Most animation software packages give some form of graphical presentation of such information.

Figure 6.4: Non-uniform distribution of spline interpolated positions for tween frames. The insert graph illustrates the relationship between distance along the curve and time (i.e., which frame).

The reason that tween frames aren't uniformly distributed along the path is that the relation between τ and time is not a simple linear one. To achieve a uniform velocity between keyframes (or as uniform as is possible given the number of tween frames) we need to parameterize the spline not by time but by *arc length*.

For the spline segment determine the constant vectors $\mathbf{K}_0$, $\mathbf{K}_1$, $\mathbf{K}_2$ and $\mathbf{K}_3$
Define the function $\mathbf{p}(\tau) = (((\mathbf{K}_3\tau + \mathbf{K}_2)\tau + \mathbf{K}_1)\tau + \mathbf{K}_0)$

Set n to the number of intervals in the summation, a value between 20
and 30 should be accurate enough in context of computer animation.

Set length $L = 0$
Set step counter $j = 0$
Repeat the following while $j < n$ {
  Calculate the incremental vector using the function $\mathbf{p}(\tau)$ as follows:
  Let $\tau_0 = \dfrac{j}{n}$ and $\tau_1 = \dfrac{(j+1)}{n}$
  $\mathbf{\Delta p} = \mathbf{p}(\tau_1) - \mathbf{p}(\tau_0)$
  Increment L by the length of $\mathbf{\Delta p}$
  $L = L + |\mathbf{\Delta p}|$
  $j = j + 1$
}

Listing 6.1: Calculating the length of a segment of a cubic spline.

The arc length is the length of the segment between two keyframes. For example, in the case of the segment between frames 14 and 18 of figure 6.4, if we let L be the length of the segment then we need to find τ's which give $\mathbf{p}$'s at distances along the curve of $L/4$, $L/2$ and $3L/4$ from the point $\mathbf{P}_0$.

The phrase "along the curve" is of key importance. The length of a curve is determined by working out the distance traveled on the curve from $\mathbf{P}_0$, to $\mathbf{P}_1$. If we represent the segment between $\mathbf{P}_0$ and $\mathbf{P}_1$ by the curve C then:

$$L = \int_C \mathbf{ds}$$

This is known as a *"line integral"* and for our purposes it to be evaluated numerically as an approximate sum with n steps. The larger n is the more accurate the approximation to L. A value for n of between $20 \sim 50$ is usually good enough for most animation calculations. Remember that any point on the curve is given by equation 2.32. An algorithm to determine L based on the simple trapezoidal numerical integration method is presented in listing 6.1.

This algorithm allows us to calculate L but suppose we were to stop adding while $j < n$. We would get a distance somewhat short of L, say d. With some trial and error we could choose to stop (say when $j = n'$) so that d (the cumulative distance along C) equals $L/4$. Suppose we let $\tau = \dfrac{n'}{n}$ and substitute this in equation 6.1. Then a point $\mathbf{p}$ (on C) will be obtained which is at a distance $L/4$ from $\mathbf{P}_0$.

Use the algorithm given in listing 6.1 to define the function $\mathbf{p}(\tau)$,
calculate the length of the segment L and evaluate the vector constants
$\mathbf{K}_j$, $0 \le j \le 3$

Calculate the distance along the spline from point $\mathbf{P}_0$ to the point where the
object should be in frame i (assuming uniform speed).

$$d = \left(\frac{i - b}{c - b} \right) L$$

Call the function $\tau_d = Bisect(d)$ to determine by iteration the parameter
for substitution in equation 6.1 to give the location on the spline during frame i.

$$\mathbf{p} = (((\mathbf{K}_3 \tau_d + \mathbf{K}_2)\tau_d + \mathbf{K}_1)\tau_d + \mathbf{K}_0)$$

Listing 6.2: An algorithm to determine the position $\mathbf{p}$ of an object during keyframe
i when it follows a path described by a spline. The spline is given by the four points
$\mathbf{P}_{-1}$ at frame a, $\mathbf{P}_0$ at frame b, $\mathbf{P}_1$ at frame c and $\mathbf{P}_2$ at frame d. Keyframes must
satisfy the condition $a < b < c < d$ and frame c and d must be chosen so that $b < i < c$.

By defining $\tau = \dfrac{n'}{n}$ the algorithm effectively provides a functional relationship
$d = f(\tau)$ but to parameterize by arc length we need to know τ given d, i.e.,
$\tau = f^{-1}(d)$. This cannot be written directly. It can only be obtained by the
systematic equivalent of trial and error, i.e., *iteration*.

There are many iterative procedures we could use to find a τ that satisfies
$f(\tau) = d$. Since we know that $\tau = 0 \Rightarrow d = 0$ and $\tau = 1 \Rightarrow d = L$, the easiest
to implement and most reliable procedure is the simple bisection method [32].
Bisection may not be the most rapidly convergent procedure for finding the root
of a non-linear equation but when we know that there is only one possible τ
and that it lies in the interval $[0, 1]$ the bisection method is guaranteed to find
the answer. *There is no point in a practical animation program issuing an error
message "root not found."*

A bisection algorithm to determine the position $\mathbf{p}$ during keyframe i by interpolation from a spline passing through points $\mathbf{P}_{-1}$ etc., subject to the same
end conditions is given in listings 6.2 and 6.3.

Figures 6.3 and 6.4 illustrated that part of the curve between the central
two points of a cubic spline fit through four points lying on the curve. A spline
path must start and end somewhere and when interpolating in the first or last
segment then the algorithm must be modified. For the example in figure 6.5
tween frames 2 through 9 and 21 through 59 fall into this category.

There are a number of possible approaches which can be applied to determine
a position near the beginning or end of a spline path. One that works well is to
introduce fictitious control points $\mathbf{P}'_{-1}$ and $\mathbf{P}'_2$ given by:

$$\mathbf{P}'_{-1} = \mathbf{P}_0 - (\mathbf{P}_1 - \mathbf{P}_0) \qquad \text{At the start of spline.}$$
$$\mathbf{P}'_2 = \mathbf{P}_1 + (\mathbf{P}_1 - \mathbf{P}_{-1}) \qquad \text{At the end of spline.}$$

Function $\mathrm{Bisect}\,(\mathrm{d})$ {
$\mathrm{Bisect}\,(\mathrm{d})$ returns a τ in the interval $[0,1]$ which when substituted in
$\mathbf{P}(\tau)$ will return a point at a distance d from $\mathbf{P}_0$. Start by settings
upper and lower bounds for the interval in which τ_d lies: $\tau_1 = 0$ and $\tau_2 = 1.0$
LOOP:
 Test whether the interval in which τ_d lies is small enough so that
 the iteration can be terminated: $\epsilon < 10^{-3}$
 if $(\tau_2 - \tau_1 < \epsilon)$ jump on to DONE:

 Call the function given in listing 6.4 to calculate the distance along
 the spline up to the point determined by $\tau_d = \frac{1}{2}(\tau_1 + \tau_2)$
 $d_m = SegLength(\tau_d)$
 if $(d_m < d)$ {
 Reduce the interval size by lowering the upper bound: Set $\tau_2 = \tau_d$
 }
 else {
 Reduce the interval size by raising the lower bound: Set $\tau_1 = \tau_d$
 }
 jump back to LOOP: to repeat iteration
DONE:
Rreturn the value of τ_d which is accurate to within ϵ of the exact
value of τ corresponding to d
}

Listing 6.3: The $\mathrm{Bisect}()$ function used by the algorithm in listing 6.2.

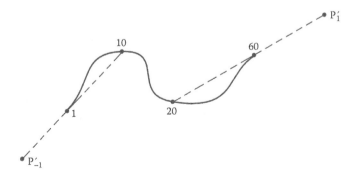

Figure 6.5: Interpolating over the first and last segments of a cubic spline.

Finally in this section it is worth stressing the following two points:

1. We have assumed that interpolation is done on groups of four keyframes
at a time. For example animating the motion over the 400 frames depicted
in figure 6.6 involves interpolation with the following groups of points:

Tween Frames	Use Key Frames
2 to 9	1, 10 and 60 (with fictitious point)
11 to 59	1, 10, 60 and 100
61 to 99	10, 60, 100 and 200
101 to 199	60, 100, 200 and 300
201 to 299	100, 200, 300 and 400
301 to 400	200, 300 and 400 (with fictitious point)

2. There is no guarantee that the motion in different segments will take place at the same velocity but at least within a segment it will be constant.

Function $SegLength(\tau_d)$ {

Use the constants $\mathbf{K}_0$ etc. and function $\mathbf{p}(\tau)$ determined
in the algorithm of listing 6.1

Set n to the number of intervals in the summation a value between 20
and 30 should be accurate enough.

Set length $d = 0$ and parameter $\tau = 0$
Calculate the increment in parameter $\Delta\tau$
$$\Delta\tau = \frac{\tau_d}{n}$$
Repeat the following while $\tau < \tau_d$ {
  Calculate the incremental vector using the function $\mathbf{p}(\tau)$
  $\Delta\mathbf{p} = \mathbf{p}(\tau + \Delta\tau) - \mathbf{p}(\tau)$

  Increment d by the length of $\Delta\mathbf{p}$ $d = d + |\Delta\mathbf{p}|$
    Increment parameter $\tau = \tau + \Delta\tau$
}
Return the calculated distance d
}

Listing 6.4: Determining the length of the part of the spline segment up to the point where the parameter $\tau = \tau_d$. This function is similar to the function given in figure 6.1.

6.2.2   Motion along 3D paths

In section 6.2.1 it was observed that it is quite difficult for an animator to describe a complex three-dimensional movement by placing the object executing that motion in appropriate locations at key times. Even when the path followed by the object is interpolated from a spline curve the motion may still appear jerky because the ratio of distance between key locations to their time interval may vary from interval to interval.

Probably the simplest way to avoid such difficulties is to dispense with the hard and fast rule that during a keyframe the object has to be located exactly at the location recorded for that keyframe. This can be achieved by defining a

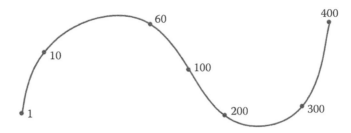

Figure 6.6: An example of position interpolation for a 400 frame animation with 7 keyframes.

path along which the object is to move during a preset interval. The shape of the path is described by as many *control points* as may be needed to push it through given locations. A model following a path will thus embark on its journey at a specific frame and arrive at its destination again at a specified time but how it behaves during its travels is determined by the computer.

To find the location of a model during the interval a calculation similar to that for a spline segment must be performed (see section 6.2.1). However, for a path the summation applies to the full length of the spline. In cases where the path is composed of several segments from different cubic splines the summation switches from spline to spline as it works out the length. For example the path shown in figure 6.7 contains seven control points; to determine its length involves repeating the summation algorithm of figure 6.1 six times using cubic splines passing through the points:

Path segment	Control points
A	(-1) 1 2 3
B	1 2 3 4
C	2 3 4 5
D	3 4 5 6
E	4 5 6 7
F	5 6 7 (8)

Points (-1) and (8) are fictitious points which influence the way in which the path approaches the points at its start and finish.

Finding where on the path any element may be during frame i uses a procedure similar to that for basic tweening as set out in figure 6.2. The only significant difference is that a path may be composed of several different spline segments and the one to be used must first be identified before the bisection algorithm is applied. Once an appropriate τ has been obtained, equation 6.1 yields the location **p** of any object following the path.

If we assume that the length of the path L is known and each control point records its distance from the start of the curve, determining on which segment **p** lies is simply a matter of comparing the distance d (from the start of the

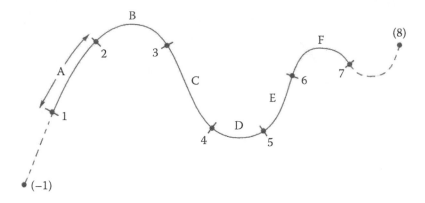

Figure 6.7: A path through seven control points.

curve to **p**) with the distance of the control points from the start of the path. When two are found which bracket d then they are the ones we need. Thus the distance d is given by:

$$d = \left(\frac{i - s}{f - s} \right) L$$

where s identifies the frame in which the object is at the start of the path and f is the frame where it reaches the end.

6.2.3   Orientation tweening

An overall transformation that places a model in the scene includes components of translation and rotation. In this section we turn our attention to how to obtain the rotation to apply in a tween frame, given known rotations (or *attitudes*) in adjacent keyframes. The transformation matrix that represents the combined translation and rotation $[T]$ may be written as the product:

$$[T] = [T_p][T_a]$$

where $[T_p]$ expresses the translational component and $[T_a]$ expresses the rotational component. Writing the matrices in this order is equivalent to applying the rotation *before* the translation. Whilst it is possible to use the reverse order, applying the rotation first means that we can interpolate orientations independently from positions.

Determining the orientation taken by model or camera in a tween frame therefore requires the interpolation of angles. However, angles *cannot* be interpolated in the same way that position coordinates are. Section 2.18 discussed this problem and introduced the quaternion as a mathematical entity with properties that are ideally suited to the specific problem of orientation tweening.

It is how $[T_a]$ is obtained during tween frame k (say $[T_a]_k$) that is the subject of this section.

We have seen already that it is *not* possible to interpolate angles (ϕ, θ, α) for frame k given angles in adjacent keyframes l and m by saying:

$$\alpha_k = \alpha_m \left(\frac{k-l}{m-l} \right) + \alpha_l$$

Therefore $[T_a]_k$ cannot be determined by composing individual rotations:

$$[T_a]_k = [R_z(\alpha_k)][R_y(\theta_k)][R_x(\alpha_k)]$$

Neither is it possible to obtain $[T_a]_k$ during frame k by interpolating directly with matrices expressing the orientation at keyframes l and m (see section 2.18).

During the keyframes l and m the matrices $[T_a]_l$ and $[T_a]_m$ are determined from the known values of $(\phi_l, \theta_l, \alpha_l)$ and $(\phi_m, \theta_m, \alpha_m)$, respectively. It may not be possible to interpolate matrices but it is possible to interpolate a quaternion associated with a rotation matrix. This was discussed in section 2.18.7 where the *slerp*() function was introduced. Section 2.18 showed how the same orientation could be expressed in terms of Euler angles (ϕ, θ, α), a quaternion $[w, x, y, z]$ or a matrix T which pivots the object into that orientation. Algorithms were given for conversion from any representation into any other.

The quaternion provides a solution to our angular interpolation problem and its use can be summarized in the following three steps:

1. Given an orientation expressed in Euler angles at two keyframes, l and m, calculate equivalent quaternions q_l and q_m, using the algorithm given in section 2.18.3.

2. Interpolate a quaternion q_k that expresses the orientation in frame k using:

$$\mu = \frac{k-l}{m-l}$$
$$\rho = \cos^{-1} q_l \cdot q_l$$
$$q_k = \frac{\sin(1-\mu)\rho}{\sin \rho} q_l + \frac{\sin \mu \rho}{\sin \rho} q_m$$

See section 2.18.7 for details.

3. Use the expressions in section 2.18.4 to obtain $[T_a]_k$ given the quaternion q_k.

And there we have it: $[T_a]_k$ so obtained is a matrix representing the orientation adopted in frame k so that the orientation of any model changes smoothly during the interval between keyframes l and m.

In practice it is not essential to record orientation explicitly with Euler angles. Most practical animation software sets up the direction in which a model is pointing interactively. In this case the keyframe could record an orientation as a matrix or possibly even as a quaternion directly; there is no need to use Euler angles. The visual feedback from a refreshed display of the object is usually sufficient for the animator to decide that the orientation they require has been adopted.

6.2.4   Hierarchical animation

Hierarchical animation occurs when *the action of one element is specified relative to the action of another element.* The simplest example of an hierarchical animation is for one model to follow another. Using recursive calls, very little programming effort is required to allow an animation program to support hierarchical behavior. The only noteworthy event from a programming point of view is that an infinite recursion must be prevented. Infinite recursion will occur if for example an element ends up following itself.

There are an almost infinite variety of ways in which hierarchical links can be established involving not only the relative positions of elements but also their orientation. For example it is usually easier for an animator to tell the camera to keep "looking at" some target which can then be instructed to move or follow a model. The result is that the model will always remain in the center of the field of view.

Here is a list of a few potentially useful hierarchical links:

1. One item follows another.

2. One item follows another at a fixed distance from the first.

3. One item follows another with the *artificial condition* that any of the x, y or z coordinates do not participate in the hierarchical link.

4. One item remains orientated so that its x axis always points at a fixed location or at another item.

5. One item rotates round an axis, without the need for orientation tweening, while it moves about.

6. One item's orientation mimics that of another item.

6.3   Character animation

The computer has proved a very effective tool in generating animated sequences. It has been particularly effective when it is the observer/camera that is moving, for example in *fly by* or *walk through* animations. The basic algorithm of section 6.2 showed how several models may be placed in a global scene and individually directed how to behave. This approach works very well provided the

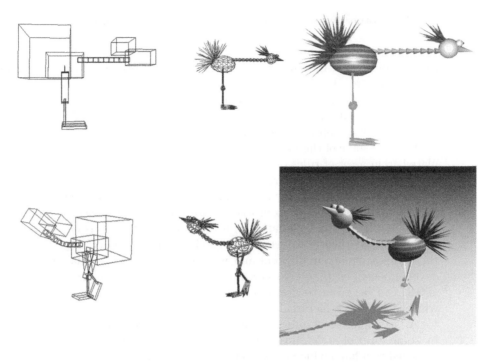

Figure 6.8: An example of the use of hierarchical links in animation. The figure illustrated has 20 separate models (boxes bounding the models, wireframe and hidden surface drawings are shown). The models are linked hierarchically. Each model has been instructed to follow another at a point offset relative to the coordinate system of the one it is following; they have then been aligned individually. Taken together, various arrangements of the models lead to the appearance of a single entity. Tweening the orientation between linked models at given key instances (keyframes) will produce an animation with the composite object moving smoothly from one pose to another.

model is rigid; in this context rigid means that its behavior is specified by setting only a few parameters.

Sadly, characters, both human and animal, usually behave in a far from rigid way and in order to make animations that include characters a way must be found to allow them to behave as realistically as possible. The motion of characters is very complex but one can think of them as having a "global" behavior similar to that of a rigid object; they move about from place to place for example. They also have superimposed on their general motion an internal (local) behavior that arises from internal flexibility. If we insisted on animating every last detail of a character's local behavior then it would quickly become quite impossible to achieve anything. Some form of compromise will have to be accepted. In many ways this is a similar problem to that in modeling the fine detail of a surface; polygonal patches cannot be made small enough to represent perfectly every detail and other techniques such as image mapping and procedural textures are required.

In animation it is possible that some types of action might be initiated algorithmically so that the animator does not have to move every vertex in a model by hand at a few keyframes. Some physical actions such as the flexible behavior of fabric, plastic deformation, flapping in the wind, twisting and bending etc., can be simulated directly from the laws of physics. Section 6.5 discusses a few examples of this approach to animation.

Perhaps some of the more autonomous behavior of a character might be simulated from a set of rules or repetitive patterns of action. Character animation is still a very active area of research in computer graphics and therefore there is at present no correct answer to the question: what is the *best* method to adopt? So, what is the best way to proceed? Obviously a stiff *wooden* performance is unacceptable and the simulation of every muscular twinge is currently impractical; the goal then is to achieve as good a result as practically possible with the equipment at our disposal and within the resources available for software development, i.e., *time*. We saw in section 6.2.4 and figure 6.8 that an internal action can be given to a character by constructing it from many components which behave in a hierarchical way.

A large number of animal species have their movements primarily controlled by some form of *skeleton* that is in essence hierarchical; for example a finger is attached to a hand which is connected to a lower arm, etc. The skeleton imposes constraints on how an animal behaves (it cannot suddenly double the length of its legs for example). For animation purposes the idea of a skeleton is very useful. In traditional clay animation a rigid wire *skeleton* is embedded in the clay and this allows the animator to manipulate the model in a realistic way. (The Oscar winning Wallace and Gromit are excellent examples of clay characters with a wireframe skeleton.) We can use a skeleton in computer animation too; it fulfills two functions:

1. It provides a rigid framework which can be pivoted, twisted and rotated. Vertices and polygons are assigned to follow a specific *bone* in the skeleton and thus the model will appear to take up various poses, just as does the clay model.

2. The hierarchical nature of the skeleton allows for natural behavior, for example pivoting the upper arm about the shoulder in a model of a human figure will cause the lower arm and hand to execute the same pivot without the animator having to do it explicitly.

Consider the example shown in figure 6.9, where the model is pictured on the left, in the center is its skeleton shown as a thick black line and on the right is a diagrammatic representation of the hierarchical links in the skeleton. Using the skeleton, the animator has the option to pivot parts of the model about the end points (nodes) of any of its bones. Taking the model in figure 6.9 as an example,

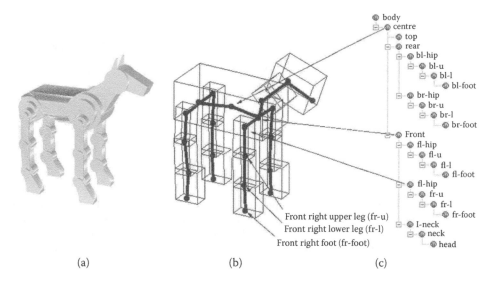

body
└ centre
    ├ top
    └ rear
        ├ bl-hip
        │   └ bl-u
        │   └ bl-l
        │   └ bl-foot
        ├ br-hip
        │   └ br-u
        │   └ br-l
        │   └ br-foot
        └ Front
            ├ fl-hip
            │   └ fl-u
            │   └ fl-l
            │   └ fl-foot
            ├ fl-hip
            │   └ fr-u
            │   └ fr-l
            │   └ fr-foot
            └ l-neck
                └ neck
                    └ head

Front right upper leg (fr-u)
Front right lower leg (fr-l)
Front right foot (fr-foot)

(a)   (b)   (c)

Figure 6.9: A model with its skeleton: In (a) the model is shown; (b) shows the skeleton (the thick lines). A pivot point is shown at the end of each *bone*. The thin lines represent boxes that contain all the parts of the model attached to each bone. In (c) a hierarchical representation of all the *bones* and how they are connected is illustrated.

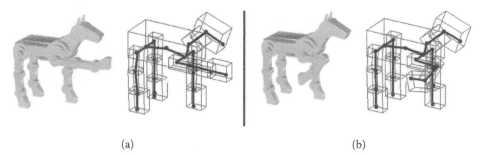

(a)   (b)

Figure 6.10: Pivoting the leg of the model shown in figure 6.9 into two poses.

a rotation of the front right upper leg around the hip joint moves the whole front right leg (see figure 6.10(a)). If this is followed by rotations of the lower leg and foot the pose illustrated in figure 6.10(b) results.

Using a skeleton in the context of well-designed interactive software which lets the animator see what is happening from multiple viewpoints, the key elements of character animation can be achieved despite the fact that control is restricted to a *mouse* and the display is only on a flat screen. In the next four subsections we will look at one possible way to describe the skeleton, record its pose and interpolate between two *keyframe* poses.

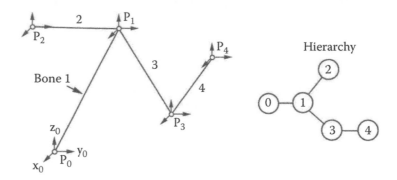

Figure 6.11: Specifying a rest pose of a skeleton with four bones $1-4$. In addition to the positions $\mathbf{P}_i$ of the nodes at the end of the bone, a local frame of reference $(\mathbf{x}_i, \mathbf{y}_i, \mathbf{z}_i)$ is attached to each node. On the right a hierarchical diagram of the skeleton is shown. $\mathbf{P}_0$ is a **root** node which has no bone attached and acts as the base of the skeleton.

6.3.1   Specifying character poses

Any skeleton has what we can term a *rest* pose, which is simply the form in which it was created, before any manipulation is applied. The skeleton illustrated in figure 6.9 is in a rest pose. With the knowledge of hierarchical *connectivity* in a skeleton, a position vector giving the location of the end (the node or the joint) of each bone uniquely specifies the skeleton's rest position. To behave like the wireframe of a clay animation figure any other pose adopted by the skeleton should satisfy the criteria:

1. Be obtained with a rotational transformation about an axis located at one of the nodes of the skeleton.

2. If a transformation is deemed to apply to a specific bone, say i, then it must also be applied to the descendant (child) bones as well.

For example consider the simple skeleton illustrated in figure 6.11; it shows four bones. Bones 2 and 3 are children to bone 1 and bone 4 is child to bone 3. Each bone is given a coordinate frame of reference (e.g., (x_3, y_3, z_3) for bone 3). (For the purpose of this example the skeleton will be assumed to lie in the plane of the page.) $\mathbf{P}_0$ is a node with no associated bone; it acts as the base of the skeleton and is referred to as the **root**.

Suppose that we wish to move bone 3. The only option is to pivot it around a direction vector passing through node 1 (to which bone 3 is attached). We saw in chapter 2, sections 2.12, 2.12.4 and 2.12.5 how to specify a rotational transformation as a 4×4 matrix, and to combine rotations round different axes to give a single matrix $[M]$ that encodes information for any sequence of rotations

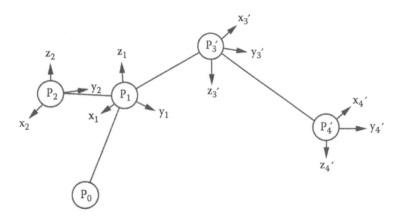

Figure 6.12: Specifying a pose for the skeleton in figure 6.11 by a rotation of bone 3 and its descendants round the node at the end of bone 1.

performed at a point. This matrix takes the form:

$$[M] = \begin{bmatrix} a_{00} & a_{01} & a_{02} & 0 \\ a_{10} & a_{11} & a_{12} & 0 \\ a_{20} & a_{21} & a_{22} & 0 \\ 0 & 0 & 0 & 1 \end{bmatrix} \tag{6.2}$$

The last row and column contain zeros because there are no translation components when manipulating a skeleton, and *all rotations are relative to a coordinate system with its origin at the point around which the skeleton is pivoted.*

Once $[M]$ has been calculated, its application to $\mathbf{P}_3$ and $\mathbf{P}_4$ will move them to appropriate locations for the new pose. The example pose in figure 6.12 was obtained by a rotation of π round axis y_2. There are a few important observations that emerge from this simple example:

1. Node 4 is affected by the transformation because it is descended from node 3.

2. Nodes 0, 1 and 2 are *unaffected* and remain at locations $\mathbf{p}_0$, $\mathbf{p}_1$ and $\mathbf{p}_2$. Importantly the node about which the rotation is made is **not** disturbed in any way.

3. The coordinate frames of reference attached to nodes 3 and 4 are also transformed. They become $(\mathbf{x}_3', \mathbf{y}_3', \mathbf{z}_3')$ and $(\mathbf{x}_4', \mathbf{y}_4', \mathbf{z}_4')$.

4. Although node 4 (at $\mathbf{p}_4$) is moved, its position is unchanged in the local frame of reference attached to node 3.

5. When $[M]$ is applied to nodes 3 and 4 it is assumed that their coordinates are expressed in a frame of reference with origin at $\mathbf{P}_1$.

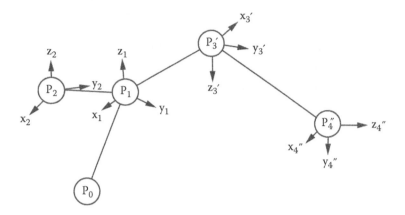

Figure 6.13: Co-positional nodes do not imply that two poses are identical. The nodes in this pose of the skeleton from figure 6.11 are at the same location as the nodes in the pose shown in figure 6.12 but the local frames of reference do not take the same orientation.

It is possible to apply additional rotational transformations until any desired pose is achieved for a specific keyframe in the animation. To attain the pose depicted in figure 6.10(b) several successive transformations from the rest position of figure 6.9 were necessary.

Note that even if the position of the nodes in two poses is identical it does **not** mean that the poses are identical. Look at figure 6.13; this shows 4 bones (4 nodes) co-positional with the nodes in the pose of figure 6.12. A close inspection reveals that the local frames of reference are very different. The skeletons look the same because they have cylindrical symmetry but a network of polygons and vertices attached to the bones would not necessarily exhibit this property and therefore the model might look quite different. (The pose depicted in figure 6.13 was obtained in two steps, a rotation round $\mathbf{x}_1$ followed by rotation round $\mathbf{x}_3'$.)

6.3.2   Interpolating character poses

Character animation using a skeleton is similar in principle to rigid body animation. Given a pose for keyframes l and m we need to determine how the skeleton is posed for some frame $k : l < k < m$.

In the last section we saw that it might take several operations to manipulate the skeleton into the desired pose. In interpolating how the skeleton changes between the two poses it does not necessarily follow that operations used to position the skeleton should be mimicked. We would like the character to *flow* from one pose to another with the *minimum of fuss*. To achieve this we will need to think of interpolating the angular change between linked bones, i.e., between a child and its parent bone.

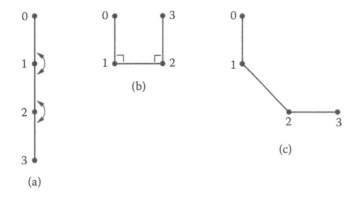

Figure 6.14: (a) and (b) show two poses of a simple skeleton with three bones. (The circles represent the nodes at the end of the bones). (c) shows an interpolated pose midway between (a) and (b).

To see how this will work look at the example in figure 6.14 where two poses of a very simple skeleton are shown. In pose (a) the second and third bones are orientated π apart from their respective parents. In (b) they are $\dfrac{\pi}{2}$ apart. Interpolation should proceed smoothly as the skeleton moves from pose (a) to pose (b). This is accomplished by changing the angle between bones 1 and 2 and between bones 2 and 3 simultaneously; in both cases from π to $\dfrac{\pi}{2}$. Interpolating in this way leads to the pose depicted in (c) half way through the move.

Note how the angular changes are always *relative* (child to parent) so that a rotation of a child is expressed in the frame of reference of the parent. The parent bone and its frame of reference may themselves be pivoting and this in turn adds an additional rotation to any children which accentuates the children's global movement. Simultaneous angular changes in two bones often leads to a realistic motion. The act of raising an arm will involve pivoting the whole arm round the shoulder whilst simultaneously bending it at the elbow.

If we extrapolate the two-dimensional concept depicted in figure 6.14 into a three-dimensional one, we will have a pretty good method of simulating "animal" behavior, with the animator required to provide only a few key poses. Indeed it is quite possible to imagine building up a library of poses from which the animator can choose the appropriate ones for the computer to link together over a specified time interval.

Thus, we return to the question of how to interpolate the difference in the angle between child to parent of the same two bones in two poses. Angular interpolation has been discussed in chapter 2, section 2.18 and in section 6.2.3 where the quaternion was introduced as the mathematical entity of choice for

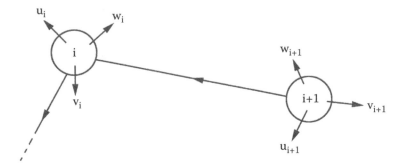

Figure 6.15: Part of skeleton at *rest*. Two bones are shown with their nodes (i and $i + 1$) and local coordinate systems.

angular interpolation. In character animation we have the little complication of determining just what are the appropriate quaternions for interpolation. This will be considered in the next section.

6.3.3   Interpolating one bone relative to its parent

Figure 6.15 shows two bones that form part of a simple skeleton that we will use in this section. The skeleton is in its *rest* position. For each bone their associated nodes i and $i + 1$ and local frames of reference given by basis vectors $(\mathbf{u}_i, \mathbf{v}_i, \mathbf{w}_i)$ and $(\mathbf{u}_{i+1}, \mathbf{v}_{i+1}, \mathbf{w}_{i+1})$ are illustrated. The local basis vectors are labeled $\mathbf{u}$, $\mathbf{v}$ and $\mathbf{w}$ so that they are not confused with the global $\mathbf{x}, \mathbf{y}, \mathbf{z}$ coordinate system.

Suppose now that a number of rotations of node $i + 1$ around the axes at node i are made so that node $i + 1$ takes up the position and orientation depicted in figure 6.16. The rotational transformation which moves node $i + 1$ between the two orientations in figures 6.15 and 6.16 can be expressed as a single matrix $[M]$ of the form given by equation 6.2. The elements a_{00} etc., of $[M]$ may be calculated from the local basis vectors in the two orientations, $(\mathbf{u}_{i+1}, \mathbf{v}_{i+1}, \mathbf{w}_{i+1})$ and $(\mathbf{u}'_{i+1}, \mathbf{v}'_{i+1}, \mathbf{w}'_{i+1})$.

Another way to think about matrix $[M]$ is that when it is applied to node $i + 1$ at $\mathbf{P}_{i+1}$ in figure 6.15, it will move node $i + 1$ to the new position at $\mathbf{P}'_{i+1}$ as shown in figure 6.16. Remember, this assumes that the position of node i is used as the origin while executing the rotation.

We can now propose that given $[M]$ (which pivots node $i + 1$ from $\mathbf{P}_{i+1}$ to $\mathbf{P}'_{i+1}$) the following three-step algorithm will return a matrix $[M_k]$ which pivots node $i + 1$ part way along an arc through $\mathbf{P}_{i+1}$ and $\mathbf{P}'_{i+1}$. How far along the arc $[M_k]$ takes $\mathbf{P}_{i+1}$ depends on the parameter:

$$\tau = \frac{k - f}{l - f} : f \le k < l$$

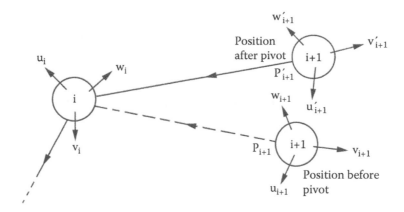

Figure 6.16: A combination of rotational movements of node $i + 1$ around node i produces another pose of the part of the skeleton given in figure 6.15.

where f and l are the frames in which the movement begins and ends, respectively.

The algorithm:

1. Convert the matrix $[M]$ to an equivalent quaternion q_m. (An algorithm for this appears in section 2.18.5.)

2. Use the *slerp* function (from section 2.18.7) to obtain a quaternion:

$$q_k = slerp(\tau, q_i, q_m)$$

q_k is a quaternion that holds the same information that in $[M]$ will pivot $\mathbf{P}_{i+1}$ into its position during frame k.

q_i is the unit quaternion. It is used here because $\mathbf{P}_{i+1}$ is the rest position for node $i + 1$.

3. Convert q_k to the equivalent rotational transformation matrix $[M_k]$ which when applied to $\mathbf{P}_{i+1}$ will pivot it round $\mathbf{P}_i$ into position (for frame k) on the arc joining $\mathbf{P}_{i+1}$ to $\mathbf{P}'_{i+1}$.

6.3.4   Hierarchical interpolation

The previous section demonstrated how angular interpolation is used to animate a child node pivoting around its parent's axes. In a skeleton there is likely to be a long chain of *parent-to-child* linkages and any parent bone is thus also likely to execute some rotation around its own parent. In this scenario we have a situation in which the frame of reference for the orientation of a child relative to its parent is a moving one. This greatly complicates the issue and it is the purpose of this

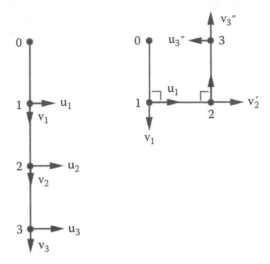

Figure 6.17: A simple skeleton in two poses with local frames of reference given by vectors **u**, **v** and **w**. All the **w** vectors are at right angles to both **u** and **v** and therefore they point into the page and thus are not visible in the diagram.

section to develop a strategy for hierarchical interpolation which minimizes the complexity.

The main difficulty with a moving frame of reference can be illustrated by looking back to the example in figure 6.14, which is reproduced in figure 6.17 with additional vectors depicting the local frames of reference at the nodes on the end of the bones.

Consider what happens to node 3 and its frame of reference as the skeleton changes from the pose on the left to the pose on the right of figure 6.17. In absolute terms the vectors $\mathbf{u}_3$ and $\mathbf{v}_3$ undergo a complete reversal, i.e., $\mathbf{u}'_3 = -\mathbf{u_3}$ and $\mathbf{v}'_3 = -\mathbf{v_3}$. Interpolating between these two sets of directions is not possible because node 3 could *swing* either clockwise or anti-clockwise since the result would be the same. It is only by considering the relative change between node 3 to its parent (node 2) that it becomes obvious that node 3 must rotate in an anti-clockwise sense by $\dfrac{\pi}{2}$ round the vector $\mathbf{w}_2$.

From this example we can see that the orientation of a child relative to its parent's frame of reference must be taken into account when performing interpolation. There are two ways in which this might be done:

1. Use the frames of reference of child and parent to calculate rotational transformations that relate:

    (a) The child's frame of reference to the parent's in the first pose, say $[T_1]$.

(b) The child's frame of reference to the parent's in the second pose, say $[T_2]$.

Interpolation proceeds as described in section 6.3.3 between quaternions representing the matrices $[I]$ and $[T_2][T_1]^{-1}$.

2. Specify every pose in terms of the rest pose. Thus if:

(a) $[T_1]$ is a transformation matrix that rotates node $i+1$ round its parent so as to adopt the first pose, and

(b) $[T_2]$ is a transformation matrix that rotates node $i+1$ round its parent so as to adopt the second pose,

then interpolation proceeds as described in section 6.3.3 between quaternions representing the matrices $[I]$ and $[T_2][T_1]^{-1}$. If $[M_k]$ is the matrix equivalent to the interpolated quaternion then the product $[T_1][M_k]$ is the matrix that pivots node $i+1$ (and all its descendants).

In either of the above approaches we will have a collection of transformation matrices (one for each node) that describe their *local* behavior, i.e. relative to their parent only. To render the model based on the pose of a skeleton, the skeleton itself and the vertices attached to each bone must be moved into position.

If we use the second approach as an example then the poses (a) and (b) shown in figure 6.18 are recoded in the sequence of transformations $[M_a]_1$, $[M_a]_2$, $[M_a]_3$ and $[M_b]_1$, $[M_b]_2$, $[M_b]_3$, respectively. (An interpolated pose would be determined by the sequence $[M_k]_1$, $[M_k]_2$, $[M_k]_3$.) To bend the skeleton into poses (a) and (b) the sequence of operations illustrated in figure 6.19 and outlined below is performed:

1. Start with skeleton at rest.

2. Multiply on the left and right the matrix $[M_a]_1$ by translations $[T(-\mathbf{P}_1)]$ and $[T(\mathbf{P}_1)]$, respectively, so that its rotation is centered on skeleton node 1 at $\mathbf{P}_1$:

$$[M'_a]_1 = [T(\mathbf{P}_1)][M_a]_1[T(-\mathbf{P}_1)]$$

Apply transformation $[M'_a]_1$ to skeleton nodes 2 and 3 and all vertices attached to bones 2 and 3.

This is depicted in figure 6.19(a); note that skeleton nodes $\mathbf{P}_2$ and $\mathbf{P}_3$ have moved to $\mathbf{P'}_2$ and $\mathbf{P'}_3$.

3. Modify matrix $[M_a]_2$ so that its rotation is centered on skeleton node 2 at $\mathbf{P'}_2$ by pre- and post-multiplying by translations $[T(-\mathbf{P'}_2)]$ and $[T(\mathbf{P'}_2)]$, respectively:

$$[M'_a]_2 = [T(\mathbf{P'}_2)][M_a]_2[T(-\mathbf{P'}_2)]$$

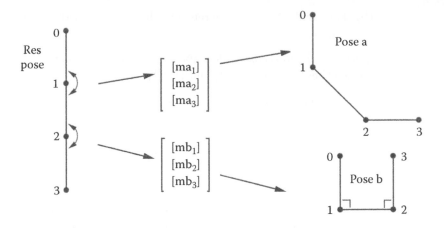

Figure 6.18: Specifying a specific pose with a series of rotational transformations based on the skeleton's rest position.

Apply transformation $[M'_a]_2$ to skeleton node 3 and all vertices attached to bone 3.

This is depicted in figure 6.19(b); note that skeleton node $\mathbf{P}'_3$ has moved to $\mathbf{P}''_3$.

4. Modify matrix $[M_a]_3$ so that its rotation is centered on skeleton node 3 at $\mathbf{P}''_3$ by pre- and post-multiplying by translations $[T(-\mathbf{P}''_3)]$ and $[T(\mathbf{P}''_3)]$, respectively:

$$[M'_a]_3 = [T(\mathbf{P}_1)][M_a]_2[T(-\mathbf{P}''_2)]$$

Apply transformation $[M'_a]_3$ to all vertices attached to bone 3.

This is depicted in figure 6.19(c); note that skeleton node $\mathbf{P}''_3$ has not moved; only the local frame of reference at node 3 and any vertices attached to the last bone in the hierarchy will be affected.

It must be stressed that it is only the final result of these successive transformations that is rendered or displayed.

6.3.5   The quest for more realistic character animation

A rigid skeleton with polygons and vertices attached to a specific bone is ideal for *robots* like the model depicted in figure 6.9. It also works pretty well for human figures but in reality the surface of an animal might well have a detailed texture, e.g., hair or fur, and this will tend to move flexibly as muscles expand and contract and skin stretches and bends.

To simulate these effects a polygonated mesh covering the surface of an object is still quite applicable provided it is fine enough and a procedure is provided to

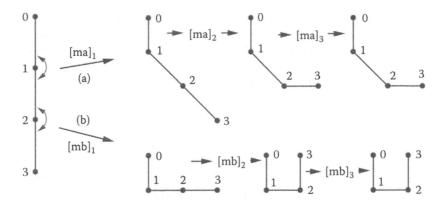

Figure 6.19: Applying the transformations down the chain. Attaining pose (a) from figure 6.18 is depicted at the top and pose (b) at the bottom. (This example is discussed in the text.)

the animator that enables them to specify appropriate behavior without having to move every vertex in the model by hand.

One approach that is used in a few commercial animation packages is to use a "field" which behaves in a way that is analogous to the effect a magnetic or electric field has on charged or magnetic materials. The effect of the field is proportional to the distance from its source and two or more sources can be called into play to provide a combined effect. In the context of a polygon/vertex/skeleton computer model the vertices attached to the bone of a skeleton can have their position perturbed by a force proportional to their distance from adjacent bones or other structures (muscles) which themselves might be attached to one or two adjoining bones in the skeleton.

Another approach to attaining realistic behavior with the minimum of amount of work on the part of the animator is to use *goal directed motion*. Using this approach the animator does not have to manipulate every bone in the structure to set up a particular pose. For example to make a figure walk, all the animator has to do is drag the feet into position and the rest of the body will follow. Perhaps this is a little bit of an oversimplification but it serves to illustrate the intention of goal directed animation. At the center of goal directed animation lies the technique of *inverse kinematics* which we will discuss in section 6.4. What we have been investigating thus far is basically called *forward kinematics*.

6.4 Inverse kinematics

Inverse kinematics or just IK for short is popular as a technique employed by animators to reduce their workload in setting up complex actions particularly those involving hierarchical motion. Just as *tweening* helps in making it much quicker to compile animations of many frames by getting the computer to fill in the gaps between keyframes, IK helps by reducing the number of adjustments an animator has to make to set up a keyframe. Animating characters with all the complexity of posing the figure springs immediately to mind as a good example but other actions can also benefit from the application of an IK engine. The term *IK engine* is often used to describe a "black box" mathematical function which applies an IK solution to a specific hierarchically linked set of models according to IK theory. For example a moving chain or any folding structure can be animated much more quickly with the help of IK. Animators also use IK to describe complex motions such as a figure riding a bicycle. The figure's feet are told to follow the pedals and its hands the handlebars. All the animator has to do is set up the motion of the bicycle itself and the character will follow it.

A good discussion of the basics of IK, the pros and cons of forward versus inverse kinematics and IK applied to skeletons is provided by Watt and Watt [86]. They also introduce the theory but leave out some of the detail. In this section we will look in a detailed way at how IK calculations are set up and solved. We will adopt a different approach to that of Watt and Watt but we will obtain the same results.

Perhaps we should begin by stating that IK calculations are *not* trivial. They involve solving non-linear systems of equations in which there are always more unknowns than equations. Thus the system is either poorly constrained or not constrained at all. As we proceed to look at IK we will see how these problems are solved and a couple of demonstrator applications are provided to allow you to see the effect of IK in practice.

A 3D computer animation's use of IK is obviously going to require a 3D IK engine. However it is much simpler to understand a 2D IK engine and therefore this is where we will begin. The solution of the 3D IK problem follows exactly the same procedure as that used in 2D. It is only in setting up the problem that differences occur; thus we will use a 2D example to present a method of solution.

6.4.1 The IK problem

Most of the work on which the concept of IK is based originated in the field of robotics, robotics in the sense of the machines used in automation and manufacturing processes. The articulated linkages that form the arms and hands of machines designed to fulfill a manipulation role must be able to reach any point within a working region and the hand at the end of the robot's arm must also be able to adopt any orientation.

For a robot used as a surrogate human on a production line an important feature of its design is that the hand can approach the working materials at the correct angle. To do this there must be enough linkages from the place where the robot is anchored to its hand and each link must have sufficient degrees of freedom. If the robot can put its hand in the correct place then the next question is: how does it get there? It may be starting from a rest position or the place in which it has just finished a previous task. From the operator's point of view it would be very helpful if they only had to move the hand, not adjust every link from base to hand. However the hand must be at the end of the articulated linkage and it is the relative orientation of the links that dictate where the hand is.

Thus, given the relative orientation of articulated linkages, say Θ (which represents the angles that establish how each link is orientated, e.g., by the set: θ_1, θ_2, ..., θ_n), the location of the end of the articulation $\mathbf{X}$ is given by some function:

$$\mathbf{X} = f(\Theta) \tag{6.3}$$

This is called **forward kinematics** because the links are set by the operator who gives values to elements of Θ.

However in the ideal operating environment the robot's operator would like to set $\mathbf{X}$; thus the problem is: given $\mathbf{X}$ can we find a suitable Θ? Posed in this way it is an **inverse** kinematic problem. To solve it we must find the inverse of the function $f()$ so that we can write equation 6.3 as:

$$\Theta = f^{-1}(\mathbf{X}) \tag{6.4}$$

Thus we can summarize in a single statement the IK problem:

> *How, given the design of an articulation and a desired position for the last linkage, do we obtain $f^{-1}()$ and hence from it the configuration of all the links?*

It must be stressed that it may not be possible for the articulation to reach the desired position $\mathbf{X}$ and hence we call it a *goal*.

Since $\mathbf{X}$ and Θ are both vectors we might hope to be able to write equation 6.3 in matrix form:

$$[X] = [A][\Theta] \tag{6.5}$$

and solve it by calculating the inverse of A and hence Θ from the set of linear equations:

$$[\Theta] = [A]^{-1}[X]$$

Unfortunately $f()$ is in most cases a non-linear function and thus it is not possible to express equation 6.3 in the form given by equation 6.5. To solve the problem we must use an iteration technique which is essentially the same as that used for finding the solution of a set of simultaneous non-linear equations. McCalla [58] describes the usual procedure. The procedure essentially linearizes equation 6.3 by expressing it in differential form:

$$\Delta\mathbf{X} = f'(\Theta)\Delta\Theta \tag{6.6}$$

and then incrementally stepping toward the solution. Since $f()$ is a multi-variable function $f'()$ is the Jacobian matrix of partial derivatives given by:

$$J(\mathbf{\Theta}) = \begin{bmatrix} \dfrac{\partial X_1}{\partial \theta_1} & \dfrac{\partial X_1}{\partial \theta_2} & \cdots & \dfrac{\partial X_1}{\partial \theta_p} \\ \dfrac{\partial X_2}{\partial \theta_1} & \dfrac{\partial X_2}{\partial \theta_2} & \cdots & \dfrac{\partial X_2}{\partial \theta_n} \\ \cdots & \cdots & \cdots & \cdots \\ \dfrac{\partial X_m}{\partial \theta_1} & \dfrac{\partial X_m}{\partial \theta_2} & \cdots & \dfrac{\partial X_m}{\partial \theta_n} \end{bmatrix}$$

By calculating an inverse for J equation 6.6 may be written:

$$\mathbf{\Delta\Theta} = J^{-1}\mathbf{\Delta X}$$

J is of course dependent on $\mathbf{\Theta}$ so an initial guess must be made for the values θ_1, $\theta_2 \ldots, \theta_n$. In the case of the IK problem the initial guess is simply the current configuration. After the first step we proceed to find a new $\mathbf{\Theta}$ by iterating:

$$\mathbf{\Theta}_{n+1} = \mathbf{\Theta}_n + \mathbf{\Delta\Theta}$$

where n is a count of the number of iterations and at each step J^{-1} is recalculated from the current $\mathbf{\Theta}_n$.

Iteration will be discussed in detail when we come to consider the procedure for two-dimensional IK in section 6.4.2, when we will also address some outstanding issues such as how an inverse of a **non-square** Jacobian matrix is obtained and how we iterate toward the desired goal.

6.4.2   Solving the IK problem in two dimensions

We will look at an example of a three-link articulation. Restricted to two dimensions it moves only in the plane of the page. When equations have been obtained for this specific case we will see how they may be extended to a system with n links. The links are fixed at one end, which we will designate as the origin $(0, 0)$. The other end, at point (x, y), is moved toward a goal point, which it may or may not reach. Where it gets to is what we hope a solution to the IK problem will reveal.

A solution of equation 6.4 gives us the orientation of each link in the chain and from that we can find out how close to the goal the end point actually gets. Figure 6.20 illustrates several possible configurations for a three-link articulation and figure 6.21 presents the notation used to specify and solve the three-link IK problem.

Figure 6.21 shows us that if we know the values of $\mathbf{P_1}$ (anchor point), l_1, l_2, l_3 (lengths of the links) and θ_1, θ_2 and θ_3 (the relative orientation between one link and the next), then the current position of every joint in the link is fully specified (including the end point $\mathbf{P_4}$).

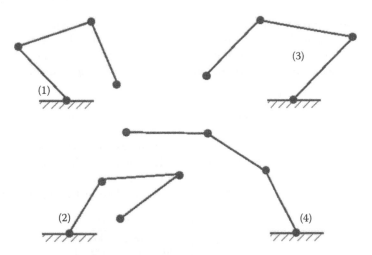

Figure 6.20: Several possible orientations for a three-link two-dimensional articulated figure. In configurations 1 and 2 the articulation reaches to the same end point. We may therefore surmise that simply specifying the location of an end point does not guarantee a unique configuration for the links.

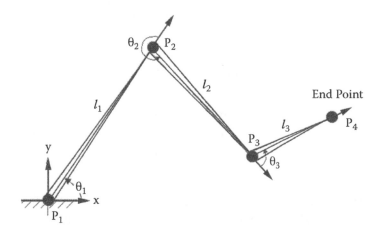

Figure 6.21: Specifying the three-link articulation. The first link is anchored at $(0,0)$ and lies at an angle of θ_1 to the x axis. The lengths of the links are l_1, l_2 and l_3 and link 2 makes an angle of θ_2 from link 1. The end point $\mathbf{P}_4$ lies at coordinate (x, y).

Since $\mathbf{P}_1$, l_1, l_2 and l_3 are constant and independent of the orientation of the linkage, it is only the θ_i that are the unknowns in our IK function, equation 6.4. For our specific example:

$$\mathbf{P}_4 = \mathbf{f}(\theta_1, \theta_2, \theta_3)$$

Note carefully how θ_i is specified as an angle measured anti-clockwise from the direction in which link $(i-1)$ is pointing to the direction in which link i is pointing. The first link angle θ_1 is referenced to the x axis. Using this information we can write an expression for the (x, y) coordinate of $\mathbf{P}_4$:

$$\left[\begin{array}{c} x \\ y \end{array} \right] = \left[\begin{array}{c} l_1 \cos(\theta_1) + l_2 \cos(\theta_1 + \theta_2) + l_3 \cos(\theta_1 + \theta_2 + \theta_3) \\ l_1 \sin(\theta_1) + l_2 \sin(\theta_1 + \theta_2) + l_3 \sin(\theta_1 + \theta_2 + \theta_3) \end{array} \right] \tag{6.7}$$

Equation 6.7 shows that $f(\theta_1, \theta_2, \theta_3)$ is as we suspected, a non-linear function. Therefore we will need to solve the IK problem by linearizing 6.7 and iterating toward the desired goal position of $\mathbf{P}_4$. The first step in this procedure is to obtain the Jacobian and for the 2D IK problem of three links, this is the 2×3 matrix:

$$J = \left[\begin{array}{ccc} \dfrac{\partial x}{\partial \theta_1} & \dfrac{\partial x}{\partial \theta_2} & \dfrac{\partial x}{\partial \theta_3} \\ \dfrac{\partial y}{\partial \theta_1} & \dfrac{\partial y}{\partial \theta_2} & \dfrac{\partial y}{\partial \theta_3} \end{array} \right]$$

The terms $\frac{\partial}{\partial \theta_i}$ are obtained by differentiating equation 6.7 to give:

$$J = \left[\begin{array}{ccc} J_{11} & J_{12} & J_{13} \\ J_{21} & J_{22} & J_{23} \end{array} \right] \tag{6.8}$$

where:

$$
\begin{array}{rcl}
J_{11} & = & -l_1 \sin(\theta_1) - l_2 \sin(\theta_1 + \theta_2) - l_3 \sin(\theta_1 + \theta_2 + \theta_3) \\
J_{12} & = & -l_2 \sin(\theta_1 + \theta_2) - l_3 \sin(\theta_1 + \theta_2 + \theta_3) \\
J_{13} & = & -l_3 \sin(\theta_1 + \theta_2 + \theta_3) \\
J_{21} & = & l_1 \cos(\theta_1) + l_2 \cos(\theta_1 + \theta_2) + l_3 \cos(\theta_1 + \theta_2 + \theta_3) \\
J_{22} & = & l_2 \cos(\theta_1 + \theta_2) + l_3 \cos(\theta_1 + \theta_2 + \theta_3) \\
J_{23} & = & l_3 \cos(\theta_1 + \theta_2 + \theta_3)
\end{array}
$$

With J calculated we are nearly ready to go through the iteration process that moves $\mathbf{P}_4$ toward its goal. An algorithm for this will be based on the equations:

$$
\begin{array}{rcl}
\mathbf{\Theta}_{n+1} & = & \mathbf{\Theta}_n + J(\mathbf{\Theta}_n)^{-1} \mathbf{\Delta X} \\
\mathbf{X}_{n+1} & = & f(\mathbf{\Theta}_{n+1})
\end{array}
$$

Before we can do this we must investigate how J^{-1} is obtained from J.

The generalized inverse The definition of the inverse of a matrix A is a matrix A^{-1} such that if $|A| \neq 0$ then A and A^{-1} satisfies:

$$AA^{-1} = A^{-1}A = I$$

This definition of the inverse only applies to square matrices. In the case of any matrix A it is possible to define a generalized inverse A^- which satisfies:

$$AA^-A = A \tag{6.9}$$

If A is square and $|A| \neq 0$ then $A^- = A^{-1}$. Post-multiplying both sides of 6.9 by the transpose of A gives us:

$$AA^-(AA^T) = AA^T$$

AA^T is a square matrix and therefore if $|AA^T| \neq 0$ we can find its *conventional* inverse $(AA^T)^{-1}$ and write:

$$
\begin{aligned}
AA^-(AA^T)(AA^T)^{-1} &= AA^T(AA^T)^{-1} \text{ or} \\
AA^- &= AA^T(AA^T)^{-1}
\end{aligned}
$$

The implication here is that for any (not necessarily square) matrix if we need its inverse we may use its (generalized) inverse A^- given by:

$$A^- = A^T(AA^T)^{-1} \tag{6.10}$$

This is exactly the expression that we need in order to invert the $n \times m$ Jacobian matrix.

For more information on generalized inverses and their properties and limitations consult Bouillion and Odell [13]. Specifically the two points most important for IK are the existence of an inverse for AA^T and the fact that normally we have more unknowns than equations (i.e., $m > n$). The practical implication of $m > n$ is that the articulation can attain its goal in more than one configuration.

Iterating toward the goal Having found a way to invert J we develop an algorithm to iterate from one configuration toward the goal. A suitable algorithm is given in listing 6.5.

Step 4 of the algorithm given in listing 6.5 provides the mechanism to test for convergence of the IK solution procedure. It is based on ensuring that the norm of the vector $\mathbf{\Delta X} - J(\mathbf{\Theta})\mathbf{\Delta\Theta}$ is smaller than a specified threshold:

$$\|\mathbf{\Delta X} - J(\mathbf{\Theta})\mathbf{\Delta\Theta}\| < \epsilon$$

If we substitute for $\mathbf{\Delta\Theta}$ and call J^- the generalized inverse of J then in matrix form:

$$\|(I - JJ^-)\mathbf{\Delta X}\| < \epsilon$$

We use this criteria to determine a $\mathbf{\Delta X}$ that satisfies the condition on the norm. We also use this to determine whether the iteration can proceed or if we must accept that the goal cannot be reached. A simple test on the magnitude of $\mathbf{\Delta X}$ will suffice: when it is less than a given threshold then either the goal has been reached or it is so small that the end will never get there.

Start with the linkage configuration defined by the set of angles:
$\theta_1, \theta_2, \theta_3 ... \theta_n$ (which we will write as $\mathbf{\Theta}$),
and end point located at $\mathbf{P}$ i.e. at coordinate (x, y)
Apply the steps below to move the end point towards its goal at $\mathbf{P}_g$
  (i.e. at :(x_g, y_g))
Step 1:
Calculate the incremental step $\mathbf{\Delta X} = \mathbf{P}_g - \mathbf{P}$
Step 2
Calculate $J(\theta_1, \theta_2, \theta_3, ... \theta_n)$ (use the current values of θ_1 etc.)
Step 3:
Find the inverse of J which we will call J^- then:$J^- = J^T(JJ^T)^{-1}$
(if J is a $2 \times n$ matrix J^- is a $n \times 2$ matrix)
Step 4:
Test for a valid convergence of the iteration:
  $\mathbf{if}$ $(\|(I - JJ^-)\mathbf{\Delta X}\| > \epsilon)$ the step towards the goal
the $\mathbf{\Delta X}$) is too large, so set $\mathbf{\Delta X} = \dfrac{\mathbf{\Delta X}}{2}$
and repeat step 4 until the norm is less than ϵ.
If the inequality cannot be satisfied after a certain number of steps then it is
likely that the goal cannot be reached and the IK calculations should be
terminated (This step is discussed in more detail in the text)
Step 5:
Calculate updated values for the parameters θ_1 etc.
$\mathbf{\Theta} = \mathbf{\Theta} + J^- \mathbf{\Delta X}$
$\mathbf{\Theta}$ is the vector of angles for each link $[\theta_1, \theta_2, ...]^T$
Step 6:
Calculate the new state of the articulation from θ_1, θ_2 etc. check the end
point $\mathbf{P}_4$ to see if is close enough to the goal. It is likely that $\mathbf{\Delta X}$ will
have been reduced by Step 4 and thus the end point will be somewhat short
of the goal. In this case *go back and repeat the procedure from* Step 1
Otherwise we have succeeded in moving $\mathbf{P}_4$ to the goal point $\mathbf{P}_g$

Listing 6.5: Iterative algorithm for solving the IK problem to determine the orientation
of an articulated linkage in terms of a number of parameters θ_i given the goal of moving
the end of the articulation from its current position $\mathbf{X}$ toward $\mathbf{X}_{goal}$.

Equations for a general two-dimensional articulated linkage At the beginning of
this section we said that it was easy to extend the problem from one involving
three links to one which can take any number, say n links. In essence we use
the same algorithm but the expressions for (x, y) and the Jacobian terms $\dfrac{\partial x}{\partial \theta_i}$
become:

$$x \;=\; \sum_{i=1}^{n} l_i \cos\left(\sum_{j=i}^{i} \theta_j\right)$$

$$y \;=\; \sum_{i=1}^{n} l_i \sin\left(\sum_{j=i}^{i} \theta_j\right)$$

$$\frac{\partial x}{\partial \theta_k} \;=\; -\sum_{i=k}^{n} l_i \sin\left(\sum_{j=1}^{i} \theta_j\right)$$

$$\frac{\partial y}{\partial \theta_k} \;=\; \sum_{i=k}^{n} l_i \cos\left(\sum_{j=1}^{i} \theta_j\right)$$

$$k \;=\; 1 \to n$$

6.4.3   Solving the IK problem in three-dimensions

All the steps in the solution procedure for the 2D IK problem presented in the algorithm of figure 6.5 are equally applicable to the three-dimensional IK problem. The calculation of generalized inverse, iteration toward a goal for the end of the articulation and termination criteria are all the same.

Where the 2D and 3D IK problems differ is in the specification of the orientation of the links, the determination of Jacobian and the equations that tell us how to calculate the location of the joints between links.

Although the change from 2D to 3D involves an increase of only one dimension the complexity of the calculations increases to such an extent that we cannot normally determine the Jacobian by differentiation of analytic expressions. In this section we will take an "engineering approach" to obtain the information we need. Watt and Watt [86] give a rigorous analysis but basically obtain the same result although they express it in a different form. No matter what way the analysis proceeds we recognize that a greater number of variables will be needed to specify the state of a 3D articulation. You will remember that one angle per link is sufficient for a 2D articulation, since in that case each link had only one degree of freedom, i.e., rotation. In a 3D system with three degrees of freedom for each link we must choose to use three parameters for each link. It turns out that indeed three parameters per link is sufficient and the three Euler angles which are sometimes used to define the orientation of objects in the scene being rendered by a computer animation program is one possibility.

For our explanation we will start by considering the three-link articulation depicted in figure 6.22.

Just as in the 2D IK problem we will obtain a differential formulation relating small changes in the orientation of the links to changes in the location of the end point. Later we will extend this to accommodate changes in the orientation of the local frame of reference at the end of the linkage. Thus as for the 2D case

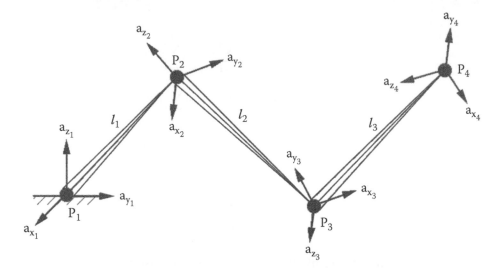

Figure 6.22: A three-dimensional articulated linkage. It has an orthogonal frame of reference given by the basis vectors $(\hat{\mathbf{a}}_x, \hat{\mathbf{a}}_y, \hat{\mathbf{a}}_z)$ attached to the joint at the end of each link. Any structure associated with a link is regarded as fixed relative to the frame of reference for that link. As the linkages move and pivot to reach toward a new goal, the local frames of reference twist and turn and their bases move. The first link is attached to a fixed base at $\mathbf{P}_1$.

we will write an equation relating a small change in end point to a change in parameters for each linkage:

$$\mathbf{\Delta X} = J(\mathbf{\Theta})\mathbf{\Delta\Theta} \tag{6.11}$$

In this case $\mathbf{X}$ is a 3D vector and $\mathbf{\Delta\Theta}$ measures, in some as yet to be defined sense, the orientation of each link. The inverse of equation 6.11 will provide the information on how to arrange the linkage so that its end point moves toward its goal.

> *As far as the iterative steps for the 3D algorithm are concerned they mirror exactly the 2D algorithm; it is only the dimensions of the vectors and matrices that change.*

With a solution procedure for the 3D IK problem based on equation 6.11 in place we need only consider how the 3D Jacobian is obtained and in what form $\mathbf{\Delta\Theta}$ must be expressed. Unfortunately the one thing we cannot do is write an analytic expression for $\mathbf{X}$ given $\mathbf{\Theta}$ and obtain J by analytic differentiation. An alternative method will have to be found. It is here that we use a so-called "engineering approach" to determine J. Hopefully the assumptions we make regarding how a rotation propagates through a linkage and how it affects the end points will be fairly obvious, but if you insist on a rigorous proof then one can be found in Watt and Watt [86].

Our goal is to write an expression that relates a small change in the orientation of each link to a small change in position of the final link: this is J. Two assumptions are made during this calculation and they are justifiable because only *infinitesimal* changes in link orientation are being considered. These assumptions are:

1. In rotational transformations the trigonometric functions $\sin\theta \mapsto \theta$ and $\cos\theta \mapsto 1$ for small θ.

2. The order in which rotational transformation are applied does not affect the outcome of a rotation.

With these assumptions in mind we proceed by considering the effect of small changes in orientation at each link of the structure shown in figure 6.22. These rotations are made by rotating all links lying farther away from the base of the linkage by $\Delta\theta$ around some axis $\hat{n}$. In section 2.18.2 it was stated that any rotation can be expressed as a single angle of rotation and an axis for that rotation. Equation 2.45 reproduced below as equation 6.12 expresses the equivalence of a rotational transformation, acting on an arbitrary vector $\mathbf{r}$, as a matrix R or a vector equation for rotation by angle θ round the direction vector $\hat{n}$ on:

$$\mathbf{r}' = R\mathbf{r} = \cos\theta\mathbf{r} + (1 - \cos\theta)(\hat{n} \cdot \mathbf{r})\hat{n} + \sin\theta(\hat{n} \times \mathbf{r}) \qquad (6.12)$$

In the limit where rotation is by a very small angle equation 6.12 may be written as:

$$\mathbf{r}' = R\mathbf{r} = \mathbf{r} + \Delta\theta(\hat{n} \times \mathbf{r}) \qquad (6.13)$$

The incremental change in the position of $\mathbf{r}$ given by:

$$\boldsymbol{\Delta}\mathbf{r} = \Delta\theta(\hat{n} \times \mathbf{r}) \qquad (6.14)$$

We are now in a position to consider the effect on the end of an articulation of incremental rotations at each link. Look at figure 6.24(a); it shows the effect on a three-link structure of a rotation of $\Delta\theta_1$ round the vector $\hat{n}_1$ based at point $\mathbf{P_1}$. From equation 6.14 we can calculate that the change in position of $\mathbf{P}_4$ by this single rotation is:

$$(\boldsymbol{\Delta}\mathbf{P}_4)_1 = (\Delta\theta_1\hat{n}_1) \times (\mathbf{P}_4 - \mathbf{P}_1)$$

Figure 6.24(b) shows the effect of subsequently rotating the linkage by $\Delta\theta_2$ round $\hat{n}_2$ which is based at the point $\mathbf{P}_2$. Again equation 6.14 lets us write an expression for the change in $\mathbf{P}_4$ due to that rotation:

$$(\boldsymbol{\Delta}\mathbf{P}_4)_2 = (\Delta\theta_2\hat{n}_2) \times (\mathbf{P}_4 - \mathbf{P}_2)$$

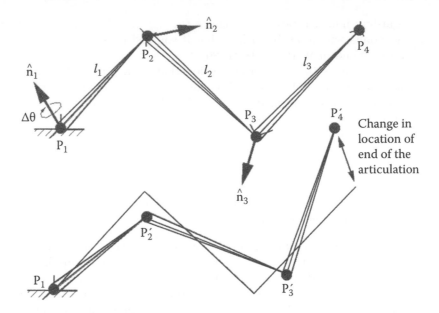

Figure 6.23: The articulated linkage from figure 6.22 before and after a small rotation is applied to each link. The rotation may be specified by giving an angle $\Delta\theta$ and an axis $\hat{n}$ around which the rotation is made.

We can see that a rotation round a vector based at $\mathbf{P}_3$ will also have an effect on the position of $\mathbf{P}_4$ and that the accumulated change in the position of $\mathbf{P}_4$ is the sum of the effects of rotations round the vectors based at points 1 to 3, that is:

$$\mathbf{\Delta P}_4 = \Delta\theta_1\hat{\mathbf{n}}_1 \times (\mathbf{P}_4 - \mathbf{P}_1) + \Delta\theta_2\hat{\mathbf{n}}_2 \times (\mathbf{P}_4 - \mathbf{P}_2) + \Delta\theta_3\hat{\mathbf{n}}_3 \times (\mathbf{P}_4 - \mathbf{P}_3) \quad (6.15)$$

Equation 6.15 gives a linear relationship between the change in position at the end of an articulation and a rotation applied to each link. We have almost achieved our goal of obtaining the Jacobian matrix.

Before making the final step little further exploration of the result of an incremental rotation defined in equations 6.13 and 6.14 is necessary. One reason for this is that we have not explained how the vectors $\hat{\mathbf{n}}_i$ are obtained. We shall now see how these are in fact not needed explicitly because we can work directly from the frames of reference (the $\hat{\mathbf{a}}_{xi}$, $\hat{\mathbf{a}}_{y_i}$ and $\hat{\mathbf{a}}_{zi}$ basis vectors depicted in figure 6.22) attached to the end of every link.

Using the components of $\hat{\mathbf{n}}$, $\mathbf{r}$ and $\mathbf{\Delta r}$ we can express equation 6.14 as a matrix:

$$\begin{bmatrix} \Delta r_x \\ \Delta r_y \\ \Delta r_z \end{bmatrix} = \begin{bmatrix} 0 & -n_z\Delta\theta & n_y\Delta\theta \\ n_z\Delta\theta & 0 & -n_x\Delta\theta \\ -n_y\Delta\theta & n_x\Delta\theta & 0 \end{bmatrix} \begin{bmatrix} r_x \\ r_y \\ r_z \end{bmatrix} \quad (6.16)$$

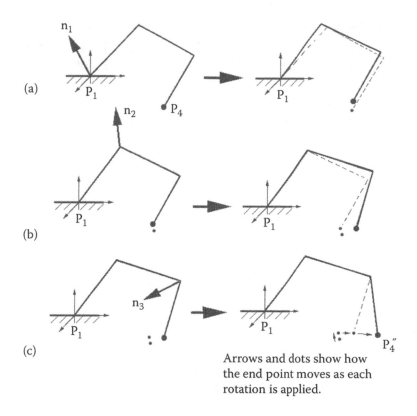

(a)

(b)

(c)

Arrows and dots show how
the end point moves as each
rotation is applied.

Figure 6.24: Accumulating the small rotations occurring at each link of a three-link articulation leads to an accumulated change in the position of the end point of the linkage $\mathbf{P_4}$. In (a) the linkage is slightly repositioned by a small rotation round $\hat{\mathbf{n}}_1$. For (b) and (c) the small rotations only apply to links lying between the point of rotation and the end of the articulation at $\mathbf{P_4}$.

In section 2.12.3 matrices were given which would rotate a vector by a specified angle around either the x, y or z coordinate axis. If rotations around all three axes are performed on a vector $\mathbf{r}$ we can write a matrix expression for the change in $\mathbf{r}$:

$$\mathbf{\Delta r} = (R_x(\Delta\theta_x)R_y(\Delta\theta_y)R_z(\Delta\theta_z) - I)\mathbf{r} \qquad (6.17)$$

$R_x(\Delta\theta_x)$ represents a rotation of $\Delta\theta_x$ radians round the x axis. I is the identity matrix.

For pure rotations R is a 3×3 matrix and if as stated in our prerequisite assumptions $cos\theta \mapsto 1$ and $\sin\theta \mapsto \theta$ then the rotation matrices for axial rotation by angles $\Delta\theta_x$ etc., become for x, y and z, respectively:

$$
\begin{bmatrix} 1 & 0 & 0 \\ 0 & 1 & -\Delta\theta_x \\ 0 & \Delta\theta_x & 1 \end{bmatrix}
\begin{bmatrix} 1 & 0 & \Delta\theta_y \\ 0 & 1 & 0 \\ -\Delta\theta_y & 0 & 1 \end{bmatrix}
\begin{bmatrix} 1 & -\Delta\theta_z & 0 \\ \Delta\theta_z & 1 & 0 \\ 0 & 0 & 1 \end{bmatrix}
$$

Using the assumption that the order of multiplication is unimportant for small angle rotations and neglecting second order product terms like $\Delta\theta_x\Delta\theta_y$ equation 6.17 becomes:

$$
\begin{bmatrix} \Delta r_x \\ \Delta r_y \\ \Delta r_z \end{bmatrix}
=
\begin{bmatrix} 0 & -\Delta\theta_z & \Delta\theta_y \\ \Delta\theta_z & 0 & -\Delta\theta_x \\ -\Delta\theta_y & \Delta\theta_x & 0 \end{bmatrix}
\begin{bmatrix} r_x \\ r_y \\ r_z \end{bmatrix}
\tag{6.18}
$$

Note the similarity between equations 6.18 and 6.16; if terms such as $\Delta\theta_x$ are identified with terms such as $\Delta\theta n_x$ there is a one-to-one correspondence. Thus we can say that in the case of incremental rotations:

A small rotation of θ around a single axis $\hat{n}$ can be accomplished equivalently by performing three small rotations around three basis vectors.

Returning now to equation 6.15 and the term associated with link i:

$$\Delta\theta_i\hat{\mathbf{n}}_i \times (\mathbf{P}_4 - \mathbf{P}_i)$$

For the specific three-link example in equation 6.15 i satisfies $1 \leq i < 4$, and we may express $\hat{\mathbf{n}}_i$ in terms of the known basis vectors for frame i as:

$$\Delta\theta_i(\alpha\hat{\mathbf{a}_{xi}} + \beta\hat{\mathbf{a}_{yi}} + \gamma\hat{\mathbf{a}_{zi}}) \times (\mathbf{P}_4 - \mathbf{P}_i)$$

where α, β and γ are constants. Now, writing $\alpha\Delta\theta_i$ as $\Delta\theta_{xi}$, $\beta\Delta\theta_i$ as $\Delta\theta_{yi}$ and $\gamma\Delta\theta_i$ as $\Delta\theta_{xi}$ we may express $\Delta\theta_i\hat{\mathbf{n}}_i \times (\mathbf{P}_4 - \mathbf{P}_i)$ as:

$$\Delta\theta_{xi}\hat{\mathbf{a}_{xi}} \times (\mathbf{P}_4 - \mathbf{P}_i) + \Delta\theta_{xi}\hat{\mathbf{a}_{yi}} \times (\mathbf{P}_4 - \mathbf{P}_i) + \Delta\theta_{xi}\hat{\mathbf{a}_{zi}} \times (\mathbf{P}_4 - \mathbf{P}_i)$$

Substituting this expression into equation 6.15 for $i = 1$, $i = 2$ and $i = 3$ gives a set of unknowns, the $\Delta\theta_{xi}$ etc. There is a simple linear relationship between them and their contribution to $\Delta\mathbf{P}_4$ which when written in matrix form gives the Jacobian that we have been seeking.

$$
[\Delta\mathbf{P}_4] = \begin{bmatrix} \mathbf{J}_{x1} & \mathbf{J}_{y1} & \mathbf{J}_{z1} & \mathbf{J}_{x2} & \mathbf{J}_{y2} & \mathbf{J}_{z2} & \mathbf{J}_{x3} & \mathbf{J}_{y3} & \mathbf{J}_{z3} \end{bmatrix}
\begin{bmatrix} \Delta\theta_{x1} \\ \Delta\theta_{y1} \\ \Delta\theta_{z1} \\ \Delta\theta_{x2} \\ \Delta\theta_{y2} \\ \Delta\theta_{z2} \\ \Delta\theta_{x3} \\ \Delta\theta_{y3} \\ \Delta\theta_{z3} \end{bmatrix}
\tag{6.19}
$$

where:

$$
\begin{aligned}
\mathbf{J}_{x1} &= \hat{\mathbf{a}}_{x1} \times (\mathbf{P}_4 - \mathbf{P}_1) \\
\mathbf{J}_{y1} &= \hat{\mathbf{a}}_{y1} \times (\mathbf{P}_4 - \mathbf{P}_1) \\
\mathbf{J}_{z1} &= \hat{\mathbf{a}}_{z1} \times (\mathbf{P}_4 - \mathbf{P}_1) \\
\mathbf{J}_{x2} &= \hat{\mathbf{a}}_{x2} \times (\mathbf{P}_4 - \mathbf{P}_2) \\
\mathbf{J}_{y2} &= \hat{\mathbf{a}}_{y2} \times (\mathbf{P}_4 - \mathbf{P}_2) \\
\mathbf{J}_{z2} &= \hat{\mathbf{a}}_{z2} \times (\mathbf{P}_4 - \mathbf{P}_2) \\
\mathbf{J}_{x3} &= \hat{\mathbf{a}}_{x3} \times (\mathbf{P}_4 - \mathbf{P}_3) \\
\mathbf{J}_{y3} &= \hat{\mathbf{a}}_{y3} \times (\mathbf{P}_4 - \mathbf{P}_3) \\
\mathbf{J}_{z3} &= \hat{\mathbf{a}}_{z3} \times (\mathbf{P}_4 - \mathbf{P}_3)
\end{aligned}
$$

From equation 6.19 it is relatively straightforward to see how a Jacobian matrix can be obtained for an articulation with any number of links. Since $\mathbf{\Delta P}_4$ is a vector the dimension of the Jacobian for an n link articulation is $3 \times 3n$ with the three terms associated to link i given by:

$$
\begin{bmatrix} \ldots & \hat{\mathbf{a}}_{xi} \times (\mathbf{P}_{n+1} - \mathbf{P}_i) & \hat{\mathbf{a}}_{yi} \times (\mathbf{P}_{n+1} - \mathbf{P}_i) & \hat{\mathbf{a}}_{zi} \times (\mathbf{P}_{n+1} - \mathbf{P}_i) & \ldots \end{bmatrix}
$$

Having found a way of calculating the Jacobian for the 3D IK problem we can summarize the procedure used to apply IK in the manipulation of a 3D articulated linkage such as that illustrated in figure 6.22. The steps are:

1. A linkage (e.g., the one shown in figure 6.22) is established in its initial configuration. The location of the end points of all links are known and the frames of reference associated with each link are defined. A goal point for the end of the link to move toward is given.

2. From the coordinates of end points of each link and the reference frames axes a Jacobian matrix is calculated and its inverse is used to determine small angles of rotation to apply to the structure.

3. The linkage is pivoted by carrying out rotation by these angles around the basis vectors. This establishes new coordinates for the end points of the linkage; it also changes the direction of the basis vectors.

4. If the end point has not reached its goal the previous two steps are repeated until either the end point does reach its goal or it is not possible for it to move any closer to the goal. The procedure given in figure 6.5 details the iterative process because it applies equally well to both 2D and 3D IK problems.

Setting a goal for the orientation at the end of the chain If you look back at figure 6.22 you will see that at the end of the chain (the point $\mathbf{P}_4$) there is a reference frame whose basis vectors are $(\hat{\mathbf{a}}_{x4}, \hat{\mathbf{a}}_{y4}, \hat{\mathbf{a}}_{z4})$. Nothing has been said about how they move as $\mathbf{P}_4$ is dragged towards its goal. If no prescription is placed on the base vectors at $\mathbf{P}_4$ they will pivot in the same way that the other base vectors pivot when the articulation is rotated in the incremental steps which take $\mathbf{P}_4$ toward its goal.

To obtain an expression for the change in direction of these base vectors consider the effect of the incremental changes in equation 6.15 for the example in figure 6.23. There:

1. A rotation around $\hat{\mathbf{n}}_1$ based at $\mathbf{P}_1$ pivots base vectors at $\mathbf{P}_2$, $\mathbf{P}_3$ and $\mathbf{P}_4$.

2. A rotation around $\hat{\mathbf{n}}_2$ based at $\mathbf{P}_2$ pivots base vectors at $\mathbf{P}_3$ and $\mathbf{P}_4$.

3. The rotation experienced by a base vector at $\mathbf{P}_4$ is subject to the accumulated rotations at all the other joints in the linkage.

To obtain an expression for the effect of accumulated rotations we consider again equation 6.13 but this time write it in the form of a small rotation round vector $\hat{\mathbf{n}}_1$:

$$\mathbf{r}' = \mathbf{r} + (\Delta\theta_1 \hat{\mathbf{n}}_1 \times \mathbf{r}) \tag{6.20}$$

A subsequent rotation of $\mathbf{r}'$ round $\hat{\mathbf{n}}_2$ can be expressed in the same terms:

$$\mathbf{r}'' = \mathbf{r}' + (\Delta\theta_2 \hat{\mathbf{n}}_2 \times \mathbf{r}') \tag{6.21}$$

Substituting for $\mathbf{r}'$ from 6.20 in 6.21 we obtain an expression for the accumulation of two rotations on $\mathbf{r}$:

$$\mathbf{r}'' = \mathbf{r} + (\Delta\theta_2 \hat{\mathbf{n}}_2 + \Delta\theta_1 \hat{\mathbf{n}}_1) \times \mathbf{r} + (\Delta\theta_2 \Delta\theta_1)(\hat{\mathbf{n}}_2 \times (\hat{\mathbf{n}}_1 \times \mathbf{r}))$$

For very small rotations second order terms may be neglected giving:

$$\mathbf{r}'' = \mathbf{r} + (\Delta\theta_2 \hat{\mathbf{n}}_2 + \Delta\theta_1 \hat{\mathbf{n}}_1) \times \mathbf{r}$$

Comparing this with equation 6.20 it is evident that the accumulation of two rotations may be expressed as a single rotation around one axis:

$$\Delta\theta \hat{\mathbf{n}} = (\Delta\theta_2 \hat{\mathbf{n}}_2 + \Delta\theta_1 \hat{\mathbf{n}}_1)$$

Extending the argument by induction results in an expression for the change in $\mathbf{r}$ due to n small rotations, it is:

$$\Delta\mathbf{r} = (\sum_{i=1}^{n} \Delta\theta_i \hat{\mathbf{n}}_i) \times \mathbf{r} \tag{6.22}$$

Applying the above results shows that the accumulated rotation at the end of a three-link articulation is equivalent to a single rotation given by:

$$\Delta\theta_4\hat{\mathbf{n}}_4 = \Delta\theta_3\hat{\mathbf{n}}_3 + \Delta\theta_2\hat{\mathbf{n}}_2 + \Delta\theta_1\hat{\mathbf{n}}_1 \qquad (6.23)$$

The $\hat{\mathbf{n}}_i$ vectors in equation 6.23 can be expanded in an analogous way to that used in the derivation of equation 6.15. When this is done equation 6.23 becomes:

$$\Delta\theta_4\hat{\mathbf{n}}_4 = \sum_{i=1}^{i=3}(\Delta\theta_{xi}\hat{\mathbf{a}}_{xi} + \Delta\theta_{xi}\hat{\mathbf{a}}_{yi} + \Delta\theta_{xi}\hat{\mathbf{a}}_{zi}) \qquad (6.24)$$

Since this involves the same incremental rotations to those of equation 6.19 it is appropriate to augment the Jacobian given in equation 6.24 and solve the position and orientation problems together. Thus equation 6.19 becomes:

$$\left[\begin{array}{c} \Delta\mathbf{P}_4 \\ \Delta\theta_4\hat{\mathbf{n}}_4 \end{array}\right] = \left[\begin{array}{ccccccccc} \mathbf{J}_{x1} & \mathbf{J}_{y1} & \mathbf{J}_{z1} & \mathbf{J}_{x2} & \mathbf{J}_{y2} & \mathbf{J}_{z2} & \mathbf{J}_{x3} & \mathbf{J}_{y3} & \mathbf{J}_{z3} \\ \hat{\mathbf{a}}_{x1} & \hat{\mathbf{a}}_{y1} & \hat{\mathbf{a}}_{z1} & \hat{\mathbf{a}}_{x2} & \hat{\mathbf{a}}_{y2} & \hat{\mathbf{a}}_{z2} & \hat{\mathbf{a}}_{x3} & \hat{\mathbf{a}}_{y3} & \hat{\mathbf{a}}_{z3} \end{array}\right] \left[\begin{array}{c} \Delta\theta_{x1} \\ \Delta\theta_{y1} \\ \Delta\theta_{z1} \\ \Delta\theta_{x2} \\ \Delta\theta_{y2} \\ \Delta\theta_{z2} \\ \Delta\theta_{x3} \\ \Delta\theta_{y3} \\ \Delta\theta_{z3} \end{array}\right]$$

$$(6.25)$$

($\mathbf{J}_{x1}$ etc., are unchanged from equation 6.19.)

By using the solution of equation 6.25 in the iterative algorithm of figure 6.5 we have a comprehensive IK solution for a 3D articulated linkage in which it is possible to specify a goal for both the position and the orientation (of the reference frame) at the end point.

An alternative view of the basis vectors Throughout this section we have described articulation in terms of a set of position vectors for the end point of each link in the articulation (the $\mathbf{P}_i$) and a set of basis vectors (the $\hat{\mathbf{a}}_x, \hat{\mathbf{a}}_y, \hat{\mathbf{a}}_z$) located there. However one can take an alternative view of how these positions and bases might be determined. Such an alternative view is sometimes useful because of the way in which most computer animation programs describe the hierarchical linking of models in an articulation.

For example one might want to animate with IK the raising of a "chain" from a heap lying on the ground until it becomes fully extended as shown in figure 6.25 for example. The chain in this example is made up from a number of "links" and since all the links look the same it is only necessary to build a vertex/polygon model for one of them. The vertices in the model are specified relative to the frame of reference used for construction, usually the global frame.

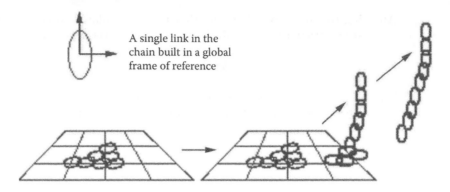

Figure 6.25: IK is used to animate the raising of a chain from a pile of links on the floor until it dangles from a hook.

To build the multi-link chain the individual model is copied and then rotated and/or translated as necessary to assemble the chain.

What we will show in this section is that it is possible to obtain all the necessary terms for the calculation of the Jacobian in equations 6.19 or 6.25 from the same series of transformation matrices used to position copies of a model in some hierarchical combination such as the chain example.

To see how this is done consider the illustrations in figure 6.26. They depict a series of actions which start from a point $\mathbf{P}_1$ located at the origin of the global frame of reference and proceed as follows:

1. A rotation (say around the vector $\hat{\mathbf{n}}_1$) is applied to $\mathbf{P}_1$ and also to a copy of the original basis axes $(\hat{\mathbf{x}},\hat{\mathbf{y}},\hat{\mathbf{z}})$. The rotation is followed by a translation that takes $\mathbf{P}$ and the rotated basis frame to $\mathbf{P}'_1$. The composite transformation $[T_1]$ is a 4×4 matrix:

$$\begin{bmatrix} r_{11} & r_{12} & r_{13} & t_x \\ r_{21} & r_{22} & r_{23} & t_y \\ r_{31} & r_{32} & r_{33} & t_z \\ 0 & 0 & 0 & 1 \end{bmatrix}$$

   The elements r_{ij} represent the rotation and the t_i the translation.

   If we imagine a link existing between $\mathbf{P}'_1$ and $\mathbf{P}_1$ the illustration labeled (b) resembles closely a 3D articulated structure with one link. It has an end point at $\mathbf{P}'_1$ and a set of basis vectors which are no longer coincident with the global frame even through they were derived from it. For the moment we will label these $\hat{\mathbf{x}}'_1$, $\hat{\mathbf{y}}'_1$ and $\hat{\mathbf{z}}'_1$.

2. Suppose we now repeat the process (i.e., apply a transformation T_2 to effect a rotation round the vector $\hat{\mathbf{n}}_2$ followed by a translation), $\mathbf{P}'_1$ will

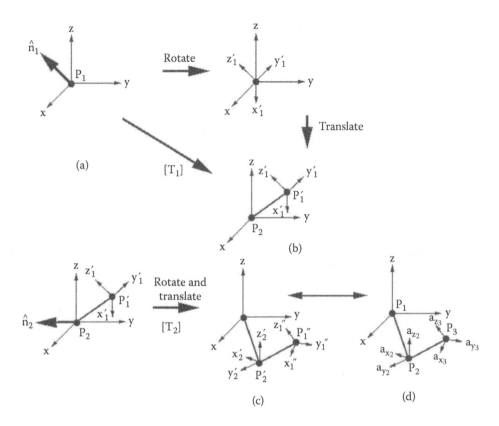

Figure 6.26: Assembling an articulation by repeated transformation of a point at the origin of a global frame of reference and a copy of the global frame's basis vectors. The illustrations are discussed in the text.

move to $\mathbf{P}_1''$ and the copy of the original base axes will reorient themselves as illustrated in (c). A point $\mathbf{P}_2$ at the origin in (b) will move to $\mathbf{P}_2'$.

Now it doesn't take too much imagination to recognize the emergence of a linkage suitable for the application of IK. A comparison between illustration (c) and figure 6.22 will show us that illustration (c) is equivalent to a two-link articulated system. A two-link system using the notation of figure 6.22 and mirroring illustration (c) is given in (d) and this illustrates the one-to-one correspondence. Figure 6.27 gives a table listing the items which correspond.

3. With a correspondence established between the points and bases used in the derivation of J and the application of a transformation to a point at the origin and global coordinate frame we can proceed to obtain $\mathbf{P}_i$ and $\hat{\mathbf{a}}_{xi}$ etc., directly from the transformation matrices $[T_1]$ and $[T_2]$.

Illustration (c)	Illustration (d)
Origin	$\mathbf{P}_1$
$\mathbf{P}_2'$	$\mathbf{P}_2$
$\mathbf{P}_1''$	$\mathbf{P}_3$
Global $\mathbf{x}$	$\hat{\mathbf{a}}_{x1}$
Global $\mathbf{y}$	$\hat{\mathbf{a}}_{y1}$
Global $\mathbf{z}$	$\hat{\mathbf{a}}_{z1}$
$\mathbf{x}_2'$	$\hat{\mathbf{a}}_{x2}$
$\mathbf{y}_2'$	$\hat{\mathbf{a}}_{y2}$
$\mathbf{z}_2'$	$\hat{\mathbf{a}}_{z2}$
$\mathbf{x}_1''$	$\hat{\mathbf{a}}_{x3}$
$\mathbf{y}_1''$	$\hat{\mathbf{a}}_{y3}$
$\mathbf{z}_1''$	$\hat{\mathbf{a}}_{z3}$

Figure 6.27: Table giving correspondence between points and axes in illustrations (c) and (d) of figure 6.26.

Point $\mathbf{P}_1$ is at the origin and is just $(0,0,0)$, point $\mathbf{P}_2$ is given by applying $[T_2]$ to $(0,0,0)$ and point $\mathbf{P}_3$ is given by applying the composite transformation $[T_{21}] = [T_2][T_1]$ to $(0,0,0)$.

A similar argument applies to the basis vectors, for example $\hat{\mathbf{a}}_{y3}$ is obtained by applying $[T_{21}]$ to the vector $(0,1,0)$.

Immediately we can see that these simple multiplications have the effect of extracting elements of rows or columns from the appropriate transformation matrix. Thus the matrix which establishes link i is effectively:

$$\begin{bmatrix} (a_x)_x & (a_x)_y & (a_x)_z & P_x \\ (a_y)_x & (a_y)_y & (a_y)_z & P_y \\ (a_z)_x & (a_z)_y & (a_z)_z & P_z \\ 0 & 0 & 0 & 1 \end{bmatrix}$$

where $(a_x)_x$ is the x component of the $\hat{\mathbf{a}}_x$ basis vector for link i and $\mathbf{P}_i = (P_x, P_y, P_z)$.

Finally it is worth just reiterating that these values are extracted from the transformations that built the linkage by moving a copy of the model from its reference frame into position along the chain. So for the point at the end of an n link system its location and base axes orientation are read from the composite transformation: $[T] = [T_n][T_{n-1}]...[T_2][T_1]$

6.4.4   The cyclic coordinate descent method

The *Jacobian* IK algorithm is well defined analytically and can be rigorously analyzed and investigated, but in practice it can sometimes fail to converge. In

Step 1:
Start with the last link in the chain (at the end effector).
Step 2:
Set a loop counter to zero. Set the max loop count to some upper limit.
Step 3:
Rotate this link so that it points towards the target. Choose an axis of rotation that is perpendicular to the plane defined by two of the linkages meeting at the point of rotation. Do not violate any angle restrictions.
Step 4:
Move down the chain (away from the end effector) and go back to Step 2
Step 5:
When the base is reached, determine whether the target has been reached or the loop limit is exceeded. If so, exit; if not, increment the loop counter and repeat from Step 2.

Listing 6.6: The cyclic coordinate descent iterative algorithm for manipulating an IK chain into position. It works equally well in two or three dimensions.

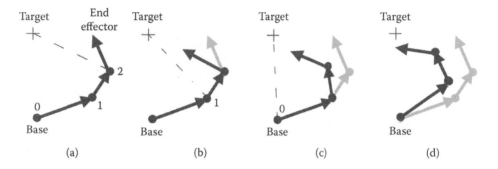

Figure 6.28: The cyclic coordinate descent algorithm. Iteration round 1 (loop count = 1). The original position of the linkage is shown in light grey.

fact, all iterative algorithms can sometimes fail to converge. However, when the Jacobian method fails to converge, it goes wrong very obviously. It does not just grind to a halt; it goes *way over the top!* For computer animation applications it would be preferable to have a *simple* algorithm that can be applied in real time and is stable and robust.

A heuristic algorithm called the *cyclic coordinate descent* (CCD) method [90] works well in practice. It is simple to implement and fast enough to use in real time, even though it doesn't always give an optimal solution. It consists of the five steps given in listing 6.6.

The algorithm is best explained with reference to the example given in figures 6.28 and 6.29. The steps are labeled (a) to (h), where (a) is the starting configuration. A line joining pivot point 2 to the target shows how the last link

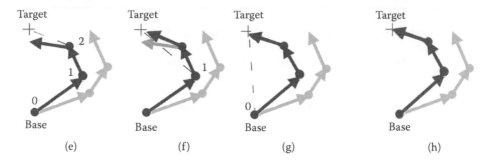

Figure 6.29: The cyclic coordinate descent algorithm. Iteration round 2 (loop count = 2) completes the cycle because the end effector had reached the target.

in the chain should be rotated about an axis perpendicular to the plane in which links 1 and 2 lie. After this rotation, the linkage will lie in the position shown in (b). Next, the linkage is rotated about point 1 so that the end effector lies on the line joining point 1 to the target point. This results in configuration (c), at which time a rotation about the base at point 0 is made to give configuration (d). This completes round 1 of the animation. Figure 6.29 configuration (e) is the same as figure 6.29(d), and a pivot at point 2 is made to give configuration (f). Further pivots about point 1 result in configuration (g). Finally, a pivot about point 0 leads to configuration (h), by which time the end effector has reached the target and the iteration stops.

Of course, there are many other configurations that would satisfy the goal of the end effector touching the target, but the configuration achieved with the CCD algorithm is the one that *feels* natural to the human observer. It is also possible that in certain circumstances, the end effector may never reach the goal, but this can be detected by the loop count limit being exceeded. Typically, for real-time work, the loop count should never go beyond five. The Jacobian method has the advantage of responding to pushes and pulls on the end effector in a more natural way. The CCD method tends to move the link closest to the end effector. This is not surprising when you look at the algorithm, because if a rotation of the last linkage reaches the target, the algorithm can stop. When using these methods interactively, there are noticeable differences in response; the CCD behaves more like a loosely connected chain linkage whilst the Jacobian approach gives a configuration more like one would imagine from a flexible elastic rod. In practical work, the CCD approach is easy to implement and quite stable, and so is our preferred way of using IK in real-time interactive programs for virtual reality applications .

A program that illustrates the CCD algorithm in practice is available from the website. It consists of a stylized representation of a pair of industrial robots designed to move their tool head to a working position and perform some form of manipulation. In the simulation, the working point's location and tool head

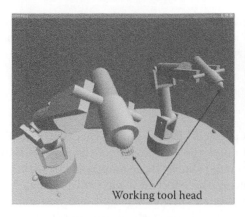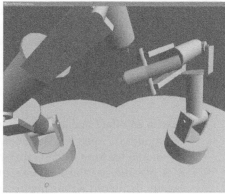

Working tool head

Figure 6.30: An inverse kinematic simulation of two idealized 5 degree of freedom robots performed using the cyclic coordinate descent algorithm.

orientation are set interactively by the user; the articulated linkage then follows these points. The angular orientation of each of the joints is determined by the algorithm. A screenshot of the program is illustrated in figure 6.30. The visualization was created using a combination of the basic primitive cylinders and cubes rendered using OpenGL and the GLUT and adapted from the basic template program presented in section 7.1.5.

6.5 Physics

When computer game programmers discuss animation they talk about *physics* because in a game the action is not usually pre-scripted and the action is supposed to mimic the real world. In the real world how things behave when they move, how they react when they are subjected to a force, for example gravity, how they stretch and bounce, and how they behave when they collide with something is determined by the basic laws of physics, or to be more precise the laws of motion.

Often the mathematical models that are to be used to simulate the physical behavior of objects and the computer codes derived from them are provided in a library or component that is added to the games engine. This section presents a few examples of an approach to animation where the action is not specified in a set of keyframes; rather models follow paths, twist, turn, deform or accelerate using the same physical laws that govern the dynamics of objects in the real world. Before looking at the examples it is worth considering how such physical processes are used in the context of 3D graphics. There are two main aspects to consider:

1. How is the effect of a physical process applied to the model?

2. How is the effect determined given that the animator wants to retain some degree of control over the action but not to the extent of violating the physical laws the effect is trying to simulate?

Let's look at each of these aspects in a little more detail.

How is an effect applied? Since a physical effect usually either moves or distorts the model in some way it should affect the coordinates of the vertices that give the model its form. There are two points in the basic animation algorithm where it is possible to consider introducing the effect of a physical process. Vertices can be displaced either before or after the model is moved into position.

For example the side to side flapping motion of a swimming fish simulated by a lateral wave should be applied to a model of a fish before the fish is directed to swim in circles. In this case the effect acts in the *local* coordinate frame of the model. Alternatively an object falling under gravity might be tumbling as it falls; tumbling is simulated by angular interpolation. In this case the effect of gravity must act in the *global* frame of reference; otherwise the object might at times appear to fall upward.

There is another important issue to consider when using an effect that moves individual vertices in a model: the number and location of its vertices. This is important because there is little point applying a distortion to a model if the vertices are located so far apart that the detail created by the effect is missed. For example, one way to simulate the animation of a wave is to take a planar mesh and apply a time dependent displacement to the vertices in it. Since a flat plane can be represented with a mesh of very few vertices the wave will appear very *rough* unless some redundant vertices are built into the original flat plane. This example is illustrated in figure 6.31.

How is an effect controlled? Let's consider the example of an effect that simulates the action of gravity on an object so that it falls to the floor and bounces a couple of times before coming to rest.

In a keyframe system the animator might direct that the whole action is to occur over a period of 100 frames and the object is to bounce twice. Unless the distance from release point to the floor and coefficient of restitution (bounciness) fit the equation of motion under gravity the object will not behave as directed and at the end of the 100 frame period it might be left hanging in mid-air.

The question then is do we let the physics overrule the animator? The answer is equivocal. For the example cited it is possible to achieve a compromise that lets the animator have control over the duration and number of bounces whilst still giving the appearance of realistic behavior by "*massaging*" the value used for g, the acceleration of gravity.

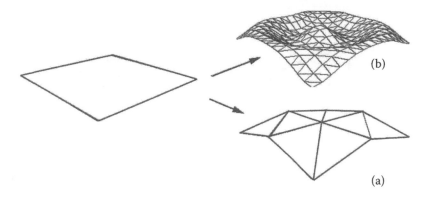

Figure 6.31: Simulating a radial wave by displacing vertices in a mesh. In (a) the wave is represented by an array of nine vertices whilst in (b) there are 225 vertices. When flat (on the left) both meshes have the same appearance whilst it is only the finer mesh that gives a good representation of the wave effect when it is applied.

6.5.1 Standardization

An important practical concern when you need to implement a large variety of effects is that they should act through some sort of a common interface.

For physically based effects implemented in the **C** or **C++** languages, one approach uses a table of pointers to functions. Each function in the table implements one effect and they all use the same parameters.

The first function parameter defines a range of frames $[f_s, f_f]$, over which the effect acts and from this calculation a parameter $\tau : 0 \le \tau < 1$ is determined by:

$$\tau = \frac{current frame - f_s}{f_f - f_s + 1}$$

Written in this form the effect can be implemented in a way that is independent of the number of integer frames in the interval during which it is to occur. The other essential parameters are the number of vertices and access to the list of vertices in the model being affected.

All functions will behave in a standard way such that when $\tau = 0$ the vertex data will be modified to reflect the initial state of the effect, and when $\tau = 1$ the final state is put into effect. The function would be called during two of the steps in the basic animation algorithm:

1. Before the model is moved into position. (In the coordinate frame of reference used for design and specification of the model.) In this frame of reference the point $(0, 0, 0)$ is the so-called *hold point*.

2. After the model has been moved into position but before the viewing transformation is applied. (In the global coordinate frame of reference.)

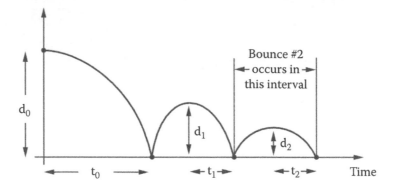

Figure 6.32: Graph of position against time for an object falling and making several bounces.

Now we turn to consider three examples of animation effects arising from some simple physical laws.

6.5.2 Falling and bouncing

On earth objects fall because they are subject to the constant gravitational force and if dropped their velocity increases linearly until they hit a solid surface at which point they may rebound. In this section we will develop a model that conforms to the constraints discussed in the previous section. Our model will allow the animator to specify parameters that correspond to useful control variables. In this case the control variables of choice are:

1. The height to fall is d_0.

2. The number of bounces to be performed is n_b.

3. The coefficient of restitution is μ.

The coefficient of restitution is a measure of how elastic the bounce is; it is defined as:

$$\mu = \frac{\text{velocity after impact}}{\text{velocity before impact}}$$

To satisfy our standardization criteria the fall must be completed when the parameter $\tau = 1$.

Figure 6.32 illustrates graphically how a dropped object behaves by plotting a curve of its height above the ground against time since dropped.

In our computer simulation we have two options as to how we apply the effect to a model built around a network of vertices. The first idea that comes to mind is to treat the model as a single entity and then use the distance from the model's center to the rebound plane for d_0. Every vertex in the model is moved by the same amount and as a result the whole model behaves as a rigid entity. An alternative idea (and perhaps a more interesting one) treats each vertex individually so that d is the distance of a vertex to the rebound plane. This can give the illusion of a *floppy* or *flexible* model.

The algorithm that we will use must be based on the standard equations for motion under constant acceleration but in order to satisfy the constraints above we will have to determine an artificial acceleration. In other words g, the acceleration due to gravity, will not be $9.8ms^{-2}$. From a visual point of view this will not be a problem because the acceleration of an object will still look quite realistic. To obtain a suitable value of g we recognize that the time to first impact t_0 is related to the distance fallen d_0, by:

$$d = \frac{gt_0{}^2}{2}$$

Thus if t_0 is known g can be found.

Determining t_0 involves calculating the time intervals $t_1, t_2, \ldots, t_{nb-1}$ (illustrated in figure 6.32) and using the fact that the overall time is scaled to unity thus we have:

$$t_0 + 2(t_1 + t_2 + t_{nb-1}) = 1$$

The relationship between t_i and t_{i+1} is known because $t_{i+1} = \mu t_i$ and thus g may be determined from:

$$t_0 = \frac{1.0}{1.0 + 2(\mu + \mu^2 + \ldots + \mu^{n_b-1})}$$

$$g = \frac{2d_0}{t_0^2}$$

The height of any rebound d_i is given by $d_i = \mu^i d_0$ and the position at any instant of time (τ) is calculated with the usual expression $d = v_i \tau + \frac{1}{2} g \tau^2$, where v_i is the initial velocity for bounce i in which τ will satisfy:

$$t_0 + 2(t_1 + \ldots + t_i) \le \tau < t_0 + 2(t_1 + \ldots + t_i + t_{i+1})$$

6.5.3 Projectiles

The behavior of a projectile forms the basis for the simulation of explosions, fireworks, etc. The same equations governing the behavior of an object falling under gravity also apply to a projectile. This time however the projectile is fired with an initial velocity in the direction $\mathbf{d}$ of magnitude $V = |\mathbf{d}|$; see figure 6.35.

Under the influence of gravitational acceleration g and assuming that the projectile is fired from the point $(0, 0, 0)$ parametric equations for the motion are written as:

$$r = V \cos \alpha t$$

$$z = -\frac{1}{2} g t^2 + V \sin \alpha t$$

Gravity is assumed to act in the negative z direction and r is a radial coordinate along the direction in which the projectile will fly.

From the point of view of describing the action in the context of practical animation software the initial velocity V and projection angle α are probably less desirable *user* controlled parameters than say the point where the projectile is to hit the ground or where it is to reach maximum height. If either of these are specified then the equations can be rearranged so that not only appropriate V and α are determined internally but the direction in which the projectile is launched is also uniquely specified.

6.5.4   Explosions

To simulate an object exploding a combination of dynamic motion applied to individual polygons in the model and some sort of post-process to add a glow or smoke clouds can result in very realistic images. Probably the four most significant elements are:

1. Each polygon from which a model is constructed is treated as a projectile and fired off with a high initial velocity in a direction away from the center of the explosion.

2. A bright *flash* of light centered on the site of the explosion is expanded radially away from its origin over a short time interval.

3. A large number of *particles* (pixels of bright color) are projected away from the center of explosion; their color is faded to black after a few frames.

4. Draw a waxing and waning bright halo around and within the polygons as they fly off; this simulates burning and fire.

The last three effects in this list do not involve polygons or vertices in the model and are created by processing the image after it has been rendered and stored in a framebuffer. Figures 6.33 and 6.34 illustrate a variety of explosions simulated by combining one or more of these elements.

Ballistic projectiles To simulate the first element in the list above involves treating each polygonal facet in a model as if it were a projectile with the center of the polygon acting as its center of mass. We can imagine several scenarios:

1. The projectiles are influenced by gravity, falling back to a *ground* plane. Some polygons will be projected downward and consequently they hit the ground at high velocity; they may bounce back up.

2. Polygons might not be affected (noticeably) by gravity, e.g., some fireworks which simply burst away radially from the center of explosion and gradually fade away.

Figure 6.33: Simulating an explosion by breaking the model up into its component polygons and ballistically firing them off from the center of the explosion. A few of the larger components are retained as single entities and a *bright* flare is painted over the image at the seat of the explosion.

3. Polygons which are not simply point projectiles will be subjected to rotational forces causing them to tumble randomly.

4. Because explosion is a time-dependent process, polygons farther away from the origin of the explosion will be projected at later times. This simulates the action of a shockwave traveling through the model.

One of the most difficult things to achieve with simulations of this type is to provide meaningful control to the animator. For the simulation it is probably desirable that the explosion occurs over a fixed-time interval, say unit time. A function executing the effect moves the polygons into appropriate positions according to some parameter τ $(0 \leq \tau \leq 1)$ derived from the frame being rendered. Other possible control parameters might include *how big* the effect is to look (this can be achieved by specifying the maximum displacement a polygon is to achieve or in the case of gravitational influence the maximum height reached by the projected polygons).

Let us consider the example of an explosion occurring at a point $\mathbf{P}_e$ somewhere inside an object built from n polygonal facets, the centers of which are located at $\mathbf{P}_i : 0 \leq i < (n-1)$. The direction in which polygon i is projected is therefore: $\mathbf{d} = \mathbf{P}_i - \mathbf{P}_e$. Assuming that gravitation forces are significant and that the animator has specified the explosion must rise to a maximum height of Δz above the model's position and then fall to a ground plane at $z = 0$ the equations of projectile motion allow us to obtain a value for g (acceleration due to gravity) that will have all the polygons on the ground at the latest when $\tau = 1$. The geometry of projectile motion is illustrated in figure 6.35.

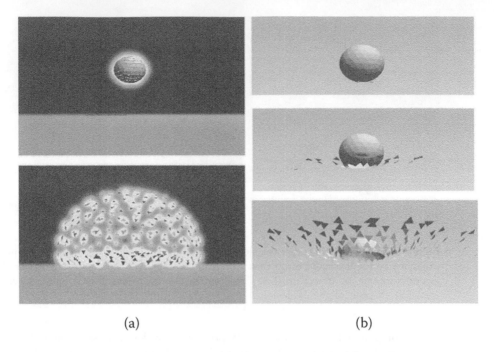

(a)   (b)

Figure 6.34: Simulating explosions: The sphere is broken up into its polygonal components and they are projected away from the point of the blast. In (a) the effect is enhanced by an image processor which uses an alpha channel to draw a *fire-like* glow round the model. The glow increases in intensity and size as the explosion progresses. In (b) the polygons are blasted out after a delay which is proportional to their distance from the seat of the explosion; this simulates a *shock* front.

The longest time of flight will occur when polygon k (the one with maximum z coordinate) is thrust vertically. Thus from the equations for parabolic motion:

$$
\begin{aligned}
r &= V\cos\alpha t \\
z &= -\frac{1}{2}gt^2 + V\sin\alpha t
\end{aligned}
$$

we can see that the time it takes a projectile to reach its apex is:

$$
\frac{V\sin\alpha}{g}
$$

As expected, this will be a maximum when $\alpha = \frac{\pi}{2}$. At the apex of its motion a projectile fired vertically will have zero velocity and the time it takes for it to fall back to the ground, a distance $\Delta z + \Delta f$ ($\Delta f = \mathbf{P}_{i_z}$ the height of polygon i

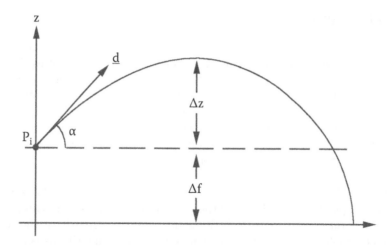

Figure 6.35: The trajectory of a projectile released from point $\mathbf{P}_i$ in direction $\mathbf{d}$.

above ground) is given by:

$$t_{fall} = \sqrt{\frac{2(\Delta z + \Delta f)}{g}}$$

The time it takes a projectile to reach the highest point is determined from the usual equations:

$$\Delta z = \frac{V \sin \alpha}{2g}$$

$$t_{up} = \frac{V^2 \sin^2 \alpha}{g}$$

Given:

$$t_{up} = \sqrt{\frac{2\Delta z}{g}}$$

By assuming that the total flight time is normalized to unity the acceleration g must be:

$$g = (\sqrt{2\Delta z} + \sqrt{2(\Delta z + \Delta f)})^2$$

and the initial velocity V is:

$$V = \sqrt{2g\Delta z}$$

Using V and g, the location of all the exploding polygons at any τ is given by substituting for t in the equations of parabolic motion. Each polygon will have a different α depending on its position relative to the center of explosion.

Polygons reaching the ground before $\tau = 1$ will need to be prevented from falling farther.

6.6   Animating cloth and hair

These two topics are considered together because some of the same mathematical principles on which their behavior is modeled have similarities. The modeling of hair and cloth is being discussed in this chapter on animation because both of these materials are generally non-rigid and move in an unscripted way according to the simple laws of motion and elasticity. Indeed, one of the simplest models for both hair and cloth envisages them as a spring mass system. Alternatively, it is possible to model hair that is soft and semi-rigid in the same way that textures like fur are simulated; see section 11.4.

Cloth The simulation of animated figures that are wearing loose fitting clothing is a major challenge. It is still the subject of ongoing research and many technical papers on new or more realistic models appear regularly in the scientific press. One problem with most of the new sophisticated algorithms is that they are not very practical. Sometimes they only work when the cloth fulfills certain design constraints, or perhaps the dynamics are fine, but the collision detection does not work well. These problems are considerably accentuated if the simulation is to be part of a real-time application program. To animate cloth realistically in real-time is still a major challenge. A good and wide-ranging introduction to the challenges of animating cloth, and some of the best mathematical models can be found in House and Breen [43]. The extensive list of references in House and Breen [43] is a good place to start following up on the latest state of research.

One approach in which the movement of a cloth texture can be simulated (and that does work very well in practice, is also good for real-time systems and is robust and mostly stable) is through an extension of the spring mass model for elastic and Jello-like deformation. In McMenemy [59] chapter 18 a practical algorithm and computer code is described for the simulation the deformation of elastic objects. This code works well for objects that enclose a volume and for objects that are sheet-like. It is the sheet-like objects that interest us here. When some sections of a sheet's boundary are free to move, as the object is pulled around by another point on or inside the sheet, the whole object produces a motion that quite closely resembles a piece of cloth being moved about. The only drawback of this spring-mass model is that *it stretches* whereas cloth is mostly an inelastic material. However it only takes a minor iterative extension of the algorithm to effectively remove the elasticity and give a resulting motion that is a pretty good representation of a piece of cloth being moved around. Before looking at the algorithm's extension, it is necessary to consider a few details of the spring-mass model.

The mathematical model The mathematical model on which the dynamics of cloth simulation will be based is that of a spring mass particle system, as illustrated in figure 6.36. In (a) a 3D shape is represented by a mesh network of interconnecting springs along each edge in the shape. The vertices are repre-

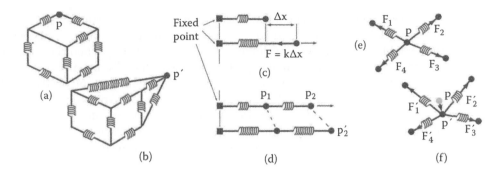

Figure 6.36: A spring mass particle system model for elastic deformation. (See the discussion in the text.)

sented by particles at points such as **p**. In (b), pulling **p** away from its original position establishes restoring forces in the springs that would tend to return the mesh to its original shape when we release the vertex at point **p′**. In a simple one-dimensional spring (c), the restoring force is proportional to the extension in the length of the spring. (d) When two or more springs are connected, all the non-fixed points such as $\mathbf{p}_1$ may move. All new positions must be obtained simultaneously; in this 1D case an analytic solution of the math model may be obtained. (e) If the springs form a complex 3D network then the effect of a distortion must be obtained using a numerical solution technique. (f) When the point **p** is moved to **p′**, the forces in all attached springs will change and the shape of the network will adjust to a new state of equilibrium.

When an object's surface is constructed as a series of polygonal faces the edges in our *mesh* correspond to the little springs in the network joining the vertices together. The original configuration of the model is its rest state, and as one or more of the vertices are pulled, the whole network of springs adjusts to take on a new shape, just as they would if the model was built out of real springs and one of them was pulled or pushed.

The behavior of this network of springs is modeled mathematically by using the well-known laws of Hooke and Newton. Hooke's law says that the restoring force **F** in a spring is proportional to the extension in the spring $\mathbf{\Delta p}$. That is, $\mathbf{F} = k\mathbf{\Delta p}$, where k is the constant of proportionality. Newton says that the acceleration **a** of a particle (in this case a vertex in the mesh) with a mass m is proportional to the force applied to it. That is, $\mathbf{F} = m\mathbf{a}$. And of course, the acceleration is given by the second derivative of the distance moved, so this equation can be rewritten as $\mathbf{F} = m\,\ddot{\mathbf{p}}$. This differential equation would be relatively easy to solve for a single vertex and one spring, but in a mesh with hundreds of vertices interconnected by springs in three dimensions, a numerical approximation to the modeling equations and a computer are needed.

Several numerical techniques can be used to solve the equations that simulate how the vertices respond to an applied disturbance (House and Breen [43] discuss this in depth). One technique that is fast and simple and has been used by physicists for solving dynamic particle problems has also been shown by computer game developers to be particularly good for our type of problem. It is called *Vertlet integration* [85], and whilst it allows us to avoid the complexity of carrying out an *implicit* solution for the equations, we can also still avoid some of the instabilities that occur in the simpler *explicit* solution techniques.

Combining the laws of Hooke and Newton gives a second order differential equation:

$$\mathbf{a} = \ddot{\mathbf{p}}_i = \frac{\mathbf{F}}{m} = \frac{k}{m} \sum_{j=1}^{n} \Delta(\mathbf{p}_j - \mathbf{p}_i) \qquad (6.26)$$

which we must solve at every vertex in the mesh. The term $\sum_{j=1}^{n} \Delta(\mathbf{p}_j - \mathbf{p}_i)$ sums the change in the length of each of the n edges that are connected to vertex i. We must discretize equation 6.26 by replacing the second order differential $\ddot{\mathbf{p}}_i$ with an approximation. The key feature of Vertlet integration recognizes that the first order differential of p, that is $\dot{\mathbf{p}}_i$, is a velocity and that if we are given initial values for position and velocity, we can write an iterative pair of equations which may be used to determine how a vertex moves in a short time interval Δt. If $\mathbf{p}$ is the current position of a vertex and $\mathbf{v}$ is its current velocity then the updated position $\mathbf{p}'$ and updated velocity $\mathbf{v}'$ are given by:

$$\begin{aligned} \mathbf{v}' &= \mathbf{v} + \mathbf{a}\Delta t \\ \mathbf{p}' &= \mathbf{p} + \mathbf{v}'\Delta t \end{aligned}$$

Normally, the velocity is not calculated explicitly and is approximated by a finite difference expression for the differential. If the previous position is given by $\overline{\mathbf{p}}$ then $\mathbf{v} = \frac{\mathbf{p} - \overline{\mathbf{p}}}{\Delta t}$. The expression may be re-written to obtain $\mathbf{p}'$ as:

$$\mathbf{p}' = 2\mathbf{p} - \overline{\mathbf{p}} + \mathbf{a}\Delta t^2$$

And of course, the previous position has to be updated once it as been used. That is, $\overline{\mathbf{p}} = \mathbf{p}$. By substituting for $\mathbf{a}$ as given in equation 6.26, the result is a remarkably simple iterative algorithm that can be used to solve for the transient behavior of a mesh. With the right choice of parameters, it offers a visually reasonable approximation to the behavior of a squashy/elastic/flexible object.

The model of equation 6.26 can be slightly improved by adding in the effect of a *damper* in parallel with the spring. This helps to make the object appear less elastic. It is easy to model this effect mathematically because the damper provides a force which is proportional to the velocity of a vertex: $\mathbf{F}_d = k_d(\mathbf{p} - \overline{\mathbf{p}})/\Delta t$. This force is added to the spring restoration force in equation 6.26.

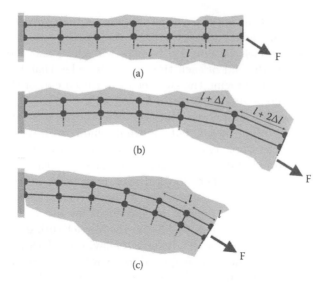

Figure 6.37: Applying the relaxation algorithm to eliminate any elasticity in the spring-mass model for cloth materials. In (a) a force F pulls the network of polygons in the direction of the force; each edge spring extends to reach an equilibrium, shown in (b). In (c) the relaxation has restored each edge to its original length, but the cloth vertices have taken up new positions.

The stability and type of behavior of the simulation is governed by the choice of values for the coefficients Δt, m, k and k_d. The code accompanying McMenemy and Ferguson [59] is a very good base from which to start to build a cloth simulator.

Stiffening things up The spring mass system and its mathematical model is ideal for simulating the behavior of a material that is elastic as it is stretched or pulled around by points along part of its boundary. There are some numerical issues relating to the stability of the equations, especially as the material becomes stiffer (the term *stiff equations* is not used without reason). This is one reason why more sophisticated simulations move from an explicit numerical integration to an implicit one. Unfortunately cloth **is stiff**; it has very little elasticity. Indeed for most types of cloth it should have no elasticity at all. However, as the stiffness tends to infinity, the problem of stability goes away and it is possible to add a very simple iterative step in the Vertlet algorithm which basically prevents any of the springs in the spring mass model from extending. Yes, it's that simple. This approach is called *relaxation* and it, and variants of it, have been used for many years in the solution of partial differential equations.

To see what this extra step entails, look at figure 6.37 which shows a few polygons making up a cloth sheet. One edge of the sheet is fixed and the edge at the other end of the sheet is subject to a force (e.g., gravity, or just an inertial force due to boundary movement) that causes the edge to move. In a spring mass elastic model the polygon vertices will move and the sheet will stretch. However, if at the end of each time step, any edge that has changed in length is pulled back, by moving the two vertices at each end of the edge back toward each other, the original length will be restored.

Of course, pulling on one edge will elongate the next and so on, with these effects reverberating throughout the whole chain, or in the case of a 2D piece of cloth, across the whole cloth. So, this process has to be repeated until stability has been restored and all the edges have relaxed to their original length. This refinement takes a number of steps. The refinement process iterates until the relaxation is complete. Fortunately iterative relaxation is a stable numerical process that converges rapidly, so it is ideal for use in real-time simulations. When successive relaxation is added to the Vertlet spring-mass model the result is a very usable model for the dynamic behavior of cloth material.

Several refinements can be applied to the relaxation process. First the Vertlet time step is usually small and consequently during each time step the change in length of any one spring will be small. Therefore, usually only one relaxation iteration is necessary at each time step. In essence, this just adds a single step to the calculation. Second, where lengths need to be calculated a square root operation is needed, because the edge lengths only change by a very small fraction at each step. An approximation can be used to obtain the root without explicitly calculating the square root. The approximation is based on a first order Taylor series expansion of the function $f(x) = \sqrt{x}$. If vertices at positions $\mathbf{p}_i$ and $\mathbf{p}_{i+1}$ are joined by an elastic edge e, then the length of e is $e = (\mathbf{r} \cdot \mathbf{r})^{\frac{1}{2}}$ where $\mathbf{r} = \mathbf{p}_{i+1} - \mathbf{p}_i$. The original length of each side e_0 is given by $e_0 = (\mathbf{r}_0 \cdot \mathbf{r}_0)^{\frac{1}{2}}$, where $\mathbf{r}_0$ is the vector between $\mathbf{p}_{i+1}$ and $\mathbf{p}_i$ in their original (undisturbed) positions.

Now consider (up to first order) the Taylor expansion for the function $f(x) = x^{\frac{1}{2}}$ in the region of a:

$$f(x) = x^{\frac{1}{2}} \approx a^{\frac{1}{2}} + (x - a)\frac{1}{2a^{\frac{1}{2}}} \tag{6.27}$$

If we let $x = e^2 = \mathbf{r} \cdot \mathbf{r}$ and $a = e_0^2$ in 6.27 then we can write an expression for e in terms e_0 and $\mathbf{r} \cdot \mathbf{r}$:

$$e \approx e_0 + (\mathbf{r} \cdot \mathbf{r} - e_0^2)\frac{1}{2e_0}$$

for a small stretch. Written in this way we avoid the calculation of a square root in determining the length of every edge during every iteration and at every time step. In an initialization phase, on a one-off basis, the values of e_0, e_0^2 and $\frac{1}{2e_0}$ are calculated for each edge. Listing 6.7 summarizes the steps in the algorithm.

The relaxation algorithm of listing 6.7 discussed in this section makes no attempt to prevent cloth-to-object or cloth-to-cloth collision. Adding inter-object collision detection, where the cloth drapes itself over solid objects, could be built

```
nVertices, (there will be one less edge.)
while(1){   while running the model
   update the vertex positions
   UpdateNextTimestep();
   Sleep(T);   wait T ms until next step
}

void UpdateNextTimestep(){
  dt = time_step;
  Mass = particle mass;
  nVertlet = dt/nSteps;   number of steps to reach dt
  for(l=0;l<nVertlet;l++){
    for(k=0;k<nRelaxations;k++)  relaxations
      for(i=0;i<nVertices-1;i++){
          Restore the edges to original length
      }
    }
    for(i=1;i<nVertices;i++){   Vertlet model
      Ccalculate vertex forces due to springs damping etc.
      Force = getForce(..);
      Calculate new vertex position.
      Xnew = 2*Xcurrent - Xold  +  (dT*dT/Mass)*Force;
      Update old and current positions
      Xold = Xcurrent;   Copy to previous
      Xcurrent = Xnew;   Update current
    }
  }
}
```

Listing 6.7: The spring-mass Vertlet algorithm with relaxation to restore the original edges of the polygons.

into the algorithm without adding too much code. Whilst adding a significant number of calculations, it is still possible to do a first order collision detection in real-time unless the colliding objects are very complex. Unfortunately adding intra-object collision detection and preventing self-intersection within the cloth mesh will increase the computation time considerably. Except for quite modestly sized cloth meshes the calculation times significantly exceed any processing that can be done in real-time.

The argument above was expressed in terms of a network of polygon edges, but the edges do not have to form the boundary of a shape. Joining edges together to form a chain of springs with small weights at each joint is just as valid and will behave stably. A chain of inextensible dynamic segments is an excellent model for the behavior of long hair when it is anchored at one end. The simulation of hair is discussed next.

Hair When discussing the practical algorithm for simulating the dynamic behavior of cloth, it was suggested the relaxation-Vertlet algorithm could be adapted to simulate the movement of hair. Thought of as a rigid chain of small segments attached at one end (at the root of the hair) and free at the other, each segment carries a small mass that is subjected to inertial and gravitational forces. As the root is moved, the rest of the hair follows with its motion determined using an algorithm similar to that used for cloth in listing 6.7. To be realistic it will be necessary to build the model with many hundreds of individual chains. Unlike the cloth model, where the polygons of the material can be illuminated in the usual way with a simple Lambertian calculation, the hairs do not have a unique surface normal vector to work with in the lighting calculations. One approach to resolving this issue is to assume that the hairs are cylindrical within each segment and to derive a lighting model based on the general appearance of a cylinder, possibly with some fraction of transparency and translucency.

One of the best real-time simulations of hair can be found in the Nalu demonstration from nVidia that is described in chapter 22 by Nguyen and Donnelly in *GPU Gems 2* [71]. Their chapter explains how a point-sphere collision detection and a dynamical simulation of a small fraction of *guide* hairs may be used to reduce the computation time. The behavior of other hairs is determined by interpolation from the guides.

At SIGGRAPH 2008 a major course called "Realistic Hair Simulation, Animation and Rendering" was organized by Bertails [9]. The notes from this course (150 pages) are readily available from several websites. The course covers the whole topic from dynamics to rendering and illumination. It is certainly the place turn next for an in-depth study of this topic.

6.7   Particle modeling

Mesh models are an excellent way of representing solid shapes; even shapes that deform internally or move in a very flexible way are well represented by a network of polygons or lines. However, some things do just not lend themselves to being rendered from a mesh model description. Flames, breaking waves, smoke, cloud and flowing fluids are all examples of elements that are found in nature and are phenomenon that should definitely be represented in the CGI world. Of course, some of these phenomena can be created using fractals [67] or volume rendering techniques, but often volume rendering techniques just take too long, and thus are very unsuitable for any real-time use. Also, many phenomenon change continuously with time, and trying to render them volumetrically gets just too complex. An example of a phenomenon that is not suitable for either mesh modeling or volumetric rendering is water flowing from a tap, hitting the ground, kicking up a spray and flowing away to form a puddle on the floor. This is where a particle-based model comes in. By thinking of a phenomenon as a collection of particles, tens, or even hundreds of thousands of particles, all acting

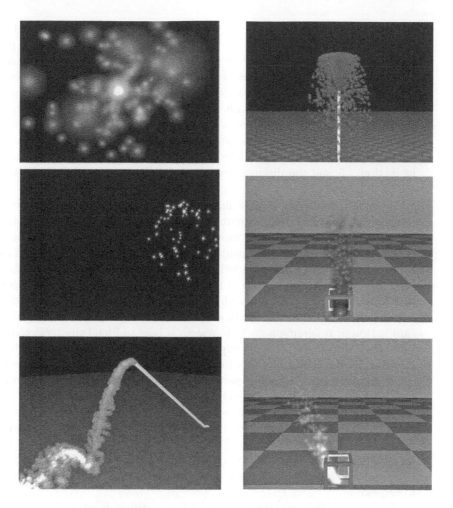

Figure 6.38: Examples of a particle model in action.

like tiny objects, it is possible to simulate some wonderful effects. The waterfall at the cliff top, the clown having a bucket of water thrown over them at the circus, the flames and smoke emanating from a pile of burning logs, or the spray from ocean waves breaking over rocks are all readily modeled by a collection of particles.

But why is it so simple? It is simple because the particles are modeled as *points* and there is no need to worry about *collision*. Each point behaves like a mini-projectile and is subject only to some very simple dynamics so their movement is easily calculated. Of course there is a very large number of particles, but this large number obscures the appearance of the individual particles and they start to look like they are a single entity. Figure 6.38 illustrates a few examples of particle models in action. Even though individual particles behave autonomously, all the particles participating in a particular effect have properties in common. Things such as their trajectory, color, transparency and how these properties vary over time (to make them eventually disappear; their lifetime) will all have been defined by the particle generator. To highlight the fact that many thousands of particles will usually collaborate, the term *a particle system* is used to describe how the group behaves and is configured. In a practical sense it allows all the properties of the particle system to be defined in a single structure which releases individual particles as and when required. See the code example in section 7.5 and the discussion on OpenFX in section 9.7.5 for greater detail about implementation.

The idea underlying the simulation of a particle system could not be simpler: Each particle is rendered as a partially transparent, image-mapped polygon that always faces the viewer. The movement of the polygon in three dimensions is governed by the equations of projectile motion using parameters such as: direction and velocity of ejection, lifetime, and the time dependence of other factors such as size, brightness color and transparency. Each particle may be subject to elastic (or inelastic) collision with other objects (but not other particles). This calculation is fast since the particle is considered to be a point. The final important action in rendering a particle system is how to blend the rendered polygons into the image buffer. For example, to render flames, additive blending would be used; to render bubbles in a liquid, replacement blending might be used.

A good way to see how a particle system is configured and controlled is to look at a specific example: The OpenFX software explored in chapter 9 includes a particle effects simulator. The examples illustrated in figure 6.38 were created with it. The OpenFX particle system emits a number of particles with a well defined set of initial attributes. The particles may be be created on a one-off or on a rolling basis. Their attributes determine how the particles will behave. As time elapses the individual particles evolve until they are finally exhausted and disappear.

In each particle system there may be anything from as few as one, to as many as 10,000 particles. The *up* (vertical or Z) direction often has a particular significance, e.g., smoke rising above a fire. The particles are the only visible parts of a particle system. They are dynamic and behave like a set of projectiles that are fired off from the center of the particle system. One good way to initially think of a particle system is as a sort of exploding firework; the bright sparks in the firework are the particles, each firework itself is a particle system. Of course a CGI particle system can do more than look like a bursting firework. It can arrange for a continuous stream of particles to be ejected from the center of the particle system. It can arrange for the particles to remain active (alive) for longer. It can arrange for the particle to be ejected with high speed or slow speed. The particles can be affected by pseudo-gravitational forces and/or appear to be affected by a degree of randomness in their ejected direction or speed, or anything else.

Figure 6.39: Typical particle image texture maps.

By carefully choosing these settings a wide range of phenomena can be simulated. For example:

- For a firework effect, a short burst of about 20–30 particles is sent off from the origin of the particle system in a random radial directions with a lifetime of about 2–3 seconds. During this time the particles are subjected to a gravitational deceleration and they change color and gradually fade away (by increasing the transparency). Note that this is a short burst of particles.

- For the flame effect, a continuous stream of particles with a small upward velocity is emitted. These have a lifetime of a few seconds. During this time the particles change color and fade away. Emitting more particles per second results in a brighter flame. As the particles near the end of their lifetime they fade away. By keeping the velocity low, the particles don't move too far away from the center of the flame. The continuous stream of particles appears to keep the fire going.

- For a fluid fountain effect, a continuous stream of quite a large number of particles are emitted with a high velocity in one specific direction. The particles have a lifetime so that they never disappear. The particles are given a fixed color and no change is made in their transparency during their lifetime. The particles are subjected to a downward gravitational acceleration and they should also bounce off the ground or objects in order to give some illusion of a splash effect.

In addition to the major properties of a particle system (lifetime, etc.) the realism is increased by adding some random fluctuations to each of the particle's parameters. For example, in the firework effect the direction in which the particles are emitted is totally random. In the case where no randomness is given to the direction of particle emission, by default they are ejected vertically. One last point concerns the particles themselves. They are not just points of color; they are actually small monochrome bitmaps, like those shown in figure 6.39.

Usually the bitmaps are also used to modulate the transparency of the polygons onto which they are painted. In the bitmaps shown in figure 6.39 the pixels that are colored white are replaced with the color specified for the particle and the bitmap's alpha channel is used to set the particle's transparency (white = opaque, black = transparent). So the controls of a particle system consist of settings for: emission rate (the number of particles generated per second), speed of emission, lifetime color alpha (how transparent a particle is), acceleration (gravity may speed the particle up, or slow it down), variation in direction of ejection, random fluctuations in the speed, lifetime and color.

The simple idea behind a particle model and its relative ease of implementation focuses attention on the 3D artist. It is up to the artist to choose the values of the parameters and settings, for example the color, number of particles etc. Getting a good looking particle system is therefore a problem of usage rather than a problem of algorithm or software design. Probably the best thing the software engineer can do is to write a very careful description of the action of each of the settings and what various values of these might achieve.

For example, the images in figure 6.40(a) and (b) illustrate what happens when a particle system moves during an animation. The particles will keep their positions relative to the moving particle system (a) or they can *detach* from the local coordinate system and become free to drift away from the moving object.

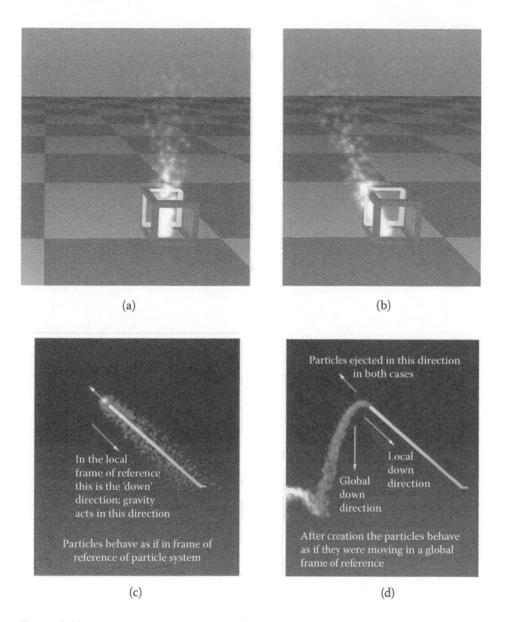

(a)

(b)

(c)

(d)

Figure 6.40: Top: A particle emitter at the center of the frame is moving from left to right. In (a) the particles remain in the local frame of reference. In (b) the particles are emitted in the local frame of reference but complete their life by moving in a global frame of reference. (c) Particles are emitted and continue to move in a local frame of reference. (d) The particles' movement switches to a global frame of reference as soon as they leave the emitter.

Part II

Practical 3D graphics

Introduction to part II

The algorithms discussed in part I are designed to be implemented in a software package that delivers everything an application needs for building, animating and visualizing a virtual world. Rather than working up the algorithms into a contrived program to demonstrate them in practice, this part leads up to a description of the code in a comprehensive tool that we have been developing for several years. Chapter 9 opens the door on OpenFX which directly uses all the algorithms of part I as well as those of the more sophisticated ideas that are coming in part III. It is our hope that it will be useful for you to see the algorithms in the context of a wide ranging practical backdrop to all aspects of 3D computer graphics. You might consider augmenting OpenFX, say by writing a radiosity-renderer, or simply use it for the exemplification of how modeling, rendering and animation algorithms can be implemented in a practical setting.

Before looking at OpenFX it would leave yawning gaps in any practical consideration of 3D graphics if we did not consider how to make use of the algorithms that are now implemented in the electronic hardware of nearly every computer, be it a powerful workstation, desktop, laptop, tablet or even a cell phone.

In this book we choose to do this using the highly respected OpenGL application programmer interface (API). Chapter 7 explains how the rendering algorithms discussed in part I fit into the OpenGL framework and gives some key pointers on how to use it. Chapter 8 follows this through for the specific approach needed when working with the hand-held and tablet devices that have much more limited resources.

Whole books cover the topics of chapters 7 and 8, so we choose to focus on only the absolute essentials as we see them: those key features that will help you map your algorithm designs onto the hardware and build them into prototype *apps* as quickly as possible. The book's accompanying website contains additional briefing documents and several highly annotated example projects to fill in the details we do not have space to put in print.

7

Real-time 3D: OpenGL

With the insatiable demand for more and more realistic computer games, attention has focused on hardware acceleration of the rendering pipeline. To derive maximum benefit from hardware implementations of such things as geometric transformations, rasterization and shading, application programmers are now commonly using standard libraries such as OpenGL and Direct 3D for their 3D programming.

The capabilities of the graphics hardware are rapidly increasing, and to keep pace with this, the software APIs are evolving at an alarming rate. Thus, one of the major challenges in writing programs is to be aware of these changes and how they affect your existing and future software creations.

For many years, workstations have had access to the very successful OpenGL API. Designed originally by the graphics specialist system manufacturer *Silicon Graphics Inc*, for UNIX based systems it first appeared on Windows PCs with the Windows NT version 3.51 release.

The only real alternative in high-level programming to OpenGL is to use Microsoft's Direct3D. This first appeared in the August 1996 release of the MSDN. Both OpenGL and the Direct3D APIs provide quite a lot of functionality in common but the way this functionality is achieved is somewhat different. Although Direct3D has evolved away from the pure Component Object Model (COM) to provide its API, the fact that it is restricted to Microsoft platforms means that we will not consider it further.

In this chapter we will highlight some essentials of the structure of OpenGL programs and point you to the book's website for up-to-date information on development processes and documented sample projects.

Why do we choose OpenGL to illustrate the practical implementation of 3D graphics? Answer: It has a long pedigree of stability, simplicity, powerfulness and most important it has cross-platform compatibility. which means that that no one manufacturer or operating system can hold you to ransom.

It is worth mentioning how OpenGL has evolved. In the initial specification OpenGL was exceptionally powerful and as a result there was little need for radical changes in the API over a long period of time. Small additions occurred in each minor version increment. The developer could call on an API that was rich in functions for manipulating geometry, lighting, image mapping and frame buffer operations. All this functionality was built into the hardware of the graphics adapters. Thus, this rendering pipeline became known as the *fixed functionality pipeline*. When (in the early years of the 21st century) the hardware manufacturers created graphics pipelines that were user programmable, OpenGL adapted by introducing a new language (called the GL Shading Language, GLSL) for driving the programmable hardware and a few additional API functions to provide access to the *programmable pipeline*.

As Silicon Graphics faded from the scene, the Kronos group *took up the baton* and the rate of change has accelerated in recent years, so that the OpenGL API keeps up with the new hardware, including mobile and embedded devices. This however does pose a challenge for the application programmer. If you look at the most recent edition of the *Red Book* [82] you will find that the it is very different from the first edition. There has been a particular revolution between editions seven and eight, and many aspects of the original philosophy have been deprecated.

Evolution continues, with added functionality that makes it more efficient for 3D CAD and modeling applications to render using the hardware acceleration and there is a convergence between the versions for workstation/desktop and embedded/mobile devices. Mobile device programming will be considered as a separate topic in chapter 8.

On the bright side, OpenGL allows for old programs to be maintained, and even developed, through what is known as the *compatibility mode*, whilst newer applications take advantage of the *core* mode using those features that best suit the graphics hardware.

It is a good idea to know a little of how the graphics hardware works before doing 3D graphics application development with OpenGL because keeping this information in the back of your mind helps in planning how you structure your programs and in what way you implement them.

Three main elements—geometry, lighting and mapping (mapping may be referred to as either texture mapping or image mapping because it makes use of pictures to add detail to the surfaces presented as a mesh of polygons)—constitute the principal stages in the original rendering pipeline; see figure 7.1. The geometry and lighting calculations apply to the vertices. The mapping calculations apply to the pixels (OpenGL calls them fragments) just before they are written into the output framebuffer. The graphics adapter's internal memory is used for the storage of images, vertex data and the output framebuffers. The main input to the pipeline is a stream of vertices. These pass through the transformation stage to determine where their two-dimensional projection is placed in the output buffers. The lighting calculations are also done at the same time on a per-vertex basis. The job of the rasterizer is to determine what pixels in the output buffer are covered by any points, lines or polygons. The rasterizer also interpolates the vertex-based attributes (such as position, normal, texture coordinate and color) and Z depth across a polygon and uses the interpolated data

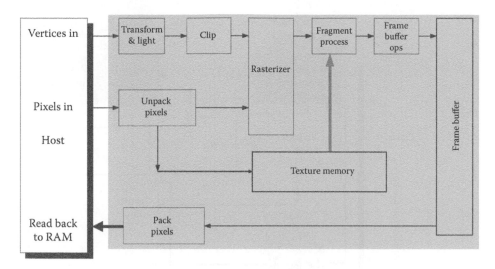

Figure 7.1: The original hardware graphics pipeline.

to present a single attribute value and depth to the fragment processing stage. In the fragment stage a texture/image lookup is performed and the pixel color modified when appropriate. The *framebuffer ops* stage combines the output of the fragment processing stage with the contents of the visible output buffer, and uses the depth buffer to determine whether that pixel should indeed be recorded or discarded.

The graphics hardware depicted in figure 7.1 is immutable, hence the description the *fixed functionality* pipeline. This was the starting point for the evolution of graphics hardware which has brought increasing stages of user programmability into the pipeline, now awarded the same status as the computer's central processing unit and given the title the GPU (graphics processing unit).

Thus the original pipeline (figure 7.1) has developed into that of figure 7.2 where short programs are written in the OpenGL Shading Language (GLSL) and loaded into their respective processors. Some of the programmable stages shown in figure 7.2 are essential for graphics and others offer enhanced actions that will not be discussed further here. It is also probable that in the future other stages in the pipeline or other functional units may become programmable to facilitate use of the massive parallelization that the GPU offers.

From our point of view it is still vertex and fragment processing that are most important. The compute unit is used for general processing (at the time of writing this is latest addition to the hardware and requires OpenGL version 4.3 or later to make use of it). This will not be discussed further.

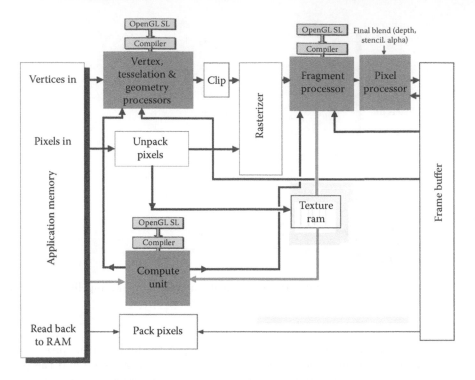

Figure 7.2: The GPU hardware graphics pipeline. Programs are written in a high-level language, compiled and loaded into their respective processing units.

7.1 The basics

This section delves into a little more detail about the OpenGL approach to geometry manipulation, lighting, and materials and texture/image mapping, and how it is evolving.

7.1.1 Geometry

The shape of a model is defined by its vertices. The polygonal surface that we see is either defined by an implicit ordering of the vertices, or can be specified using a list similar to that described in section 3.2. Individual object models are built relative to a local frame of reference (called object coordinates). Several objects can be combined by applying different transformations to arrange them in a global frame of reference (called world coordinates). To setup a viewpoint and direction of view, a further transformation is applied that has the effect of moving all the objects so that the viewpoint is located to $(0, 0, 0)$ and the direction of view is along the $-z$ axis. Figure 7.3 illustrates this frame of reference. OpenGL calls this frame of reference eye coordinates.

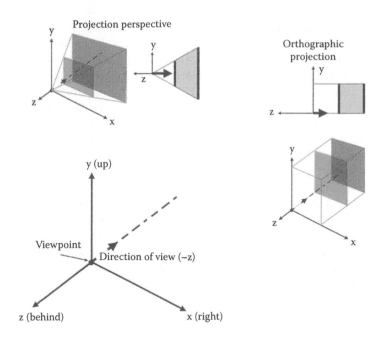

Figure 7.3: The OpenGL coordinate system and default viewing position and direction. The two main types of projection are shown with the shaded front and back clipping planes.

To produce a 2D picture of the scene a projection matrix is used. There are two forms of projection, perspective and orthographic (again illustrated in figure 7.3). OpenGL calls the coordinates (after projection) clip coordinates. In the compatibility mode of operation the projection matrix is stored and manipulated separately, and simply called the *Projection* matrix. After the projection transformation is applied the coordinates are still three dimensional; in other words the division by the depth (the z) coordinate in a perspective projection has not yet occurred. OpenGL then clips the polygons so that only those parts of the model lying inside the clipping volume are retained. The clipping volume is a cuboid in the case of an orthographic projection, and a frustum in the case of a perspective projection.

The final stage of geometry processing is to carry out the perspective division (see section 2.12.8). In the case of an orthographic projection the Z coordinate is simply ignored. This coordinate division results in each vertex having a two-dimensional coordinate (called normalized device coordinates) that is then converted to the integer window coordinates. Figure 7.3 illustrates this process.

A number of interesting effects can be achieved with the projection matrix by varying its elements: for example, different fields of views, different camera aspect ratios, and left-right stereoscopic asymmetry. Originally, and when working in compatibility mode, this can be handled by some utility functions, `gluPerspective( )`, `glOrtho()`; and `glFrustum()`; but in the *core* mode the task of building these various matrices is left to the application program.

How the projection is mapped into the integer window/screen coordinates is defined by the API function `glViewport();`. Correctly matching the aspect ratio with the window size is important so that circles don't become ellipses if the user changes the dimensions of the output window. This is an essential part of any OpenGL program and will require an adjustment to the Viewport and the projection's properties in response to a change in window size.

Turning to consider the model and view matrix, suppose we wish to use the same model in two different locations in the world coordinate system. Then suppose that $\mathbf{p}_i$ is a vertex in the model (represented as a column vector). We can re-position and re-orientate this to represent the first instance of the object with a homogeneous transformation $[T_{m1}]$. The second instance's position (in world coordinates) will be determined by the transformation, $[T_{m2}]$. If the transformation required to view the objects is $[T_v]$ and the camera projection transformation is given by $[T_p]$, then the coordinates for vertex $\mathbf{p}_i$ in the first instance of the object prior to perspective division will be given by:

$$[p'] = [T_p][T_v][T_{m1}][p]_i$$

and for the second instance it will be given by:

$$[p''] = [T_p][T_v][T_{m2}][p]_i$$

As an example of the application of a projection matrix, suppose that the coordinates of $\mathbf{p}''_i$ are $(0.5, 0.5, 2.0, 1.0)$ and the window viewport is 100×100 pixels. Then in an orthographic projection the window coordinates of $\mathbf{p}''_i$ will be $(50, 50)$ and for a perspective projection it would be $(25, 25)$.

In *compatibility mode*, the matrix $[T_{mv}] = [T_v][T_{m1}]$ is termed the *ModelView* matrix. OpenGL's transformations take the same form as that discussed in section 2.12, and going forward it is essential that you know how to construct your own matrices and use them in the programmable stages of the OpenGL pipeline.

In the *compatibility mode*, and in any hardware that only supports fixed functionality, the current transformation is accumulated by successive multiplications of an identity matrix by the matrices representing the basic operations of translation, scale and rotation, using functions like `glRotatef(...)`. When you have access to the programmable pipeline the transformation matrices are computed directly by the application itself and fed into the *vertex processing* stage (as `uniform` variables).

This discussion sums up the major points about geometry operations in OpenGL, but as a final comment let us consider again the order of the transformations.

Transformation ordering Section 2.12.4 explained that the order in which a transformation is applied is crucial in getting the desired result. As just mentioned, the correct projection onto the viewing plane of a vertex is determined by the combination of three transformation matrices:

$$[T] = [T_p][T_v][T_m] \tag{7.1}$$

When working in *compatibility mode* the first transform to be defined in the code is the last to be applied to a vertex $[p]_i$. Thus the viewing transformation must be defined first (by a call to `gluLookat(..)` for example). And, if the vertex is first translated and then rotated within the world coordinate system with a composite transformation $[T_m] = [T_{m_r}(\theta)][T_{m_t}](\mathbf{dx})$ then the order of the function calls to set up the same transformation must be given as:

```
glOrtho(..);   //for an orthographic projection
gluLookat();
glRotate( ..);
glTranslate();
...draw the vertex
```

When working in *core mode* and creating your own transformation matrices, say $[MVP]$ for the combined model, view and projection matrices, they must be assembled in the same order as given in equation 7.1. So for the steps in the code above:

$$[MVP] = [P][V][M_{r(\theta)}][M_{t(dx)}] \tag{7.2}$$

where $[V]$ is the viewing matrix, $[M_{r(\theta)}]$ is a rotation matrix and $[M_{t(dx)}]$ is a translation matrix. This can be done in either the application program itself or in a vertex shader program.

One of the most important aspects of this internal ordering comes about when we want to pass any transformation matrices into the rendering pipeline, as must now be done in the core mode of operation. The functions that send the transformation matrices into the pipeline pass their values as a linear array of 16 elements. In all computer languages a two-dimensional array is stored linearly in memory, and in C and C++ the ordering is called *row major*. This means that the order of the storage of a 4×4 array:

$$\begin{bmatrix} a_{00} & a_{01} & a_{02} & a_{03} \\ a_{10} & a_{11} & a_{12} & a_{13} \\ a_{20} & a_{21} & a_{22} & a_{23} \\ a_{30} & a_{31} & a_{32} & a_{33} \end{bmatrix}$$

is $a_{00}, a_{01}, a_{02}, a_{03}, a_{10}, a_{11}, \ldots$, etc. where the first subscript identifies the row.

Because OpenGL expects its matrices to be presented in *column major* order, any 4×4 matrix declared in C or C++ code as `M[4][4];` must first be transposed before it is passed into either the fixed functionality pipeline or to a GLSL vertex shader program. **This is a very important concept.**

(The robot simulator project on the website is a good example of combinations of transformations in action.)

7.1.2   Lighting

In compatibility mode, when polygons are dispatched into the rendering pipeline the surface normal vector that accompanies them is used in a basic Lambertian illumination model to generate a light intensity for that vertex. OpenGL only allows up to eight lights, and very few hardware systems support that full number. The light intensity calculated at the vertices of a polygon is interpolated in the rasterizer so that when processing moves into the fragment processing stage it is combined with the material settings to calculate a color value to be written into the output framebuffer.

The fixed function pipeline has the option to perform a Gouraud shading during rasterization and a very simple specular model may also be used. In the programmable pipeline the programmer has complete freedom to define any lighting model they choose. The application must pass information about the position and attributes of any lights to the appropriate shader programs. Nevertheless:

> Grouping vertices by their surface color, or by transparency, or texture/image map is a useful pre-processing step, because it reduces the traffic between host computer and adapter. Also, several repetitions of the rendering process for the same sets of vertices may be required in order to achieve a particular effect (e.g., a fur texture).

7.1.3   Texture mapping

As discussed in section 4.6 pictures from image files are often painted across a mesh of polygons to provide texture detail that would otherwise not be possible to see using different materials because the mesh cannot be made sufficiently detailed. To position the picture in the desired location, the polygons must be metricized with a two-dimensional coordinate frame of reference. A surface's 2D frame of reference is defined by specifying *texture coordinates* at each vertex of the surface's mesh. Texture coordinate values must be passed into the graphics pipeline. In the fixed functionality pipeline and when using a GPU in compatibility mode the the texture coordinates are normally set using the function `glTexCoord2f(...);` for each vertex in the object. Again in this mode texture coordinates can also be generated automatically; one of the built-in automatic texture coordinate generators produces coordinates suitable for mapping an image to give the illusion that the surface is reflecting any image mapped onto it. In the core mode the texture coordinates for a vertex or a group of vertices are passed to the vertex shader using the same mechanism as the vertex position coordinates and any other vertex attribute such as its surface normal or a surface color.

To use a texture map, the image has first to be loaded into the video card's memory. Then, before any polygon is rendered with a mapped image, the texture must be selected and texturing enabled. Shrinking the code down to the absolute

```
GLuint nTexture;

glEnable(GL_TEXTURE_2D);
// load the texture from a file into computer RAM
pix=LoadBmp("picture.bmp",&w,&h);
glGenTextures(1, &nTexture);
glBindTexture(GL_TEXTURE_2D, nTexture);
// install the image into the texture RAM
glTexImage2D(GL_TEXTURE_2D, 0, GL_RGB, w, h,
             0, GL_RGB, GL_UNSIGNED_BYTE, pix);
// how is texture to blend with underlying color
glTexEnvf(GL_TEXTURE_ENV, GL_TEXTURE_ENV_MODE, GL_MODULATE);
// how is the texture to be scaled
glTexParameteri(GL_TEXTURE_2D, GL_TEXTURE_MAG_FILTER, GL_LINEAR);
glTexParameteri(GL_TEXTURE_2D, GL_TEXTURE_MIN_FILTER, GL_LINEAR);
// how is the texture to appear outside interval [0,1]
glTexParameteri(GL_TEXTURE_2D, GL_TEXTURE_WRAP_S, GL_REPEAT);
glTexParameteri(GL_TEXTURE_2D, GL_TEXTURE_WRAP_T, GL_REPEAT);
free(pix);  // the computer's memory copy is no longer required
glDisable(GL_TEXTURE_2D);
```

Listing 7.1: Loading a texture map image into graphics memory.

```
glEnable(GL_TEXTURE_2D);
glBindTexture(GL_TEXTURE_2D, nTexture);

// draw the object

glDisable(GL_TEXTURE_2D);
```

Listing 7.2: Using a texture loaded in texture memory and identified by an image identifier handle. When using the programmable shaders in the GPU there is a little more work involved because the texture must be sampled and the value from it applied to the fragment.

minimum required to setup and display an image we end up with a two-step process. The two steps in texturing are performed with code such as that shown in listings 7.1 and 7.2, (you can find the whole working program on the website).

Basic texture maps only permit one map to be applied to one group of vertices at one time. This is something of a limitation, especially if you want to simulate a surface that is partially reflective (using a reflection map) and rough (using a bump map). Most graphics hardware now supports *multi-textures*, where several maps can be used at the same time on the same vertex group.

7.1.4 Output buffers

A set of framebuffers records several pieces of information about each pixel.

- The Z buffer contains the value of the Z coordinate after the transformations have been applied. This depth is used in the hidden surface determination algorithm. It is possible to configure it so that writing to it, or reading from it can be enabled or disabled as required.

- The stencil buffer can be used to form a mask into the output buffers.

- The accumulation buffer is typically used in an algorithm that renders motion blur.

- There are at least two output image buffers to record RGB values for each pixel. Often a transparency value (an alpha) that allows transparent polygons to be mixed into the scene is also stored. One of these buffers (the G_FRONT) buffer is used by the display hardware to present output images to the user. The other (the GL_BACK) buffer is targeted for output by the rendering pipeline (thus the assembly of the image is hidden from the user). There might also be one or more GL_AUX0 buffers that can be used for temporary output, and to facilitate stereoscopy some hardware will provide front and back versions of a GL_LEFT and GL_RIGHT buffer.

One point worth highlighting about the output buffers: They will have the same dimensions as the window they are supporting. Thus the largest window that can be created is equal to the size of the desktop display. This is quite a limitation and OpenGL now supports framebuffer objects (FBOs) and renderbuffer objects (RBOs) to circumvent this limitation. FBOs and RBOs are discussed later in section 7.4. The various buffers can be enabled and disabled as required, with code such as:

```
glEnable(GL_DEPTH_TEST);
glClear(GL_COLOR_BUFFER_BIT|GL_DEPTH_BUFFER_BIT);
glFrontFace(GL_CW);
```

7.1.5   Practical implementation

When it comes to desktop programs that use OpenGL there are two approaches: write native platform specific code or use one of the environments that abstract the platform away allowing the application to focus on the core drawing tasks. Currently there are two good libraries that we use for the examples accompanying the book (references to these can be found on the website). The GL Utility Toolkit (GLUT) has been around for many years but has not been updated recently. A *like-for-like* replacement called FreeGLUT is well maintained and is recommended in the Red Book. Any application program that is written for the GLUT can be adapted to use FreeGLUT simply by changing libraries. The GLUT/FreeGLUT is readily available for all platforms. Pre-built DLLs are available for Windows and pre-built packages can be readily installed on all the GNU/LINUX flavors. On Apple Mac OSX the original GLUT is installed by default with the developer tools package.

Another platform encapsulating library the GLFW can be an alternative to using the GLUT/FreeGLUT. It has the slight advantage that it is available for OSX platforms as well as Windows. Currently it does not support menus but this may change.

In all the abstraction libraries the programming metaphor is for the developer to provide callback handler functions for such things as: a change of screen resolution, a re-drawing of the OpenGL enabled display window and handling mouse and keyboard events. A simple cross platform example package for the fixed function pipeline using the GLUT/FreeGLUT libraries can be obtained from the website.

A third and pretty-much essential library to include with your OpenGL programs is the GLEW (The GL Extension Wrangler). Many of the functions introduced into OpenGL after version 1 have not found their way into the stub libraries on Windows or X-Windows or OSX or within the mobile development tools. The only way to gain access to these (extension functions as they are called, even though they are mainstream functionality) is to use a few special platform dependent functions that delve into the OpenGL drivers and return pointers to the functions so that the functions can be called. Under Windows this function is `wglGetProcAddress()`.

It would be a significant chore to have to call this function repeatedly for each of the functions now in the OpenGL core model and resolving this issue is precisely the function of the GLEW library. Once initialized it makes available to the programmer all the OpenGL API functions under their API name whether a particular platform has them in its DLL or SO library.[1]

7.2 Native programming

7.2.1 Native Windows

Two approaches may be used to develop a native Windows application:

1. Follow a basic template program that calls directly to the Window's Application Programming Interface (the Win32 API) functions as described in the Software Development Kit (SDK). Such a template will exhibit the core features of message loop, Window Class and message handling function. The API functions are provided in a set of libraries that are implemented as *dynamic link libraries* (DLLs). Most of the DLLs that an application will use are components of the operating system itself. `SHELL32.DLL`, `GDI32.DLL` and `USER32.DLL` are examples of these components. The SDK also includes a large number of "header" files which define constants and provide prototypes for the myriad of API functions.

---

[1] The GLEW is recommended in the *Red Book* and is likely to be maintained for the foreseeable future. On Windows it, at time of writing, supports functions at least up to OpenGL version 4.3.

```
..
case WM_CREATE:{
// create the OpenGL display context
// based on the normal Windows GDI context
HGLRC hRC;
HDC hDC;
hDC = GetDC(hWnd);
// the properties of surface are defined
// in a PixelFormat
bSetupPixelFormat(hDC);
hRC = wglCreateContext( hDC );
wglMakeCurrent( hDC, hRC );
...
}
break;
```

Listing 7.3: Create a display context for OpenGL, specify a pixel format for the underlying display surface and carry out any further initialization specific for the application (analogous to that shown in listing refglcode:glutinit).

2. The Microsoft Foundation Class (MFC) library [75] provides a framework for constructing programs by deriving classes from an extensive class hierarchy that encapsulates all the WIN32 API functionality such as toolbars and dialog boxes. It includes suitable default processing so that an application program can be built with quite a sophisticated user interface with only minimal effort on the part of the developer.

These approaches present code that looks very different to the programmer.

An application based on calls to functions in the SDK libraries has an entry point in the conventional **C** language sense. In programs that use the MFC library the main elements of a Windows application are hidden inside the library classes.

However, whether one is using the native API or the MFC classes, all the OpenGL code is the same and it can be divided up into the same basic tasks covered in section 7.1.

In native mode the initialization requires a display surface to be created and this must be attached to the window that is to view the surface. *The term display surface is a generic one and applies to all platforms. The window in which the OpenGL output appears can be thought of as a view of this surface.* The best place in the code to perform this initialization is in response to a **WM_CREATE** message in the message handler function for the window. The steps are shown in listing 7.3. To set up a pixel format, the function shown in listing 7.4 is used. The PixelFormatDescriptor provides the programmer with the opportunity to request that the display windows are assigned particular properties like stereoscopy and color depth. Two Windows API functions **ChoosePixelFormat(..)**; and **SetPixelFormat(..)'** are used to configure a Windows drawing surface.

```
static BOOL bSetupPixelFormat(HDC hDC){
// define the requested format
static PIXELFORMATDESCRIPTOR pfd = {
 sizeof(PIXELFORMATDESCRIPTOR),
  1,                    // version number
 PFD_DRAW_TO_WINDOW |  // support window
 PFD_SUPPORT_OPENGL |  // support OpenGL
 PFD_DOUBLEBUFFER,     // double buffered
 PFD_TYPE_RGBA,        // RGBA type
  24,                  // 24-bit color depth
 0, 0, 0, 0, 0, 0,     // color bits ignored
 0,                     // no alpha buffer
 0,                      // shift bit ignored
 0,                      // no accumulation buffer
 0, 0, 0, 0,             // accum bits ignored
 32,                   // 32-bit z-buffer
 0,                    // no stencil buffer
 0,                    // no auxiliary buffer
 PFD_MAIN_PLANE,          // main layer
 0,                   // reserved
 0, 0, 0                // layer masks ignored
 };
int pixelformat;
if (WantStereo)pfd.dwFlags |= PFD_STEREO;
if ( (pixelformat = ChoosePixelFormat(hDC, &pfd)) == 0 ) {
//..  error ...
 return FALSE;
}
if (SetPixelFormat(hDC, pixelformat, &pfd) == FALSE) {
//... error..
 return FALSE;
}
 return TRUE;
}
```

Listing 7.4: Create a pixel format for the display surface. This example shows how to setup a stereoscopic surface.

A third API function `GetPixelFormat(..);` may be used to check what pixel format is currently in use by the window.

Note: It is at the context creation stage that you can choose to configure your display surface for OpenGL operating in the *compatibility mode* or the *core mode*.

To render the 3D scene using OpenGL library functions, appropriate code is added in the `WM_PAINT` message handler. In the case of an MFC program the same code is added to the `OnPaint();` handler method. In the example shown in listing 7.5 the `drawObjects(..);` function will apply a transformation for the left or right eye of a stereoscopic view, or for a monoscopic view, and then call on other code to draw all the objects in the scene.

```
//
case WM_PAINT:
 HDC hDC;
 PAINTSTRUCT ps;
 BeginPaint(hWnd, &ps);
 // OpenGL code
 glClearColor(gbRed,gbGreen,gbBlue,1.0);
 glClear(GL_COLOR_BUFFER_BIT | GL_DEPTH_BUFFER_BIT);

 drawScene(.);

 // show the back buffer
 hDC = wglGetCurrentDC();
 SwapBuffers(hDC);
 // end of OpenGL code
 EndPaint(hWnd, &ps);
 break;
```

Listing 7.5: Render the scene using OpenGL.

7.2.2 Native OSX

Using OpenGL natively on OSX is a little more involved than using the GLUT, but there is a built-in Cocoa class that handles most of the work for us. Deriving an application's View class from `NSOpenGLView` will enable that View as an OpenGL rendering surface and provide methods that can be delegated in order to endow the window with the properties required. Simply by starting with a new Cocoa project in Xcode and adding a view class derived from `NSOpenGLView` is all that is required to start building a native OSX OpenGL application.

A commentary on, and code for, a basic OSX application may be found on the website. It is worth mentioning briefly what happens as a Mac OSX application prepares to execute. OSX does not use a single .EXE program to store all the executable code and resources. It uses a folder called a bundle which is given the filename extension .APP. OSX hides the contents of the bundle from the user, making it look like a single file. Inside the bundle are two important components: the executable program's binary code and a NIB file (now called an XIB file). As well as describing menus and dialog boxes the XIB file can contain instructions to tell the loader to create instances of important objects for the application; *the language of Cocoa is called Objective C after all.* The `main();` function of an OSX Cocoa program usually only consists of one line of executable code:

```
#import <Cocoa/Cocoa.h>
int main(int argc, char *argv[]) {
    return NSApplicationMain(argc, (const char **) argv);
}
```

The immediate call to `NSApplicationMain()` causes an object of the application class that is described in the XIB file to be created and its delegated method `applicationDidFinishLaunching()` to be called. With the chain of execution to `applicationDidFinishLaunching()` confirmed an object of a class derived from NSOpenGLView is created. The creation of the object also leads to the automatic execution of the intiWithFrame :   method where the pixel format for the display surface is defined and applied to the display surface. The developer is saved some work through the use of the library class NSOpenGLView which hides much of the very low level detail. Once the OpenGL View has been created any Setup(..) method can be called from applicationDidFinishLaunching : to complete the application's own specific initialization.

Unless you are familiar with the Objective-C language and have some Cocoa programming experience it might be worth reading Hillegass and Preble [42] which will help build up your knowledge. For a comprehensive explanation of how to to use OpenGL on the Mac take a look at the book by Kuehne and Sullivan [51].

7.2.3 Native GNU/Linux

OpenGL was devised originally to run on Silicon Graphic's workstations and so it sits very naturally with the X windows Linux environment. To setup and render the ubiquitous teapot using OpenGL into an X window mapped onto an OpenGL drawing surface takes just a few simple function calls; see the accompanying example and commentary on the website.

7.3   The GL shading language

The way forward for OpenGL is now firmly established along the lines of the hardware pipeline described in figure 7.2. Introduced in OpenGL version 2 the programmable pipeline opened phenomenal potential in the world of real-time 3D applications. Because of the programmability of the pipeline the hardware has a lot of the attributes that we would attribute to a computer, thus the programmable graphics processor is generally referred to as the GPU. To enable programs using OpenGL to access this powerful feature of the hardware, a special programming language was devised to control the new hardware. The language has a C-like syntax with some additions to allow programs to match onto hardware features like vector and matrix arithmetic.

The current syntax of the shading language is fully documented in the *Red Book* but its syntax has changed since its introduction and it continues to evolve as the hardware improves. Fortunately older shader codes can still be used in *compatibility mode*. So far, the most significant changes concern the way data (vertices, etc.) is introduced into the pipeline and the way it is passed from stage to stage. Other stages in the pipeline have been endowed with programmability in addition to the original vertex and fragment processing steps.

However, for most applications that deal with rendering triangular polygons the vertex and fragment processors remain the most important. Fortunately too, nearly all the syntax of the executable statements in the language have remained constant, so it does not take a lot of effort to upgrade a shader program for use with the most recent syntax or make it ready for enhancement with tasks performed in the newer processing stages, such as the tessellation and geometry processors.[2]

With regard to the GLSL syntax, it should not be difficult to follow the logical statements for anyone who is familiar with C. In our book on virtual reality [59] there is a comprehensive introduction to using the GL shading language in compatibility mode, and our OpenFX software offers a GPU version of its renderer that provides all the same features as the software renderer. OpenFX will be examined in chapter 9.

However, because of the way in which the hardware is designed the GPUs are not just CPUs, and while this offers advantages it also means that you cannot just approach the design of a GPU shader program as if it was a normal CPU algorithmic texture, such as those examined in chapter 11.

So, it is important to appreciate the special features and restrictions which arise in the GPU because of the close relationship with the language of 3D graphics and the need to prevent a shader code from doing anything that does not match well with the GPU hardware, for example, trying to access vertex data in a fragment shader. This is because at the fragment processing stage in the rendering pipeline, the vertex data has been interpolated by rasterization and the fragment does not know from which polygon it came. So it is not possible to determine whether the fragment came from a triangular polygon, or a quadrilateral polygon, or what the coordinates of the polygon's vertices were.

Perhaps the most important concept in basic shader programming is this:

> *The output from the vertex shader, which includes all the globally defined output variables that have been calculated in the vertex shader or set on a per-vertex basis, are interpolated across a polygon and passed to the fragment shader as a single value specifically for that fragment (or pixel) alone.*

Looking back at figure 7.2 the two most important stages in the pipeline are:

1. Programmable vertex shaders perform calculations that relate to *per-vertex* operations, such as transformations, transients, lighting mapping coordinates.

2. Programmable fragment shaders do the calculations for *per-fragment* operations, such as coloring and texturing. Some lighting can be done in these processors as well.

The term *programmable shader* is used for all these, even though a vertex shader may modify the geometry (as in mesh skinning) and have nothing to do with

---

[2]We will not discuss any of these new features in this book. Good examples of using the geometry and tessellation shaders can be found in the *Red Book*, or at the time of writing in Wolff [92].

surface shading at all. The fragment shader is usually combined with a pixel shader, and they both can be referred to as either *fragment* or *pixel* shaders.

Having this hardware picture clear in our minds is very useful when designing GPU programs. It makes it clear why there are restrictions regarding what can and can't be done in a shader program. It also illustrates why the flow of execution is as follows: *Run the vertex program first for every vertex and then, later on in the pipeline, run the fragment program.* The fact that all vertices have the same function applied to each of them and that fragment processing can be done simultaneously allows for massive parallelism to be employed.

Different GPUs from different manufacturers, such as nVidia, Intel and AMD, will require different machine codes to drive the hardware, and so the GLSL compiler needs to be implemented as part of the graphics device driver which is supplied with a specific GPU. After compilation, the device driver forwards the machine instructions to the hardware.

7.3.1 Sending information into the pipeline

In the original concept of OpenGL vertex data was passed into the pipeline one vertex at a time using functions like `glVertex3fv(...)`. This can be quite inefficient for various reasons and it soon became clear that it is better to transfer blocks of vertices (and other vertex data, like normal vectors) together, hold them in buffers in the GPU and draw them as a single unit using functions like `glDrawArrays(...)` or `glDrawElements(...)`. In version 3 and later this approach is defined as *core* and the old drawing functions have been deprecated. Whilst it is still possible to drive the pipeline in the compatibility model, the preferred wisdom is to pass the geometry of a model into the pipeline using the process of:

- Create one or more vertex array objects (VAO) and/or one or more vertex buffer(VBO). These buffers exist in graphics memory and are filled with vertex attribute data.

- Fill the vertex buffers with vertex attribute data, e.g. position, normals, colors, texture coordinates, etc.

- Connect the vertex attribute data to named (or indexed) global variables in the vertex shader code.

- Command the pipeline to draw the contents of a buffer using one of the `Draw...()` functions.

Whilst this is a simplification, with some necessary detail omitted, it conveys the essence of the core process.

Listing 7.6 presents an example of a minimal piece of code that an application program could use in order to load a group of vertices into the rendering pipeline and draw them.

```
GLfloat vertexbufferdata1[] = { .. }; // some data
GLfloat vertexbufferdata2[] = { .. }; // some data

// create a vertex array object (VAO)
glGenVertexArrays(1, &VertexArrayID);
glBindVertexArray(VertexArrayID);

// set up a buffer bind it to the VAO
glGenBuffers(1, &vertexbuffer);
glBindBuffer(GL_ARRAY_BUFFER, vertexbuffer);
vertexbuffersize=sizeof(vertexbufferdata1);
glBufferData(GL_ARRAY_BUFFER,
  vertexbuffersize,
  vertexbufferdata1,
  GL_STATIC_DRAW);
glEnableVertexAttribArray(0);
glVertexAttribPointer(
  0,
  3,
  GL_FLOAT,
  GL_FALSE,  0, (void*)0 );
// repeat for any other buffers as necessary

// draw the vertices in groups of 3 as triangles
glDrawArrays(GL_TRIANGLES, 0, vertexbuffersize/3);

//reload the buffer and draw again with different data
// does not have to be the same side

vertexbuffersize=sizeof(vertexbufferdata2);
glBufferData(GL_ARRAY_BUFFER,
  vertexbuffersize,vertexbufferdata2,GL_STATIC_DRAW);
glDrawArrays(GL_TRIANGLES, 0, vertexbuffersize/3);

// unbind and delete buffers when not needed
```

Listing 7.6: Setting up vertex data using a Vertex Array Object and one or more Vertex Buffer Objects.

The preceding itemized steps can pass large quantities of data to the vertex processor of the pipeline where it is subjected to the actions of the vertex shader code. To send smaller items of data, for example the transformation matrices that move the vertices into position within the global coordinate system, another special type of variable, called a **uniform** variable, may be used. Any **uniform** variables set in the application program's code are readable in all the processors in the pipeline.

7.3.2   Passing information from one shader to another

Within any shader simply qualify global variables that you want to pick up from an earlier stage in the pipeline with the keyword **in**, and global variables that you want to pass down the pipeline with the keyword **out**.

Variables that you want to pick up from a buffer that that has been filled by the application program's code are further identified with a location that they have been given by the application program.

Any uniform variables that you want to use are declared as global variables, qualified with the keyword `uniform`. In the shaders programs `uniform` variables are read-only. The code in listing 7.7 shows the form of a pair minimal shaders.

7.3.3   The GLSL syntax and built-in variables

The GLSL supports the usual C data types of `float`, `int` etc. To these it adds various types of vector and matrix, which are declared as `vec3` (a 3×1 vector), `vec2`, `mat4` (a 4×4 array) for example. Vectors and matrices are particularly pertinent for 3D work. Whilst these additional data types occur frequently in shader codes, perhaps the most interesting part of a GLSL variable is its *qualifiers*, e.g., `uniform`. The qualifiers are important because when applied to global variables (declared outside the `main` or other functions) they provide a mechanism for parameters to be passed to the shader code from the application. They also provide a mechanism for the vertex shader to pass information to the fragment shader and to interact with the *built-in variables* which provide such things as the transformation matrices calculated in the fixed-functionality pipeline.

A good understanding of the meaning and actions of the qualifiers is essential if one wants to write almost any kind of shader. We will now consider a brief outline of each:

- `const`. As the name implies, these are constants and must be initialized when declared,

- `uniform`. Variables declared with this qualifier are available in both vertex and fragment shaders because they are uniform across the whole primitive. They are expected to change infrequently. For example, a vertex and fragment shader might declare `uniform vec3 BaseColor;`. The application program would set this uniform variable with a call to `glUniform3f(getUniLoc(Prog, "BaseColor"), 0.75, 0.75, 0.75);`.

- `in` Global variables with this qualifier are used to acquire data that has been set in a previous stage of the rendering pipeline.

- `out` Global variables with this qualifier carry information on the next stage in the pipeline.

In both vertex and fragment shaders the ability to *read from* and *write to* a few predefined (called built-in) qualified variables provide an interface with the pipeline. The built-in variable `vec4 gl_Position;` must be assigned a value at the end of the vertex shader so as to pass the vertex coordinates into the rest of the pipeline. A vertex shader must also apply any transformations that are

```
#version 330 core

layout(location = 0) in vec3 vertexPosition;

uniform mat4 MVP;

void main(){
 gl_Position =  MVP * vec4(vertexPosition,1);
}
```

```
#version 330 core

layout(location = 0) out vec4 color;

uniform vec4 Colour;

void main(){
        color = Colour;
}
```

Listing 7.7: Minimal shader programs.

in operation. In compatibility mode this can be done with a built-in function called `ftransform()`; but to conform to the core approach. The best approach is to **do-it-yourself** by passing in a 4×4 matrix through a uniform variable containing the appropriate transformation.

In the early versions of the GLSL, named built-in variables played a more significant role, but many of these have now been withdrawn.

Thus a minimal pair of shaders can consist of just a couple of lines of code; see listing 7.7.

7.3.4   Template shader codes

The book's website contains a number of template and example shader codes that execute in both compatibility and core modes. These demonstrate in principle how to set up Phong's illumination model; some more advanced shader codes are discussed in chapter 11 and in relation to the OpenFX program of chapter 9.

Image mapping In the GLSL, information from texture maps is acquired with the use of a *sampler*. We will keep it simple in our example, and show the minimal code required so a shader program pair can paint image texture maps on fragments. The code for these shader programs is given in listing 7.8.

Reflection mapping Many objects exhibit reflection of their environment. Listing 7.9 shows the outline of a suitable fragment shader. For reflection maps, we do not want to use any surface lighting models, and so this is omitted.

```
// Vertex Shader  - for traditional image mapping
#version 330 core
layout(location = 0) in vec3 Vertex;
layout(location = 1) in vec3 Normal;
layout(location = 2) in vec2 Texture;

uniform mat4 MVP;
uniform mat4 MV;
uniform mat4 NM;
uniform vec3 LightPos;

out float Diffuse;   // diffuse light intensity
out vec2  TexCoord;  // texture coordinate (u,v)

void main(){
 gl_Position =  MVP * vec4(Vertex,1); // buit in variable
 vec3 PP = MV * vec4(Vertex,1); // vertex position world coodinates
 vec3 PN = normalize(NM * Normal);// normal vector
 // light direction vector
 vec3 LV = normalize(LightPos-PV);
 Diffuse = max(dot(LV, PN), 0.0); // diffuse illumination
 // Get the texture coordinates - choose the first -
 // we only assign one set anyway
 TexCoord = Texture; // pass to fragment shader
}
```

```
// Fragment Shader - simple 2D texture/image map, diffuse lighting

#version 330 core

layout(location = 0) out vec4 Color;

in  float Diffuse; // from vertex shader
in   vec2 TexCoord; // from vertex shader

uniform sampler2D Rsf;  // from calling program

void main (void){
 // Get the fragment color by addressing the texture map pixel
 // date - the "texture2D" built in function takes the texure
 //sampler "Rsf"  // and fragment interpolated texture
 // coorinates as arguments and the ".RGB" (what SL calls
 // a "swizzle") extracts the RGB values from the
 // texture2D() return value.
 vec3 color = (texture2D(Rsf, TexCoord).rgb * Diffuse);
 // promote the 3 element RGB vector to a 3 vector and output
 Color = vec4 (color, 1.0);
}
```

Listing 7.8: The image mapping shader program pair.

```
// Fragment Shader - reflection mapping
#version 330 core
// pass on the Color into the next pipeline stage
layout(location = 0) out vec4 Color;

const vec3 Xunitvec = vec3 (1.0, 0.0, 0.0);
const vec3 Yunitvec = vec3 (0.0, 1.0, 0.0);

// this is our sampler to identify the iamge map
uniform sampler2D RsfEnv;

varying vec3 Normal; // from vertex shader
varying vec3 EyeDir; // from vertex shader

void main(){
  // Compute reflection vector - built-in function :-)
  vec3 reflectDir = reflect(EyeDir, Normal);
  // Compute the addess to use in the image map - we need an
  // address in the range [0 - 1 ] (angles of looking up /down)
  vec2 index;
  index.y = dot(normalize(reflectDir), Yunitvec);
  reflectDir.y = 0.0;
  index.x = dot(normalize(reflectDir), Xunitvec) * 0.5;
  // get the correct range [0 - 1]
  if (reflectDir.z >= 0.0) index = (index + 1.0) * 0.5;
  else{
  index.t = (index.t + 1.0) * 0.5;
  index.s = (-index.s) * 0.5 + 1.0;
  }
  // copy the addressed texture pixel to the output
  Colour = texture2D(RsfEnv, index);
}
```

Listing 7.9: The reflection map fragment shader.

Bump mapping Our portfolio of shader programs would not be complete without the ability to use an image texture as a source of displacement to the surface normal, i.e., bump mapping. Bump mapping requires us to use a `sampler2D` and provide a tangent surface vector. Vertex and fragment shaders for bump mapping are given in listing 7.10 and listing 7.11. A few of comments are pertinent to the bump mapping procedure:

- To minimize the work of the fragment shader, the vertex shader calculates vectors for light direction and viewpoint (eye location) direction in a coordinate frame of reference that is in the plane of the polygon which will be rendered by the fragment shader (this is called *surface-local space*).

  Figure 7.4 illustrates the principle; in the world (global) coordinate frame of reference, the eye is at the origin. The polygon's normal ($\mathbf{n}$), tangent ($\mathbf{t}$) and bi-normal ($\mathbf{b}$) are calculated in the global frame of reference. Transformation of all vectors to a surface-local reference frame allows the fragment shader to perform position-independent lighting calculations because the surface normal is always given by the vector $(0, 0, 1)$.

```
// Vertex Shader - Bump mapping
#version 330 core
// input vertex attributes
layout(location = 0) in vec3 Position;
layout(location = 1) in vec3 Normal;
layout(location = 3) in vec3 Tangent;
layout(location = 4) in vec2 Texture;
layout(location = 5) in vec3 Color;

uniform mat4 MVP; // full transform
uniform mat4 MV;  // model and view
uniform mat4 NM;  // normal transform
uniform vec3 LightPos;

// These two vectors pass the direction from vertex to light
// and viewpoint (IN A COORD REFERENCE FRAME of the polygon!!!)
out vec3 LightDir;
out vec3 EyeDir;
// this passes surface texture coords to fragment shader
out vec2 TexCoord;
// pass on surface color
out vec3 Vcolor;


void main(){
 gl_Position =  MVP * vec4(Position,1); // must pass on
 // get a coordinate system based in plane of input surface
 vec3 n = normalize(NM * Normal);
 vec3 t = normalize(NM * Tangent);
 EyeDir = vec3 (MV * vec4(Position,1));
 // pass on texture coords to fragment shader
 TexCoord = Texture;
 // Get normal, tangent and third vector to make curviliner coord frame
 // of reference that lies in the plane of the polygon for which we are
 // processing one of its vertices.
 vec3 n = normalize(gl_NormalMatrix * gl_Normal);
 vec3 t = normalize(gl_NormalMatrix * Tangent);
 vec3 b = cross(n, t);
 // get the light direction and viewpoint (eye) direction in this new
 // coordinate frame of reference.
 vec3 v;
 vec3 LightPosition=vec3(gl_LightSource[0].position);
 v.x = dot(LightPosition, t);
 v.y = dot(LightPosition, b);
 v.z = dot(LightPosition, n);
 LightDir = normalize(v);
 v.x = dot(EyeDir, t);
 v.y = dot(EyeDir, b);
 v.z = dot(EyeDir, n);
 EyeDir = normalize(v);
```

Listing 7.10: Bump mapping vertex shader program.

By doing this, we ensure that the surface normal vector is always given by coordinates $(0, 0, 1)$, and thus it is easily displaced (or bumped) in the fragment shader by adding to it the small changes Δu and Δv obtained from the bump map.

```
// Fragment Shader  - Bump mapping
#version 330 core

layout(location = 0) out vec4 color;

in vec3 LightDir;  // input from vertex shader
in vec3 EyeDir;
in vec2 TexCoord;
// pass on surface color
in vec3 Vcolor;

uniform sampler2D Rsf;

// fraction of light due to specular hightlights
const float SpecularFactor = 0.5;
// range [4.0 - 0.1]  bump gradient [large - small]
const float Gradient = 4.0;

void main (void){
 vec3 SurfaceColor = Vcolor;  // get the color
 // get the surface normal perturbation vector
 // - it is encoded in the texture image
 vec2 grad = (texture2D(Rsf, TexCoord).rg);
 // calculate the new surface normal - perterb in (x,y) plane
 vec3 normDelta=normalize(vec3((grad.x-0.5)*Gradient,
  (grad.y-0.5)*Gradient,1.0)));
 // now apply the lighting model
 vec3 litColor = SurfaceColor* max(dot(normDelta, LightDir), 0.0);
 vec3 reflectDir = reflect(LightDir, normDelta);
 float spec = max(dot(EyeDir, reflectDir), 0.0);
 spec *= SpecularFactor;
 litColor = min(litColor + spec, vec3(1.0));
 color = vec4(litColor, 1.0);
}
```

Listing 7.11: Bump mapping fragment shader program.

To obtain the surface-local coordinates, we first set up a rectilinear coordinate system with three basis vectors. We have two of them already: the surface normal $\mathbf{n} = (n_x, n_y, n_z)$ and the tangent vector $\mathbf{t} = (t_x, t_y, t_z)$ (passed to the vertex shader as a vector attribute from the application program). The third vector $\mathbf{b} = (b_x, b_y, b_z)$ (known as the *bi-normal*) is defined as $\mathbf{b} = \mathbf{n} \times \mathbf{t}$. Vectors $\mathbf{d}_w$ (such as viewpoint and light directions) are transformed from world coordinates to the surface-local frame by $\mathbf{d}_s = [T_{ws}]\mathbf{d}_w$ where $[T_{ws}]$ is the 3×3 transformation matrix:

$$[T_{ws}] = \begin{bmatrix} t_x & t_y & t_z \\ b_x & b_y & b_z \\ n_x & n_y & n_z \end{bmatrix}$$

(More details of this transformation can be found in section 2.12.6.)

- The normal displacement is usually encoded as an image map. This is done by preprocessing the image pixel map after it is read/decoded and

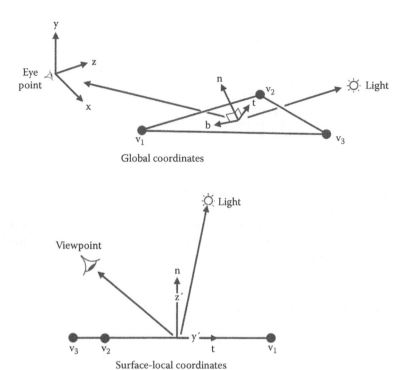

Figure 7.4: Surface local coordinates.

before it is copied into texture memory. It is first converted to a gray-scale and then the gradient is encoded by storing the $\frac{\partial \mathbf{n}_u}{\partial u}$ as the *red* pixel component and the v gradient ($\frac{\partial \mathbf{n}_v}{\partial v}$) as the *green* component. The gradient map is copied to texture memory and thus the surface normal displacement vector is easily extracted from the texture by $\boldsymbol{\Delta}\mathbf{n} = (\Delta n_1, \Delta n_2, 0) = (M_r(u, v), M_g(u, v), 0)$ (where $M_r(u, v)$ is the red component of map M at texture coordinate (u, v)). Because we are working with a normal now relative to the surface-local coordinates $\mathbf{n} = (0, 0, 1)$ the coordinates of the displaced normal ($\overline{\mathbf{n}} = \mathbf{n} + \boldsymbol{\Delta}\mathbf{n}$) vector are $(\Delta n_1, \Delta n_2, 1)$.

- An alternative method of generating the displacement vector allows it to be calculated within the fragment shader program. This eliminates the preprocessing step, at the expense of a little extra GPU processing in the fragment shader. By sampling the texture map at four points that have a small texture coordinate offset, the image's intensity gradient can be obtained. The following shader code fragment illustrates the idea:

```
const float d=0.01;
// Assumes gray color,  get value
float y1 = (texture2D(Rsf, TexCoord+vec2( 0.0, d)).r);
// above and below sample point.
float y2 = (texture2D(Rsf, TexCoord+vec2( 0.0,-d)).r);
// and to left
float x1 = (texture2D(Rsf, TexCoord+vec2( d, 0.0)).r);
// and right
float x2 = (texture2D(Rsf, TexCoord+vec2(-d, 0.0)).r);
vec3 normDelta=normalize(vec3((y2-y1)*Gradient,
        (x1-x2)*Gradient,1.0));
```

Procedural textures It is in the area of procedural textures that the real power of the programmable GPU becomes evident. More or less *any* texture that can be described algorithmically can be programmed into the GPU and rendered much faster than with any software renderer. Chapter 11 provides a rich collection of algorithms for procedural textures that are quite amenable to implementation as GPU textures.

7.3.5 Setting up the transformation matrices

With the removal of the internally handled matrix transformations through the GL_MODELVIEW and GL_PROJECTION matrices it is important to be able to replicate their behavior in an application's code. The elements of projection matrices arising from calls to either glOrtho(...) and glFrustum(..) are defined in the *Red Book* but the utility functions that previously helped us set up a projection based on a field of view and a viewpoint that looks at a specific target are not quite so readily available. To achieve the same result of these functions requires the functions given in listing 7.12.

The only point worthy of note about listing 7.12 is in the LookAt(..) function where the *LookAt* transformation is made up of a translation, which positions the eye point at $(0, 0, 0)$ and a rotation that aligns the frame of reference of the camera (defined by the direction between eye and target and an *up* direction). The rotation matrix is basically the same as that derived in section 2.12.6, however OpenGL defines the y axis to be vertical, so, if we express the *up* direction as the vector $(0, 1, 0)$ (i.e., along the y axis) we must reverse the order of rows 2 and 3 and change the sign of the elements in row 3 (as is done in listing 7.12).

Finally for this section, two very important reminders:

1. The OpenGL world is mapped with a right-handed coordinate system, the y axis is vertical, and we observe from $(0, 0, 0)$ looking down the $-z$ axis.

2. Transpose any $C/C++$ transformation matrices before passing them into the pipeline.

```
#define DEGRAD  .. // converts devress to radians
#define CROSS(v1,v2,r) .. // vector cross product r=v1*v2
#define LENGTH2(a) ... // length of vector
// copy matrix toiut=tin
static void c4to4(GLfloat tin[4][4], GLfloat tout[4][4];
//multiply matrix tr=t1*t2
static void m4by4(GLfloat t1[4][4],GLfloat t2[4][4],GLfloat tr[4][4]);
// set to Identity matrix t = I
static void null_transform(float t[4][4]);

void gl_Ortho(GLfloat m[4][4], GLfloat l, GLfloat r,
 GLfloat b, GLfloat t, GLfloat n, GLfloat f ){
 // l=left r=right b=bottom, t=top, n=near f=far
 null_transform(m);
 m[0][0]= 2.0f/(r-l);      m[0][3]= -(r+l)/(r-l);
 m[1][1]= 2.0f/(t-b);      m[1][3]= -(t+b)/(t-b);
 m[2][2]= -2.0f/(f-n);     m[2][3]= -(f+n)/(f-n);
}

void gl_Frustum(GLfloat m[4][4], GLfloat l, GLfloat r,
 GLfloat b, GLfloat t, GLfloat n, GLfloat f ){
 // l=left r=right b=bottom, t=top, n=near f=far (clip planes)
 null_transform(m);
 m[0][0]= 2.0f*n/(r-l);    m[0][2]= (r+l)/(r-l);
 m[1][1]= 2.0f*n/(t-b);    m[1][2]= (t+b)/(t-b);
 m[2][2]= -(f+n)/(f-n);    m[2][3]= -2.0f*f*n/(f-n);
 m[3][2] = -1;             m[3][3]= 0;
}
```

```
void glu_Perspective(GLfloat m[4][4], GLfloat fovy,
 GLfloat a, GLfloat n, GLfloat f ){
 // fovy = horizontal field of view a = aspect ratio width/height
 // n = near f = far (clipping planes)
 GLfloat t,b,l,r;
 t = n*(GLfloat)tan(DEGRAD*fovy/2.0);
 b = -t;   l = -a*t;  r =  a*t;
 gl_Frustum(m,l,r,b,t,n,f);
}

void glu_LookAt(GLfloat m[4][4],
 GLfloat ex,GLfloat ey,GLfloat ez, // eye
 GLfloat cx,GLfloat cy,GLfloat cz, // target
 GLfloat ux,GLfloat uy,GLfloat uz){// up
 GLfloat f[3],s[3],u[3],l,m1[4][4],m2[4][4];
 null_transform(m); null_transform(m2);
 f[0]=cx-ex; f[1]=cy-ey; f[2]=cz-ez;
 u[0]=ux; u[1]=uy; u[2]=uz;
 l=1.0/LENGTH(f);  VECSCALE(l,f,f)
 CROSS (f,u,s)
 l=1.0/LENGTH(s);  VECSCALE(l,s,s)
 CROSS (s,f,u)
 translate(m1,-ex,-ey,-ez); null_transform(m2);
 m2[0][0]= s[0]; m2[0][1]= s[1]; m2[0][2]= s[2];
 // re-order because Y Z axes are reversed (Y is UP! )
 m2[1][0]= u[0]; m2[1][1]= u[1]; m2[1][2]= u[2];
 m2[2][0]= -f[0]; m2[2][1]= -f[1]; m2[2][2]= -f[2];
 m4by4(m2,m1,m);
}
```

Listing 7.12: Creating transformation matrices that match the functionality of the old GLU utility functions.

7.4   The P-buffer and framebuffer objects

It was mentioned earlier that in addition to the front and back output buffers OpenGL may offer a few additional buffers, AUX0, AUX1 etc. However, many display adapters do not support these buffers. Even if the AUXn buffers are supported they have a major limitation in that they cannot exceed the current size of the output window. More specifically, they cannot exceed the size of the underlying *drawing surface*. An output window is just a system dependent view of the drawing *surface* OpenGL renders onto a drawing surface attached to a window. This is a problem if you want to render a scene at a resolution that is greater than the desktop size. It is also a major problem if you want to render to a texture (an image map) to be used later (for example, an image may be required at a resolution of twice the maximum window size, and include an automatically generated mip-map, taking its resolution even higher). Being able to render to very large off-screen buffers of any size has advantages. The modern way to render into large output buffers that can also be used as textures for subsequent mapping is through the use of framebuffer objects (FBOs). The older way was through the use of Pixel (or P) buffers. Both of these techniques are used in the OpenFX renderer (see chapter 9), and a document describing how to use framebuffer objects is available on the website.

7.5   Rendering a particle system using OpenGL

To round off this chapter on OpenGL programming we return briefly to consider the practical implementation of a real-time particle system. Section 6.7 looked into the very powerful contribution that particle models can play in enriching CGI movies and computer games. Because of the simplicity of the concept, particle models are ideal for use in real-time applications and OpenGL provides all the capabilities needed for rendering a particle system, i.e. alpha blended texture mapping, integrated transformations and a wide range of framebuffer combiner operations.

In this short section a couple of listings provide a framework that can act as a progenitor for a comprehensive particle system. Indeed, the OpenFX particle actor, as described in section 9.7.5, is little more than a scaled up version of the ideas given in listings 7.13 and 7.14. Listing 7.13 draws attention to the importance of a couple of data structures, one for the particle system itself, where its image texture, its number of particles and an array of particles are defined. The second structure represents each particle and is needed so that the particle can evolve from its generation by the particle system. The two functions in listing 7.13 perform the tasks of (1) setting up the particle texture and particle system parameters, and (2) updating the position and attributes of each particle as time elapses. The most significant steps in rendering the particle system are presented in listing 7.14. Each particle is a small texture mapped GL_QUAD

```
// Structures for a particle system

typedef struct ParticleTag {
 GLfloat p[3]; // position
 float c[3]; // colour
 Alpha; //transparency
 ..
 .. // other properties
} Particle;

typedef struct ParticleSystemTag {
 int type; // image blending type
 int np; // number of particles
 Particle *P;// list of particles
 int iid; // texture map image
} ParticleSystem;

// global texture IDs
GLint g_particle_textures[NTEXTURES];

void MakeParticleTextures(void){ // Setup particle textures
 ..
 // ask for the number of particle image textures needed
 glGenTextures( nParticleImages, &g_particle_textures[0]);
 ..
 // load image and copy to GPU txture memory.
 ..
}

void UpdateParticle(double time, ParticleSystem *Ps){
 ..
 // Timed function to take each particle through its
 // evolution. Details will depend on the nature of
 // the particle system.
 for(i=0;i<Ps->np;i++){ // process each particle
   ..
 }
 ..
}
```

Listing 7.13: Data structures for a particle system.

that is rendered by modulating how it is blended into the output buffer with the texture map. How the QUAD is blended is the secret of producing the appearance of *hot fire* or the *spray* form breaking waves on the sea shore. The geometry transformations must place the particles in the correct location with respect to the viewpoint and any objects associated with the particle system. However, the transformations must ensure that no rotation is applied to the textured QUAD and that it is always perpendicular to the viewing direction.

When these simple guidelines are followed, the full beauty of many natural phenomenon can be brought to the computer screen in real-time, like those in figure 6.38 for example.

```
void DrawParticleSystemGL(ParticleSystem *Ps){
..
// activate texture mapping
glBindTexture(GL_TEXTURE_2D,g_particle_textures[Ps->iid]);
glTexParameterf(GL_TEXTURE_2D, GL_TEXTURE_WRAP_S, GL_REPEAT);
glTexParameterf(GL_TEXTURE_2D, GL_TEXTURE_WRAP_T, GL_REPEAT);
glEnable(GL_BLEND);
if(Ps->type == 1)glBlendFunc(GL_SRC_ALPHA, GL_ONE_MINUS_SRC_ALPHA);
else glBlendFunc(GL_SRC_ALPHA,GL_ONE);
glDepthMask(GL_FALSE);
glBegin(GL_QUADS);
for(i=0;i<Ps->np;i++){ // process each particle
..
p=Ps->P[i];
// set the particle's attrubue
glColor4f(p->c[0],p->c[1],p->c[2],p->Alpha);
..
// get the particle's position
xc=p->p[0]; yc=p->p[0]; zc=p->p[2];
// rectangle is alwaays draw perpendicular to the viewing direction
// and filling the textured QUAD
glTexCoord2f(1.0f, 1.0f); glVertex3f(xc+psize, yc+psize, zc);
glTexCoord2f(0.0f, 1.0f); glVertex3f(xc-psize, yc+psize, zc);
glTexCoord2f(0.0f, 0.0f); glVertex3f(xc-psize, yc-psize, zc);
glTexCoord2f(1.0f, 0.0f); glVertex3f(xc+psize, yc-psize, zc);
}
glEnd();
glDepthMask(GL_TRUE);
glDisable(GL_BLEND);
glBindTexture(GL_TEXTURE_2D,0);
..
}
```

Listing 7.14: Draw a particle system.

7.6   Summing up

This chapter has shone the spotlight onto how to do a number of the most useful tasks in 3D graphics by using the OpenGL 3D real-time graphics library. In the limited space available we have not been able to consider in depth a couple of interesting examples that you can find via the book's website:

1. The dual robot manipulation simulator that demonstrates how to use inverse kinematics and a complex combination of transformation systems.

2. The fly-by demonstrator that shows how an OpenGL application can be made seamlessly compatible across desktop and mobile platforms.

3. The metaballs demonstrator that illustrates how to implement a marching cubes algorithm and render it using OpenGL in either the compatibility or core .rendering models.

For a full presentation of many more things that you can do with OpenGL consult the *OpenGL SuperBible* [78] which covers just about everything you are ever likely to want to know how to do with OpenGL.

8

Mobile 3D: OpenGLES

This chapter investigates how to extend the power and simplicity of OpenGL in the world of mobile devices, smart phones and tablets. *Apps*, as they are popularly known, can be endowed with the same high-powered 3D graphics that we have become used to on the desktop and laptop platforms. The distinction between traditional laptop/notebook computers and mobile devices like the Apple iPad or the Google Nexus phone is getting more and more blurred. Is there a significant difference between a notebook using an Intel i7 processor with detachable keyboard and touch screen, say running Windows 8, and an iPad with an ARM processor and bluetooth keyboard? Both of these devices have a similar look and feel, both run the same range of programs, e-mail clients, browsers, presentation software etc. Many Apps depend on high-speed 3D graphics, and not just the computer game Apps. The powerful geometric transformations of 3D graphics can endow applications and even operating systems with lively effects like spins, page turns, image flips etc.

From the program developer's perspective there is a very significant difference between building apps for the desktop platform and apps for a mobile device. *It is **not** possible to develop programs for a tablet or phone on the tablet or phone themselves.* It is perfectly possible to develop programs for any Windows 8 computer on a Windows 8 computer, but it is not possible to develop programs for a Windows Phone 8 on a Windows Phone! The same applies to Apple's devices and to the Android devices, so this is quite a useful way to classify a platform as either desktop or mobile. Since OpenGL is designated a cross-platform graphics library, the way we will choose to designate a host as a mobile is to say: those platforms that offer the full OpenGL specification are desktops and notebooks, and those that use OpenGLES as tablet/phones/hand-held devices.

OpenGLES [63] (or OpenGL for Embedded Systems) has a much shorter pedigree than OpenGL. A powerful graphics library capable of rendering in 3D requires a significant hardware resource; unless a program requires the full power of a high-end device all mobile devices already do an excellent job. With the exception of a few restrictions, once an application has carried out the specific platform dependent initialization then the same OpenGL drawing function calls can be used in OpenGLES.

OpenGLES is the 3D drawing system used by Apple's iOS devices and by Google's Android systems. It was also used by Nokia in the Symbian smartphones. Unfortunately Microsoft's current Windows phone uses their Direct3D graphics and will not be discussed further here. In this chapter we will briefly review the few differences between OpenGL and OpenGLES and then look at a couple of examples that can be used to form templates for some iOS and Android apps making use of 3D graphics.

8.1 OpenGLES

In the short history of OpenGLES (GLES) the specification has undergone quite a rapid development. This is mainly because the graphics hardware available for embedded systems is catching up fast on the hardware that has been available on the desktop PCs for some time. Perhaps the most significant change in GLES has occurred during the introduction of version 2 when the GLES rendering pipeline became programmable.

As the OpenGLES and OpenGL APIs converge, the fixed functionality functions in the API are being deprecated. However, the GLES never offered the display list, or the `glVertex(..)` family of functions, and so it should not require such a radical change in the coding of applications to update them to use the version 2/3 API as would be required for a very mature desktop program.

The GLES-2 (and subsequent versions, version 3 being the most recent at time of writing) pipeline does not support any fixed functionality, and all application programs must create a minimal set of shaders. Even GLES 1 uses the modern method of specifying geometry, with polygon lists and/or vertex buffers providing a better way of defining geometry. These types of structures were discussed in chapter 3 and therefore OpenGLES (and indeed the latest version of OpenGL) match very well the data structures used in the algorithms described in part III.

The source codes and projects that accompany this chapter provide examples of how to use these modern data structures.

An OpenGLES application has to create and initialize a drawing surface and obtain a handle to a rendering context in much the same way that an application would do for the full OpenFX. We will elaborate on the setup phase because, once a GLES surface has been defined and a drawing/device context obtained for it, the actual process of rendering is platform independent and we can *pretty much* use the same code that we use on the desktop. For example, the usage of texture mapping lighting and shader codes will be identical. Indeed, if you have built your desktop programs using the `VertexPointer()` and `glDrawElements()` or `glDrawArrays(..)` functions then OpenGL programs should port seamlessly to GLES.

Listings 8.1, 8.2 and 8.3 highlight the key steps in rendering with the `DrawElements()` function, that is, the geometry, topology and surface attributes

```
// The vertices give the model
// its shpae
int num_model_vertices=0;
GLfloat *model_vertices=NULL;

// The surface normals are
// needed by the lighting model
GLfloat *model_normals=NULL;

// The indices list the vertices associated
// the the faces the give the model its
// surface.
int num_model_indicies=0;
short *model_indicies=NULL;

// The simplest surface attibute is its
// color which is specified for each
// vertex
GLubyte *model_colours=NULL;
```

Listing 8.1: A minimal set of data is needed to describe a 3D model. These variable are used to reference it.

```
FILE *fp;
..
// how much data
fread(&num_model_vertices,sizeof(),1,fp);
fread(&num_model_indicies,sizeof(),1,fp);
// provide memory buffers of suffficent size
// to hold the data for vertices and triangular faces
if((model_vertices=(GLfloat *)malloc( // 3 coords per vertex
  num_model_vertices * 3 * sizeof(GLfloat))) == NULL){ ... /* error */ }
if((model_normals=(GLfloat *)malloc(  // one vector per vertex
  num_model_vertices * 3 * sizeof(GLfloat))) == NULL){ ... /* error */ }
if((model_colours=(GLubyte *)malloc( // RGBA color
  num_model_vertices * 4 * sizeof(GLubyte))) == NULL){ ... /* error */ }
if((model_indicies=(short *)malloc( // Triangles have 3 vertex IDs each
  num_model_indicies * 3 * sizeof(short))) == NULL){ ... /* error */ }
// obtain the main data
fread(model_vertices,sizeof(GLfloat),num_model_vertices * 3,fp);
...
```

Listing 8.2: Before any 3D data can be drawn it must be assembled in a form that may be passed to the rendering functions. The source of the data might be anything. In this piece of code it is simply assumed to be obtained from a file previously opened for reading.

must be specified in memory buffers in the correct order. In some ways, loading data into graphics memory with the `VertexPointer()` and `glNormalPointer()` functions is similar to setting up a display list. Using `DrawElements()` fulfills many of the actions that might otherwise be done by calling an old style display list.

```
..
// indicate that the data also contains some
// basic surface attribites
glEnableClientState(GL_COLOR_ARRAY);
// Load the data into the GPU
glVertexPointer(3 ,GL_FLOAT, 0, model_vertices);
glNormalPointer(GL_FLOAT, 0, model_normals);
glColorPointer(4,GL_UNSIGNED_BYTE,0,model_colours);

//apply any transformations here

glDrawElements(GL_TRIANGLES, // data represents triangles
  num_model_indicies*3,  // how may triangles
  GL_UNSIGNED_SHORT,     // format of each uumber
  &model_indicies[0]);   // pointer to the first one

...
```

Listing 8.3: Pass geometry and attribute data to the pipeline and render it. Repeat as necessary.

In the next sections we illustrate how to use OpenGLES on iOS and Android platforms. Our aim is to provide a minimum of code on which to base applications, so that it is easy to extend them into a wide spectrum of potential apps.

8.2   3D on iOS

To develop iOS applications there is no real alternative but to use the Xcode tools suite on an Apple computer. There are many similarities between an iOS application and a Cocoa program for OSX (as described in section 7.2.2), including the detail of the way in which a container window is created in code or an object is loaded from a NIB/XIB file. Developing for a real iOS device can be quite awkward because the programs must be electronically signed before they may be executed on a device. Device signing requires a *profile* generated on the Apple developer's website for specific devices. Before this can be done the developer must be a registered developer, which costs real money. However, the emulator does an excellent job of simulating the operation of 3D graphics without the need for registration.

The code examined in this section demonstrates how to render using either GPU shaders in GLES versions ≥ 2 or switch back to the fixed functionality behavior. The example is based on a program from the SDK that has been edited to bring the essential detail of a GLES iOS App into sharp focus. The full project codes and a commentary on the development process can be obtained from our website with versions that are set up for the various form factors of the iOS devices, iPad, iPhone etc.

One of the nice things about a program that uses OpenGL is that once a drawing surface has been established the need to interact with the host system can be kept to a minimum.

Any iOS App that is going to use GLES may be built by extending on code associated with the following basic steps:

1. Create the code for a class, derived from the `UIView` API class (e.g., called `EAGLView`), to represent the View.

2. Add an object of this class to the XIB file using interface builder (Xcode).

3. Provide code in the AppDelegate class for the delegated functions.

4. Provide code for the class that will represent the OpenGL view. Since an object of this class has been defined in the XIB file, an instance of it will be created and its method called automatically:
   `(id)initWithCoder:(NSCoder*)coder`.
   It is within `initWithCoder` that the properties of the OpenGL display should be established. Also, since the `EAGLView` class is derived from the `UIView` class the delegated method `(void)drawView:(id)sender` will be called automatically when the display needs to be refreshed. It is in `drawView` that we can place all our OpenGL drawing code.

Once these iOS specific tasks have been completed the addition of two (non-iOS specific) functions that

1. do anything that can be done as a one-off set up and

2. draw whatever is needed (this function is called in response to a regular timer)

will give a complete template for any App that wants to present itself on a 3D canvas. Listings 8.4 to 8.14 fill in a little more of the detail.

The `AppDelegateClass` of listings 8.4 and 8.5 provides overridden methods that are called when the application object is created and when it is destroyed. This gives us the opportunity to control the behavior of the View object which is defined in the XIB and linked to the `glView` member variable of the `AppDelegateClass`.

Our View object is an instance of the `EAGLView` class, which is derived from the standard iOS class `UIView`. To endow the `EAGLView` class with an OpenGL rendering surface a standard documented process has to be followed. In this example we are going to enhance the basic properties by offering the potential to use either the OpenGLES version 1 or version 2 approach. (Remember that the GLES version 2 does not have a fixed functionality pipeline and all programs must render through a pair of GPU shader codes.)

The derived View class is specified in listing 8.6 with its most relevant members and methods highlighted in listing 8.7. Since the View object is

```
#import <UIKit/UIKit.h>

// forward class reference to main application class
@class EAGLView;

@interface glesIosAppDelegate : NSObject <UIApplicationDelegate> {
 UIWindow *window;
 EAGLView *glView; // will point to the OpenGL View object
}

// connect to object in XIB file
@property (nonatomic, retain) IBOutlet UIWindow *window;
@property (nonatomic, retain) IBOutlet EAGLView *glView;

@end
```

Listing 8.4: The application delegate header file defines sub-class with its application specific members.

defined in the XIB (resource) file the standard approach of iOS is to call its `initWithCoder:` method during creation. It is in this method that all the hard work of configuring the View is done.

Before looking at the configuration of the rendering surface for either GLESv1 (version 1, fixed functionality) or GLESv2 (version 2 GPU shader) we shall consider the methods in the `EGALView` class that start and stop the timed display update. In listing 8.8 the `startAnimation:` method starts a timer that calls the `drawView:` method, when the timer fires. The timer function then instructs the appropriate renderer (for GLESv1 or GLESv2) to draw the scene.

Returning to consider the drawing code, the objects that perform either fixed function or programmable rendering are of classes that have similar form; the version 2 class is presented in listing 8.9. The difference between a class representing a version 1 (fixed function) drawing surface and one to be used with the programmable version 2 pipeline lies not in their members but in what commands the initialization and rendering method have to issue. Under iOS, rendering is done into a framebuffer object (FBO) with attached renderbuffer. FBOs and renderbuffers were discussed in section 7.4 for desktop platforms and their use in the mobile context is no different, except that the actual presentation of the rendered output is done by calling the display context's method `presentRenderBuffer;` as in:

```
// GLES version 1
[context presentRenderbuffer:GL_RENDERBUFFER_OES];
// GLES version 2
[context presentRenderbuffer:GL_RENDERBUFFER];
```

In listing 8.10 the preparation of a drawing surface to receive output rendered through the programmable pipeline is shown. It includes a call to a method to

```
#import "glesIosAppDelegate.h"  // class definition
#import "EAGLView.h"  // main class definition

@implementation glesIosAppDelegate // over-ridden methods

@synthesize window; // link pointer to object in XIB
@synthesize glView; // link pointer to object in XIB

// This method is called by system when object is created
- (BOOL)application:(UIApplication *)application
   didFinishLaunchingWithOptions:(NSDictionary *)launchOptions {
 // Apply any launch specific code here.
 [window makeKeyAndVisible];
 // Start the timer associated with the view, to refresh
 // the display
 [glView startAnimation];
  return YES;
}
// The class also delegates method that are called by the system
// when other events occur, such as activation of another app.
// They are omitted here for brevity.

// IOS programs call this method on exit to allow for clean-up.
// We release the resources in the usual way.
- (void)dealloc {
 [window release];
 [glView release];
 [super dealloc];
}

@end  // end of the class
```

Listing 8.5: The application delegate source.

load, compile and install the shader programs. (The code for a `loadShaders;`
method would be similar to those used on a desktop with the exception that the
source will either be explicitly given in a text string in the code or a file within
the application bundle.)

If the drawing window's dimensions change then the View's dimensions have
to be change. On mobile devices with their small screens a change of window size
is much less likely to occur than in a desktop program; however, the possibility
must still be serviced, not least because a change of size always happens when a
window is first created. As one would expect there are slight variations between
resizing a FBO for fixed-function and for GPU-programmable rendering. Since
the output surface is represented as a FBO, it and its attached renderbuffers have
to be resized accordingly. Fortunately, the same code can be used for every app,
so the brief template, taken from the iOS API reference examples and shown in
listing 8.11, is sufficient to handle all re-sizing eventualities.

It is always good programming practice to perform a smooth shutdown and
release of resources; listing 8.12 shows the way.

And now, after all the preamble we come to the actual drawing. Everything
that you draw using OpenGLES—geometry, transformations, texture maps—can

```
#import <UIKit/UIKit.h>
#import <QuartzCore/QuartzCore.h>
#import <OpenGLES/EAGL.h>
#import <OpenGLES/EAGLDrawable.h>

// methods that are implemented by the rendering class
@protocol ESRenderer <NSObject>
- (void)render;
- (BOOL)resizeFromLayer:(CAEAGLLayer *)layer;
@end

// This class wraps the CoreAnimation CAEAGLLayer
@interface EAGLView : UIView
{
@private
 id <ESRenderer> renderer; // will point at renderer object
 BOOL displayLinkSupported;
 NSInteger animationFrameInterval;
 id displayLink;
 NSTimer *animationTimer;
 // add any other members would go here
}

@property (readonly,nonatomic,getter=isAnimating) BOOL animating;
@property (nonatomic) NSInteger animationFrameInterval;

// overridden methods
- (void)startAnimation;
- (void)stopAnimation;
- (void)drawView:(id)sender;

@end
```

Listing 8.6: The GLES derived class `EGALView`. The listing presented here follows the instructions set out in the developer's documentation and Apple's distributed examples.

be done with the same code that you would use in a desktop application; even the GPU shaders are identical. Rendering is done in the `render:` method of the respective GLES version classes, `ES1Renderer` and `ES2Renderer`. Remember, `render:` is called via the timer created during initialization; see listing 8.8. The code required for rendering, apart from drawing the application specific components, only requires that the display context is first set, the framebuffer object is bound, and the renderbuffer content is presented to the user. Listing 8.13 exemplifies these salient points in the case of a version 2 rendering context. GLES 2 has no fixed-function capability and therefore a pair of GLSL shaders must be activated and used. Listing 8.14 presents a short pair of shaders that perform the bare minimum of transforming the vertices into position. The color assignment highlights the process of passing attributes on a per vertex basis to the vertex shader, which then passes the vertex colors on through the rasterizer which interpolates them for the fragment shader. (Note: There is usually a one-to-one correspondence between fragments and pixels.)

```
#import "EAGLView.h" // class definition
#import "ES1Renderer.h" // GLES version 1 renderer class
#import "ES2Renderer.h" // GLES version 2 renderer class

@implementation EAGLView

@synthesize animating;
@dynamic animationFrameInterval;

+ (Class)layerClass{ // class method must be implemented
 return [CAEAGLLayer class];
}

// The EAGL view is stored in the XIB file.
// When it's loaded -initWithCoder: is called
- (id)initWithCoder:(NSCoder*)coder {
 if ((self = [super initWithCoder:coder])){
  // Get the layer and set its properties
  CAEAGLLayer *eaglLayer = (CAEAGLLayer *)self.layer;
  eaglLayer.opaque = TRUE;
  eaglLayer.drawableProperties = [...] // properties
  // try to allocate a GLES version 2 renderer
  renderer = [[ES2Renderer alloc] init]; // call the init method
  if(!renderer){ // no version 2 renderer
   // try to allocate a version 1 renderer
   renderer = [[ES1Renderer alloc] init]; // and call "init"
   if(!renderer){ // no renderer available
     [self release]; return nil;
   }
  }
  ... // any other code for this method
 }
 return self;
}
// other overridden methods
- (void)drawView:(id)sender { // draw the view
 [renderer render]; // call the chosen drawing method
}
- (void)layoutSubviews { // resize the view
 [renderer resizeFromLayer:(CAEAGLLayer*)self.layer];
 [self drawView:nil];  // and draw again
}
... // other methods
}
@end
```

Listing 8.7: Initialising the GLES view and preparing the surface for OpenGLES rendering using either GLES version 1 or version 2.

8.2.1   Some example iOS 3D projects

The iOS application we have described is very basic. It does not use any texture maps or elaborate shaders; however it is readily extended. The View class and the appDelegate class afford opportunities to access the device's internal sensors, accelerometers, compass etc., and to make use of the multi-touch screen. In this book we don't have the space to work through a number of interesting applications, but there is no page limit on the website, and there you will find

```
- (void)startAnimation {
 if (!animating){
   animationTimer =
    [NSTimer scheduledTimerWithTimeInterval:(
    NSTimeInterval)((1.0/60.0) * animationFrameInterval)
     target:self selector:@selector(drawView:)
     userInfo:nil repeats:TRUE];
 }
 .. // call any "execute once" OpenGL configuration from here
 animating = TRUE;
 }
}

- (void)stopAnimation {
 if (animating){ // remove the timer
   [animationTimer invalidate];
   animationTimer = nil;
 }
 animating = FALSE;
 }
}

- (void)drawView:(id)sender {
 // call the render function in the active GLES class object
 [renderer render];
}
```

Listing 8.8: A system timer mechanism is used to re-draw the display at regular intervals, thus achieving an animated view.

the code for a few projects that elaborate on the basics covered in this section and use a few more of the features of the *iDevices*.

Two of the examples are:

- *Porting the SanAngles city:* The SanAngles program (figure 8.1) is a widely available OpenGL program which uses no external data, no image maps and a pre-programmed set of camera changes and object movement. It also has a high polygon count and no unusual aspects of OpenGL rendering are used. For these reasons the program is a good benchmarking example across platforms. The SanAngles examples was one of the first applications used to demonstrate how to use native code on the Android platforms. On the book's website you will find projects and code for our implementations of the program for iOS (as well as for Nokia's Symbian Smartphone OS and Windows, Mac OSX and Ubuntu Linux).

- *The 3D map:* This example demonstrates how to render a 3D map using terrain data and textured with a satellite image. The challenge in this example does not come from the OpenGL rendering of a polygonal mesh and texture map. It comes from the combination of a 3D display with standard on-screen dialog buttons and edit boxes, how to change the viewpoint and

```
// File ES1Renderer.h // for GLES version 2
#import "EAGLView.h"

#import <OpenGLES/ES2/gl.h>
#import <OpenGLES/ES2/glext.h>

@interface ES2Renderer : NSObject <ESRenderer>
{
@private
 EAGLContext *context; // the device context
 // The pixel dimensions of the CAEAGLLayer
 GLint backingWidth,backingHeight;
 // The OpenGL ES names for the framebuffer and
 // renderbuffer used to render to this view
 GLuint defaultFramebuffer, colorRenderbuffer;
 // The identity of the GPU shader program
 // required by GLES version 2 (or greater)
 GLuint program;
}

s- (void)render; // srawing method
- (BOOL)resizeFromLayer:(CAEAGLLayer *)layer;

@end
```

Listing 8.9: The classes that encapsulate the rendering process are very similar for both GLES versions 1 and 2. This listing presents the specification of the version 2 classes.

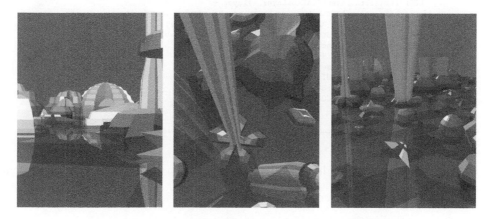

Figure 8.1: The SanAngles application rendered on iPad.

view direction using the touch screen interface, and how to load the map and 3D data from the application bundle. The application's code, which is available from the website, should be readily followed and will build into a product (see figure 8.2) for either the emulator or any of the iOS devices.

```
- (id)init { // (class ES1Renderer) called from the initWithCoder:
if ((self = [super init])) {
  context = [[EAGLContext alloc] initWithAPI:kEAGLRenderingAPIOpenGLES2];
  if (!context ||
      ![EAGLContext setCurrentContext:context] ||
      ![self loadShaders]) { // NOTE: Call to load shaders
    [self release]; // If this point is reached then something
    return nil;      // went wrong - no renderer available.
  }
  // Create default framebuffer object.
  // The backing will be allocated for the current
  // layer in method "-resizeFromLayer"
  glGenFramebuffers(1, &defaultFramebuffer);
  glGenRenderbuffers(1, &colorRenderbuffer);
  glBindFramebuffer(GL_FRAMEBUFFER, defaultFramebuffer);
  glBindRenderbuffer(GL_RENDERBUFFER, colorRenderbuffer);
  glFramebufferRenderbuffer(GL_FRAMEBUFFER,
     GL_COLOR_ATTACHMENT0,
     GL_RENDERBUFFER,
      colorRenderbuffer);
}
return self;
}
```

Listing 8.10: Initializing the display surface to receive output rendered using GLES version 2 or greater (with programmable shaders).

```
// Code for resizing a GLES version 2 layer
- (BOOL)resizeFromLayer:(CAEAGLLayer *)layer {
// Allocate color buffer backing based on the current layer size
glBindRenderbuffer(GL_RENDERBUFFER, colorRenderbuffer);
[context renderbufferStorage:GL_RENDERBUFFER fromDrawable:layer];
glGetRenderbufferParameteriv(GL_RENDERBUFFER,
  GL_RENDERBUFFER_WIDTH, &backingWidth);
glGetRenderbufferParameteriv(GL_RENDERBUFFER,
 GL_RENDERBUFFER_HEIGHT, &backingHeight);
if (glCheckFramebufferStatus(GL_FRAMEBUFFER)
   != GL_FRAMEBUFFER_COMPLETE){ ... } // fail
return YES;
}
```

Listing 8.11: Resize the display window, code taken from the GLES version 2 rendering classes.

8.3   3D on Android

Android has proved very popular as a smart-phone operating system, and there are a wide variety of tablet devices that use the Android OS. Android is an open-source project and therefore development is not handicapped by needing to pay to run your program on your devices as it is on the iOS platforms. The principle environment in which apps are executed is a JAVA virtual machine (VM) called Dalvik. In the devices themselves, the VM executes on top of a

```
// Code to smoothly release the GL buffers and drawing contexts
// for GLES version >= 2

- (void)dealloc {
  // Delete GL buffers
  if (defaultFramebuffer) {
    glDeleteFramebuffers(1, &defaultFramebuffer);
    defaultFramebuffer = 0;
  }
  if (colorRenderbuffer) {
    glDeleteRenderbuffers(1, &colorRenderbuffer);
    colorRenderbuffer = 0;
  }
  if (program){
    glDeleteProgram(program);
    program = 0;
  }
  // Release context
  if ([EAGLContext currentContext] == context)
    [EAGLContext setCurrentContext:nil];
  [context release];
  context = nil;
  [super dealloc];
}
```

Listing 8.12: Closing down: Before an iOS application terminates, the framebuffers and any GPU shader programs should be deleted so that no resources are lost for other apps.

Figure 8.2: A mapping application.

UNIX/Linux kernel; thus it is also possible to write Android applications in a native language, and execute them outside the VM. The Native Development Kit (the NDK) provides all the information the developer needs to write and execute apps written in C. Writing an app that uses some JAVA code running in the VM and some C code compiled and used natively is also possible. Whilst the Android API provides a rich collection of JAVA classes for making use of any

```
- (void)render{
 // bind the frame buffers
 [EAGLContext setCurrentContext:context];
 glBindFramebuffer(GL_FRAMEBUFFER, defaultFramebuffer);

 // Set up the display  - this code could be ued in "init"
 glViewport(0, 0, backingWidth, backingHeight);
 glClearColor(0.5f, 0.5f, 0.5f, 1.0f);
 glClear(GL_COLOR_BUFFER_BIT);

 // Choose the vertex and fragment programs to run
 glUseProgram(program);

 /* DRAW USING OPENGL FUNCTION CALLS **/

 glUseProgram(0);  // Release GPU shader program
 // bind the buffer that has been rendered and display it in the View
 glBindRenderbuffer(GL_RENDERBUFFER, colorRenderbuffer);
 [context presentRenderbuffer:GL_RENDERBUFFER];
 }
```

Listing 8.13: Render function of class ES2Renderer. Note the function call used to specify which GLSL program to run.

specialized device hardware, it is also possible to write native apps that access the underlying hardware, e.g., the accelerometers, the wireless and bluetooth networks, but this is undesirable. Accessing the hardware natively is complex and often depends on the specific hardware. One thing that is easy to do natively, however, is to render to the screen using OpenGL; thus if you are developing a game app for say both iOS and Android doing everything using OpenGL you should be able to maximize the amount of common code used.

Three-dimensional graphics is a very small corner of the Android realm and apps that depend on it may not be so well known. Getting started with Android application development is a little harder than with iOS and Cocoa touch because documentation and example programs are not so centrally controlled and devices available from a wide range of suppliers tend to have their little quirks. A good book that covers the basics is worth looking for if you have not written an Android app before. Which one to choose can be a matter of personal taste. Darcy [18] worked for me. Any others that become available after we go to press will get a mention on the website.

One unfortunate consequence of the unbelievably rapid change in the mobile-phone/tablet arena (from zero to sophisticated multi-sensor image processing computer in less than four years) is that the developer's tools and the SDKs can change unrecognizably in less than a year. Every few months there is a new iOS or Android version. However in both cases, the fundamentals that are of interest to us have been established and when you look beyond the superficial changes in developer's tool appearance, everything we discuss in this chapter should remain relevant so long as there is an iPhone or Android tablet still on sale.

```
// Vertex Shader ////
#version 150 core
// passed in from App to shader on a per-vertex basis
layout(location = 0) in vec3 vertexPosition;
layout(location = 1) in vec4 color;

uniform mat4 MVP;  // vie and projecton transformation

//pass this to fragmet shader
out vec4 colorVarying;

void main() {
 // set the built in variable
 gl_Position =  MVP * vec4(vertexPosition_modelspace,1);
 colorVarying = color;
}

// Fragment shader ////
#version 150 core

in  vec4 colorVarying;
layout out (location = 0)gl_FragColor;

void main(){
    // set the output
    gl_FragColor = colorVarying;
}
```

Listing 8.14: The minimal code needed for a pair of shaders to render scene geometry.

We have two choices when it comes to using OpenGLES on an Android platform: use the JAVA class wrappers for OpenGL, or go native and write in C using the native development kit (NDK). In this section the key stages of code development for both approaches will be outlined. As with all our examples in the book, the listings will identify significant fragments whilst the full programs will be are available with added commentary on the website.

8.3.1 Rendering with the `GLSurfaceView` class

Android apps are based around the activity and possibly several activities. Often, each activity is associated with a specific task with a specific screen layout, showing buttons, text boxes and other user interface elements. As the user switches from activity to activity, the display switches from screen to screen.

The screen layout is defined as an XML script located in one of the project's resource folders. Apps can contain several activities and it is possible to put the 3D elements in their own activity with their own full screen display. A GLES activity can access hardware (e.g., accelerometers) and use the touch screen interface in the same way as any other activity. To make the developer's work easier, the Android SDK provides a JAVA wrapper class for OpenGL functions and a straightforward way of defining the drawing surface.

No special permissions are required to draw on the display and a default manifest file covers all necessary application settings.

For an activity to make use of OpenGL the additional API imports required are:

```
import javax.microedition.khronos.egl.EGLConfig;
import javax.microedition.khronos.opengles.GL10;
import android.opengl.GLSurfaceView;
```

Setting up the activity to use the programmable shader pipeline, available in GLES version 2 or later, is not that different from setting up for a GLES version 1.x output.[1] A few method changes are required, but perhaps the most significant addition is the need to compile, link and install the shader programs.

For an activity that makes use of OpenGLES 2 a couple of extra API imports are needed:

```
import android.opengl.GLES20;  // additional include
import android.opengl.Matrix;  // for matrix operations
```

A pair of very basic shaders need be defined. The easiest way to do this is as a couple of JAVA strings:

```
public final String vertexShaderCode = "     ";
       "uniform mat4 uMVPMatrix;" +
       "attribute vec4 vPosition;" +
       "void main() {" +
       "  gl_Position = vPosition * uMVPMatrix;" +
       "}";

public final String fragmentShaderCode =
       "precision mediump float;" +
       "uniform vec4 vColor;" +
       "void main() {" +
       "  gl_FragColor = vColor;" +
       "}";
```

Transformation matrices must be built in the application and passed to the shaders because OpenGL is phasing out the use of the built-in matrix stack. Listings 8.15 and 8.16 show how to implement the three most important methods of the GLSurfaceView interface.

Listings 8.17 and 8.18 provide a few lines of code to exemplify how a user-defined class might define a mesh that can be rendered using the glDrawElements(..) function. Note that in Android the `glXXX()` functions are wrapped as methods of the `gl.glXXX()` and `GLES20.glXXX` classes.

At the time of writing GLES version 3.01 has been released. Whilst it adds some features, the basic principles described here remain valid.

8.3.2   3D rendering with the NDK

Using OpenGL through the Android SDK wrapper class is fine for most applications but if you have an app that is only based around 3D graphics and you

---

[1]A document describing setting up a GLES version 1 display can be found on the website.

```
class PA3DRenderer implements GLSurfaceView.Renderer {

  private MyMesh mMesh; // the mesh
  // the projection matrices
  private final float[] mProjMatrix = new float[16];
  private final float[] mVMatrix = new float[16];
  private final float[] mMVPMatrix = new float[16];

  private final int mProgram; // the shader program
  // define a pair of simple shaders as strings
  public final String vertexShaderCode = "  ...  ";
  public final String fragmentShaderCode = "... ";

  public void onSurfaceCreated(GL10 gl, EGLConfig config) {
    // defnine the GLES surface background
    GLES20.glClearColor(0.0f, 0.0f, 0.0f, 1.0f);
    // load and compile the shaders
    int vertexShader = loadShader(GLES20.GL_VERTEX_SHADER,vertexShaderCode);
    int fragmentShader = loadShader(GLES20.GL_FRAGMENT_SHADER,fragmentShaderCode);
    // create/attach/link the shader program
    mProgram = GLES20.glCreateProgram();
    GLES20.glAttachShader(mProgram, vertexShader);
    GLES20.glAttachShader(mProgram, fragmentShader);
    GLES20.glLinkProgram(mProgram);
    // load a mesh
    mMesh = new MyMesh();
    // put any other initialization code HERE
  }

  public static int loadShader(int type, String shaderCode){
    // create a vertex shader type (GLES20.GL_VERTEX_SHADER)
    // or a fragment shader type (GLES20.GL_FRAGMENT_SHADER)
    int shader = GLES20.glCreateShader(type);
    // add the source code to the shader and compile it
    GLES20.glShaderSource(shader, shaderCode);
    GLES20.glCompileShader(shader);
    return shader;
  }
}
```

Listing 8.15: The rendering class and its method create the OpenGL output surface and define a couple of very simple shaders.

want to execute on several platforms then avoiding as much use of the Java VM as possible is a worthy alternative. It is possible to build an app based entirely on OpenGL and that makes no connection with a JAVA Activity class. However there may be occasions where it will be necessary to make use of some standard JAVA activity type classes. For this type of app, it is still possible to perform all the major tasks in a native library with its functions accessed from a JAVA activity. Such an app is readily organized so that the native code provides three functions to perform the tasks of initialization, drawing (in response to a timer) and release of resources.

All Android native code is compiled into a shared object library (a .SO library) using the Android NDK tools and libraries. The functions that are re-

```
public void onSurfaceChanged(GL10 gl, int w, int h) {
 // Adjust the viewport based on geometry changes,
 // such as screen rotation
 GLES20.glViewport(0, 0, width, height);
 float ratio = (float) width / height;
 // this projection matrix is applied to object coordinates
 // in the onDrawFrame() method
 Matrix.frustumM(mProjMatrix, 0, -ratio, ratio, -1, 1, 3, 7);
 // put any view dependent code HERE
}

public void onDrawFrame(GL10 gl) {
 // Draw background color
 GLES20.glClear(GLES20.GL_COLOR_BUFFER_BIT);
 // Set the camera position (View matrix)
 Matrix.setLookAtM(mVMatrix, 0, 0, 0, -3, 0f, 0f, 0f, 0f, 1.0f, 0.0f);
 // Calculate the projection and view transformation
 Matrix.multiplyMM(mMVPMatrix, 0, mProjMatrix, 0, mVMatrix, 0);
 // Draw the mesh
 mMesh.draw(mMVPMatrix,mProgram);
}
```

Listing 8.16: The rendering class and its method create the OpenGL output surface and define a couple of very simple shaders.

quired to be externally visible have special wrapper methods written for them using the notation of the Java Native Interface (the JNI) that makes them executable within any Java program where they are declared as `private static native void MethodName(...)` ... class methods.

Our NDK example project is based on a slightly modified version of the SanAngeles program that ships with the NDK. (The SanAngles example is a well-known benchmark program for OpenGLES. It has already been referenced in section 8.2.1 and multiple platform versions may be found on our website.)

Full details on the development process and code descriptions are given in the commentary that accompanies the project's downloadable archive but it is worth highlighting the details of the function naming and argument referencing that must be adopted when linking Android JAVA VM code with code compiled into a native shared object library. This is the JNI.

JNI nomenclature and NDK naming conventions   The Java Native Interface (JNI) is not an Android-specific specification. It applies to any situation where Java code running in a VM wishes to access native code written in a native language, typically C. The NDK uses the JNI as its definition of how to define function names and arguments in native code so that they can be used with the method names and calling conventions in the Java code. Because Java uses very different storage conventions for its variables (for example, Java strings are not simply *byte character arrays*,) the matching of parameters passed back and forth will need to undergo translation and use a highly structured naming convention. This is well documented in the JNI specification [55].

```
class MyMesh {

    private final FloatBuffer vertexBuffer;
    private final ShortBuffer drawListBuffer;

    private int mPositionHandle;
    private int mColorHandle;
    private int mMVPMatrixHandle;

    // some mesh data;
    // number of coordinates per vertex in this array
    static final int COORDS_PER_VERTEX = 3;
    static float Coords[] = { ...};
    // order of the vertex data
    private final short drawOrder[] = { ....};
    // 4 bytes per vertex
    private final int vertexStride = COORDS_PER_VERTEX * 4;

    // Set color & alpha
    float color[] = { .. };

    public MyMesh() { // set up the mesh
        // initialize vertex byte buffer
        ByteBuffer bb = ByteBuffer.allocateDirect(
          // (# of coordinate values * 4 bytes per float)
          Coords.length * 4);
        bb.order(ByteOrder.nativeOrder());
        vertexBuffer = bb.asFloatBuffer();
        vertexBuffer.put(Coords);
        vertexBuffer.position(0);
        // initialize byte buffer for the draw list
        ByteBuffer dlb = ByteBuffer.allocateDirect(
        // (# of coordinate values * 2 bytes per short)
                drawOrder.length * 2);
        dlb.order(ByteOrder.nativeOrder());
        drawListBuffer = dlb.asShortBuffer();
        drawListBuffer.put(drawOrder);
        drawListBuffer.position(0);
    }

}
```

Listing 8.17: The geometry of a 3D scene is typically rendered with the use of `glDrawArrays()` or `glDrawElements()`.

One of the trickiest things to do with the NDK is to pass data and make function calls back and forth between the native functions and the Android API. The rules of the JNI describe how to interpret data passed to the native functions, and how to package data to be returned to the JAVA code. In terms of function calls it is also likely that one would want to:

- Call native functions from JAVA class methods

- Call JAVA class methods from the native code

- Create JAVA objects from the native code

```
public void draw(float[] mvpMatrix, int mProgram) {
    // Use our shader to render
    GLES20.glUseProgram(mProgram);
    // get handle to vertex shader's member
    mPositionHandle = GLES20.glGetAttribLocation(mProgram, "vPosition");
    // Enable a handle to the vertices
    GLES20.glEnableVertexAttribArray(mPositionHandle);
    // Prepare the  coordinate data
    GLES20.glVertexAttribPointer(mPositionHandle, COORDS_PER_VERTEX,
                                 GLES20.GL_FLOAT, false,
                                 vertexStride, vertexBuffer);
    // get handle to fragment shader's vColor member
    mColorHandle = GLES20.glGetUniformLocation(mProgram, "vColor");
    // Set color for drawing the mesh
    GLES20.glUniform4fv(mColorHandle, 1, color, 0);
    // get handle to mesh's transformation matrix
    mMVPMatrixHandle = GLES20.glGetUniformLocation(mProgram, "uMVPMatrix");
    MyGLRenderer.checkGlError("glGetUniformLocation");
    // Apply the projection and view transformation
    GLES20.glUniformMatrix4fv(mMVPMatrixHandle, 1, false, mvpMatrix, 0);
    // Draw the mesh
    GLES20.glDrawElements(GLES20.GL_TRIANGLES, drawOrder.length,
                          GLES20.GL_UNSIGNED_SHORT, drawListBuffer);
    // Disable vertex array
    GLES20.glDisableVertexAttribArray(mPositionHandle);
}
```

Listing 8.18: The geometry of a 3D scene is typically rendered with the use of `glDrawArrays()` or `glDrawElements()`.

The best way to see the steps involved is to look at a minimalist example that does the things needed and that can provide template code snippets that we can call on when we ask *how can I do that*.

This example illustrates how to do some of the things you might wish to do using the NDK. The code has been kept to a minimum but it illustrates how to call a native method, and how to call object and static class methods from a native function.

We do not have space to explain the full JNI notation and refer you to the specification [55]; however the example we have chosen to describe includes passing integers, floats, and text strings, so with a bit of intelligent guessing you should be able to work out how to use two, three, or more arguments in the functions.

Using the JNI notation Listings 8.19 and 8.20 present an example of how to use the JNI in an Android activity. Listing 8.20 defines a class with a static method that will be called from the native functions. The main activity indicates that three native functions in a shared object library called libndk1 will be used. The AndroidNDK1SampleActivity has four methods. The first three are attached to three buttons on the screen and they execute when one of the buttons is pressed. The fourth method is used to illustrate how to call an object method from a function in the native library. The method in **class CRsf;** (listing 8.21) is used to illustrate how to call a static method in a class that has not been instantiated with any objects. Method **onCallNative1** passes a text string to the native function **helloLog**. Method **onCallNative2** passes two integers to the native function **getString** that returns a string. Method **onCallNative3** calls the native function **setup** that calls back to the two JAVA methods: **onRSFinstance** and **onRSFstatic**.

Listing 8.22 contains two functions. The first **JNI_OnLoad()** is called whenever the native library is loaded and affords the developer the opportunity to perform any tasks that must be done before any of the exported functions are called. The second function **getString()** serves two purposes. First it illustrates the rather odd naming convention that must be used for functions that are to be called from the JAVA code. The naming convention is relatively easy to work out because it is made up by using these instructions:

> Start with **Java_**, then append the name of package that is to contain the functions (but replace the "." with an "_") then append the name of the activity (with "_"s pre-pended and appended,) and finally add the name of the function. Thus, for example, to call a native function using the method name **setup** from an activity called **AndroidNDK1SampleActivity** contained in a package called **org.openfx.sample.ndk1**, the native code function name will need to be:

```
Java_org_openfx_sample_ndk1_AndroidNDK1SampleActivity_setup (...)
```

Quite a mouthful.

The second function in listing 8.22 (**getString**) demonstrates how to convert a C language string into the form required by JAVA and pass that back to the method that called it.

Listing 8.23 completes the code for this short demonstration. Here **setup()** uses the NDK's API functions to demonstrate how to get access to a method in a JAVA class and call that method with appropriate parameters. For example the **AndroidNDK1SampleActivity** class' method **onRSFinstance(...)** requires one integer argument passed by reference. The JNI code for a single integer argument is "(I)I".

8.4 Summing up

This chapter has lifted the lid and peeped into the future of 3D graphics because mobile computing is almost certainly going to be where the future is for most people's use of computers. By being there at the start, OpenGL is likely to dominate the 3D mobile app market for the foreseeable future. And the reason that OpenGL can be delivered on these platforms is down to the skillful, efficient

```
// the app will be packaged here
package org.openfx.sample.ndk1;

import android.os.Bundle;
import android.util.Log;
import android.view.View;
import android.widget.Toast;

public class AndroidNDK1SampleActivity extends Activity {
 private static final String DEBUG_TAG = "RSF-NDK1";
  /** Called when the activity is first created. */
 @Override
 public void onCreate(Bundle savedInstanceState) {
 super.onCreate(savedInstanceState);
 setContentView(R.layout.main);
 }

 // class methods go here

 // Native fuctions that will be called are listed
 // here with their return and argument data types.
 private native void helloLog(String logThis);
 private native String getString(int value1, int value2);
 private native void setup();

 // the NDK library to load is
 static {
   System.loadLibrary("ndk1");
 }

} // end of class
```

Listing 8.19: The main activity code.

design and implementation of the GLES. Our single chapter can only scratch the surface of everything that can be done with the OpenGL for embedded systems. Check out Munshi et al. [63] to delve in more deeply. The significant change of approach that has been seen in moving from GLES version 1 to version 2 points to quite a bit of work in re-coding application programs. Fortunately in moving from version 2 to version 3 (the latest at time of writing) there are no significant changes and version 2 programs should update without a problem (because version 3 adds rather than deprecates functionality).

However, just because you can draw in 3D on a mobile device doesn't mean that you should. Directly porting a successful 3D app from a desktop to a different media rarely works. While a tablet device may be forgiving, the much smaller screen on a phone or media player is so different that any app that has buttons, controls or displays text should be re-thought. Touch and multi-touch, and an exciting range of sensors are also likely to revolutionize the way the user interacts with their device and its applications.

Of critical importance in the mobile world is the awareness of battery life, and the the need for an application to *give way*, for example when receiving a phone call.

```
// methods to be included in main Activity class

public void onCallNative1(View view) {//Act on button
 // call to the native method
 helloLog("This string will go to the log");
 }

 public void onCallNative2(View view) {// Act on button
 String result = getString(5,2);  // native method
 long
 Log.v(DEBUG_TAG, "Result: new "+result);
 result = getString(105, 1232);
 }

 public void onCallNative3(View view) {// act on button
 // call to the native method
 Log.v(DEBUG_TAG, "Calling Setup new");
 setup();
 }

 public int onRSFinstance(int i) { // called from NATIVE
 String d=String.format("%d",i);
 Log.v("RSF-C new", "Result:"+d);// c
 return i+8; // return something
 }
```

Listing 8.20: The main activity's methods.

```
package org.openfx.sample.rsf1;

import android.os.Bundle;
import android.util.Log;

// a second class with a "static" method
// to be called from the native code

public class CRsf {
 // called from ntive function
 static public int onRSFstatic(int i) {
 Log.v("RSF-CA new", "Result: ");
 return i+8;  // return something
 }

}
```

Listing 8.21: A class with a static method declared in a second JAVA file.

Like all 3D apps this chapter has, I hope, shown that the coding is the easy part. In reality the appeal of any 3D app is going to be in its models, artwork and animation. Good programming only helps by delivering high-speed performance to make the models dance.

```
#include <jni.h>
#include <string.h>
#include <stdio.h>
#include <android/log.h>
#define DEBUG_TAG "NDK_AndroidNDK1SampleActivity"

// pointers and references used in the native code
JavaVM *vm;
JNIEnv *env;
jclass manager_class;
jclass rsf_class;
jobject self;

// Always called on library load
jint JNI_OnLoad(JavaVM *curVM, void *reserved) {
 return JNI_VERSION_1_4;
}

//function name and return value (helloLog)
void Java_org_openfx_sample_ndk1_AndroidNDK1SampleActivity_helloLog
// arguments
 (JNIEnv * env, jobject this, jstring logThis) {
jboolean isCopy;
const char *szLogThis;
  *szLogThis = (*env)->GetStringUTFChars(env, logThis, &isCopy);
 (*env)->ReleaseStringUTFChars(env, logThis, szLogThis);
 __android_log_print(ANDROID_LOG_DEBUG,DEBUG_TAG,"NDK:LC: [%s]",
     szLogThis);
}

//function name and return value (getString)
jstring Java_org_openfx_sample_ndk1_AndroidNDK1SampleActivity_getString
// arguments
(JNIEnv * env, jobject this, jint value1, jint value2) {
 char *szFormat = "The sum of the two numbers is: %i";
 char *szResult;
 // add the two values
 jlong sum = value1+value2;
 // malloc room for the resulting string
 szResult = malloc(sizeof(szFormat) + 20);
 // standard sprintf
 sprintf(szResult, szFormat, sum);
 // get an object string
 jstring result = (*env)->NewStringUTF(env, szResult);
 // cleanup
 free(szResult);
 return result;
}
```

Listing 8.22: The native code: Loading function and examples of sending and receiving a text string.

Tablet and mobile devices do open up a brave new world because they give the 3D app developer access to unique features like the accelerometers and compass that have no real meaning for the desktop. Location-based services, GPS sensors, 3D maps etc. can be the progenitor of many novel 3D-enabled applications.

```
//function name and return value
void Java_org_openfx_sample_ndk1_AndroidNDK1SampleActivity_setup
// arguments
(JNIEnv * env, jobject this){
 int id = 88; // test value to be passed to JAVA methods
 ..
 // call instance method
 // get pointer to class
 manager_class = (*env)->FindClass
     (env,"org/openfx/sample/ndk1/AndroidNDK1SampleActivity");
 // get the method
 jmethodID mid = (*env)->GetMethodID
    (env,  manager_class, "onRSFinstance", "(I)I");
 // call the method (the "this" parameter is used here because
 // we are calling a method in the object that called this funciton)
 id=(*env)->CallIntMethod(env, this, mid, id);
 ..
 // calling class static method
 // get pointer to class
 rsf_class = (*env)->FindClass
     (env,"org/openfx/sample/rsf1/CRsf");
 // get the method
 jmethodID mids = (*env)->GetStaticMethodID
     (env, rsf_class, "onRSFstatic", "(I)I");
 // call the method
 id=(*env)->CallStaticIntMethod(env, rsf_class, mids, id);
 ..
}
```

Listing 8.23: The native code: Example of native code calling static and instance methods in a JAVA class.

9

The complete package: OpenFX

The aim of this book is to put the algorithms of computer graphics into a practical setting and make them usable. There can be no better way to do this than by showing how this is done in a comprehensive application program with all the features that one expects to find in a mainstream 3D animation tool. I have chosen to do this by examining the open source application suite called OpenFX.[1] It is mature software, having been in continual development for over 10 years. It has a reputation of being robust and very comprehensive, and it has wide range of support materials available on its OpenFX.org website. The code is documented extensively and there are many briefing notes on the OpenFX website, so this chapter aims to act as a description of how all the parts of OpenFX fit together to turn it into a practical modeling, animation and rendering program.

There are two advantages of using OpenFX. First it covers almost everything one needs to consider in a book such as this. It has modules for building polygonal 3D models, animating them and rendering images of the scenes using conventional software algorithms and a near-real-time GPU engine. Second, despite an immediate reaction you might have that an application written by one man and a dog will be a big disadvantage, we disagree! Precisely because it is the product of a small team working part time, the code is short (enough), the implementation efficient and it will be much easier for you to follow than it would otherwise be if it was the product of hundreds of person years of programmer time. So that's the rationale for shifting the focus in the second edition to examine the code of a really useful 3D authoring tool. We will be able to see how all the theory and algorithms that you've been reading about can be made practical.

It's not unreasonable to expect that after reading this chapter you will be able to take the code and adapt it for your own specific needs, for example to read, modify and write an editor for almost any polygon based 3D data.

---

[1] I designed the software architecture and engineered most of the code.

OpenFX is written in ANSI C and uses the Windows native API and the OpenGL API. No other libraries, APIs or third-party software are required in order to build it. It has been compatible with all version of Windows since Windows NT version 3.1 and is just at home on Windows 8. We originally built the code using the Watcom C compiler and had DOS batch and makefiles to bring everything together.[2] However, as the industry standard for Windows applications development is now Visual Studio, that's what we use. Our preferred IDE is Visual Studio 2003. (We much prefer this to the later versions, but the VS2003 solution and project files can all be easily upgraded for use with the later editions of Visual Studio. OpenFX builds just as happily with an upgraded solution file in Visual Studio 2012 as it did in VS2003.)

OpenFX is not a single program. It is based around three executable programs, a collection of dynamic link libraries, and a number of other stand-alone utility programs. The three core applications behave (and appear to the user) as if they are one single application program. They are:

1. *The Animator* is where animations are staged and directed. Every element on the stage is called an actor. Polygonal models move and turn in front of a camera. Lights, backgrounds, non-mesh actors, for example a particle system, and even several cameras are also scripted in the Animator. The action is rehearsed and previewed in real-time, using wireframe visualization and when the director is satisfied with the clip, a script is written for the Renderer to turn into a shaded image or movie. The Animator is the program that the user first sees. It loads the Designer and other programs as needed.

2. *The Designer* is used to design and build the polygonal mesh models that will be used as *costumes* for the Animator's main actors. The models use conventional triangular polygons to represent the surfaces of the object. The Designer uses three main lists to record the geometry and its topology: (1) the polygonal faces, (2) the network of vertices that the faces are attached to, and (3) the edges in the model. The edges are not borders on the polygonal faces; any two vertices can be connected by an edge even if they are not part of a face. The Designer is also used to build a list of materials and texture maps and apply them to the polygonal surfaces.

3. *The Renderer* is the module that creates the photographic images of models built in the Designer and animated in the Animator. The Renderer performs most of its work in the background using either a software scanline Z-buffer hidden surface algorithm with an optional hybrid ray-tracing algorithm, or the GPU accelerated hardware accessed through the OpenGL library. The Renderer is used by both the Animator and Designer and will continue to execute in the background while activity continues in the other

---

[2]Yes! The program actually ran under DOS (in its first version).

modules. The Renderer module can be used in a mode (called the Script Renderer) that does not need either the Animator or Designer modules to be loaded. The Script Renderer may also be run on several other platforms at the same time.

OpenFX can be said to conform to the *Document-View* architecture of many application programs. Word, Excel and Photoshop are all applications of this type. The Microsoft Foundation Class (MFC) discussed in section 7.2.1 uses the Document View design as one of its core concepts.

In the case of the Animator, the document is a description of a scene and the action in the scene. The document is represented in memory as a collection of objects arranged as a tree structure held together using doubly-linked list data structures. The view comes in two forms: a diagrammatic view of the tree and a three-dimensional map of the scene with a director's camera view. The user can use either view to alter the scene's data and its inter-relationships.

In the case of the Designer the document is a description of a polygon mesh model, its spatial design and the appearance of its surfaces. This document is represented in memory by lists of vertex positions, mesh topologies and surface materials. The view does just what it says; it allows the user to see the mesh and alter it through a three-dimensional plan and oblique view.

This chapter begins with a brief review how OpenFX works from the user's perspective. Then we will focus on the three main modules in turn, examining their key data structures, how the plug-in modules work and how the code is constructed. The whole book could have been devoted to exploring the OpenFX code, and in a way it is. The theory on which computer graphics is based, the rendering, modeling and shading algorithms, the structures used for describing 3D models and the hardware visualization using OpenGL that preceded this chapter **are** OpenFX. Of course, we don't have space to forensically examine every one of the lines of code in the program but we can look at the most important components of the data structures, the core program variables and the flow of execution through the algorithms. The story that this tells is not available on the OpenFX website, but to make the most of this chapter it should be read in conjunction with the code itself and especially the links provided on the book's website which hook into the OpenFX developers' web pages and Doxygen-generated reference documentation.

9.1   Using OpenFX

For reasons of space, we will say only a very little about the usage of OpenFX. There is no substitute for trying things yourself, so before we explore the code, why not download and install OpenFX and grab a copy of the source code too.

The best way to set up a development environment and explore the source code is to start by installing the binary release and then superimpose the source code onto the same folder structure.

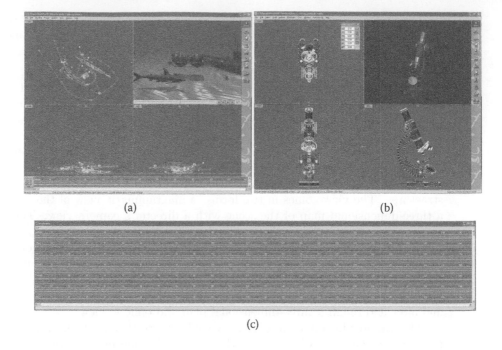

(a)   (b)

(c)

Figure 9.1: The OpenFX user interfaces. (a) Animation, (b) Design and Modeling, (c) Timelines and Keyframes.

9.1.1 The OpenFX approach to animation and modeling

The program observes the standard conventions of:

- Click on an item to select it.

- Double click for extended information.

- Click and drag to move the item.

All the user actions take place in a cubic volume called the *working-volume*. A 3D cursor may be placed anywhere inside the working-volume by moving it in one or more of the view windows.

The Animator and Designer modules have two main user interface components, (1) tools and (2) actions. Tools are appropriate for repeated use and actions are usually applied one at a time. When a tool is activated it stays active until another tool is selected. In the Designer, actions are normally prohibited unless the default tool is in use.

The language of animation and modeling A mesh of triangular polygons represents the objects that are to be animated. Objects can be anything, a car, a plane, a dog or a human figure. Deciding how many triangles to use in the model is not an exact science. The triangular faces can be given additional attributes such as color and texture. They can also have a picture or movie painted onto their surface.

The triangular facets (faces of the model) are positioned using a vertex at each corner. Each triangular face is surrounded by three edges. The edges make up a "wireframe" description of the model. The mouse (or stylus) is used to move the vertices of the model in 3D space and thus change the shape of the model. Models are built inside a cubic region of space know as the working-volume. The size and position of the "working-volume" is easily changed.

Animation takes place over a number of frames. A *Keyframer* tool specifies costume, movement, orientation and scale in *keyframes*. In an animation the term *actor* is used to describe each directable element. An actor can be: a *star* that performs in front of the camera, or a camera from which the animation is filmed, or one of a number of lights, or a path along which other actors can move. The actors wear a *costume* which is a model created in the Designer. Actors can change costume during the animation; this allows model morphing (changes of shape). For example, a fish can turn into a bird.

Actors fulfill all the roles in an animation and as a consequence they take a number of specific forms. The most common actor is a *normal* actor that can *wear* any mesh model as its costume. These actors will be the principal visible elements in the rendered movies. Actors also represent other key elements: The *Camera* actor does what its name implies. The *Sky* actor represents the background. The *Ground* is a flat plane that extends to the horizon in all directions. A *Director* coordinates camera switching. The *Post-process* applies an image filter to the output. The last type of actor, and possibly the most interesting, is called a *Robot*. It is a special form of the *Normal* actor specifically used for character animation.

Animating The Animator module is where animations are set up. Three orthogonal views and a camera view show the world where the action takes place. The visible region of the world, the working-volume, may be moved through space and changed in size. A major component of the Animator is the *Keyframer*. The Keyframer shows the timelines and keyframes for all the actors in a spreadsheet-like format.

Keyframer To direct the activity of an actor during an animation requires the use of timelines and keyframes. The Keyframer is a module where the timelines and keyframes of all actors can be viewed and edited in one display. Normally timelines and keyframes are created implicitly as actors are added and the tools are used to move them into position and tell them what to do. In the Keyframer window, time runs in the horizontal direction and for each actor the extent of timelines and position of keyframes is displayed. The timelines are the red horizontal lines and the colored dots at the end of the timelines are the keyframes.

Designing The Designer module is where polygonal models are built. Three orthogonal views give working access to the working-volume, where vertices, edges and faces may be placed. The mesh of polygons and vertices gives a triangular faceted model for real or imagined objects. The orthogonal view in the upper right corner of the screen displays a rendered preview of the contents of the working volume.

9.2   The OpenFX files and folders structure

Figure 9.2 shows a list of the sub-folders within the OpenFX main folder in which the source code is located. It is very important when building the application that these folders retain their names and relative path locations. Preferably the OpenFX main folder should be located in the root on drive C:; however all the build files use relative path specifications and therefore building OpenFX on an alternative drive or in a sub-folder of some other path should only throw up minor issues.

There are a number of other folders used during the execution of the program, and to hold sample models, animations, images, movies etc. However, these do not contain code and they have been omitted in figure 9.2.

As mentioned in the chapter's opening remarks, although OpenFX appears to the user as one application it is in fact structured as three main .EXE programs, plus a number of other utility programs that play movies, display images or convert from one data format to another. The appearance of an integrated application is achieved by launching one application from another using the `WinExec()` API function. Using the knowledge that each application is based around a window of a unique Windows Class and that when an application is loaded it will respond to messages sent to its window. For example, the designer module (main window class name of `OFX:ModelerClass`) can be instructed to become active using the code:

```
..
if((hWnd=FindWindow("OFX:ModelerClass",NULL)) != NULL){
  SetForegroundWindow(hWnd);
  BringWindowToTop(hWnd);
}
else{
  strcpy(modulename,gszHomeDir);strcat(modulename,"design.exe");
  result=WinExec(modulename,SW_SHOW);
  if(result < 32){ ... /* error */    }
  if((hWnd=FindWindow("OFX:ModelerClass",NULL)) != NULL){
    SetForegroundWindow(hWnd);
    BringWindowToTop(hWnd);
  }
  else .. // eror did not start
}
...
```

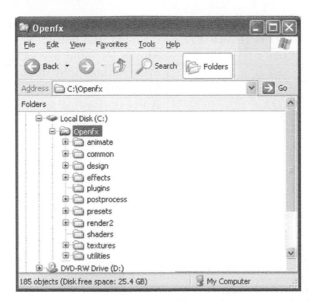

Figure 9.2: The main folders containing the OpenFX code.

And the renderer module (with a main window class name of `OFX:RenderClass`, which is based around a window of window class `OFX:RenderClass`, can be instructed to terminate itself by sending it a message with the code:

```
..
if((hWnd=FindWindow("OFX:RenderClass",NULL)) != NULL){
   SendMessage(hWnd,WM_COMMAND,IDM_CALLBACK_SHUTDOWN,0);
 }
..
```

Each of the three main executable programs of OpenFX uses a number of additional dynamic link libraries (.DLLs). They are either loaded with the main program when it is loaded, or they are loaded and unloaded as necessary. The DLLs that are loaded at the start contain essential components of the programs. Resources for the menus, dialog boxes and text strings are provided to the Designer, Animator and Renderer in separate files: des_res.dll, ani_res.dll and rnd_res.dll. Providing resources in this way allows for easy internationalization of the application. It has been translated for use with the Japanese language just by changing these three files. Many essential modeling tools (boolean modeling for example) are also provided through DLLs. These DLLs apply to optional components, material shaders, animation effects and image post-processors. For example, many of the modeling actions in the Designer are loaded, executed and released through calls to the DLL handling functions in the Win32 API, using the code:

.BMP .GIF .TGA .JPG .PNG .TIF	Image file formats supported for input and output
.AVI	Movies for input and output
.STL	Stereo lithography data
.3DS	Mesh objects in 3D Studio format
.DXF	Autocad drawing format.
.WRL	VRML formats.

Table 9.1: Well-known file types that OpenFX supports.

```
BOOL LoadInternalAction(char *library){
 ..
 HMODULE hLib;
 FARPROC fpFun;
 X__STRUCTURE *Evs;
 BOOL (*fpFun1)(HWND, HWND, X__STRUCTURE *);
 Evs=&EviStructure;
 strcpy(lname,gszHomeDir); strcat(lname,library);
 if((hLib=LoadLibrary(lname)) != NULL){
   if((fpFun=GetProcAddress(hLib,"_Xmodeler")) != NULL){
     fpFun1 = (void *)fpFun;
     status=(*fpFun1)(ghwnd_main,ghwnd_info,Evs);

   }
   else return FALSE;
   FreeLibrary(hLib);
 }
 else return FALSE;
 return TRUE;
}
```

OpenFX uses a special structure, in this case an X__STRUCTURE, to pass pointers that give access to most of its global variables and functions to the attaching DLL. This is discussed in detail in section 9.8 on building plug-ins.

9.2.1 Filename extensions

Like all application programs OpenFX uses filename extensions to hint at the type of information a file contains. A number of file extensions are used in addition to the well-known file types that the program supports. The well-known filenames are mainly used to contain images and movies. Tables 9.1 and 9.2 show the list of filename extensions used and supported by OpenFX. The rendering module uses a temporary *script file* (filename extension .SCR) that is created by the Animator. It is not normally of any concern to the user because it is written automatically and removed when the program terminates. However it can be created for off-line rendering on multiple hosts.

.OFX	An animation.
.MFX	A mesh model.
.SCR	Intermediate Renderer's file.
.EFX	An animation plug-in effect.
.AFX	A Designer action plug-in.
.DFX	A Designer tool plug-in.
.XFX	An image post processor.
.PFX	An Animator's preset animation.
.TFX	A plug-in-shader.
.RSQ	A robot actor sequence.
.PTH	A path for actors to move along.

Table 9.2: OpenFX specific file formats.

9.3 Coordinate system and units

Before one can make sense of the code of OpenFX it is essential to know how OpenFX represents its data in three-dimensional space. The most significant feature of the coordinate system is that it is *integer* based. Floating point (either `float` or `double` type) numbers are used in intermediate calculations and during final transformations in the renderer and depth buffer. The reasons that the mesh models have their vertex coordinates recorded as integers is because comparisons can be done exactly. Many geometric algorithms can be done more robustly when using integers for coordinates and the optimizing step made prior to ray-tracing can be made much more efficient.

Given these advantages there is the disadvantage that the scale of objects is limited to the maximum size of a 32-bit integer, about 4×10^9. Since the animator can scale models up by many orders of magnitude a compromise has to be accepted and the models built in the Designer are limited to sizes between ± 2048 and ± 33554432 integer units. The zoom function is limited to work within these limits. In the Animator the limits are ± 2048 and ± 1073741824. The lower limit allows for some detail to be presented at higher detail than maximum zoom permits and the upper limit gives space for movement at maximum *zoom out*. These restrictions really only limit the level of detail that can be recorded in a scene, and pose no practical limitations on the scope of animations or models that can be used.

The coordinates used by OpenFX differ from those used in OpenGL. In OpenFX the Z axis is vertical; models are built so that they face forward along the $+Y$ axis. In the animator, when models move forward they move in the direction of their local $+Y$ axis. The coordinate system is right handed and this defines the direction of the X axis as lying toward the right.

Figure 9.3 illustrates how the 2D screen is arranged so that the user can work in a 3D volume, and how the windows into to the working-volume relate to the coordinate system. There are two important reference points highlighted in figure 9.3. First, the coordinate axis has to be defined. This is called the center point and it is the point by which the model is positioned and moved in the animator. Second, because it is necessary to use a 2D computer screen, via mouse or pen, a way must be found to move and work at a 3D location in the working-volume. This can be done by defining a 3D cursor. To move the 3D cursor to a 3D location, the user has to position it using at least two of the view windows. The program variables `NpointerX`, `NpointerY` and `NpointerZ` hold this value.

9.4   User interface implementation

To build 3D models and set up animated scenes, an application program requires a fairly comprehensive user interface. The Animator and Designer programs present a very similar similar appearance to the user, but there are minor differences. The Animator's fourth view window presents a wireframe representation of the scene as visualized by a camera. The Designer's fourth window shows the object as seen from an arbitrary view pointer. The Designer's fourth window may be optionally rendered using the OpenGL shading library (the other wireframe views are rendered using Win32 GDI[3] functions) and most of the interactive tools can be used in this window. The Animator's camera view is purely passive. However, the renderer, which is a completely separate program, can be commanded to draw a 3D shaded view into the Animator's camera view windows (demonstrating the power of the inter-process communication outlined in section 9.2).

The Renderer does not need a sophisticated user interface, so its presentation is simply that of a tabbed Windows dialog box. The Renderer's dialog layout is loaded from a resource file. The majority of the Renderer's code is platform independent, and porting this module to other hosts would be a fairly simple task.

The user interfaces of the Animator and Designer modules is based on a collection of hierarchical windows. The application's main windows has a blank client area and a menu. The three rectangular view windows and the perspective/camera windows are created as child windows. The toolbar buttons are implemented as child windows of another window representing the toolbar, which itself is a child window of the main window. The main window receives and processes messages from the application's menu bar.

The window class names and their message processing functions are given in table 9.3 for the Animator, and in table 9.4 for the Designer.

---

[3]Future versions of OpenFX will render all views using OpenGL at some point.

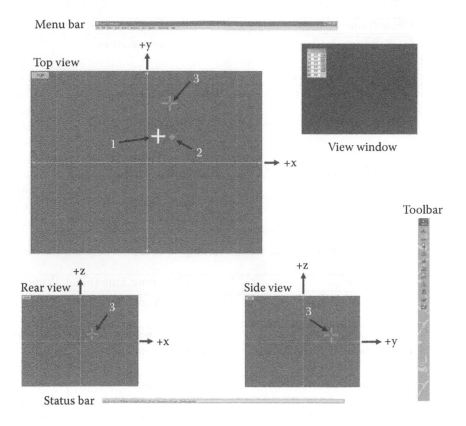

Figure 9.3: The OpenFX screen layout depicts three main user windows showing views into the working volume. The views show a view from the top looking down, a view from the rear looking forward and a view from the right side looking to the left. In the coordinate system used by OpenFX the Z axis is vertical and the X axis points to the right. This figure also shows the other main screen elements and identifies three important markers. (1) The center (hold) point, (2) an offset point, and (3) the 3D cursor used to move the work position in 3D space.

The Animator's menu commands are handled by the function called `AnimatorMenuCmd(... LOWORD(wparam), hwnd, lparam);`, and the Designer's menu commands are processed in `DesignMenuCommand(LOWORD(wparam), hwnd, lparam);`. These functions take the standard Windows message parameters as arguments, and dispatch actions, tools and all the major tasks undertaken by the program.

Other window messages are handled in the window functions for each class of windows, for example the mouse button, mouse move and keyboard messages.

Class Name	Message Handling Function	Window
OFX:AnimatorClass	MainAnimatorWndProc	Main application
OFX:AnimatorViewClass	AnimatorViewWndProc	Camera
OFX:AnimatorTriViewClass	AnimatorTriViewWndProc	Working volume view
OFX:AnimatorQuicktimeClass	QuicktimeWndProc	Frames progress bar.
OFX:AnimatorToolboxClass	ToolboxWndProc	Tool panel container
OFX:AnimatorToolBtnClass	ToolBtnWndProc	Button in tool panel

Table 9.3: Window class names, message handling functions in the Animator.

Class Name	Message Handling Function	Window
OFX:ModelerClass	MainModelerWndProc	Main application
OFX:ModelerViewClass	ModelerViewWndProc	Oblique view
OFX:ModelerTrivViewClass	ModelerTriViewWndProc	Each working volume
OFX:ModelerToolboxClass	ToolboxWndProc	Tool panel container
OFX:ModelerToolBtnClass	ToolBtnWndProc	Button in tool panel

Table 9.4: Window class names, message handling functions in the Designer.

The three windows that show the top, rear and side views are all handled by the same window function.

Rendering of the client areas of all the windows is not done directly in response to a WM_PAINT message because for very large meshes this would be too slow, especially when re-sizing a window. Instead, only when a tool is used or an action is performed rendering takes place using the GDI API functions into an off-screen bitmap. The off-screen bitmap is rendered to the display using PatBlt() when a WM_PAINT message occurs, or is generated internally.

The Designer's optional shaded perspective/orthographic view, rendered using OpenGL, is created in a DLL (built with project "gldesign") loaded at runtime. The OpenGL window replaces the OFX:ModelerViewClass window with one of class OFX:OpenGL. All its messages are processed by the handler function OpenGLWndProc(), whose source code can be found in the file "gldesign.c", that is one of the build files for the DLL gldesign.dll.

In addition to the program's main windows there are a small number of modeless dialogs used for defining user-specified units, some of the tools, and in the Designer for working with materials and image maps.

A few other window classes are used to handle some floating tool panel windows, for example the coordinates dialog box.

9.5 The Animation module

The Animator program is the launching point for all the other applications of OpenFX. It provides a window into a four-dimensional world where the actions of the actors are directed in space and time. The Animator's interface implementation is described in section 9.4. This section provides a commentary on the way the Animator organizes its data structures and a tour of the main route in the path of execution.

9.5.1 The data structures

The numerical description of the action and the scene is recorded externally in the .OFX file, and stored internally in a series of data objects for the various components. These are arranged in a series of doubly linked lists that are interconnected via object pointers that topologically resemble a tree. Figure 9.4 illustrates how the data is organized. Each actor in a scene is represented by an instance of a **node** object whose data structure is presented in listing 9.1. The key program variable **FirstNp** points to the first node in the doubly linked list of nodes and may be used to gain access to every piece of data used in the Animator. There must always be at least one actor in a scene; this must be a camera actor. In figure 9.4 the list of nodes can be see at the left-hand side.

For each node, the behavior of the actor is fully specified by providing up to four additional linked lists for the key events. The list of key events map onto a timeline with each event being described to the user as a key frame. The four types of key events are:

- Costume: This type of event is defined by the variables in an **object** (or sky or director) data structure and the first item is pointed to by the variable **fobj / fsky/ fposition** in the actor's node structure.

- Position: This list of events, stating that the actor will be located at (x, y, z) in frame i, is pointed to by the variable **fpos** in the actor's node structure.

- Alignment: This list of events, stating that the actor's local y axis will be rotated by angles (ϕ, θ, ρ) around the global (world) (x, y, z) axes in frame k, is pointed to by the variable **fali** in the actor's node structure.

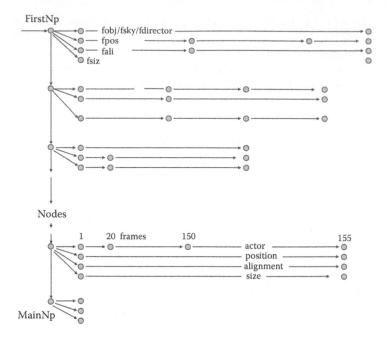

Figure 9.4: The Animator's scene is specified by and represented by a tree-like structure, where each actor is based on a node. The actions of the actor is described by up to four other types of data objects that exist.

- Size: This list of events, stating that the actor's dimensions will be scaled by a factor of $(\Delta x, \Delta y, \Delta z)$ in frame k, is pointed to by the variable `fsiz` in the actor's node structure.

The common data structure members `firstframe` and `lastframe` identify the segment of the animation throughout which the costume/position/alignment/size applies. The information presented to the user carries the implication that a *keyframe* lies at the end of each of these segments. Although not essential, it is assumed that the order of the timeline objects is the same as their temporal progression. For example, a timeline segment (also known in the program as a channel) covering the interval between frames 1 and 30 precedes a segment covering frames 31 and 51. Note, however, that gaps in the time sequence are quite normal and some timelines may have no keyframe channels/segments at all. For example, in a 100-frame animation a camera may have two position channels from frames 10-90 and 100-100 (i.e., a single frame specification).

The costume or `object` data structure is used to specify actors of several types. The members of the structure are shown in listing 9.2. The structure applies to all objects that use a mesh model, including the ROBOT actor type.

```
typedef struct Animator_NODE {
 struct Animator_NODE   *last;  /* pointer to previous object */
 struct Animator_NODE   *next;  /* pointer to next object */
 struct Animator_SKY    *fsky;  /* pointer to the first sky object
                                    for SKY actors otherwise NULL */
 struct Animator_DIRECTOR_tag
                        *fdirector; /* pointer to the first director
                                        if not DIRECTOR then  NULL */
 struct Animator_OBJECT   *fobj; /* pointer to the first OBJECT object
                                    represents all other actor */
 struct Animator_POSITION *fpos; /* pointer ot the first POSITION
                                    timeline segment for this actor */
 struct Animator_ALIGN    *fali; /* pointer ot the first ALIGNMENT
                                    segment for this actor */
 struct Animator_SIZE     *fsiz; /* pointer ot the first SCALING
                                    segment for this actor */
 short  type,  /*  Identifies the type of actor
                    e.g. NORMAL CAMERA etc. */
        ID;    /*  Unique identifier given by
                    Animator to represent the actor*/
 char actorname[128]; /*  Text string for the Actor's name  */
} node;
```

Listing 9.1: The `node` data structure is a doubly linked list of actors in the scene. It contains pointers to the other objects that describe what the actor is doing, where it is doing it and when it is doing it.

The ROBOT actor type, PATH actors and even the *PostProcessor* actor use this structure. Any member variable that is not used for a particular actor is set to NULL.

The costume object is the largest object in OpenFX because it has to encompass such a disparate range of data. Listing 9.2 highlights the most important data pointers. Two of the pointers and two `long` structure members require further consideration. These are `npoints`, `nedges`, `*points` and `*edges`. These members are significant because they are associated with the wireframe data for costumes based on mesh models that have been built in the Designer and loaded from an .MFX type file (points are equivalent to vertices). The arrays these pointer address can be large (perhaps $> 100,000$ vertices) and will occupy a large block of RAM memory. Some animations might need to instance thousands of these meshes and so, to save memory, if different actors use the same mesh *only one instance of each model* (loaded from an MFX file) is held in memory. Since the same memory might be used by several costumes careful reference counting is required to ensure that this memory is only released when the last costume, that was using it, is deleted. Care also needs to be taken when costumes are being changed (i.e., a different mesh is being loaded into the costume). There is also the question of when a costume is being changed does the change only apply to the selected actor, or does it apply to all actors using this mesh. The functions `CreateCostume()` and `DeleteCostume()` handle this reference counting.

```
typedef struct Animator_OBJECT {
// for all actor types
struct Animator_OBJECT *last; // Doubly-linked lsit of timeline
struct Animator_OBJECT *next; // segments (last and next pointers)
short type; /* Actor type  NORMAL ROBOT GROUND PATH etc */
short firstframe, /* The first frame of this segment of the timeline */
      lastframe;  /* The last frame of this segment of the timeline */
short morph; /* Indicates Actor's costume is morphing */
// Followed by actor type specific members
..
// Selected other members
long nNurbs; /* Number of NURBS patches inNORMAL actor */
nurbs *Nurbs; /* NURBS patch data for any NURBS in OBJECT */
/* If this is a particle system actor then thi smember is valid */
ParticleSystem particles;
/* for IMAGEPROCESS actors the name of the effect*/
char *xip;
 object;
```

Listing 9.2: The Costume (object) data structure. Some members have been removed from this listing to help highlight the most important items. (Consult the web references for a link to a full list of member variables.) Listings 9.3, 9.4 and 9.5 contain details of the actor-specific structure members.

```
// NORMAL AND SKELETON specific members
point origin, /* origin of a mesh object */
      offset; /* offset point */
long npoints; /* Number of vertices in the model */
long nedges; /* Number of edges in the model */
long nskeleton; /* For ROBOT actors number of skelton bones */
point *points;  /* Array of vertices MAIN DATA FOR MESH OBJECT */
Sedge *edges;   /* Array of edges MAIN DATA FOR MESH OBJECT */
long *skid; /* Vertx -> skeleton node it is attached to*/
skel *skeleton; /* pointer to skeleton structure */
char name[255]; /* The name of the MFX file for NORMAL and ROBOT */
awire w_frame; /* A wireframe for use a bounding box */
point outline[8]; /* Corners of the bounding box of the object */
// external effect
char *effect; /* The name of any Animation effect */
HMODULE hEffect; /* Handle to any animation effect DLL */
```

Listing 9.3: Members of the costume (object) structure specifically for NORMAL and ROBOT actors.

Two types of actors have customized costume objects, the Sky and the Director. Neither of these actors have any connection with a mesh or extended data, whereas, a Path for example uses extended data to define its control points. The key members of the Sky and Director actors are highlighted in listing 9.6.

Looking back at the object (costume) data structure (listing 9.2), it can be seen that some members use instances of other data structures. The Robot actor uses an array of skel (see listing 9.7) types to specify the location and

```
// light and ground specific members
unsigned char colour[3], /* colour */
acolour[3]; /* secondary colour */
short groundtype; /* Type (PLAIN/TEXTURED etc.) */
short lighttype; /*  OMNIDIRECTION SPOTLIGHT NOSHADOW etc. */
double light_intensity; /* light intensity [0 - 1] */
short depth_cue; /* Is the light intgensity to fall off */
..
short self_shadow, /* This actor self shadows */
cast_shadow, /* This actor does or does not cast a shadow. */
show_shadow; /* Show or do not show shadows  */
RAMIMAGE image; /* Any image that is needed by a GROUND */
```

Listing 9.4: Members of the costume (object) structure specifically for LIGHT and GROUND actors.

```
// Path specific members
short pathtype, /* type of path OPEN CLOSED etc. */
double *v; /* pointer to velocity profile array */
npathpoints; /* this holds the number of pathpoints. */
pathpoint *firstpathpoint; /* pointer to their first pathpoint */
double pathlength; /* path length (in internal units) */
int npec; /* Number of pathedit control points */
PATHEDITCONTROL *pec; /* Pointer pathedit control points */
```

Listing 9.5: Members of the costume (object) structure specifically for PATH actors.

orientation of the bones in the skeleton. It also uses a list to identify which mesh vertex is attached to which bone. A ground actor might require an image map and this is defined in a RAMIMAGE structure. Path type actors require a list of path control points (data type **pathpoint**, see listing 9.8) and a further set of spline control points (data type **patheditcontrol**) are used to determine how fast objects following the path travel along the path, where they accelerate or decelerate etc. Particle system actors have their own special structure to hold the parameters and settings that define that particle system's behavior.

The particle system implemented within OpenFX follows very closely the principles set out in section 6.7 but some special circumstances need to be taken into account. These are the position, orientation and scale of the system, as well as the time interval over which the effect takes place. No temporal scaling is applied. The effect plays out in absolute time, but it may be curtailed if the timeline segments are too short, or have finished completely if the segments are too long. Each costume timeline segment is designated as one performance of the particle system. The behavior starts in frame one of the segment and continues for the duration of the segment. Some particle systems may have the appearance of a flow that continues until the end of the segment. Some may burn themselves out and have to be reignited with another segment.

```
typedef struct Animator_SKY {
 char name[128]; /* The name of the Sky actor */
 short type; /* The type of sky (simple Backdrop etc. ) */
 unsigned char colour[3], /* The sky's horizon colour */
  zcolour[3]; /* The Sky's zenith colour */
/* The first and last frames of this segment of the timeline */
 short firstframe,
       lastframe;
 long aff,/* For animated Sky this is the first frame */
      alf,/* For animated Sky this is the last frame */
      ast;/* For animated Sky this is the frame interval */
 RAMIMAGE image; /* the image associated with this sky. */
  ..
} sky;

typedef struct Animator_DIRECTOR_tag {
/* The first frame of this segment of the timeline */
 short firstframe, lastframe;
/* Pointer to the Camera actor that is to be used */
 struct Animator_NODE *ActiveCamera;
  ..
} director;
```

Listing 9.6: The Sky and Director costume structures. Some members have been removed from this listing to help highlight the most important items. (Consult the web references for a link to a full list of member variables.)

Listing 9.9 presents the particle system actor's data structure. Since this actor is only represented by a bounding box in the Animator's view windows, the structure needs to do little more than record the properties that the user has set. By default the particle effect is located at $(0, 0, 0)$ and enclosed in a unit cube. In the Animator the unit cube is 32768 integer units on each side. ("Enclosed" is a loose term here because the particles could travel beyond the enclosing cube but the great majority of the action of the actor will take place within the cube.)

9.5.2 The OFX file format

The animation file format is based on the idea of a series of chunks. A chunk has a four byte identifier and a four byte size block. By grouping data in this way it is possible for file readers to jump over chunks that it cannot recognize. However, the .OFX format records most of its information in a single chunk. The first four bytes of a .OFX file always contains the four byte character sequence "OFXA" followed immediately by a long integer giving the size of the file. OpenFX always stores integer data so that the high order byte of a two or four byte integer occurs first in the file. The main chunk that records the internal data structures is identified by the characters "STAG" (short for stage). The specific details of this chunk are best obtained by looking at the functions `SaveAnimationFile(...)` and `LoadAnimationFile(...)` in the file "loader.c".

```
typedef struct Animator_SKELETON {
  long    id;         /* index of parent node in skeleton */
  char    name[16];   /* name for skeleton element        */
  vector  u,v,w,      /* u,v,w are original axes          */
          uu,vv,ww;   /* transformed axes directions      */
  double  R[4][4],    /* R is the rotational matrix       */
          Q[4][4],    /* Q quaternion tweened R matrix    */
          T[4][4];    /* T is the transformation matrix   */
  point   p,          /* p is original skeleton vertex    */
          pp,         /* transformed point                */
          pt,         /* pp after Actor's transformation  */
          wk,         /* work point                       */
          bx[8];      /* bx is original bounding box       */
  double  weight;     /* bone weight                      */
  double  wrange;     /* bone weight range in % of length */
  double  wzone ;     /* bone weight falloff zone %       */
  ...
}skel;
```

Listing 9.7: The Robot actor data structure. Some members have been removed from this listing to help highlight the most important items. (Consult the web references for a link to a full list of member variables.)

```
typedef struct Animator_PATHPOINT {
struct Animator_PATHPOINT *last;  /* previous item  */
struct Animator_PATHPOINT *next;  /* to next item   */
short status;
point p;   /* The coordinates of the path point.*/
double distance; /* The distance of the point from path start */
double ptheta,    /* Tension related parameter - not used */
       pfi;       /* Tension related parameter - not used */
/* Between path points the path curve is drawn as a spline
   under tension these parameters holds the tension parameter
   to both sides of the point*/
double tension_p,
       tension_n;
} pathpoint
```

Listing 9.8: The pathpoint data structure. Some members have been removed from this listing to help highlight the most important items. (Consult the web references for a link to a full list of member variables.)

9.5.3   Program execution

The program begins at the usual Windows WinMain(..) entry point (file Animate.c) where the classes for the user interface windows are registered and the message processing loop executes. In this respect, OpenFX is nothing more than a standard Win32 API program. Messages from the main window menu are processed as described in section 9.4 by function `MainAnimatorWndProc(..)`. When the user engages a tool from the tool menu a command is passed up through its hierarchical windows to the function `AnimatorMenuCmd(...)`. Tools and ac-

```
typedef struct Animator_PARTICLESYSTEM_tag {
long id;   /*    Integer identifier */
long NumP; /*    Number of particles in the particle system */
long iid;  /*    Type of particle system */
char ImageName[256]; /*  Name of particle's texture map */
/* The remainder of the values in this structure hold parameters
 * that define the particle system. */
...
} ParticleSystem;
```

Listing 9.9: The particle system and particle structure. Some members have been removed from this listing to help highlight the most important items. (Consult the web references for a link to a full list of member variables.)

tions behave slightly differently. When a tool button is activated by the user (by clicking on it in the toolpanel) it remains active and the mouse cursor takes up an icon that is representative of the tool's behavior. Tools have to be explicitly turned off by the user. All the tool initiation commands are eventually passed to function **EngageTool(..)** and tool termination-of-use commands to **DisengageTool(...)**.

The commands from tools and menu actions will commonly influence the animation stored in memory, for example, by creating or deleting nodes, or by creating or deleting one or more timeline segments. Some of the tools change the viewpoint (zooming or panning) or allow actors to be selected and moved. The other key functions in the code are those already mentioned for loading and saving the .OFX file and for creating the intermediate script files (.SCR) that pass the description of the scene to the Renderer.

The .SCR files are simple text files that describe each frame in the animation in terms of which actors are to be included (mostly loaded from .MFX mesh files), where they are to be located and to what direction are they to be turned. The script files are written by function **MakeScript(...)** in file "writescript.c". Once the Animator writes a script, the Renderer can be instructed to load it and execute it by posting a message to the Renderer's main window as follows:

```
// get a handle to the Renderer's window
if((hWnd=FindWindow("OFX:RenderClass",NULL)) != NULL){
 // tell the renderer to load the script file and act on its contents
 PostMessage(hWnd,IDM_CALLBACK_SETUP_ANIMATOR,0,
    MAKELPARAM((WORD)CurrentFrame,(WORD)Nframes));
 }
// show and activate the Renderer's dialog
SetForegroundWindow(hWnd);
BringWindowToTop(hWnd);
ShowWindow(hWnd,SW_SHOW);
```

The important clues given in this section and the description of the data structures in the last section should be all you need to jump in and follow the logic of the program's code (with the help of the on-line code documentation of course too).

```
typedef struct Animator_POSITION {
/* First frame of the 'bar' of this segment of the timeline
   for specified actor. */
 short firstframe,
/* Last frame (at the time of keyframe) of bar in timeline */
      lastframe;
  short type;    /* Linear or Quadratic tweening */
  point finish;  /* Position of actor in keyframe */
  struct Animator_NODE *onpath;  /* This actor is following a path */
/* When following a path this is the name of the followed object */
  char pnodename[128];
/* When positions are being determined using spline tweening
     these set hhe Spline parameter at start/end of the timeline */
  double tension_s,
         tension_e,
  ..
} position;

typedef struct Animator_ALIGN {
  short firstframe,lastframe;  /* same as position */
  short type, /* Linearly or Quadratic interpolion */
        im;   /* Internal rotation (=0) or about an axis (= 1/2/3 ) */
  double theta, /* Banking (angles are in degrees) */
         phi,   /* Direction (around)  0 along +x X to right
                   range is (-180 to +180 ) degrees */
         alpha, /* Elevation */
         ima;   /* Internal rotation 0=none 1=clock 2=anti-clock */
/* When aligned to a path this points to the path object */
  struct Animator_NODE *topath;
/* When aligned to another actor this string is the name of the
   actor this one uses for alignment */
  char anodename[128];
  ..
} align;

typedef struct Animator_SIZE {
/* The scaling values in X Y Z (local coordinates) */
 double Sx,Sy,Sz;
/* Type of interpolation - linear to last keyframe, or
    quadratic back to last two keyframes */
     short firstframe, lastframe; /* same as position */
 short tweentype; /* Linear or Quadratic tweening */
  ..
} size;
```

Listing 9.10: The Position Orientation and Size data structure. Some members have been removed from this listing to help highlight the most important items. (Consult the web references for a link to a full list of member variables.)

9.5.4 Character animation

The Robot is a type of actor introduced in version 2 specifically to facilitate character animation. Because it is based on a mesh model it uses the same basic costume structure (listing 9.2 with the skel pointer playing an important role). Each bone in the skeleton is specified by the structure given in listing 9.7. The member variables R[4][4], Q[4][4] and T[4][4] play the pivotal role of representing the rotational transformation of the bone in its parent's frame of

Skeleton hierarchy view and editor   Skeleton pose preview

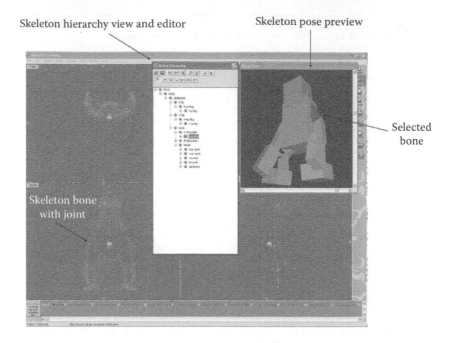

Selected
bone

Skeleton bone
with joint

Figure 9.5: The Robot actor manipulator. The hierarchy viewer is implemented using a TreeView dialog box control and the pose preview is rendered in a floating window using OpenGL in function `DrawViewRobotGL(...)` or the GDI in function `DrawViewRobot(...)`. All Robot actor code is grouped together in file "robot.c".

reference. The Animator's vertex manipulator tool offers the user two modal dialog boxes to allow them to select view and alter the appearance of a robot actor as shown in figure 9.5. The presentation of this dialog occurs through a call to `SkeletorOn()` which in turn is called from `EngageTool(...)`. The global variable `tool` identifies which tool has been selected from the tool panel.

The costume data structure records every joint orientation for a specific keyframe. The linked list of costume timeline segments can then be used to interpolate the joint orientations during the inter-keyframe intervals, thus delivering smooth kinematic animation within the Robot actor. All the functions relating to the Robot actor are grouped together in the file "robot.c".

Creating a script for the renderer from an animation that includes Robot actors requires a number of additional temporary files. These are stored in a temporary folder (one for each robot) along side the script file. Within the temporary folder, the pose orientations for every joint in the robot are written into a separate file for each keyframe.

9.5.5   Extending the animation module

When the desire to add new functionality cannot be satisfied through the production of new plug-ins as discussed in section 9.8 then it is necessary to modify the Animator's source code directly. How this is done would of course depend on what that task is. The most likely additions might be the inclusion of a new tool or command action, or possibly a new type of actor.

Adding a command action is probably the least complex modification, not because the action itself is less complex but because the changes to the code would be minimal. Adding a menu item and handler is relatively simple, the steps involved being: (1) create identifiers for a menu item and text string hint to the resource header files, (2) add the menu and string themselves to the resource DLL (project "ani_res"), (3) add a `case` in the function `AnimatorMenuCmd(...)`, (4) add a new function (possibly in a new file) to perform the action, (5) call it from the added `case` block and when it returns and (6) call the functions that update the display and status information by:

```
ReDrawStageDisplay(TRUE); // Update the view windows
PerspectiveView(0,1);            // Update the camera window
UPDATETIMELINES(IDC_TIMEL_UPDATE)  // Update the keyframe window.
```

Adding a tool would require an extra tool button to be inserted into the tool panel. Bitmaps to represent the tool would need to be added to the tool images (located in the resource folder, e.g., tools-b.bmp), but it would not be difficult to extend the number of number of tools in the tool panel. Modifying the `N_ICONS` define statement, adding to the `aTools[ ]` array and providing a defined command message (e.g., `IDM_ACTOR_TOOL_MYTOOL` will augment the user interface. The new message should be handled in the `AnimatorMenuCmd(...)` function and the actual tool code executed via the `EngageTool(...0` function. Of course the tool will need to know what to do with the particular type of actor that is selected and how to respond to mouse messages in the view windows (handled in the `AnimatorTriViewWndProc(...)` function.

9.6   The Designer module

The Designer program is normally launched from the Animator but can operate independently. It provides a window into the three-dimensional world where its tools are used to build mesh models of almost any complexity. The Designer's user interface is implemented using similar coding to that described in section 9.4 and differs from the Animator's user interface only because the idea of a camera viewing a scene makes no sense and there is no aspect that needs to be a function of time.

In the Designer the fourth window is used to provide a view, from any direction, of the contents of the working-volume. The fourth view is normally presented using a hidden surface and shaded drawing implemented using OpenGL.

The functions that deliver the shaded view have been implemented within a self-contained DLL (called glview.dll) that also gives the user a real-time indication of the alignment of any image maps or material shaders.

Like the Animator, the Designer uses integer coordinates for its vertex locations and other key points. Each vertex is assigned a selection state from the list: *selected, deselected, hidden or ineditor.* This status is recorded in the vertex object and is used by the tools and actions, and the drawing functions. Tools and actions only apply to selected vertices, or faces or edges. An edge is deemed to be selected if the vertices at both ends are selected. Faces are deemed selected if all three face vertices are selected.

9.6.1   The main data structures

The data that describes the mesh models in OpenFX mirrors almost exactly the structures discussed in chapter 3. The model data fall into two classes. First, the geometry is specified using lists of vertices, edges, faces and skeleton bones. Second, the appearance of the visible surfaces are defined by assigning the polygons an identifier for either a material, or an image map. The material's properties and the image map's images are recorded in two lists.

In other software from which OpenFX evolved the lists of vertices etc., were built as doubly linked lists of individual objects. This data arrangement makes it much easier to add, delete and re-order the data but the Windows implementation of the memory management functions were not fast enough to use this approach in models that might contain in excess of 100,000 vertices and 500,000 faces. Chapter 3 showed how such limitations could be overcome with a little effort, thus the OpenFX Designer uses dynamically allocated arrays of objects to store the data. The structures that represent the objects are described in this section. The global variables that give access to the data are listed in table 9.5. Note that the skeleton bone structure is a much shorter list and therefore the skeleton bone data is represented as a doubly linked list of objects each one of which represents a single bone.

Geometry data structures Whilst there are a few data structures used for minor purposes the essentials of the geometry are described by lists of vertices, edges and faces. The most important members of these structures are presented in listings 9.11, 9.12 and 9.13. Consult the online references for a link to a full list of member variables.

The Skeleton data serves two purposes. First, because it describes a hierarchical relationship that allows groups of vertices in a model to be associated with a node (or bone) in the hierarchy it can make the process of vertex selection significantly more convenient for the user. Vertex selection (and the implied edge and face selection that goes with it) is the first step the program user has to do before applying tools or actions. Anything that eases this task for the user is useful in itself. Second, because the skeleton's nodes can also be given a 3D position that is meaningful to the vertices attached to that node, it is pos-

Name	Data type	Function
Nvert	int	Number of vertices
Nedge	int	Number of edges
Nface	int	Number of faces
Nskel	int	Number of skeleton bones
MainVp	vertex *	Pointer to array of vertices
MainEp	edge *	Pointer to array of edges
MainFp	face *	Pointer to array of faces
iMap[]	IMAGEMAP	Array of image maps
iMat[]	SURFACEMATERIAL	Array of surface materials
nImaps	int	Number of image/texture maps
nMats	int	Number of materials
MainSp	skel *	Pointer to the end of skeleton bone list
FirstSp	skel *	Pointer to start of skeleton bone list

Table 9.5: The global variables that give access to the Designer's main data most of which is represented as user-defined data types.

```
typedef struct Designer_VERTEX_tag {
/*  This vertex belongs to this Skeleton node  */
struct Designer_SKELETON_tag *sp;
/*  The status of the vertex SELECTED DESELECTED HIDDEN etc.*/
char  status,status_undo;
float x,y; /* Vertex texture coords */
long  xyz[3]; /* vertex coordinates */
} vertex;
```

Listing 9.11: The vertex data structure. Some members have been omitted to help highlight the most important items.

sible to apply rotational transformations to those vertices using a local frame of reference attached to that bone. The hierarchical (parent–child etc.) skeleton arrangement also allows the same rotation transformations to be applied to any descendant nodes and their associated vertices. The same effect of these transformation would be exceptionally difficult to obtain using only rotations about one of the coordinate axes or even any about any arbitrary axis. Building a hierarchical skeleton into a model gives it the potential to be articulated. This forms the basis of the manipulation of a Robot actor in the Animator.

Having a hierarchical data relationship facilitates the potential for future developments, for example allowing the Skeleton to become part of an IK chain (see section 6.4) or be part of a muscle/skin deformation model where vertices representing the surface of a limb of an animal moves as the skeletal bones change their relative orientations.

```
typedef struct Designer_EDGE_tag {
 long V[2]; /*  List of vertices at the end of the edge. */
} edge;
```

Listing 9.12: The edge data structure. Some members have been omitted to help highlight the most important items.

```
typedef struct Designer_FACE_tag {
 long V[3];   /*  The vertices around the face. */
 /*  Which material is to be applied to this face */
 short material;
 /*  Which Image/Texture map is to be applied to this face*/
 short imagemap;
 /*  These are the Image/Texture coordinates for the vertics
    of the face, they are done on a PER FACE basis so that
    adjacent faces cna have a different mapping*/
 float x[3],y[3];
 BOOL gp; /*  The mapping coordinates are valid for this face*/
 ..
} face;
```

Listing 9.13: The face data structure. Some members have been omitted to help highlight the most important items.

Looking at the Skeleton's data structure in listing 9.14 one should especially note the local frame of reference vectors u,v,w and the rotational transformation matrix t. The axis vector u is always aligned with the bone (from the node at the end toward the parent node to which it is attached). The other axes are orthogonal to u and are also mutually orthogonal. The user can change the rotation orientation of the v and w axes relative to u. Once the nodes at the ends of the bones have been positioned and the bone's local frame of reference has been defined, then this is considered as the *rest pose* of the skeleton. The rest pose is used in the animator when a Robot actor is animated.

The Designer's Skeleton can also fulfill a third function, when no vertices are assigned to a specific bone. This phenomenon is known as *rubber-bones* and it is based on the idea of a potential field surrounding the bones. When the rubber-bones tool is in use, the vertices are said to be influenced by their proximity to the bones. If a bone is moved, it appears to pull the vertices with a strength that is proportional to their distance from the bone. Of course, all the bones influence the vertex and any bones that are not moved opposes this pull effect. How this effect works out depends on the weights and range parameters that the user can assign to each bone. Member variables that record this information are also present in the Skeleton node data structure (listing 9.14).

The functions in the Designer's code that provide all the Skeleton manipulation and data management are located in the file "skeleton.c".

```
typedef struct Designer_SKELETON_tag {
 struct Designer_SKELETON_tag *at,      /*  The parent of this bone  */
                      *next,*last;       /*  Doubly linked list items */
 /*  The bone's frame of reference at the end of the bone */
 vector u,v,w;
/*  Transformation and Inverse Transformation applied to the Bone */
 double t[4][4],tr[4][4];
 point xyz; // coordinate of endpoint
 point bx[8]; // bounding box
 char name[16]; //name
 ..
 // bone attributes
 double wrange,wzone;  // range(in % of length of bone influence)
 double weight,r_scale; // bone influence weight
 ..
} skel;
```

Listing 9.14: The Skeleton/Hierarchy data structure. Some members have been omitted to help highlight the most important items.

Material and image map data structures The geometry of a mesh model only tells half the story. The surface's appearance is just as important. This could be as simple as a basic color, but to achieve any form of realism something more sophisticated is required. OpenFX provided two ways to describe the appearance of a surface: its materials and image maps. Each polygonal face carries two integers that identify the index into the two lists of surface materials and image maps. If these integers in the **face** data structure are set to -1 then no material or image map is applied. For legacy reasons each face also carries values for surface color and a couple of other attributes but it is uncommon for these to have much usage in any model.

In OpenFX the materials cover basic settings properties, transparency etc. The image maps provide a way of layering up to four images over the surface. The materials also provide the mechanism for assigning procedural shaders to the surface. Up to four shaders (implemented as external plug-in DLLs or GLSL programs) can be combined in a single material. All image maps and some materials require texture coordinates. OpenFX records texture coordinates on a per-vertex **and a per-face** basis. The reason for the per-face storage is because two faces that may share common vertices could require different texture coordinates at a common vertex. Materials do not use a 2D texture coordinate system based on vertices or faces. They use a 3D system based on a unit cell defined by a **MATERIALAXIS** structure that is part of the material. The **ax** member of the **SURFACEMATERIAL** structure (listing 9.15) holds the details of the reference cell. The concept of a texture is explained in section 11.1.1.

Listing 9.15 identifies the main members of the material data structure. Worthy of note is the four element array of shader objects. The shader objects are implemented as external DLLs that are loaded when required. The persistent information that is needed for each shader is the name of the DLL and its user-

```
typedef struct Designer_SURFACEMATERIAL_tag {
 char name[32]; /* Name of the material */
 // material colors Integer in [0 - 255]
 unsigned char mcolour1[3],mcolour2[3];
 // other properties integer [0 - 255]
 unsigned char gloss; // specularity
 unsigned char refl;  // reflectivity
 unsigned char transp; // transparency
 long refractive_index;
/* The axis in use for this material */
 struct Designer_MATERIALAXIS_tag ax;
 /* The list of up to 4 external shaders per material */
 struct Designer_XSHADER_tag Shader[4];
 // On/Off switches
 BOOL bSmooth,bShiny,bClear,bGlassEdge,bUseSurfaceMapping;
 ..
} SURFACEMATERIAL;
```

Listing 9.15: The material and shader data structures. Some members have been omitted to help highlight the most important items.

```
typedef struct Designer_IMAGEMAP_tag {
 ..
char     N[32],*S,*R,*B,*T;/*   ImageMap name and filenames */
RAMIMAGE si,ri,bi,ti;     /*  Image Is stored in RAM */
short    sp,rp,bp,tp;     /*  Fraction of map mxsed with material*/
char     TypeR,TypeB,TypeT,/*  Is it an Amim/Still map */
         Map,             /*  Planar/Cylindrical/Spherical  */
point    P,X,Y;           /*  Map position */
long     Vlock[3];        /* control point locked to vertex */
 ..
} IMAGEMAP;
```

Listing 9.16: The image map data structure. Some members have been omitted to help highlight the most important items.

defined parameters. The user's parameters are stored as a text string because this method allows external developers to choose the format of the parameters (for their plug-ins) but still permit them to be recorded in the Designer's memory space and data file.

The image map structure, of listing 9.16, provides up to four classes of map. Starting with OpenFX version 2, the image source files are stored in memory and also in the .OFX file so that there is no danger of the user losing them or having path location problems if they send models to another use. The images are stored as a byte-for-byte copy of the original file and thus there is no need to decode them in the Designer.

The oblique shaded view window has the option to display the model superimposed with its surface image maps. To achieve this, small thumbnail images are made whenever the image maps are updated. The thumbnail images are stored in a list of `GLMAP` structures. The global pointer variable `GLMAP *glMapList;` locates this list and it is updated in the "gldesign.dll" function `BuildMapList();` called from `GluCommands(..)`, which in turn is driven by sending a `WM_LOAD_MAPS` message to the `OpenGLWndProc(..)` window message handler for window class `OFX:OpenGL`.

9.6.2 The MFX file format

The format used for the file to record the mesh models is based on the idea of a chunk of data. In this it behaves in a similar way to the animation .OFX file, described in section 9.5.2. The file itself begins with a four character header "FORM" followed by a long integer giving the size of the file. The integer is stored with the high byte stored first. (This is not the natural order for Windows platforms and so an internal function is used for reading and writing long integers.) The fact that the file contains an OpenFX mesh model is evident by another four character sequence "OFXM" following immediately. After that, the file contains a number of chunks holding the appropriate data to describe the mesh geometry, the materials and image maps, and a few other essentials, like the coordinate origin point and the coordinate scaling between internal and user units.

Each chunk of data begins with a four byte identifier and a long integer that gives the length of the chunk. The code functions that handle reading and writing of the .OFX files is located in file "loader.c" with `SaveObject(..)` writing the data and `LoadObject(...)` reading it.

Other functions in file "loader.c" support the *undo* functionality. Some operations that only involve moving vertices are easily undone by simply copying their position before the action and replacing the current location with the backup if the operation is to be undone. Operations that increase the number of vertices can be easily undone by discarding the extra data that is always added to the end of the data lists. Other operations, those that involve the deletion of parts of the data, cannot be so easily undone. For those, the saving and loading functions make, and restore, temporary copies of the data.

9.6.3 Program execution

The Designer program is very similar in many respects to the Animator. The tool panel and its buttons, the menu commands, status bar and orthogonal view windows are all created using very similar code in both programs. Execution of the Designer begins at the usual Windows WinMain(..) entry point (file design.c) where the classes for the user interface windows are registered and the message processing loop executes. Messages from the main window menu are processed as described in section 9.4 by function `MainModelerWndProc(..)`. When the user engages a tool from the tool menu a command is passed up through its hierarchical windows to the function `DesignMenuCommand(...)`. Tools and actions behave differently. When a tool button is activated by the user (by clicking on it in the toolpanel) it remains active and the mouse cursor takes up the representative of the tool's behavior. Tools have to be explicitly turned off by the user. All the tool initiation commands are eventually passed to function EngageDesignerTool(..). The Skeleton tools are engaged from a menu command and they call EngageSkeletonTool(..) to commence execution. The one-shot actions are initiated in function ExecuteDesignerAction(..). Some of the actions are built as external DLLs and their action is performed in LoadExternalAction(...).

The commands from tools and menu actions will commonly influence the model geometry data stored in memory. Some of the tools change the viewpoint (zooming or panning) or allow vertices to be selected and moved. When tools are engaged, the mouse and keyboard messages sent to the message handler function have to be interpreted and appropriate actions taken. For example, when the *pan-view* tool is engaged (the global variable tool takes the value PAN) and if the user left-clicks the mouse in the client area of one of the view windows, a WM_LBUTTONDOWN message is sent to the handler ModelerTriViewWndProc(..), where the code:

```
else if(tool == PAN){
 SetCapture(hwnd);  // capture mouse messages to this window
 ClipCursor(...);  // keep the mouse within the window
 PanToolDown( ... ); // start the tool action
 bTrackPan=TRUE; // flag that tool is in working
```

is executed. Now, when the mouse is moved and the WM_MOUSEMOVE message is received, the code checks for the bTrackPan flag and executes:

```
else if(bTrackPan){  // using the pan tool
   PanToolMove(...); // change the working volume reference point
   ..
}
```

When the user releases the mouse button the WM_LBUTTONUP message results in the capture being released and the bTrackPan flag lowered:

```
else if(bTrackPan){
  ClipCursor(NULL); // release the cursor
  ReleaseCapture();  // stop capturing messages
  PanToolUp( );  // fully re-draw
  bTrackPan=FALSE;  // flag that tool is no longer working
}
```

The response to receipt of mouse messages for the other tools is handled in other branches of the if (...) then ... else if (..) else ... code groups.

9.6.4   GLdesign

The provision of a window into the working-volume that provides an orthographic view from a user-defined direction is provided in the external DLL "gldesign". This DLL is built with its own project in the design solution. The DLL's exported function `_AttachViewOpenGL()` is called by the Designer to create an OpenGL window as a child of the main applications window and although implemented in its own DLL it has access to all the Designer's global variables and main functions through the mechanism to be discussed in section 9.8. Rendering a network of triangular polygons using OpenGL was discussed in section 7.2.1 and the "gldesign" module follows those basic principles. The window's messages are handled in `OpenGLWndProc(...)` where the Designer's tools can perform their functions in response to the mouse move and button messages in the same way that they do for the rectangular view windows. The shaded view is drawn in function `drawScene(...)` which provides the option for stereoscopic rendering. To maintain as high a refresh rate as possible, the geometry, material and image maps are written into a display list which only needs to be updated if the contents of the working-volume change. A basic change of viewing direction does not require the display list to be re-created.

The display lists are rebuilt in response to a `WM_UPDATE` message being sent from the Designer's refresh functions:

```
case WM_UPDATE:
  if(!bCanUseShaders)Make3dDisplayList(); // Fixed functionality version
  else          Make3dDisplayListProg(); // Programmable shader version
  InvalidateRect(hWnd, NULL, FALSE);
  break;
```

This code fragment initiates the shaded rendering which is done using either the OpenGL fixed functionality or programmable pipeline. By supporting both OpenGL pipelines OpenFX maintains the widest applicability possible. Building the display list is simply a matter of looping through all the `Nfaces` faces in the `MainFp` list. Since the Designer does not record vertex normals these have to be created and stored in a temporary array.

9.6.5   Extending the Designer module

Unless a tightly integrated tool is required, the best approach to extending the Designer module is through an external tool or action. The material shaders library can also be extended through the use of the plug-ins. In this case the Designer is only peripherally involved. All it has to do is to load and display a modal dialog box for the user to define parameters. Writing plug-ins is discussed in section 9.8.

9.7   The Renderer module

The Renderer application program is a Windows Win32 application controlled by the user through a dialog box from which the output image/movie file, image size and format can be set. Normally the Renderer is loaded implicitly from either the Animator or Designer by executing the .EXE file using the Wind32 API function `WinExec(..)`.

The Renderer program uses DLL library files loaded as necessary to:

- Unpack texture maps

- Render specific texture effects (shaders)

- Generate animation effects (such as flapping, morphing)

- Write output image or movie files in a number of formats

- Post-process the image, e.g., to add blurring, lens/optical effects and 3D fog

Within the renderer there are actually two renderers:

1. A software scan-line, Phong shading, hidden surface renderer with a ray-tracing extension.

2. A hardware-based engine for use with graphics cards that have a programmable OpenGL pipeline.

The GPU renderer is implemented using the OpenGL techniques introduced in chapter 7. It relies on an off-screen P-buffer or renderbuffer and framebuffer object (FBO) in order to render at a resolution that is larger than the output window. The GPU renderer renders in near real-time because there are still a number of steps that need to be executed in the CPU, things like loading the data files and the need to read back from the GPU the rendered images so that they can be written to a file using a well known image/movie file format. However, even at resolutions in excess of 2048 by 2048 it still takes a fraction of a second to render a frame, even when an accumulation buffer is used eight times per frame for the purposes of anti-aliasing.

Most of the work of the Renderer is done without the need for any visible presentation and user interaction. Although written as a Windows application all the Windows platform dependent functions are located in one file "winmain.c". The user interface is implemented as a dialog-based application, two buttons on the dialog run either the GPU or CPU renderer by calling `render(...)` with a list of arguments that mimic the way a C or C++ `main(int argc, char **rgv);` is passed its command line arguments by the system. The reason for this unusual way of passing data is that the Renderer used to be a completely platform independent command line application program only. The path of execution through the application will be explored in section 9.7.2 after the data structures needed for the application are introduced.

Stepping from frame to frame The Renderer is driven from a script file created in the Animator. The script lists all the actors that are to appear in a scene on a frame-by-frame basis. The Renderer reads the scene description, loads the mesh actors from their OFX file, positions them according to the instructions in the script, renders the frame, then discards the scene data and returns to read again from the script file to process the next frame. Often a single frame is all that is required; however in an animated sequence the Renderer may have to re-load mesh models and texture map images, if they are needed in subsequent frames. Re-loading models and images from disk is a slow process and it could take up to 99% of the rendering time when using the GPU. To alleviate this inefficiency, the Renderer does not discard mesh models and image maps when working on an animation of more than one frame; instead it caches the models, and before loading data from a file it checks the cache to see whether there is a copy already there. The mechanism by which the cache is implemented can be found in file "loadscpt.c". When the script calls for a mesh object to be loaded a call is made to `CheckForExistingObject(..)` . If it returns a non-negative identifier then that identifies the object (see listing 9.17) in the object list that has already been used and is cached. If a model is loaded, it is added to the cache by calling `CopyObjectToBackup(ObjectID);` The object cache does not exist in a separate list. Each object maintains a copy of the original vertex and face list. When the Renderer has finished rendering the script it calls `FreeAllObjects()` to empty the cache and release the memory buffers.

9.7.1 The main data structures

The Renderer does not need to use such a rich set of data structures as are needed in the Designer or Animator modules. All the mesh models used in a scene give rise to the addition of an object to the object list which is pointed to by the global variable `object *Object`. The number of mesh models that are held in the cache is given by the global variable `ObjectCount`. When a scene is being rendered, the member variable `in_use`.of the `object` structure is used to indicate whether that particular object is needed in that particular frame. Using a flag in this way avoids including mesh models when rendering a frame in which that mesh is not required. Listing 9.17 presents the mesh object data structure. In any frame there will only be one active camera, and up to one ground plane, and one background sky, so the specifications of these actors is recorded as single instances of ground and sky objects, in global variables `Ground` and `Sky`. The edge data in a .MFX file is not used in the Renderer so the edge chunks in the .MFX file are bypassed.

Listing 9.18 highlights the most significant members in the principle geometric data needed in the Renderer.

The Renderer also needs to load and store the material properties and image maps associated with the mesh objects. Structures similar to those used in the Designer are used in the Renderer. Each object identifies its material list

```
typedef struct Renderer_OBJECT_tag {
BOOL in_use; /* Used to indicate object already loaded */
// position information
vector Centre; /* Coordinate of centre */
axis Abase; /* The object's base axis */
// Counts of each type of data
long NoFaces,NoVertices,NoNurbs, NoMaps,NoMats, NoSkeleton;
long NoTraceVertices,NoTraceFaces;
long NoFbackup,NoVbackup,NoTbackup;
..
// Pointers to key object data
vertex *Vbase,*Vbackup; /* Pointers to the vertices*/
face *Fbase,*Fbackup; /* List of faces with back up */
long *Skids; /* Points vertices at their skeleton bone */
skel *Skeleton; /* The object's skeleton */
imap *Mbase; /* Materials used in object */
matl *Tbase,*Tbackup; /* Image (Texture) maps */
nurbs *Nbase; /* Nurbs in model */
..
// Vertices and faces used in ray-tracing to traverse the octree
tvertex *Vtracebase;
tface *Ftracebase;
..
/* Bounds for this object when projected onto framebuffer */
 long xmin,xmax,ymin,ymax;
/* Transformation applied to this object and its inverse */
 double trpos[4][4],trinv[4][4];
 double fi,theta,alpha,ima; /* Orientation */
 double sx,sy,sz; /* Scaling */
 ...
} object;
```

Listing 9.17: The mesh object data structure. Some members have been omitted to help highlight the most important items.

```
typedef struct Renderer_VERTEX{/*   structure for each vertex   */
vector p;                      /*   real position  3D space    */
ivector ip;                    /*   integer vertex coordinates */
double u,v;                    /*   texture coordinates        */
double x,y;                    /*   screen location pixel space */
 ...
} vertex;
```

Listing 9.18: The vertex structure as used during rendering.

through the pointer ***Tbase**, and its image map list via ***Mbase**. Loading and uncompressing image data from files of type JPG, PNG and GIF can also slow the rendering process significantly and so the Renderer caches the image data in a list called **ImageStoreList** which is a pointer to a dynamically allocated array of **ImageStoreEntry** structures that store the uncompressed image data in a raw 24 bit format. The functions and variables that relate to image map management are located in code file "loadmaps.c".

```
typedef struct Renderer_FACE {
 UNSIGNED V[3];     /*  Vertex identifier                       */
 ..
 short ffmap;       /*  identifies which image map is in use.  */
 short ffmat;       /*  identifies which material is in use.   */
 /*  screen bounds for projected face  0 -> XMAX 0 -> YMAX   */
 short top,bottom,left,right;
 vector n;          /*  normal to face                         */
 vector pn[3];      /*  The phong normals                      */
 double uu[3],vv[3];/* mat/map coordinates of face vertices    */
 double ww[3];      /* volume material coordinate              */
} face;
```

Listing 9.19: The face structure as used during rendering.

The image cache is built up as each model's image maps are created. It is emptied by calling `ReleaseImageStore()`; when rendering of the script is complete. The task of reading and decoding an image file format is carried out in an external DLL and so it would not require a major code revision to add an additional type of image to the supported list.

The scanline software renderer is multi-threaded. The way OpenFX uses the full power of the processor is to dispatch rendering of all pixels in a scanline to a thread of execution. Normally the Renderer determines how many processors/-cores are available and breaks up the number of rows in the output image into $n = H/N_c$ threads, where H is the output image height and N_c is the number of processors or cores. The operating system is then responsible for scheduling thread execution. The Renderer groups the scanlines in an interlaced pattern so that alternate lines are sent to different cores. This usually helps in balancing the rendering load without any additional scheduling. (There is an argument for organizing the rendering into a tile based rasterization as that might be more cache friendly, but this does not fit in well with the scanline rendering approach.)

Of course there are some stages in the rendering process that are not practical to carry out concurrently, (reading the script and loading the mesh and image data are good examples,) so the Renderer performs all loading and transformation stages in a single thread. It then dispatches N_c threads to render a group of n scanlines each. The dispatching thread waits until all the threads have completed. It then runs the post-processors and cleans up.

To render a scanline, a number of temporary buffers are needed: a Z depth buffer, and object and face lists. The buffers are sized to the width of the output image. If several scanlines are going to be rendered concurrently it will be necessary to use different temporary storage locations for each thread. The Renderer does this by setting aside memory blocks, breaking them up into the necessary buffers, assigning pointers to appropriate locations, recording these pointer values in a special object (its structure is shown in listing 9.20) and passing a pointer to copies of these objects to each worker thread.

```
typedef struct THD_tag {
/*  Pointer to the base memory, other variables offset from here*/
UCHAR  *ram;
/*  Array: identity of face visible in each pixel on the scanline */
long   *Zbuffer,
/* Array: identifying face on previous line. Used in anti-aliasing */
       *Xbuffer,
/* Array: identity of object visible in each pixel on the scanline */
       *Zobject,
/* Array: face on previous line */
       *Xobject,
/* Identity of face in glass layer */
       *Zglass[NGLASS],
/* Identity of object in, up to NGLASS, glass layers */
       *Zglass0[NGLASS];
/* Depth buffer value in pixels on scanline */
double *Zdepth,
/* fractional pixel offset in pixels on scanline */
       *Zposn,
/* Depth buffer for glass faces in pixels on scanline */
       *Zglassd[NGLASS],
/*  Fractional ratio for ground pixels (accelerate calculation */
       *Zground;
/*  The scanline renderer's output buffers for THIS thread. */
/*  over 3 anti-alias rows.  */
UCHAR  *Red,    *Green,   *Blue,    *Alfa,
       *L_Red, *L_Green, *L_Blue, *L_Alfa,
       *LL_Red,*LL_Green,*LL_Blue,*LL_Alfa;
} THD;
```

Listing 9.20: The thread structure.

9.7.2 Program execution flow

All the Windows specific code is located in file "winmain.c". The resources are built using a separate project into the dynamic link library called "rnd_res.dll". An instance handle to the dialogs etc., is obtained by calling `ResourceX()` in the DLL that is linked with the renderer using its stub library.

The GPU renderer code is held in files "rendergl.c", "rendergl1.c" and "rendergl2.c". Program execution begins at the traditional `WinMain(..)` entry point; a window of class `OFX:RenderClass` is created in `RendererMainLoop(..)` where the message processing loop keeps the application alive and dispatches messages. The `OFX:RenderClass` window does not have a menu and serves only as a container for three dialog based windows. Its window message handler, `RendererMainWndProc()`, has the task of handing messages that are passed to and from the Animator or Designer and dispatching the rendering task and presenting the appropriate contained dialog depending on the context, e.g., rendering is in progress. The functions handling the behavior of the three dialog sub-windows are listed in table 9.6. The tabbed dialog `DLG_TAB` provides the interface which allows the user to tell the Renderer what to do. It divides the user settings into four dialog tab pages that are implemented in the standard

Window Handle	Resource ID	Dialog Function	Comment
hwndcontrol	DLG_TAB	TabbedDlgProc	Tabbed dialog
hwndupdate	RD_UPDATE	UpdateDlgProc	Progress bars
hwndupdageX	RD_UPDATEX	UpdateXDlgProc	Progress with preview

Table 9.6: The embedded dialog windows used by the Renderer to present its user interface.

way described in the Win32 API documentation. The user settings are recorded in an instance of the PARAMLIST structure. These settings are passed to the function `render(...)` when it is called to commence the rendering process.

The tabbed dialog container has two large buttons that pass the command message `MENU_FILE_RENDERN` to `RendererMainLoop()` to initiate the rendering process. It is at this point that there is an exchange of messages with the Animator: The Renderer sends a message `IDM_CALLBACK_ASCRIPT` to the Animator to instruct it to write a .SCR script file. When the Animator has written the script file, it sends back a message to the Renderer `IDM_CALLBACK_SETUP` telling it (the Renderer) that the script is written and rendering should commence. On receipt of the callback message the Renderer sends itself the *go-code* via message `IDM_CALLBACK_SETUP` and function `render(...)` is called.

This seemingly convoluted message exchange allows the Renderer to appear to the user as if it is seamlessly integrated with the Animator. It can even render its output image into the camera window within the Animator without appearing to have any user involvement at all.

Once `render(...)` gets started the rendering process needs no further intervention. The script is written and the remainder of the code is pretty much independent of the platform on which it operates. Inside `render(..)` the command parameters are processed, variables are initialized, the script is read frame by frame, mesh data loaded, and either the software or hardware renderer executed. Listing 9.21 presents the key steps of function `render(..)`.

9.7.3 The software renderer

This was the first renderer written for OpenFX and it has evolved over the years to include hybrid ray-tracing and concurrent rendering.

The arguments of the `render()` function are in the form of a list of text strings (a legacy from the non-Windows entry point). These arguments specify things like: image resolution, output format, controlling script file name, and ray-tracer parameters. In function `render()` the script file is opened, and its description of each frame in an animation or the objects in a specific scene are loaded. Then for each frame (or a single scene) the following steps are performed:

- `GetCommand()` (file loadscpt.c) reads all the .MFX files and assembles the

```
int render(int argc, char **argv){
..
while(i < argc) /* process arguments */ .. i++;  }
}
..
if(AllocateRamBuffers() == FAIL)return FAIL // Allocate memory buffers
}
// open script file
if((CF=fopen((char *)scriptfile,"r")) == NULL)goto EXITPOINT;
..
NEXTFRAME:
.. // process the script, load meshes etc.
GetCommand(  ...  );
SetPerspectiveView(); /* build view transformations */
TransformSceneForRendering(..); /* move objects */
// Rrender the scene using either the GPU or Software
if(bRenderOpenGL){
  RenderGL( ...); // GPU renderer
  ..
}
else{ // Software Renderer
  if(RenderHide() == FAIL)failure=FAIL;
  ..
}
// store image in output buffer and output files
..
FREEPOINT:
.. // end of frame
FreeFrameObjects();
if(Lights != NULL){X__Free(Lights); Lights = NULL;}
if(trace_reflections || trace_refractions || trace_shadows)freeBST();
goto NEXTFRAME;
EXITPOINT:
.. // clean up
FreeAllObjects();
FreeRamBuffers();
free_render_discarded_list();
ReleaseImageStore();
if(CF != NULL)fclose(CF);
return (int)failure;
}
```

Listing 9.21: The render(..) function's key steps.

data that describes the 3D models into the Renderer's data structures (see later). Objects are loaded in function R_LoadObject() (file loadmesh.c).

- Once the objects have been loaded their vertex coordinates are transformed into the coordinate system used by the Renderer. This is done in function TransformSceneForRendering(). The coordinate system places the viewpoint at $(0,0,0)$ with the direction of view $(0,1,0)$ and the *up* vector $(0,0,1)$. After this, the scene is rendered into the image memory buffer. This is done by function RenderHide() (file render.c).

- The RenderHide() function is responsible for breaking up the scene into scanline groups and dispatching them to each processor for rendering. It also applies some tricks to try and speed up the rendering process by switching between two versions of the actual rendering algorithm: one for use when anti-aliasing is to be applied, and one for use when anti-aliasing is not to be used.

Each scanline is passed to a function that does the actual rendering of the pixels in that scanline. Ultimately, the outcome of the calculations at a pixel level are combined to form the final image.

- The function that carries out the rendering of a single scanline is `RenderMultiThreaded()`.

  Function `RenderMultiThreaded()` (file Render.c) is responsible for working through the pixels on the given scanline. `RenderMultiThreaded()` begins by obtaining any background value (e.g., from the sky or ground plane). It then loops through each object determining first strike polygons, and writing into the scanline buffer the identity of the polygon and object that are visible at each pixel on the scanline. (This process implements the hidden surface algorithm).

- Once the hidden surface algorithm determines what is visible, the rendering process can begin to determine the color values for the pixels on the scanline. On completion of the rendering task the pixel image values are stored temporarily so that anti-aliasing can be applied; they are then written into the output buffer. (Functions `AntiAliasLine()` and `ScanlineToZbuffer()` and `ScanlineToZobject()` carry out this task.)

- The core of the rendering process takes place in function `ShadedScanLine()` and its anti-aliasing equivalent `FastAntiAliasedSchadedScanLine()`. `ShadedScanLine()` uses the information abut which object and polygon are visible in a pixel to commence the pixel rendering process.

- For every pixel on the scanline, the function `GetRowPixelValue()` is called. The arguments passed to this function contains all the information necessary to render what is visible in this pixel. `GetRowPixelValue()` is a thin wrapper for `GetPixelValue()` which renders each individual pixel. The arguments to `GetPixelValue()` are:

  1. the (i,j) image coordinates (of the pixel),
  2. an identifier of the surface material properties of the polygon that is visible in pixel (i,j),
  3. the surface normal vector, and
  4. the Z depth of that point.

It returns the (RGB) value to be written into the final output image.

- `GetPixelValue()` (file Material.c) applies the lighting model and determines the surface properties using information recorded about the surface materials data.

  The pixel lighting model used in OpenFX is a simple diffuse illumination model like that described in chapter 4 with the surface color being determined from either a material specification (possibly including an algorithmic shader) or an image map that has been painted over the surface. Surface image maps, reflection maps, bump maps or transparency maps are other possible options.

- When ray tracing is turned on, any surface with a material that has reflectivity > 0 or transmissivity > 0 is further processed by calling one of the functions: `trace_transmission_ray()` or `trace_reflection_ray()` to complete the rendering process. The `trace_xxx_ray()` (file Raytrace.c) functions are recursive. They call the function `GetSurfaceValue()` which in turn calls `GetPixelValue()` to obtain the surface values.

  An additional ray tracing function is used to determine shadows by tracing shadow rays from the surface point to each light source.

This brief tour through the Renderer's code should give you all the clues you need to augment the software or to see how the algorithms described in chapters 4 and 5 can be applied in practice.

9.7.4 The hardware renderer

The GPU renderer is called into action after all the scene descriptions of a frame in an animation have been read, the mesh models and picture maps loaded, material settings configured and geometric transformations applied. Thus, the coordinates of all polygon vertices, and even the ground and sky, are positioned relative to a frame of reference with the viewpoint located at $(0, 0, 0)$ an *up* axis vertical along the z axis and the direction of view along the y axis. Of course OpenGL uses a different arrangement of a right-handed coordinate system so in order to maintain the same sense an additional axis mapping has to be included: $x \to x$, $y \to -z$ and $z \to y$.

The GPU renderer can target its output to an on-screen window, but since this limits the resolution it also offers an option to target its output to either a p-buffer or a renderbuffer attached to a FBO. It uses code based on the ideas explained in section 7.4. In order to achieve an image quality to match the software renderer only hardware that supports a programmable pipeline can be used for this renderer. The choice of output is made in the function `RenderGL(..)` which then dispatches execution to configure the output buffers. Again, most of the code required to prepare the output media has been discussed in chapter 7 and it will not be discussed here again. Since OpenFX offers the simultaneous use of four textures, surface, reflection, transparency and bump, a larger number of two-dimensional textures have to be initialized. When rendering has been completed the OpenGL color buffers (and the depth buffer) have to be copied into the CPU buffers for writing to the output files. This done in two of the functions in the file "renergl.c", `CopyGLtoFSB()` and `CopyGLtoZdepth()`.

Irrespective of which output target is chosen, the scene is rendered from the camera view in function `RenderCameraView(...)` in file "rendergl1.c". As all the vertices were transformed to match a camera located at $(0, 0, 0)$ the scene can be rendered without the need for any further transformations. However, to be able to deliver an anti-aliased result, the scene is drawn using a function `Draw3dScene()` so that its output can be captured in an OpenGL *display list* that is run several times with appropriate viewpoint pixel jitter. This approach to performing anti-aliasing on OpenGL generated images is discussed in the *Red Book* [82].

Function `Draw3dScene(...)` is the heart of the GLSL rendering engine. It relies on a number of sub-functions to render the mesh models: the ground and the sky backdrop. The ground is presented as a flat quadrilateral. Using the first light and a reflection transformation, a shadow and reflection of the mesh models may be rendered on the ground. By switching to an orthographic projection, a quadrilateral that fills the viewport is rendered into the background to represent the sky.

The rendering of the mesh models is achieved by partitioning their faces into those that use (1) materials, (2) image maps or (3) neither materials nor maps. Faces exhibiting materials are further subdivided into those that are opaque and those that are transparent or semi-transparent, with those that are opaque being rendered first. Within this subdivision the polygons are rendered in the order of their material or image map. This allows external textures or image maps to be set up only once per frame. The small overhead of looping through all the faces in the mesh for every map and material is a small overhead when compared to switching images in a 2D texture. The vertex and fragment shader codes that are needed for the GPU renderer are located in the *shaders* folder. They are read and compiled as part of the initialization process (at the same time as the renderbuffer or p-buffer are created, function `SetupRenderOpenGL()`) by calling `ShadersInit(..)` which may be found in file "shaders.c".

This brief tour of the code of the GPU renderer has brought into focus how OpenFX deploys the GLSL and off-screen rendering to deliver a renderer that almost matches for quality, and exceeds for speed its software renderer. Hopefully it will help you drill down into the code and follow it in detail so that you see how the GLSL can be used in a real practical program.

9.7.5 The particle systems

The particle-system actors in OpenFX behave in a very similar way to the general principle described in section 6.7 but with the extension that they are positioned, scaled and orientated using values obtained from the position, alignment and scaling timelines. If the script file, written by the Animator, directs a particle system to be present in a scene it will also define the properties of the system. However, a particle system actor is not like a normal actor because its appearance in a frame also depends on the time difference between the time of the frame and the time at which the effect was initiated (e.g., in a burst of fireworks, where each particle of fire is located, during frame k depends on what frame the fireworks were set off). Particle systems *evolve*; the position of the particles at frame n are usually determined from their positions during frame $n-1$ often with a random element thrown in. Thus, in order to work out the appearance of a particle system for frame n, even when only rendering frame n, it is necessary to follow the evolution of the particle system, frame by frame, from its creation, right up to, and including frame n, even to the extent of making sure that the sequence of any random numbers used gives the same result. This makes the task for the Renderer much harder.

The Renderer resolves the difficulties, outlined in the previous paragraph, by performing a full particle system evolution for every particle system that exists during the rendering of frame n. Thus, for example, suppose a particle system has a costume that spans frames 10 to 20. When the renderer is working on frame 12 it starts by working out the particle positions in frame 10 (at the start). It then uses the frame 10 positions as the starting point for working out the positions in frame 11. Then it uses the frame 11 particle states to work out the positions in frame 12. Having calculated what particles are where, what they look like, even if if they still exist (in frame 12), it will render them into the output image buffer.

In any animation there could be many particle systems, these are recorded in a dynamically allocated list of `ParticleSystem` objects pointed to by the global pointer variable `*ParticleS` . The global variable `Nparticles` gives a count of the total number of particle systems. The `ParticleSystem` and `particle` object structures are summarized in listing 9.22.

As each frame is loaded and while the objects are being moved into their global position the particle systems are initialized by calling `SetupParticles(..)` from within the `TransformSceneForRendering(..)` function. Particle images are also loaded before rendering starts and if the OpenGL renderer is used, the images are converted into 2D textures. The set-up functions also perform the task of moving the state of the particle systems (and their particles) into the state that they should be in during the frame being rendered, by calling `UpdateParticleSystem(..);`. (This step will take an increasing calculation time as the animation progresses.)

All the code related to particle systems can be found in the file "particles.c". Whilst there are a significant number of lines of code needed to deliver OpenFX's particle system's behavior, it is basically repetition of the steps set out in the OpenGL example presented in section 7.5. The GPU and CPU renderers use common code to initialize and update the particle systems but they have to call their different functions to draw in their respective image buffers. The drawing functions are named `RenderParticlesGL(...)` and `RenderParticles(..)` and

```
typedef struct Renderer_PARTICLE_tag{
  vector p,p1;  /*   position */
  vector v,g,dg;/*   velocity and gravity */
  vector c;  /*   colour ( 0 - 1) */
  double fAlpha, ... ;/*  Transparency */
  ..
} Particle;

typedef struct Renderer_PARTICLESYSTEM_tag {
  vector pin; /*  Base Position */
  ..
  /*  Transformation of particle system object */
  double particle_object_transformation[4][4];
  long Rate;  /*   rate of creation per second */
  long NumP;  /*  number of particles */
  char ImageName[256]; /* Image filename */
  ...
  /*  Pointer to the particles in this particle system */
  Particle *particles;
  ...
} ParticleSystem;
```

Listing 9.22: The particle system and particle data structures. Some of the member variables have been omitted from this listing to force focus onto the Renderer significant member variables.

they are called after the rendering of all the other elements in the scene have been completed.

9.7.6 Loading plug-ins

The Renderer uses three types of plug-ins: the Animator's motion effect, the surface material shaders and the image post-processors. All of these plug-ins are loaded as needed and released after rendering is complete. All are implemented as DLL libraries. The surface material shader differs from the other two types of plug-ins because it has to remain active during the rendering process, and functions in the DLL will need to be called on a per-pixel basis. The motion effect only need to be accessible during the preprocessing stage when the vertices of the mesh models are moved into their positions in the global frame of reference. By their very name, the image post-processors are only needed once rendering has been completed and just before the image buffer is dumped into a picture or movie file. Within the Renderer's code all the plug-in modules are handled in the file "plugins.c". The mechanism of loading, accessing functions and unloading DLL modules mimics that for the Animator and Designer.

The External material shader DLLs are loaded at the same time as the mesh models are loaded by calling (`LoadExternalTexture(...)`. At the same time as the DLLs are attached, pointers to the external functions that render the shader during pixel calculations are obtained and stored in a **shader** structure so that rendering of pixel is not penalized by having to find the function's address every time it is needed. The `shader` structures are stored in a list that is pointed to by the global variable `*Shader`. If an external shader needs to be applied to a polygon's surface while rendering a pixel, the `Shader` list provides a direct lookup for a pointer to the right function in the right library. Rendering of a pixel that requires an external shader is done through `RenderExternalTexture(...)` called from the core rendering function `GetPixelValue(...)`.

The animation motion effect is loaded and executed in `ExternalFX(...)` is called from `EffectObjectVertices(..)` which executes as part of the set up phase. Image post-processing is done from within `ExternalImageProcess(..)` which is called after all rendering has finished (at the end of function `render(...)`).

Any DLL loaded by the Renderer remains attached until all frames have been rendered. The number of loaded libraries is recorded by static variable `nLibraryHandleListItems` in file "allocmen.c". Each library handle is recorded in a list of objects containing information about all the loaded DLLs. The list is addressed by the static pointer `LibraryHandleList`. All external DLLs remain attached until the Renderer terminates, at which time they are released by calling `FreeLibraryHandleList()`.

9.8   Adding to the software

To enhance the the range of modeling tools, imaging and animation effects, it is not necessary to work directly with OpenFX's Animator, Designer or Renderer codes. The software is designed in such a way that most of its functionality can be enhanced by writing plug-in modules. It is relatively easy to provide the following additional components. The plug-in components are:

1. Modeling tools, used exclusively by the Designer.

2. Modeling actions, used exclusively by the Designer.

3. Animation templates, used exclusively by the Animator.

4. Material surface shaders, used by the Designer and the Renderer.

5. Animation motion effects, used by the Renderer and the Animator.

6. Image processors, used by the Designer and the Animator.

All instances of these plug-ins are created as Window's DLLs that are loaded at runtime. Some may remain attached until the parent program terminates; others may complete their task and then be unloaded.

Full details of how to write these plug-ins are given on the OpenFX website, but it is worth explaining a couple of the important principles of this process. The most important thing to be able to do in a plug-in module is to gain access to the data that the parent program is holding. It is also important to be able to use some of the functions that exist within the main program. Sometimes this is called an API or library. In the case of OpenFX there is a mechanism in place that provides access to most global variables and functions of the parent programs, without the need to link any of the DLLs with an API or other library.

9.8.1 Accessing global variables and main program functions

OpenFX uses a pointer mechanism for granting the plug-ins access functions in the parent program and the parent program's global variables. Since all OpenFX plug-ins are DLLs that are loaded into the main application's address space, all global functions and variables can be accessed by any loaded DLL. It is only a matter of knowing where they reside in memory. OpenFX facilitates this by providing a collection of C/C++ pointers. The plug-in DLLs are **not** loaded when the main application starts.[4] They are loaded when required and unloaded when the user is finished using them. In the case of plug-ins that are used in the Designer or Animator **and** are needed by the Renderer (e.g., procedural textures) then the Renderer loads all the needed plug-ins when it reads the script file during initialization. The Renderer unloads the plug-ins when it is finished with the script.

In the case of an external animation template plug-in, when the Animator wishes to use the template it calls the `_ExternalPreset(..)` function with two arguments: (`HWND parent`, and `ANI_STRUCTURE *lpevi`). The first argument is a handle to the container's window that is used in the generation of the modeless dialog box that allows the user to enter the template's parameters. The third parameter, the `lpevi` parameter, is a pointer to the instance of the `ANI_STRUCTURE` data structure. This instance contains pointers to the Animator's global variables and its most useful functions. Part of this structure is shown in listing 9.23.

Full details of the members of the `ANI_STRUCTURE` structure can be found in the code documentation; here we mention the most important. The global variables and functions referenced in this structure allow the developer to programmatically generate animations of any complexity and length. Some of the variables and function arguments refer to other OpenFX specific data types. Definitions for these as well as many useful constants are included in the "struct.h" file. The Animator keeps only one copy of this structure. It is initialized at start-up, and passed to the preset plug-in. By using the members of this structure any plug-in can access the functions used internally by the Animator. This method is a very simple and a very flexible method of allowing plug-ins to access global data and functions in the calling programs.

In order that the contents of structures like `ANI_STRUCTURE` can be made available to all functions and files in a plug-in the pointers passed to the functions are normally transferred to a global variable. The global variable is then

---

[4]Many of the built-in actions are also implemented as DLLs that are loaded when the program starts.

```
typedef struct tagANI_STRUCTURE {
..
short *Nnodes,*Nground,*Nrobots,
        *Nskys,*Ncameras;
struct NODE **MainNp,**FirstNp,
                    **SelectedCamera,**SelectedNode;
..
long   *Nframes,*CurrentFrame;
short (*fpGetTransform)(short, ... );
void (*fp_scal)(double [4][4], double, double, double);
struct OBJECT * (*fpCreateActor)(struct NODE *, long, long);
struct NODE * (*fpCreateNode)(void);
..
void *dummyf[64];
} ANI_STRUCTURE;
```

Listing 9.23: The Animator's structure used for passing API information to a *Preset* template.

symbolically substituted into variable references and function calls using a number of #defines of the same name. For example, in the Designer an external action is initiated through a call to:

```
BOOL _Xmodeler(HWND parent_window,HWND info_window,X__STRUCTURE *lpevi){
```

The **X__STRUCTURE** structure pointer is immediately copied into the global variable:

```
X__STRUCTURE *lpEVI;
```

by a statement `lpEVI=lpevi;`.

Accessing the Designer's global variables and functions in a DLL module through direct use of a pointer to the **X__STRUCTURE** (or through the **ANI_STRUCTURE** in the Animator) is very tiresome. For example, to use the Designer's number of selected vertices global variable (called NvertSelect), it would be necessary to refer to it using the code ((*(lpevi->NvertSelect))). This is very messy! To overcome this issue and provide an interface to the functions so that they can be made to look (in the code) just like normal function calls, a number of #defines are included in the header files: "define.h" for the designer, "dstruct.h" for the animator, and "defines.h" for the plug-in shaders.[5] A similar strategy is used by the memory management functions in the Designer and Animator to make its functions accessible to all the plug-ins through the **X__MEMORY_MANAGER** structure and its defines in file "memdef.h". Table 9.7 summarizes the structures used to pass access pointers to the different types of plug-ins.

By using these #defines, calls to functions and access to global variables can be made as if they were part of the module code.

---

[5]This is located in folder "textures" to match the **X__SHADER** structure which is used by the Renderer to make its internal variables and functions accessible in a shader.

Structure	Modules	Used with
X_STRUCTURE	Designer	Tools and Actions
ANI_STRUCTURE	Animator	Presets and Post-processor
X_MEMORY_MANAGER	Designer, Animator and Render	All plug-ins
X_SHADER	Renderer	Shaders
XIMAGE	Renderer	Post-processors
SFXINFO	Animator and Renderer	Animation Effects
SFXDATA	Animator and Renderer	Animation Effects

Table 9.7: Structures used to pass internal references from main module functions and variables (Animator, Designer and Renderer) to the plug-ins.

9.8.2 Post-processor plug-ins

Two of the OpenFX post-processor plug-ins, discussed in this section, afford good examples of the wide range of extensions to OpenFX that it is possible to create using an image post-processor alone. This flexibility comes about because the XIMAGE structure passes to the plug-ins not only pointers to the output color and depth buffers, but also details of the viewing transformation with camera viewpoint and viewing direction, and details of all the lights and targets in the scene. With this information it would be possible to carry out a further rendering pass that inserts a collection of additional elements that, as far as the viewer is concerned, look like they are an integral part of the image. The most significant entries in the XIMAGE structure are highlighted in listing 9.24. A pointer to an instance of this structure is passed to the function exported by the DLL called:

```
   // text string with process' parameters
   long _RenderImageProcess(char *PrmList,
   // pointer to structure that gives access to Renderer global variables
   XIMAGE *lpXimage
){  ....}
```

The function is called once rendering is complete.

Lens flare camera effect The lens flare effect is a good example of how to use the lights in the scene, how they are geometrically arranged relative to the viewpoint and how to draw into the color buffers. It also illustrates how to use the depth buffer to determine whether a light source is actually visible or is obscured behind objects already renderd. Figure 9.6 illustrates two variants of a lens flare effect.

The appearance of a lens flare is obtained by mixing a series of programmatically drawn shapes, mostly circles and faded lines, into the output image buffer. The shapes are arranged so that they are spaced out along a line from the center

```
typedef struct Renderer_XIMAGE_tag {
double ViewTransform[4][4]; /* viewing transformation matrix     */
double Xscale,Yscale;      /* scaling for  camera field of view  */
long Frame;                /* frame being rendered               */
long Xmax,Ymax;            /* dimensions of the image            */
long Nlights;              /* number of lights present           */
light *Lights;             /* pointer to array of light structures*/
long Ntargets;             /* not used yet                       */
vector *Targets;           /* not used yet                       */
fullscreenbuffer *Screen;  /* pointer to screen buffer           */
double *Zbuffer;           /* pointer to Z depth buffer          */
.... (omitted)
double *ViewPoint;         /* Camera viewpoint  (vector)         */
double CamPhi;             /* Camera setting                     */
double CamTheta;           /*         "                          */
double CamAlpha;           /*         "                          */
double CamSx;              /*         "                          */
double CamSy;              /*         "                          */
double CamSz;              /*         "                          */
char *aParameters;         /* parameter list for current effect  */
char *mParameters;         /* morph parameters (morphing from)   */
long version;              /* version LITE / PRO /DEMO           */
short (*fp_Terminate)(void);/* test for termination              */
void  (*fp_Yield)(void);   /* yield for app messages             */
.. (omitted)
} XIMAGE;
```

Listing 9.24: The structure used to pass references for the Renderer's data to the post-processor plug-ins.

of the image to the location of the light that is giving rise to the effect. Drawing shapes is probably not the best way to render the visual elements of a lens flare; a better approach would be to design the lens effect in an art program, divide it up into a number of elements, save these as individual images and then scale and blend the images into the output buffer.

The lens flare effect is delivered in two source files: "lens.c" and "lens1.c". The effect's entry point in is "lens1.c". Three types of flare are simulated and most of the code is contained within the entry function _RenderImageProcess(..). In a case where the position of a light is specified as a parameter of the effect, its coordinates have to be transformed to match the camera view point and orientation. This is done using the viewing transformation made available through the XIMAGE structure. It is applied in the utility function TransformIntoView(..) which performs a straightforward 4×4 matrix multiplication. Any lights in the scene will have already been moved by the Renderer and if one of those is involved in the effect then its identity will have been stored as part of the parameter settings.

Most of the remainder of the code is associated with (1) drawing the parts of the effect into the framebuffer which is referenced through the XIMAGE pointer lpXimage->Screen, or (2) providing a modal dialog for use by the Animator to define the parameters of the effect. The user's configuration dialog is created and used in response to a call from the Animator to the exported function: `_SetExternalParameters(...)`. This effect's dialog is relatively complex because it offers tabbed pages in which the user can set multiple parameters. It also offers a small window in which the appearance of the lens flare can be simulated. Despite these complexities, the dialog coding conforms very closely to that of a standard Win32 API tabbed dialog.

An example atmospheric effect The atmospheric effect is a good example of how an additional rendering step can be added in post-production. Post-production can add a volume rendering step, in which the depth buffer and the spotlight shadow buffers can be used to provide the appearance of a dusty atmosphere. To render the volume effect, a ray originating at the viewpoint is traced through the scene until it passes beyond the rear-clipping plane. Each ray is traced in small incremental steps gradually accumulating a small (and randomly generated) increase in the proportion of scattered light seen in that pixel. This is a very approximate model, to be physically accurate, a real model for scattering would need to be made. However, tracing a ray in small steps even with only a few steps, for every pixel is a considerable computational burden, and therefore this approximation is made.

Figure 9.6 illustrates a couple of examples of the use of this effect where a spotlight shines into a dusty (highly scattering) environment. The effect offers a few variants. This section will only discuss the model in the case of spotlights. Spotlights are the only type of light that can usefully be used in OpenFX because in order to simulate the appearance of the shadowing one sees in a dusty environment it is necessary to determine the shadow state that applies at each point along the line that is traced out into the scene. Using the shadow state, the fraction of the scattered light to be mixed into the image from dust/particles/water vapor etc., in the environment may be determined. The shadow state of any point along a ray may be determined by working out where that segment lies in 3D space and (for spotlights) looking up their shadow depth buffer to see if that point is in the shadow of some object or not.

Using this explanation of the concept that underlies the method of rendering the effect, it is not difficult to follow the logic of the code. `_RenderImageProcess(..)` is the entry point. Each light is then considered in turn, followed by execution of the nested loops to work through every pixel in the image. In the case of spotlights, the tracing ray is checked to see if it passes through the cone of illumination. When it does not, there is no need to proceed further as the viewing ray is not illuminated and therefore does not scatter any light. When the viewing ray does pass through the spotlight cone, it is necessary to integrate along the ray summing up the scattering component over those stretches in which it is not obscured from the light source by any intervening objects. Any point that falls within a spotlight's shadow volume can have its shadowing state determined without tracing a shadow ray through the scene.

Figure 9.6: Examples of OpenFX post-processors: a lens flare effect and an atmospheric effect.

All that we have to do is compare its distance from the light with the shadow depth recorded in the light's depth buffer.

Looking into the code, as each pixel (i, j) is processed, the line-of-sight ray is integrated over its passage through the spotlight cone for light k in function `TracePixel(...)`. Within *TracePixel(...)* `Nsamples` steps are taken along the ray; at each step the shadow relationship is checked by `PointInShadow(...)`. If no shadowing object is present the scattering fraction is increased. Once the ray has been traced out to a point in the far distance, the accumulated scattering fraction is used to blend the current value in the image buffer with the color of the scattered light. Of course this model is still very approximate because the scattered light color is simply assumed to be a constant value. Nevertheless, the appearance is reasonable (as can be seen in the images at the bottom of figure 9.6) and the execution time is still practically usable even for large image sizes.

9.9   Continuing to dissect OpenFX

This chapter has provided the major clues that should let you get to grips with the OpenFX program code and follow the fine detail of algorithm implementation that we don't have the space to cover here in great, or even modest, detail. OpenFX is a fully practical code and implements most of the algorithms discussed in the rest of this book. It even uses the OpenGL coding concepts of chapter 7. The code presents a complete picture of how to do it in practice—and remember, this 3D package probably has the shortest and most compact code of any 3D application program of comparable power.

I hope that this chapter and the preceding ones in part II will provide you with a good reference on how to do what you want to do with 3D graphics and gives you some practical code that you can plug and adapt in your own applications.

Part III

Practical algorithms for modeling and procedural textures

Introduction to part III

The two chapters in part III leave behind basic principles and introduce some specific and more sophisticated, yet still practically useful, topics.

The modeling algorithms described in chapter 10 were chosen because they constitute some of the most essential tools for constructing polygonal models algorithmically (as opposed to a simple tool that allows a program's user to draw a curve in 3D); for example, triangulating an arbitrary polygon (that might contain holes) is a very tedious job when done manually. As another example, the boolean operations that are easy to perform on a model made up from a collection of procedurally defined primitives are very difficult to create in an arbitrary network of triangular polygons. But since many shapes are very difficult to build using any other method, it is something that we must be able to do.[6] These algorithms pose an interesting technical challenge (due mainly to the inability of any computer to perform arithmetic to arbitrary precision) as opposed to something simple, but still useful, like duplicating parts of a model.

The textures developed in chapter 11 have been chosen, first, because they are visually appealing and have some novelty. But they are presented primarily because they cover a comprehensive range of classes of textures:

- Geometric: with well defined shapes and patterns, e.g., dots.

- Periodic: based on oscillatory functions, sinusoids, or combinations of sinusoids, e.g., water waves.

- Random: based on pseudo random numbers, the famous *fractal* textures are a form of these. However in chapter 11 the textures show how to extend the Perlin noise based textures by mixing in some regularity.

And of course all these classes can be subdivided into those that perturb the surface color, those that perturb (bump) the surface normal vector, or those that do both. Equipped with the code for these classes of shader it should be easy for you to combine them, or adapt them to build your own unique designs.

Note: Consult the website to obtain the annotated code listings for these algorithms and both C and GLSL code versions of the shaders. Examining the OpenFX package source code is also a good way to see how these algorithms fit into a fully equipped practical package.

---

[6]Even deciding whether a polygonated 3D model has a hole in it or not is considerable challenge in practice—something that is necessary for boolean operation.

10

Modeling with polygonal datasets

In creating models of objects for use in computer animation and visualization programs the most popular and versatile approach is to build them from a large number of very simple primitive planar polygons. Highly successful professional 3D animation programs and most computer games use this approach. It would be quite impractical to build polygonated models by entering lists of facets and vertex positions on a keyboard. In all *useful* programs the computer provides pre-built collections of flat triangular or rectangular polygons to represent primitive shapes such as cylinders, spheres and torii. It is rarely sufficient to limit the modeling process to a simple combination of primitive shapes and therefore application programs must provide a wide variety of algorithmic procedures to help the user combine and manipulate the basic shapes as well as creating other more complex ones.

It is within this context that we may state: The primary goal of a modeling algorithm is to construct medium to high complexity shapes automatically from basic planar polygons. For example the helical tube illustrated in figure 4.27 and the ribbon in figure 4.38 were both constructed algorithmically by creating and combining many triangular polygons.

Any algorithm which builds models by combining polygonal shapes (triangles or quadrilaterals) must do so within a framework imposed by the way the specification of the model is recorded. Chapter 3 investigated a number of commonly used recording strategies and data structures to hold the specification of the model. Those components of a model's specification that are essential for the procedures described in this chapter are: the vertex, the edge and the (planar polygonal) facet. Since any planar polygonal facet can be reduced to a set of triangular facets (by the first algorithm to be discussed) all the remaining algorithms we will consider use triangular polygons.

Even the longest and most involved procedures can be broken down into a number of steps which themselves can usually be further subdivided. All of them will be written as a sequence of logical steps that are readily translated into whatever computer language happens to be currently in favor. Most call upon the geometric mathematics discussed in chapter 2.

In order to keep the length of each algorithm as short as possible it is appropriate to define a few procedures that perform basic tasks. The most fundamental of these create new elements in the description of a model, a vertex, an edge, or a facet (polygon). These procedures which we call:

$newV(x, y, z)$ Create a new vertex at coordinates (x, y, z).
$newE(v_0, v_1)$ Create a new edge joining vertices v_0 and v_1.
$newF(v_0, v_1, v_2)$ Create a new facet with v_0, v_1 and v_2 as its vertices.

belong to a group that manages data structures of the type described in chapter 3. Each function returns an index for the new item in the array of items. In an alternative implementation the same functions might instead return a pointer to a new item at the end of a linked list. We will assume that in practice these procedures handle any internal failure, possibly as a result of shortage of storage space. In the same class of function, procedures to remove one or more objects of each type from the database will be needed. A neat way to do this is to use a flag in the data structure for each element which if set will cause that element to be deleted during the execution of a *deleting* procedure (for that type of element). This is discussed in section 3.3 and figure 3.7.

$deleteV()$ Remove all flagged vertex objects from the description database.
$deleteE()$ Remove all flagged edge objects from the description database.
$deleteF()$ Remove all flagged facet objects from the description database.

Other *helper* procedures will be called upon to make lists, for example, make a list holding the identity of a group of vertices connected together, or make a path among a list of connected edges as illustrated in figure 10.1.

10.1   Triangulating polygons

This is one of the longer algorithms to be considered in this chapter, but it plays a key role in a number of others too. It is used not only to reduce an n sided polygon to a combination of triangular polygons but also to add facets that cover or *cap* the inside of a curve recorded as a set of edges. Capping is a vital step in building 3D models of text characters, such as those shown in figure 2.30. TrueType or postscript font systems describe their characters as a set of outlines. For a 3D model of a text character to be of any use the interior of the characters must be filled with facets so that they can be colored, textured and interact with the lighting. Incidentally, reducing an n sided polygon to a set of triangles to all intents and purposes requires the same algorithm as one that caps a closed path of n line segments. So we really only need to consider one algorithm.

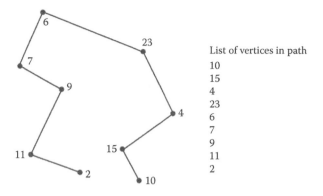

Figure 10.1: The action of a *helper* function $GetPath(s_{id})$ to build a list (shown on the right) which sequentially identifies each vertex starting at s_{id} and is connected by edges forming a path. The procedure will stop when the path can go no further or a loop back to the start occurs.

One final comment in the preamble to this chapter: an enormous simplification can be made in cases where a polygon to be triangulated is convex. However, a significant complication is introduced if the polygon has a hole in it, so much so that a discussion about capping of polygons with holes is postponed until section 10.2.

10.1.1 The case of convex polygons

Let's look at the simple case first: Section 4.2 gave a definition of a convex polygon, say called P, the implication of which is that a triangulation may be simply obtained by adding a vertex V anywhere inside the polygon, edges joining V to all vertices of P, and facets between V and two adjacent vertices of P. This forms a structure known as a *triangle fan*, one of which is illustrated in figure 10.2. The algorithm given in listing 10.1 creates a triangle fan.

10.1.2 Non-convex polygons

When it comes to filling non-convex (concave) polygons the approach described in section 10.1.1 will not work. Figure 10.3 illustrates the problem. Some of the new edges fall outside the polygon and some of the new facets overlap each other. A strategy must be devised that does not let new edges or facets fall outside the original boundary of the polygon. It does not really matter whether additional vertices are added or not.

Before developing an algorithm for a capping procedure that applies to non-convex polygons consider the following tentative procedure for capping the 8 sided polygon shown in figure 10.4. Start with the 8 sided polygon, then: (a) Add an edge between vertices $0-2$. This makes a facet with vertices $0-1-2$. (b) Add

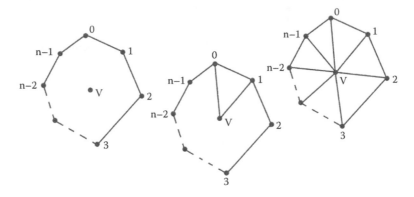

Figure 10.2: Triangulating a convex n sided polygon. Once additional vertex V is created, edges and facets are added linking V to the original n vertices.

Find a point (x_c, y_c, z_c) that lies inside the polygon.
(Possibly, a point halfway between vertices 0 and $\frac{n}{2}$)
Add a vertex: $newV(x_c, y_c, z_c)$
(This is vertex number n.)
Repeat for $0 \le i < n$ {
   Add edge between vertices n and i: $newE(n, i)$
}
Repeat for $0 \le i < n - 1$
  Add facet: $newF(n, i, (i + 1))$
  }
Add facet (linking back to the start): $newF(n, (n - 1), 0)$

Listing 10.1: Algorithm to replace an $n > 2$ sided convex polygon with n triangular facets. The vertices are labeled $0, 1, 2, \ldots, (n - 1)$.

another edge, $2 - 4$. Again a facet is made between vertices $2 - 3 - 4$. Similarly add edges $4 - 6$ and $6 - 0$. (c) Having returned to vertex 0 this completes the first pass through the algorithm. The original 8 sided polygon has been partially capped but a hole is left in the center.

Suppose we now consider the edges joining vertices $0 - 2 - 4 - 6 - 0$ as a 4 sided polygon. To cap this all we would have to do is go back and repeat the process. Joining vertices $0 - 4$ adds a facet with vertices $0 - 2 - 4$. This leaves a single three sided polygon $0 - 4 - 6$ which can be immediately turned into a facet to complete the capping procedure as shown in figure 10.4(d).

With a little refinement this simple idea can be automated to give an algorithm that will cap (triangulate) any nearly planar (convex or concave) outline (polygon boundary) provided that there are no holes in it. The '*little*' refinement mentioned is necessary because it is not always possible to join vertices like $0 - 2$

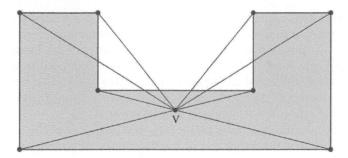

Figure 10.3: A concave polygon cannot be triangulated by simply joining its vertices to an extra vertex placed somewhere inside. In fact there is **no** point inside that would be satisfactory.

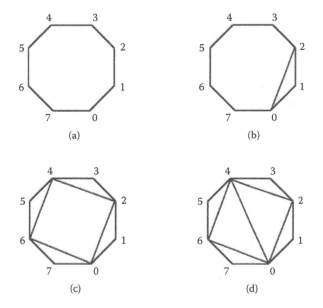

Figure 10.4: Steps in a possible capping procedure for a convex 8 sided polygon.

without that edge lying *outside* the polygon. However because the boundary of the polygon is closed there must exist some place where it is possible to make a connection between some vertices i and $i + 2$ and thus reduce the number of sides in the polygon by 1. Consequently after at most $n - 2$ repetitions of the above procedure the polygon will be capped.

From this tentative set of instructions it is now possible to write a general algorithm that follows the ideas set out in the example of figure 10.4. However it is not easy to write specific logical instructions that are equivalent to some rather

vague statements. For example, to comply with the wishes of the instruction "...
*this reduces the number of sides by one, repeat the procedure with the remaining
sides ...*" some way of logically recognizing that an edge has been removed from
the polygon must be found. Probably the best approach to resolve this specific
issue is to design and use temporary data structures. The temporary structures
will be used only during the execution of a particular algorithm. When it finishes
resources allocated temporarily will be released.

The advantage of using temporary structures is that the primary vertex, edge
and facet structures that record the description of a model don't have to change
to facilitate specific needs of the procedure.

A suitable format for recording the temporary information is a list of n structures, $List(i)$. Each structure ($List(i)$) will correspond to one of the vertex/edge
pairs that constitute the border of the outline to be capped and it will record
the following information:

V_{id}	A *pointer to* (identifier for) the vertex associated with this item.
L_l	An index into the list indicating the previous vertex that has not yet been eliminated.
L_n	An index into the list indicating the next vertex that has not yet been eliminated.
f_f	A flag to indicate whether this item needs no further consideration.
$\mathbf{p}$	The position vector recording the location of the vertex V_{id}.
$\hat{\mathbf{n}}$	The normal to the edge associated with this item.

The n items in $List(i)$ will be ordered sequentially round the border of the
polygon (a border which must form a closed loop). The edge associated with
item i in the list joins the vertex for item i to the vertex for item $i+1$. The edge
associated with item $n-1$ joins the vertex for item $n-1$ to the vertex for item
0. For the example illustrated by figure 10.4 the initial state of the list is shown
in figure 10.5.

The purpose of the entries L_l and L_n are to allow the algorithm to skip over
those edges that have been eliminated as the reduction continues. The members
$\hat{\mathbf{n}}_i$ and $\mathbf{p}_i$ are important in determining whether it is possible to join vertex i
with vertex $i+2$ (i.e., determining whether the candidate edge lies inside the
border). The normal to the plane in which the polygon lies, $\hat{\mathbf{n}}$, is also necessary
for this determination.

At first sight it would appear that it should be obvious whether an edge
joining vertices i and $i+2$ lies inside or outside a closed polygon (see figure 10.4)
but there are two problems:

1. In three dimensions what does it mean to say: Inside of a polygon? The
   answer is: There is no meaning, unless we assume that the curve is planar
   and the concept of inside and outside is applied in the two-dimensional
   sense to the plane in which the polygon lies.

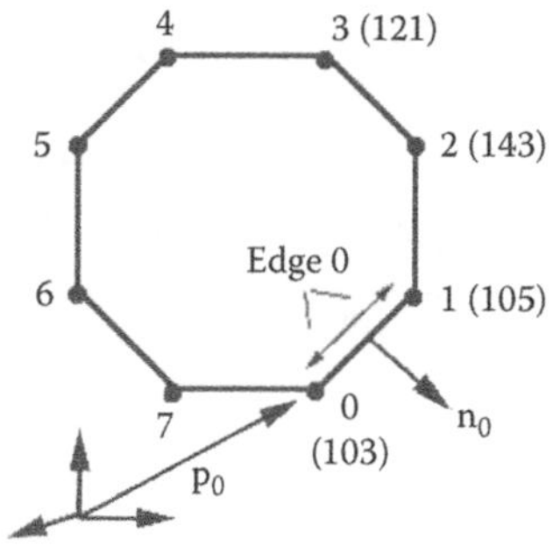

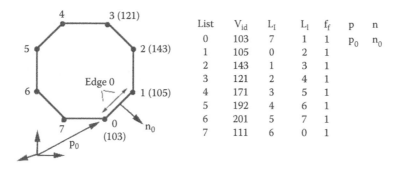

List	V_{id}	L_I	L_l	f_f	p	n
0	103	7	1	1	p_0	n_0
1	105	0	2	1		
2	143	1	3	1		
3	121	2	4	1		
4	171	3	5	1		
5	192	4	6	1		
6	201	5	7	1		
7	111	6	0	1		

Figure 10.5: The contents of the temporary vertex/edge list before the first step of the example given in figure 10.4. The numbers shown in brackets beside the list of indices are vertex identifies; for example the first vertex in the list is vertex number 103.

2. Even in two dimensions how does one algorithmically tell if a point lies inside or outside a curve? A human observer seems to find this a simple thing to do provided the curve is not too convoluted.

To test whether an edge joining vertices i and $i+2$ lies inside the boundary or not it is sufficient to test the mid-point, given by:

$$\mathbf{p}_m = \frac{1}{2}(List(i).\mathbf{p} + List(i+2).\mathbf{p})$$

lies inside the boundary. A test should be made to see if this new edge intersects other edges in the boundary. The latter requirement need only be satisfied by edges not adjacent to either vertices i or $i+2$. Edges adjacent to vertices i and $i+2$ cannot possibly intersect an edge joining vertices i and $i+2$.

Thus, referred to a two-dimensional plane containing a closed curve C, the test of whether a point P lies inside C is a three-step process:

1. From P draw a line in any direction until it is far away from C. (Say out to a circle which is large enough so that it encloses all of C and contains P.)

2. Move along the line from P counting the number of times C crosses the line.

3. If the count is an odd number then P is inside C; otherwise P is outside the curve.

This is called the *Jordan curve theorem* (see Haines [33]). Figure 10.6 illustrates some examples of the use of this test. This simple procedure works because: To go from being inside to being outside C (or vice versa), C must be crossed. To go from inside to outside and back to inside, or outside to inside to outside C has to be crossed an even number of times.

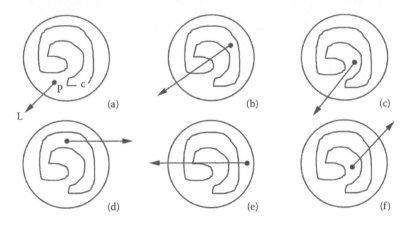

Figure 10.6: Some examples of testing whether the point P lies inside the curve C. (a) 0 crossings outside. (b) 3 crossings inside. (c) 0 crossings outside. (d) 1 crossing inside. (e) 4 crossings outside. (f) 2 crossings outside.

It is important to keep in mind that in all the algorithms described in this chapter curves are represented by a finite number of straight line segments. Thus to test how many times the line L, from P, crosses C we have to only to check L against each segment of C. There is no need to worry about going far enough along L because we are essentially checking every point on C. Since L can in theory be any line at all it is appropriate to choose something simple, say a line at right angles to the edge for which $\mathbf{p}_m$ is the mid-point.

Unfortunately, the accuracy of computer calculations can cause even this simple test to go wrong. To see this look at the example in figure 10.7(a). Does the test line cross C within edge i or edge $i+1$? The answer is critically important because if the calculation shows that it crosses both then the test will deliver an erroneous result. The only way to ensure a correct answer is to be very careful in determining intersections that occur near the ends of the edges that make up C. For example one might say that if L intersects edge i within a very small distance of the end joined to edge $i+1$ the test for intersection with edge $i+1$ would not be done. This would work for cases like figure 10.7(a) but in 10.7(b), *alas*, another mistake would occur.

To avoid all these problems the following action can be taken: If the intersection between L and C is near the end of edge i don't check edge $i+1$, instead check to see if vertices V_i and V_{i+2} are on the same side of L. If they are, then L does not cross C, otherwise it does. One final complication: If a piece of C is parallel to L ignore it, e.g., as in Figure 10.7(c), but don't forget that the vertex comparison now applies to V_i and V_{i+3}.

In the preceding discussion it was assumed that containment was tested for in two dimensions. The capping algorithm requires that the polygon be planar but

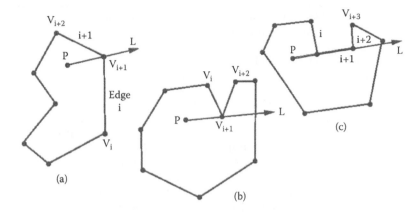

Figure 10.7: The tricky question: Does line L cross C in segment i or segment $i+1$ or not at all?

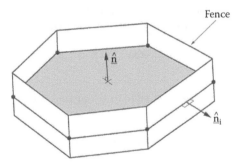

Figure 10.8: Fencing in a polygon prior to testing whether or not an edge lies inside a polygon's boundary.

not necessarily lying in the (x, y) plane, i.e., that all the vertices lie in some plane so that it is possible to determine a single $\hat{n}$ for the plane of the polygon. The plane may however be oriented in any direction. Therefore, all the calculations for containment must be performed in the plane of the polygon. One could imagine finding an inverse transform that brings $\hat{n}$ in line with say the z axis, apply it to the vertices around the polygon and make the edge crossing tests in the xy plane. The alternative is to make the edges take on a three-dimensional character by placing small rectangular planes parallel to $\hat{n}$ and lying along each edge of the polygon, what might be described as *fencing* it in; see figure 10.8. It doesn't really matter how the test is done; both approaches are subject to the same problems of accuracy and the result they deliver is the same.

Once allowance is made for these complications we can set out an algorithm for capping any closed polygon C, given that it is recorded as n straight edges in an array of structures $List(i)$. The algorithm is presented in listing 10.2.

For the n edges making up C build the array holding
$List(i)$, the temporary data discussed in the text.

Set the current index indicator $i = 0$.
Set the number of edges remaining to be eliminated: $m = n$.

Repeat the following while $m > 3$ {
    Get the next two entries in the list. $j = List(i).L_n$ and $k = List(j).L_n$
    Test whether an edge joining vertices $List(i).V_{id}$ and $List(k).V_{id}$
    lies inside the polygon. If it does then: {
        Add an edge: $newE(List(i).V_{id}, List(k).V_{id})$
        Add a facet: $newF(List(i).V_{id}, List(j).V_{id}, List(k).V_{id})$
        Flag list entry j as begin invalid: $List(j).f_f = 0$
        Switch it out of the list: $List(i).L_n = k$ and $List(k).L_l = i$
        Reduce the number of valid entries in the list: $m = m - 1$

        Update the normal $List(i).\hat{\mathbf{n}}$ to take account of the fact that
        edge i replaces edges i and j and therefore
        joins vertices $List(i).V_{id}$ and $List(k).V_{id}$.

        Move on to the next edge. Set $i = k$
    }
    Otherwise   {
        Move on to the next edge to try again. Set $i = j$
    }
}
Make a facet with the remaining three valid edges.
(with the vertices for those entries for which $List().f_f = 1$)

Listing 10.2: An algorithm to cap a planar polygon. It can also be used to cap a single closed piecewise linear curve, one that does not loop or consist of several pieces.

Revisiting the inside outside question Associated with the decision as to whether an edge falls inside or outside the bounding outline are two problems that warrant additional comment. They are illustrated in figure 10.9.

1. In the case of the polygon illustrated in figure 10.9(a) an edge e, joining vertices i and $i + 2$, lies along the border of the polygon C. If inserted it would create a triangle with zero area. To prevent the need to ask the question whether the mid-point of e is inside or outside C (which is not an easy question to answer) a preemptive test for co-linearity between lines joining vertices i to $i + 1$ and i to $i + 2$ should be performed. This can be done by creating vectors for the direction of these lines and testing that the dot product $> (1 - \epsilon)$ where ϵ is of the order of magnitude of the precision of the calculation.

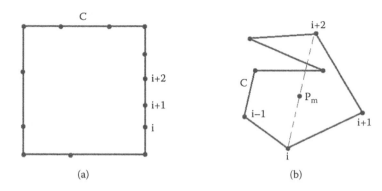

(a)   (b)

Figure 10.9: Additional tests will need to be added to the procedure for determining whether a point lies inside an polygon. In (a) an edge joining vertices i with $i+2$ would form a triangle with zero area. In (b) the edge joining vertices i with $i+2$ is partially outside the polygon.

2. In the situation illustrated in figure 10.9(b) the mid-point of the edge joining vertices i and $i+2$, $\mathbf{p}_m$ is inside C but other edges of C intersect it. In this case vertex i should not be joined to vertex $i+2$. To prevent edges being falsely labeled as internal an additional test should be performed to check whether any edge in C crosses the proposed edge (the one between vertices i and $i+2$). In making this test all the edges in C should be checked except those linked to vertices i and $i+2$, i.e., the edges $i-1$, i, $i+1$ and $i+2$.

Notes:

1. For a polygon that is planar any three vertices which are not co-linear can be used to determine the normal $\hat{\mathbf{n}}$ of the plane in which the polygon lies.

2. No matter how careful one is in making the calculation there will always be the potential for the algorithm to make a mistake. So in any practical implementation care should be taken to build in an escape mechanism.

O'Rourke [65] and De Berg [19] offer a rich source of algorithms for computational geometry problems like capping.

10.2 Triangulating polygons with holes

The algorithm developed in section 10.1 was restricted to capping an area enclosed by a single curve. It would very useful if it were possible to extend it to automatically cope with more elaborate situations. Three typical examples are depicted in figure 10.10. The first labeled (a) shows three simple closed curves.

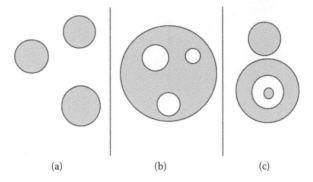

Figure 10.10: Some examples of more elaborate shapes that commonly arise and need to be capped. The shaded areas are the parts of the figures that should be covered with triangular polygons.

A fairly straightforward extension of the basic procedure could cope with this. In the second, diagram (b), a closed outline is shown containing three holes. This is a much more difficult case to cap satisfactorily and a procedure to accomplish this is the subject we will turn to now. The third, illustration (c), shows another potentially troublesome situation with three separate pieces to be capped one of which lies inside the hole in another. In fact it turns out that once an algorithm capable of capping separate pieces which have holes is developed any of the examples in figure 10.10 can be capped successfully.

Most of the steps described in section 10.1 can be used again here by carefully preprocessing the set of outlines to be capped. Consider the example in figure 10.11 where the shaded area represents the interior of the outlines that are to be capped. The example shows two separate shapes, labeled A and B, which if they could be treated separately would be directly amenable to capping with the algorithm of section 10.1. Note that piece B lies inside a hole, and that the holes themselves could be described as an outline associated with the boundary of the shape that contains the hole.

Using these ideas as a guide we can write down three preprocessing steps that will prepare almost any combination of shapes for capping with the algorithm we have just discussed:

1. Make a list of all separate pieces in the outline; call these C_i. Check that each piece forms a closed curve. Checks could also be done to make sure that the curve does not cross itself or bifurcate, but these are probably less necessary. Record the information about each piece in an array, say $List(i)$, of the data structures described in section 10.1.

2. After step 1 each piece in the outline will either be the outline of a hole or the outline of part of the shape. Determine into which category all the

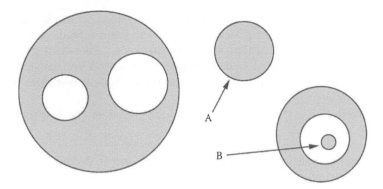

Figure 10.11: Example of a complex outline to be capped. The shaded area represents the interior. Curves labeled A and B are referred to in the text.

pieces fall. Deciding whether a curve C_i is the outline of a hole or the outline of a shape or indeed the outline of a shape lying within a hole is essentially the same as determining whether a point P (any point on C_i) lies inside a curve.

3. If the piece C_k is the outline of a hole determine which of the curves C_i is holed by C_k. Then amalgamate curves C_k with C_i and any other holes inside C_i to form a single curve. Order the structures in the list $List(i)$ so that a continuous path occurs round the augmented outline.

After preprocessing each separate piece of the outline can be passed to the algorithm given in figure 10.2 for capping.

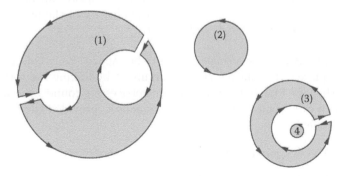

Figure 10.12: Preprocessing the example in figure 10.11 to eliminate holes and prepare for capping each piece of the outline by using the algorithm of figure 10.2.

Taking the outlines shown in figure 10.11 as an example the preprocessing steps will reduce 7 discrete pieces to the 4 outlines shown in figure 10.12. The pieces labeled A and B in figure 10.11 become the outlines labeled 2 and 4.

The holes lying inside outline 1 have been joined to it. A consistent direction has been assigned to the outline and at the joins a small *gap* has been inserted to emphasize the fact that there are **no** holes. The small gap does not really exist but it is essential to include it in the position vectors that are part of the $List(i)$ structures. This is so that the *inside/outside* test does not get confused by coincident edge segments.

Well, that's the theory, we should now consider the preprocessing steps in a little more detail.

Listing the pieces of the outline   The simplest way to do this is to define an array of $List()$ structures. Let's call it $ListOfLists()$. Each entry records the following:

$List(i)$	Array of $List$ structures. The $List$ structure is defined in section 10.1.
n	The number of $List$ structures in this piece of the outline.
f_i	Identity of closest enclosing piece if this is the outline of a hole.
f_d	A flag to indicate whether this piece has been processed.
$\hat{\mathbf{n}}$	A normal vector for the plane in which this piece lies.

Determining the status of a piece of the outline   This procedure follows closely the arguments used to determine whether a point lies inside or outside a closed polygon. For this situation the test does not have to be quite so rigorous because we can assume that the pieces of the outline don't overlap. The test can take the coordinates of the vertex at the start of the first edge in each piece (i.e., $ListOfLists(i).List(0).\mathbf{p}$) as the point to determine whether or not it lies inside the other outlines (i.e., those which are $\neq i$).

If the point $ListOfLists(i).List(0).\mathbf{p}$ lies inside an odd number of pieces then it is the boundary of a hole and the identity of the piece $\neq i$ closest to it is recorded in the variable $ListOfLists(i).f_i$.

Joining holes to make a single outline to be capped   Each hole H should be joined to the piece of the outline B, surrounding it by linking the vertices V_h and V_b in each that are closest together. These vertices are found by comparing distances between every pair and choosing the smallest, provided the following conditions are satisfied:

1. An edge joining V_h to V_b does not cross H.

2. An edge joining V_h to V_b does not cross B.

3. An edge joining V_h to V_b does not cross any other hole inside B.

Once a valid V_h and V_b have been found a new outline B' that combines B and H is constructed by building a replacement for the $ListOfLists()$ entries holding curves H and B. The combined list will contain two additional edges in the outline. These link V_b to V_h as the path goes from B to H and V_h to V_b as the path rejoins B.

After that, as hinted earlier, the vertices at the ends of the two additional edges are *pulled back* by a small displacement to prevent numerical problems in the capping stage. The distance to pull back can be a small fraction of the length of the edges. This perturbs some of the $ListOfLists(i).List(j).\mathbf{p}$ vectors but because they are copies of vertex positions the vertices themselves will not be moved.

Completing the jigsaw A **C** language code for this algorithm is included with the book. It takes as input an array of n of the $ListOfLists$ data structures described earlier and uses the functions $newE$ and $newF$ to create the edges and facets that complete a triangulation of the outlines described by the $List$ members of each structure in the $ListOfLists$ array.

The code uses the approach of bounding the outline with a series of planes parallel to the normal $\hat{\mathbf{n}}$ as illustrated in figure 10.8. This means that the calculations to determine whether or not a piece of the outline is part of a hole, or if an edge joining two vertices lies inside or outside, must find the intersection between a line L and a bounded plane P:

> L is a *feeler ray* designed to detect the number of times it crosses a boundary. It starts at the point to be tested for containment, $\mathbf{p}_m$, which is usually the mid-point of an edge between two vertices. L is directed at right angles to the edge and to $\hat{\mathbf{n}}$. P (the piece of the *fence*) is a plane perpendicular to the plane in which the curves lie. For any edge i it is given by the equation: $(\mathbf{p} - List(i).\mathbf{p}) \cdot List(i).\hat{\mathbf{n}} = 0$.

The piece of the *fence* along edge i is bounded by two lines parallel to $\hat{\mathbf{n}}$ (perpendicular to the plane of the curve) and passing through $List(i).\mathbf{p}$ and $List(i+1).\mathbf{p}$, respectively. The geometry is pictured in figure 10.13.

The test is divided into two parts:

1. Find $\mathbf{p}_i$ the point of intersection between L and P.

2. Establish whether $\mathbf{p}_i$ lies between the vertices i and $i+1$. Specifically in this case we know that $\mathbf{p}_i$ will lie on the line through the points $\mathbf{p}_a = List(i).\mathbf{p}$ and $\mathbf{p}_b = List(i+1).\mathbf{p}$. Therefore a parameter μ may be determined from:

$$(\mathbf{p}_i - \mathbf{p}_a) = \mu(\mathbf{p}_b - \mathbf{p}_a) \qquad (10.1)$$

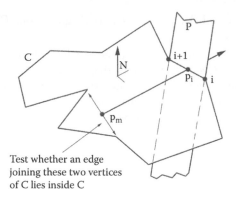

Test whether an edge
joining these two vertices
of C lies inside C

Figure 10.13: Part of the test for containment of a point $\mathbf{p}_m$ inside a piecewise linear curve C. The test line L is checked for intersection with a piece P of the *fence* bounding the curve.

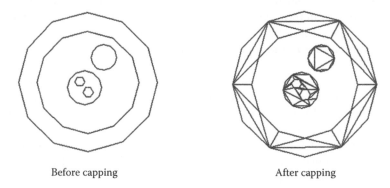

Before capping   After capping

Figure 10.14: Triangulating the shape shown on the left gives the result on the right. The shape contains nested holes.

If $0 \le \mu \le 1$ then C is crossed by L in C's edge segment between vertices i and $i+1$. Note that in equation 10.1 any one of the components of the vectors could be used to determine μ. To prevent division by zero, we choose the component of $(\mathbf{p}_i - \mathbf{p}_a)$ with the largest magnitude. To determine $\mathbf{p}_i$ use the expressions given in section 2.6.

When all the preceding steps are combined the algorithm is complete. The results of its action when presented with an outline containing multiple nested shapes and holes is shown in figure 10.14.

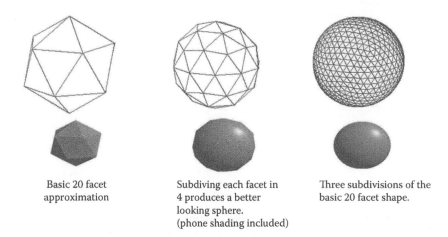

Basic 20 facet
approximation

Subdiving each facet in
4 produces a better
looking sphere.
(phone shading included)

Three subdivisions of the
basic 20 facet shape.

Figure 10.15: Approximating a sphere by repeated subdivision of the facets of which it is composed.

10.3   Subdividing polygonal facets

The major reason to subdivide a polygon is to provide additional mesh elements so that finer detail in a model may be included. For example: A sphere might be represented by 20 carefully arranged triangular polygons. However such an approximation is very coarse and if rendered from a nearby viewpoint it would be hard to convince any observer that it actually represented a sphere. Dividing each edge of the 20 polygons will produce an approximation to the sphere with 80 triangular facets. After moving the additional vertices at the mid-point of the edges to the surface of a sphere a much better, *but still faceted*, approximation is produced. Subdividing these 80 facets in the same way and repeating the operation once more produces an excellent approximation to a sphere which after rendering is hard to distinguish from a mathematically perfect CSG sphere.

> *CSG: Constructive solid geometry, is a method of building models from the functional description of a number of simple primitives. A CSG sphere is represented by its mathematical equation and thus will appear perfectly spherical when rendered at all resolutions and from all viewpoints.*

The example of constructing better and better approximations to a sphere by repeated subdivision of a faceted model is illustrated in figure 10.15.

Interior subdivision places a vertex at the center of each triangular facet and thus divides it into three. The important thing to note about this is that no edges in the model are divided. Thus in this form of subdivision, changes made to one facet has no effect on facets sharing a common edge. Interior subdivision is illustrated in figure 10.16.

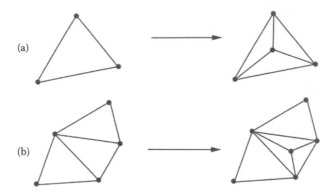

Figure 10.16: (a) Subdividing the interior of a triangular facet. In (b) it may be seen that a subdivision in one facet does not affect the vertex network of other facets. Compare this to the subdivision shown in figure 10.17.

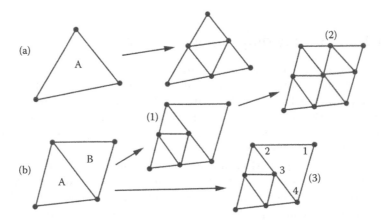

Figure 10.17: Subdividing a facet: (a) Vertices are added along the mid-points of the edges of the facet. This necessarily effects adjacent facets if a triangulated polygonal network is to be maintained. Part (b) shows the effect of subdividing a facet on its neighbors; either the facet labeled B is subdivided or it becomes a quadrilateral (which may not be planar). The cases labeled (1), (2) and (3) are the outcomes discussed in the text.

Subdividing internally a triangular polygon is straightforward since (as illustrated in figure 10.16) there are no knock on effects in adjacent facets. It is simply a matter of modifying the data structure for the facet being subdivided (to re-vector its vertex entries). Two additional facets with appropriate vertex data are created and if an edge list is required then three new entries go into that too.

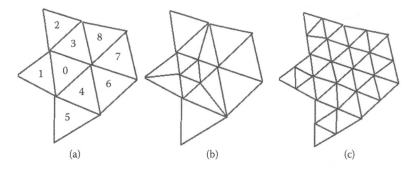

Figure 10.18: The *knock on* effect of subdividing one facet at a time.

A subdivision that involves the insertion of a vertex at the mid-point of the edges of a facet is more difficult to accomplish since we want to avoid creating a polygon with more than three vertices. The case shown in figure 10.17(b) illustrates one aspect of the problem. For the facet labeled B there are three possible outcomes:

1. Only the edge common with facet A is divided.

2. All its edges are divided.

3. It is not divided but is modified to become a quadrilateral with four vertices.

The last outcome is undesirable because if the vertex labeled 3 is moved then the quadrilateral facet B will no longer be planar and it is possible to open up a gap in the previously closed network of facets. The first two outcomes will ensure that the subdivisions of B are triangular and planar but the second case has knock on implications for any facets attached to B along the edges not common to A.

Before the algorithm can be declared complete there is another practical problem that needs to be addressed. To see what this is look at figure 10.18(a). It shows a connected network of 8 triangular facets each one of which is to be subdivided. They have to be processed in order, but subdividing facet 0 also affects facets 1, 3 and 4. It would not be a good idea to modify facets 1, 3 and 4 as illustrated in (b) because when it comes time to subdivide them it would then not be possible to obtain the optimal subdivision shown in (c). Yet another minor annoyance is that every facet must know the identity of its neighbors (e.g., facet 0 is a neighbor of facets 1, 3 and 4). If this information is not available then every facet will have to be tested against every other facet to see if they share a common edge, or equivalently, have two vertices in common.

The algorithm given in listings 10.3 and 10.4 builds a subdivision by using an auxiliary list to record the identity of vertices which divide the edges of the

Establish a temporary list, $List(j)$, to record for each facet the identity of the vertices that may be inserted in the three sides of a facet. Each entry in the list will record up to three items.
1) The ID of vertex inserted between $Poly(i).Vid(0)$ and $Poly(i).Vid(1)$
2) The ID of vertex inserted between $Poly(i).Vid(1)$ and $Poly(i).Vid(2)$
3) The ID of vertex inserted between $Poly(i).Vid(2)$ and $Poly(i).Vid(0)$
Use the algorithm of section 3.6 to find the identity of the facets adjacent to the edges in the network.

Repeat the following for all edges i in the network   {
    Create a vertex, say V_n at the mid point of edge i
    Create an edge between V_n and $Edge(i).Vid(1)$
    Modify edge i so that it now connects vertices
    $Edge(i).Vid(1)$ and V_n
    if $Edge(i).Fid(0) \geq 0$ {
        If edge i joins vertex $Poly(Edge(i).Fid(0)).Vid(0)$ to
        vertex $Poly(Edge(i).Fid(0)).Vid(0)$ record V_n in the first
        item in the temporary list for facet $Edge(i).Fid(0)$.
        If it does not try the other two sides.
    }
    Do the same thing for facet $Edge(i).Fid(1)$
}

Listing 10.3: Part 1 of the key steps in an algorithm to subdivide a network of connected triangular facets. $Edge(i)$ is a list of structures that defines the edges. $Edge(i).Fid(j)$: $j = 0, 1$ are the identities of the facets adjacent to edge i. $Edge(i).Vid(j)$: $j = 0, 1$ are the identities of the vertices to which edge i is connected. $Poly(i)$ is a list of structures that describe each facet in the network.

facets. This list is called on to provide vertex information as new facets are added; three for each original facet. The algorithm assumes that a list of facets adjacent to edges has been prepared using the procedure given in section 3.6.

10.4   Lofting

The name lofting is given to the procedure that takes a set of closed curves lying in parallel planes and joins them up to form a surface. For example the curves shown on the left of figure 10.20 can be automatically linked with edges and facets to form the solid surface shown on the right. The curves are recorded as a list of vertex-edge pairs. (This data structure was introduced in the discussion on capping in section 10.1.)

The core part of the algorithm involves linking two adjacent curves with edges and facets. The whole set of curves is then linked by considering pairs of curves in turn. For example in figure 10.20 the *loft* was produced by linking curves 1

Repeat the following for all facets j in the network   {
[Note that at this stage the list $List(j)$ will have a
[vertex identity for all three items in each element because
[every side of all facets will have been subdivided.
[Note also that it is very important that a consistent ordering
[of vertices for new facets is maintained so that the surface
[normal vectors will point in the outward direction for all facets.
Add three facets between the vertices below:
Facet 1) $List(j).V_{01}$, $List(j).V_{12}$, $List(j).V_{20}$
Facet 2) $List(j).V_{01}$, $Poly(j).Vid(1)$, $List(j).V_{12}$
Facet 3) $List(j).V_{12}$, $Poly(j).Vid(2)$, $List(j).V_{20}$
And three edges between the vertices below:
Edge 1) $List(j).V_{01}$, $List(j).V_{12}$
Edge 2) $List(j).V_{12}$, $List(j).V_{20}$
Edge 3) $List(j).V_{20}$, $List(j).V_{01}$
[These are illustrated in figure 10.19
Modify facet j and so that it is attached to vertices
$Poly(j).Vid(0)$, $List(j).V_{01}$ and $List(j).V_{20}$.
}

Listing 10.4: Part 2 of the key steps in an algorithm given in listing 10.3 that subdivide a network of connected triangular facets.

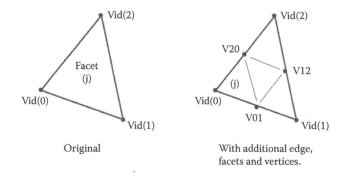

Figure 10.19: Labeling of vertices for the subdivision algorithm given in Figure 10.3.

and 2, then curves 2 and 3, then curves 3 and 4, followed by curves 4 and 5 and finally curves 5 and 6.

For any two planar closed curves with n and m vertex/edge pairs respectively it is essential that the *join* is made with triangular facets and that vertices near each other are connected together. In other words: vertices from one side of the first curve must not be connected to the far side of the second. It would also be desirable to make the connections so that the triangular facets are as near equilateral as possible. For some curves it is almost impossible to automatically

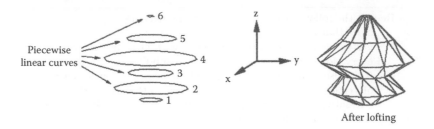

Figure 10.20: Lofting involves joining a set of closed curves to form a solid surface. In this example the curves lie in xy planes and are displaced from one another in the z direction.

decide what form the join should take. Even *by eye* it can sometimes be none too easy either. Figure 10.21 illustrates how the simple act of displacing two curves can lead to very different arrangements of edges and facets in a join.

Given the above caveats the following procedure will loft a set of k planar curves recorded in an array of lists identifying the vertex/edge pairs that make up each closed curve. For example the two curves depicted in figure 10.21 are composed of 11 and 20 vertex/edge pairs in the upper and lower curves respectively.

The algorithm consisting of 8 main steps is:

1. Pick the curves in pairs, 0 and 1, 1 and 2 etc., and repeat the following steps to join them. We will think of these curves as paths with a starting point that may or may not be the first vertex/edge in the list. The paths will be labeled P_n and P_m with n elements (vertex/edge pairs) in P_n and m in P_m.

2. Find the elements in P_n and P_m that are closest together. Label these f_n and f_m.

3. Re-make the lists for P_n and P_m so that f_n and f_m are the first elements in each list. This is the step that requires the curves to be closed. (It is possible to modify this algorithm to loft a set of open curves by arranging the elements in the list so that the first ones are f_n and f_m.)

4. The procedure requires that P_n has fewer elements than P_m so if $m > n$ swap the curves.

   This completes the preparation, but before we can build the join which involves simultaneously moving along the paths stitching together elements that are "close", we must decide in which directions to move.

5. To decide in which direction to move compare the distance l_x between the second vertices in P_n and P_m with the distance l_y between the second

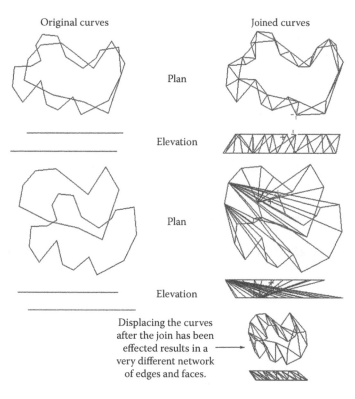

Original curves   Joined curves

Plan

Elevation

Plan

Elevation

Displacing the curves
after the join has been
effected results in a
very different network
of edges and faces.

Figure 10.21: The effect on the join between two curves when one is displaced from the other before the join is executed. The curves are shown in plan and elevation view.

vertex in P_n and the last vertex in P_m. If $l_x > l_y$ then the curves are oriented the wrong way round so one of them must be reversed; reverse P_m. This is illustrated in figure 10.22.

Getting the curves the right way round allows us to follow both curves in ascending vertex order and basically join them up, vertices 1 to 1, 2 to 2 etc. Because P_m may have more vertices than P_n a protocol will have to be adopted to allow the extra ones to *join in*. These actions occur in the next two steps.

6. For every element i, in P_n, find the element j in P_m so that vertex j is closest to the vertex for i. Element j must be chosen so that **no** vertex further along P_m is already connected to any vertex in P_n. (This is very important.) While this step is proceeding record in the data structure for the elements of P_n the identity of the element in P_m to which each one is attached.

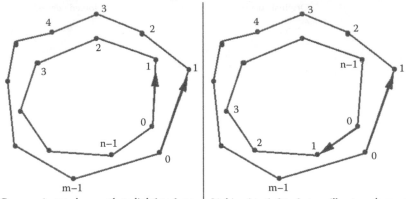

Curves orientated correctly to link 1 to 1 etc. | Linking 1 to 1, 2 to 2 etc. will not work correctly

Figure 10.22: If curves are not orientated appropriately then the join will not work.

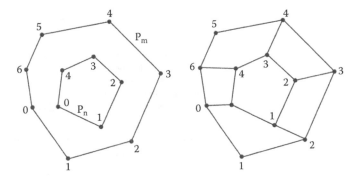

Figure 10.23: An example of joining two curves before and after the execution of step 6 in the algorithm.

After this step every vertex in P_n will be connected to a vertex in P_m. There may be some vertices in P_m not connected and triangular facets need to be created but we have achieved a framework that has a reasonable geometry and no overlapping edges. Figure 10.23 illustrates an example of the state of the join after this step.

7. Make a second pass along path P_n to join in the unconnected vertices of P_m and build the facets. For each element i in P_n do the following:

   (a) Set an index, i_0, to the identity of the element in P_m to which the vertex i is attached. If i is not at the end of P_n set another index, i_1, to the element in P_m to which vertex $i + 1$ in P_n is attached. If i is at the end of P_n set i_1 to some value $> m$.

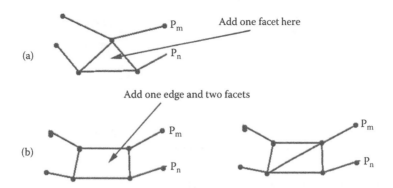

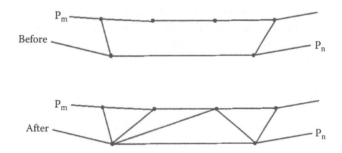

Figure 10.24: Inserting one or two facets to make up the join. (a) Adding one facet. (b) Adding two facets requires an edge too.

Figure 10.25: Linking a longer gap in P_m to two adjacent vertices in P_n.

(b) If $i_1 = i_0$ then vertices i and $i + 1$ in P_n are attached to the same vertex in P_m and it is only necessary to add one facet as illustrated in figure 10.24(a).

(c) If $i_1 = i_0 + 1$ then two facets are required as shown in figure 10.24(b).

(d) If $i_1 > i_0 + 1$ then a variable number of facets and edges need to link i and $i + 1$ in P_n to j in P_m such that $i_0 + 1 \le j < i_1$. There are a number of arrangements that can accomplish this. In the example shown in figure 10.25 the vertices in P_m are joined to vertex i until one of them gets closer to vertex $i + 1$. After that they are linked to vertex $i + 1$.

8. The final step is to add the facets where the ends of P_n and P_m link back to the start.

This procedure will work in the vast majority of cases but it may run into problems where one oriented curve has a very large number of points whilst the one next to it has only a few.

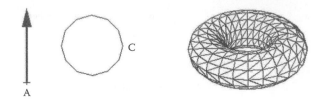

Figure 10.26: The surface of revolution on the right was produced by revolving the curve C around the axis A, shown on the left.

10.5   Surfaces of revolution

A surface of revolution is the formal way to describe the shape produced in a workshop with a lathe. It has an axis around which some curve is rotated to build a network of vertices and facets. The curve could be expressed analytically or it could be a piecewise linear approximation to a smooth curve. An analytic description is often used in constructive solid geometry applications but in the context of the polygon faceted description of surfaces used in this chapter it is appropriate to use a piecewise linear description of the curve.

A typical example of a model built with a single surface of revolution is the torus illustrated in figure 10.26.

Typically the axis of revolution will be parallel to one of the Cartesian axes. Other parameters required are:

1. The angle through which the revolution occurs. A positive angle will result in a counter-clockwise direction of rotation. A full revolution of 360° will produced a closed surface; in this case the direction of rotation is irrelevant.

2. Because the surface is to be approximated by a finite number of polygonal pieces the number of steps (*sections*) in the rotation must be specified. For a 360° rotation more steps will result in a better approximation to a smooth surface of revolution. (The example of figure 10.26 used a section placed every 15° which is about the minimum acceptable.)

Producing a surface of revolution is one of the most fundamental actions in constructing 3D models because some of the most commonly used primitive shapes are surfaces of revolution. The sphere, ellipse and torus may all be constructed by revolving the appropriate curve.

An algorithm that builds a 3D surface of revolution will need to construct a network of connected facets and edges from vertices placed at the position of the sections. The algorithm proceeds one section at a time and if the revolution is for a full 360° a final step will add facets to connect the last section back to the first. Care will also be needed to account for the revolution of a curve which is closed (such as that in figure 10.26) because in those cases the last vertex in the piecewise representation is assumed to be connected to the first.

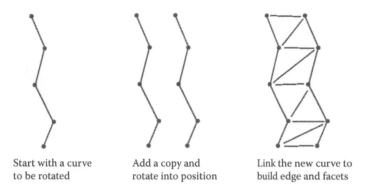

Start with a curve
to be rotated

Add a copy and
rotate into position

Link the new curve to
build edge and facets

Figure 10.27: Link on the next section as part of the process of building a surface of revolution.

Starting with a curve (in the form of a set of vertices and edges) for the outline of one half of the final shape each section is added by the following actions:

1. Copy the original curve: Its vertices and edges.

2. Rotate the copied vertices into position; the copied edges will automatically follow.

3. Build edges and facets to link the new curve onto the old one as illustrated in figure 10.27.

The code for a function to implement this algorithm is included with the book. The input takes: an ordered list of n vertex identifiers $List(i)$ describing the curve, a flag f_{loop} indicating if the curve is closed, a vector $\mathbf{p}$ which is a point on the axis of rotation $\hat{\mathbf{d}}$, the direction of the axis of rotation, n_s, the number of steps in the revolution and finally θ, the counter-clockwise angle of revolution. It is important that the algorithm creates facets with a consistent ordering so that all the facet normal vectors point outward. Of course if a full revolution is not completed then there will be a viewpoint from which the rear of the facets will be visible.

10.6 Beveling

Beveling (alternatively called filleting) removes sharp corners from objects. As such it therefore plays an important role in many CAD application programs. In 3D graphics beveled edges are commonly used to enhance the appearance of models of text strings.

Adding a bevel to a model built from triangular polygons is difficult because it involves cutting and modifying polygons. It is much easier to build the bevel

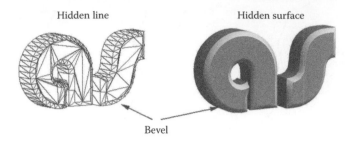

Figure 10.28: Models for the letters *A and S* showing a bevel on the front face.

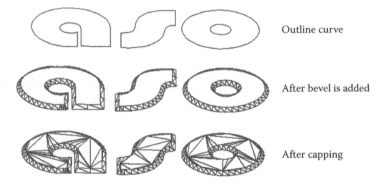

Outline curve

After bevel is added

After capping

Figure 10.29: Beveling an outline.

into the model as it is constructed. This is the way the model of the *letters* shown in figure 10.28 was constructed.

The generation of a beveled shape can begin with a set of closed curves using a modified version of the triangulation algorithm described in section 10.1. Once the curve has been beveled it can be capped with the triangulation algorithm to produce a closed shape; see figure 10.29 for an example.

To create a bevel from a series of closed outlines there are two issues to be addressed:

1. To which side of the curve is the bevel formed? This is tied in with the idea of a curve with a hole in it because the bevel round a hole should slant in the opposite direction to the bevel round the outside of the curve. The curves shown in figure 10.29 contain both a series of outside outlines and a hole; you should be able to see how the bevel is made accordingly.

2. How does the bevel behave as it goes round a bend? This will depend on whether:

   (a) The bevel is to appear on the inside of the bend as you go round (shorter path).

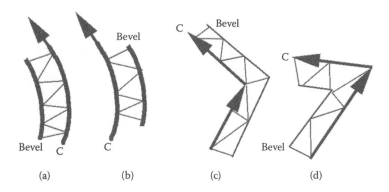

Figure 10.30: Beveling a curve that goes round a bend. (a) The bevel is on the inside of the curve C. (b) The bevel is on the outside of C. (c) On the outside of a hairpin bend. (d) On the inside of a hairpin bend.

    (b) The bevel is to appear on the outside of the bend as you go round (longer path).

These cases are shown in figure 10.30(a and b). Since all the curves used in this chapter are built from straight edges (piecewise linear) the problem of how to arrange the facets in the bevel is accentuated when the curves go round a bend that is greater than about 270°. The question therefore is: How to how to build the bevel?

A first guess for a procedure might be: Add one edge lying parallel to each edge in the original curves, offset it by the depth of the bevel and link it to the main curve with edges and facets. However, this won't work for curves with hairpin bends, Figure 10.30(c and d), because the repositioned edges overlap or leave a gap as shown in Figure 10.31. Even though this first idea may not work immediately it is a good starting point for a better procedure because an edge can be inserted to fill any gap and edges that would overlap can be shortened. This approach leads to satisfactory looking bevels; see figure 10.32.

  A reasonable algorithm that produces such a bevel round a set of outline curves requires the following three steps:

1. Given a list of closed curves (closed curves are needed so that the bevel can be placed to the *inside*) determine whether each curve represents the outline of a hole or an outside edge.

2. For each vertex/edge pair V_i, determine a normal to the edge; call it $\hat{\mathbf{n}}_i$. Choose $\hat{\mathbf{n}}_i$ so that it lies in the plane of the curve and points in the direction in which the bevel is to be made. In addition, for each V_i obtain the average

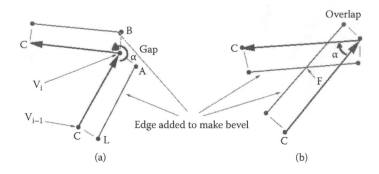

Figure 10.31: Beveling a hairpin bend either leaves a gap or causes an overlap.

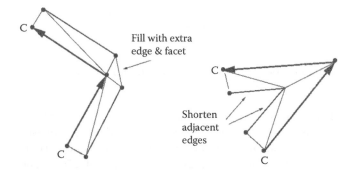

Figure 10.32: Beveling a hairpin bend with the gap filled in and overlapping edges shortened.

of the normals to the curve at V_i and its neighbor V_{i-1}; call this $\hat{\mathbf{v}}_i$. Use $\hat{\mathbf{v}}_i$ to obtain the necessary extension or shortening for the edges in the bevel.

3. Travel round each curve and consider in turn the individual vertex/edge pairs V_i making up the curve. With each V_i (we assume that the bevel has been constructed up to V_{i-1}), check the angle α between V_i and V_{i-1} (on the side where the bevel is to be built) and do the following:

If $\alpha > 270°$ (figure 10.31(a)), add a vertex in the bevel beside V_i, (labeled A) and link it with an edge to the *last* vertex in the bevel (labeled L beside V_{i-1}). Add another vertex, B, again beside V_i (but offset in a direction perpendicular to the edge V_i). Join B to A with an edge and add appropriate facets. The vertex B becomes the *last* vertex in the bevel.

If $\alpha < 270°$, determine the position of the point labeled F in figure 10.31(b). Add a vertex at F, join it to the *last* vertex and add other edges and facets as appropriate to build the bevel. The case shown in Figure 10.31(b) has an α for which the edge of the bevel is shorter than the edge parallel to it in the

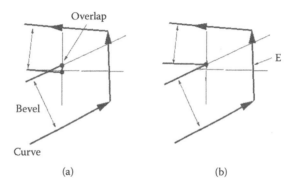

Figure 10.33: Resolving the problem that can occur if the curvature is too great to accommodate the required bevel depth. In (a) the edges in the bevel overlap. By preventing the creation of a vertex and edge associated with edge E in the original curve, the overlap is avoided (b).

curve C. This will be true for cases where $\alpha < 180°$. If $180° < \alpha < 270°$ the edge in the bevel will be longer than the one it is parallel to in the curve C.

Figure 10.32 illustrates the result of applying this procedure to the curve fragments of figure 10.31.

There is one irritating complication when beveling part of a curve like that shown in figure 10.31(b). What happens if the edge segments are shorter than the depth of the bevel? In such cases the location of the point F (figure 10.31(b)), determined from two consecutive edges would cause an overlap as shown in figure 10.33(a). To avoid this a test should be inserted before creating a vertex at F to see if an overlap is going to occur. If the result of the test is positive then F should not be created and the algorithm will just skip forward to consider the next edge.

10.7 Orienting surface normals

Sometimes the order in which the vertices to which a polygon is attached is not listed in a consistent order. That is, if you look at a plan of a network of facets, some facets have their vertices listed in a clockwise sense and some have their vertices listed in a counter-clockwise sense. An example is illustrated in figure 10.34. If this happens a renderer cannot determine if the front or back of a polygonal is the one facing the camera. Thus it is not possible to perform a back-face cull (see section 4.2.7) because this might lead to holes appearing in the model. Consequently all facets have to be rendered and this slows the rendering procedure. A further complication of inconsistent orientation

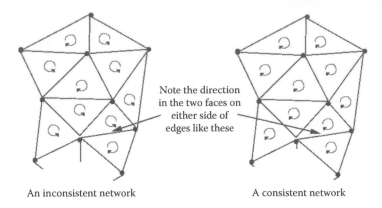

An inconsistent network   A consistent network

Figure 10.34: The order in which the vertices bordering a polygon are recorded can produce a consistent or an inconsistent network. A consistent network is one in which the surface normals (formed by a vector cross product between two non co-linear edges) of connected polygons are directed toward the same side of the network.

in surface patches is that it is very difficult to calculate appropriate normal vectors and as a consequence unpleasant artifacts can appear when the Phong or Gouraud shading procedures are used to simulate curved surfaces.

This section presents a procedure that will orientate a network of connected triangular facets by making the order in which the vertices of any facet are recorded consistently counter-clockwise when looking at the facets from the "*out-side*" of the model. Although some models do not have a definite inside or outside (a flat sheet of facets for example) one side can be arbitrarily designated the outside. Models that consist of several pieces can be orientated simply by treating each piece as a separate network.

For the purposes of this algorithm a facet is part of a network only if it is connected to other facets along at least one of its edges. Facets that meet only at a vertex are considered as separate networks.

The algorithm which is recursive can be summarized in the following five steps:

1. Add an integer identifier s_{id} to the data structure describing each polygon. This will be used to identity separate pieces in the model.

2. Flag every polygon as being unidentified, i.e., set $s_{id} = -1$.

3. For every polygon work out the identity of the polygons adjacent to it, i.e., those that have a common edge will have two of their vertices the same as the polygon being checked. A suitable procedure is given in section 3.5.

4. For each polygon k, check if it is unidentified. If it is, then call the recursive function $IdentifyConnected(LastOneSet, SetThisOne)$ to assign it and

all facets connected to it. The function also makes all connected facets adopt the same counter-clockwise vertex ordering scheme.

The function will be called with the identity of the polygon to be checked (the parameter $SetThisOne$), and the identity of the last one that has been checked (parameter $LastOneSet$). Since $0 \leq k$ we can use -1 as the starting value for $LastOneSet$. The initial call then takes the form $IdentifyConnected(-1, k)$. A counter c is initialized $c = 0$ which will count the number of discrete pieces in the model. On execution $IdentifyConnected()$ performs the following functions:

(a) For polygon $SetThisOne$ check if its flag $s_{id} \geq 0$. If it is then return from the functions because facet $SetThisOne$ has already been set and therefore this test stops further recursion.

(b) If $LastOneSet \geq 0$ make the orientation of polygon $SetThisOne$ the same as $LastOneSet$ by swapping two vertices in the vertex list if necessary. However if $LastOneSet < 0$ then increment the count c because *as yet* there are no adjacent facets.

(c) Assign the flag $s_{id} = c$ for polygon $SetThisOne$.

(d) Call $IdentifyConnected()$ once for the polygons adjacent to polygon $SetThisOne$, with of course the $LastOneSet$ parameter now specifying the polygon identified by $SetThisOne$.

5. With each individual piece, i.e., all those facets having the same values of s_{id}, do the following:

(a) Find a bounding box.

(b) Choose an arbitrary point P outside the bounding box. (If rendering is taking place the best choice for P is the viewpoint.)

(c) Find the polygon closest to P, say k. If k's normal is directed so that the back of k is visible from P reverse all the normal vectors and vertex orderings of polygons identified with the same s_{id} as k.

10.8 Delaunay triangulation

Sometimes an arbitrary collection of points is encountered without any details as what happens between them. Perhaps they represent samples from a scientific experiment for example. To be able to visualize them (by rendering) they must be connected together by a network of polygons. This specific problem occurs frequently in engineering design and analysis. If the number of points is large, then doing it by hand, say in an interactive design application, is out of the question and an automated procedure must be sought.

For any set of more than three points building a network of triangular polygons is always possible. Grouping more than three points to form the basic polygonal unit has the advantage that fewer polygons will need to be rendered. However there are many drawbacks, not the least of which is the complexity of the procedure to determine the polygonization.

Invariably the triangulated mesh used in a mathematical analysis requires that it should be as regular as possible, that is: The triangles should be approximately *equiangular* (or to put it another way: No long thin triangles). This requirement is exactly the one we strive to attain in producing models for 3D visualization because it makes the writing of a good quality renderer so much easier. All the numerical pitfalls that occur because of long thin facets are avoided when the triangles are nearly equiangular. A method that guarantees to deliver a locally equiangular arrangement of edges and facets has been devised. It goes by the name of *Delaunay triangulation.*

The Delaunay triangulation technique is particularly helpful in visualizing functions of two variables: $z = f(x, y)$, especially when the sample points (x, y) are arranged randomly. A very good example of this is: Geographic Information Systems (GIS) which record topographic data. The height z is sampled at a set of (x, y) coordinates. A triangulation based on the (x, y) coordinates with the z coordinate derived from the height value at each point gives a 3D surface that can be sent to a standard renderer to produce informative images such as that illustrated in figure 10.35. The locations of the data points for the scene in figure 10.35 and mesh created by Delaunay triangulation are shown in figure 10.36. A GIS therefore does not need to record any edge or facet information.

Many other scientific and engineering disciplines find this approach to visualizing information very useful and it is one use for 3D graphics. Another reason for us to consider the Delaunay procedure for triangulating a set of points is that it forms an important step in the construction of faceted models using the technique of Boolean operations to be discussed in section 10.9.

The algorithm presented in this section will follow the approach of Sloan [83] with the exception that we will allow the plane in which the triangulation is built to lie in any orientation rather than a horizontal xy plane. (An arbitrary plane of triangulation is essential for the Boolean procedure of section 10.9.) Delaunay triangulations are produced on a flat plane. The third dimension is irrelevant because a surface cannot be assigned to an arbitrary collection of points in three dimensions.

The essence of the Delaunay triangulation algorithm is relatively straightforward. The basic premise is:

> *Take one point from the data set at a time and insert it into a pre-existing triangulation making any necessary adjustments to the* edge/facet *information so that all the facets remain as equiangular as possible.*

Figure 10.35: Making a Delaunay triangulation from a collection of geographic data allows a 3D renderer to produce a visualization of the landscape that the data represents. An animation of the *fly by* type is readily generated over a model of a landscape from earth or some other world.

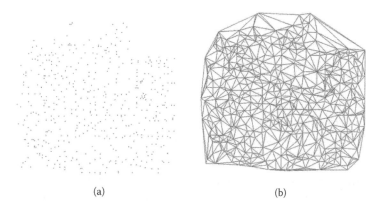

(a) (b)

Figure 10.36: The data points and mesh from which the image in figure 10.35 was generated. (a) The location of the sample points. (b) The mesh generated by Delaunay triangulation.

The process is started by making a dummy facet big enough to enclose all the points. After completing the Delaunay triangulation the vertices of this *enclosing* triangle are removed and consequently any edges or facets attached to them disappear too. The basic idea of the algorithm is illustrated in figure 10.37.

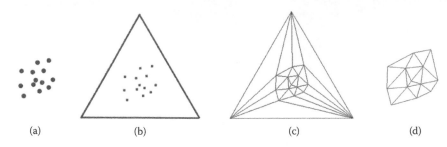

Figure 10.37: The triangulation of a set of points. (a) The points, (b) enclosed by a supertriangle, (c) triangulated and (d) with the supertriangle removed (enlarged view).

The basic steps are:

1. Add a triangular facet in the same plane in which the points lie. Make it large enough so that all points are inside it. Thus the initial triangulation contains just a single triangle. Call this the **supertriangle**.

2. With each point P in the list of points to be inserted, do the following:

   (a) Find an existing triangle that encloses P, say it is triangle k.

   (b) Form three new triangles by connecting P to the vertices of k. The net gain of triangles is two and three new edges are created.

   (c) The new triangulation is updated so that the properties of a Delaunay triangulation again apply to the whole network of edges and facets. *This is the main step in the algorithm and it will be discussed below.*

3. Once all the points have been inserted in the triangulation the vertices that form the supertriangle are removed. Any edge or facet attached to one of these supertriangle vertices must also be removed. Figure 10.37 illustrates the outcome after the main steps in the algorithm.

In step 2 above it was stated that: *After a point P is inserted in the triangulation the triangulation is updated so that the properties of a Delaunay network are re-established.* This is accomplished by the following three steps:

1. All the triangles that have a common edge with one of the three triangles adjacent to P are placed on a last-in, first-out stack. The facets labeled X, Y, and Z in figure 10.38 are adjacent to P and the facets A, B and C are opposite to P.

2. If the stack is empty this phase of the algorithm is complete. Otherwise, a triangle is popped off the stack and a test made to see if the edge common to it and its neighbor with P as a vertex should be switched, e.g., pairs A and X, B and Y etc. (See figure 10.38.) This test effectively decides

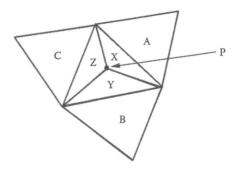

Figure 10.38: The triangles A, B and C, share a common edge with the (three) triangles X, Y and Z, which have P as one of their vertices. A,B and C are said to be *opposite* P.

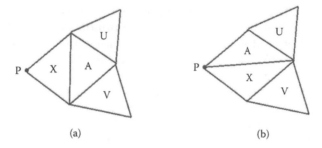

Figure 10.39: Should the edge common to triangles A and X shown in (a) be swapped to give the configuration shown in (b)? If configuration (b) is adopted then the triangles labeled U and V will need to be reconsidered because they will now be *opposite* P and we need to check whether their common edge needs to be swapped.

whether the internal angles of the triangles X and A in figure 10.39 are closer to being equiangular in configuration (a) or configuration (b).

If a swap from configuration (a) to configuration (b) is made then two triangles replace two triangles so no new edges or facets are created. However the action of making such a swap will have implications for the other triangles adjacent to that labeled A in figure 10.39(a) and this must be accounted for in the next step.

3. If a swap is made any triangles that become opposite P are **pushed** onto the stack. There will be at most two; see those labeled U and V in the example of figure 10.39.

Execution then loops back to step 2 to continue processing the (possibly extended) stack.

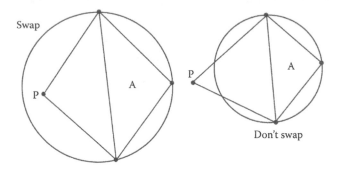

Figure 10.40: Swap the common edge if P lies inside the circumcircle of the triangle, A, opposite P.

Finally, to complete the description of the algorithm we must discuss the test that determines whether to swap the **common edge**. In two dimensions this is equivalent to deciding whether P lies inside the circumcircle of the triangle opposite P. If it does the edge is swapped, if it does not then no change is necessary; see figure 10.40.

The point P (in figure 10.41) lies on the circumcircle of the triangle V_1, V_2, V_3 if $\alpha + \beta = \pi$. It lies inside the circumcircle if $\alpha + \beta > \pi$ and outside if $\alpha + \beta < \pi$. To calculate α and β directly would involve inverse trigonometric functions (which is always undesirable) but since $\alpha + \beta < 2\pi$ the point P will lie inside the circumcircle if $\sin(\alpha + \beta) < 0$. Using this formulation avoids the inverse trigonometric function but there are some numerical difficulties due to round off errors when $\alpha + \beta \approx \pi$; however the four-step algorithm due to Cline and Renka [16] can solve such problems. We can extend their two-dimensional procedure to apply to any plane where the points P, V_1 etc., in figure 10.41 are given by position vectors $\mathbf{v}_1$, $\mathbf{v}_2$, $\mathbf{v}_3$, and $\mathbf{p}$. This algorithm is presented in listing 10.5.

In the coding of the Delaunay algorithm that accompanies the book the following points should be noted:

1. For this implementation the plane in which the points to be triangulated lie may be selected to be parallel to the xy, yz or zx planes.

2. The supertriangle, which may be specified arbitrarily, is chosen by first finding the rectangle enclosing all the points in the plane. Let the center of this rectangle be (x_c, y_c) and d its longest dimension. An equilateral triangle with the circle, radius d center (x_c, y_c), inscribed inside it will also enclose all the points. The vertices of the supertriangle are therefore located at $(x_c, y_c + 2d)$, $(x_c - \sqrt{3}d, y_c - d)$ and $(x_c + \sqrt{3}d, y_c - d)$.

3. In order to swap an edge the data structure representing the facets needs to keep a record of which facets are adjacent to which facets; and which edge

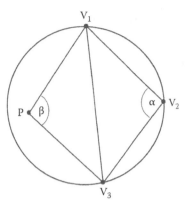

Figure 10.41: The geometry used to test whether P lies inside the circumcircle of the triangle V_1 - V_2 - V_3.

is adjacent to which facet. When an edge is swapped it is not only vital to update the adjacency information in the facets directly affected but also to update the information in those adjacent to the modified facets both before and after the swap. For example: Swapping the edge E shown in figure 10.42 will affect the adjacency information not only in the triangles labeled A and B but also in triangles X and Y. The triangle Z is not affected because it remains adjacent to A.

4. Care must be taken when swapping edges so that the order in which the vertex data is recorded remains consistent. We don't want some of the normal vectors pointing to one side of the plane and the remainder pointing to the other.

5. The code for this algorithm will generate a mesh from 10,000 points in a few seconds on a standard personal computer.

10.9 Boolean modeling

Boolean modeling is the name given to a procedure for building models from a combination of primitive shapes or indeed from other models. The name is taken from the algebra of mathematical logic devised by George Boole in 1847 because its operations provide a very useful analogy to describe the way in which shapes may be combined.

The simplest way to combine two models is to add them together. This can be represented by a Boolean operation called an **or** operation which is written using the $+$ symbol. For example if we let the symbol A represent an eight sided

Start by calculating the vectors below:

$$\hat{\mathbf{v}}_{13} = \frac{\mathbf{v}_1 - \mathbf{v}_3}{|\mathbf{v}_1 - \mathbf{v}_3|}$$

$$\hat{\mathbf{v}}_{23} = \frac{\mathbf{v}_2 - \mathbf{v}_3}{|\mathbf{v}_2 - \mathbf{v}_3|}$$

$$\hat{\mathbf{v}}_{1p} = \frac{\mathbf{v}_1 - \mathbf{p}}{|\mathbf{v}_1 - \mathbf{p}|}$$

$$\hat{\mathbf{v}}_{2p} = \frac{\mathbf{v}_2 - \mathbf{p}}{|\mathbf{v}_2 - \mathbf{p}|}$$

Then make the scalar products:

$\cos \alpha = \hat{\mathbf{v}}_{13} \cdot \hat{\mathbf{v}}_{23}$
$\cos \beta = \hat{\mathbf{v}}_{1p} \cdot \hat{\mathbf{v}}_{2p}$

Now apply the test:

if ($cos\alpha \geq 0$ and $\cos \beta \geq 0$) Do **not** swap.
else if ($\cos \alpha < 0$ and $\cos \beta < 0$) **Do** swap.
else {
  Calculate:
  $\sin \alpha = |\hat{\mathbf{v}}_{13} \times \hat{\mathbf{v}}_{23}|$
  $\sin \beta = |\hat{\mathbf{v}}_{2p} \times \hat{\mathbf{v}}_{1p}|$
  Then: **if** ($\sin \alpha \cos \beta + \sin \beta \cos \alpha < 0$) **Do** swap.
  else Do **not** swap.
}

Listing 10.5: Algorithm to test whether the edge of the triangle between $\mathbf{v}_1$ and $\mathbf{v}_2$ should be swapped to join $\mathbf{p}$ to $\mathbf{v}_3$; see figure 10.41.

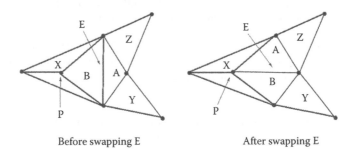

Before swapping E   After swapping E

Figure 10.42: Swapping the edge E will alter which triangles are adjacent to which other triangles not only in those directly affected, those labeled A and B, but also those labeled X and Y. However triangle Z is *not* affected because it remains adjacent to A irrespective of the orientation of edge E.

polygonal cube then a model made from two cubes can be described symbolically as $A + TA$ (where T represents a translation). If you need a model of a cylinder C with a sphere S sitting on top of it you can build a model for C and a model for S and then **or** them together, result $C + S$.

Suppose however you want a model where C pokes through S; something like the illustration of figure 10.43(a). It would be quite difficult to design by hand a

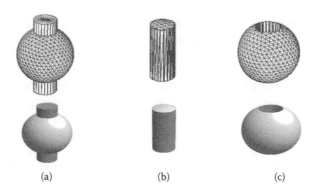

(a)   (b)   (c)

Figure 10.43: (a) *OR-ing* a sphere and cylinder, expressed in Boolean algebra $S + C$. (b) *AND-ing* a sphere and cylinder, Boolean notation: $S \cdot C$. (c) The result of the Boolean expression $S\bar{C}$. We can think of this as *subtracting a cylinder from a sphere*. Notice that the cylinder, which is not visible, appears to cut a hole in the sphere.

mesh of facets to cover such a surface. However since this shape is just another manifestation of $S + C$ if there was an automatic way to go from the meshes for S and C to one for $S + C$ a very useful modeling procedure would result.

Incidentally: To generate an image of the combination $S + C$ with a hidden surface renderer there is no need to work out a mesh for $S + C$. The two components can be used in their original form and the renderer will avoid drawing those parts of the facets of C that lie inside S because they are obscured by S.

If $S + C$ was the only Boolean combination then (from a 3D modeling point of view) there would be no advantage in using it. However $S + C$ is not the only possibility that *Boolean algebra* allows. The other relevant Boolean operations are:

- **not**, written as $\bar{A}$. It's *not* possible to show a picture of $\bar{S}$ or $\bar{C}$ because such a solid fills the whole universe **except** that small volume occupied by S or C. You might argue that **not** is *not* a very useful operation; on its own that's true but when it is used in conjunction with the next operation the true power of "Booleans" as a 3D modeling tool is evident.

- **and**, written as $S \cdot C$ or simply SC. Again **and** is an unfortunate name. The symbols +, and . are much more revealing as to the actual effect of operations if you liken them to the *add* and *multiply* operations of basic algebra. So what of SC (S AND C): This is a solid that occupies the space where S and C overlap; an example is illustrated in figure 10.43(b).

The real power of a Boolean operation as a modeling idiom is that it allows shapes like that shown in figure 10.43(c) to be produced from simple primitives, S and C in that example. We can think of the shape Figure 10.43(c) being the result of the removal of that part of S where S and C overlap. One might call it a **subtractive** operation but strictly speaking it is $S\bar{C}$ (that part of the universe occupied by the sphere and **not** by the cylinder). This *subtractive* operation is exceptionally useful. A number of very important constructional methods are based on the principles of *drilling a hole* or *cutting a bit off*.

In theory it should be possible to build a model of any shape by emulating some combination of Boolean operations on a very small subset of primitive shapes. Indeed this topic is so important it is given the name *constructive solid geometry*. Most CAD applications use some CSG. A number of ray tracing programs are based on the CSG concept because it can reduce the number of elements that need to be rendered in any one scene whilst not restricting the models to a few textured spheres or cubes.

One way to model an object using boolean primitives is to use Boole's notation for combination of primitives and build the model out of primitives. A ray-tracing algorithm is just at home tracing rays through a model described with functional primitives (spheres, cylinders etc.) as it is tracing rays through a set of planar polygonal faces. Alternatively, the surface of a model described by a Boolean combination of primitives can be readily turned into a network of polygonal faces using the marching cubes algorithm described in section 10.10.2.

In the context of a model made with polygonal faces it is more difficult to use the Boolean concept on the mesh because:

1. The models are not based on a relatively small number of primitive shapes but on a large number of flat planar pieces. Therefore there are many more possible configurations that need to be considered and this can take a long time.

2. CSG objects always have a very well defined sense of inside and outside. Faceted models do not necessarily have that sense. Suppose we build a faceted model for a sphere but decide to remove a few facets from one side of it. How could we then use this *open* sphere in Boolean operations?

3. Whereas a CSG representation of say a sphere and a cylinder will produce an intersection that is smooth, if we try the same thing with faceted models the line of intersection will be a jagged edge. This is especially noticeable when the faceted approximation is a coarse one. There is nothing much can be done about this except increase the resolution of the mesh.

4. The facets that result from a *Boolean cutting* operation tend to be poorly shaped, long thin facets. These often occur and tend not to render very well and preclude a lot of additional processing.

5. The algebra of the intersections of bounded planes in three dimensions is very sensitive to the round off errors that occur in computer calculations.

Despite these difficulties some shapes are much more easily modeled using a Boolean *subtraction* operation; for example, the holes in a Swiss cheese. It

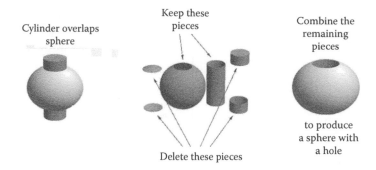

Figure 10.44: The intersection of the faceted models for a sphere S and a cylinder C cuts them into three pieces each. By discarding unwanted pieces a model of the Boolean subtraction $S\bar{C}$ is obtained.

is therefore essential to devise an algorithm that can provide Boolean-like functionality to as good an approximation as possible.

Such an algorithm is presented in this section. The algorithm takes care to produce a triangulation that minimizes the number of small and thin facets and to avoid (where possible) the problems due to round off errors. The algorithm is quite long but it is possible to break it up into a number of sections that can be considered separately and a relatively simple overview of the strategy it uses can also be given. The procedure owes some of its heritage to the ideas of Laidlaw et al. [52].

Before presenting the strategy of the procedure there are a few points that are worth considering:

1. For a computer graphics application we do not need to consider an operation equivalent to Boolean addition. Indeed because a polygonated model might not have a definite inside *subtraction* is also meaningless in some cases. A better way to think of the process is of a model being cut into pieces, some of which will be discarded to leave the appropriate shape; see figure 10.44.

2. With a model made from a collection of triangular facets we must know which facets are doing the cutting and which are being cut. This can be accomplished by making a list of facets that fall into these two groups, we will call these lists:

    (a) The Work list

    (b) The Tool list

    For the example shown in figure 10.44 the facets that make up the sphere S are placed in Work list while those in the cylinder C belong to the Tool list.

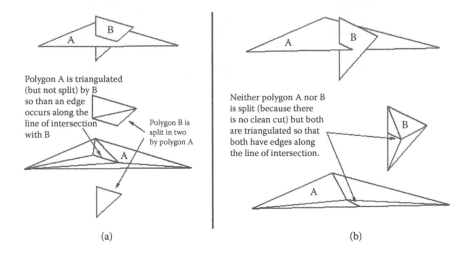

Polygon A is triangulated (but not split) by B so than an edge occurs along the line of intersection with B

Polygon B is split in two by polygon A

Neither polygon A nor B is split (because there is no clean cut) but both are triangulated so that both have edges along the line of intersection.

(a)   (b)

Figure 10.45: An intersection between two triangular polygons. In (a) the polygon labeled B is split in two by polygon A. In (b) neither polygon is split.

3. Breaks in the model occur where the facets from these two lists intersect each other and both sets need to be divided. We can achieve this by first breaking the facets in the Work list along the line of intersection with the facets in the Tool list. When that has been done the lists may be swapped and the algorithm repeated.

4. The intersection occurs along one or more piecewise linear sections which form a path across the surface. Each linear segment occurs as the result of the intersection of two planes. Some of these paths might form closed loops. For example the *line of intersection* between cylinder and sphere in figure 10.44 will consist of two circles on the sphere and two circles on the cylinder.

5. The $S\bar{C}$ operation depicted in figure 10.44 results in both S and C being completely cut into 3 pieces each. However, any Boolean modeling procedure that is based on a network of planar polygons must be able to cope with the possibility that some shapes may not be completely dissected. For example an intersection between two triangular facets might not split either or might split just one of them; see figure 10.45.

Taking these observations into account we can propose a possible algorithm to cut two sets of facets along their line(s) of their intersection as follows:

1. With all facets in the model make two lists: (1) the Work list and (2) the Tool list.

2. Find the line of intersection through the facets of the Work list due to intersection with the facets in the Tool list. Since all the facets are planar the line of intersection will consist of a finite number of straight line segments.

3. Build the line of intersection into the facets of the Work list.

4. Split the facets in the Work list along the line of intersection.

5. Swap the facets in the Tool and Work list and repeat the previous three steps.

Steps 2, 3 and 4 above cover the main actions of the algorithm. However, adding a series of edges into a network of facets is very difficult and so it is preferable to carry out the actions of creating and inserting (steps 2 and 3) at the same time. Thus the line intersection is built into the facets from the Work list at the same time as it is determined.

If we are able to implement these ideas we will have an acceptable procedure for creating separated pieces that are the best approximation to Boolean products one can obtain from a network of polygonal facets. The next sections will expand on the detail of the two main stages (2 and 3).

10.9.1   Determining and incorporating the line of intersection

The first main action of the algorithm is to determine the line of intersection between facets in the Tool and Work lists and to make sure that this is built into the network of Work facets. To see how this works consider the small network shown in plan view in figure 10.46. In (b) the line of intersection is shown and for ease of illustration we will assume that facets in the Work list lie in the plane of the page and facets in the Tool list lie perpendicular to it. Hence they appear as a line in the diagram. Note that the intersection line appears as a number of straight line segments.

Consider now how the line of intersection is determined: It is made up from a number of line segments. So finding the points where these segments begin and end determines the line of intersection. Thus the algorithm is based on the idea that:

> *The segments that go to make up the line of intersection have their end points at the locations where either an edge of a facet in the Work list intersects a facet in the Tool list or where an edge of a facet in the Tool list intersects a facet in the Work list.*

Once we know where these points are everything else follows fairly readily from that; we proceed in two phases:

- Phase 1: For every edge of a facet in the **Tool** list find its point(s) of intersection with a facet in the **Work** list.

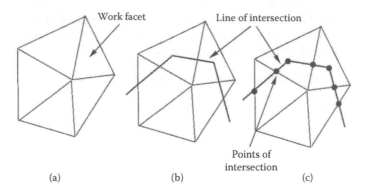

Figure 10.46: (a) A plan view of some facets in the Work list. (b) Adding the (*edge on*) view of facets in the Tool list shows the *line of intersection*. (c) The line of intersection will pass through the points of intersection between edges of facets in the Tool list and facets in the Work list and vice versa. There are **no** other places where it can change direction.

- Phase 2: For every edge of a facet in the **Work** list find its point(s) of intersection with a facet in the **Tool** list.

Figure 10.46(c) highlights where these points are for that particular example.

Now consider another question: How is the line of intersection built into the triangular polygon network given we know the points through which it must pass? And the answer:

> The line of intersection **emerges** *automatically if we insist that as vertices are inserted at the points where edges meet facets the network is constantly updated to make sure that all the facets in it remain triangular.*

Figure 10.47 illustrates the progress of these phases of the algorithm for the example of figure 10.46 and shows how the line of intersection becomes evident with edges along it. In figure 10.47(a) is the initial network; the line of intersection is shown dotted. (b) and (c) insert the two points where the edge of the facets in the Tool list intersect facets in the Work list. In (d), (e), (f), (g) and (h) five points are inserted where the edges of facets in the Work list intersect facets in the Tool list. By the time all points have been inserted, at (h), edges along the full length of the intersection have been created. Diagram (i) highlights the resultant line of intersection along these edges.

All of this looks quite straightforward and for the example shown it is. Unfortunately however both phases can be plagued by the creation of too many edges and facets. To see how this might occur consider again the example shown in figure 10.47. After Phase 1 is complete, in diagram (c), six new edges are associated with facets in the Work list; there are four additional facets too. These edges must themselves be used during Phase 2 to check for intersection with the

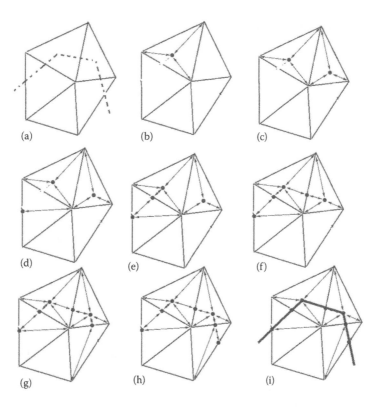

Figure 10.47: Inserting the points of intersection between the edges of facets in the Work and Tool lists one at a time into the network of Work facets produces edges lying along the line of intersection. Illustrations (a) to (i) are discussed in the text.

Tool facets. In the example of figure 10.47 they don't intersect any of the tool facets but that's just the case in this particular example.

There is another problem that is manifest in Phase 1 itself. Look at the example in figure 10.48. The Work list consists of one facet only and all the facets in the Tool list intersect it. Inserting the points of intersection in the order 1, 2, 3, 4 gives configuration (d) at the end of Phase 1. Phase 2 completes the triangulation but at the price of the inclusion of another point P as shown in (e).

To be specific: In (a) the single facet is cut by facets in the Tool list (shown edge on, this is equivalent to the line of intersection too). This gives rise to four intersection points as shown in (b) and labeled in the order in which they are to be inserted. After the first point is inserted the Work facet is shown divided in three (c). When Phase 1 is completed the triangulation (d) is the result. After checking **all** the edges in the work facet for intersection with facets in the Tool list the final triangulation with edges along the full length of the intersection line is

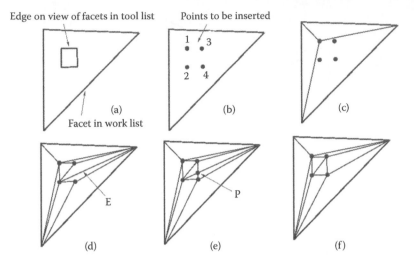

Figure 10.48: Triangulating an insertion in the Boolean algorithm. Details of illustrations (a) to (f) are discussed in the text.

produced (e). However, if the edge E in (d) had been "flipped" the triangulation (f) would have been produced. None of the edges in (f) intersect any of the Tool facets and the full length of the line of intersection is completely covered without the need for the extra point P.

Configuration (e) is unsatisfactory because the extra point P is unnecessary. Configuration (f) is much more acceptable but to achieve it the edge labeled E had to be flipped so that it joined points 3 and 4. Fortunately we have already discussed an algorithm that does just this (Delaunay triangulation) in section 10.8. To apply the Delaunay procedure to Phase 1 of this stage in the Boolean algorithm we consider each facet in the Work list separately. Every facet in the Work list is considered as a Delaunay supertriangle and is used to produce a *best* triangulation with any intersection points that fall inside it. After all the intersection points are inserted however the supertriangle is not deleted. Figure 10.49 illustrates the result of performing two Delaunay triangulations in two work facets A and B.

Thus the algorithm for Phase 1 may be summarized as follows:

Repeat the following with all the edges i of the facets in the Tool list   {
    Repeat the following with all the facets j in the Work list   {
        if edge i intersects facet j at point P {
            Add P into a Delaunay triangulation with
            facet j as the original supertriangle.
        }
    }
}

Edge on view of facets in the tool list

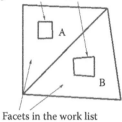
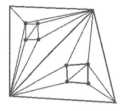

Facets in the work list

Build Delaunay triangulation
in both triangles A and B

Figure 10.49: Delaunay triangulations are built (independently) in facets A and B which are the entries in the Work list at the start of the algorithm.

There are a couple of observations that we will need to consider carefully when implementing the algorithm for Phase 1:

1. If it turns out that a point to be inserted just happens to hit an edge e of the growing Delaunay triangulation it must be left out. We do this because in Phase 2 the intersection of e with a facet in the Tool list will create a point at the same place and if it were inserted in Phase 1 it would create an infinitesimally thin facet which might not be removed by the Delaunay procedure.

2. We must also be careful to use not only edges from Tool facets that cross Work facets but also edges where the vertex at one end actually lies in the plane of the Work facet.

These two observations are made because they are significantly influenced by round-off error in calculations. *Numerical problems caused by the limited accuracy to which computers calculate implies that there are always going to be a few configurations of Work and Tool facets that result in a Boolean operation failing.*

Now consider the actions of Phase 2:

> *Take each edge of the facets in the Work list (including the edges and facets added in Phase 1), find their point of intersection with the facets in the Tool list and build these points into the network of Work facets.*

We cannot use a Delaunay procedure in this phase because the intersections are occurring at the edge of a facet rather than in its interior. This will affect facets on both sides of the edge and they will have to be divided so that both remain triangular. We will also have to be careful because when an edge is created in Phase 2 it has the potential to intersect other facets in the Tool list, indeed possibly one that has already been checked.

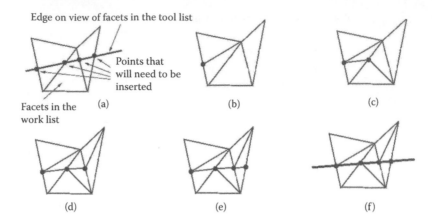

Figure 10.50: The first part of Phase 2 finds the point of intersection between Tool facets and the edges of Work facets. If an intersection occurs then the edge is divided in two and the facets on both sides are split.

It turns out that by a careful re-arrangement, somewhat analogous to the Delaunay *triangle flipping* procedure, it is possible to ensure that edges created in Phase 2 will not intersect any facet. They will either:

1. stop short of a facet, or

2. lie in the plane of a Tool facet and thus be part of the line of intersection.

In Phase 2 the edges associated with facets in the Work list are processed twice. In the first pass those edges arising from facets in the Work list as it stands after Phase 1 are tested. If an intersection occurs a vertex is added at the point of intersection and the facets on both sides of the edges are split. Note that the four facets and two edges created by the split are considered to be in the Work list but they play no role in the first pass. This process is illustrated in figure 10.50.

In the first pass any edges that lie in the plane of a Tool facet are marked because they contribute a segment to the line of intersection. The second pass uses an iterative procedure to rearrange the edges added in the first pass and it terminates when no edges of a Work facet cross any of the Tool facets.

To see what the iterative procedure does consider the example shown in Figure 10.51. In (a) a single facet is held in the Work list and the facets in the Tool list form two separate pieces. In this example no edge of any facets in the Tool list intersects a facet in the Work list and therefore the only points of intersection arise in Phase 2 at the four points indicated in (b). The points are to be inserted in the order 1, 2, 3, 4. The triangulations shown in (c), (d), (e) and (f) illustrate the network as each point is built in.

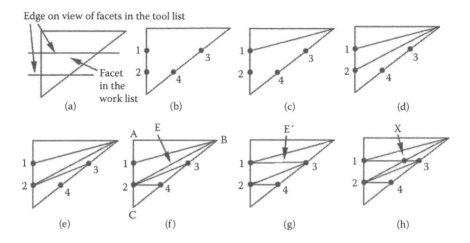

Figure 10.51: This example is discussed in the text.

On comparing triangulation (f) (figure 10.51) with the view (a) it can be seen that the edge joining points $(2-4)$ lies in the plane of one of the Tool facets and is therefore part of the line of intersection. Of the other internal edges created in Phase 2 it is only the edge E, joining point 2 to vertex B (B is a vertex of the original triangle), which still intersects a facet in the Tool list. All the other edges do not cross a facet in the Tool list. For the next step the edge labeled E will either have to be split, as in diagram (h), or flipped, as in diagram (g) so that E' joins vertices $(1-3)$. Triangulation (h) with its extra vertex X is obviously less desirable than triangulation (g) and it is the job of the iterative procedure to seek out edges like E and flip them.

Unfortunately, simply looking for internal edges created in the first part of Phase 2 which intersect a Tool facet and then flipping them is not satisfactory in some cases. The example shown in figure 10.52 illustrates the problem. Both edges, e_1 and e_2, intersect a facet in the Tool list. However if edge e_1 is flipped the resulting triangulation will have overlapping facets and this is **most** undesirable. The reason that facets overlap is that after flipping, the edge e_1 no longer lies inside the quadrilateral formed by facets f_1 and f_2. In fact a flip will result in overlapping facets if either of the angles α or β are $\geq \pi$. Thus we must not allow edges such as e_1 to be flipped if $\alpha \geq \pi$ or $\beta \geq \pi$.

Of course it is unacceptable to leave e_1 so that it crosses a Tool facet. Fortunately the edge e_2 can be flipped and when that is done it becomes possible to also flip edge e_1. As a result an appropriate triangulation is created with edges along all parts of the line of intersection. This is illustrated in figure 10.53.

These sections of the line of intersection
are completed. They should be joined but
edges e_1 and e_2 are in the way.

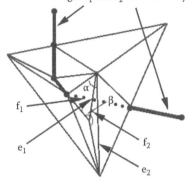

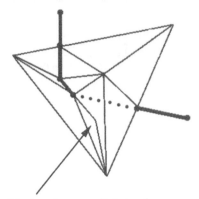

Flipping edge e_1 results in two faces
overlapping here which has unsatisfactory
consequences.

Figure 10.52: A configuration in which the edges e_1 and e_2 intersect a facet in the
Tool list. Flipping e_1 will result, at best, in a triangulation with overlapping facets or
at worst cause subsequent steps to get stuck in an infinite loop!

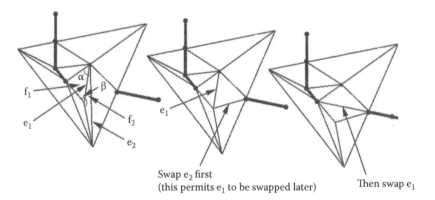

Swap e_2 first
(this permits e_1 to be swapped later)   Then swap e_1

Figure 10.53: Flipping edge e_2 first allows edge e_1 to be flipped without creating an
overlap and produce a triangulation with edges covering the line of intersection.

Because an algorithmic procedure can only consider edges in the order in
which they are stored and cannot *know* which edge to flip first, it must *iterate*.
All candidate edges are tested for intersection with a Tool facet. If they intersect
but can't be flipped a flag is raised and the process continues trying to flip the
remainder. After all the edges have been tested and if the flag is raised the tests
are repeated (iterated) until no edges intersect a Tool facet. This process relies on
the fact that if an edge to be flipped does not currently satisfy the interior angle

First pass of Phase 2
Repeat the following for each Tool facet i {
    Repeat the following for each edge j of the Work facets   {
        if edge j lies in the plane of facet i {
            Mark edge j as a boundary edge
          }
        else if edge j intersects facet i {
            Split j in two at the point of intersection and divide the
            two facets that lie on either side of j
          }
      }
}

Second pass of Phase 2
Repeat the following for each Tool facet i {
    LOOP: This is the loop back to point of the iteration.
    Set iteration flag: $f = 0$
    Repeat the following for each edge j of the Work facets {
        Skip any edge that was not added during the first part of Phase 2
        Skip any edge that is part of the line of intersection.
        (Both these type of edges must be left in place because
        they are important in defining the outline shape of the model.)
        if edge j lies in the plane of facet i {
            Mark edge j as a boundary edge
        }
        else if edge j intersects facet i {
            if edge j cannot be flipped raise the flag: $f = 1$
            else {
                Flip edge j so that it becomes *the other* diagonal of the
                quadrilateral formed by the two facets on either side of edge j.
                If (after flipping) edge j lies in the plane of facet i mark it as
                part of the line of intersection.
            }
        }
      }
    if $f = 1$ (flag raised) jump back to LOOP
}

Listing 10.6: The procedure for Phase 2 of the first part of the *Boolean cutting algorithm*.

constraint then flipping another edge will cause conditions to change making it possible to achieve the required flip (in a subsequent iteration). Fortunately this will always happen because of the way in which the original configuration was derived.

Taking all these features into account Phase 2 of this part of the algorithm is summarized in listing 10.6.

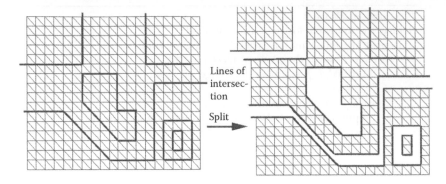

Figure 10.54: Lines of intersection that split a network of facets. Note that the part of the line of intersection labeled X does not cause a split.

10.9.2   Splitting facets along the line of intersection

Having built the line of intersection into the facets in the Work list it only remains to split them along it. Of course the network or *Work* facets will not be split unless segments of the line of intersection form a complete cut, either by forming loops or crossing from one outside edge to another. This is illustrated in figure 10.54.

This stage of the algorithm is quite straightforward because the procedure of section 10.9.1 has already marked which edges in the model are part of the line of intersection. With this knowledge the following steps will cut the facets in the work list along the line(s) of intersection if they split the network:

1. Set a counter l (initially to: $l = -1$). This will be used to count the number of pieces and identify to which piece each facet belongs. Label all facets in the work list as unidentified. This can be done by assigning a member of the facet data structure $Facet(i).l = l$.

2. Repeat steps (a) and (b) below until all Work facets are identified. (This procedure is very similar to the "orienting" algorithm of section 10.7.)

   (a) Increment l and pick an unidentified facet, say it is k. We could choose it to be the first one for which $Facet(k).l = -1$. Assign $Facet(k).l = l$.

   (b) Find the neighboring facets to facet k; this information is recorded in the $Fid(j)$ member variables for the facet data structure. Let $n = Facet(k).Fid(j)$ with $0 \leq j < 3$ in turn. If the edge common to facets n and k (given by $Facet(k).Eid(j)$) is **not** part of the line of intersection then n is in the same piece as k and we repeat (recursively) this step in facet n and in n's neighboring facets until progress is blocked either by the line of intersection or the edge of the model.

Note that the Eid and Fid can be determined by the algorithm given in section 3.5 and that they are also kept up to date by the Delaunay algorithm, as it flips edges and facets around.

3. Once all facets have been identified as belonging to one of the l pieces repeat step (a) below for each $i : 0 \leq i < l$.

   (a) Make a copy of all the facets with $Facet(k).l = i$.

   When copying facet k remember that the vertices it is attached to and the edges which bound it must also be copied. Care will be needed to make sure that no edge or vertex is copied twice, for example from adjacent facets with a common edge.

4. Remove from the database all the facets, edges and vertices recorded in the Work list.

   Note: It may be easier to make copies of all the relevant bits and remove the originals rather than to try and copy the structure along the line of intersection.

Figure 10.55 illustrates the identification of facets up to a boundary or line of intersection. Note that if the edge of intersection does not completely split the network of facets then they will be identified as part of the same piece; this is desirable. To be specific: In figure 10.55: (a) The edges that form the line of intersection are highlighted. (b) Choose any facet at random and label this as being part of the first piece. (c) Label the facets adjacent to the first one chosen unless that facet is on the other side of the outline. (d) Finish labeling all facets adjacent to those identified with a 0; remember a boundary may not be crossed. When there are no facets adjacent to 0 remaining choose another at random and label this 1. (e) Label with a 1 the facets adjacent to the facet labeled 1 in (d). (f) Label with a 1 the facets adjacent to the facets labeled 1 in (e). (g) Finish labeling all possible facets adjacent to those facets labeled 1 in (f). Pick another at random and label this 2. (h) Label all possible facets adjacent to the one labeled 2 in (f). Since there are no unidentified facets left the identification is complete. (i) Copy all the facets labeled 1, 2 and 3 as separate pieces and delete the originals. This gives us the three pieces formed by the cutting operation.

10.10   Metaball modeling and marching cubes

There are shapes that do not lend themselves to modeling with any of the algorithms considered in this chapter, or even with an interactive design tool in which the user has a free hand. This is especially true of many organic shapes. Another source of three-dimensional data, laser scanners and stereoscopic imaging systems produce a *point cloud* of data that represents the shape of the object. Before a point cloud of 3D data can be visualized the surface needs to be *meshed* into

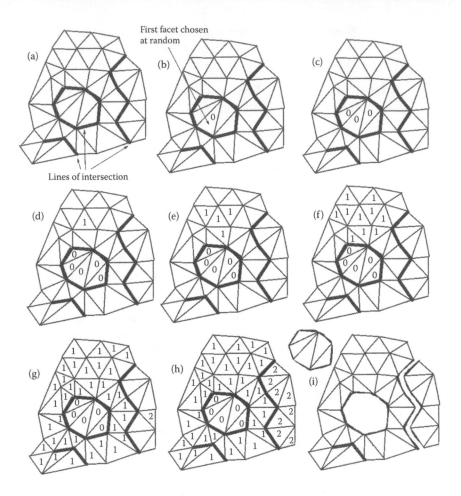

Figure 10.55: Identifying the pieces to be split up. Illustrations (a) - (i) are discussed in the text.

a network of polygonal faces. This is not a trivial task, and a mesh generated in this way can be very messy. Some manual tidying up is often inevitable. A third source of data that is often visualized as a 3D model is a potential field, where the visualization takes the form of a triangular mesh built across an equi-potential surface. Several layers may be superimposed with transparency. Medical image data and the results of scientific experiments are excellent examples of this sort of problem.

This section will dive into the concept and the algorithms of two techniques that allow us to visualize volume data and build mesh models through a combination of potential fields. Some of the plug-in modules of OpenFX (chapter 9)

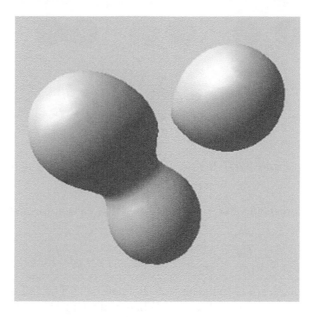

Figure 10.56: An example of a metaball model. Three metaballs are shown here, with two of them overlapping to form an amalgamated shape.

offer source code examples for the algorithms discussed here. We start by looking at metaballs and move on to consider the marching cubes algorithm for meshing and rendering equi-potential surfaces. The visualization of a metaball (or as it is sometimes known, blobby modeling) requires the visualization of an equi-potential surface, which is done using marching cubes.

10.10.1   Metaballs

A metaball model (see figure 10.56) is made up by combining a number of potential fields and generating a surface that joins up every place where the field takes the same value. This is known as an equi-potential or iso-surface. Each metaball is defined as a function in n-dimensions. In three dimensions this is simply a function of position $f(x, y, z)$. Metaballs can also be used to generate two-dimensional contours, in which case the function is $f(x, y)$.

The algorithm starts by specifying a threshold value and potential function to define the surface of the metaball, thus,

$$\sum_{i=1}^{n} f_i(x, y, z) \leq t \tag{10.2}$$

represents the volume enclosed by the surface. (f is the potential function and

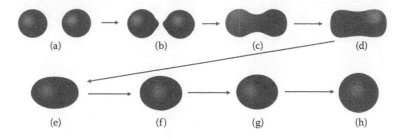

Figure 10.57: Metaballs form by amalgamating potential fields.

t is the threshold value.) A typical function chosen for metaballs is:

$$f(x,y,z) = \frac{1}{((x-x_0)^2 + (y-y_0)^2 + (z-z_0)^2)} \qquad (10.3)$$

where (x_0, y_0, z_0) is the center of the metaball. The fall-off function should go to zero at a maximum distance. When evaluating the metaball field, any points beyond the maximum distance from the center point are ignored. Because the iso-surface is the result of adding the fields together, its smoothness is dependent on the smoothness of the fall-off curves. When metaball fields start to interact the result is shown in figure 10.57.

The arrangement of metaballs shown in figure 10.56 was created by three metaballs using the field function $p_{(x,y,z)}$ given by:

$$\left(\sum_{i=1}^{n} \frac{r_i^2}{|\mathbf{d}_i^2|} \right) - t = 0 \qquad (10.4)$$

where: r_i is the radius of the metaball, and $\mathbf{d}^i$ is the vector between $P_{(x,y,z)}$ and the center of the metaball.

Metaballs do not have to be based on spherical fields surrounding a point. They can be based on a cylindrical field surrounding a line, or even lie around an planar polygon, or any 3D shape, and they can be very effective when animated. Figures 10.58 and 10.59 illustrate how a set of metaballs can be visualized; this is taken from OpenFX.

10.10.2   Marching cubes

At the core of the visualization of metaball generated equi-potential surfaces is the marching cubes algorithm. The same algorithm will render any equi-potential surface in a potential field, and can be used to render a non-convex hull around a point cloud, such as that shown in figure 10.59.

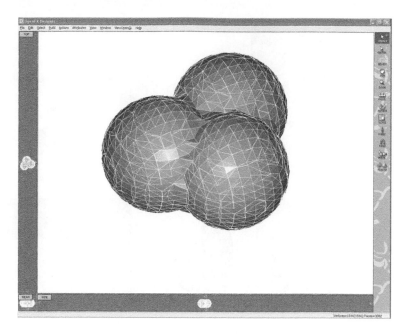

Figure 10.58: Three spherical metaballs are triangulated using the marching cubes algorithm of section 10.10.2.

The marching cubes algorithm is a natural extension of the two-dimensional marching squares algorithm that is used to draw a contour at a specific value of a 2D potential field. Marching squares has great utility in drawing height contours on a map or isobars on a weather map. It is much easier to understand the algorithm's concept in two dimensions and there are many fewer configurations that have to considered.

To appreciate the marching squares algorithm consider the grid shown in figure 10.60. Each point of this grid is given a weight (a potential value), and in this example the reference potential value is 5. To draw a curve whose value is constant and equal to the reference value, each square in the grid is individually considered. Those grid squares where every one of its four vertices is either below the reference value, or every one of its four vertices have a value above the reference value, will have no segments of the contour passing through them.

Where some corner potential values lie above and below the reference value then the contour will pass through that square. Careful consideration of all possible combinations (above/below) indicates there are only 16 possible configurations required to represent all possible ways the contour can pass through the 2D squares. There are some possible combinations illustrated in figure 10.61 that are ambiguous; these are labeled A. The ambiguity, which is illustrated in figure 10.62, does not imply any real error because the contours remain closed.

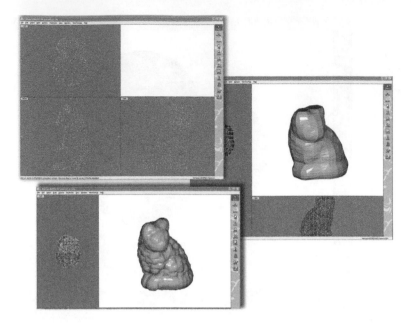

Figure 10.59: A point cloud of vertices gives rise to a meta-surface by placing a metaball at each vertex and meshing the equi-potential surface.

The concept of the marching squares algorithm can be naturally extended to three dimensions where the squares become cubes that have 8 vertices per cube and the line segments that made up the contour become polygonal faces that make up the equi-potential surface (iso-surface). Each cube will either lie inside the iso-surface, or outside the iso-surface, or it will straddle the iso-surface. With each cube having 8 vertices there are 256 (i.e., 2^8) possible arrangements of its corners being inside or outside the volume enclosed by the iso-surface. However, taking into account symmetries (rotation, mirroring and re-labeling) this reduces to only 16 possibilities. Figure 10.63 depicts the possible combinations and the triangulations that have to be constructed to produce the closed surface for that part of the iso-surface that lies inside the cube.

In order to be able to determine which of the 16 cases apply to a specific set of vertex potential values, each of the 16 cases is assigned an index formed from a binary interpretation of whether a corner (vertex) potential value is above or below the equi-potential surface; see figure 10.64.

In this way, vertices from 1 to 8 are weighted from 1 to 128 (v1 = 1, v2 = 2, v3 = 4, etc.); for example, the case 3 (figure 10.63) corresponds to the number 5 (v1 and v3 are outside, $1 + 4 = 5$). By using the corner weights in this way a fast look-up table can be constructed to define how many polygons need to be created for each of the 16 possible configurations and along which edges of the

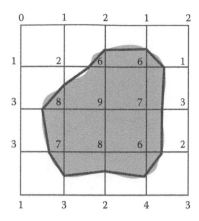

Figure 10.60: A square grid with potential field values (of some nominal unit) at each grid point. A contour with the value of 5 is shown after interpolation. The shaded area equates to the area where the potential field's value is greater than 5.

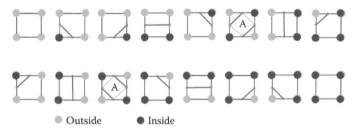

Outside   Inside

Figure 10.61: The 16 combinations of grid square crossings that depend on the values of the field at the corner vertices relative to the contour.

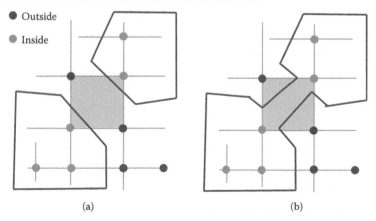

Outside

Inside

(a)   (b)

Figure 10.62: In the ambiguous cases the contours could be connected in two different ways for the same pattern of vertex potential field values.

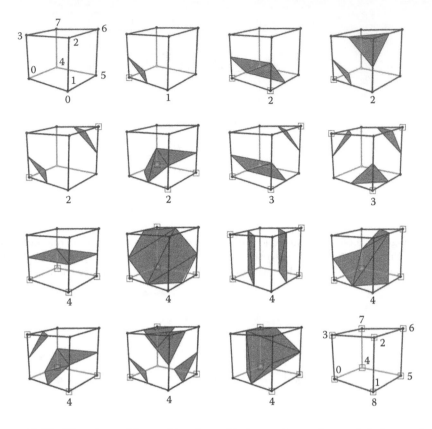

Figure 10.63: The 16 possible combinations of in/out cube vertices and their associated triangulation.

cube, and where their surface vertices have to be positioned. Thus the algorithm can be expressed in a few simple steps:

1. Break up space into small cubes (> 1,000,000,000).

2. Consider each cube in turn.

3. Calculate an index by comparing the 8 corner density values with the iso-surface value.

4. Using this index look up the list of edges from a pre-calculated table (the edges around each triangle).

5. Interpolate the position of the intersection along the edge using the density values at the vertices at each end of the edge.

6. Calculate a normal at each vertex.

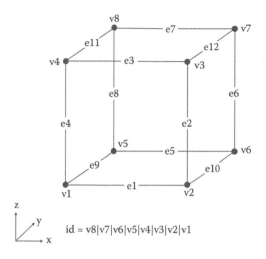

Figure 10.64: Weights assigned to each cube's vertices.

7. Output the triangle vertices and normals.

To implement this algorithm in practice we need to define some data structures, first a 3D vector. There are many ways to do this, for this example we choose:

```
typedef struct {
  float x;
  float y;
  float z;
} VECTOR3D;
```

Next, a structure is needed for each grid point in the cubic lattice. This structure might include other data that is interpolated across the cell.

```
// cube grid vertex
typedef struct {
  VECTOR3D position; // position of the grid vertex
  float value;  //the value of the scalar field
  .. // other data
} CUBE_GRID_VERTEX;
```

New vertices will be inserted along edges where the potential values at either end of the edge bracket the iso-surface value. This structure might include the identity of the CUBE_GRID_VERTICES that it separates.

```
//vertex created from the linear interpolation along edge
typedef struct {
  VECTOR3D p; // position
  .. ..other data
```

```
} SURFACE_VERTEX;
```

Each cube in the lattice will need to identify which vertices (data points) surround it.

```
typedef struct {
  CUBE_GRID_VERTEX  *vertices[8];  //pointers to vertices
} CUBE_GRID_CUBE;
```

And finally we will use a structure to reference the whole system by providing references to the vertices and cubes in the lattice.

```
typedef struct {
  int numVertices;  // number of vertices
  CUBE_GRID_VERTEX * vertices;  // list of vertices
  int numCubes;  // number of cubes
  CUBE_GRID_CUBE * cubes;       // list of cubes
} CUBE_GRID;
```

The full code is available as a download. Here we highlight the important structures that map onto the algorithm. Probably the most important data structures are the lookup tables that allow us to use the inside/outside data for each cube's vertices to build the surface triangles on the part of the iso-surface lying within that cube. Listing 10.7 shows a few of the entries in these three vital tables.

The verticesAtEndsOfEdges[] table has two entries for each of the 12 edges of the cube. Each pair indicates which of the eight vertices, numbered 0 to 7, lie at the ends of the edges. It is used in interpolating the position of any surface vertex that will lie somewhere along the edge.

The edgeTable[] uses the inside/outside code (the ID value in figure 10.64) calculated from the combination of field values at the vertices to identify which of the 12 cube edges will cross the iso-surface. The pattern of triangles to be built among the vertices added on the cube edges due to its intersection with the iso-surface, is given in the last table: triTable []. In triTable [], there are up to 5 triples of identifiers for the list of iso-surface vertices that will be positioned somewhere along the edges of the cube. A (-1) in the data indicates that there are no further triangles needed for this inside/outside arrangement of cube vertex potential values.

A single instance of the CUBE_GRID structure is used to define the cubic lattice that fills the space around the region of the potential field that is to have one of its equi-potential surfaces (iso-surface) triangulated. A maximum grid size needs to be defined so that we can determine the resolution of the surface mesh, and memory buffers for this data can be created dynamically:

```
// maxGridSize defines the dimensions of the lattice
// enclosing the potential field
BOOL CUBE_GRID_CreateMemory(CUBE_GRID *g){
  g->vertices=(CUBE_GRID_VERTEX *)
```

```
//Table gives the vertices at the end of each edge
int verticesAtEndsOfEdges[24]=
{0, 1,
 .. ,
 3, 7};
```

```
// Table identifies which of 12 cude edges will cross the iso-surface.
// Each entry is a bit pattern corresponding with an edge either crossing
// or not crossing the threshold value. There is one entry for each of
// the 256 possible arrangements of the 8 vertex states (in/out)
int edgeTable[256]={
0x0   , 0x109, 0x203, 0x30a, 0x406, 0x50f, 0x605, 0x70c,
0x80c, 0x905, 0xa0f, 0xb06, 0xc0a, 0xd03, 0xe09, 0xf00,
..
0x70c, 0x605, 0x50f, 0x406, 0x30a, 0x203, 0x109, 0x0   };
```

```
//This table gives which of the vertices, added along the cube edges where
//they cross the iso-surface, to join to form triangles for the surface
//(-1) indicates no more groups of 3 (max of 5 triangles per cube
int triTable[256][16] ={
{-1,-1,-1,-1,-1,-1,-1,-1,-1,-1,-1,-1,-1,-1,-1,-1},
{0,1,9,-1,-1,-1,-1,-1,-1,-1,-1,-1,-1,-1,-1,-1},
..
{1,8,3,9,8,1,-1,-1,-1,-1,-1,-1,-1,-1,-1,-1},
..
{2,8,3,2,10,8,10,9,8,-1,-1,-1,-1,-1,-1,-1},
..
{-1,-1,-1,-1,-1,-1,-1,-1,-1,-1,-1,-1,-1,-1,-1,-1}
};
```

Listing 10.7: The lookup tables for the marching cubes algorithm.

```
malloc(sizeof(CUBE_GRID_VERTEX)*
(maxGridSize+1)*(maxGridSize+1)*(maxGridSize+1));
if(!g->vertices) { return FALSE; }
g->cubes=(CUBE_GRID_CUBE*)malloc(sizeof(CUBE_GRID_CUBE)*
 maxGridSize*maxGridSize*maxGridSize);
if(!g->cubes) {  return FALSE; }
return TRUE;
}
```

The instances of the structure representing the cubes need to be initialized, the vertices at the lattice points within each cube need to be positioned and given a value or the potential field, and each cube needs to have its list of corner vertices assigned. This is done in listing 10.8.

```
BOOL CUBE_GRID_Init(CUBE_GRID *g, int gridSize){
  int i,j,k;
  int currentCube;
  int currentVertex=0;
  g->numVertices=(gridSize+1)*(gridSize+1)*(gridSize+1);
  // assign lattice vertex positions, this example is based on a cubic
  // lattice centred on (0,0,0) and filling the cube [-10,10]
  for(i=0; i<gridSize+1; i++) {
   for(j=0; j<gridSize+1; j++){
    for(k=0; k<gridSize+1; k++){
     g->vertices[currentVertex].p.x=
        (i*20.0f)/(gridSize)-10.0f;
     ..    // other positions
     currentVertex++;
    }
   }
  }
  g->numCubes=(gridSize)*(gridSize)*(gridSize);
  currentCube=0;
  // assign the vertices around each cube
  for(i=0; i<gridSize; i++) {
   for(j=0; j<gridSize; j++) {
    for(k=0; k<gridSize; k++)    {
     g->cubes[currentCube].vertices[0]=
       &g->vertices[(i*(gridSize+1)+j)*(gridSize+1)+k];
     g->cubes[currentCube].vertices[1]=
        &g->vertices[(i*(gridSize+1)+j)*(gridSize+1)+k+1];
     ...    // other vertex assignments
     currentCube++;
    }
   }
  }
  return TRUE;
}
```

Listing 10.8: Setting up the lattice coordinates with their field values.

Once the lookup tables are established and the preparatory work done in listings 10.7 and 10.8 completed, the implementation of the marching cubes algorithm in listing 10.9 can be executed.

The implementation of the algorithm proceeds by considering each cube in turn as a individual entity. The code in listing 10.9 fulfills the following logic:

1. Work out which of the patterns (using the ID value of figure 10.64) of iso-surface faces is required for the cube, based on the value of the field at the cube's vertices. This is the variable cubeIndex.

```
void CUBE_GRID_DrawSurface(CUBE_GRID *g, float threshold){
 //local storage up to 12 possible vertices for any iso-surface in cube
 static SURFACE_VERTEX edgeVertices[12];
 for( i=0; i<g->numCubes; i++){//loop through cubes
  //calculate which vertex pattern to apply
  //based on cube vertex values
  if(g->cubes[i].vertices[0]->value < threshold)
    cubeIndex |= 1;
  if(g->cubes[i].vertices[1]->value < threshold)
    cubeIndex |= 2;
  ... // set indices for the other vertices
  //look-up this value in edge table to see which edges to interpolate along
  usedEdges=edgeTable[cubeIndex];
  //if the cube is entirely within/outside surface, or has no faces
  if(usedEdges==0 || usedEdges==255)continue;
  //check each edge to see if it should have an iso-surface vertex
  for(currentEdge=0; currentEdge<12; currentEdge++) {
   if(usedEdges & 1<<currentEdge) {
    CUBE_GRID_VERTEX *v1,*v2; // get the cube edge's vertices
    ve1=verticesAtEndsOfEdges[currentEdge*2];
    ve2=verticesAtEndsOfEdges[currentEdge*2+1];
    v1=g->cubes[i].vertices[ve1];
    v2=g->cubes[i].vertices[ve2];
    // intepolate to put iso-surface vertex along cube edge
    delta=(threshold - v1->value)/(v2->value - v1->value);
    edgeVertices[currentEdge].position.x= . . . .
   }
  }
  //make the triangular faces in this cube 3 vertices per face
  for(k=0; triTable[cubeIndex][k]!=-1; k+=3){
   MakeTriangleFaceAt(
      &edgeVertices[triTable[cubeIndex][k+0]].p,
      &edgeVertices[triTable[cubeIndex][k+1]].p,
      &edgeVertices[triTable[cubeIndex][k+2]].p)
  }
 }
}
```

Listing 10.9: Executing the marching cubes algorithm.

2. Using cubeIndex, look up the edge table to identify which of the cube's edges will cross the iso-surface.

3. Consider each edge of the current cube in turn: If it crosses the iso-surface determine where, and record this in the edgeVertices [] list. If none of the cube's edges cross the iso-surface just ignore this cube.

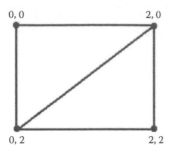
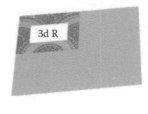

Figure 10.65: The result of assigning texture coordinates to the vertices of two triangular facets.

4. Finally, build the triangular mesh by using the pattern of faces appropriate for the cube's ID. Table triTable [] holds the triangular face information by indexing the edgeVertices [] list. The coordinates of the triangles' vertices will be found in the edgeVertices [] list.

In this implementation of the marching cubes algorithm each polygon is created as a separate face. The network is not connected and each face's vertices are independent of all the other vertices. To be useful in a 3D modeling package where vertices from neighboring faces occur at the same point, the faces should really share the same vertices, and where the edges of a face are common to other faces then only one edge should be inserted into the data structures. This could be done in a post-creation sorting stage, but it would be preferable if the code presented here were modified to do this as the face data is being created. To do this would require that each cube keeps a record of its 26 immediate neighbors so that when a new face is added a check is made to see whether any of its edges or vertices have been created before in a neighboring cube. The use of an integer based coordinate system for vertices makes this step very much more robust.

10.11   Texture coordinate generation

In section 4.6 the use of texture coordinates was discussed. It was not stated there how texture coordinates are generated. It was stated that images were applied to a two-dimensional *texture* coordinate system (X, Y) (commonly referred to as (u, v) coordinates) and that a single copy of the image occupied the region in which the coordinates satisfied: $0 \leq X < 1.0$, $0 \leq Y < 1.0$.

One obvious way to assign texture coordinates is by hand. The example in Figure 10.65 shows two triangular facets with texture coordinates and a rendered picture with the image shown mapped across the facets.

Manual assignment is however only satisfactory if very few facets are involved. An automatic procedure that assigns mapping coordinates according to some

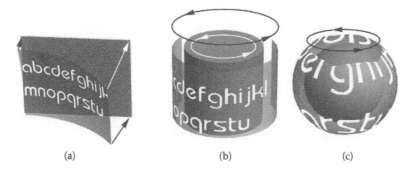

Figure 10.66: Projected image texture mapping: (a) A planar map. (b) A cylindrical map. (c) A spherical map.

more usable scheme is essential if we are to apply maps to models with many facets and non-planar geometry. It turns out that three basic formats provide map coverage for almost all situations. They are:

1. Planar mapping

2. Cylindrical mapping

3. Spherical mapping

These are illustrated in figure 10.66.

Planar mapping is the most appropriate method of application when the surface to be covered is approximately flat. Cylindrical and spherical mapping are most appropriate when the surfaces to be painted are approximately cylindrical or spherical. Since it is impossible to achieve an undistorted mapping from a plane to a cylinder or plane to a sphere it is obvious that at least these three types of mapping must be available. Most potential uses for an image map are covered by one of these three cases.

From a usability point of view each of these mapping methods requires only a few parameters for their specification. Texture coordinates for each vertex are readily calculated from one of these mapping methods.

10.11.1 Planar mapping

Figure 10.67(a) illustrates the mapping relationship. A network of triangular facets is shown overlapped by a rectangle R, which is assumed to bound the image being mapped. The question then is: What are the mapping coordinates of any vertex, V, in the network of facets?

The case shown in figure 10.67(a) doesn't tell the whole story because the facets are located in three dimensions and whilst ideally they should be planar so that the map is not distorted, they don't have to be. Neither do they have to

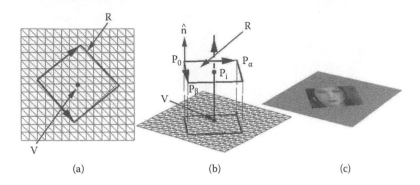

(a)   (b)   (c)

Figure 10.67: (a) A rectangle bounding the image to be mapped is shown overlapping a network of facets. (b) A three-dimensional view of the same situation that shows how the mapping rectangle R is projected on to the surface at right angles to R. (c) Rendering the facets after assignment with mapping coordinates.

lie in the plane of R and therefore to obtain mapping coordinates for V we must assume that the mapping coordinates are determined by a projection in three dimensions from R to V; this is illustrated in figure 10.67(b).

The procedure for determining mapping coordinates at V is as follows: A straight line through V (given by position vector $\mathbf{P}_v$) is constructed in the direction of the normal to the plane of R, i.e., parallel to the normal to R (say $\hat{\mathbf{n}}$). It intersects the plane in which R lies at the point $\mathbf{P}_i$. Since $\mathbf{P}_i$ is in the plane of R it can be expressed as a linear combination of the two vectors along the sides of R. Thus if R is defined by the three points $\mathbf{P}_0$, $\mathbf{P}_\alpha$ and $\mathbf{P}_\beta$, the vectors along the edges are: $\mathbf{P}_\beta - \mathbf{P}_0$ and $\mathbf{P}_\alpha - \mathbf{P}_0$. The algorithm from section 2.11.1 will allow us to find an α and β which satisfy:

$$\mathbf{P}_i = \mathbf{P}_0 + \alpha(\mathbf{P}_\alpha - \mathbf{P}_0) + \beta(\mathbf{P}_\beta - \mathbf{P}_0)$$

$\mathbf{P}_i$ is obtained by calculating the intersection point in the plane of R: $(\mathbf{p} - \mathbf{P}_0) \cdot \hat{\mathbf{n}} = 0$ and the line: $\mathbf{p} = \mathbf{P}_v + \alpha\hat{\mathbf{n}}$. (See Section 2.6.)

The mapping coordinates of V follow by assuming that at $\mathbf{P}_0$ the mapping coordinates are $(0,0)$, at $\mathbf{P}_\alpha$ they are $(1,0)$ and at $\mathbf{P}_\beta$ they are $(0,1)$ and therefore at V the (X_v, Y_v) are simply:

$$X_v = \alpha$$
$$Y_v = \beta$$

If this procedure to assign texture coordinates to all vertices is followed, an image will be painted on the facets so that it lies inside the projection of R in a perpendicular direction to the plane in which R lies. The top left corner of the image will occur at $\mathbf{P}_0$, the top right corner of the image at $\mathbf{P}_\alpha$ and the bottom left corner of the image at $\mathbf{P}_\beta$.

Note that the planar mapping described here uses three points to define the location of the map and therefore the opposite sides are always parallel even though the angle between $\mathbf{P}_\alpha$ and $\mathbf{P}_\beta$ does not have to be $90°$.

It would be possible to define a map using four points, one at each corner of the rectangle but it is considerably more complex to determine the mapping coordinates from such a map because the opposite sides would not necessarily be parallel. Haines [33] gives expressions (without derivation) for a *convex quadrilateral* mapping that could form the basis of the necessary procedure.

10.11.2 Cylindrical mapping

In cylindrical mapping one imagines that the picture is wrapped around a cylinder enclosing the surface to be textured (see figure 10.66(b)). The texture coordinates are assigned to a vertex V by finding the point on the cylinder where a line from the axis of the cylindrical map passing through V (at $\mathbf{P}_v$) intersects the cylindrical surface, at $\mathbf{P}_i$. This is illustrated in figure 10.68. Since $\mathbf{P}_i$ lies on the cylinder its position in a frame of reference associated with the cylinder can be specified as a fraction of the distance between the top and bottom of the cylinder d and a fraction of a full rotation round the cylinder θ. The angle of rotation is specified relative to a line where the left hand edge of the image is stuck to the cylinder.

To define a cylindrical map the radius of the cylinder used to define the map is not important. We can assume $r = 1$, but the following must be specified:

- The axis of the cylinder. The best way to do this is with a point on the axis at the top of the cylinder $\mathbf{P}_1$ and a point at the bottom of the cylinder $\mathbf{P}_2$. We will assume that the Y mapping coordinate is zero at the top of the cylinder and unity at the bottom.

- The location of the left-hand edge of the map on the curved surface of the cylinder. An easy way to do this is by specifying some point $\mathbf{P}_L$ which may be any point that is **not** on the axis of the cylinder.

  The left-hand edge is a line running parallel to the axis of the cylinder through a point unit distance from the cylinder's axis in the direction of $\mathbf{P}_L$.

- The angle of rotation, ϕ, from the left-hand edge of the map round the cylindrical axis which is to be equivalent to one copy of the image. This is the location where the X mapping coordinate is unity. When $\phi = 2\pi$ it takes one copy of the map to go all the way round the cylinder. If $\phi = \dfrac{\pi}{4}$ the map occupies one eighth of the cylinder, or to put it another way, it takes eight copies to paint all around it.

This geometry is illustrated in figure 10.68.

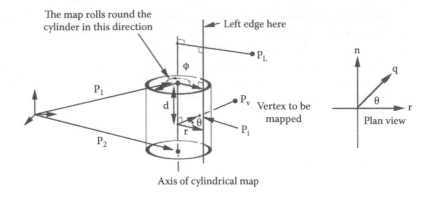

Figure 10.68: Cylindrical mapping.

In view of the discussion above the assignment of mapping coordinates at any vertex is made using the following procedure:

> Given that ϕ is the angle round the cylinder equivalent to an X mapping coordinate of unity and the distance between the top and bottom of the cylinder is assumed to cover one unit of the Y mapping coordinate, vertex V will be assigned texture coordinates according to:

$$X_v = \frac{\theta}{\phi}$$
$$Y_v = d$$

d and θ are illustrated in figure 10.68. They may be calculated in terms of $\mathbf{P}_1$, $\mathbf{P}_2$ and $\mathbf{P}_L$ using the algorithm given in listing 10.10. Here $\mathbf{P}_v$ is the position vector for vertex V.

10.11.3   Spherical mapping

A spherical mapping can be described in a very similar way to a cylindrical mapping except that the central axis serves only to define the position of the north or south poles of the sphere. One can imagine the image being *squeezed* onto the sphere as illustrated in figure 10.66.

To map the image to the sphere we use the angular components (ϕ, θ) of spherical polar coordinates (defined in section 2.1.2) where θ and ϕ satisfy: $0 \leq \theta < \pi$ and $-\pi < \phi \leq \pi$. The parameters θ and ϕ will need to be equated to mapping coordinates (X, Y) in the range $0 \leq Y < 1$ and $0 \leq X < 1$. For any vertex V a ϕ and θ are obtained by drawing a line from V (with position vector $\mathbf{P}_v$) to a point at the center of the spherical map, and calculating the point where this line intersects the unit sphere.

Firstly find d:
Let $\mathbf{y} = \mathbf{P}_2 - \mathbf{P}_1$ (the axis of the cylinder)
Thus d is the projection of $(\mathbf{P}_V - \mathbf{P}_1)$ onto the axis of the cylinder.
$$d = \frac{(\mathbf{P}_V - \mathbf{P}_1) \cdot \mathbf{y}}{\mathbf{y} \cdot \mathbf{y}}$$

Secondly find θ:
Let $\mathbf{x} = \mathbf{P}_L - \mathbf{P}_1$ (a direction towards the 'seam')
Let $\mathbf{q} = (\mathbf{P}_V - \mathbf{P}_1) - d\mathbf{y}$
($\mathbf{q}$ is the direction of $\mathbf{P}_V$ from the cylinder's axis)
Set $\hat{\mathbf{q}} = \dfrac{\mathbf{q}}{|\mathbf{q}|}$
We need a direction perpendicular to the cylinder's axis that is towards
the seam: Let $l = \dfrac{(\mathbf{P}_L - \mathbf{P}_1) \cdot \mathbf{y}}{\mathbf{y} \cdot \mathbf{y}}$
and $\mathbf{r} = (\mathbf{P}_L - \mathbf{P}_1) - l\mathbf{y}$
($\mathbf{r}$ is the direction of $\mathbf{P}_L$ from the cylinder's axis)
Set $\hat{\mathbf{r}} = \dfrac{\mathbf{r}}{|\mathbf{r}|}$
Then $\theta = \arccos(\hat{\mathbf{q}} \cdot \hat{\mathbf{r}})$

This only specifies θ in the range: $0 \le \theta < \pi$ we need to know
whether θ lies in quadrant 3 or 4. Determine this by forming
the vector $\hat{\mathbf{n}}$ which is perpendicular to the plane in which
$\mathbf{P}_1, \mathbf{P}_2$ and $\mathbf{P}_L$ lie.
$$\hat{\mathbf{n}} = \frac{\mathbf{x} \times \mathbf{y}}{|\mathbf{x} \times \mathbf{y}|}$$

if $\hat{\mathbf{q}} \cdot \hat{\mathbf{n}} < 0$ then $\theta = -\theta$

This algorithm gives θ in the range $-\pi < \theta \le \pi$ other ranges
can be obtained by appropriate scaling.

Listing 10.10: Algorithm to determine the cylindrical mapping parameters d and θ for the geometry illustrated in figure 10.68.

Once the point where this line intersects a unit sphere is known in terms of angle θ (from the north pole) and ϕ (longitude) the mapping coordinates for vertex V, (X_v, Y_v), are given by:

$$Y_v = \frac{\theta}{\pi}$$

$$X_v = \begin{cases} \dfrac{\phi}{2\pi} & : 0 \le \phi \le \pi \\[2mm] \dfrac{2\pi + \phi}{2\pi} & : -\pi < \phi < 0 \end{cases}$$

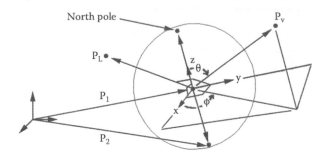

Figure 10.69: Spherical mapping.

This maps a picture with its top located at the north pole and its bottom at the south pole. Angles θ and ϕ are obtained by following an argument similar to the one used to derive the cylindrical mapping coordinates. This geometry is illustrated in figure 10.68.

In the geometric specification illustrated in figure 10.69 the center of the mapping sphere is at $\mathbf{P}_1$. We will assume that the south pole is located at $\mathbf{P}_2$ and that $\mathbf{P}_L$ is an arbitrary point, not on the polar axis. In an analogous way to the way it was used for cylindrical mapping $\mathbf{P}_L$ specifies where the "seam" of the map lies. Given this information the algorithm presented in Figure 10.11 will determine the θ and ϕ.

10.11.4   Automatic map coordinate generation

Generating image map coordinates is not always easy in a modeling tool. Projections such as those just discussed can provide a great starting point because many objects have a high degree of topological similarity with the plane or cylinder. When it is possible to start with a basic surface texture coordinate system, an interactive design tool that unrolls the mapping coordinates onto a 2D display can be written so that its user may interactively tweak the 2D texture coordinates corresponding to a 3D vertex so that it is positioned at the place in the image map that they desire. The OpenFX software has such a tool; figure 10.70 illustrates it in action. For this tool to be successful a good initial guess of the mapping coordinates is essential, otherwise many 2D coordinates will overlap and it will be impossible for the artist to separate them.

Sometimes however it is not possible to get a good initial texture coordinate mapping, and another approach is worth exploring. When a surface is modeled by a mesh of polygons that are connected together in a coherent way, that is, there are no gaps in the mesh, and it does not twist back on itself, or bifurcate in a strange way, then it is possible to use the 2D mapping coordinates of just one polygon to establish a mapping over the whole surface of an object.

Of course there are going to be cases where this will not work very well; for example trying to texture-map a cube made up from six quadrilaterals, when

First a right handed frame of reference relative to the given spherical map must be established.

Let:

$\mathbf{z} = \mathbf{P}_1 - \mathbf{P}_2$

$\mathbf{y} = \mathbf{z} \times (\mathbf{P}_L - \mathbf{P}_1)$

$\mathbf{x} = \mathbf{y} \times \mathbf{z}$

normalize:

$\hat{\mathbf{x}} = \dfrac{\mathbf{x}}{|\mathbf{x}|}$

$\hat{\mathbf{y}} = \dfrac{\mathbf{y}}{|\mathbf{y}|}$

$\hat{\mathbf{z}} = \dfrac{\mathbf{z}}{|\mathbf{z}|}$

Now determine ϕ:

Let: $\mathbf{r} = \mathbf{P}_v - \mathbf{P}_1$

and : $\hat{\mathbf{r}} = \dfrac{\mathbf{r}}{|\mathbf{r}|}$

then: $\phi = ATAN2((\mathbf{r} \cdot \mathbf{x}), (\mathbf{r} \cdot \mathbf{y}))$

To determine θ use:

$\theta = \arccos(\mathbf{r} \cdot \mathbf{z})$

Listing 10.11: Determining θ and ϕ relative to a specification of the spherical map for a vertex at $\mathbf{P}_v$.

just one of them is initially mapped, is unlikely to produce a pleasing result. In this case a spherical map centered within the cube is likely to come much closer to the desired result.

In principle the automatic generation of a 2D coordinate system over a curved surface is relatively simple if we make the assumption that two adjacent faces can be unrolled, by rotating the second face around the common edge so they they lie in a plane. Once unrolled the coordinate system can be mapped out across the adjacent face and mapping coordinates assigned to the non-common vertex. Figure 10.71 illustrates the idea: (a) shows a flat mesh of triangular polygons in which vertices 1, 2 and 3 of triangle A have been assigned mapping coordinates using a frame of reference with the x axis lying along the edge from vertices 1 to 3 and the y axis lying along the edge from 1 to 2. Since triangles B and E are adjacent to A their non-common vertices 4 and 7 can have their mapping coordinates assigned using the local frame of reference in triangle A. Now, as triangle B has a full 2D frame of reference its vertices' mapping coordinates can be used to establish a frame of reference relative to triangle B, which in turn can then be used to assign mapping coordinates to the non-common vertices in the triangular faces adjacent to B.

Once triangle B has been mapped, the algorithm can simply recurse across the connected mesh establishing mapping coordinates at every vertex until the

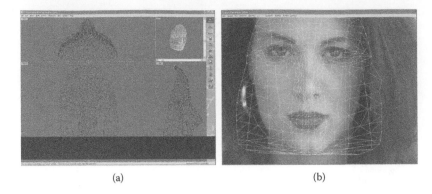

(a)   (b)

Figure 10.70: Interactively moving the texture map coordinates by superimposing the 2D texture coordinates mesh over an image. (a) The 3D mesh model. (b) The 2D texture coordinates and image to be wrapped around the mesh.

whole mesh is triangulated. When the mesh represents a non-planar surface, the faces adjacent to the reference frame will need to be temporarily rotated around the common edge with the reference face, so that both faces lie in a plane. Once aligned in a plane, a 2D mapping coordinate can be generated at their non-common vertex. A suitable transformation can be obtained by recognizing that it has to align the faces' normal vectors by a rotation around the vector joining the vertices at the ends of the common edge. For example, in figure 10.71(b) the vectors $\mathbf{n}_A$ and $\mathbf{n}_B$ should be aligned by rotation around the vector $\mathbf{d}$; section 2.12.5 describes suitable algorithms to achieve this.

In figure 10.71(a) the surface triangulation is totally consistent, because each triangle is only adjacent to a maximum of three other triangles and the surface is flat. This algorithm would not work for the case shown in figure 10.71(c) because of the single vertex joining the two pieces.

If we now imagine folding the mesh in figure 10.71(a) around a surface to take the shape, shown in cross-section in (b), there is no reason why the vertices cannot carry the same texture coordinates. Indeed there is no reason why the texture coordinate generation has to start with a flat mesh because the connections among the faces remains the same. For example faces A and B virtually lie in the same plane and it is easy to see that an assumption of continuing to apply the frame of reference from A into B is not a bad one.

The cross-section in figure 10.71(b) illustrates a mapping on to a spiral object in which the map (defined in just one triangular face) winds round the spiral, something that could not be achieved with the use of a cylindrical map for example. There are, of course, some cases where this algorithm will not work very well. A triangle that is joined to two others along a common edge could lead to inconsistencies, figure 10.71(d). Applying the algorithm, starting at face A, to the three sides of a cube shown in (e) could lead to different mapping coordinates

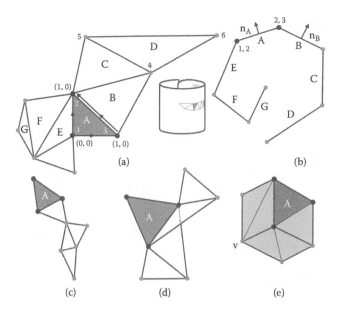

Figure 10.71: Recursively generating texture coordinates using the local frame of reference established in an adjacent polygon. (a) Flat mesh, (b) rapping mesh around a curved surface, (c) a mesh that cannot be mapped, (d) and (e) cases that could result in an inconsistent mapping.

assigned to vertex V, depending on the order in which the adjacency is processed by the recursive algorithm.

But, all-in-all, the algorithm can provide a very useful tool to the 3D artist when it comes to painting 2D mapping coordinates onto their 3D models, or at least starting to assign a model's vertices with 2D mapping coordinates.

10.12   Building polygonal primitives

Most primitive shapes are readily constructed using one or more of the algorithms we have now considered.

In general it is therefore only necessary to specify a very small amount of structural information because the automatic procedures will do the bulk of the work. For example we saw that a torus can be constructed by specifying a circle of edges and vertices followed by the generation of a surface of revolution.

The following list suggests how the most basic primitives might be constructed:

- **Cube**
  Start with a square, 4 vertices, 5 edges, 2 facets, copy it, move the copy and loft the two outlines.

- **Pyramid**

  Start with a square, add the rest by hand, one vertex, 4 edges and 4 triangular facets.

- **Cone**

  Start with an angled line, 2 vertices, 1 edge. Construct a surface of revolution about an axis that passes through one of the vertices. If necessary, cap the base of the cone (which is a convex polygon).

- **Tube**

  Start with a line (2 vertices, 1 edge). Construct a surface of revolution about an axis parallel to, but offset from, the line.

- **Cylinder**

  Build a tube as above then proceed to cap the top and bottom; both are convex polygons.

- **Sphere**

  Two possible methods:

  1. Start with a set of vertices and edges describing a semi-circle. Then build a surface of revolution around an axis passing through both ends of the semi-circle.

  2. Start with a very basic approximation to a sphere. Subdivide the edges and facets and move the additional vertices radially until they lie on a sphere. If necessary repeat this process until the faceted appearance is reduced to an acceptable degree.

- **Disk**

  Start with a set of vertices and edges describing a circle, then cap the circle.

- **Torus**

  Start with a set of vertices and edges describing a circle, construct a surface of revolution about an axis outside the circle.

11

Algorithms for procedural textures

In chapter 4 the basic idea of the procedural (or algorithmic) texture was introduced. In this chapter we will look at some examples that take advantage of those ideas to produce a collection of interesting surface textures. We will concentrate on what one might describe as following the basic principles of mixing geometric and noise patterns.

It is important to realize that the procedural textures described in this chapter do not have any basis in physical or biological principles; they are essentially just "computer hacks" that look good and do the job.

All the textures considered in this chapter have been implemented as either DLL plug-ins or as GLSL shaders for OpenFX. After reading this chapter and chapter 9 you should be able to follow the finer details of a practical implementation of the algorithms in the OpenFX code. Since the first edition of this book was printed it has become routinely possible to make use of the hardware acceleration offered by the GPU, so algorithmic textures can now be generated in real-time and with increasing sophistication. Despite their programmability, GPUs are still specialized processors that are nowhere near as flexible as the CPU of a traditional general purpose processor. They also have quite a limited memory, especially for storing the shader codes. Despite the C like form of the GLSL it is usually necessary to re-engineer an algorithm's implementation, from the way it would be written in a standard high level language, to the way it must be structured as a pair of GLSL shader programs. For example, rather than generate a noise value using the Perlin algorithm an image map is used as a lookup table.

Another reason for adopting a different approach to texture implementation is the fact that the GPU is expected to render textures repeatedly in real-time, and therefore, moving as many operations as possible into a *execute once* set-up step becomes essential. For these reasons we offer two versions of the procedural texture algorithms in this chapter, one that is usable within the limits imposed by the GPU hardware and another for the general software approach where there are no limits.

Almost any natural pattern can be simulated with a procedural texture. Perlin has greatly extended his original work and others have developed the procedural texture so that now almost any surface appearance can be simulated. For example: Turk [84] and Witkin and Kass [91] have shown that *reaction diffusion* is a very successful technique for developing fascinating procedural textures including many animal skin patterns (giraffe, zebra), coral and weaved surfaces. Other useful sources of information may be found in the book by Ebert et al. [23].

The range of possible uses of algorithmic is not limited to painting patterns on 2D surfaces. Perlin and Hoffert [68] and Kajiya and Kay [48] introduced the concept of the hypertexture which one could describe as a three-dimensional equivalent of the procedural texture. Rather than applying a texture to a meshed surface a volume of some sort is specified and calculations proceed to determine the opacity at points within that volume. To determine what is visible when looking at a hypertexture the opacity must be calculated at a number of sample points along the viewing direction (or ray as it passes through the hypertexture volume). As a result hypertextures are extremely slow to compute and therefore very careful thought is needed before embarking on their use. In this chapter we do not discuss hypertextures but for more information the aforementioned references are a good place to look.

11.1   A standard interface

It is a good idea to arrange that procedural textures interface to their host renderer with a few standard parameters. All those rendering applications that offer their users the ability to write plug-in textures communicate with their plug-ins through a standard interface. It is also useful to design a standard set of variables to communicate with the GPU shader programs so that different shaders can be called into action without having to call on a whole collection of special cases.

11.1.1   An interface for procedural textures

For a renderer that uses textures through shared object libraries or DLLs, a comprehensive interface can be achieved with the function prototype and argument set given in listing 11.1.

The function returns the Boolean value FALSE if the function fails for any reason, otherwise TRUE is returned. The function's parameters fall into five groups:

1. (Vectors: $\mathbf{p}$, $\mathbf{n}$)
   $\mathbf{p}$ is a position vector of the spot on the textured surface for which we wish to calculate the texture value, i.e., the surface color.

```
BOOL TextureProcedure(
 VECTOR p,  // coordinate of surface point
 VECTOR n,  // surface normal at "p" (unit length)
 VECTOR P,  // position vector to origin of texture parallelepiped
 VECTOR U,  // normalized basis vectors of texture parallelepiped
 VECTOR V,
 VECTOR W,
 float   u,  // relation between "p" and texture parallelepiped
 float   v,  // i.e. p = P + uU + vV + wW
 float   w,

 MATRIX3 T,  //Transform vector from (x,y,z) to (U,V,W) coordinates
 float  *opacity,    //Opacity of surface
 float  *reflectivity,  // Reflectivity of the surface
 VECTOR color    // return the surface RGB color (0.0 - 1.0)
)
{
 .. Body of the texturing procedure
 ..
 //Return FALSE if function fails, otherwise return TRUE
 return TRUE;
}
```

Listing 11.1: A prototype for a wide variety of texturing functions.

$\mathbf{n}$ is a unit direction vector normal to the surface being textured at $\mathbf{p}$. Many textures redirect $\mathbf{n}$ away from its input direction. Some bend it in combination with a color variation but a number of the most effective textures involve shifts in the direction of $\mathbf{n}$ alone.

2. (Vectors: $\mathbf{P},\mathbf{U},\mathbf{V},\mathbf{W}$, and scalars: u,v,w)
   These important parameters allow a texture to be applied in a way that is relative to a coordinate system that may move, be non-orthogonal or differentially scaled. Perhaps this frame of reference follows an object in an animation so that we don't get the unpleasant appearance of the object *moving through a sea of texture*! Many textures are repetitive. A regular checkerboard or wallpaper pattern for example is readily simulated with an appropriate use of u, v and w. Section 11.1.1 discusses these parameters further.

3. (Matrix: $[T]$)
   A 3×3 transformation matrix that allows direction vectors (such as the surface normal $\mathbf{n}$) which are specified in a global (x, y, z), frame of reference to be used in the $(\mathbf{U}, \mathbf{V}, \mathbf{W})$ frame. Whilst it is possible to calculate $[T]$ in the body of a texture function from $\mathbf{U}$, $\mathbf{V}$ and $\mathbf{W}$ it is much more efficient

to do this only once, before rendering the image, rather than every time a pixel is rendered.

If the components of $\mathbf{U}$ etc., are (U_x, U_y, U_z) etc., then $[T]$ is given by:

$$[T] = \begin{bmatrix} U_x & V_x & W_x \\ U_y & V_y & W_y \\ U_z & V_z & W_z \end{bmatrix}^{-1}$$

In those cases where $\mathbf{U}$, $\mathbf{V}$ and $\mathbf{W}$ form an orthogonal basis there is no need to calculate an inverse matrix because $[T]$ may be written immediately as:

$$[T] = \begin{bmatrix} U_x & U_y & U_z \\ V_x & V_y & V_z \\ W_x & W_y & W_z \end{bmatrix}$$

4. (Scalars: *opacity and *reflectivity)

   If the client renderer is a ray tracer then modifications to the opacity or reflectivity of the surface by a procedural texture might have interesting practical use. For example a texture simulating "clouds" would have zero opacity in the *gaps* between the clouds, a rapid transition to a unit value at the edge and unit opacity in the cloudy areas. Passing a pointer to these floating point values allows the texture function to modify the value or just leave it alone (in C++ a reference could be used). Both parameters lie in the range $[0, 1]$.

5. (Vector: color)

   This is a floating point triple (specified as a vector purely for convenience) that returns the red, green and blue (RGB) components of the texture color observed at $\mathbf{p}$. Each component is scaled into the range $[0, 1]$. When TextureProcedure() is called this parameter should hold a basic underlying surface color that for certain textures (e.g. bumpy) will remain unchanged.

Also consult the OpenFX code in the "textures" folder (see chapter 9) which implements all the algorithms described in this chapter.

A reference frame The vector parameters $\mathbf{P}$, $\mathbf{U}$, $\mathbf{V}$ and $\mathbf{W}$, introduced in section 11.1, are illustrated in figure 11.1. They define a unit texture cell (or parallelepiped) that we regard as being a bounding volume inside which the essential features of the texture will be created. The basis vectors $\mathbf{U}$, $\mathbf{V}$ and $\mathbf{W}$ do not have to be orthogonal and this allows skewed or sheared texture patterns to be readily simulated. The base vectors have an origin at $\mathbf{P}$ and if $\mathbf{U}$, $\mathbf{V}$, $\mathbf{W}$ and $\mathbf{P}$ are transformed in the same way as any object the texture is applied to then the texture will look as if it is fixed to the object and not like some *field* through which the object is moving; see figure 11.2.

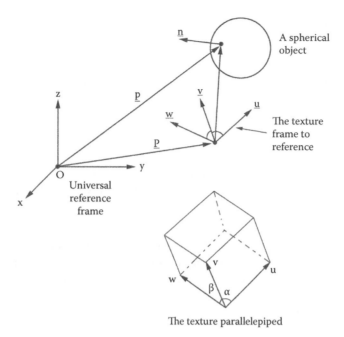

Figure 11.1: A frame of reference in which to specify a volume texture.

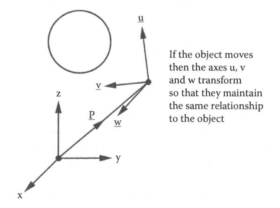

Figure 11.2: Transforming the texture cell keeps it in the same relative position to the object whose surface exhibits the texture.

Any point $\mathbf{p}$ on the surface of an object is specified relative to the texture cell by:

$$\mathbf{p} = \mathbf{P} + u\mathbf{U} + v\mathbf{V} + w\mathbf{W}$$

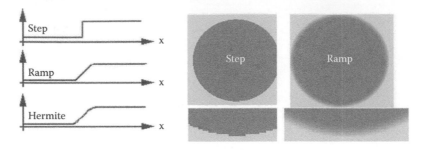

Figure 11.3: Applying a ramp transition between the colored dot and the background removes the unpleasant aliasing effects that are very noticeable when a step transition is used.

The coefficients u, v and w are used as texture coordinates in calculating the surface shading. To make the texture appear larger or smaller or be distorted, they can be scaled before calling the texture function.

As we have seen, if $\mathbf{U}$, $\mathbf{V}$ and $\mathbf{W}$ form an orthogonal basis then u, v and w may be easily calculated. For a non-orthogonal basis a set of three simultaneous equations must be solved every time the u, v and w are needed.

Color blending Textures that include color changes exhibit unpleasant aliasing effects when change is abrupt. On the other hand if the change is blended over a small distance the aliasing effect is much less noticeable. Several blending functions have been proposed but a simple ramp is often acceptable although some texture developers recommend using Hermite interpolation. Figure 11.3 illustrates alternative ramp shapes and the effect of a simple ramp on the edges of a large colored *dot*.

Noise functions Many textures make use of the Perlin noise generators which were introduced in chapter 4, section 4.5.2. Four fundamental functions were introduced there. In the algorithms described in this chapter and the code that accompanies them single and vector valued *Noise* and *Turbulence* functions are specified in listing 11.2.

Note that in this case the position coordinates x,y,z are specified as three separate values rather than as a VECTOR data type.

The implementations of fNoise() etc., used in producing the textures illustrated in this chapter were written to return single values in the range $[0, 1]$ or vectors that are of unit length. There are many other codes that could be used to generate noise with the necessary statistical properties.

It is important to appreciate that these noises are adjusted so that they give a reasonable correlation between returned values when the input points are spaced one unit apart. That is v1 (given by v1 = fNoise (0.0,0.0,0.0)) will be fairly close to v2 (given by v2 = fNoise (1.0,0.0,0.0)) whereas v3 (given by

Return a "Noise" value in the range [0.0 - 1.0]
float fNoise (
 float x , //Coordinates of the point at which the Noise value
 float y , //is to be calculated.
 float z);

Return a " 1/f Noise" value in the range [0.0 - 1.0]
float fTurbulence (
 float x , //Same as for fNoise function. Note that each
 float y , //function will return the same number if called
 float z // with the same "x y z" values.
);

Return a normalized random vector with the
void vNoise (
 VECTOR v , //Returned vector
 float x , //Coordinates of the point at which the vector
 float y , //is to be calculated.
 float z);

Return a " 1/f" random vector
void vTurbulence (
 VECTOR v , //Returned vector
 float x , //Same as for fNoise function.
 float y , // ""
 float z // ""
);

Listing 11.2: Noise function definitions.

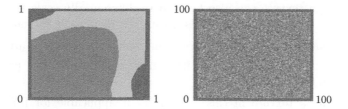

Figure 11.4: (a) Noise texture at a resolution of one unit. (b) The same noise texture at a resolution of 100 units.

$v3 = $ fNoise $(100.0,0.0.0))$ will be virtually independent of v1. This point is illustrated in figure 11.4 which shows a texture based on the same noise function viewed at two different scales.

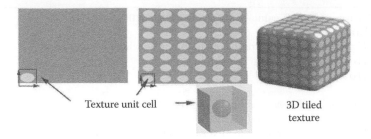

Figure 11.5: Tiling a texture by repeating the unit texture cell shown on the left produces a *wallpaper* effect.

Repetitive patterns To repeat a texture pattern the idea of the texture unit cell is a useful one. The unit cell depicted in figure 11.1 can be tiled to fill space. Three of the sides of the cell lie in planes formed by pairs of the vectors $\mathbf{U}$, $\mathbf{V}$ and $\mathbf{W}$ with the others lying in parallel planes. Thus the texture cell is a parallelepiped with edges of unit length. Any point $\mathbf{p}$ with texture coordinates (u, v, w) may be tiled by first calculating:

$$
\begin{aligned}
u' &= u - \mathrm{floor}(u) \\
v' &= v - \mathrm{floor}(v) \\
w' &= w - \mathrm{floor}(w)
\end{aligned}
$$

where *floor(x)* returns the nearest lowest integer to x. The (u', v', w') are then substituted in the remainder of the texture calculation in place of (u, v, w).

This technique of modifying $\mathbf{p}$ through its (u, v, w) coordinates before calculating a texture can also be used to differentially scale the appearance of a texture. For example the dots illustrated in figure 11.3 can appear flattened along one or two of their axes if the values of u and v are prescaled by $\frac{1}{2}$. Figure 11.5 illustrates a repetitive array of elliptical dots produced using the function given in listing 11.3.

Tiling a texture in this way makes it applicable for filling 3D space and not just covering a two-dimensional surface. On those surfaces where mapping coordinates (section 4.6) are available at $\mathbf{p}$ they can be used to determine the value returned by a procedural texture, however since there are only two mapping coordinates we must choose to set the third to some arbitrary value, say zero.

As you have probably guessed, the example dot texture is generated by placing a colored *sphere* at the center of the texture cell and making the calculations in three dimensions. As a result the dots on the surface appear because the visible surfaces cut through the array of texture cells, the *voxels*.

```
#define EDGE 0.05 // give the spot a soft edge

BOOL TextureProcedure(
 VECTOR   p, VECTOR n,
 VECTOR   P,VECTOR U, VECTOR V, VECTOR W,
 float    u, float v, float w,
 MATRIX3  T,
 float    *opacity, float *reflectivity,
 VECTOR   color
){
 double r;
 VECTOR spot_color = {1.0,0.0,0.0};// Red spot
 double radius =0.25;// Spot occupies half the unit cell

 u *= 0.8;              // Apply differential scaling
 v *= 0.8;              // for elliptical shapes

 u=(u-floor(u))-0.5;// Leave these lines out
 v=(v-floor(v))-0.5;// for a single dot at the
 w=(w-floor(w))-0.5;// center of the texture cell

 if((r=sqrt(u*u+v*v+w*w)) < radius) {
  color[0]=spot_color[0];// Inside the spot copy the spot color
  color[1]=spot_color[1];
  color[2]=spot_color[2];
 }
 else if(r < radius+EDGE){// blend the colors at the edge of
                          // the spot to avoid aliasing.
  r= (r-radius)/EDGE;
  color[0] = color[0]*r + spot_color[0]*(1.0-r);
  color[1] = color[1]*r + spot_color[1]*(1.0-r);
  color[2] = color[2]*r + spot_color[2]*(1.0-r);
 }
 return TRUE;
}
```

Listing 11.3: A repetitive "dot" texture.

11.1.2 An interface for GPU shaders

If you are not familiar with GPU shader programming please read section 7.3 before continuing.

When a texture function is to be implemented through GPU programs, the interface to the shader codes will require the same information to be communicated to it that would be passed to a function executing in a CPU DLL. However, the GPU shaders do not pick up its parameters through function arguments. The shader's parameters are passed by using memory locations in the GPU that the application program can write into. All our shader examples will use GLSL `uniform` qualified variables that can be referenced through their names by the application program.

The main geometric data (vertex positions and normal vectors) are passed to the shader through GLSL built-in variables, 2D or 3D texture maps are passed though a small collection of samplers, a texture's frame of reference is passed as three `uniform` variables and the texture coordinate of each vertex is passed through a buffer attached to a vertex array object.

The other major differences in using a GPU texture are (1) the need to use a texture map as a lookup table for the self-similar noise function, and (2) the need to also implement other aspects of the rendering process, e.g., lighting.

In all the GLSL code examples the following GLSL code is included in the vertex shader:

```
//Input of the vertex position relative to the texture base axes
layout(location = 4) in vec3 ShaderPosition;

// Input of material base axes for the texture unit cell
uniform vec3 Uvector;
uniform vec3 Vvector;
uniform vec3 Wvector;
```

In the fragment shader, the map that will be used as a noise lookup needs to be made available:

```
uniform sampler3D NoiseMap;      // Map for 3D noise
```

It is also necessary to declare several variables that are assigned values in the vertex shaders and are used (after interpolation in the rasterizer) in the fragment shader:

```
out  vec3 tnorm;   //normal vector
out vec4 PP;        //position
out vec3 texpos;   //texture position

out vec3 uvec;      //the three texture cell axes
out vec3 vvec;
out vec3 wvec;
```

Note: These in/out variables are assigned on a per-vertex basis in the vertex program, but when used in the fragment shader they apply to the location on the surface visible in the fragment being rendered.

The GPU is highly efficient at carrying out interpolation and generating repeating patterns. GLSL functions floor(..), roof(..), mix(..) and clamp(..) are provided to facilitate the tasks of blending color and determining fractional positions within a texture's unit cell.

11.2 CPU textures

In this section we will examine algorithms to generate seven classes of procedural textures built using three principles: regular patterns, irregular patterns, perturbation to surface normal vectors or a combination all three. The algorithms do not assume any particular restriction on their implementation. Versions of some of them for GPU use will be examined further in section 11.3.

11.2.1 Regular dots

In section 11.1.1 we saw how to produce a repetitive pattern of dots by embedding a sphere in the basic texture cell. It would take only a small modification to place cubes or other patterns at the center of the cell. We can think of an analogy with the crystallographic arrangement of atoms in a solid. A dot at the center of the texture cell corresponds to a body centered cubic (BCC) structure. There are other crystallographic arrangements that produce regular patterns of dots. In fact an hexagonal close packing (HCP) arrangement has proved to be very useful because quite a few of the textures to be described later are based on it.

On their own neither the HCP nor the face centered cubic (FCC) are particularly exciting but they do raise an interesting and important issue:

> *Neither the FCC or HCP packaging arrangements can be tiled in a way so that all the spheres making up the basic repeat unit lie completely within the unit cell.*

This complicates the task of producing repetitive patterns because when we need to determine what texture feature occurs at some coordinate (u, v, w) we must take account of adjacent texture cells so that the patterns match along their borders. If the patterns from neighboring cells don't match exactly some dots in the pattern might look like they have been cut in half. (A problem analogous to aligning the wallpaper pattern when hanging adjacent strips.)

11.2.2 FCC dots

In an FCC pattern there is one spherical dot at the center of each face of the texture cell. Thus to determine the color at (u, v, w) six spherical intersection tests must be performed for each cell. In addition we must remember that each sphere is shared with an adjacent texture cell. To make sure that no discontinuity occurs the dots on opposite faces of the texture cell need to be the same size and color.

This introduces another important point that we should remember as other textures are developed:

> We are determining the texture at one given point (either **p** or equivalently (u, v, w)) on each function call, **not** the texture of many points that satisfy some given property of the texture.

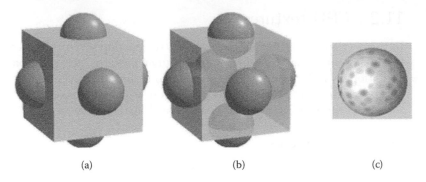

(a)   (b)   (c)

Figure 11.6: The unit cell for an FCC dots texture and an example of its application to a solid object. (a) Solid cell showing spheres protruding into adjacent cells. (b) Semi-transparent unit cell showing the 6 spheres. (c) Soft edged dots applied to a sphere.

For example we cannot set the color of all points inside a dot in one call to the texturing function. This may seem like a trivial point but it is very significant in practice and for many textures, especially those based on random dots. It can significantly complicate the coding.

Figure 11.6 illustrates the relation of the FCC dots to the texture cell and pictures an example of the texture applied to a solid object. Details of the algorithm which consists of a simple test as to whether a point lies inside one of six spheres can be found by following the code that accompanies the book.

11.2.3   HCP dots

In contrast to BCC and FCC dots an hexagonal close packed (HCP) arrangement of spheres forms the closest packing that it is possible to obtain. This pattern is of particular interest mainly because the hexagonal mesh, leopard, amphibian, honeycomb and vein textures are derived from it.

Like the FCC dots we must be careful to remember that spheres from one cell will overlap into adjacent texture cells. In this case to obtain a repeatable texture cell we require 22 spheres. Compare this to the single test required for a BCC dot pattern. Figure 11.7 visualizes the arrangement of the spheres in the unit HCP cell. Because of the regularity, any spheres that lie partly outside the texture cell exactly overlap spheres in adjacent cells and thus when working in adjacent cells they are automatically considered. That is, a sphere on the right of cell i overlaps one from the left of cell $i + 1$.

The HCP unit cell is not rectilinear. For a cell of unit width its length and height are both $\frac{\sqrt{3}}{2}$. Three layers of spheres are needed to fill the texture cell; the middle layer is an offset copy of layer one and the top layer is a repeat of the bottom one. This arrangement of spheres in the layers is depicted in figure 11.8

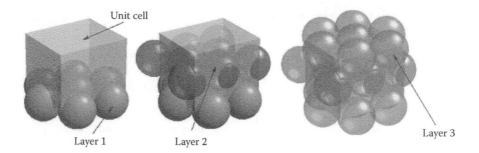

Figure 11.7: Visualizing the spherical units that make up the HCP unit texture cell.

where the dimensions are also presented. Note that this illustration depicts the case where the spheres just touch (as would be the case in a real HCP crystal). As we will see later some very interesting textures arise when the sphere radii vary from this nominal value, a situation that is of course impossible in a real crystal. Seven spheres are needed for layers 1 and 3; eight spheres must be used in layer 2.

In the HCP texture (as with those considered earlier) the actual pattern seen on any given surface is that which appears as the surface cuts through an infinite lattice of texture cells. This is depicted in figure 11.9 where an angled plane is shown cutting through a single texture cell.

The implementation of the algorithm for an HCP dot pattern follows closely the same principles used in the FCC procedure. It basically tests to see if the point **p** lies inside (or on the edge of soft edges) any of the 22 spheres in the unit cell. If the test proves positive then the color or other surface attribute assigned to the dot is returned.

11.2.4   Regular bumps

The BCC, FCC or HCP dot pattern can be used to generate regular arrays of raised bumps or sunken dimples if the surface normal vector is pushed off the vertical at points lying inside the dots. For example the bumps illustrated in figure 11.10 were produced from a basic BCC dot pattern but instead of changing the color of the surface inside the dot the surface normal was perturbed in the way illustrated in the cross-sections. It is relatively straightforward to make bumps on a surface when the bumps are derived from a two-dimensional function that covers the surface. However, more thought is necessary when the bumpy surface is to be derived from a texture that fills a 3D volume. In this case the surface bumps are formed at those locations where the surface intersects spheres in the texture cell. We must ensure that not only is the normal bent in the desired direction (bump or pimple) but also that the direction is consistent for adjacent points on the surface. For example the bumps on the left, right, top and bottom

Layers 1 and 3 shown in plan view

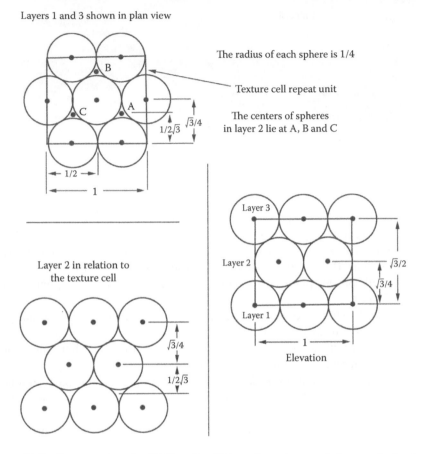

The radius of each sphere is 1/4

Texture cell repeat unit

The centers of spheres
in layer 2 lie at A, B and C

Layer 2 in relation to
the texture cell

Elevation

Figure 11.8: Constructing the HCP unit cell from three layers of close packed spheres. Each sphere is of radius $\dfrac{1}{4}$ but the unit cell is not a precise cube.

surfaces of the cubes in figure 11.10 must all *bump* outward irrespective of on which side they lie.

In figure 11.11 a cross-section is shown through the texture cell so that it also intersects one of the spheres inside it. The normal at any point **p** on the surface between points a and b is pushed away from the perpendicular in proportion to its distance from the center of the texture cell sphere at c. Working from a specification of the geometry of the cell a little vector algebra determines c. Once c has been found the direction in which to bend **n** is calculated; call this $\mathbf{\Delta n}$. The new normal vector ($\mathbf{n}_b$ after *bumping*) is given by:

$$\mathbf{n}_b = \mathbf{n} + \gamma \mathbf{\Delta n}$$

where γ is the proportion of the bump to apply at **p**.

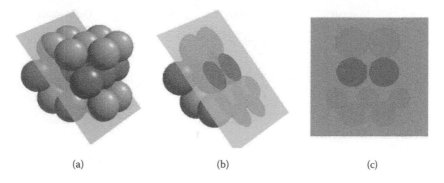

(a)   (b)   (c)

Figure 11.9: (a) The texture cell with the planar surface cut through. (b) A cut away view. (c) The pattern as it appears in the surface.

Since the surface normal $\mathbf{n}$ is determined with respect to a global frame of reference but the texturing algorithms require that all calculations are done in the $(\mathbf{U}, \mathbf{V}, \mathbf{W})$ reference frame we must transform $\mathbf{n}$ and $\mathbf{p}$ so that they can be used relative to the $(\mathbf{U}, \mathbf{V}, \mathbf{W})$ frame. The surface normal $\mathbf{n}$ in the $(\mathbf{U}, \mathbf{V}, \mathbf{W})$ frame of reference is obtained by applying:

$$\mathbf{n}' = [T]\mathbf{n}$$

To obtain an equivalent for $\mathbf{p}$, say $\mathbf{p}'$ we use the *known* texture coordinates (u, v, w) at $\mathbf{p}$ and by letting $\mathbf{p} = (u', v', w')$ with:

$$
\begin{aligned}
u' &= u - \mathrm{floor}(u) \\
v' &= v - \mathrm{floor}(v) \\
w' &= w - \mathrm{floor}(w)
\end{aligned}
$$

Account is taken of the fact that the texture cells repeat ad infinitum.

After transformation, $\mathbf{p}'$, like $\mathbf{n}'$, can be manipulated relative to the texture cell coordinate system. If calculation for the *bumped* surface normal proceeds with respect to the texture cell axes then the repetition of the texture cell will occur automatically.

To determine the change in surface normal due to the *bumps* we proceed as follows: Let $r < 0.5$ be the radius of a sphere at the center of the texture cell, i.e., at: $\mathbf{C} = (0.5, 0.5, 0.5)$. Find the point $\mathbf{p}'_c$ (at c in figure 11.11(a); c is the point on the surface closest to $\mathbf{C}$) using $\mathbf{p}' = (u', v', w')$ (the position vector relative to the texture cell for the point p). We can write:

$$\mathbf{p}'_c = \mathbf{C} - ((\mathbf{p}' - \mathbf{C}) \cdot \mathbf{n}')\mathbf{n}'$$

and therefore the direction in which we must bend the surface normal, relative

Normals   Raised bumps   Normals   Depressions

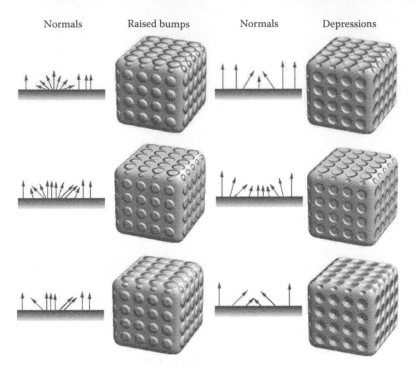

Figure 11.10: Regular bumps and depressions formed by modulating the surface normal of a solid object. The amplitude and direction of the modulation at a point **p** is determined by its distance from a sphere placed at the center of a *texture cell*. The figure illustrates how the surface normal behaves in a cross-section through one of the bumps. Bumps are shown on the left and depressions on the right.

to the texture cell axes, is given by:

$$\mathbf{\Delta n}' = \frac{\mathbf{p}' - \mathbf{p}'_c}{|\mathbf{p}' - \mathbf{p}'_c|}$$

If $|\mathbf{C} - \mathbf{p}'| < r$ then the point of interest lies inside the sphere and the normal will be pushed in the direction of $\mathbf{\Delta n}'$ by an amount that depends on the proportion of the distance γ, at which p' lies between the points labeled a and c in figure 11.11(a). γ is given by:

$$\gamma = 1 - \frac{|\mathbf{p}' - \mathbf{p}'_c|}{\sqrt{r^2 - (|\mathbf{C} - \mathbf{p}'_c|)^2}}$$

$\gamma = 1$ when p is at c and $\gamma = 0$ when p is at either a or b.

The form of the rule used to mix $\mathbf{\Delta n}'$ with $\mathbf{n}$ determines the apparent shape of the bump, but before it is added to $\mathbf{n}$ it must be transformed back to a global

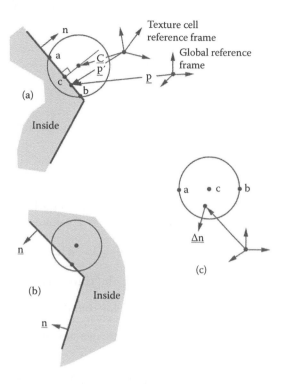

Figure 11.11: A cross-section through a surface intersecting one of the spheres in the texture cell. (a) Case where the inside of the surface is on the left and (b) when it is on the right. (c) Shows a plane view and again $\mathbf{\Delta n}$ is the direction in which $\mathbf{n}$ is bent at $\mathbf{p}$.

frame of reference using:

$$\mathbf{\Delta n} = \Delta n'_u \mathbf{U} + \Delta n'_v \mathbf{V} + \Delta n'_w \mathbf{W}$$

11.2.5 Pimples

The raised bump (or pimple) textures illustrated on the left of figure 11.10 were produced by adding $\mathbf{\Delta n}$ with $\mathbf{n}$ when $\gamma < 1$ according to the equation:

$$\mathbf{n} = \alpha \mathbf{n} + (1 - \alpha)\mathbf{\Delta n}$$

The parameter α is determined as follows for the three cases illustrated in the figure with the rules:

1. Rounded pimples

$$\alpha = \sin \frac{\pi}{2}\gamma$$

2. Buttons

$$\alpha = \begin{cases} 1 & : \gamma < 0.5 \\ \frac{1}{2}\left(1 - \cos 4\pi\gamma\right) & : \gamma \geq 0.5 \end{cases}$$

3. Studs

$$\alpha = \begin{cases} 0.5 & : \gamma < 0.5 \\ 1 & : \gamma \geq 0.5 \end{cases}$$

11.2.6 Dimples

The depression (or dimple) textures illustrated on the right of figure 11.10 were produced by adding $\Delta\mathbf{n}$ with $\mathbf{n}$ when $\gamma < 1$ using:

$$\mathbf{n} = \alpha\mathbf{n} - (1 - \alpha)\Delta\mathbf{n}$$

Again α is determined as follows for the three cases:

1. Rounded dimples, the same as for rounded pimples above: $\alpha = \sin\frac{\pi}{2}\gamma$

2. Flat dimples, the same as for buttons above:

$$\alpha = \begin{cases} 1 & : \gamma < 0.5 \\ \frac{1}{2}\left(1 - \cos 4\pi\gamma\right) & : \gamma \geq 0.5 \end{cases}$$

3. Conical pits

$$\alpha = 0.5$$

In all cases if $\gamma \geq 1$ no modulation is applied to $\mathbf{n}$.

11.2.7 A hexagonal mesh

Producing an hexagonal ridge pattern such as that illustrated in figure 11.12 is relatively straightforward on a flat two-dimensional plane. To construct an equivalent pattern that fills three-dimensional space and at the same time satisfies the repetitive requirements of a procedural texture is a bit harder. One interesting method that leads to the 3D hexagonal honeycomb texture of figure 11.12 and has potential as a technique for further development (e.g., the textures of section 11.2.23) arises from the same ideas that produced the dimpled texture.

In essence the procedure is: Spheres used to produce the bumps of an HCP dimple pattern are expanded until they start to overlap. If the overlap is prevented the rounded edges of the dimples flatten out so that hexagons start to appear. A $\mathbf{Z}$ buffer (which only needs one value) may be used to prevent spheres overlapping. This process is illustrated in figure 11.13.

Figure 11.12: An hexagonal ridge pattern produced by overlapping the HCP texture spheres.

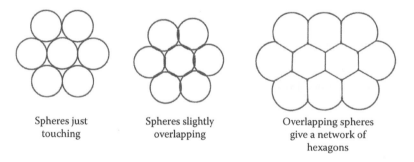

Spheres just touching

Spheres slightly overlapping

Overlapping spheres give a network of hexagons

Figure 11.13: A 3D hexagonal mesh produced by growing spheres.

In the case of the unit texture cell illustrated in figure 11.7 spheres of radius 0.25 give maximum space filling, i.e., they just touch. If the radius is increased to $\frac{\sqrt{3}}{2}$ perfect hexagonal shapes are the result. The algorithm presented in listing 11.4 uses a **Z** buffer to determine inside which of the texture cell's 22 spheres (one sphere equates to one hexagon) any point p lies.

To produce the ridges along the edges of the hexagonal cells we need to determine whether a point lies within a small distance from the edge of the cell, i.e., inside the ridge. We can do this by considering the value in the **Z** buffer. When p lies near the edges of the hexagon its **Z** buffer value (call it Z_p) will be of similar magnitude to the values in the **Z** buffers of adjacent spheres. Thus if the difference in value for two adjacent spheres is within some small tolerance then p is said to be on the ridge between hexagons.

To bend the normal on the beveled sides of the hexagon the change in normal direction is approximated with a vector $\mathbf{\Delta n}$ derived in a manner analogous to

Set the depth buffer $Z = 0$

Given point of intersection $\mathbf{p}$ check each of the 22 spheres (i),
to see if it lies inside. i.e. is $(\delta_i = |\mathbf{p} - \mathbf{c}_i|) < r$?
  If it does and $\delta_i > Z$ then   {
      Set $Z = \delta_i$ and record the identity of sphere $i : id = i$
      (after all the sphere have been checked this reveals which
      sphere has its center closest to $\mathbf{p}$)
  }

Set another depth buffer $Z_b = 0$

To determine how close to the edge of the hexagon $\mathbf{p}$ is work through
all spheres (i) again.
  if $(i \neq id)$ {
    if $(\delta_i > 0$ and $(r - \delta_i) > Z_b$) {
      Set $Z_b = (r - \delta_i)$
    }
  }
  if $(|Z_b - Z| < a_1)$ {
      $\mathbf{p}$ lies on the hexagonal ridge.
  }
  else if $(|Z_b - Z| < a_2)$ {
      $\mathbf{p}$ lies on beveled side.
  }
  else {
      $\mathbf{p}$ lies in the hexagonal depression.
  }

Listing 11.4: Algorithm to generate the basic elements of an hexagonal mesh pattern. a_1 and a_2 are parameters that determine the width of the ridges and their sloping sides.

that used for the regular dimples. Strictly speaking this will not exhibit a crease at the point where two edges of the hexagon meet but this will hardly be noticed. The ridges in figure 11.13 do not have such a crease.

11.2.8   Textures derived from the noise functions

Apart from the basic *bozo* texture (section 4.5.2) and those simply derived from it by color blending and added turbulence (e.g., wood, marble etc.) a number of interesting patterns can be produced by passing the output from Perlin's noise generators through a number of functions.

Figure 11.14: A contour pattern which with some added turbulence and appropriate blend of color could resemble a three-dimensional wood grain pattern.

11.2.9 Contours

The contour pattern illustrated in figure 11.14 is derived from the basic bozo texture by passing it through a periodic function, in this case a sinusoid, and then thresholding the result as follows:

Given the point of interest as a (u, v, w) coordinate.

$$n_{u,v,w} = \tfrac{1}{2}(1 + \sin(2\pi f_q \ \text{fNoise}(u, v, w))$$

```
if (n_{u,v,w} > (1.0 - t)) {
    return the color of the contour
}
else return the background
```

The parameter t governs how thick the contours appear and f_q is a measure that can be most accurately described as a sort of *frequency* of the contours. Values of about 0.1 for t and 20 for f_q usually give good results, as illustrated in figure 11.14.

11.2.10 Plasma

The texture illustrated in figure 11.15 resembles the appearance of a brightly colored plasma field. It is produced by adding differently scaled noises and passing the result through a sinusoidal function to generate red, green and blue color components with different frequencies and phases. If the phases and frequencies are the same for each color a monochrome pattern will be observed.

Red, green and blue (r, g, b) values of the plasma at coordinate (u, v, w) are determined by the algorithm in listing 11.5.

Figure 11.15: A texture that gives the illusion of a plasma field.

//Given the point of interest as a (u, v, w) coordinate.
//the r, g, b color values are obtained as follows:

$n_1 = \text{fNoise}(u, v, w)$
$n_2 = \text{fNoise}(\frac{1}{2}u, \frac{1}{2}v, \frac{1}{2}w)$
$n_3 = \text{fNoise}(\frac{1}{4}u, \frac{1}{4}v, \frac{1}{4}w)$
$N = n_1 + n_2 + n_3$

$r = \frac{1}{2}(1 + \cos(2\pi f_r N + \phi_r))$
$g = \frac{1}{2}(1 + \cos(2\pi f_g N + \phi_g))$
$b = \frac{1}{2}(1 + \cos(2\pi f_b N + \phi_b))$

Listing 11.5: Algorithm to generate a plasma texture.

11.2.11 Underwater (caustics)

The caustic pattern that appears on the bottom and sides of swimming pools and underwater surfaces can be simulated by another modification of the basic noise pattern with appropriate color mixing. In the underwater pattern the noise is passed to a function that *folds* high values down to lower values and then scales and mixes the color of the caustic with a background shade. Two parameters govern the appearance of the caustics: the sharpness (s) controls the rapidity of color transitions, and the coverage (c) gives an overall increase in the percentage of the surface area covered by the caustic. The algorithm used to produce the caustic pattern in figure 11.16 and return an RGB triple on the interval $[0, 1]$ is given in listing 11.6.

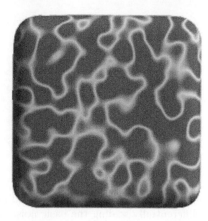

Figure 11.16: A caustic pattern gives the appearance of the patterns of light that play on underwater surfaces. The features have a sharpness of 0 and a coverage of 0.8.

//Given the point of interest as a (u, v, w) coordinate.

$n = \text{fNoise}(u, v, w)$
//Use a triangular function on the noise value:
if $(n > 0.5)n = 2(1 - n)$
else $n = 2n$
//Rescale the noise as follows:
$n = 0.3 + 0.9n$
//Mix the caustic color with the background:
if $(n > c)$ {
$\quad n = \dfrac{n - c}{1.2 - c}$
$\quad n = n(1 + s)$
$\quad$ **if** $(n > 1)\ n = 1$
$\quad r = nR_c + (1 - n)R_b$
$\quad g = nG_c + (1 - n)G_b$
$\quad b = nB_c + (1 - n)B_b$
}

Listing 11.6: Algorithm to generate a caustic texture.

11.2.12 Other worlds

A simple combination of the basic noise and turbulence functions with differential scaling can give a very good approximation to the appearance of a gas planet, like Jupiter. It is especially effective when applied to a spherical object such as that depicted in figure 11.17.

The algorithm in listing 11.7 (where n, β, f_f and f_s are parameters that affect visual appearance) outlines the main steps in producing the textured surface of figure 11.17.

Figure 11.17: Simulating the appearance of the banding in the atmosphere of a large gaseous planet by differentially scaling the basic noise function.

//Given the point of interest as a (u, v, w) coordinate.
//Note the differential scaling applied to the w coordinate.

$t = \text{fTurbulence}(20u, 20v, 10w)$
$w' = w + f_f t$
$s = \text{fNoise}(\frac{u}{1000}, \frac{v}{1000}, \beta w')$
$s' = s + n(\ \text{fNoise}(50u, 50v, 25w') - 0.5)$
//Limit s' to lie in range $[0, 1]$
$s = 0.5 + (s' - 0.5) * f_s$
//Finally blend the banding color with the background:
$r = sB_r + (1 - s)C_r$
$g = sB_g + (1 - s)C_g$
$b = sB_b + (1 - s)C_b$

Listing 11.7: Procedure to create the texture illustrated in figure 11.17. If $f_f > 0$ eddies and vortices appear in the atmosphere. If $b = 10$ then approximately 10 bands of gas lie in the unit cell. If $n > 0$ local perturbations in the atmospheric color appear. As $f_s \to 0$ the bands tend to fade. The input point is at coordinate (u, v, w) and the RGB triple r, g, b is the result of mixing the background color (B_r, B_g, B_b) with the band color (C_r, C_g, C_b).

11.2.13 Clouds

Another simple use of the noise function is to simulate a cloudy sky. Appropriate color mixing gives the clouds white edges and dark gray centers. Wispy clouds can be produced by differential scaling and the degree of shearing (a blustery day) is simulated by adding some turbulence. A point of interest is the way in which the turbulence is put into effect. Given a (u, v, w) coordinate at which a color is to be determined the turbulence is added to the position $(u+\Delta_u, v+\Delta_v, w+\Delta_w)$ before it is passed to the position dependent noise generator. This approach to modifying a texture, i.e., pre-modulating the position, is a useful one with utility

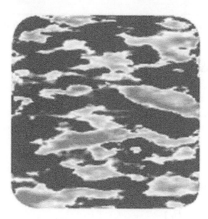

Figure 11.18: A cloudy day.

for generating other interesting textures. Figure 11.18 illustrates the cloudy texture.

The algorithm in listing 11.8 outlines the main steps in producing the textured surface of figure 11.18.

11.2.14 Regular dots perturbed by noise

In the discussion of the cloud texture it was pointed out that perturbing the position coordinate before passing it to the noise function was a useful way of producing textures. The following sections look at three textures produced by perturbing the (u, v, w) coordinate before passing it to an HCP dot or bump generator.

11.2.15 Leopard

The pattern illustrated in figure 11.19 was generated from a regular cell of HCP spheres by perturbing the position (u, v, w) with a number of sinusoids prior to testing for containment within one of the 22 HCP spheres.

The algorithm in listing 11.9 outlines the main steps in producing the textured surface of figure 11.19.

11.2.16 Reptile

If the regular bump pattern (of section 11.2.4) is changed to an HCP arrangement and the radius of each bump is increased and allowed to overlap, then a texture resembling a "scaly" skin is the result. Modulating the pattern with a combination of sinusoids adds to the realistic appearance which can be further enhanced by color blending near the edges of the bumps as shown in figure 11.20. The algorithm used to produce the texture is given in listing 11.10.

```
//Given the point of interest as a (u, v, w) coordinate.

//Displace the sampling point (u, v, w) by obtaining a turbulence vector Δp
vTurbulence(Δp, u, v, w, )
u' = u + tΔp_u
v' = v + tΔp_v
w' = w + tΔp_w
//Sample the noise function at (u', v', w') and blend colors:
n = fNoise(u', v', w')
if (n < 0.5) //return the background color
else if (n < 0.6) {
    //Blend to white from background: B
    f = 10(n - 0.5)
    r = r + f(1 - B_r)
    g = g + f(1 - B_g)
    b = b + f(1 - B_b)
}
else {
    //Blend to gray:
    f = 1 - 5(n - 0.6)
    r = fr
    g = fg
    b = fb
}
```

Listing 11.8: Procedure to create the texture illustrated in figure 11.18. The parameter t governs the *wispiness* of the clouds.

11.2.17   Veins

The regular honeycomb pattern of section 11.2.7 is readily transformed into the veined pattern of figure 11.21 if the point of interest, (u, v, w), is perturbed by a noise value before executing the algorithm of listing 11.4. The beveled sides of the hexagonal ridges are organized so that they form a trough rather than a ridge.

The changes shown in listing 11.11 transform the regular hexagonal mesh of figure 11.12 into the veined surface of figure 11.21.

11.2.18   Random dots and crystals

One might think that producing random dots would be one of the easier textures to create. After all one is just laying out a few spheres randomly in space and then determining whether a point $\mathbf{p}$ or (u, v, w) lies inside one of them. Unfortunately however because the texture must extend throughout an infinite volume we would need to make an infinite number of tests to see whether $\mathbf{p}$ lies inside one of the random dots or not. Clearly this is not a practical proposition and another method will have to be found.

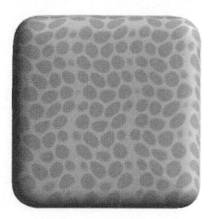

Figure 11.19: An animal skin pattern.

//Given the point of interest as a (u, v, w) coordinate.

//Displace the sampling point (u, v, w)
$u' = u + 0.11 \sin(\text{fmod}(3u, 2\pi))$
$u'' = u' + 0.2 \sin(\text{fmod}(0.1v, 2\pi))$
$v' = v + 0.15 \cos(\text{fmod}(4u'', 2\pi))$
$v'' = v' + 0.2 \sin(\text{fmod}(0.1w, 2\pi))$
$w' = w + 0.15 \cos(\text{fmod}(5v'', 2\pi))$
$w'' = w' + 0.2 \sin(\text{fmod}(0.1u'', 2\pi))$

//Check each of the 22 spheres of radius 0.25 in the HCP texture cell,
//if (u'', v'', w'') lies inside sphere i at a distance r from its center then mix
//from the background color to the texture's color.

Listing 11.9: Procedure to create the texture illustrated in figure 11.19. The $\text{fmod}(a, b)$ function returns the remainder of $\dfrac{a}{b}$.

Again one might think that considering the texture as a repetition of the unit cell would help because then we could confine our tests to a finite number of randomly placed dots inside the cell. Unfortunately there are two problems here. First, dots placed near the edge of the cell will overlap adjacent cells and unless we organize things so that the arrangement of dots within the cell allows it to tile seamlessly then a disjoint pattern will be visible. This is analogous to what happens when the adjacent strips of patterned wallpaper are not lined up correctly. Second, even when a wallpaper tiling is correctly set or if the dots are kept away from the edges of the cell then the pattern will not appear random and areas near the edges of the unit cells will stand out visually. Thus, to create a random array of dots an approach is needed that can be used on a texture cell

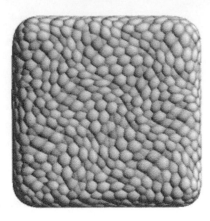

Figure 11.20: A perturbed regular array of overlapping HCP bumps can resemble a scaly skin.

//Given the sampling point as the (u, v, w) coordinate.

//Displace the sampling point: (u, v, w)
$u' = u + 0.16 \sin(\text{fmod}(2w, 2\pi))$
$v' = v + 0.16 \cos(\text{fmod}(3u, 2\pi))$
$w' = v + 0.16 \cos(\text{fmod}(4v, 2\pi))$

//Check each of the 22 spheres of radius 0.5 in the HCP texture cell stopping
//when (u', v', w') lies inside one of them, say at a distance r from its center.
//Bend the surface normal in proportion to r.

If $(r > 0.15)$ //blend from the background color to the texture color.

Listing 11.10: Procedure to create the *scaly* texture illustrated in figure 11.20.

basis whilst still allowing the random placement of dots, at least to the tolerance of a visual inspection.

Consider a single dot of radius $r \leq 0.5$ placed randomly in a unit cell, say as that shown in figure 11.22. Unless it is placed dead center it will overlap into adjacent cells. However at most it will only intrude into the immediate neighbors. Therefore if we construct a random dot texture by placing one sphere somewhere in every unit cell when the time comes to check whether a point at (u, v, w) lies inside the sphere (which forms the dot) only the spheres from the cell in which (u, v, w) lies and its 26 immediate neighbors need be considered. Since one dot is put somewhere in each texture cell the pattern will be quite pleasing to the eye because there will be no large gaps between dots nor will the dots tend to cluster. Each dot in the texture cell is readily drawn with different colors or radii to add to the effect.

Figure 11.21: This veined texture could be used to represent leaded glass when the surface is partially transparent.

//Given the point of interest is the coordinate (u, v, w).

//Get the random vector $\mathbf{d}$ from the noise function: vNoise$(\mathbf{d}, u, v, w)$
//Disturb the input point:
$u = u + 0.7d_u$
$v = v + 0.7d_v$
$w = w + 0.7d_w$
//Proceed with the honeycomb pattern.
//Note: $\mathbf{d} = (d_u, d_v, d_w)$ is a vector in the texture cell's frame of reference.

Listing 11.11: Procedure to create a veined texture.

There are two apparent difficulties in implementing the algorithm suggested in the previous paragraph. These are:

1. The first is that the random placement of dots must be done in a reproducible manner. To put it another way: If points (u, v, w) and (u', v', w') both lie in cell i, j, k the set of spheres used throughout the algorithm (which will basically be the same as that discussed in section 11.2.14) must be consistent. We must also remember that in practice points will not be passed to a texture generating function in any particular order (this was one of the criteria under which Perlin's noise function was developed).

2. Our second difficulty is that in considering points lying in texture cell i, j, k we must consider the effect of cells $i-1, j, k$ etc., and therefore we need to be able to reproduce the random placements of the dots in these cells as well.

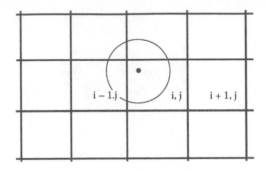

Figure 11.22: A random dot in texture cell i, j will overlap into at most cell i, j's nearest neighbors. (In this two-dimensional example the dot in cell i, j could lie in at most 9 cells.)

The solution to both of these problems is straightforward in practice because the numbers that emerge from a pseudo random number generator are a reproducible sequence based on some *seed* value. Therefore if a seed is derived from the identity (the i, j, k) of the cell under test the random position of the sphere within it may be reproduced exactly. Two alternative ways to generate such a seed are:

1. Use fNoise(i, j, k).

2. Use i, j, k and a hashing function to generate a pointer to an entry in a table of random numbers.

The first way is easier to implement but the second is faster and can be used in cases where we need more than one dot per unit cell.

11.2.19   Random dots

The random dots illustrated in figure 11.23 are the results of the implementation of the method described above with an index into a table of 2000 random vectors obtained by the hashing functions:

```
#define IMOD(z,a)  ((z) - ((z)/(a))*(a))
#define PATTERN(x,y,z)   ( ((z)+16384L)*64536L +  \
                           ((y)+16384L)*32768L +  \
                           ((x)+16384L))

index=IMOD(PATTERN(i,j,k),1999);
```

Once selected a random vector is used to place each sphere at some point in the texture cell. Random vectors from the same table are also used to vary the color and radius of the dot. Blending dot and background color near the dot edge helps to alleviate aliasing artifacts.

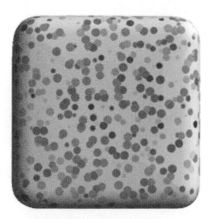

Figure 11.23: Variably sized random colored dots.

Figure 11.24: Random colored crystals. (Basically a random dot texture but with a dot radius that exceeds the size of the unit cell.)

11.2.20 Crystals

By allowing the dot radius to increase until adjacent dots overlap and then bringing into effect a **Z** buffer as used in section 11.2.7 the dots will appear to lock together into a matrix of colored *crystals*. Figure 11.24 illustrates a basic one sphere per unit cell texture after crystallization with the color of each dot chosen at random.

11.2.21 Blisters

Blisters are another example of the extension of the random dots texture. In this case the surface normal inside the dots is perturbed in much the same way as was done for the case of the regular bumps. Blisters are flatter than bumps but this

Figure 11.25: Random blisters: Raised random dots.

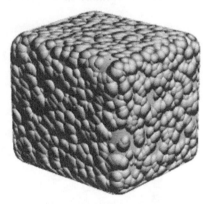

Figure 11.26: Peas: Rounded high density blisters.

is readily produced by using a slightly different mix of normal and perturbing vectors. Points that lie near the center of the dots can be colored differently for added effect.

11.2.22   Peas

The pea texture is yet again another version of the blisters texture. A greater density of random bumps is produced by placing 3 spheres in each unit cell. No flattening of the bumps is used, but by changing the sphere radius, the surface can be covered to a lesser or greater extent; see figure 11.26.

11.2.23   Sharply edged features

These textures are constructed by a combination of the ideas already derived and include the honeycomb and paving stones.

Figure 11.27: Honeycomb: a hexagonal mesh.

Figure 11.28: Paving stones and chipped fragments.

Honeycombs The honeycomb cube shown in figure 11.27 uses the steps from the hexagonal mesh algorithm (section 11.2.7), but without applying an inner limit to the extent of the beveled edge.

Paving stones The paving stone and fractured texture (figure 11.28) are derived from the crystal texture (section 11.2.20). By simply beveling the edges of the crystals the cracks between the paving stones appear. Points near the crystal edges are identified using the same calculation that identified whether points were on the ridges of a regular hexagonal mesh. In the case of the cracked texture very wide ridges were used.

A neat trick is to make the interior of the paving stones look dirty or weathered by mixing in a dark color modulated by $fNoise(u, v, w)$. Additionally, if each stone is given a slight color variation (a toned down multi-colored crystal) the whole surface looks more natural.

Figure 11.29: Some examples of basic undulating textures.

11.2.24 Rough surfaces

Rough surfaces fall into two categories:

1. Those with smooth changes to the direction of the surface normal, which are derived from combinations of vector noises.

2. Those with sharp changes to the surface normal direction vector. Often some smooth undulations are mixed with the more pronounced sharp features.

A basic rough surface is a straightforward mix of surface normal $\mathbf{n}$ and output from $vNoise(\mathbf{\Delta n}, u, v, w)$. Many different appearances are achieved by:

1. Scaling: calculate $\mathbf{\Delta n}$ from $vNoise(\mathbf{\Delta n}, su, sv, sw)$ after scaling the input coordinate (u, v, w) by s.

2. Amplification: vary the *bumpiness* through the parameter α and perturb $\mathbf{n}$ by:

$$\mathbf{n} = \mathbf{n} + \alpha \mathbf{\Delta n}$$

The bumpy cubes shown in figure 11.29 represent examples of different s and α values.

An almost infinite variety of other *continuous* rough and bumpy surfaces can be achieved by adding $vNoise()$ and $vTurbulence()$ vectors in different proportions and at different scales. Experimentation is very often the best way of finding pleasing effects.

The remaining three rough textures discussed next are primarily based on the algorithm for the *Pea* (section 11.2.22), which is a discontinuous bumpy surface. Each adds a new component to $\mathbf{\Delta n}$ either a $vNoise()$ or a scaled version of the *Pea* itself with minor features superimposed on it.

 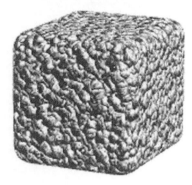

Figure 11.30: Crusted surfaces.

11.2.25 Crusts

The crusted texture shown in figure 11.30 is the result of the following modifications to the *Pea* texture algorithm:

1. Add a vector noise displacement to (u, v, w) before applying the **Pea** algorithm.

2. The radius of the *peas* are chosen from a random distribution in the range $[0.6 - 1.8]$ (relative to the size of the unit texture cell).

3. A power law, $(a' = a^2)$, is applied to the fraction of $\mathbf{\Delta n}$ mixed with $\mathbf{n}$ by:

$$\mathbf{n} = a'\mathbf{n} + (1 - a')\mathbf{\Delta n}$$

4. A continuous noise at a magnified scale is added to the final result. This adds a little fine detail to the gnarled look of the crusted texture.

The overall appearance will change depending on the resolution at which the texture is rendered as is evident from the examples illustrated in figure 11.30.

11.2.26 Crumpled

A crumpled surface that can resemble *used aluminum foil* is an example of an angular texture and is produced by adding **inverted** *Pea* textures at smaller and smaller scales and with different amplitudes. Usually there is no need to go beyond about three overlapping textures. The illustration in figure 11.31 was produced by perturbing (u, v, w) prior to computing the second and third components. Each component is calculated at a scale which is twice as small as the previous one and added in the proportions: 1.0, 0.8 and 0.95.

Figure 11.31: Scaly skin surface showing ridge features at decreasing scales.

11.2.27 Faceted

Crumpled surfaces exhibit features of a combination of basic rough surfaces with decreasing amplitudes and reducing scales. A faceted texture uses the same idea of summing effects at decreasing scales but without changing the amplitudes. Flat surfaces (which give the texture the appearance of some sort of naturally occurring mineral) are produced by quantizing Δn using integer arithmetic before mixing it with the surface normal.

The *Pea* texture (11.2.22) forms the basis for this texture. This time the hemispherical peas are inverted so that they appear to be pushed into the surface. The normal vector is quantized as shown in the following **C/C++** code fragment. This example gives approximately 16 flat quadrilaterals per hemispherical depression:

```
dn  //is the vector that bends the surface normal.
Normalize(dn);
dn[0]=0.5*(double)((int)(dn[0]*2.0));  //Quantize the 3 components
dn[1]=0.5*(double)((int)(dn[1]*2.0));  //components of "dn" using
dn[2]=0.5*(double)((int)(dn[2]*2.0));  //integer arithmetic.
Normalize(dn);
```

Faceted rectangular surfaces are illustrated in figure 11.32. The sample on the right depicts an alternative version in which three unquantized faceted textures are mixed by offsetting their position and only making a slight change of scale. The following code fragment documents the offset and scale change made during each of the 3 steps in the original version:

```
//offset the (u,v,w) coordinate and scale
//it before adding the next 'inverted Peas'
u += 20.0;  v += 21.0;  w += 22.0;
u *= 1.2;   v *= 1.2;   w *=1.2;
```

Figure 11.32: Two example of a faceted surface with angular and rounded features.

Plateau   Canyons   Ridges

Figure 11.33: Stucco surfaces.

11.2.28 Stucco surfaces

Stucco textures are very useful in situations where rich surface detail is desirable but without it becoming the center of attention. All the stucco textures involve bending the surface normal to form ridges, troughs or raised plateau-like features. Figure 11.33 illustrates three typical variations. The curved edges of the features may themselves twist gently, tightly or be very ragged indeed.

Stucco surfaces are simulated by thresholding the noise function:

$$n = fNoise(u, v, w)$$

For example: In the plateau effect, illustrated in figure 11.33, points on the surface where $n > 0.5$ are on the plateau and points where $0.55 < n < 0.6$ are on the slope. The ridge effect requires points satisfying $0.4 < n < 0.45$ to be on the up slope and points where $0.55 < n < 0.6$ to be on the down slope.

Determining the direction in which to bend the normal on the slopes requires the calculation of the gradient of $fNoise()$ at the point (u, v, w), i.e., $\Delta \mathbf{n} = -\nabla f_{u,v,w}$ or:

$$\Delta \mathbf{n} = -\left(\frac{\partial f}{\partial u} \hat{\mathbf{u}} + \frac{\partial f}{\partial v} \hat{\mathbf{v}} + \frac{\partial f}{\partial w} \hat{\mathbf{w}} \right)$$

Figure 11.34: Leather: (a) A derivative of Stucco textures and (b) Truncated Peas.

In practical terms this means using finite differences to determine the partial differentials. Thus the change in surface normal $\mathbf{\Delta n} = (\Delta n_u, \Delta n_v, \Delta n_w)$ is given by:

$$\Delta n_u = -(fNoise(u + \delta, v, w) - fNoise(u - \delta, v, w))$$
$$\Delta n_v = -(fNoise(u, v + \delta, w) - fNoise(u, v - \delta, w))$$
$$\Delta n_w = -(fNoise(u, v, w + \delta) - fNoise(u, v, w - \delta))$$

δ is a small increment in the coordinates of magnitude about 0.01. This value is chosen because the texture cell is of unit size and we are only interested in features whose sizes are of the order of about 0.05 units on this scale.

The steepness of the slopes of the features are governed by a parameter α which scales $\mathbf{\Delta n}$ before adding it to $\mathbf{n}$:

$$\mathbf{n} = \mathbf{n} + \alpha \mathbf{\Delta n}$$

Applying a turbulent perturbation to (u, v, w) before proceeding with the stucco algorithm will give very ragged and irregular boundaries and mixing the stucco surface with other bumpy textures also makes interesting surfaces.

11.2.29 Leather and cauliflower

In this section we will look at a couple of interesting combination textures. Leather is a natural material in common use and it would be nice to have a computer-generated texture that approximates to it. There is no one *correct* leather pattern so we will look at two variations. The first is produced by mixing stucco textures and the second is yet another variant of the ubiquitous *Pea*. In some circumstances the *cauliflower* pattern, so called because it resembles the florets of that vegetable, could even be used as a leather texture. The leather textures are illustrated in figure 11.34 and the cauliflower in figure 11.35.

The stucco leather is composed with the sum of 4 stucco (*canyon*) textures (using thresholds of 0.48, 0.54, 0.60 and 0.66) preprocessed by perturbing (u, v, w) with a little turbulence, viz.:

Figure 11.35: A Cauliflower.

```
vTurbulence(D, u, v, w);
u += D[0] * 0.4;
v += D[1] * 0.4;
w += D[2] * 0.4;
```

As each of the texture layers are added they are scaled and offset by:

```
u += 30;   v += 40;   w += 50;    // offset
u *= 1.01; v *= 1.02; w *= 1.03;  // scale
```

The only slight complication in this texture compared with a basic stucco is that special consideration must be given to those points where the canyons overlap. *A canyon within a canyon* must not be allowed to develop. One way to achieve this is by using a flag to indicate if point (u, v, w) is on the floor or side of a canyon; the floor takes precedence. After all 4 patterns have been processed the flag is used to select the correct $\Delta \mathbf{n}$.

The second potential leather pattern follows the **Pea** algorithm until the slope α of the pea at (u, v, w) is determined. Then α is modified as follows:

1. Thresholded: (if $\alpha < 0.4$ do not bend $\mathbf{n}$).

2. Subjected to a functional transformation $\alpha = \alpha^{0.25}$.

3. Perturbed by an attenuated standard noise vector $vNoise()$ at $\frac{1}{5}$ scale.

For the cauliflower surface the *Crumpled* algorithm is followed with the following exceptions:

1. The point (u, v, w) (input coordinate) is not perturbed after the addition to $\Delta \mathbf{n}$.

2. The "bumps" are inverted so that they bump out.

3. The amplitude of $\Delta \mathbf{n}$ is not attenuated during the phase in which the *Pea* procedure is repeated 3 times.

4. The feature size is reduced much more rapidly; 4 times on each loop.

Vertex position, normal and color (input)
```
layout(location = 0) in vec3 VertexPosition;
layout(location = 1) in vec3 VertexNormal;
layout(location = 2) in vec4 VertexColour;
```
Vertex position relative to the texture base axes
```
layout(location = 3) in  vec3 ShaderPosition;
```

Material base axes for the texture unit cell
```
uniform vec3 Uvector;
uniform vec3 Vvector;
uniform vec3 Wvector;
```

geometric Transformations
```
uniform mat4 NormalMatrix;
uniform mat4 ModelViewMatrix;
uniform mat4 ModelViewProjectionMatrix;
```

Variables to pass to fragment shader
```
out vec3 tnorm;   Vertex normal vector
out vec4 PP;      Vertex position
out vec3 texpos;  Texture position
out vec3 Color;   Vertex color
```
The three texture cell axes
```
out vec3 uvec;
out vec3 vvec;
out vec3 wvec;
```

Listing 11.12: The global variables used for input and output to a GLSL vertex shader for all algorithmic and procedural textures.

11.3 GPU textures

The texture algorithms described in section 11.2 can, for the most part, be adapted to execute as part of a pair of GPU shader codes. Like the CPU procedural textures the GPU textures make use of a repeating unit cell, and some other attributes that are passed to the GPU from the CPU application programs. In this section, the GPU specific features of an algorithm that has already been discussed in section 11.2 will be elaborated.

Most of the work in surface texturing which has to be done on a *per-pixel* basis takes place in the GPU's pixel (or fragment) program. The vertex program has usually to do little more than pass on the texture cell coordinates, vertex position, and surface normal vector. Listings 11.12 and 11.13 gives a GLSL vertex shader that is sufficient to work for all the textures in this chapter.

Note: The code that follows from the fragment programs makes use of the output variables defined in listing 11.12.

```
void main(void){
  Compute the transformed normal
  tnorm  = NormalMatrix*VertexNormal ;
  Set the built in variable with the vertex position
  gl_Position = ModelViewProjectionMatrix*VertexPosition;
  Copy the vertex position
  PP= ModelViewMatrix * VertexPosition;
  Pass the vertex position in the texture cell and
  the texture cell edge vectors to fragment program
  texpos = ShaderPosition;
  vvec = normalize(NormalMatrix * Vvector);
  wvec = normalize(NormalMatrix * Wvector);
  uvec = normalize(NormalMatrix * Uvector);
  Set color ouptut variable
  Color = VertexColor;
}
```

Listing 11.13: The code for the GLSL vertex shader that is used for all the algorithmic and procedural textures.

11.3.1 Regular patterns

Dots and checks and many other regular patterns are easily generated in a few lines of fragment shader code, for example, a 3D space filling checker texture that repeats once per unit cell can be coded as:

```
//Assign interpolated input to a shader variable
vec4 surface_colour=gl_Color;
//Offset into cell (from varying variable)
vec3 p=floor(texpos);
int id = int(p.x)+int(p.y)+int(p.z);   which octet ?
//Override shader color value
if(((id/2)*2) != id) {
  surface_colour=vec4(second_color,1.0);
}
//other code and pass on value of  surface_colour
```

The FCC dots pattern of section 11.2.2 requires a static array of six vectors vec3 ppp[6]. During execution each vector is tested against the texture cell coordinate. When the texture coordinate of the pixel lies within a spherical volume centered on one of the list of vectors (*ppp[]*) it is colored according to the code in listing 11.14.

11.3.2 Regular bumps

Equivalent GPU textures for the bumps, pimples and dimples (section 11.2.4) require an array of 35 cell relative positions for the center of the bumps, and

```
vec3 p = texpos;    p=fract(p);
vec4 surface_colour=gl_Color;
float e= // the edge fraction
for(i=0; i<6 ; i++){ // for each sphere
  if((a=length(p-ppp[i])) < Size){ // built in length function
   if((Size-a) > zb){
    zb=(Size-a);
    if(i == 0 || i == 2){
     surface_colour=vec4(Colour1,1.0); // alternative colors
    }
    else if(i == 1 || i == 3){
     surface_colour=vec4(Colour2,1.0); // for the crystal layers
    }
    else{
     surface_colour=vec4(Colour3,1.0);
    }
    if(a > e){ // use mix function to blend sphere edges
     surface_colour=mix(surface_colour,gl_Color,
     (a-e)/(Size-e));
    }
   }
  }
 }
}
```

Listing 11.14: Generating a volume dot pattern.

a procedure for bending the surface normal. The perturbation of the normal vector can follow closely the form of the code in the non-GPU C code whilst taking advantage of the GLSL's vector operations and built in functions. A few key lines in the shader are shown in listing 11.15.

11.3.3   Textures involving noise

Noise-based textures in a GPU require the use of a texture lookup. A 3D texture can be thought of as a large table of random numbers that will give a reproducible and periodic random number when *looked-up* for a 3D texture coordinate. Our noise texture array contains $64 \times 64 \times 64$ entries; the OpenFX code in file "gldesign_noise.c" that can be found in folder "render2" shows how to build a suitable noise texture for shaders using Perlin's algorithm.

In the case of the contour texture of section 11.2.9 the noise value from the 3D noise texture lookup at the texture cell coordinate is passed through a cyclic smoothing function to amplify/attenuate the underlying surface color as given in listing 11.16.

This texture lookup will naturally repeat for any input coordinate outside the range $[0, 1]$. Other textures like clouds and caustics follow this approach closely in their GPU implementations.

```
vec3  vnorm   =  normalize(tnorm);   // use built in function
  ..
p = texpos;  // texture cell relative position
for( ii=0;  ii<35  ; ii++){// find which sphere is holding the bump
  if(length(p-ppp[ii]) < BumpSize)pnn=ppp[ii];
}

  ..
nw=abs(dot(vnorm,wvec));// get normal vector's direction
nu=abs(dot(vnorm,uvec));   // relative to the texture cell
nv=abs(dot(vnorm,vvec));    // axes and assume surface local frame
// Calculate the direction to bend the normal vector
// relative to the cells base axes.
vec2  c=p.xy;
nDelta = nw*(c.x*uvec + c.y*vvec);
c=p.yz;
nDelta = nDelta + nu*(c.x*vvec + c.y*wvec);
c=p.zx;
nDelta = nDelta + nv*(c.x*wvec + c.y*uvec);
// bend the normal vector
vnorm += nDelta*sfactor;   // add normal displacement
```

Listing 11.15: Generating regular bumps in a GPU fragment shader.

```
float  sintab(in float  value){// periodic smoothing function
  return  0.5*(1.0+ sin ((value-floor(value))
                    *3.141592657*2.0));
}
  ..
 vec4  surface_colour;
 // look up the 3D texture
 vec4  Ns=texture3D(NoiseMap,texpos);
 float  noiseH=(Ns[0]*2.0);  // just use the first value
 noiseH = sintab(noiseH*10.0);
 if(noiseH > 1.0- Thickness){
    surface_colour=vec4(noiseH*C1,1.0);
 }
  ..
```

Listing 11.16: A contour texture shader.

11.3.4 Perturbation of regular textures

The leopard and reptile textures are obtained by perturbing a regular pattern, such as that set up in section 11.3.1. The GPU implementation can then follow the logic given in figures 11.9 and 11.10.

```
#define PATTERN(x,y,z)    (  ((z)+127.0)*511.0 +  \
                             ((x)+127.0)*255.0 +  \
                             ((y)+127.0))
  . . .
  float zb = 4;   // maximum value of texture Z buffer
  vec3 pf = texpos;   // texture position from varying variable
  vec p=fract(pf);   // fractional part
  pf=floor(pf);
  // 27 cell patterns are needed to fill the texture cell
  int ii; for(ii=0;ii<27;ii++){
  // choose a random pattern using hashing functions..
  // ppp[] is the centre of pattern cell
  float pat=PATTERN(ppp[ii].x+
              pf.x,ppp[ii].y+pf.y,ppp[ii].z+pf.z);

    . . .
  // NoiseData is a 2D table of random numbers to make different
  // crystal sizes using uniform variables "bradius" and "lradius"
  // that define the user's choice texture properties
  vec3 vclri=texture2D(NoiseData,pat).rgb;
  radius=bradius+lradius*(vclri[1]-0.5);
  pl=ppp[ii]+vclri;  // offset the pattern entry
  pl=p-pl;
  if((dl=length(pl)) < radius){ // inside the cell
    // is this a larger value ?
    if(dl < zb){   // zb is the Z-buffer
      zl=zb;
      zb=dl;  // update cell Z buffer
      id=float(ii);   // which pattern
      clr=vclri;
      pnn=ppp[ii];    // which pattern cell center
    }
  }
 }
```

Listing 11.17: A crystal texture.

The crystal-like textures of figure 11.24 are obtained by randomizing the pattern of cell positions and using a random number from a lookup table to give a variability to the size of the crystals in the pattern. Listing 11.17 highlights the main steps in a suitable shader implementation.

By also varying the direction of the surface normal vector throughout the cell, as was done in section 11.3.2, textures based on the peas of figure 11.26 are obtained.

Having now written GPU programs for the the crystal and pea textures then the other texture discussed in section 11.2 (the paving stones, the cracked,

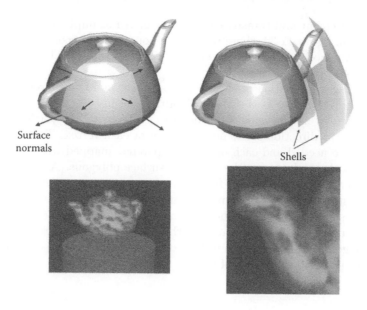

Figure 11.36: A fur texture. Shells around the surface of the object are displaced along the surface normal (a part of the shell is shown with exaggerated displacement). The shell is transparency mapped using a noise texture to give random regions of dense and light fur.

crusted, crumpled and faceted surfaces, and the cauliflower) may be generated by extension of the GPU codes for the crystal and pea, as was done for the CPU code.

In this section only the key feature of the fragment program have been highlighted. To gain a full appreciation of the details of the code, and see how to deploy them in a powerful rendering engine, the GPU programs on the website (and those of the OpenFX program) should be studied.

11.4   Fur and short hair

The challenge in rendering a texture like animal fur and short stubbly hair arises because the boundary silhouette of an object cannot be changed by simply altering the appearance of the faces, or the surface normal vector, and unfortunately this is the most significant visual cue used by an observer to tell that the surface is furry. When viewing a furry material back down the local surface normal there is also a perception of depth with some places on the surface being farther away; however this is a second-order effect. Despite these difficulties, and provided that the fur or hair does not have any dynamic properties, a very reasonable approximation to a furry texture can be created using the a combination of surface displacement and transparency mapping. An example of a furry texture can be seen in figure 11.36 where the edge silhouette has become streaked and blurred and the normal view gives a depth perception that is only really discernible in a stereoscopic rendering.

The combination of surface displacement and transparency mapping is generally referred to as the *Shells* algorithm because the idea is to build a series of surface layers, shells, around the object by moving the vertices a small distance along the direction of the normal vector at each vertex. Typically 10 to 20 shells may be needed and each one is transparency mapped with a noise texture that alters the *alpha* across the displaced surface polygons. As the additional surface attenuations build up, the fur takes on the appearance of growing out of the original surface with a random orientation. Since the vertices **are** being moved for each shell, the object's silhouette loses its uniform appearance and looks blurry. The realism of fur generated in this way could be improved by adding a few polygons extending in the normal direction from the object's surface and image mapped with side views of the fur.

Bibliography

[1] T. Akenine-Möller and E. Haines. *Real-Time Rendering.* Natick MA: A. K. Peters, 1999.

[2] V. B. Anand. *Computer Graphics and Geometric Modeling for Engineers.* New York NY: John Wiley and Sons, 1993.

[3] E. Angel. *Computer Graphics.* Reading MA: Addison Wesley, 1990.

[4] A. A. Apodaca and L. Gritz. *Advanced Renderman: Creating CGI for Motion Pictures.* San Francisco CA: Morgan Kaufmann, 1999.

[5] Ian Ashdown. *Radiosity: A Programmer's Perspective.* New York NY: John Wiley and Sons, 1994.

[6] J. Avro (Ed.). *Graphics Gems II.* Cambridge MA: Academic Press, 1991.

[7] F. Ayres. *Theory and Problems of Matrices (Schaum's Outline Series).* New York NY: McGraw-Hill, 1975.

[8] R. H. Bartles, J. C. Beatty, and B. A. Barsky. *Introduction to Splines for Use in Computer Graphics and Geometric Modeling.* Los Altos CA: Morgan Kaufmann, 1987.

[9] J. Bertails. "Realistic Hair Simulation, Animation and Rendering." In *SIGGRAPH Course Notes, SIGGRAPH Course Notes.* Los Angeles CA: SIGGRAPH, 2008.

[10] J. Blinn and M. E. Newell. "Texture and reflection in computer generated images." *Communications of the ACM* 19:10.

[11] J. Blinn. "Simulation of wrinkled surfaces." *Computer Graphics* 12.

[12] J. Blinn. *Jim Blinn's Corner: A Trip Down the Graphics Pipeline.* San Francisco CA: Morgan Kaufmann, 1996.

[13] T. Boullion and P. Odell. *Generalized Inverse Matrices.* New York NY: John Wiley and Sons, 1971.

[14] J. E. Bresenham. "Algorithm for computer control of a digital plotter." *IBM Syst J.* 4:1 (1965), 25 – 30.

[15] P. Burger and D. Gillies. *Interactive Computer Graphics.* Reading MA: Addison Wesley, 1989.

[16] A. K. Cline and R. L. Renka. "A storage efficient method for construction of a Thiessen triangulation." *Journal of Mathematics* 14.

[17] R. H. Crowell and R. E. Williamson. *Calculus of Vector Functions.* Englewood Cliffs NJ: Prentice Hall, 1962.

[18] L. Darcey. *Android Wireless Application Development.* Upper Saddle River, NJ: Addison-Wesley, 2010.

[19] M. De Berg. *Computational Geometry: Algorithms and Applications.* Germany: Springer Verlag, 2000.

[20] M. DeLoura (Ed.). *Game Programming Gems.* Rockland MA: Charles River Media, 2000.

[21] D. H. Eberly. *3D Game Engine Design.* San Francisco CA: Morgan Kaufmann, 2000.

[22] D.S. Ebert and S. Worley. *Texturing and Modeling a Procedural Approach.* Cambridge MA: Academic Press, 1994.

[23] D. Ebert, F. Musgrave, D. Peachey, K. Perlin, and S. Worley. *Texturing and Modeling a Procedural Approach.* Cambridge MA: Academic Press, 1994.

[24] W. Engel (Ed.). *Shader X^3: Advanced Rendering Techniques with DirectX and OpenGL.* Hingham MA: Charles River Media, 2005.

[25] W. Engel (Ed.). *Shader X^4: Advanced Rendering Techniques.* Hingham MA: Charles River Media, 2006.

[26] W. Engel (Ed.). *Shader X^5: Advanced Rendering Techniques.* Boston MA: Charles River Media, 2007.

[27] W. Engel (Ed.). *GPU Pro.* Natick MA: A. K. Peters, 2010.

[28] W. Engel. *Programming Vertex and Pixel Shaders.* Boston MA: Charles Rivers Media, 2004.

[29] G. Farin, D. Hansford, and G. E. Farin. *The Essentials of CAGD.* Natick MA: A. K. Peters, 2000.

[30] R. Fernando (Ed.). *GPU Gems.* Boston MA: Addison Wesley, 2004.

[31] A. Foley, S. Van Dam, S. Feiner, and J. Hughes. *Computer Graphics: Principles and Practice,* Second Edition. Reading MA: Addison-Wesley,, 1990.

[32] C. F. Gerald. *Applied Numerical Analysis.* Reading MA: Addison Wesley, 1978.

[33] A. S. Glassner (Ed.). *An Introduction to Ray Tracing.* London U.K.: Academic Press, 1989.

[34] A. Glassner (Ed.). *Graphics Gems.* Cambridge MA: Academic Press, 1990.

[35] N. Greene. "Environment mapping and other applications of world projections." *IEEE Computer Graphics and Applications* 6:11.

[36] J. Gregory. *Game Engine Architecture.* Natick MA: A. K. Peters, 2009.

[37] W. R. Hamilton. "On quaternions: Or on a new system of imaginaries in algebra." *Philosophical Magazine* 25 (1844), 10–14.

[38] A. Hanson. *Visualizing Quaternions.* San Francisco CA: Morgan Kaufmann, 2006.

[39] R. Hartley and A. Zisserman. *Multiple View Geometry in Computer Vision.* Cambridge U.K.: Cambridge University Press, 2011.

[40] J. Hartman and J. Wernecke. *The VRML 2.0 Handbook: Building Moving Worlds on the Web*. Reading MA: Addison Wesley, 1996.

[41] P. Heckbert (Ed.). *Graphics Gems IV*. Cambridge MA: Academic Press, 1994.

[42] A. Hillegass and A. Preble. *Cocoa Programming for Mac OS X*. Upper Saddle River NJ: Pearson Education, Inc., 2012.

[43] D. H. House and D. E. Breen (Ed.). *Cloth Modeling and Animation*. Natick, MA: A. K. Peters, 2000.

[44] Adobe Systems Inc. *Postscript Language Reference Manual*. Reading MA: Addison Wesley, 1990.

[45] T. L. Janssen. "A simple efficient hidden line algorithm." *Computers and Structures* 17:4 (1983), 563 – 571.

[46] H. W. Jensen. *Realistic Image Synthesis Using Photon Mapping*. Natick, MA: A. K. Peters, 2001.

[47] F. June. *An Introduction to Video Compression in C/C++*. On Demand Publishing LLC: Create Space, 2010.

[48] J. T. Kajiya and T. L. Kay. "Rendering fur with three-dimensional textures." *Computer Graphics* 23:3.

[49] J. H. Kindle. *Plane and Solid Geometry (Schaum's Outline Series)*. New York NY: McGraw-Hill, 1950.

[50] D. Kirk (Ed.). *Graphics Gems III*. Cambridge MA: Academic Press, 1992.

[51] R. P. Kuehne and J. D. Sullivan. *OpenGL Programming on Mac OS X*. Upper Saddle River NJ: Addision Wesley, 2008.

[52] D. H. Laidlaw, W. B. Trumbore, and J. F. Hughes. "Constructive solid geometry for polyhedral objects." *Computer Graphics* 20:4.

[53] S. St Laurent. *Shaders for Game Programmers and Artists*. Boston MA: Thompson Course Technology, 2004.

[54] E. Lengyel. *Mathematics for 3D Game Programming and Computer Graphics*. Boston MA: Course Technology (Cengage), 2012.

[55] S. Liang. *The Java Native Interface: Programmer's Guide and Specification*. Palo Alto CA: Sun Microsystems Inc., 1999.

[56] C. Lindley. *Practical Ray Tracing in C*. New York NY: John Wiley and Sons, 1993.

[57] S. Lipschutz. *Linear Algebra (Schaum's Outline Series)*. New York NY: McGraw-Hill, 1975.

[58] T. R. McCalla. *Introduction to Numerical Methods and FORTRAN Programming*. New York NY: John Wiley and Sons, 1967.

[59] K. McMenemy and S. Ferguson. *A Hitchhiker's Guide to Virtual Reality*. Wellesley MA: A. K. Peters, 2007.

[60] Moller and Trumbore. "Journal of Graphics Tools." www.acm.org/jgt, 1990.

[61] M. E. Mortenson. *Mathematics for Computer Graphics Applications: An Introduction to the Mathematics and Geometry of CAD/CAM, Geometric Modeling, Scientific Visualization*. New York NY: Industrial Press Inc., 1999.

[62] M. E. Mortenson. *Geometric Modelling*. New York NY: Industrial Press Inc., 2006.

[63] A. Munshi, D. Ginsburg, and D. Shreiner. *OpenGL ES 2.0*. Upper Saddle River NJ: Addision Wesley, 2009.

[64] H. Nguyen (Ed.). *GPU Gems 3*. Upper Saddle River NJ: Addison Wesley, 2005.

[65] J. O'Rourke. *Computational Geometry in C*. Cambridge U.K.: Cambridge University Press, 1993.

[66] A. Paeth (Ed.). *Graphics Gems V*. Cambridge MA: Academic Press, 1995.

[67] H.-O. Peitgen, H. Jurgens, and D. Saupe. *Chaos and Fractals New Frontiers of Science*. New York NY: Springer-Verlag, 2011.

[68] K. Perlin and E. M. Hoffert. "Hypertexture." *Computer Graphics* 23.

[69] K. Perlin. "An image synthesizer." *ACM SIGGRAPH Computer Graphics* 19:3 (1985), 287 – 296.

[70] M. Pharr and G. Humphreys. *Physically Based Rendering from Theory to Implementation*. Burlington MA: Morgan Kaufmann, 2010.

[71] M. Pharr (Ed.). *GPU Gems 2*. Upper Saddle River NJ: Addison Wesley, 2005.

[72] B. T. Phong. "Illumination for computer generated pictures." *CACM* 18:6.

[73] Majenta PLM. "Solid Edge." www.majentaplm.com/solidedge/, 2012.

[74] W. H. Press, S. A. Teukolsky, W. T. Vetterling, and B. P. Flannery. *Numerical Recipies in C++*. Cambridge U.K.: Cambridge University Press, 2002.

[75] J. Prosise. *Programming Windows with MFC*. Redmond WA: Microsoft Press, 1999.

[76] D. F. Rogers and J. A. Adams. *Mathematical Elements for Computer Graphics*. New York NY: McGraw-Hill, 1990.

[77] W. Schroeder, K. Martin, and B. Lorensen. *The Visualization Toolkit and Object-Orientated Approach to 3D Graphics*. New Jersey: Prentice Hall PTR, 1996.

[78] G. Sellers, R. S. Wright Jr., and N. Haemel. *OpenGL SuperBible,* sixth edition. Upper Saddle River NJ: Addison Wesley, 2013.

[79] A. Sherrod and W. Jones. *Beginning DirectX 11 Game Programming*. Boston MA: Course Technology (Cengage), 2012.

[80] P. Shirley. *Realistic Ray Tracing*. Natick MA: A. K. Peters, 2000.

[81] K. Shoemake. "Animating rotation with quaternion curves." In *Proceedings of SIGGRAPH-85*, pp. 245–254. ACM, 1985.

[82] D. Shreiner, G. Sellers, J. Kessenich, and B. Licea-Kane. *OpenGL Programming Guide: The Official Guide to Learning OpenGL Version 4.3* eighth edition. Upper Saddle River NJ: Addision Wesley, 2013.

[83] S. W. Sloan. "A fast algorithm for constructing Delaunay triangulations in the plane." *Advances in Engineering Software* 1.

[84] G. Turk. "Generating textures on arbitrary surfaces using reaction-diffusion." *Computer Graphics* 25:4.

[85] L. Vertlet. "Computer experiments on classical fluids." *Physics Review* 159:6 (1967), 98–103.

[86] A. Watt and M. Watt. *Advanced Animation and Rendering Techniques: Theory and Practice.* Reading MA: Addison Wesley, 1992.

[87] A. Watt and M. Watt. *3D Computer Graphics.* London U.K.: Longman Higher Education, 1999.

[88] A. Watt. *Fundamentals of Three-Dimensional Computer Graphics.* Reading MA: Addison Wesley, 1989.

[89] A. Watt. *3D Computer Graphics.* London U.K.: Longman Higher Education, 1999.

[90] C. Welman. "Inverse Kinematics and Geometric Constraints for Articulated Figure Manipulation." MSc Thesis, Simon Frazer University.

[91] A. Witkin and M. Kass. "Reaction-diffusion textures." *Computer Graphics* 25:4.

[92] D. Wolff. *OpenGL 4.0 Shading Language Cookbook.* Birmingham U.K.: PACKT Publishing, 2011.

Index

aliasing, 110, 129
ambient reflection, 117
Android, 304
angular interpolation, 238
animal skin texture, 477
animation, 187
anti-aliasing lines, 111
anti-aliasing points, 111
arc length, 194
articulated linkage, 222
articulated linkage (2D), 223

Bézier curves, 47
Bézier patch, 69
ballistics, 242
beveling, 401
bilinear interpolation, 137
bisection method, 196
blending curves, 44
bones, 73, 204
Boolean modeling, 413
bouncing, 240
bounding volumes, 172, 173
bozo texture, 472
Bresenham's algorithm, 156
bump mapping, 139, 284

camera, 188
capping, 376
Cartesian coordinates, 11
cauliflower texture, 490
caustics texture, 474
character animation, 202
character poses, 206
child-parent hierarchy, 206
circumcircle, 412
clay animation, 206

clipping, 106
clipping plane, 107
closest distance, 19
cloth modeling, 246
cloud texture, 476
CMYK, 116
Cocoa, 277
codec, 90
color blending, 458
color model, 115
combining transformations, 31
compatibility mode (OpenGL), 268
constructive solid geometry, 391, 416
convex polygons, 94, 377
coordinate conversion, 13
coordinate system, 11
coordinates (OpenGL), 267
core mode (OpenGL), 264
crazy paving texture, 485
crumpled texture, 487
crystals texture, 483
culling, 104, 405
cyclic coordinate descent, 234, 235
cylindrical mapping, 443

Dalvik, 304
degrees of freedom, 223
Delaunay triangulation, 81, 407
depth cueing, 120
depth sorting, 95
diffuse reflection, 117
direction vector, 14
directional light source, 115

edge, 73, 375
encrusted texture, 487
environment mapping, 141

Euler angles, 59, 141, 201
explosions, 242

facet, 73, 375
face (see facet), 73
falling under gravity, 238
feeler ray, 168
fireworks, 241
flexible model, 241
fly by, 189
forward kinematics, 216
fractal, 132
fractal textures, 130
fragment shader, 278
fragments, 264
frame buffer objects(FBO), 272, 290
framebuffer, 90, 110
FreeGLUT, 272
frustum, 38
fur texture, 497

generalized inverse, 220
geographic information systems, 408
geometric textures, 130
GLES, 293
GLEW, 273
GLFW, 273
GLSL, 277, 281, 453
GLUT, 272
goal directed animation, 215
Gouraud shading, 122
GPU, 6, 87, 91, 265, 266, 320, 350, 461
great circle, 66

hair simulation, 246
hashing, 146
heading, 188
hexagonal mesh texture, 470
hidden line, 158
hidden surface, 92
hierarchical animation, 202, 204
hierarchical interpolation, 211
hierarchy, 73, 188
homogeneous coordinates, 14, 27
honeycomb texture, 485
HSV, 116
hybrid tracing, 172
hypertexture, 454

ill-conditioning, 44
illumination, 115
image mapping, 134, 282
integer coordinates, 69
interior subdivision, 391
interpolation, 42, 188, 208
inverse kinematics, 187, 215, 292
iOS, 296
iteration, 196, 221

Jacobian matrix, 218
jaggies, 110
JAVA virtual machine, 304
JNI, 310
joints, 205

keyframe, 187, 191, 203, 237
kinematics, 216

lathing, 400
leather texture, 490
lens flare, 365
lighting, 114
line drawing, 154
line segment, 17
line, equation of, 16
linear interpolation, 45, 191
lofting, 394

marching cubes, 429
materials, 75, 128, 270, 453
metaballs, 429
mip-mapping, 141
mirror surfaces, 118
moiré patterning, 154
mosaic pattern, 136
multi-threading, 184

NDK, 308
nested holes, 390
node, 204
noise, 132, 458
non-convex polygons, 377
non-linear equations, 217
NURBS, 55, 56, 69

Objective C, 277
octree decomposition, 176

OpenFX, 70, 166, 319, 430, 453
OpenGL, 6, 91, 97, 129, 263, 293
OpenGLES, 293
optimized ray tracing, 171
orientation, 188, 189, 405
orientation tweening, 200
orthogonal basis, 458

P-buffers, 290
painter's algorithm, 95
parametric curves, 41
Particle System, 252, 290, 359
paths, 198
pea texture, 484
Perlin noise, 132, 144, 454
Phong shading, 122, 125, 406
physical animation, 237
pipeline, 90, 92, 264
pitch, 188
pivot, 189
pixels, 89
planar mapping, 443
planar shadows, 150
plane, equation of, 17
planet texture, 475
plasma texture, 473
point light source, 115
polygon, 24, 69, 375
polygonal data sets, 375
position vector, 14
PostScript font, 47, 376
primitive shapes, 23, 171, 451
procedural textures, 128, 131, 453
projectiles, 241
projection transformation, 38
pseudo shadows, 149

quadratic interpolation, 46, 192
quaternion, 60, 200

random dots texture, 482
raster, 89
ray tracing, 168
reaction diffusion, 454
recursive ray tracing, 169
recursive subdivision, 178
reflection, 21, 118, 140, 170
reflection mapping, 140, 141, 282

refraction, 22
regular bumps texture, 465
regular dots texture, 463
rendering, 88
RGB, 115
rigid body animation, 189
Rodrigues' rotation formulae, 34
roll, 188
rotational transformation, 29, 190, 206
rough surface texture, 486

scaling transformation, 29
scan line, 100, 101
scripts, 187
seed filling, 101
shaders, 128, 270, 277, 300, 350, 453
shading, 121
shading errors, 127
Shading language, 277
shadow maps, 151
shadows, 149, 151
skeleton, 73, 204
SLERP function, 67
snapshot, 188
spatial subdivision, 172, 174
specular reflection, 118
spherical mapping, 443
spherical polar coordinates, 11
splines, 50, 55, 192
spotlights, 115, 151
standard texture interface, 454
stucco texture, 489
subdividing polygons, 391
supersampling, 113
supertriangle, 410
surface local coordinates, 287
surface normals, 81, 405
surface of revolution, 400
surface patches, 69

tessellation, 376
texture cell, 460
texture coordinates, 73, 129, 135, 442, 460
texture patterns, 459
texture reference frame, 456
textures, 75, 128, 270, 453
tiling pattern, 136

transformations, 26
translational transformation, 28, 190
transparency, 101, 138
transparency mapping, 138
triangulation, 376
TrueType font, 376
TrueType fonts, 47, 376
turbulence, 132
tweening, 187, 203, 216
type quantifiers, 281

uniform qualifier, 281

vectors, 14
veins texture, 478
vertex, 14, 69, 375
vertex array object (VAO), 279
vertex buffer object (VBO), 279
vertex shader, 278
Vertlet integration, 248
view transformation, 36
viewing transformation, 168, 190
viewpoint, 189
volume rendering (atmospherics), 367
voxel, 180
VRML, 61

walk through, 189
wireframe, 71, 79, 154, 160
wrap mapping, 448

Z buffer, 96, 100, 106, 159, 171, 320

Printed and bound by CPI Group (UK) Ltd, Croydon, CR0 4YY

22/10/2024

01777636-0010